CELTIC LANGUAGE, CELTIC CULTURE

CELTIC LANGUAGE, CELTIC CULTURE:
A Festschrift for ERIC P. HAMP

edited by
A. T. E. Matonis and Daniel F. Melia

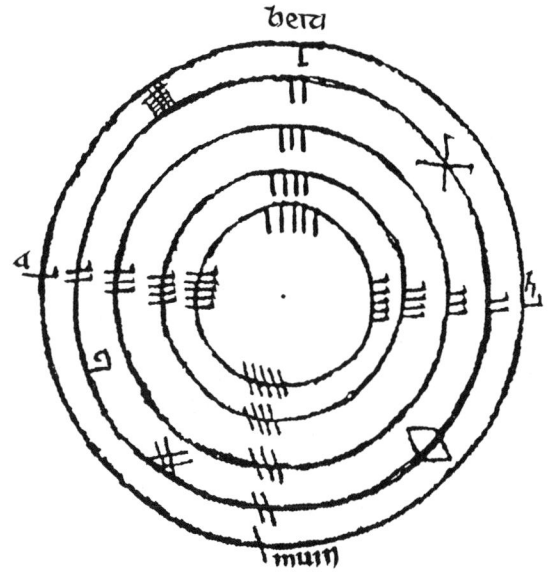

Ford & Bailie, Publishers,
Van Nuys, California
1990

© Ford & Bailie and the contributors 1990

Published by
Ford & Bailie, Publishers
P. O. Box 2156
Van Nuys, CA 91404-2156

Design by Paula Powers Coe

Library of Congress Cataloging-in-Publication Data

Celtic language, Celtic culture.
  "Bibliography of Eric P. Hamp" : p. 345
  1. Celtic languages. 2. Hamp, Eric P. I. Hamp,
Eric P. II. Matonis, A. T. E. III. Melia, Daniel F.
PB1002.A44 1990   491.6   90-3040
ISBN 0-926689-01-0 (alk. paper)

The Ogham device on the cover and title page is reproduced from the *Book of Ballymote* by kind permission of the Officers of the Royal Irish Academy.

"A Grief Ago" and six lines from "Altarwise by Owl-light" from Dylan Thomas, *The Collected Poems of Dylan Thomas,* © 1939 by New Directions Publishing Corporation. Reprinted by permission of New Directions Publishing Corporation. U.S. Rights. Acknowledgement is made to J. M. Dent and Sons, Ltd. and to the Trustees for the Copyrights of the late Dylan Thomas for permission to reprint "A Grief Ago" and six lines from "Altarwise by Owl-light" from *Collected Poems: Dylan Thomas, 1934–1952,* 1952, and for permission to reprint 171 words from Dylan Thomas, *Collected Letters,* ed. Paul Ferris, 1985. Rights in the English language throughout the world except the U.S.A. Acknowledgement is made to Macmillan Publishing Company, *The Collected Letters of Dylan Thomas,* ed. Paul Ferris, 1985, for permission to reprint 171 words.

Printed on acid-free paper and bound in the United States of America

All rights reserved

Contents

Foreword ix
Tabula Gratulatoria xi

Part I: Comparative and Continental Celtic

1 Some Proleptic Pronouns in Gaulish 3
  Joseph F. Eska

2 Celtiberi: A Note 13
  Henry M. Hoenigswald

3 Zum plomb du Larzac 16
  Karl Horst Schmidt

4 Einige Beobachtungen zu indogermanische /w/ im Keltischen 26
  Patrizia de Bernardo Stempel

5 Some Celtic Phrasal Echoes 47
  Calvert Watkins

6 Some Celtic Otherworld Terms 57
  Patrick Sims-Williams

Part II: Irish

7 Notes on the Diminutive Suffix *-ín* in Modern Irish 85
  Tomás de Bhaldraithe

8 Vowel Hiatus in Early Modern Irish 96
  Brian Ó Cuív

9 Another Look at Old Irish *imbúaruch* 'this morning', *imbárach* 'tomorrow morning' 108
  Anders Ahlqvist

10	Old Irish *cú*: A Naïve Reinterpretation *Lionel Joseph*	110
11	Sword as *Audacht* *Joseph Falaky Nagy*	131
12	*Noínden*: Its Semantic Range *Edgar M. Slotkin*	137
13	The Semantic Fields of Early Irish Terms for Black Birds and Their Implications for Species Taxonomy *Maria Tymoczko*	151
14	"Men Will Die": Poets, Harpers, and Women in Early Irish Literature *Joan N. Radner*	172
15	A Poetic Klein Bottle *Daniel Frederick Melia*	187

Part III: Scottish Gaelic

16	A Brief Historiography of Scottish Gaelic Dialect Studies *Anna Bosch*	199
17	An Impersonal Usage in Scottish Gaelic *William Gillies*	207
18	Writing Without Reading: An Illiterate Imperfect Speaker's Adventures in Writing Gaelic *Nancy C. Dorian*	218

Part IV: Welsh

19	Constituent Order in the Negative Declarative Sentence in the White Book Version of *Kulhwch ac Olwen* *T. Arwyn Watkins*	247
20	Word-Order in Old Irish and Middle Welsh: An Analogy *Proinsias Mac Cana*	253

21	Where Was *Rhaeadr Derwennydd (Canu Aneirin,* Line 1114)? R. Geraint Gruffydd	261
22	Twin Mystery Verbs of the *Canu i Gadfan* Catherine A. McKenna	267
23	Problems Relating to the Composition of the Welsh Bardic Grammars A. T. E. Matonis	273
24	A Highly Important Pig Patrick K. Ford	292
25	A Note on a Possible Anglo-Saxon Pun in *Branwen* Kathryn A. Klar	305
26	An Early Work on Irish Folklore and Dylan Thomas's "A Grief Ago" Katharine T. Loesch	308

Part V: Breton

27	Welsh *ar bwys* : Breton *war-bouez* J. E. Caerwyn Williams	325
28	The Semantics of the Simple Tenses of the Verb at Plougrescant Jean Le Dû	336

Bibliography

Bibliography of Eric P. Hamp   345

Foreword

Displaying a breadth of vision and a depth of knowledge more easily associated with an earlier and grander age of scholars, Eric Hamp's linguistic scholarship spans most subjects of language study and most of the Indo-European languages in each of their historical stages. The readers of this volume will be familiar with all of this, with many of his individual labors, with the copiousness of his knowledge, and with the unconfinable generosity of the man himself. He is living proof that there need be no contradiction between rigorousness of mind and generosity of spirit. Given the polymath that Eric Hamp is, no single volume could pay adequate tribute to him or to his accomplishments. Certainly no prefatory summary can pretend to offer more than a synopsis of any great scholar's achievements, and fall short even at that. Such is the case here. This volume, therefore, is intended to honor Eric Hamp's contributions to Celtic studies, which began with one of his earliest essays, "Morphophonemes of the Keltic Mutations" (1951), and which continue today in his frequent publications in Celtic journals and in his efforts to record the spoken Gaelic of St. Kilda's and other dying dialects of Scottish Gaelic. An index of Professor Hamp's uninterrupted interest in Celtic is provided by his bibliography, which is here published for the first time.

To say that Eric Hamp's friends are legion would probably be an understatement, nominal Roman legionary strength being only six thousand. Had the resources been available, this volume, likewise, would have contained not tens, but hundreds of contributions from scholars helped, influenced, and stimulated by Eric and by his work. Many will also have had the pleasant but slightly unnerving experience of meeting Eric in some totally unexpected part of the world, an experience so widespread as to give rise to the speculation that there is more than one of him.

While his publications are the most obviously classifiable record of Eric Hamp's contribution to Celtic studies, he has left his imprint in other important ways as well: in his kind and enthusiastic encouragement of junior scholars and, most significantly for us in North America, in the role he played in the formation of the Celtic Studies Association of North America. This volume attempts to reflect some of the academic interests of the man to whom it is a tribute, but it also tries to reflect, if only imperfectly, a more personal historical academic record. To this end it contains articles written by Professor Hamp's students; by cofounders of the Celtic Studies Association of North America; and by those colleagues in Celtic studies with whom Eric has over the years formed a close collegiality and abiding friendship. We think it is appropriate and not too fulsome to say that its preparation has been a labor of love.

A. T. E. MATONIS
DANIEL FREDERICK MELIA

Tabula Gratulatoria

ADKINS, ARTHUR W. H., *Department of Classical Languages and Literatures, University of Chicago*

YR ADRAN GYMRAEG, *University College of North Wales, Bangor, Gwynedd*

AHLQVIST, ANDERS, *Galway and Helsingfors; University College, Galway*

ANTTILA, RAIMO, *Department of Linguistics, University of California, Los Angeles*

BAILIE, CHADINE P. (FORD), *13840 Kittridge St., Van Nuys, California*

BAMMESBERGER, ALFRED, *Richard Strauss Strasse 48, Eichstätt*

BAYLESS, MARTHA, *Department of English, University of Oregon, Eugene*

BEVAN, GARETH A., *Geiriadur Prifysgol Cymru, Aberystwyth, Dyfed*

BOK, ABIGAIL, *Center for Medieval and Renaissance Studies, University of California, Los Angeles*

BOLLARD, JOHN K., *Department of English Language and Literature, Smith College, Northampton, Massachusetts*

BOSCH, ANNA, *University of Chicago*

BRAIDWOOD, ROBERT J., *Oriental Institute, University of Chicago*

BREATNACH, PÁDRAIG A., *University College Dublin, Belfield*

BROWN, WILLIAM R., *19C North Front St., New Paltz, New York*

CAREY, JOHN, *Department of Celtic Languages and Literatures, Harvard University*

CELTIC COLLOQUIUM, *University of California, Berkeley and Los Angeles*

CENTER FOR THE STUDY OF COMPARATIVE FOLKLORE AND MYTHOLOGY, *University of California, Los Angeles*

CENTRE FOR ADVANCED WELSH AND CELTIC STUDIES, *University of Wales, Aberystwyth*

COE, PAULA POWERS, *Folklore and Mythology Program, University of California, Los Angeles*

CORTHALS, JOHAN, *Institut für Allgemeine Sprachwissenschaft und Indogermanistik, Universität Hamburg*

CRAM, DAVID, *Jesus College, Oxford University*

CREMIN, AEDEEN, *Department of History, University of Sydney, Australia*

DAHLSTROM, AMY, *Department of Linguistics, University of Chicago*

DE BERNARDO STEMPEL, PATRIZIA, *Sprachwissenschaftliches Institut der Ruhr-Universität Bochum*

DE BHALDRAITHE, TOMÁS, *Royal Irish Academy, Dublin*

DE HOZ, JAVIER, *Departamento de Filología Griega, Universidad Complutense, Madrid*

DEPARTMENT OF IRISH FOLKLORE, *University College, Dublin*

DORIAN, NANCY C., *Bryn Mawr College, Bryn Mawr, Pennsylvania*

DUNLEAVY, GARETH W. and JANET E., *University of Wisconsin, Milwaukee*

DURAN, JAMES J., *634 Cedar Ave., No. 9, Long Beach, California*

EDEL, DORIS, *Institute for Celtic Languages and Literature, University of Utrecht*

EMBLETON, SHEILA, *Department of Languages, Literatures and Linguistics, York University, Toronto*

ESKA, JOSEPH F., *Dublin Institute for Advanced Studies*

ESTRADA, JACQUELYN L., *Department of History, University of California, Los Angeles*

EVANS, D. ELLIS, *Jesus College, Oxford University*

EVANS, D. SIMON, *St. David's University College, Lampeter, Dyfed*

FIFE, JAMES, *6655 La Jolla Blvd., No. 11, San Diego, California*

FORD, PATRICK K., *Department of English, University of California, Los Angeles*

FREEMAN, PHILIP M., *Department of Celtic Languages and Literatures, Harvard University*

FRIEDMAN, VICTOR A., *Department of Slavic Languages, University of North Carolina, Chapel Hill*

GEIRIADUR PRIFYSGOL CYMRU, *Aberystwyth, Dyfed*

GEROW, EDWIN, *Reed College, Portland, Oregon*

GIANNAKIS, GEORGIOS, *Indo-European Studies Program, University of California, Los Angeles*

GILLIES, WILLIAM, *Department of Celtic, University of Edinburgh*

GIMBUTAS, MARIJA, *Institute of Archaeology, University of California, Los Angeles*

GLEASURE, JAMES W., *Department of Celtic, University of Glasgow*

GOLDSMITH, JOHN A., *Department of Linguistics, University of Chicago*

GORROCHATEGUI, JOAQUIN, *Departamento de Estudios Clásicos, Universidad del País Vasco, Vitoria, España*

GRAGG, GENE, *Department of Linguistics/Oriental Institute, University of Chicago*

GRUFFYDD, R. GERAINT, *University of Wales Centre for Advanced Welsh and Celtic Studies, Aberystwyth, Dyfed*

GUILLAUME, GABRIEL, *Université Catholique, Angers Cédex, France*

GÜTERBOCK, HANS G., *Oriental Institute, University of Chicago*

HANKS, WILLIAM F., *Department of Linguistics, University of Chicago*

HAYCOCK, MARGED, *Adran y Gymraeg, Coleg Prifysgol Cymru, Aberystwyth, Dyfed*

HENNESSEY, JOHN S. JR., *Sacramento, California*

HOENIGSWALD, HENRY M., *University of Pennsylvania, Philadelphia*

HOFFNER, HARRY A., *Oriental Institute, University of Chicago*

HOLLAND, GARY, *Department of Linguistics (and Celtic Studies Program), University of California, Berkeley*

HULD, MARTIN E., *Deparment of English, California State University, Los Angeles*

INDO-EUROPEAN STUDIES PROGRAM, *University of California, Los Angeles*

INOUE, TOMOYUKI, *Indo-European Studies, University of California, Los Angeles*

IRELAND, COLIN A., *Dublin Institute for Advanced Studies*

JACOBS, NICOLAS, *Jesus College, Oxford University*

JONES, LESLIE, *Venice, California*

JOSEPH, LIONEL, *95 Montgomery Street, Cambridge, Massachusetts*

KAZAZIS, KOSTAS, *Department of Linguistics, University of Chicago*

KELLY, PATRICIA, *Royal Irish Academy, Dublin*

KLAR, KATHRYN A., *Celtic Studies, University of California, Berkeley*

KLAUSNER, DAVID N., *Center for Medieval Studies, University of Toronto*

KNAB, PETER, *Sprachwissenschaftliches Seminar, Philipps-Universität Marburg*

KNOBLOCH, JOHANN, *Sprachwissenschaftliches Institut, Universität Bonn*

KOCH, JOHN T., *Department of Celtic Languages and Literatures, Harvard University*

KÖDDERITZSCH, ROLF, *Sprachwissenschaftliches Institut der Universität Bonn*

KRAHWINKLER, HARALD, *Institut für österreichische Geschichtsforschung, Wien*

LAMBERT, PIERRE-YVES, *Ecole Pratique des Hautes Études, Sorbonne*

LAVER, JOHN D. M. H., *Department of Linguistics, University of Edinburgh*

LAZAR-MEYN, HEIDI ANN, *810 Moose Hill Road, Guilford, Connecticut*

LE DÛ, JEAN, *Université de Bretagne Occidentale, Brest*

LEHMANN, RUTH P. M. and WINFRED P. LEHMANN, *The University of Texas, Austin*

THE LIBRARY, *Queen's University, Belfast, Northern Ireland*

THE LIBRARY, *University College, Cork, Ireland*

LLYFRGELL GENEDLAETHOL CYMRU/THE NATIONAL LIBRARY OF WALES, *Aberystwyth*

LOESCH, KATHARINE T., *Department of Communication and Theater, University of Illinois, Chicago*

MAC CANA, PROINSIAS, *Dublin Institute for Advanced Studies, Ireland*

MACQUEEN, JOHN, *School of Scottish Studies, University of Edinburgh*

MCCAWLEY, JAMES D., *Department of Linguistics, University of Chicago*

MCCAUGHEY, TERENCE, *Department of Irish, Trinity College, Dublin*

MCINTOSH, ANGUS, *Gayre Institute, University of Edinburgh, Scotland*

MCKENNA, CATHERINE A., *Department of English, Queens College, CUNY, Flushing, New York*

MCLEAN, HUGH, *Slavic Department, University of California, Berkeley*

MCNEILL, DAVID and NOBUKO, *Departments of Psychology and Linguistics, University of Chicago*

MCQUOWN, NORMAN A., *Department of Anthropology, University of Chicago*

MALKIEL, YAKOV, *Department of Linguistics, University of California, Berkeley*

MATONIS, A. T. E., *Department of English, Temple University, Philadelphia*

MECKLER, MICHAEL LOUIS, *Department of Classical Studies, University of Michigan, Ann Arbor*

MEID, WOLFGANG, *Institut für Sprachwissenschaft der Universität, Innsbruck*

MELIA, DANIEL F., *Department of Rhetoric, University of California, Berkeley*

MITCHELL, DAVID H., *Department of English, Friends Select School, Philadelphia*

NAGY, JOSEPH FALAKY, *Department of English, University of California, Los Angeles*

THE NEWBERRY LIBRARY, *Chicago*

NÍ CHATHÁIN, PRÓINSÉAS, *Department of Early and Medieval Irish, University College, Dublin*

NICOLAISEN, W. F. H., *Department of English, State University of New York, Binghamton*

NILSEN, KENNETH E., *St. Francis Xavier University, Antigonish, Nova Scotia*

Ó BROIN, TOMÁS, *13 Newcastle Park, Galway, Ireland*

Ó BUACHALLA, BREANDÁN, *Department of Modern Irish, University College, Dublin*

Ó CONCHEANAINN, TOMÁS, *2, Valleyview, Delgany, Co. Wicklow, Ireland*

Ó CATHASAIGH, TOMÁS, *Department of Early Irish, University College, Dublin*

Ó CORRÁIN, AILBHE, *Keltiska Avdelningen, Uppsala Universitet*

Ó CORRÁIN, DONNCHADH, *Department of Irish History, University College, Cork*

Ó CUÍV, BRIAN, *Dublin Institute for Advanced Studies*

Ó FIANNACHTA, PÁDRAIG, *St. Patrick's College, Maynooth*

ÖLBERG, HERMANN, *Institut für Sprachwissenschaft, Universität Innsbruck*

PADEL, O. J., *2, Edward St., Truro, Cornwall*

PENZL, HERBERT, *Department of German, University of California, Berkeley*

PERRY, JOHN R., *Department of Near Eastern Languages and Civilizations, University of Chicago*

POLOMÉ, EDGAR C., *Department of Oriental Languages and Literatures, University of Texas, Austin*

POPPE, ERICH, *Sprachwissenschaftliches Seminar, Philipps-Universität Marburg*

PUHVEL, JAAN, *Department of Classics, University of California, Los Angeles*

RADNER, JOAN N., *Department of Literature, American University, Washington, D.C.*

RAUCH, IRMENGARD, *Department of German, University of California, Berkeley*

REJHON, ANNALEE C., *Celtic Studies (UIDS), University of California, Berkeley*

RICHTER, MICHAEL, *Fachgruppe Geschichte, Universität D 7750 Konstanz*

ROBERTS, BRYNLEY F., *National Library of Wales, Aberystwyth, Dyfed*

ROIDER, ULRIKE, *Institut für Sprachwissenschaft, Universität Innsbruck*

ROSE, NANCY H., *Department of Modern Languages, Hampden-Sydney College, Hampden-Sydney, Virginia*

RÖSSING, HANS, *Sprachwissenschaftliches Seminar, Philipps-Universität Marburg*

ROYAL IRISH ACADEMY, *Dublin*

SADOCK, JERROLD M., *Department of Linguistics, University of Chicago*

SAYERS, WILLIAM, *Council of Ontario Universities, Toronto*

SCHMIDT, KARL HORST, *Sprachwissenschaftliches Institut der Universität Bonn*

SCHOOL OF CELTIC STUDIES: THE STAFF, *Dublin Institute for Advanced Studies*

SCHWARTZ, MARTIN, *Department of Near Eastern Studies, University of California, Berkeley*

SIMS-WILLIAMS, PATRICK, *St. John's College, Cambridge University, England*

SILVERSTEIN, MICHAEL, *Departments of Linguistics and Anthropology, University of Chicago*

SLOTKIN, EDGAR M., *Department of English and Comparative Literature, University of Cincinnati, Ohio*

SPECIAL COLLECTIONS: ANGUS L. MACDONALD LIBRARY, *St. Francis Xavier University, Antigonish, Nova Scotia*

SPEITEL, HANS H., *Linguistic Survey of Scotland, University of Edinburgh, Scotland*

SPRACHWISSENSCHAFTLICHES INSTITUT, *Ruhr-Universität Bochum*

STACEY, ROBIN CHAPMAN, *Department of History, University of Washington, Seattle*

STUMP, GREGORY T., *Department of English, University of Kentucky, Lexington*

SWARTZ, DOROTHY DILTS, *Lexington, Massachusetts*

SWEETSER, EVE, *Department of Linguistics (and Celtic Studies Program), University of California, Berkeley*

TERNES, ELMAR, *Phonetisches Institut, Universität Hamburg*

THOMSON, DERICK S., *Department of Celtic, University of Glasgow*

TIMM, LENORA A., *Linguistics Program, University of California, Davis*

TYMOCZKO, MARIA, *Department of Comparative Literature, University of Massachusetts, Amherst*

UBO FAKULTETSBIBLIOTEKET HF, *Institutt for Lingvistikk og Filosofi, Universitetet I Oslo*

UNTERMANN, JÜRGEN, *Universität Köln*

VAN STRIEN, M., *Celtic Institute, University of Utrecht*

WATKINS, CALVERT, *Department of Linguistics, Harvard University*

WATKINS, T. ARWYN, *University College, Belfield, Dublin*

WELSH, ANDREW, *Rutgers University, New Brunswick, New Jersey*

WERT, ELLEN L., *Department of English, Lafayette College, Easton, Pennsylvania*

WILLIAMS, J. E. CAERWYN, *Centre for Advanced Welsh and Celtic Studies, University College of Wales, Aberystwyth*

ZBIGNIEW, GOLAB, *Department of Slavic Languages, University of Chicago*

ZIMMER, STEFAN, *Seminar für Vergleichende Sprachwissenschaft, Freie Universität Berlin*

PART I

COMPARATIVE AND CONTINENTAL CELTIC

Some Proleptic Pronouns in Gaulish

§1. INTRODUCTION

There is in Insular Celtic a not uncommon construction in which an infixed or suffixed proleptic object pronoun anticipates the direct object, which follows later in the sentence,[1] for example:

duda·ánaic inna ríga "which had come to *them*, the kings"[2]

mani·thobrea día dó a n-accobor "unless God gives *it* to him, the desire"[3]

foilsigth-i in spirut and-som a rrath "the Spirit manifests *it* in him, the grace"[4]

neu's goreu o gadeu gewilid "he made *it*, disgrace on armies"[5]

ny's gweles dyn eiryoet y sawl dynyon "no one ever saw *them*, so many people"[6]

mi a'e dywedaf itt yr ystyr "I shall tell *it* to you, the reason".[7]

In Old Irish, which distinguishes the three grammatical genders in the singular of the third person, one sometimes finds that a neuter pronoun anticipates a substantive of another gender, for example:

cresaigth-i in fer medónach in lagin móir sin "the middle man brandishes *it* (neut.), that great spear (fem.)"[8]

ni·thucat beos rúin ind rechto "they do not understand *it* (neut.) yet, the mystery (fem.) of the law".[9]

There is one commonly recognised example of such a construction in Gaulish, namely, that in the inscription from Chamalières in which *sos* (masc. acc. pl.) anticipates the list of names that follows:

*loṭites-snI eθθi-c-sos, briχtIa aṇderon, c̨. lucion floron nigrInon adgarion, aemilIon paterin(on), claudIon legitumon, caelion pelign(on), claudIo(n) pelign(on), marcion uictorin(on), asiatIcon aθθedillI "Quicken us [i.e., them] by the magic of underworld spirits,[10] C. Lucios Floros Nigrinos the invoker, Aemilios Paterinos, Claudios Legitumos, Caelios Pelignos, Claudios Pelignos, Marcios Victorinos, Asiaticos son of Aθθedillos."[11]

I have now tentatively identified two further examples of such a construction in Gaulish, which, aside from their inherent interest, may provide some evidence for the investigation of the development of the order of constituents in the early Celtic sentence from the strict SOV order of Hispano-Celtic to the fundamental SVO order of Gaulish to the basic VSO order of Insular Celtic.

§2. The Bilingual Inscription of Vercelli

In May 1966 a Latin–Gaulish bilingual inscription was discovered near the town of Vercelli in northern Italy.[12] The Latin text reads,

FINIS CAMPO QVEM DEDIT ACISIVS ARGANTOCOMATERECVS COMVNEM DEIS ET HOMINIBVS ITA VTI LAPIDES IIII STATVTI SVNT[13] "[This is] the boundary for the field that Acisius Argantocomaterecus gave to gods and man in common; thus four stones are placed (here)."

The Gaulish text, written in the Lugano script (on which see Lejeune 1977, 594–97) and meant to translate the Latin text (more or less), reads,

aKisios arKaToKo⟨K⟩maTereKos TosoKoTẹ ạTos TeuoχTonion eu.[14]

The most convincing interpretation of the Gaulish text offered among the primary treatments is that of Lejeune (1977, 600) who, though he does not offer an interpretation for the verb, renders: "A. A. institutit fines deorum-et-hominum ex uoto."[15] Koch (1983, 187–88) has now offered an interpretation of the Gaulish verb as a direct translation of Lat. *dedit*, suggesting that we have a formation *to-kon-de* 'has given' and comparing the Old Irish (*to-ro-ad-d-*) and Brittonic (*to-ro-d-*) formations. This is very probably correct, with *ko(n)-* either serving as a perfective augment, or with the reduplication characteristic of the perfect suppressed due to the presence of two preverbs (cf. Thurneysen 1946, 431 §694 [b]); cf. Gaul. δεδε

(Narbonensis) < *de-dh$_3$-e[16] and Lep. *TeTu* (Prestino) < *de-dh$_3$-u. As for the morpheme *śo*-, Koch (1983, 188-89) regards it, rightly I think, as an infixed pronoun, and offers the following remarks:

> In the present interpretation, an acc. N(oun) obj. co-occurs with an infixed pron. Since the latter precedes the former, a resumptive strategy is ruled out. Possibly, ŠO(N)/ŠO(Š) like Lat. *ille* and, for that matter, like Gaul. *sosin*[17] . . . could be either an independent or dependent demonstrative. Where dependent, it would have to cliticise to some word other than its head N(oun) (itself phonologically empty). Here, though the head is expressed, ŠO(-) is infixed as a sentential clitic detached from its N(oun) P(hrase). Perhaps such "tmesis" was the regular old construction, or the coreferent N(oun) P(hrase) may figure as a "marked" afterthought. Less probably, SO(-) might be a relative here, (cf. the OIr. nasalising rel. ptc. *sa*"), so that TO-ŠO·KOTE would mean exactly "quem dedit." . . . the obj. pron. shuns the S(entence)-initial element and is enclitic to an element of the internal verbal complex, thus disobeying W(ackernagel's) L(aw).

He translates, "Akisios Argantokomaterekos has given these boundaries for [*lit.* of] gods and men."

The treatment of the pronoun *śo*-[18] as either dependent or relative seems unlikely to me. One may note that a demonstrative is not to be found in the Latin text, and that the constituent order of the Gaulish text, with *śo*- appearing before *aTos*́, does not support a relative interpretation. Instead, I prefer to understand it as proleptic in function, which is more in accordance with Insular Celtic facts. I would also disagree with Koch on a further point and assert that Wackernagel's Law has not been disobeyed. The subject is to be interpreted as a *nominativus pendens*, fronted to emphasize the donor's name.[19] Indeed, because the semantically empty preverb *to*- is in origin a sentence connective, it is syntactically impossible to interpret *To-śo·KoTe* as occupying any but sentence-initial position (at the deep-structure level). A literal translation of the inscription would then be, "Acisios Argantocomatereco, he gave them, boundaries[20] of gods and men."

§3. A Graffito from La Graufesenque

On the side of one of the Gaulish production lists found at La Graufesenque is the following inscription:

sioχti albanos panna extratuθ ccc.[21]

The only detailed interpretation undertaken is that by Thurneysen (1927, 302), who believed that the inscription means "Entweder 'Albanos hat ausser den *tuθθos* (noch) 300 *pannas* geliefert' oder 'übernommen' oder 'zur Verfertigung, als Pensum erhalten,' oder auch präsentisch 'übernimmt' usw., je nachdem man an Lieferungs-Listen . . . oder an Verteilungs-Listen denkt."[22] He rightly identified *sioχti* as the verb and noted that every Celticist would immediately think to OIr. *siächt*, the preterite of *saigid* 'seeks, makes for'. After a comparison of the two forms, however, he concluded that "die lautliche Ähnlichkeit von *sioχti* und *siacht* wird . . . trügerisch sein" (303). Since that time Meid (1963, 80) has commented that the "auslautende -*i* ist zweifellos identisch mit dem *i* der Primärendung," which is in accordance with Koch's new prosodic theory on the development of the early Celtic verbal complex.[23]

But I am not yet convinced that *sioχti* and *siächt* are not to be connected in some way. *Siächt* has an aberrant history: originally a perfect form, it was remade into a *t*-preterite; see Watkins (1962, 167). From all appearances, it is likely that *sioχti* also has an aberrant, but not necessarily identical, history.[24]

Whatever the verb means, nevertheless, the context—that of keeping accounts—seems fairly clearly to call for the preterite tense. Therefore, I view *sioχti*, whatever its origin, as a 3. sg. asigmatic aorist in form, which requires a secondary verbal desinence. I understand the remaining -*i* to be the neuter nom.-acc. sg. pronoun *id*, which is well attested in the inscription from Chamalières, here in a proleptic function, and which has dropped its -*d*.[25] Because the neuter proleptic pronoun -*i* anticipates the masc. acc. sg. *tuθ(θon)*, we must have a case of a neuter proleptic pronoun anticipating a substantive of another gender, as is sometimes found in Old Irish (see §1 above). This leads me tentatively to translate the La Graufesenque inscription literally as "Albanos supplied(?) it, an additional lot, [i.e.,] 300 vessels."

§4. Synthesis

Sims-Williams (1984, 176) has argued that the proleptic pronouns found in Insular Celtic are not simply redundant, but serve to reinforce the definiteness of the following object. In view of the examples that are found in Insular Celtic and the contexts of the three that appear to exist in Gaulish, there would seem to be much to recommend such an explanation. It is possible, then, that the proleptic construction originally arose (in part) to mark this semantic reinforcement. But more important still are its syntactic implications.

It appears from the inscription *buscilla-sosio legasit in alixie magalu* (Séracourt à Bourges) "Buscilla placed this in Alisia for Magalos" that Vendryes' Restriction (1911–12 [as modified by Dillon 1943]), which limited object pronouns to position after the first preverb of compound verbs, after particles, and after simple verbs in Insular Celtic, was not fully operational in Gaulish.[26] But it is clear from Koch's recent survey of the syntax and constituent order of the Gaulish sentence (1983) that there was a strong tendency for a direct object to be closely bound to its governing verb. That is, it generally follows immediately after the verb. It is legitimate to conclude, therefore, that *To-śo·KoTe*, with infixed object pronoun, and *sioχt-i*, with suffixed object pronoun, have been drawn to sentence-initial position by the presence of those pronouns and by the necessity for them to comply with Wackernagel's Law.[27] Had they not been present, the constituent orders **To- aKisios arKaToKomaTereKos -KoTe* . . . and *albanos sioχt . . . would have emerged at Vercelli and La Graufesenque, respectively.

§5. Coda

The syntactic mechanism whereby the presence of a proleptic object pronoun brings about the fronting of the verb to sentence-initial position has been invoked by Sims-Williams (1984, esp. 174–80) to account for the development of absolute verbal desinences and the basic sentence-initial position of the verb in Insular Celtic. He proposes that proleptic constructions as seen in the Gaulish sentences discussed in the present paper proliferated throughout the verbal system, thus drawing the verb to sentence-initial position due to the constraints of Vendryes' Restriction, and also, in simple verbs, providing protection from apocope of primary *-i by the presence of suffixed pronouns. These proleptic pronouns, when not serving in any reinforcing or adverbial capacity, were later deleted (in the third person, at least). While I would not want to exclude the possibility that the proleptic construction played a role in the development of basic VSO order in Insular Celtic, it does seem that a theory that postulates the proliferation and subsequent deletion of a morphological entity for which there is very little direct evidence in Celtic[28] is in conflict with William of Ockham's maxim that *entia non sunt multiplicanda praeter necessitatem*. Inasmuch as the Gaulish proleptic constructions that have been tentatively identified can be construed as having a reinforcing character, I am given not to regard this function as secondary. Until further evidence is produced, it is prudent to conclude no more than that proleptic object pronouns may well have played a role in the development of basic sentence-initial verbal position and absolute verbal flexion in Insular Celtic; but not, I think, to the degree that Sims-Williams has suggested.[29]

JOSEPH F. ESKA
Rutgers University

NOTES

1. See Thurneysen 1946, 266 §421; and D. Simon Evans 1964, 56–57 §60, from which most of the following examples have been drawn.
2. Ml. 123c3, in Stokes and Strachan 1901, 418.
3. Wb. 4c20, in Stokes and Strachan 1901, 521.
4. Wb. 12a7, in Stokes and Strachan 1901, 571.
5. *Canu Aneirin*, gol. Williams 1938, 5.98.
6. *Buched Dewi*, gol. D. Simon Evans 1959, 21.13.
7. *Breudwyt Ronabwy*, gol. Richards 1948, 4.29.
8. *Togail Bruidne Da Derga*, ed. Knott 1936, 37.1232–33.
9. Wb. 15a34, in Stokes and Strachan 1901, 600.
10. The interpretation of the gen. pl. substantive *anderon* has been the subject of much discussion. But in view of the recent remarks of Lejeune 1985, 87, it seems more likely that *andero-* refers to 'underworld spirits' rather than 'young women'. For an opposing view see Fleuriot 1987, 201–2. One may also note that in the inscription from Larzac, *andernados brictom* (1a9) is now found beside *bnaṇom bricto[m]* (1a1) 'the magic of women'.
11. For a different interpretation of this passage, see Lambert 1987, 14–15.
12. Relevant bibliography: Tibiletti Bruno 1976; Lejeune 1977; Pisani 1979; Koch 1983, 187–89. See now also Meid 1989, 7–16.

13. The readings of Tibiletti Bruno and Lejeune differ in some details. I print a composite text. (This reading has now been confirmed by the personal inspection of Meid 1989, 8-9.)
14. As note 13. The angled brackets indicate a superfluous character. (This reading has now been confirmed by the personal inspection of Meid 1989, 9-12.)
15. Tibiletti Bruno, in the end, does not offer a final opinion on the meaning of the verb and even speculates that the form may be substantival. The suggestion of Pisani (1979, 50-51) that the base is a delabialised variant of *sek^w- 'speak, say' and that the meaning of the verb is 'indicit' or 'indixit' is ad hoc and unconvincing and, as had already been noticed by Tibiletti Bruno (1976, 360), does not show the appropriate grade of the thematic vowel. (Meid 1989, 14-16, is unsure whether to treat *To-śo·KoTe* as a verbal or a nominal form. He tentatively translates the inscription "Akisios Argantoko(m)materekos hat dieses (durch die Grenzsteine markierte) Gebiet für einen Hain der Götter und Menschen gewidmet" or ". . . hat diese Grenzsteine für einen Hain der Götter und Menschen gestiftet." I intend to address his objections [36] to the analysis presented in this paper elsewhere.)
16. With noncolouration by the laryngeal across a strong morpheme boundary.
17. In the inscription APR[ONIOS] IEV[RV S]O[SIN] ESVM[ARV] (Lezoux [Puy-de-Dôme]). But see note 19.
18. Probably standing for /sōs/ < *sons*, as attested at Chamalières (cited in §1 above). Compare the treatment of the stem vowel in *aToś* /antōs/ < *antons < *h_2ent- 'front, brow'.
19. As is perhaps also found in the inscription APR[ONIOS] IEV[RV-S]O[SIN] ESVM[ARV] (Lezoux [Puy-de-Dôme]) "Apronios, he dedicated this to Esumaros," if it is properly so restored. A further example might also be attested in the inscription *vercobretos readdas* (Argentomagus [Argenton-sur-Creuse]), concerning which Sims-Williams (1984, 190[22]) suggests that *re-* might be understood as *pro + *ed and the inscription translated as "Vercobretos, he has shaped(?) it," with *vercobretos* in the *nominativus pendens* position. Koch 1983, 204, notes that IE *d in auslaut is retained in a number of Gaulish neuter nom.-acc. sg. pronouns; but one may also note that it has fallen in the Gaulish future imperative desinence *-(n)tutu(s)* < *-(n)tōttōd* (+ *-s) attested at Larzac (I discuss this desinence in a paper to appear in *Die Sprache*). Sims-Williams's proposal, therefore, remains tenable. Fleuriot 1981, 97-98, however, has called attention to early examples of apparently reduced forms of *ro-* that appear as *re-*.

I would, however, disagree with Sims-Williams's tentative translation of the verb as 'shaped' and his comparison with OIr. *ásaid* 'grows'. One would expect a verb of such meaning to be formed on the base *$\acute{g}enh_1$- 'produce' (cf. OIr. *do·gní*) or *werǵ- 'do, make' (cf. MW *gwneuthur*; that the base originally had an -r- is evident from the residual 1. sg. pret. *gwreith* [*Canu Aneirin* 44.1102]). The ritual archaeological context described by Fleuriot (93-95) lends support to his proposal that the verb is formed on the base *h_2es- 'burn, glow' with a *d*-enlargement; one may compare Gk. ἄζα 'heat, dryness; dry sediment' < *h_2es-d- and, without the enlargement, Lat. *āra* 'altar', which is significant for its semantics. Then *-dd-* would be a digraph representing the development of *-s- plus dental to the *tau gallicum* phoneme, on which see D. Ellis Evans 1967, 410-20; *addas*, then, may be interpreted as an athematic s-aorist factitive in *-ā-* (< *-e-h_2-) and represent /aˈsās(s)/ < *aˈsāst. It would mean 'made burnt', i.e., 'sacrificed'. When we further learn from Caesar, *Gallic War* 1.16, that *vergobretos* is a Gaulish title ("convocatis eorum principibus . . . in his Diviciaco et Lisco, qui summa magistratui praeerat, quem Vergobretum appellant Aedui, qui creatur annuus et vitae necisque in suos habet potestatem" ["(Caesar) called together the (Aeduan) leaders. . . . Among them were Diviciacus, and Liscus, too. He held the highest office, which the Aedui call Vergobretus; he is elected annually, and has the power of life and death over his countrymen."]), it becomes all the more probable that the inscription means "the *vergobretos* sacrificed (it)," or, with infixed object pronoun and *nominativus pendens*, "the *vergobretos*, he sacrificed it." On *vergobretos*, see further the references listed by Holder 1907, 213–14; and Fleuriot 1984, esp. 38–40.

In a paper recently delivered at a joint meeting of the Celtic Studies Association of North America and the California Celtic Colloquium (Los Angeles, 7–10 April 1988), Wolfgang Meid has suggested that *readdas* may be analysed as *ro-* (> *re-* by reduction) + *ad-* prefixed to the base $*deh_3$- 'give' (> Celt. $*dā$-). In view of the Old Irish formation cited in §2 above, Meid's proposal seems quite alluring, and it certainly is worthy of serious consideration. The inscription would then be translated as "the *vergobretos* gave (it)" or, perhaps better in light of the archaeological context, "the *vergobretos* offered (it)."

20. In view of the syntagm FINIS CAMPO in the Latin text, it is worth considering whether Gaul. *aTos̀* should be translated as 'lands'; Lat. *finis* can have the same meaning in the plural, as can OIr. *crích*.
21. Hermet 1923, no. 22; Whatmough 1970, no. 114.
22. One may also take note of the translation of Koch 1985, 3: "Albanos supplied a lot of 300 vessels"(?).
23. Koch 1987, 161–62 argues that simple verbs in sentence-initial position, whether or not an enclitic was present, had oxytone accentuation, and that, therefore, primary *-i* was not apocopated in such forms at an early date in Celtic, as suggested by Cowgill 1975, 56–58, and since generally accepted. Koch (163) believes that this is actually attested by sentence-initial *sioχti*, but see my subsequent arguments for a different interpretation of this form. I would also view as misplaced his belief (163[23]) that the Hispano-Celtic compound verbal forms *ueŕsoniTi, amPiTiśeTi*, and *ŕo-PiśeTi* from Botorrita probably indicate that apocope of primary *-i* was not a Common Celtic innovation due to the consistent *i*-colour of the final syllabic character, regardless of the preceding vowel. Graphemic vowel harmonisation of dead vowels in the semisyllabic Iberian script is always progressive, never regressive. Thus, for example, in *ConśCiliTom* /konsklitom/ (Botorrita A3) the first *-i-* is a dead vowel whose colour anticipates that of the next etymological vowel; /konsklitom/ would never be spelled **ConśColiTom*. This means, of course, that it is improbable that we will ever know whether the Hispano-Celtic verbal forms in *-Ti* represent -/ti/ or -/t/. We may note, however, that the only Hispano-Celtic verbal form written in Latin characters that may be relevant to the question, namely, *sistat* (Peñalba de Villastar), which I understand as probably continuing $*si-sth_2-ti$, shows the apocope of primary *-i*. This form, though, may be two hundred years younger than those in the Botorrita text. On *sistat* see, in the last place, Ködderitzsch 1985, 218–19, with wider bibliography.
24. I hope to discuss this form at greater length in a future study on the preterite in Continental Celtic.

25. Instead of masc. acc. sg. *in, which would agree in gender with tuθ(θon), for n in auslaut seems to be preserved in the language of La Graufesenque. A less likely alternative is that -i represents the neuter nom.-acc. pl. pronoun *ī (< *i-h₂) and anticipates the fem. acc. pl. *panna(s)*.
26. I am sceptical that *sosio* in this inscription is to be interpreted as an independent pronoun, and therefore as evidence for the existence of SOV order in Gaulish. It is true, however, that *sosio* as an enclitic would be expected to generate the constituent order *legasit-sosio buscilla* . . . or, with *buscilla* in *nominativus pendens* position, *buscilla legasit-sosio*. . . .
27. We must recognise that the deep-structure of the Vercelli inscription, with subject in *nominativus pendens* position at surface-level, is *To-śo·KoTe aKisios arKa-ToKomaTereKos* . . . ; and that there is no apparent motivation for the sentence-initial position of the verb in the La Graufesenque graffito if -i is not a suffixed pronoun.
28. Though, as Sims-Williams demonstrates, there are parallels in other languages.
29. I should like to thank Harry Roe for reading an early version of this paper and suggesting some improvements. Patrick Sims-Williams also read a version of this paper, and I am grateful to him for his comments. Responsibility for the argument, of course, lies with me.

REFERENCES

Cowgill, Warren. 1975. The Origins of the Insular Celtic Conjunct and Absolute Verbal Endings. In *Flexion und Wortbildung*, Akten der V. Fachtagung der Indogermanischen Gesellschaft (Regensburg, 9–14. September 1973), ed. Helmut Rix, 40–70. Wiesbaden: Dr. Ludwig Reichert.

Dillon, Myles. 1943. On the Structure of the Celtic Verb. *Language* 19: 252–55.

Evans, D. Ellis. 1967. *Gaulish Personal Names: A Study of Some Continental Celtic Formations*. Oxford: Clarendon Press.

Evans, D. Simon, gol. 1959. *Buched Dewi*. Caerdydd: Gwasg Prifysgol Cymru.

———. 1964. *A Grammar of Middle Welsh*. Dublin: Dublin Institute for Advanced Studies.

Fleuriot, Léon. 1981. A propos de deux inscriptions gauloises, formes verbales celtiques. *Études celtiques* 18: 89–108.

———. 1984. Noms propres ou noms de fonctions sur quelques monnaies celtiques. In *Keltische Numismatik und Archaeologie/Numismatique celtique et archéologie*, part 1. Veröffentlichung der Referate des Kolloquiums Keltische Numismatik vom 4. bis 8. Februar 1981 in Würzburg, ed. G. Grasmann, W. Janssen, and M. Brandt, 34–42. Oxford: British Archaeological Reports.

———. 1987. Brittonica et gallica. 28. Gaulois BNANOM BRICTOM 'magie des femmes', BRIXTIA ANDERON 'magie des jeunes femmes', irlandais moyen BRICHTA BAN 'magie des femmes', vieux-breton BRITH 'magie', gallois moyen LLED-FRITH 'magie', BRITH-RON 'baguette de magie'. *Études celtiques* 24: 201–2.

Hermet, Frédéric. 1923. *Les graffites de la Graufesenque près Millau (Aveyron)*. Rodez: Carrère.

Holder, Alfred. 1907. *Alt-Celtischer Sprachschatz*, vol. 3. Leipzig: B. G. Teubner.

Knott, Eleanor, ed. 1936. *Togail Bruidne Da Derga*. Dublin: Dublin Institute for Advanced Studies.
Koch, John T. 1983. The Sentence in Gaulish. *Proceedings of the Harvard Celtic Colloquium* 3: 169–215.
———. 1985. Emphasis and Movement in the Gaulish Sentence. *Bulletin of the Board of Celtic Studies* 32: 1–37.
———. 1987. Prosody and the Old Celtic Verbal Complex. *Ériu* 38: 143–76.
Ködderitzsch, Rolf. 1985. Die große Felsinschrift von Peñalba de Villastar. In *Sprachwissenschaftliche Forschungen. Festschrift für Johann Knobloch zum 65. Geburtstag am 5. Januar 1984 dargebracht von Freunden und Kollegen*. Innsbrucker Beiträge zur Kulturwissenschaft 23, ed. Hermann M. Ölberg and Gernot Schmidt with the cooperation of Heinz Bothien, 211–22. Innsbruck: AMŒ.
Lambert, Pierre-Yves. 1987. A Restatement on the Gaulish Tablet of Chamalières. *Bulletin of the Board of Celtic Studies* 34: 10–17.
Lejeune, Michel. 1977. Une bilingue gauloise-latine à Verceil. *Comptes rendus de l'Académie des Inscriptions et Belles-Lettres* 582–610.
———. 1985. Notes d'étymologie gauloise. IX. Gaulois *VXEDIOS*. *Études celtiques* 22: 81–87.
Meid, Wolfgang. 1963. *Die indogermanischen Grundlagen der altirischen absoluten und konjunkten Verbalflexion*. Wiesbaden: Otto Harrassowitz.
———. 1989. *Zur Lesung und Deutung gallischer Inschriften*. Innsbrucker Beiträge zur Sprachwissenschaft: Vorträge und kleinere Schriften 40. Innsbruck: Institut für Sprachwissenschaft der Universität Innsbruck.
Pisani, Vittore. 1979. La Bilingue di Vercelli. *Die Sprache* 25: 49–53.
Richards, Melville, gol. 1948. *Breudwyt Ronabwy*. Caerdydd: Gwasg Prifysgol Cymru.
Sims-Williams, Patrick. 1984. The Double System of Verbal Inflexion in Old Irish. *Transactions of the Philological Society* 138–201.
Stokes, Whitley and John Strachan, ed. 1901. *Thesaurus Palaeohibernicus*, vol. 1. Cambridge: Cambridge University Press.
Thurneysen, Rudolf. 1927. Zu den Graffiti von La Graufesenque. *Zeitschrift für celtische Philologie* 16: 285–304.
———. 1946. *A Grammar of Old Irish*. Dublin: Dublin Institute for Advanced Studies.
Tibiletti Bruno, Maria Grazia. 1976. La nuova iscrizione epicorica di Vercelli. *Atti della Accademia Nazionale dei Lincei, Rendiconti di scienze morali, storiche e filologiche*, 8th ser. 31: 355–76.
Vendryes, Joseph. 1911–12. La place du verbe en celtique. *Mémoires de la Société de Linguistique de Paris* 17: 337–51.
Watkins, Calvert. 1962. *Indo-European Origins of the Celtic Verb*, vol. 1: *The Sigmatic Aorist*. Dublin: Dublin Institute for Advanced Studies.
Whatmough, Joshua. 1970. *The Dialects of Ancient Gaul*. Cambridge, Mass.: Harvard University Press.
Williams, Ifor, gol. 1938. *Canu Aneirin*. Caerdydd: Gwasg Prifysgol Cymru.

Celtiberi: A Note

The literature on the history and language of the Celtiberians has been extensive, both before Botorrita and certainly since. As a label for the "particularly archaic Celtic language"[1] of Spain, the ethnic term is so convenient as to let us forget that it has a history of its own. While the Celtiberians had generally been seen as Celts who had migrated into Iberian territory, A. Schulten wanted them to be Iberians who had penetrated from the east coast into Celtic lands. Certainty, it used to be said, was not to be had.[2]

Insofar as this was a question of how to interpret the term it is extraordinary that scholars should have felt so free to deal with it a priori. The designation is after all Greek, and we ought to ask first of all what its Greek originators could have meant by it, given the word-formation rules of their language. Even if no definitive answer were possible, it would still have been a gain to realize that this is where the problem begins.[3]

Ethnic names have an old affinity for compounding. It is a significant affinity inasmuch as the compounds in question are of a type which, however much it strikes a modern speaker as ordinary, was quite restricted and somewhat secondary in archaic Indo-European, including Greek: they are not exocentric like, for instance, the many possessive compounds of the bahuvrīhi (he who *has* much rice) sort but simply determinative, with the first part narrowing down the second (tatpuruṣa and karmadhāraya). In Homer there are three instructive examples: Πανέλληνες 'all of the Hellenes (in the wider sense)', Παναχαιοί 'all of the Achaeans (in the wider sense)', and Ἐτεόκρητες 'true (that is, original) Cretans'.[4] The three names, Ἕλληνες, Ἀχαιοί, and Κρῆτες, share the common feature that they are ambiguous in a characteristic way. The first two have, or once had, both a narrower meaning, designating a tribe, and a wider one, 'Greeks, Achaeans (in the Homeric sense)'. The third will normally refer to ordinary, in other words, Hellenic Cretans; when the autochthones are meant, this needs to be specified. It is under these special circumstances that the unusual compound formation is resorted to—even, despite its technical flavor, in epic poetry.[5]

The Homeric words are probably to be classified as karmadhārayas with attributive adjectives as first members.[6] Later there emerges in Greek word-formation the type that Ernst Risch has called *Mischungskomposita*.[7] These fall mostly into small semantic groups that suggest manipulated subvocabularies, including names for fantastic animals (τραγέλαφος) and indeed for somehow "mixed" populations: Ἑλληνομεμφῖται (*PSI*, third century B.C.), Ἑλληνογαλάται (Diodorus), Κελτοσκύθαι, Κελτολίγυες (Strabo). The Κελτίβηρες (Strabo, Catullus) belong here as well.[8]

"Mixture" is at best a noncommittal term; we can rarely know what the realities behind each of these ethnic compounds were, and the same was no doubt already true to some extent in antiquity.[9] Only in one case has a lucky accident left us with a clue: Λιβυφοίνικες (Polybius) forms a pair with Συροφοῖνιξ (Lucan; Juvenal; Συροφοίνισσα [*NT*]), the former referring to the Carthaginians, the latter to the eastern Phoenicians. This looks like a repetition of Πανέλληνες or Παναχαιοί, if by different formal means and with a different (namely, a geographic) content: Φοῖνιξ too, is ambiguous in referring to two populations and may, therefore, need tatpuruṣa compounding for precision. If the name of the Κελτίβηρες had an analogous origin we may understand it as 'Iberians (or inhabitants of Spain) (of the particular kind) that are (really) Celts' or the like. This does not exactly present us with a full historical canvas. It merely indicates what a concrete history ought to be compatible with.[10] Also, it concerns only the terminological distinction itself and not its foundation in ethnographic fact. That foundation was of course entirely different in the case of the two kinds of Phoenicians on the one hand and in that of the Celtiberians and the remaining Iberians on the other.[11]

HENRY M. HOENIGSWALD

University of Pennsylvania

NOTES

1. Schmidt 1987, 112-14. See also Schmidt 1979, 101.
2. Koch 1979, 400[5] alludes to oral discussion by R. Nierhaus and J. Untermann at the Tübingen session ("bleiben zu prüfen").
3. As late as Grosse 1975, 1103.
4. All is not clear in post-Homeric usage. I am greatly obliged to M. H. Jameson

for giving me the benefit of his discussion of the Ἐτεοβουτάδαι as well as the Ἐτεοκαρπάθιοι.
5. Hoenigswald 1940, 1977.
6. In certain other παν-compounds, παν- is the adverbial neuter as in πάμπαν 'altogether'. See also Leumann 1950, 101-5.
7. Risch 1981, 57.
8. The recurrence, in our material, of the same stems (the Celts, the Scythians [though Ἰνδοσκυθία refers to the Indus River; see note 10 on the Ebro]) may well be a reflection of bits of ethno-historiographical jargon in specific contexts. See also Koch 1979, 397. On Lt. *Celtiberi, Celtiberes*, see Kroll 1959, 74.
9. See next note.
10. Koch 1979, 389 (with discussion of the older literature) believes that the term is simply meant to contrast Hispano-Celts with the Gaulish Celts. But, as pointed out above, this is only indirectly the case; Greek compounds are not built that way. Half correct is Koch's formulation (1979, 401), "*Celtiberi* ist möglicherweise zunächst als allgemeine Unterscheidung von Nichtkelten Hispaniens und[!] Kelten Galliens gedacht, sehr bald aber, wenn nicht ausschließlich, eine regionale Fixierung [*sic*]." And he is certainly right in saying that ancient attempts at interpreting the term, such as Strabo's (1.2.27), are etiological constructions, only that this (*pace* Koch 1979, 389) also goes for Isidore, for whom *(H)iber(o)-* is primarily the name of the river (Sp. *Ebro*, with Greek accentuation [Meyer-Lübke 1890 (1972), 498]), not of the country and any of its inhabitants; hence, quite naturally (*Etymologiae* 9.2.114), *nam ex flumine Hispaniae Ibero ubi considerunt et ex Gallis . . . Celtiberi nuncupati sunt*.
11. Of course none of this has anything to do with the Iberians of the Caucasus, on whom see Schmidt 1979.

REFERENCES

G[rosse], R[obert]. 1975. Celtiberi. In *Der kleine Pauli* 1102-3. Munich: Deutscher Taschenbuch Verlag.
Hoenigswald, Henry M. 1940. Παν-Compounds in Early Greek. *Language* 16: 183-87.
———. 1977. Diminutives and Tatpuruṣas: The Indo-European Trend Toward Endocentricity. *Journal of Indo-European Studies* 5: 9-13.
Koch, Michael. 1979. Die Keltiberer und ihr historischer Kontext. *Acta Salmanticensia, Filosofia y Letras* 113: 387-419.
Kroll, Wilhelm, ed. 1959. *C. Valerius Catullus³*. Stuttgart: B. G. Teubner.
Leumann, Manu. 1950. *Homerische Worter*. Basel: Verlag Friedrich Reinhardt.
Meyer-Lübke, Wilhelm. 1890. (Reprinted 1972.) *Grammatik der Romanischen Sprachen*, 1, *Romanische Lautlehre*. Leipzig: Fues' Verlag (B. Reisland); reprinted Darmstadt: Wissenschaftliche Buchgesellschaft.
Risch, Ernst. 1981 (repr.). Griechische Determinativkomposita. In *Kleine Schriften*, 1-111. Berlin, New York: Walter de Gruyter.
Schmidt, Karl Horst. 1979. Probleme des Keltiberischen. *Acta Salmanticensia, Filosofia y Letras* 113: 101-15.
———. 1987. Die beiden antiken Iberiae, sprachwissenschaftlich gesehen. *Zeitschrift für vergleichende Sprachforschung* 100: 109-34.

Zum plomb du Larzac

Der *plomb du Larzac* wurde 1983 in der Nekropole einer galloromanischen Siedlung aus dem 1.-5. Jh. entdeckt. Fundstelle der in lateinischer Kursive geschriebenen Inschrift (Is.) von ca. 1000 Buchstaben in über 160 Wörtern ist ein La Vayssière genannter Ort, nördlich der Gemeinde l'Hospitalet-du-Larzac (Aveyron, arr^t de Millau, Canton de Nant), 15 Kilometer südlich von *La Graufesenque* im Gebiet der *Ruteni* an der Straße von *Luteva* (Lodève) nach *Condatomagus* (Millau) gelegen. Der Text der Is. befindet sich auf einer doppelseitig beschriebenen Bleitafel, die eine *urne cinéraire* abschließt und in zwei Stücke zerbrochen ist. Aus dieser Überlieferungssituation ergeben sich vier Textstücke (1a, 2a, 1b, 2b), deren Verhältnis zueinander ungeklärt ist; die Zeilen 2b 1-6 wurden von einem zweiten Schreiber hinzugefügt. Sektor 1a, dessen Vokabular z. T. durch 2a, 1b, 2b bestätigt wird besteht aus dem Einleitungstext (1-9) und dem Katalog weiblicher Namen (9-16). Der Text läßt sich weiter unterteilen in die Einleitungsformel (1-4) und eine zu den Namen überleitende Anweisung (4-9).

Unter M. Lejeunes Federführung erfolgte 1985 eine kollektive Bearbeitung der Is., an der sich außer Lejeune u. a. Fleuriot(†), Lambert, Marichal und Vernhet beteiligten.[1]

Der Text gehört in den Bereich der *defixiones*, wie bereits bei oberflächlicher Betrachtung aus einer Reihe von Schlüsselwörtern hervorgeht: *brictom* (1a 1, 1a 9), *brictas* (1b 7); *anuana sananderna* (1a 2-3), *andernados brictom* (1a 9) vs. *in das mnas ueronadas brictas* (1b 6-7); Ableitungen von den keltischen Verbalwurzeln *sag-*:[2] *adsagsona* 1a 4, *sagitiontias* 2a 8-9 (Nom. Pl. fem.), 2b 10 (Akk. Pl. fem.), **adsaxs(o)na* 2b 8; **(s)teig-* 'stechen':[3] *tigontias* 1a 4 (Gen. Sg. fem.), *ni-tixsintor* 1a 7, 2a 4-5; **u̯eid-/u̯oid-* 'wissen': *uidluias uidlu̯[a] tigontias* 1a 3-4. Lejeune et al. 1985, 122f. vermutet, daß sich in der durch Bruch und Durchbohrung willkürlich beschädigten Urne als 'tablette de malédiction' die Überreste einer Zauberin *Gemma* befunden haben und daß die Is. 'une manifestation de magie féminine' darstellt: "Des femmes ont mis en branle des maléfices, et le texte vise à en retourner l'éffet contre elles. Il s'agit donc d'une démarche de contre-magie" (30). Fleuriot 1985, 139 sieht in dem Text einen Kontrast zu Chamalières:[4] "S'il est question de magie dans les deux cas, il est à peine besoin de rappeler que la magie a deux aspects principaux: elle protège l'invocateur ou attaque ses ennemis: la tablette de Chamalières est du premier type; celle du Larzac, on va le voir, du second."

Die folgende Besprechung konzentriert sich auf den Sektor 1a; 2a, 1b, 2b werden lediglich zur Ergänzung herangezogen. Aus Raumgründen können Syntax, Grammatik und Etymologie nur auszugsweise kommentiert werden. Dies geschieht vornehmlich dann, wenn ich von Lejeune, Fleuriot und Lambert abweiche.

1. Text 1a

```
1  in      sinde    se       bnanom[5]   bricto[m]
   gegen   diesen   dieser   Frauen      Zauber

2  [i]n    eianom   anuana   sana            ander̯-
   gegen   deren    Namen    die (Akk. Pl.)  unterwelt-

3  na (Akk. Pl.)[6]   brictom   uidluias          uidlu[a]
   lichen (der)       Zauber    der Vidluia       Magien (Akk. Pl.)

4  tigontias              so[7]   adsagsona              seuę [rim]
   (der) stechenden (ist) dies.   Die Gegenwirkende      Severa
                                  (Nom. Sg.)             (Akk.)

5  tertionicnim           lidssatim          liciatim
   (und) Tertionicna (Akk.) lidssata (Attr.) liciata (Attr.)[8]

6  eianom[9]  uo-duno-derce[10]              lunget-
   deren      unter-(Grab)hügel-Öffnung      sie-soll-le-

7  [ut]u    ton-id       ponc     nitixsintor   si[es]
   gen,     außerdem,    wenn     zaubern       diese

8  dus-celinatia                  in       eanon    anuan̯[a][11]
   mit-bösem-Vorzeichen,          gegen    deren    Namen (Akk. Pl.)

9  esi   andernados         brictom   bano[na]
   ist   (der)Unterwelt     Zauber.   Banona

10 flatucias                     paulla   dona potiti[us]
   (Tochter) der Vlatucia;       Paulla,  Frau des Potitus;
```

11 aiai[12]   duxtir   adiegias   poti̯[ta
   Aiai,   Tochter der   Adiega;   Potita,

12 m]atir   paullias   seuera   du[xtir]
   Muter.   der Paulla;   Severa, Tochter

13 ualentos   doṇa   paulli[i]uṣ
   des Valens, Frau   des Paullus;

14 adiega   matir   aiias[13]
   Adiega,   Mutter der Aiia;

15 potita   dona   prim[ius   duxtir]
   Potita,   Frau des   Primus,   Tochter

16 abesias.
   der Abesa.

Als Übersetzung ergibt sich demnach:[14]

> Gegen diesen Zauber dieser Frauen, gegen deren (*eianom*) unterweltliche Namen[15] [ist] dies (*so*) der Zauber der Magien/ Zaubereien (uidlu[a] = Akk. Pl.) stechenden (*tigontias*) Vidluia (Gen. Sg.).[16] Die Gegenwirkende (*adsagsona*) soll legen/halten Severa und Tertionicna, die *lidssata* und *liciata* sind,[17] unter ihrem (*eianom* 'deren') Grabdeckel. Außerdem, wenn (*ponc*) sie (*si[es]* 'diese', bezogen auf die Namen von 9–16) mit bösen Vorzeichen zaubern, ist gegen dieser [folgenden] (sc. Zauberinnen) Namen (*in eanon anuan[a]*) der Zauber der Unterwelt: Banona, (Tochter) der Vlatucia; Paulla, Frau des Potitus; Aiia, Tochter der Adiega; Potita, (Mutter) der Paulla; Severa, Tochter des Valens (und) Frau des Paullus; Adiega, Mutter der Aiia; Potita, Frau des Primus [und Tochter] der Abesa.

2. Analyse von 1a

I. *Syntax. Basic Word Order* (BWO) SOV wird attributiv und prädikativ bestätigt: *attributiv* durch die (vermutlich alten Formeln *se bnanom bricto[m]* (1a 1), *eianom uo-duno-derce* (1a 6), *eianom anuana* 1a 2; 1a 8), *andernados brictom* (1a 9); Vgl. außerdem *se mnanom sagitiontias* (2a 8–9), *se mnanom *adsaxs(o)na* (2b 7–8);[18] *prädikativ* durch *adsagsona tertionicnim lidssatim eianom uo-dunoderce lunget[ut]u* (1a 4–7); vgl. außerdem *ne incitas biontutu* (1b 6), *ne incitas biontutuṣ* (1b 11); *eian nepi andigi ne lisatim ne liciatim ne rodatim biontutu* (2a 5-8); *semnanom sagitiontias seuerim lissatim liciatim anandognam ạcoḷụt[ut]u* (2a 8-10); *tiopritom biietutu* (1b 9).

Abweichungen von der BWO SOV: attributiv: (a) *brictom uidluias uidlu[a] tigontias so* (1a 3-4) bildet zusammen mit dem vorangehenden *bnanom bricto[m]* . . . (1a 1-3) einen Chiasmus; (b) *eianom anuana sana anderna* (1a 2-3) mit vorangestelltem pronominalen Genetiv-Attribut und nachgestelltem adjektivischem Attribut; (c) Namenformeln (1a 9-16); prädikativ: (a) *ponc nitixsintor sies* (1a 7; 2a 4-5); vgl. auch *suet petidsiont sies* (2b 9) 'si elles épargnent' (Lambert 1985, 173) mit nachgestelltem subjektiven Personalpronomen *sies*; (b) *peti sagitiontias* (2b 10) 'Schone die Gegenwirkenden' (Akk. Pl.).[19]

Die Einleitungsformel (1a 1-4), *insinde . . . so*) verweist auf das durch einen Nominalsatz ausgedrückte Thema (*topic*) der Is. Es folgt eine Anweisung an die *adsagsoṇa* im Imperativ 3. Sg. *lunget[ut]u* (1a 4-7), ergänzt durch die Konstruktion *tonid . . . andernados brictom* (1a 7-9), in die der durch die Konjunktion *ponc* eingeleitete Konditionalsatz mit Verbum im Konjunktiv (*ponc nitixsintor sies duscelinatia*) eingebettet ist (1a 7-8; vgl. 2a 4-5; vgl. auch 2b 9 *suet petidsiont sies*).

Die Konjunktion *ponc* < $*k^w omk^w e$ ist auch in Chamalières belegt: *meion ponc sesit buetid ollon* 'The small thing will become great, when he has sown it' (Schmidt 1981, 260) mit *sesit* als 3. Sg. *s*-Aorist. Die 'Konjuntion' *suet*[20] <*sue + id*(?) bleibt hypothetisch: vgl. lat. *sī*, alt *sei*, volsk. *se pis* 'si quis'; osk. *svaí, suae*, umbr. *sve* 'sī', osk. *nei suae* 'nisī' vs. *suve nei*, umbr. *sue neip* 'sī non';[21] 1b 1 wird durch die letztlich von Koch 1985, 1ff. behandelte Konjunktion *etic* 'und' eingeleitet; *etic* 1b 3 ist wahrscheinlich von dem vorangehenden *co* zu trennen: *etic . . . etic* (1b 1-3). *tonid* (1a 7) 'außerdem' vergleicht sich mit *toni* (La Graufesenque), *senit* (2a 1) und *tanit* (2a 11): *Tritos duci Deprosagi(los) toni Felixx* (Thurneysen 1927, 287); *se mnanom sagitiontias seuerim lissatim liciatim anandognam ạcoḷụt[ut]u tanit aṇdognam: tanit* geht vielleicht auf **tonid* zurück. Begründung: (α) *tan-* < **ton-* durch Einfluß der syntagmatisch benachbarten Wörter *anandognam* und *aṇdognam*, die offensichtlich ein Oppositionspaar bilden (**ṇ-andognam* vs. *andognam*);[22] (β) Auslautverhärtung von -*d*(?): vgl. *suet* 2b 9 und *senit* < **se-n-id*(?) wie *tonid* < **to-n-id*.

Dem Nominalsatz ohne Kopula, aber mit Prädikatsnomen *so*

in 1a 1-4 entspricht in 1a 8-9 ein Nominalsatz mit Kopula: *in eanon anuana esi (*esti) andernados brictom*. In 2a 5-8 liegen Verbote vor: die Prohibitivkonstruktion wird ausgedrückt durch den Imperativ *biontutu* 'sie sollen schlagen' in Verbindung mit wiederholtem *ne* plus Akkusativobjekt: *eian nepi andigi ne lisatim ne liciatim ne rodatim biontutu* "den (*eian* 'ihn', bezogen auf *boca* 'Mund' 2a 2-3) eines (*nepi* < $*kek^w\bar{\imath}$) Nicht-*digos*[23] sollen sie weder *(ne) lisata* noch (*ne) liciata* noch (*ne) rodata* schlagen."

II. *Morphologie, Etymologie*. (a) *Nomen*: Die Akkusative *lisatim, liciatim rodatim* sind auf *boca* (2a 2-3) bezogen. Etymologisch klar ist *rodatā* < $*pro\text{-}dhh_1\text{-}teh_2$;[24] bei $*lis\bar{a}t\bar{a}$ und $*lici\bar{a}t\bar{a}$ handelt es sich um Part. Perf. Pass. von denominativen *ā*-Stämmen,[25] die von *lissina* und *licina*, vermutlichen Abstraktbildungen im Instrumental (zur Agensbezeichnung), nicht zu trennen sind: *in das mnas uerondadas brictas lissinaue seuerim licinaue tertioni[cnim]* (1b 6-8)[26] "gegen die beiden Frauen, die irdischen,[27] die verzauberten durch *Lissina*, (d. h. gegen) Severa, oder durch *Licina*, (d. h. gegen) Tertionicna."

Das Namenverzeichnis (1a 9-16) enthält die Appellativa *duxtir* (11), *matir* (14) und *dona* (10; 13; 15); *duxtir* 'Tochter' bestätigt O'Brien 1956, 178f. und Hamp 1975: $*dukt\bar{\imath}r > *duxtir > Ter\text{-}$. Der wichtige Fund gibt einen *terminus post quem* für die Institutionalisierung der keltischen Neubildungen $*merk(k)\bar{a}$, $*eni\text{-}gen\bar{a}$ (vgl. auch gall. *genetā* und *gnātā*)[28] und widerlegt das von Meillet 1908, 38 gegebene *argumentum e silentio*: "Les anciens noms du 'fils' et de la 'fille' ont disparu et ont été remplacés par de nouveaux mots." Hypothetisch bleibt die Identifikation von *dona*: Fleuriot 1985, 143 verbindet das Wort mit *donicon* (1b 14) und führt beide Belege zurück auf gallisch *gdonios* 'Mensch' (Vercelli, cf. Lejeune 1977, 603f.). Die Verbindung scheint semantisch möglich (vgl. althochdtsch. *brūti-gomo*), als Stammbildung wäre jedoch eher **donia* zu erwarten. Schwierigkeiten bereitet auch der Genetiv auf *-ius*, der in *paulli[i]us* (1a 13) vorliegt und vielleicht auch bei *potiti[us]* (1a 10) und *prim[ius]* (1a 15) zu ergänzen ist. Die Rückführung von *-us* auf $*\text{-}\bar{o}is$ (Instrum. Pl.) durch Lejeune et al. 1985, 134 überzeugt wegen fehlender lautgesetzlicher Parallelen nicht. Außerdem fordert der Kontext eher einen Gen. Sg. und schließlich fehlen bisher Belege für den *o*-stämmigen Instrum. Pl. im Kelt.[29] Könnte in *-iūs* eine graphische Analogie zu dem *ias* des Gen. Sg. fem. im Namenkatalog vorliegen?

Unter den teils keltischen, teils lateinischen Namen[30] findet sich *Banona* < $*g^w\mathring{n}h_2\text{-}o\text{-}n\text{-}eh_2$, ein weiblicher Personenname, dessen

Belege auf Oberitalien und die Ostalpen konzentriert sind.[31] *Banona* gehört zu dem in Larzac auch sonst belegten Etymon von *benā* 'Frau': Gen. Pl. *se bnanom bricto[m]* (1a 1), *se mnanom sagitiontias* (2a 8–9), *se mnanom adsaxs[o]na* (2b 7–8); Akk. Pl. *in das mnas ueronadas brictas* (1b 6–7) mit Assimilation aus **bnas* (Lejeune et al. 1985, 123). Als Gen. Pl. wäre *banom* < *$*g^w\n̥h$-om* (vgl. altir. *ban*) zu erwarten.[32]

Das eingefügte *n* in gall. *bnanom* erklärt Bernardo Stempel 1987, 83 überzeugend durch Analogie (vgl. etwa **bnas* > *mnas* (Akk. Pl.). Die Vollstufe des Paradigmas ist in altir. *ben*, Akk. *bein* und den gall. PN *Sacro-bena* und *Seno-bena* belegt.[33] *Banona* entspricht in der Wortbildung dem Typus *Eponā* usw. Das Suffix *-onā* mit Themavokal *o* wurde von den *o*-Stammbildungen abstrahiert. Bereits F. de Saussure, *Cours*, 4.3 hat die Funktion der Bildung *-no-* bestimmt als 'chef de telle ou telle communauté'.[34] *Banona* ist demzufolge von der oskischen *n*-Stammbildung *Nerō* (als Ableitung von *ner-* 'Mann') zu trennen. Solmsen und Fraenkel[35] definieren die Funktion der *n*-Stämme bei Namen als *individualisierend*, während Hoffmann 1955, 35–40 an possessive Funktion denkt.

Leumann 1977, 362 sieht "die ursprüngliche idg. Verwendung der *n*-Flexion bei personalen *o*-Adjektiven als i n d i v i d u a l i s i e r e n d - substantivierend, nahezu namen-bildend" (vgl. στράβων und Στράβων 'Schieler' von στραβός). Trotz dieser in historischer Zeit feststellbaren Unterschiede in der Wortbildung von *Ban-on-ā* und *ner-ō* fällt es schwer, in den beiden Antonymen keine späteren Realisierungen einer vergleichbaren älteren Konzeption zu sehen.

(b) *Verbum*: Aus Raumgründen muß dieser Abschnitt besonders kurz gefaßt werden: (α) In den weiteren Rahmen der Verbalmorphologie gehört das Element *sies* (*ponc nitixsintor sies*: 1a 7, 2a 4–5; *suet petidsiont sies*: 2b 9), das von Lambert 1985, 163 überzeugend als "le nom. pl. tiré du pron. féminin **sī* 'elle' " interpretiert worden ist. Allerdings wird es sich dabei trotz Lamberts Feststellung "Ce pluriel n'est pas conservé en celtique insulaire" (1985) eher um eine späte Bildung des Gallischen handeln, worauf auch die Analogie zum Nom. Pl. der nominalen Konsonantenstämme hinweist; vgl. als typologische Parallele oskisch *pús* (Nom. Pl.) < *$*k^woi$* (in Analogie zu den *o*-Stämmen).

(β) Von den modalen Bildungen entspricht *petidsiont* (2b 10) den in Chamalières nachgewiesenen *si̯e/o*- Futura: *bissíet* 'er wird spalten', *pissíiu mi* 'ich werde sehen', *ṭonçnaman tonsiíontío* 'die den Eid schwören werden' (cf. Schmidt 1986, 174f.).

(γ) Schwierigkeiten bereitet dagegen das Affixagglutinat */sī/ in *ni-tixsintor* (1a 7; 2a 4–5), bei dem es sich um eine Kontamination aus */si̯e-/si̯o-/* und dem Optativ-Formans */i̯ē/ī/* zu handeln scheint.[36] Das Präfix *ni-* bestätigt zudem, daß eingeschränkte Verwendung von *ne* (*ni*) 'davon' im Altirischen (cf. Thurneysen 1946, §846) das Ergebnis einer jüngeren Sprachentwicklung darstellt.

(δ) In *Lunget[ut]u* (1a 6–7), *ạcoḷụt[ut]u* (2a 10–11), *biietutu* (1b 9), *bi(i)ontutu* (2a 7–8; 1b 6; 2b 7), vgl. auch *biontutuṣ* (1b 11), sehe ich mit Lejeune et al. 1985, 138 und Fleuriot 1985, 141 Imperativbildungen. Von den vorgeschlagenen Deutungen im Detail scheint jedoch Lejeunes Hinweis auf umbrisch *fututo* '('soyez!', 'qu'ils soient!')' wegen des unterschiedlichen Numerus nicht überzeugend zu sein, während Fleuriots Rückführung des zweiten *-tu* auf *tōd 'par ceci' den gallischen Auslautgesetzen widerspricht. Vielleicht läßt sich *-tutu* ganz einfach als expressive Doppelung der Personalendung des Imperativs 3. Sg. erklären.

(ε) Abschließend sei noch ein Hinweis gestattet auf die Belege des Part. Präs. fem., über die ich bereits an anderer Stelle gehandelt habe:[37]

1. *tigontias* (1a 4) 'der stechenden' < **tig-ont-i̯eh₂-s*, als thematischer Ableitung vom Aoriststamm der Wurzel **(s)teig-* 'stechen' (Pokorny 1959, 1016f.), zu der auch *ni-tixsintor* (1a 7; 2a 4–5) gehört.[38]
2. *sagitiontias* 'die Gegenwirkenden' (2a 8–9: Nom. Pl.; 2b 10: Akk. Pl.): *biontutu semnanom sagitiontias* (2a 7–9) 'die Gegenwirkenden dieser Frauen sollen schlagen'; der Verbalstamm *sagiti-* geht zurück auf eine Weiterbildung Wurzel *sag-* (s. oben Note 2).
3. . . .]*ictontias* (2b 13) fragmentarisch.

Zusammen mit den lexikalisierten Resten des *nt*-Partizips im Inselkeltischen[39] bestätigt der Befund von Larzac die Existenz der Kategorie für das Keltische.

Die gallo-britannische Spracheinheit läßt zudem vermuten, daß es sich bei dem Verlust der Formation um einen konvergenten Prozeß innerhalb der inselkeltischen Sprachen gehandelt hat.[40]

KARL HORST SCHMIDT

Universität Bonn

NOTES

1. Vgl. besonders Lejeune et al. 1985; Fleuriot 1985; Lambert 1985.
2. Cf. air. *saig-* 'chercher à atteindre, tendre vers, rechercher, réclamer en justice, attaquer, s'appliquer à' (Vendryes, Bachellery und Lambert 1959-, S. 9ff.).
3. Pokorny 1959, 1016f.
4. Vgl. zu Chamalières Fleuriot 1976-77, 1979; Lejeune und Marichal 1976-77; Lambert 1979; Schmidt 1979-80, 1981; Henry 1984.
5. Statt: *bnarcom.*
6. Geschrieben: *sanander̥* (2) *na* (3) ; als Akk. Pl. bezogen auf *anuana.*
7. Oder: (gegen) den Zauber der Vidluia, dieser (*so*) Magien/Zaubereien stechenden.
8. Severa Tertionicna wirkt *prima vista* wie Praenomen + Patronymicon. Wegen 1b 6-8 *in das mnas ueronadas brictas lissin̥a[ue] seuerim licinaue tertioni[cnim]* (vgl. die Übersetzung unter II) ist aber eher von zwei Personen auszugehen; vgl. auch 1a 6 *eianom* 'deren', 1b 9 *eiabi.* Die Attribute im Akk. Sg. fem. (*lidssata* und *liciata*) sind auf Severa und Tertionicna bezogen.
9. Statt: *elanom.*
10. Überzeugende Lesung von Fleuriot 1985, 142, statt: *uoduiuoderce.*
11. Statt: *inteanon anuan̥[.*
12. Statt: *iaia* (vgl. 1a 14).
13. Statt: *alias* (vgl. 1a 11).
14. Die Übersetzung weicht in Einzelpartien von Lejeune, Fleuriot und Lambert ab. Die drei französischen Gelehrten unterscheiden sich aber z. T. ebenfalls in ihren Interpretationen.
15. Oder: "gegen die (unteren =) nachfolgenden Namen," bezogen auf 9-16; die Übersetzung 'unterweltlich' scheint mir durch *andernados* (9) gestützt zu werden.
16. Vidluia dürfte Ableitung zu dem auch *uidlu[a]* zu Grunde liegenden *u*-Stamm *uidlu-* sein.
17. *lidssata* und *liciata* sind Part. Perf. Pass. zu *ā*-stämmigen Verben.
18. Vgl. *semn̥i* (2b 7), *anom adsaxs nadoc[* (2b 8).
19. Imperativ vorgeschlagen von Lambert 1985, 173: "épargne celles qui se plaignent."
20. Lambert 1985, 173; anders Fleuriot 1985, 150.
21. Walde und Hofmann 1954, 530.
22. Zur Diskussion der Etymologie von *-gna-* vgl. Bernardo Stempel 1987, 116.
23. Lautgesetzlich möglich wäre eine Verbindung mit der Wurzel *$dhei\hat{g}h$- (Pokorny 1959, 244f.).
24. Cf. Lejeune et al. 1985, 124[18]: "appartenant à *pro-də₃-to-* (*dō*-) ou plutôt à *pro-dhə₁-to-* (*dhē*-)."
25. Vgl. auch *incarata* 1b 15.
26. Cf. auch Lejeune et al. 1985, 124f.
27. *ueronadas* im Gegensatz zu *anuana sana andern̥a* (1a 2-3).
28. Cf. Schmidt 1979.
29. Vgl. letztlich Tovar 1984 [1985], 40.
30. Vgl. dagegen die überwiegend lat. Namen in Chamalières.
31. Vgl. Holder 1896, 342 mit Belegen aus *Corpus inscriptionum latinarum* III, V und XII 566 (Pompeiae Banonae).
32. Vgl. Hamp in Winter 1965, 233.
33. Cf. Schmidt 1958, 59f.

34. Vgl. weiter Krahe 1954, 73; Watkins in Birnbaum und Puhvel 1966, 45; Meid 1957.
35. Vgl. Solmsen 1922, 133.
36. Lamberts Interpretation "3ᵉ pers. du pl. d'un optatif en -si- (cf. *marcosior* sur un peson de fuseau lui aussi déponent)" (1985, 163) erklärt nicht die Sprachgeschichte der Form.
37. Vgl. Schmidt 1988.
38. Auf die etymologische Verbindung von *tigontias* und *ni-tixsintor* hat auch Lejeune et al. 1985, 124 hingewiesen, der in *ni-(s)teig-* einen *calque linguistique* nach lat. *dē-fīgere* zu erkennen glaubt. Die Wurzel *tig-* kann jedoch aus lautgesetzlichen Gründen nicht mit Lambert 1985, 164 (vgl. auch 177) auf **dhīgh-* (vgl. ggf. eher **dhēigʷ-* usw. bei Pokorny 1959, 243f.) zurückgeführt werden.
39. Vgl. Vendryes 1955, 229–34.
40. Zur Diskussion von altir. *car(a)e* 'Freund' vgl. Hamp, 1976, 4f.; Bernardo Stempel 1987, 94f.

REFERENCES

Bernardo Stempel, P. de. 1987. *Die Vertretung der indogermanischen liquiden und nasalen Sonanten im Keltischen*. Innsbruck: Institut für Sprachwissenschaft der Universität.
Birnbaum, H. und J. Puhvel, hrsg. 1966. *Ancient Indo-European Dialects*. Berkeley and Los Angeles: University of California Press.
Fleuriot, L. 1976–77. Le vocabulaire de l'inscription gauloise de Chamalières. *Études celtiques* 15.1: 173–90.
———. 1979. Note additionelle sur l'inscription de Chamalières. *Études celtiques* 16: 135–39.
———. 1985. Essai d'interprétation analytique. *Études celtiques* 22: 138–55.
Hamp, E. 1975. **dhugHtēr* in Irish. *Münchener Studien zur Sprachwissenschaft* 33: 39–40.
———. 1976. On Some Gaulish Names in -*ant*- and Celtic Verbal Nouns. *Ériu* 27: 1–20.
Henry, P. L. 1984. Interpreting the Gaulish Inscription of Chamalières. *Études celtiques* 21: 141–50.
Hoffmann, K. 1955. Ein grundsprachliches Possessivsuffix. *Münchener Studien zur Sprachwissenschaft* 6: 35–40.
Holder, A. 1896. *Alt-celtischer Sprachschatz*, Band 1, A–H. Leipzig: B. G. Teubner.
Koch, J. T. 1985. Movement and Emphasis in the Gaulish Sentence. *Bulletin of the Board of Celtic Studies* 32: 1–37.
Krahe, H. 1954. *Sprache und Vorzeit*. Heidelberg: Quelle & Meyer.
Lambert, P.-Y. 1979. La tablette gauloise de Chamalières. *Études celtiques* 16: 141–69.
———. 1985. Le Plomb du Larzac. Essai d'interprétation suivie. *Études celtiques* 22: 155–77.
Lejeune, M. 1977. Une bilingue gauloise-latine à Verceil. *Comptes rendus de l'Académie des Inscriptions et Belles-Lettres* 582–610.
——— et al. 1985. Textes gaulois et gallo-romains en cursive latine: 3. Le plomb du Larzac. *Études celtiques* 22: 95–138.

———— und R. Marichal. 1976-77. Textes gaulois et gallo-romains en cursive latine. *Études celtiques* 15.1: 151-71.
Leumann, M. 1977. *Lateinische Laut- und Formenlehre.* München: C. H. Beck.
Meid, W. 1957. Das Suffix *-no-* in Götternamen. *Beiträge zur Namenforschung* 8: 72-108, 113-26.
Meillet, A. 1908. *Les dialectes indo-européens.* Paris: Champion.
O'Brien, M. A. 1956. Etymologies and Notes. *Celtica* 3: 168-84.
Pokorny, J. 1959. *Indogermanisches etymologisches Wörterbuch.* Bern: Francke.
Saussure, F. de. 1955. *Cours de linguistique générale.* 5e édition. Paris: Payot.
Schmidt, K. H. 1958. Gallisch *nemeton* und Verwandtes. *Münchener Studien zur Sprachwissenschaft* 12: 49-60.
————. 1979. Zur Entwicklung einiger indogermanischer Verwandtschaftsnamen im Keltischen. *Études celtiques* 16: 117-22.
————. 1979-80. Gallica. *Studia celtica* 14-15: 285-89.
————. 1981. The Gaulish Inscription of Chamalières. *Bulletin of the Board of Celtic Studies* 29.2: 256-68.
————. 1986. Zur Rekonstruktion des Keltischen. Festlandkeltisches und inselkeltisches Verbum. *Zeitschrift für celtische Philologie* 41: 159-79.
————. 1988. Zur Entwicklung indogermanischer Partizipien im Keltischen. *Linguistique Balkanique* (in memoriam V. Georgiev): 25-29.
Solmsen, F. 1922. *Indogermanische Eigennamen als Spiegel der Kulturgeschichte,* hrsg. E. Fraenkel. Heidelberg: Carl Winter.
Thurneysen, R. 1927. Zu den Graffiti von La Graufesenque. *Zeitschrift für celtische Philologie* 16: 285-304.
————. 1946. *A Grammar of Old Irish.* Dublin: Dublin Institute for Advanced Studies.
Tovar, A. 1984 [1985]. Review of *Le lingue indoeuropee di frammentaria attestazione. Kratylos* 29: 36-42.
Vendryes, J. 1955. Restes d'anciens participes présents en irlandais. In *Corolla Linguistica: Festschrift Ferdinand Sommer,* hrsg. Hans Krahe, 229-34. Wiesbaden: O. Harrassowitz.
————, E. Bachellery und P.-Y. Lambert. 1959-. *Lexique étymologique de l'irlandais ancien.* Dublin: Dublin Institute for Advanced Studies.
Walde, A. und J. B. Hofmann. 1954. *Lateinisches etymologisches Wörterbuch* II. 3. Auflage. Heidelberg: Carl Winter.
Winter, W., hrsg. 1965. *Evidence for Laryngeals.* The Hague: Mouton.

Einige Beobachtungen zu indogermanische /w/ im Keltischen[1]

§1. Anlautendes #w- und lep. *Uvamokozis* und *Uvltiauiopos* (Prestino)

Anlautendes #w- vor Vokal ist im Festlandkeltischen und in den älteren inselkeltischen Denkmälern erhalten; im Irischen entsteht später #f- bzw. im Sandhi b- hinter Nasal und 0- hinter Vokal, für das Britannische ist die Velarisierung zu *gw*- bzw. leniert *w*- charakteristisch.

Zwar ist die Stellung #wC-, woraus #uC- entsteht, für unsere Betrachtungen uninteressant, es ist aber dennoch bemerkenswert, daß anlautendes *w* vor den Liquiden (#wR- < *#wRV[2] und *#wRC) im Keltischen konsonantisch realisiert wird und im Prinzip die gleiche Behandlung wie vor den Vokalen erfährt, wobei m. E. ky. *wrth* und ir. *olann* und *olc* nicht als Beispiele dieser Entwicklung zu zählen sind.[3]

Beispiele: kib. *uersoniti* (Bo. A3), *uertai* (Bo. A6), *uertatosue* (Bo. A8), *Uicanocum* (Bo. B5), *ueramos* (Vill.).[4]

Gall. *Uindulos* (Grauf.), *Vindo-* zu ky. *gwynn* : ko. *guyn* : br. *gwenn* : air. *find* 'weiß'; *Vidu-*, *vidubium* 'Hacke, Haue' zu aky. *guid*, ky. *gwydd, gwydden* : ako. *guiden*, ko. *gueyth, gvethen* : br. *gwez, gwézen* : air. *fid* 'Baum, Holz' bzw. ky. *gwyddyf* : mir. *fidbae* 'Sichel'; *uidluias, uidlu/tigontias* (Larzac 1a Z.3/4); *ueronadas* (Larzac 1b Z.7).[5]

Altbrit. *Vindocladia*[6] ON; *Vagniacis* ON zu aky. *guoun*, ky. *gwaun* 'moorland' : br. *geun* 'marsh' : air. *fán* 'slope, valley' < *wâgnâ*.[7]

Og. *Velitas* (G.): ir. *fili, filed*; vgl. ky. *gweled* 'sehen,' br. *guelet* 'la vue'; *Vergoso* (G.) : ir. *Fergus* : aky. ako. *Gurgust*, abr. *Uurgust*; *Vorrtigurn* (G.) : ir. *Foirtchern* : aky. *Guorthigirn* : abr. *Gurtiern*.[8]

Gall. *[ου]λατιαβο*[9] (D. Pl. 'Potentibus' *RIG*-G-184), *Vlatucia/Flatucias*[10] (Larzac 1b5/1a10), *Vlato-*, *Vlattius*; og. *Vlatiami* : air. *flaithem*; air. *flaith* 'lordship' : ky. *gwlad* 'country' : ako. *gulat*, ko. *gulas* : mbr. *gloat* zu *IEW* 1112; gall. ουριττακος (*RIG*-G-68), (-)*vritu(s/-), Vrittius, Vritea, Vrittia*; og. -*vritti* (G) zu air. *fríth* 'a find, found,' abr. *angruit·* lucrum, *emgruit·* questionem (*IEW* 1160).[11]

Fleuriot (1978, 80f.) möchte den Wandel *v-* > *gw-* schon für das Spätgallische ansetzen "surtout devant /a/ et /o/"; als Evidenz führt er aber lediglich "mots dialectaux de régions réculées, mots qui ont toutes chances d'être d'origine celtique" an. Dieser s. E. spätgallische Prozeß habe die Entwicklung von #*gw-* bei germanischen Lehnwörtern begünstigt. Eine derartige Annahme verliert jedoch an Wahrscheinlichkeit—so Schmidt (1979a, 287)—wenn man die Verbreitung der Velarisierung bei germanischen Lehnwörtern in der Romania im einzelnen bedenkt.

Die sporadische Anlautentwicklung zu *br-*, die Fleuriot (1978, 79, 81) für das Gallische postuliert, ist aller Wahrscheinlichkeit nach nicht dem Keltischen zuzuschreiben: die von ihm angeführte Evidenz ist nicht primär, sondern besteht aus Glossen und erst romanisch belegten gallischen Rekonstrukten, so daß hier mit vulgärlateinischem *v-/b*-Wechsel[12] zu rechnen ist, zumal *vr-* im Lateinischen nicht vorkam.

In einigen gallischen Belegen erkennen wir womöglich "an unrounding of **o* > *a* similar to what happens regularly in British Celtic":[13] *Vasso-, (-)vassus, vassos* (*KGPN* 285; Do 296; *DAG* 220, p. 914) zu aky. *guas*, ky. *gwas* : ko. *guas* : br. *gwaz* : ir. *foss* 'Diener'.

Im Britannischen wird #*gwo-* häufig zu #*go-*[14] und #*gww-* (bisweilen aus #*wi-*, das sich zu #*wu-*assimiliert hat)[15] zu #*gw-* vereinfacht. Die erwähnte Dissimilation *(g)wo-* > *(g)wa-* vollzog sich nach Hamp (1972) "in British in originally stressed syllables."[16]

Sehr selten läßt sich eine Alternanz #*gw-*/#*chw-* feststellen,[17] nach Jackson vermutlich "from a confusion of [w] with [hw] < *sw*, perhaps in external sandhi after -*s*" (*LHEB* 367) entstanden, "nevertheless it did not result in setting up a regular spirant mutation" (*HPhBr* 429). Daraus ergibt sich für die relative Chronologie:

I. *swV* > *chw*   II. #*w-* > #*gw-*.

Die britannische Entwicklung zu #*gw-* (wie auch die irische zu #*f-*) wurde von Sommerfelt (1954, 103f.) als eine "comparatively late" Eingliederung des Halbvokals *w*[18] in die für die konsonantischen Laute geltende Opposition *fortis* C : *lenis* c (d. h. unleniert vs. leniert) erklärt, die zu der Herausbildung eines 'fortis W' nach dem Muster X : w führte.[19] Obwohl diese Erklärung plausibel wirkt und der Vorgang vermutlich aus dem Inlaut hervorging, lassen sich Parallelen für einen derartigen Lautwandel auch aus idg. Sprachen anbringen, die kein System von aus der Lenierung entstandenen Oppositionen kennen;[20] außerdem "There was no CC. internal double -ww-, and w in contact with consonants is always of the weak variety" (*LHEB* 547).

Aus der Feststellung, daß das Aufkommen des *g* in der Orthographie der britannischen Sprachen um jeweils ein Jahrhundert differiert,[21] und daß brit. Namen in angelsächsischen Quellen mit bloßem anlautenden *v* belegt sind, schließt Jackson, daß zum Zeitpunkt der Abspaltung lediglich "the faint tendency towards velarization had already begun," während "The full *gw*- may have been reached at varying rates in the three dialects" (*LHEB* 390). Er räumt jedoch ein, daß als Ursache auch die Art der br. und ko. Evidenz sowie der orthographische Konservativismus beider Sprachen in Frage kommt, und datiert den Vorgang vom frühen 6. bis zum frühen 8.Jhdt.[22]

Als absolute Datierung für die irische Entwicklung zu #*f*- wird im allgemeinen das Ende des 6. bzw. der Anfang des 7. Jhdt. angesetzt,[23] wobei Watkins (1966, 71; Anm. 2) darauf aufmerksam macht, daß ein Ansatz wie A.D. 600 "is in any case too late; it rests wholly on the evidence of proper names, which are notoriously conservative in spelling." Es ist fraglich, ob in den späteren Ogam-Inschriften #*V* für #*f*- < #*w*- steht[24]—und zwar obwohl ein Zeichen für *f* vorhanden war—oder ob nicht eine bewußte Lautsubstitution vorgenommen wurde.[25]

Bereits Jackson (1950–51) hatte Einwände gegen die u. a. von Thurneysen vertretene Meinung, nach der (#)*w* zunächst (im "Primitive Irish") über (#)*β*- zu #*f*- geworden sei, vorgebracht: die Unterscheidung des Ogam-Alphabets zwischen vokalischem und konsonantischem *w* sei noch kein Beweis dafür, zumal wir im Irischen keine Verwechselung von *β* (aus leniertem *b*) und der Fortsetzung von *w finden; "and as *w* is a sound made with less friction than *β* the loss is more likely to have occurred in the form *w* than in that of *β*" (l.c. 111).

Der Übergang läßt sich allerdings am besten[26] mit Watkins (1966, 70f.) als Übertragung erklären: "The passage of *w*- to *f*- is actually generalized from . . . (so-called 'gemination') position," d.h.

etwa hinter Formen auf *s* des Artikels[27] oder des Pronomens[28] mit hoher Textfrequenz, wobei das System im Sinne Sommerfelts seine Rolle gespielt haben mag, d. h.:

-s#w : *-n#w-* : *-C#w-* : *-V#w-* >
#f- : *#β-* : *-C#W-* : *-V#w-*

nach dem Muster *-C#C-* : *-V#c-*, wobei *f-* für W- eintrat.

Die Weiterentwicklung zu air. *#f-* und ky. *#gw-*, die auch die lateinischen Lehnwörter erfaßt (z. B. lat. *vigilia* > air. *féil(e)* bzw. ky. *gwyl*, br. *guil* 'Fest'), kann erst nach der Übernahme der ersten Schicht stattgefunden haben: (a) Die Substitution des lateinischen *#f-* der ersten Lehnwörter im Air. durch *#s-* (lat. *fornus* > Air. *sornn*) weist darauf hin, daß zu dem Zeitpunkt im Air. noch kein *f* vorhanden war;[29] Thurneysen (*GOI* §921) nimmt an, daß das Altirische bereits *f* kannte, allerdings nur als lenierte Variante der Gruppe *sw*: man habe den lat. Anlaut *f* als lenierte aufgefaßt und eine "unlenierte" Variante (etwa **sworn) dazu gebildet, in der das *w* später verloren gegangen sei.[30] Dagegen spricht, daß "*f-* is not retained in the lenited forms of these words, having been replaced by *š*" (*GOI* §921). Eine einfache Lautsubstitution von *f* durch *s* scheint demgegenüber eher plausibel, da das Irische zu dem betreffenden Zeitpunkt nur *s* als einzigen Reibelaut kannte und dieses die größte phonetische Ähnlichkeit zu *f* hatte. (b) Alle Lehnwörter weisen in dieser Hinsicht die gleiche Behandlung auf.[31]

Vor diesem Hintegrund muß die lepontische Evidenz betrachtet werden: *Uindupale* FN (*Lep* 24, 86f.; *KGPN* 296), vermutlich als Ableitung vom gleichen Vorderglied *Uitilios* (so *Lep* 66, Anm. 232), wenn [vindilios] zu lesen;[32] *Uenia, Uenu* zu air. *fine* 'Familie' (*Lep* 62; Tibiletti Bruno 1981, 175, 158; *KGPN* 289); *uinom* (*Lep* 19) oder *uinoš* (?) (Tib. Bruno 1981, 163f.); *Ualaunal* (*Lep* 65, Anm. 229; Tib. Bruno 1981, 174);[33] *Uerkalai* (*Lep* 62); *Uasekia* (*Lep* 51, 65; Tib. Bruno 1981, 165) mit Grundform *vasso-* < **upo-stH-o-*;[34] dazu evtl. auch *Uaδsileos* (Tib. Bruno 1981, 161f.; *Lep* 65 mit Anm. 230 liest *Uarsileos*).

Angesichts dieser Belege werfen die Lesungen *uvamokozis* und *uvltiauiopos* Probleme auf: Für das erste Glied des PN *uf/vamokozis*[35] liegen drei Deutungen vor: (1) Der zweite Buchstabe wird *v* gelesen und als Gleitlaut zwischen **U-amo-* < **upamo-* interpretiert (*Lep* 116); dagegen spricht, daß kein Gleitlaut in Fällen wie *Uasekia* (und nicht **uvasekia, s.o.) vorliegt. Von vornherein auszuschließen ist im übrigen die hier und da geäußerte Annahme, *v* stelle eine "Lenierung" von *p* dar (dazu Schmidt 1980, 181f.). (2) Die ersten beiden Buchstaben werden von Lejeune (l.c.) als Schreibung für #*w*- gewertet; dagegen spricht, daß ansonsten, wie Lejeune selbst bemerkt, "U continue à noter" sowohl "la voyelle *u*" wie auch—in derselben Inschrift!—"la semivoyelle *w* quand elle est intervocalique" (*Lep* 100; vgl. auch *Lep* 13 §7). (3) Der zweite Buchstabe wird von Tibiletti Bruno (1981, 178ff.) als *f* gedeutet: *ufamo-* < **upsamo-*, vgl. den kib. ON *Uxama*[36] sowie gall. *Οὐξισάμη, Uxellodunum, Uxsellus* und kib. *Uśamus*.; die lepontischen und keltiberischen Belege stellen mit ky. *uchaf*[37] eine keltische Neubildung **upsamo-* gegenüber idg. **upamo-* (ai. *upama-*, ags. *ufemest*) dar, während gall. *Ουχισαμη* mit dem Suffix *isamo-* weiter geneuert hat.

Analog vermutet Tibiletti Bruno im Dat. Pl. *ufitiauiopos* aus derselben Inschrift (von Lejeune; *Lep* 98, 100, als *uvltiauiopos* gelesen, "quelle qu'en soit l'explication"[38]) eine Grundform **upsidia-* zu gall. *summa ux(s)edia* (Grauf.).[39] Der Vorzug ihrer Theorie besteht darin, daß sie beide Formen mit ⟨ꟻ :⟩ erklärt und etymologisch plausibel macht, auch wenn die dem *p*-Schwund vorausgehende lautgesetzliche Entwicklung von **ps* somst kelt. *Xs* ist "perhaps first to *fs*" (*LHEB* 529), parallel mit **pt* zu *Xt* (über **ft*).[40]

Es bliebe zu klären, ob ⟨ꟻ :⟩ das mögliche Zwischenstadium *fs* darstellt oder ob es lediglich Schreibung für [X] ist; für letzteres spricht vielleicht, daß ⟨X⟩ im Lepontischen neben ⟨K⟩ für [g] geschrieben wird, vgl. u. a. *Eripoxios* vs. *Setupokios* und *Anokopokios*, dazu bes. *Lep* 20f. Dann wäre für den Schreiber die phonetische Nähe zwischen [X] und [f] ausschlaggebend gewesen. Man denke auch an die vielfältigen Schreibvarianten für die Wiedergabe einer ursprünglichen Gruppe von zwei Dentalen (*KGPN* 101, *GPN* 410ff.) oder für die Verbindung **ps* selbst, wie aus den oben gegebenen Beispielen ersichtlich ist.

§2. Postkonsonantisches /w/ im Keltischen und das Sievers'sche Prinzip

Hinter Konsonant sind folgende Stellungen zu unterscheiden: (A) -VC*w*V-, (B) -CC*w*V-, (C) -V:C*w*V-,[41] (D) #C*w*V- bzw. #R*w*V-.

Ad A. Bekanntlich fällt noch gemeinkeltisch die Gruppe **k'* + *w* mit dem Labiovelar **k^w* zusammen. Lep. *Atekua/Atecua* (*Lep*

59, Tib. Bruno 1981, 170f.) ist, wenn mit Pisani (bei Tib. Bruno 1981, l.c.) zu *Atepa* zu stellen, als Archaismus zu werten, vgl. gall. *Equos* vs. *Epona*. Der gall. GN *Ucuete*, *-in* wird jetzt von Schmidt (1986b) als *uk^w-e-tis* "angerufenes Wesen" angesetzt.[42] Gall. *tecuan* (Grauf.) ist nach wie vor unklar. Es wird von Fleuriot (1980, 114ff.), Thurneysen folgend, zur Wurzel *tek^w-* 'laufen, fließen' (*IEW* 1059f.) gestellt: sein Ansatz *tek^wu-wom* > *tekuwom* > *tekuon* > *tecuan* als Gen. Pl. ist wegen der ad hoc-Annahme von *-om* > *-an* nicht haltbar. Koch (1985, 21f.), gefolgt von Eska 1988b, nimmt es als Akk. f. Sg. mit der Bedeutung 'beverage', erwähnt aber das Problem des dann in einem Appellativum bewahrten *k^w* nicht. Der Beleg entfällt, wenn Lamberts (1987a, 531) neue Trennung *tecu andoedo* richtig ist.

Für das Festlandkeltische können wir im allgemeinen vom Erhalt des *w* hinter C ausgehen, vgl. (1) hinter Verschlußlaut : gall. *petuar[ios]*[43] : abrit. πετουαρία ON, abr. *petguare* : mky. *petwerydd* '4', zu aky. *petguar*, ky. *pedwar* usw. '4': *Boduognatos/-genos* zu air. *Bodb* 'war goddess' : abr. *bodou·* auis . . . inmunda, *Bodu-uan, Eu-boduu*;[44] *Epomeduos*[45] zu og. *Medvvi*[46] (G.) : air. *Medb* 'enivrant' : ky. *meddw*, ko. *medhow*, br. *mezo, mezv* 'drunk'; kib. *Luguadici* (Segovia), *Luguei* (D. Sg. Peñalba Z.3u.5);[47] letzteres wird auf *lugewei/lugowei* zurückgeführt, da wir aber *ou* in kib. *Lugoues, Lugouibus* erhalten finden, stellt sich die Frage, ob ein kib. nach den Konsonantenstämmen geneuerter Ansatz *lugwei* nicht vorzuziehen wäre.

(2) hinter *s*: gall. *Nantosvelta* GN (*DAG* 213 p. 798; *KGPN* 274, 248),[48] *Coriosvelites* VN (*KGPN* 274, 183).

(3) hinter Sonant: gall. *Banuus* (<*Banwos* mit der häufigen latinisierenden Nominativendung), *Banuillus, Banui* (G.) (*GPN* 149) zu air. *banb* 'young pig' : ky. *banw*;[49] gall. *tarvos* (*DAG* 170 p. 514f.), *Tarvenna, Tarvessedum* ONn, abrit. *Tarvedunum* ON (Rivet und Smith 469f.) zu air. *tarb* 'Stier' : ky. *tarw*; gall. *arverṇatin* (Cham. 2, Schmidt 1981a, 261), *Arvernicus* (Grauf. *DAG* p. 320); gall. *Dervo-* (Do 251), abrit. *Derventio* FN (Rivet und Smith 333ff.) zu air. *derb* 'Eiche' : ky. *derw*; gall. *Luguselva* (*KGPN* 266, 233) zu air. *selb* 'possession' : ky. *helw*; zum gall. Namenelement *Elvo-, Elvio-* vgl. *KGPN* 203f. und *GPN* 347ff.

Gall. *Covirus* (*KGPN* 177) zu ky. *cywir* 'true' ist besser aus *ko-wêro-* als aus *kom-wêro-* herzuleiten. Da in Gruppen von Verschlußlaut + *w* und von Sonant + *w* auch im Inselkeltischen in der Regel kein Ausstoß des Konsonanten zu beobachten ist, bliebe die u.a. von Thurneysen (*GOI* 123) angenommene Entwicklung *mw* > *w* ohne Parallelen, so daß hier wohl mit einer—vielleicht durch falsche Trennung entstandenen—Kompositionsform *ko- zu rechnen ist (vgl. auch *GPN* 183 Anm. 2 und die Beispiele 184f.).

Angesichts dieser insgesamt eindeutigen, durch die Stellungen B-D (s. u.) noch gestärkten Evidenz müssen Fälle, in denen *w* nicht erhalten zu sein scheint, neu überprüft werden: gallolat. *petorritum/petôritum* "Wagen": Schwund des *w* vielleicht in proklitischer Stellung vor dem Hauptakzent, der wahrscheinlich im Gallischen zunächst auf dem Determinatum *ritu*- lag und erst im Lateinischen auf -*o*- zurückgezogen wurde.[50]

Nicht sicher ist die Zugehörigkeit von einigen wenigen Bildungen mit -*taro*- (*KGPN* 275) zum Etymon kelt. *tarwos 'Stier'; Gorrochategui (1984, 279) macht darauf aufmerksam, daß -*taro*- stets nur als zweites Kompositionsglied vorkommt. Wenn überhaupt, könnte -*taro*- eine Vereinfachung von *tauro*- sein, das im Festlandkeltischen ebenfalls belegt ist (*GPN* 261ff., 473f.) und zu *tarwo*- durch Metathese, vielleicht in Analogie zu *karwo- 'Hirsch', im gall. PN *Carvus* (Neumann 1983, 1070; de Bernardo Stempel 1987, 152f.), abrit. VN *Carvetii* (Rivet und Smith 301f.) umgestaltet wurde.

Fraglich ist, ob die mit *Bodo*- zusammengesetzten Namen zu *boduo*- zu stellen sind oder nicht besser zu *Boudus, Bodi-, -bodiaci, -boudio-* und air. *buaid* 'Sieg' (*IEW* 163), eine Möglichkeit, die schon von Evans (*GPN* 59f., vgl. auch 157) unter Vergleich mit den abr. PNN *Budgen, Budien, Budian* erwogen wird.

Für gall. *ueidiíu* 'I honour' (Chamalières Z.1) zu mir. *fíad* 'honour' ist eine Rekonstruktion *weid-w-i-yô vorgenommen worden (Schmidt 1981a, 267 und bes. 1984, 17ff.), bei der allerdings der *w*-Schwund im Inlaut Schwierigkeiten macht; es bliebe zu erwägen, ob ein *weidw-yô > *weiduyô sich zu *weidiyô assimiliert haben könnte. In jedem Falle muß diese Form im Zusammenhang mit dem dreimal in derselben Inschrift belegten *luge* (Z.11/12)[51] gesehen werden. Dieses wird von Schmidt (1981a, 263) als 'to Lugus' gedeutet, ebenfalls mit *w*-Schwund "by dissimilation" aus einer Vorform *luguei, wie keltiberisch belegt.

Für das Inselkeltische lassen sich folgende Feststellungen treffen: (1) Erhalt von *w* hinter C in den ältesten Sprachstufen, vgl. die oben angeführte Evidenz; (2a) Erhalt von konsonantischem *w* hinter *t, d, r, l, n* im Britannischen und Übergang zu Vokal im Auslaut erst in nachmittelkymrischer Zeit;[52] (2b) Erhalt von *w* in diesen Positionen im Irischen mit Weiterentwicklung zu *b* [β]. Jackson (1950-51, 109; *LEHB* 414) macht darauf aufmerksam, daß es sich um den umgekehrten Wandel handelt wie im Britannischen—und, wie wir jetzt wissen, im Gallischen—wo sich *m* hinter *n* zu *w* entwickelt: vgl. gall. *anuana*, ky. *anw*, abr. *-enuen* (vgl. de Bernardo Stempel 1987, 69f.); es gibt auch Beispiele hinter Liquida und mit ursprünglichem *b*, wie ky. *elwissen* und *syberw* aus lat. *eleemosyna* und *superbus*.

Jackson (1950-51, 110 Anm. 1) nimmt für air. *be(i)the* 'Birke' < **betwyâ*, zu ky. *bedw* < **betwâ*, Sg. *bedwen*, Schwund von *w* hinter *t* im Irischen an;[53] da wir aber wissen, daß bei der Bildung des Silbengipfels das Wortende eine maßgebliche Rolle spielt,[54] könnte hier auch eine Entwicklung **betuyâ* > **bethuyâ* > **bethyâ* > *be(i)the* vorliegen.

Air. *cethair* '4' reicht nicht als Zeugnis für einen *w*-Schwund hinter *t*—der dann nur irisch wäre—da mit Analogie nach dem fem. *cetheoir* < **k^wetesores*, evtl. auch mit einer dissimilierten Vorform **k^wetores* (vgl. westgr. *tetores*) gerechnet werden kann.

Aus dem Gegensatz zwischen Bildungen wie air. *fedb* 'Witwe' vs. air. *ard* 'hoch' (s. u. ad B) statt ***ardb* wird häufig der Schluß gezogen,[55] daß im Ir. nur hinter leniertem *d* altes *w* als *b* erscheine und daß demnach diese Entwicklung jünger als die Lenierung sei. Da diese Erklärung aber auf das Britannische nicht anwendbar ist, wo ebenfalls der Gegensatz ky. *gweddw* vs. *ardd* (mit leniertem *d*) besteht, liegt die Vermutung nahe, daß die dem *w* vorangehende Doppelkonsonanz in beiden Zweigen—wenn auch unabhängig—zu dessen Schwund geführt hat.

Für air. *fedb* ist im übrigen besser **widhwâ* als das häufig angenommene **widhewâ* anzusetzen, und zwar wegen der Senkung von **i* zu *e* vor *a* in der Folgesilbe im Air. wie auch wegen der aky. Entwicklung, so daß diese Etymologie keine Schlußfolgerungen in Bezug auf die intervokalische Entwicklung des *w* zuläßt. Dies veranlaßt Thurneysen,[56] eine sehr frühe Elision des Vokals anzusetzen, die noch vor der eigentlichen irischen, nach der Umfärbung der Vokale erst eintretenden Synkope stattgefunden hätte. Der angeblich elidierte Vokal hätte aber zumindest im Brit. unter dem Ton gestanden (vgl. auch ai. *vidhávâ*).

Ferner können wir vermuten, daß die Umfärbung der Vokale nach dem Übergang von *w* zu *b* [β] erfolgt ist, da die Gruppe keine *u*-Färbung aufweist. Gleiches gilt für *w* hinter Sonant, da wir keine *u*-Färbung, wohl aber gegebenenfalls *i*-Färbung beobachten, vgl. air. *ainb* < **n̥-wid-* 'ignorant' (de Bernardo Stempel 1987, 72). Die arch. ir. belegte Vorform *Conual* (*GOI* 19) zu *Conall* (og. *Cunovali* G.) deutet auf eine Entwicklung **Cunovalos* > *Conowalos* > *Conowal* > *Conwal* > *Conall*[57] hin, d. h. intervokalisches *w* wäre hier bis nach der Synkope bewahrt, und die sekundäre Gruppe *nw* würde zu *n* vereinfacht, da wir kein **Conbal* haben. Die Verhältnisse im Inlaut sind allerdings sehr komplex, und man möchte eine Entwicklung wie die folgende nicht von vornherein ausschließen: **Cunowalos* > *Cunoalos* > *Conoalos* > *Conoal*, wofür *Conual* bloße Schreibung wäre, > *Conal(l)*.

Bei air. *nónbor* '(Gruppe von) 9 Mann' vs. *Noíndruimm* (ON) und späteres *noídécde* '19 years' wird man, wenn es als **newn̥ + wirom* zu interpretieren ist, mit einer Umverteilung der Silbigkeit rechnen müssen: etwa **newnwirom* > **nownbirom* > **nónberom* > *nónbor, nónbur*.[58] Wenn man mit Tovar (1972-73, 413) der Ansicht ist, daß es sich bei den Personalzahlwörtern ursprünglich um Kollektiva auf *-r* handelt, muß man hier das *b* als einen bereits alten volksetymologisch bedingten Einschub erklären. Lambert (1978, 119) setzt dagegen ein Suffix **war* wie in air. *arbor* an.

(3a) Umstritten ist die Entwicklung von inlautendem *sw* im Britannischen: (i) > *ch* wegen ky. *gwych* 'excellent' < **weswo-* zu air. *feb* < **wesw-â* 'Vortrefflichkeit' (nur als Dat. 'as' belegt, *GOI* §911, vgl. *IEW* 1174) und bestimmter Formen des Personalpronomens der 2. Person Plur. bei *CCCG* (p. 18). Da *gwych* auch zu flk. *Vecco-* < **wikko-* gestellt werden kann (*GPC* s.v.), ist dieser Ansatz nicht zwingend (vgl. *LEHB* 526f.). (ii) Hamp[59] geht wegen unterschiedlicher Reflexe in bretonischen Dialekten von **sw* > **hw* > *w* aus, vgl. unten ad C sowie ky. *blew* 'hair,' nach ihm < **blesw-* < **mles-wo-* oder **mles-wâ*. Fälle von *Vch* bei der 2. Plur. des Verbums führt Hamp auf eine ursprünglich "clustered" Stellung VC + *sw-* zurück.

(3b) Klarer sind dagegen die Ergebnisse von *-sw-* im Irischen, wo sich das daraus entstandene *-f-* im Silbenauslaut zu *-b-* sonorisiert (*GOI* §132 u. 202).

(4a) Hinter *m* scheint sich *w* im Britannischen gehalten zu haben, allerdings unter Schwund des vorangehenden *m*, also etwa **mw* > **μw* > *w*, wenn aky. *couid*, ky. *cywydd* 'poème, chant' keine von air. *cubaid* 'harmonieux' (< **kom + fid* 'Holz; Buchstabe', etwa **kom- widu-*, *LEIA*-C-263f.) unabhängige Bildung ist. Der Schwund von *w* in der Folge *m + w*V in ky. *amygaf, amwg,* *amwyn* 'to fight with' (zu idg. 2. **weik- IEW* 1128f.) ist auf unterschiedliche Weise von Lindeman 1980 und Hamp 1982 auf die Anlautsstellung zurückgeführt worden. Das Zusammentreffen von *m* und *w* ist hier jedenfalls zu einem späteren Zeitpunkt erfolgt als im Falle von aky. *couid*.

(4b) Von einer Entwicklung des *w* zu *b* hinter einem geschwundenen *m* im Irischen zeugt neben dem angeführten *cubaid* auch air. *cubus* 'Gewissen' < **kom + fius* 'connaissance', etwa **kom-wid-tu-* (*LEIA*-C-265), während man für *coïr* 'gerecht', das zu ky. *cyweir* 'bereit' (*LEIA*-C-152) gestellt wird, eher geneigt wäre, von einer Nebenform **ko-* auszugehen, vgl. oben zu gall. *Covirus*.

Ad B. Auch in dieser Position verhält sich die Gruppe $k'/k + w$ wie labiovelares k^w, vgl. hinter *s* ky. *hysp* 'sterile, dried up': br. *hesp* 'siccus' : mir. *sesc* < **si-sk-wo-* zur Wurzel 1. **sek-* 'abrinnen, versiegen' (*IEW* 894f.; *GPC* s.v.; *LEIA*-S-96); zu gall. *Sparnomagus, Sparnacum* zu ko. *spern* 'thornbush' usw. (womöglich < **skwrno-*) vgl. de Bernardo Stempel (1987, 60; Anm. 90). Air. *scé* 'buisson d'aubépine' : aky. *ispidatenn*, ky. *yspyddaden* : ko. *spethes* : mbr. *spezadenn* 'groseille' zu einer Grundform **skwi(y)-at-* (*LEIA*-S-37; Schmidt 1985, S. 28). Diese Belege zeigen die gleiche Entwicklung wie z. B. air. *cosc* 'Strafe' : ky. *cosp* < **kom-sk^{w}o-m* und lassen einen unmittelbaren Ansatz ky. *chwedl* < **sk^{w}etlo-* (zu air. *scél* 'Geschichte') problematisch erscheinen;[60] während Vendryes—Pokorny folgend—eine Entlehnung "au proto-gaélique" (*LEIA*-S-40; *IEW* 897f.) vermutet, postuliert Campanile (1961, 77) eine britannische Entwicklung zu *Xw* für die Gruppe *sk* vor palatalem Vokal, weswegen er ky. *chwedl* usw. zu einer Wurzel mit einfachem Velar stellen möchte, was wiederum Probleme aufwirft, zumal die labiovelarhaltige Wurzel im Kelt. sehr gut vertreten ist.

Im Festlandkeltischen stellen wir hier ebenfalls den Erhalt von *w* fest: gall. *exvertin* (Thiaucourt);[61] gall. *artuaš* 'Steine' (Todi) zu air. *art* 'Stein';[62] gall. *Arduenna silva, Arduunnus* PN[63] vs. air. *ard* 'high' und ky. *ardd* 'hill' (s. o.); im Irischen lag der Schwund des *w* vor der Umfärbung der Vokale (Jackson 1950–51, S. 111).

In air. *tengae* 'Zunge' vs. mky. *tauaut*, ky. *tafod* (mit **-ng'hw-*) und in air. *ingen* 'nail' vs. aky. *eguin*, ky. *ewin*[64] (mit **-nghw-*) können wir den hinter Doppelkonsonanz erwarteten Schwund des *w* beobachten. Die scheinbar unterschiedlichen britannischen Realisierungen werfen dagegen Probleme auf: *n* ist vor der Gruppe *gw* verloren gegangen, was relativchronologisch vor dem Verlust des *w* hinter Doppelkonsonanz erfolgt sein müßte; das sich dann im Inlaut befindende *gw* wird in einer späteren Sprachstufe—zusammen mit -V*gw*V- < *w—zu inlautendem -w- vereinfacht worden sein. Das ohnehin häufig tabuistisch entstellte Wort für Zunge weist darüber hinaus den sporadisch belegten Ersatz von *w* durch *f* auf, hier vielleicht durch das Verb *llyfu* 'lecken' begünstigt.[65]

Ad C. Einige Belege sind gall. *Suaduilla* zu air. *Sadb*;[66] air. *fíadu* 'witness' < *weidwôts* (*GOI* 124, 212). Aky. *gwiw*: abr. *uuiu*, vann. *gwiù*, br. *gwiou* 'gai, vif' ist nach Hamp (1975–76, 69) auf *wêswo-, nicht auf *wêsu-[67] zurückzuführen (vgl. oben ad A sub 3a); ähnlich ist ky. *rhew* 'frost' : br. *rev, reo*, vann. *reù* nach Hamp (1973; 1975–76, 69) mit "metathesis of *-ws-" anzusetzen; br. *riou, riv* 'cold' < *(p)rêuso-* über *rêhwo- > *rihwo- (Hamp 1982b).

Ad D. Der allgemein beobachtete Zusammenfall von k^w und *k* + *w* liegt beim Etymon für 'Hund' (*IEW* 632f.). air. *cú*, ky. *ci*, ako. br. *ki*, nicht vor, was zu der Annahme zwingt, daß noch vor dem Übergang von *kw* zu *p* im p-Keltischen *w* vor *û* < *ô* geschwunden war: *k'wô(n)* > *kwû* > *kû*.

Die Gruppe #*sw* ist im Festlandkeltischen erhalten, vgl. z. B. gall. *Suaduilla* (s. o.), *suexos* '6.' (Grauf.),[68] kib. *śua, śueś* (Bo. A1 bzw. 5).[69]

Im Britannischen wird die Gruppe zu *chw* entwickelt (*LHEB* 525f.), ein Wandel, der nach dem Übergang von *s* zu *h* im Anlaut liegen muß[70] und vor der Diphthongierung von *ê* zu *wy* (vgl. mky. *hwy* 'länger' < *sê-is* und *hwyr* ? < lat. *sêrus*).

Im Irischen ist bekanntlich *w* in der Gruppe #*sw* ausgestoßen, jedoch erst nach der Lenierung, da im Sandhi V#*swV* > #*f*- wird.[71] In den Ogam-Inschriften scheint die Gruppe noch bewahrt zu sein, vgl. *Svannuci* (Korolev 1984, 189f.) zu air. *Sannuch* (*Thes.* 2.263).

In abrit. Ὠκεανὸς δουηκαληδονίος (Rivet und Smith, 44, 338) ist #C*w* offenbar noch bewahrt, ebenso in gall. *buet* (Cham. 8f.),[72] weswegen das in derselben Is. belegte *bissiet* (11) mit Schmidt (1986a, 174) nicht zu *bhû-*,[73] sondern zu *bheid-* zu stellen ist. Wenn gall. *-dallus* (*KGPN* 187) zu air. ky. *dall* (s. u.) und das PN-element *Donno-* (*GPN* 194f.) zu air. *donn* 'dunkel', ky. *dwnn* < *dhwosno-* (*IEW* 270f.) gehört, müßten Gründe für den Erhalt von *u* in *buetid* gesucht werden.

Ansonsten ist *w* hinter #C im Inselkeltischen geschwunden, vgl. z. B. air. *dorus* 'Tür' < *dhworestu-* (*IEW* 278f.), dazu wohl auch ky. *drws* 'id.', ky. ko. abr. *dor* 'Tür'; air. ky. ko. br. *dall* 'blind' <

*dhwl̥no- über *dwalno- > *dwallo- (*IEW* 266), air. *baile* 'Ort' < *bhwəlio-* (*LEIA*-B-7). Im Kymrischen liegt auch diese Entwicklung vor dem Übergang von brit. *ê* > *wy*, vgl. ky. *dwywes* 'Göttin' zu *dei-*.

Nicht überzeugend erscheint Vendryes' (1912) Versuch, Reste des *w in der Farbe des Vokals hinter *t* und *d* in air. *tul(-)* neben *taul* 'protuberance' (vgl. de Bernardo Stempel 1987, 146) und *duliu* Ml (Variante zum Komparativ *diliu* zu *dil* 'dear') zu finden. Gleiches gilt für Cowgill (1985, 20ff.), der für das Zahlwort '2', air. *dáu, da* usw., aky. *dou*, f. *dwy* (*CCCG* §327) nicht den traditionellen Ansatz *dwôu* (*IEW* 228ff.) gelten lassen will, sondern von *duwo* ausgeht. U. a. muß er ad hoc für air. *da* Schwund von *u* und *w* in zwei Etappen annehmen (*duwo* > *duva* > *dva* > *da* p. 25), was nicht durch Parallelen abgesichert werden kann, für ky. *dwy* (p. 23) eine Entwicklung *duway* > *duwî* > *duy* mit ebenfalls ad hoc angenommenem *w*-Schwund im Inlaut.

Im Falle von B, C und D handelt es sich um sogenannte Sievers-Edgertonsche Stellungen,[74] d. h. um Lautfolgen, in denen wir nach der Edgertonschen Formulierung des Sieversschen Prinzips die Realisierung #CuwV- des Sonanten erwarten würden (d. h. R̥ ″V).[75]

Die angeführte Evidenz zeigt jedoch nicht nur keine Gleitlaute, sondern deutlich unsilbische, konsonantische Realisierung, die vielfach bis zum Schwund geht oder Sonderentwicklungen hervorbringt.

Fälle wie ky. *cystrawen* < lat. *construenda, distrywio* < lat. *destruo* oder *rhewin* < lat. *ruina* verdanken ihren Gleitlaut demnach nicht britannischer,[76] sondern schon vulgärlateinischer Entwicklung, vgl. ital. *rovina, manovale* < lat. *manualis* oder lat. *vidua* > ital. *vedova*, frz. *veuve*. Vielmehr können wir uns für *w* wie auch für die Liquiden und Nasale (de Bernardo Stempel 1987, 47ff.) Seebold (1972, 122) anschließen, daß ''Beweismaterial für die Sieverssche Regel . . . aus dem keltischen Material nicht zu gewinnen'' ist.

§3. Zur relativen Chronologie im Irischen

(1) CCwV > CCV kann zeitlich nicht fixiert werden und ist vielleicht alt. (2) Die erste Schicht lateinischer Lehnwörter, darunter auch solche mit #s- für #f-, (3) die Lenierung, darunter VswV > -f- und -Vs#wV- > #f- (4) der Übergang VRwV > VRβV, darunter -Vn#wV- > #β- und (5) VδwV > VδβV sowie (6) die Umfärbung der Vokale

folgen aufeinander. Erst danach erfolgt (7) #f- : #ß- : -C#w- : -V#w- > #f- : #ß- : #f : #w-.⁷⁷

Vermutlich später schwindet w in (8a) #swV- > #sV- und (8b) #CwV- > #CV-, denn wenn (8) vor (7) stattgefunden hätte, wäre womöglich auch w im Sandhi hinter C# geschwunden. Laut Pokorny⁷⁸ hat (7) erst nach der Synkope stattgefunden, wegen Ogam *Svannuci* würde man aber annehmen, daß (9?) Apokope und (10?) Synkope erst nach #swV- > #sV stattgefunden haben. Auf jeden Fall ist (8a) nach (3) anzusetzen, während (8b) auch älter sein kann. Es folgen (11) lat. Lehnwörter mit bewahrtem #f- (zweite Schicht), erst danach wird (12) #w- in lenierter Anlautstellung als leniertes *f* [0] aufgefaßt⁷⁹ und schwindet. Wenn nämlich (12) zur Zeit von (3) stattgefunden hätte, hätte kein so klares Motiv für (7) vorgelegen, abgesehen von der Tatsache, daß wir auch sonst bei den Sonanten *r, l, n* und *y* keine echte Lenierung vorfinden.⁸⁰

Air. Gr. 28 wird (12) zwar erst zur Zeit der Synkope, aber doch vor (7) eingereiht; ähnliches gilt für Jackson (1950-51), der (12) gleichzeitig zu -VwV- > 0 und ebenfalls vor (7) ansetzt. Außerdem läßt die Tatsache, daß auch spätere lat. Lehnwörter #w- zu #f- entwickelt haben, vermuten, daß die Alternanz (C) #f- : (V) #w- noch bestand, d. h. daß die lat. Wörter als leniert aufgefaßt und ihr Anlaut entsprechend umgewandelt wurde.

In dieses Raster müßte sich nun die für den intervokalischen Schwund des *w* erarbeitete Chronologie einfügen.⁸¹ Eric Hamp schrieb 1953-54: "I hope to return to the whole problem in greater elaboration at another date." Wir wünschen ihm und uns. daß diese Hoffnung in Erfüllung gehen wird.

PATRIZIA DE BERNARDO STEMPEL
Sprachwissenschaftliches Institut
der Universität Bochum

NOTES

1. Für Unterstützung und Diskussion danke ich Prof. K. H. Schmidt, Dr. R. Ködderitzsch und besonders meinem Mann.
2. Ein Gegenstück mit #y- gab es im Idg. nicht: Mayrhofer 1986, 162 und Lindeman 1987, 31.
3. De Bernardo Stempel 1987, 115f. u. 134f.

4. Beltrán und Tovar 1982, 66, 70, 72, 79; Schmidt 1976a, 391; Tovar 1986, 88f.; Eska 1988, 120ff., 155.
5. Thurneysen 1927, 286; *GPN* 387; Do 299; *KGPN* 295f.; Schmidt 1983, 758f.; Fleuriot 1985, 57; Lambert 1985, 75.
6. Mit der Variante *Bindocladia*: "Ravenna . . . has Vulgar Latin *b* for *v*, as often" (Rivet und Smith 500).
7. Rivet und Smith 485; *GPC* s.v. *gwaun*.
8. "*V* is len[ited] after *Magi*" (Harvey 1987, 254). Korolev 1984, 69, 73, 89, 92, 115f., 197, 200; Campanile 1961, 73.
9. Auf gall. Inschriften in griechischem Alphabet findet sich die Schreibung ου für #w- (*RIG* 1.441f.): ουηβρουμαρος (*RIG*-G-27) neben *Vebrullus* (Grauf., *GPN* 384) u. ä., beides zu ky. *gwefr* 'Bernstein' wie auch der aky. PN *Guebrgur* (vgl. *KGPN* 285; *GPN* 118f., 272). Vgl. noch *RIG*-G-61, 109, 113.
10. Die einmalige Variante *Flatucias* erklärt sich sicherlich mit Lejeune (1985b, 27) als lat. Einfluß, wodurch sich (trotz Fleuriot 1985, 57) ebenfalls das keltische Lehnwort fr. *flanelle* erklären läßt: d. h. durch lateinische Substitution des *#wl- durch fl-.
11. *KGPN* 141, 298, 301; Watkins 1955, 11; Korolev 1984, 117, 199; *Lep*: 42; *DAG*, p. 420; Motta 1978, 302; *DGVBr* 65, 158; de Bernardo Stempel 1987, 113.
12. Die festlandkelt. Belege für eine graphische Alternanz *v/b* vor Vokal (vgl. *GPN* 397) können zum Teil auf Hyperkorrektismen beruhen (Do 61f.); da dieses Phänomen "era frecuente también en el latin vulgar, es dificil precisar su origen en los testimonios hispánicos" (Albertos Firmat 1966, 301).
13. Hamp 1969, 150. Vgl. auch Do 96 Anm. 1 und *KGPN* 94.
14. *GrMW* 5f.; *GEW* 149ff.; *CCCG* 11; *WGr* 152; Strachan 1909, 4; *VGKS* 1.59; Fleuriot 1964, 23; Parry-Williams 1914, 322ff.; *LHEB* 367; *HPhBr* 427ff.; Ernault 1898, 208f.; Loth 1911, 7.
15. *CCCG* 4; Fleuriot 1964, 47f.; *HPhBr* 126 u. §621. Für ky. *(g)wrth* 'gegen' vgl. aber die von de Bernardo Stempel (1987, 115) bevorzugte Erklärung. Zu mky. *ugeint* '20' (de Bernardo Stempel 1987, 110f.) vgl. *IEW* 1177 sowie zu vann. *uigent HPhBr* 141, 144. Für eine gemeinsame Erklärung mit ky. *ucher* 'Abend' siehe Morris Jones (*WGr* 89) und Hamp 1966. Zu letzterem vgl. auch *IEW* 1173 und Lindeman 1980, 406 Anm. 6.
16. Vgl. auch Fleuriot 1964, 36, 37 Note; *HPhBr* 432ff.
17. Parry-Williams 1914, 321 mit ky. und br. Beispielen.
18. Vgl. auch Hamp 1958, 213.
19. Vgl. *HPhBr* 443.
20. Vgl. Poultney 1963, 402; *LHEB* 363.
21. 8. Jhdt. für das Aky., 9. Jhdt. für das Abr. und 10. Jhdt. für das Ko.; vgl. *GEW* 154; *LHEB* 388f.; Fleuriot 1964, 22, 23, 26, 91; *HPhBr* 428.
22. So auch Fleuriot 1978, 80.
23. Vgl. Korolev 1984, 30; Thurneysen 1918, 411 und 1937, 203f.; Jackson 1950-51, 113 Anm. 1.
24. So McManus 1986, 8.
25. Zu der Wiedergabe #B- Für lat. #v- in og. *biga* als Gen. sg. zu air. *fích, fícha* 'vicus', vgl. Motta (1978, 320) und oben Anm. 10.
26. Jackson selbst hatte (1950-51, 113) von einem "unvoicing, for whatever reason" gesprochen: Parallelen dafür fänden sich im Englischen aus SW Irland und aus

Aberdeen (114 Anm. 1). Sommerfelts Ansatz (s. oben) stehen für das Ir. größere phonetische Schwierigkeiten entgegen (vgl. Watkins 1966, 71). Nicht zu überzeugen vermag schließlich auch Hammerich (1948, 33f., 59), der den ir. Lautwandel #*w-* > #*f-* durch ein Zwischenstadium *#*wh-* < *#*Hw-* erklären möchte, wobei in keltisch (und armenisch) *#*Hw-* sowohl *#*Hw-* wie auch *#*w-* zusammengefallen wären, anders als in allen anderen idg. Sprachen, in denen *#*Hw-* und *#*w-*in #*w-*zusammenfielen.

27. Watkins 1966, 71: "this sequence *hw* [aus *-s#w-*] went to *f along with* original *hw*, the lenited form of *sw*, and represents the first introduction of *f* into the Irish phonological system."
28. Vgl. etwa Hamp 1982a, 39.
29. Vgl. auch Watkins 1966, 71 Anm. 1.
30. Vgl. auch *LHEB* 126, 143. Hier kann nicht auf die Problematik der Lehnwortschichten eingegangen werden; es sei nur vermerkt, daß auch McManus (1984 §§24, 44) sich hier der alten Auffassung anschließt.
31. Vgl. *GOI* §922. *LHEB* 364. Ausgenommen sind im Irischen einige späte, gelehrte Entlehnungen mit erhaltenem #*v-*, z. B. *uigil* neben älter entlehntem *féile*. Zu den wenigen späteren brit. Lehnwörtern mit #*b-* < lat. *v* vgl. Parry-Williams 1914, 336; Lewis 1943, S. 16; *VGKS* 1.214 Anm. 1; *CCCG* §80(1); ferner den Hinweis von Albertos Firmat oben Anm. 12.
32. Vgl. Fälle mit Unterdrückung des Nasals in der Schrift aus den Iss. von Vercelli und Briona.
33. Die von Tibiletti Bruno gegebene Vorform *walamno-* läßt sich vielleicht als Partizipialbildung mit idg. *-mno-* zur Wurzel *wal-* 'herrschen' (*IEW* 1111f.) interpretieren, wie auch Lambert (Vortrag in Eichstätt, Oktober 1988) für brit. *-uellaunos* annimmt, vgl. auch gall. *barnaunom* (Larzac 2a4; s. de Bernardo Stempel 1987, 81 mit Literatur, dazu jetzt Schmidt 1988, 27f.).
34. K. H. Schmidt macht mich darauf aufmerksam, daß hier eine Suffixform *-ekio-* für erwartetes *-ikio-* vorläge, weshalb eher eine Deutung *upo-sego-* zu erwägen sei, vgl. *KGPN* 299f.
35. *Lep* 23, 51, 60f., 99ff.; vgl. auch Prosdocimis Forschungsbericht (1986).
36. Tovar 1986, 90; von Tibiletti Bruno 1981 fälschlich als gallisch bezeichnet.
37. Dazu de Bernardo Stempel 1989, 226. Zu den Superlativsuffixen vgl. de Bernardo Stempel 1987, 107f.
38. Unhaltbar ist die Hypothese Prosdocimis (1986, 240f.), hier handle es sich noch um ein vokalisches *l* vor der Entwicklung der Sproßvokale. Vgl. de Bernardo Stempel 1987, 50f.
39. Vgl. Tovar 1983, Lejeune 1985a.
40. Schmidt 1979b, 56; *CCCG* 19.
41. Anstelle des (ersten) Konsonanten kann in A-C auch ein konsonantisch realisierter Sonant auftreten.
42. Somit wird Lejeunes Vermutung (1979, 254), das Wort sei als Viersilbler zu betrachten, hinfällig. Lamberts Vorschlag (1987a, 530) vermag wegen der Semantik ("l'Aiguiseur") und der größeren lautlichen und morphologischen Schwierigkeiten (*u-* für **o-* wenn aus *aku-/*oku-*, sowie *-e-* "voyelle thématique du thème verbal [dénominatif]") nicht zu überzeugen.
43. *IEW* 642f.; *LEIA*-C-86f.; Schmidt 1980, 178 mit Liter.; Thurneysen 1927, 297; Do 359 (ad P. 219); Hermann 1923 §368.

44. *GOI* 123; *KGPN* 152; *DGVBr* 88; *GPN* 151, 60, 156f.; *IEW* 113f. 1. *bhedh-* 'stechen'.
45. *KGPN* 209; Korolev 1984, 177; *LEIA*-M-27 u. 48.
46. "Whether the VV here means *w* or *β* it is impossible to say; but in view of the use of V to spell *β* in . . . [some] Ogam names, . . . there is no reason why it should not already stand for *β*" (Jackson 1950–51, 110).
47. Ködderitzsch 1985, 216; Schmidt 1976b, 337.
48. Zum Vorderglied vgl. auch *GPN* 236 Anm. 6; de Bernardo Stempel 1987, 158.
49. De Bernardo Stempel 1987, 151; *GOI* §201.
50. Eine von der lateinischen verschiedene Betonung im Gallischen nehmen Ch. A. Williams (1891, 15) und Wolf (1982, 284) an, vgl. auch Fleuriot (1982, 66f.). Sonst wäre an Dissimilation von *$*k^w$ . . . *tw-* zu *kw* . . . *t-* zu denken, vgl. westgr. τέτορες.
51. Daneben die rätselhafte Form *luxe*. Das Problem des fehlenden *w* wird von Kowal (1987, 252) gar nicht erwähnt.
52. Loth 1910, 134; Fleuriot 1964 §34.VI; *GrMW* §13. Im Bretonischen "The *-w* may also appear to be lost, as early as the Catholicon," *HPhBr* 466; Ernault 1886, 308.
53. Keine Angabe einer unmittelbaren Vorform in *LEIA*-B-28.
54. De Bernardo Stempel 1987, 49.
55. U. a. Jackson 1950–51, 110.
56. *GOI* §108. Jackson (1950–51, 109) setzt als Grund- oder Vorform *$*widwâ$ an, ohne dazu besonders Stellung zu nehmen.
57. Vgl. Jackson 1950–51, 110f. Zum Auslaut vgl. noch de Bernardo Stempel 1984, 64f.
58. Vgl. Hamp 1953–54, 288. Pokorny (1917, 17) nimmt dagegen eine erste Zwischenstufe *$*newanwiro-$ an, die ebenfalls eine Komposition noch vor Entwicklung der Sproßvokale voraussetzt. Thurneysen (*GOI* §388) und Meid (1970, 206) erklären mit ihrem Ansatz *$*newn̥-wirom$ nicht die fehlende Palatalität der ersten Silbe.
59. 1973, 218ff.; 1974, 145f.; 1975–76, 69f.; 1982b. Ähnlich bereits O'Rahilly 1946, 6.
60. Vgl. auch *LHEB* 535: "Whether either sq^w or *sk'w* ever became WCB. *chw* is not proved beyond dispute"; ibid. §123; Foy 1896, bes. 315f. u. 323f.; Foy 1901; *LEIA*-S-39f.; *GPC* s.v.
61. Vielleicht zu air. *esert, esirt* 'one who neglects his holding' < *$*eks-wert-$, vgl. Schmidt 1981b, 83 mit Literatur; Schmidt 1986a, 178 m. Anm. 53.
62. So *LEIA*-A-91. *Lep* 37 und Tibiletti Bruno 1981, 196ff. lesen dagegen *arduas*.
63. De Bernardo Stempel 1987, 76f.; Rivet und Smith 257.
64. De Bernardo Stempel 1987, 146f. bzw. 122. Vgl. *WGr* 131; *GEW* 153.
65. *WGr* 131; *GEW* 153; *GPC* s.v. *llyfaf*; *CCCG* 34; *LHEB* §65.
66. Watkins 1955, 11; *GPN* 113, 258; Korolev 1984, 189f.; *CGSHib* 303; zu ky. *hawdd* < *$*swâdu-$ (?) vgl. de Bernardo Stempel 1989, 227.
67. U. a. Weisgerber 1969, 70.
68. Vendryes 1924, 36; Thurneysen 1927, 300.
69. Beltrán und Tovar 64, 69.
70. Vgl. Schmidt 1979b, 58; Foy 1896, 314. Zu ky. *hwyad* vgl. Lindeman 1983.
71. *GOI* §132; Schmidt 1979b, 58.
72. 'It will be': "subjonctif en *e/o* propre aux verbes athématiques sur la racine *$*bhu-$" (Lambert 1979 bei Schmidt 1981a, 262; vgl. jetzt Lambert 1987b, 17). Eine Form *-buetid* ist auch in Lezoux belegt (Fleuriot 1980, 134f.).

73. Trotz Hollifield 1983.
74. De Bernardo Stempel 1987, I.1.C. bes. p. 16; vgl. auch I.2.C.
75. Zur Notation vgl. de Bernardo Stempel 1987, 16.
76. Ähnlich *LHEB* §44. Zum Vulgärlateinischen vgl. C. Smith 1983, 940.
77. S. oben S. xxx.
78. *Air. Gr.* §89 S. 29.
79. *GOI* §231.7; *Air. Gr.* §7 Anm. 1.
80. De Bernardo Stempel 1987, 12.
81. Dazu Pokorny 1917, 1918, 1921; Hamp 1953-54; Cowgill 1967; Kortlandt 1986.

BIBLIOGRAPHIE

Air. Gr. = Pokorny, J. 1969^2. *Altirische Grammatik*. Berlin: de Gruyter.
Albertos Firmat, M. L. 1966. *La onomástica personal primitiva de Hispania Tarraconense y Betica*. Salamanca: Theses et Studia Philologica Salamant. 13.
Beltrán, A. und A. Tovar. 1982. *Contrebia Belaisca I (Botorrita, Zaragoza)*. Zaragoza: Departamento de Prehistoria y Arqueología de la Facultad de Filosofía y Letras, Universidad de Zaragoza.
de Bernardo Stempel, P. 1984. Einige Bemerkungen über das Mac Neillsche Gesetz. *Zeitschrift für celtische Philologie* 40: 64-73.
———. 1987. *Die Vertretung der indogermanischen liquiden und nasalen Sonanten im Keltischen*. Innsbruck: Innsbrucker Beiträge zur Sprachwissenschaft 54.
———. 1989. Britannischer Komparativ und Konsonantenverdoppelung. *Indogermanische Forschungen* 94: 207-33.
Campanile, E. 1961. Il nesso *s* + *tenue* in britannico. *Studi e saggi linguistici* 1: 72-78.
CCCG = Lewis, H. and H. Pedersen. 1974^3. *A Concise Comparative Celtic Grammar*. Göttingen: Vandenhoeck & Ruprecht.
CGShib = Ó Riain, P. 1985. *Corpus genealogiarum sanctorum Hiberniae*. Dublin: Dublin Institute for Advanced Studies.
Cowgill, W. 1967. On the Fate of *w in Old Irish. *Language* 43: 129-38.
———. 1985. PIE *duwo '2' in Germanic and Celtic, and the Nom.-Acc. Dual of Non-Neuter *o*-Stems. *Münchener Studien zur Sprachwissenschaft* 46.3: 13-28.
DAG = Whatmough, J. 1970. *The Dialects of Ancient Gaul*. Cambridge, Mass.: Harvard University Press.
DGVBr = Fleuriot, L. 1964. *Dictionnaire des gloses en vieux breton*. Paris; repr. Toronto: Precorp, 1985.
Do = Dottin, G. 1920. *La langue gauloise*. Paris; repr. Geneva: Slatkine, 1980.
Ernault, E. 1886. Études bretonnes. IV. Sur la chute des sons *u, w, v, f*. *Revue celtique* 7: 308-16.
———. 1898. Études bretonnes. XI. Le *j* dans la conjugaison et l'indéfini ou passif. *Revue celtique* 19: 180-211.
Eska, J. F. 1988a. *Towards an Interpretation of the Hispano-Celtic Inscription of Botorrita*. Toronto: Ph.D. diss.
———. 1988b. Notes on a Graffito from La Graufesenque. *Bulletin of the Board of Celtic Studies* 35: 33-36.

Fleuriot, L. 1964. *Le vieux breton: Éléments d'une grammaire.* Paris: Klincksieck.
———. 1978. Brittonique et gaulois durant les premiers siècles de notre ère. *Étrennes Lejeune,* 75-83. Paris: Klincksieck.
———. 1980. Inscriptions gauloises sur céramique et l'exemple d'une inscription de La Graufesenque et d'une autre de Lezoux. *Études celtiques* 17: 111-44.
———. 1982. *Les origines de la Bretagne.* Paris: Payot.
———. 1985. Essai d'interprétation analytique. M. Lejeune et al., *Le plombe magique du Larzac et les sorcières gauloises,* 44-61. Paris: Centre National de la Recherche Scientifique.
Foy, W. 1896. Die indogermanischen s-Laute (*s* und *z*) im Keltischen. *Indogermanische Forschungen* 6: 313-39.
———. 1901. Zur keltischen Lautgeschichte 2. Urkelt. *skw* im Britannischen. *Zeitschrift für celtische Philologie* 3: 274.
GEW = Baudiš, J. 1924. *A Grammar of Early Welsh.* Oxford: Milford.
GOI = Thurneysen, R. 1946. *A Grammar of Old Irish.* Dublin: Dublin Institute for Advanced Studies.
Gorrochategui, J. 1984. *Estudio sobre la onomástica indígena de Aquitania.* Bilbao: Servicio editorial, Universidad del País Vasco.
GPC = *Geiriadur Prifysgol Cymru.* 1967ff. Cardiff: Gwasg Prifysgol Cymru.
GPN = Evans, D. E. 1967. *Gaulish Personal Names.* Oxford: Clarendon Press.
GrMW = Evans, D. S. 1976³. *A Grammar of Middle Welsh.* Dublin: Dublin Institute for Advanced Studies.
Hammerich, L. L. 1948. Laryngeal Before Sonant. *Danske Videnskabernes Selskab, hist.-fil. Meddelelser* 31.3.
Hamp, E. P. 1953-54. Primitive Irish Intervocalic *w. *Études celtiques* 6: 281-88.
———. 1958. Consonant Allophones in Proto-Keltic. *Lochlann* 1: 209-17.
———. 1966. Three Armenian Etymologies. 3. Armenian *gišer,* Latin *uesper. Revue des études arméniennes* n.s. 3: 13-15.
———. 1969. Some Remarks on Gaulish Phonology. *Indogermanische Forschungen* 74: 147-54.
———. 1972. Miscellanea I. British *war* and *wor-,* *wa* and *uo-. Studia celtica* 7: 155-56.
———. 1973. Another Lesson from 'Frost'. *Journal of Indo-European Studies* 1: 215-23.
———. 1974. The Major Focus in Reconstruction and Change. In *Historical Linguistics,* J. M. Anderson and C. Jones, eds., 2.141-67. Amsterdam: North-Holland.
———. 1975-76. Miscellanea Celtica IV. The British 2 Pl. Ending and *-sw-. *Studia celtica* 10-11: 69-73.
———. 1982a. *amygaf, amwyn. Bulletin of the Board of Celtic Studies* 30: 39-41.
———. 1982b. Varia IX. Breton *riou,* OIr. *reod.* 1. Breton *riou, riv. Études celtiques* 19: 140.
Harvey, A. 1987. The Ogam Inscriptions and Their Geminate Consonant Symbols. *Ériu* 38: 45-71.
Hermann, E. 1923. *Silbenbildung im Griechischen und in den anderen indogermanischen Sprachen.* Göttingen: Vandenhoeck & Ruprecht.
Hollifield, H. 1983. A Note on Gaulish *bissiet* and *buetid. Études celtiques* 20.1: 95-99.
HPhBr = Jackson, K. 1967. *A Historical Phonology of Breton.* Dublin: Dublin Institute for Advanced Studies.

IEW = Pokorny, J. 1959. *Indogermanisches etymologisches Wörterbuch*. Bern: Francke.

Jackson, K. 1950-51. Primitive Irish *w* and *b*. *Études celtiques* 5: 105-15.

KGPN = Schmidt, K. H. 1957. *Die Komposition in gallischen Personennamen*. Tübingen: Niemeyer.

Koch, J. T. 1985. Movement and Emphasis in the Gaulish Sentence. *Bulletin of the Board of Celtic Studies* 32: 1-37.

Ködderitzsch, R. 1985. Die große Felsinschrift von Peñalba de Villastar. *Festschrift für J. Knobloch*, 211-22. Innsbruck: Innsbrucker Beiträge zur Kulturwissenschaft 23.

Korolev, A. A. 1984. *Drevnejšie pamjatniki irlandskogo jazyka*. Moscow: Nauka.

Kortlandt, F. 1986. Posttonic **w* in Old Irish. *Ériu* 37: 89-92.

Kowal, B. 1987. Beobachtungen zur Inschrift von Chamalières. *Indogermanische Forschungen* 92: 243-55.

Lambert, P.-Y. 1978. Restes de la flexion hétéroclitique en celtique? *Étrennes Lejeune*, 115-22. Paris: Klincksieck.

———. 1985. Essai d'interprétation suivie. M. Lejeune et al., *Le plombe magique du Larzac et les sorcières gauloises*, 61-83. Paris: Centre National de la Recherche Scientifique.

———. 1987a. Notes linguistiques gauloises. *Mélanges . . . J.-B. Colbert de Beaulieu*, 527-34. Paris: Le léopard d'or.

———. 1987b. A Restatement on the Gaulish Tablet from Chamalières. *Bulletin of the Board of Celtic Studies* 34: 10-17.

LEIA = Vendryes, J., E. Bachellery, et P.-Y. Lambert. 1959ff. *Lexique étymologique de l'irlandais ancien*. Dublin, Paris: Dublin Institute for Advanced Studies and Centre National de la Recherche Scientifique.

Lejeune, M. 1979. La dédicace de Martialis à Alise. *Revue des études anciennes* 81: 251-60.

———. 1985a. Notes d'étymologie gauloise. IX. Gaulois *UXEDIOS*. *Études celtiques* 20: 81-87.

———. 1985b. Approche du texte. Lejeune et al., *Le plomb magique du Larzac et les sorcières gauloises*, 24-44. Paris: Centre National de la Recherche Scientifique.

Lep = Lejeune, M. 1971. *Lepontica*. Paris: Les Belles Lettres.

Lewis, H. 1943. *Yr elfen Ladin yn yr iaith Gymraeg*. Caerdydd: Gwasg Prifysgol Cymru.

LHEB = Jackson, K. 1953. *Language and History in Early Britain*. Edinburgh: Edinburgh University Press.

Lindeman, F. O. 1980. Welsh *amwyn*. *Bulletin of the Board of Celtic Studies* 28: 603-5.

———. 1983. Welsh *hwyad*. *Bulletin of the Board of Celtic Studies* 30: 303-4.

———. 1987. *Introduction to the "Laryngeal Theory."* Oslo: Norwegian University Press.

Loth, J. 1910. Remarques et additions à l'*Introduction to Early Welsh* de John Strachan. *Revue celtique* 31: 129-81.

McManus, D. 1984. The So-Called *Cothrige* and *Pátraic* Strata of Latin Loan-Words in Early Irish. *Irland und Europa. Die Kirche im Frühmittelalter*, ed. P. Ní Chatháin and M. Richter, 179-96. Stuttgart: Klett-Cotta.

———. 1986. Ogam: Archaizing, Orthography and the Authenticity of the Manuscript Key to the Alphabet. *Ériu* 37: 1-31.

Mayrhofer, M. 1986. *Indogermanische Grammatik*. Band I. 2. Halbband: *Lautlehre*. Heidelberg: Winter.
Meid, W. 1970. *Die Romanze von Froech und Findabair. Táin Bó Froích*. Innsbruck: Innsbrucker Beiträge zur Kulturwissenschaft 30.
Motta, F. 1978. Contributi allo studio della lingua delle iscrizioni ogamiche (A–B). *Studi e saggi linguistici* 18: 257–333.
Neumann, G. 1983. Die Sprachverhältnisse in den germanischen Provinzen des Römischen Reiches. *Aufstieg und Niedergang der Römischen Welt* II.29.2, 1061–88. Berlin: de Gruyter.
O'Rahilly, T. F. 1946. Ir. *aobh, aoibheall*, etc. W. *ufel, uwel*. Gall. *Ēsus. Ériu* 14: 1–6.
Parry-Williams, T. H. 1914. Some Points of Similarity in the Phonology of Welsh and Breton. *Revue celtique* 35: 317–56.
Pokorny, J. 1917. Streitfragen zur altirischen Grammatik. 7. Vokalkontraktion und Synkope. *Zeitschrift für celtische Philologie* 11: 15–18.
———. 1918. Zur Chronologie der Umfärbung der Vokale im Altirischen. *Zeitschrift für celtische Philologie* 12: 415–26.
———. 1921. Einiges zur irischen Synkope. *Zeitschrift für celtische Philologie* 13: 31–42.
Poultney, J. W. 1963. Evidence for IE Alternation of Initial $/g^w/$ and $/w/$. *Language* 39: 398–408.
Prosdocimi, A. L. 1986. L'iscrizione leponzia di Prestino: Vent'anni dopo. *Zeitschrift für celtische Philologie* 41: 225–50.
RIG = Lejeune, M. 1985. *Recueil des inscriptions gauloises*, I: *Textes Gallo-Grecs*. Paris: Centre National de la Recherche Scientifique.
Rivet und Smith = Rivet, A. L. F. and C. Smith. 1982[2]. *The Place-Names of Roman Britain*. London: Batsford.
Schmidt, K. H. 1976a. Zur keltiberischen Inschrift von Botorrita. *Bulletin of the Board of Celtic Studies* 26.4: 375–94.
———. 1976b. The Contribution of Celt-Iberian to the Reconstruction of Common Celtic. *Actas del I Col. sobre leng. y cult. prerrom.* . . . , 329–42. Salamanca: Ediciones Universidad de Salamanca.
———. 1979a. Besprechung von *Étrennes de septantaine*. *Zeitschrift für celtische philologie* 37: 287–90.
———. 1979b. Probleme der relativen Chronologie. *Incontri linguistici* 5: 55–59.
———. 1980. Continental Celtic as an Aid to the Reconstruction of Proto-Celtic. *Zeitschrift für Vergleichende Sprachforschung* 94: 172–97.
———. 1981a. The Gaulish Inscription of Chamalières. *Bulletin of the Board of Celtic Studies* 29.2: 256–68.
———. 1981a. Grundlagen einer festlandkeltischen Grammatik. *Le lingue indoeuropee di frammentaria attestazione*, 65–90. Pisa: Giardini.
———. 1983. Handwerk und Handwerker in altkeltischen Sprachdenkmälern. *Das Handwerk in vor- und frühgeschichtlicher Zeit*, hrsg. v. H. Jankuhn et al., Teil II, 751–63. Göttingen: Vandenhoeck & Ruprecht.
———. 1984. Celtic Phonology. [Im Druck für E. Polomé and W. Winter, eds., *The Phonology of the Early Dialects of Indo-European*.]
———. 1985. Keltisch, Baltisch und Slavisch. *Festschrift für L. Mitxelena*, 23–29. Vitoria: Universidad del País Vasco.
———. 1986a. Zur Rekonstruktion des Keltischen. Festlandkeltisches und inselkeltisches Verbum. *Zeitschrift für celtische Philologie* 41: 159–79.

———. 1986b. Keltiberisch *Tocoitos/Tocoitei* und gallisch *Ucuete/Ucuetin*. *Zeitschrift für celtische Philologie* 41: 1-4.

———. 1988. Zur Entwicklung indogermanischer Partizipien im Keltischen. *Linguistique balkanique* 31 (in memoriam V. Georgiev): 25-29.

Seebold, E. 1972. *Das System der indogermanischen Halbvokale*. Heidelberg: Winter.

Smith, C. 1983. Vulgar Latin in Roman Britain: Epigraphic and Other Evidence. *Aufstieg und Niedergang der Römischen Welt* II.29.2, 893-948. Berlin: de Gruyter.

Sommerfelt, A. 1954. Consonant Quantity in Celtic. *Norsk Tidsskrift for Sprogvidenskap* 17: 102-18.

Strachan, J. 1909. *An Introduction to Early Welsh*. Manchester: Manchester University Press.

Thes. = Stokes, W. and J. Strachan. 1901-3. *Thesaurus Paleohibernicus*. Vols. 1-2. Oxford; repr. Dublin: Dublin Institute for Advanced Studies, 1975.

Thurneysen, R. 1918. Miszellen. 4. Der Übergang von *v-* in *f-* im Irischen. *Zeitschrift für celtische Philologie* 12: 410-11.

———. 1927. Zu den Graffiti von La Graufesenque. *Zeitschrift für celtische Philologie* 16: 285-304.

———. 1937. Zum Ogom. *Beiträge zur Geschichte der deutschen Sprache und Literatur* 61: 188-208.

Tibiletti Bruno, M. G. 1981. Le iscrizioni celtiche d'Italia. *I Celti d'Italia*, 157-207. Pisa: Giardini.

Tovar, A. 1972-73. Kollektiva auf *-r* im Keltischen. *Études celtiques* 13: 411-27.

———. 1983. Bilingüismo en La Graufesenque: *"summa uxsedia,"* latín y galo. En *Bivium (Festschrift für M. C. Díaz y Díaz)*, 279-84. Madrid: Gredos.

———. 1986. The Celts in the Iberian Peninsula: Archaeology, History, Language. In *History and Culture of the Celts*, 68-101. Heidelberg: Winter.

Vendryes, J. 1912. A propos des groupes initiaux *dentale + v*. In *Miscellany presented to K. Meyer*, 286-90. Halle: Niemeyer.

———. 1924. Remarques sur les graffites de Graufesenque. *Bulletin de la Société de Linguistique de Paris* 25: 34-43.

VGKS = Pedersen, H. 1909-13. *Vergleichende Grammatik der keltischen Sprachen*. Göttingen: Vandenhoeck & Ruprecht.

Watkins, C. 1955. The Phonemics of Gaulish: The Dialect of Narbonensis. *Language* 31: 9-19.

———. 1966. The Origin of the *f*-future. *Ériu* 20: 67-81.

Weisgerber, L. 1969. *Rhenania Germano-Celtica*. Bonn: Rohrscheid.

WGr = Morris Jones, J. 1913. *A Welsh Grammar*. Oxford: Clarendon.

Williams, C. A. 1891. *Die französischen Ortsnamen keltischer Abkunft*. Strassburg: Heitz.

Wolf, H. J. 1982. Quantité vocalique et accentuation de quelques types de toponymes gaulois. *L'onomastique, témoin des langues disparues*, p. p. G. Taverdet, 277-85. Dijon: Association bourguignonne de dialectologie et d'onomastique.

Some Celtic Phrasal Echoes

In his linguistic reconstructions and comparisons Eric Hamp has never confined himself to single speech sounds, single morphemes, or single words; over many years he has consistently included within the purlieu of linguistic comparison and the comparative method higher syntactic units, ranging from noun and verb phrases to sentences and entire texts. For someone who made his scholarly debut with the morphophonemics of the Celtic mutations, such an approach was as obvious and natural as it was necessary. I offer him here some scattered gleanings of textual comparisons, *phrasal echoes*, sentential similarities between Celtic and other Indo-European traditions.

For the most part, such phrasal equations may be attributed just to "funny coincidence," or to the simple principle that like circumstances may call forth like utterances. Yet sometimes the comparison of like syntactic structures also involves nontrivial lexical equations at the same structure points, or nontrivial syntactic and semantic matches under shared or common thematic context suitable for projection back in time. At this point it is legitimate to speculate whether the similarity may be ultimately genetic in character. That is to say that this is the way certain people having certain traditions, "un certain peuple ayant certaines origines" in Saussure's memorable phrase (Benveniste 1963, 13), under certain recurrent circumstances, produced certain particular utterances, which were pretty much the same across significant stretches of time and space.

"I have treated elsewhere," to use a formulaic phrase recurrent in the works of the Jubilar, two cases in Celtic (Watkins, 1989): one probably just remarkable coincidence,[1] but the other a good candidate for genetic filiation. Because the latter case now requires discussion of a conflicting view that appeared after my original version, I recapitulate it here in somewhat fuller compass, as the first of two case studies.

1

Every beginning student of Old Irish is familiar with the formulaic oath

tongu do dia toinges mo thúath[2]
"I swear by the god my people swear by,"

with its variants *tongu(-sa) do dia toingte Ulaid* (TBC Rec. I, 798, 808, 4099) "I swear by the god the Ulstermen swear by," *toingthe mo thúath* (938), and the later *luigim luigi luigis mo thúath* (2749), *luigim-sa a luigend mo t[h]úath* (2871). The phrase was familiar enough to the scribe of our earliest manuscript, Lebor na hUidre (ca. A.D. 1100), that he could just write *tongu et reliqua* (2559, 4010) or *tongu do dia* (1180, *et reliqua* add. Yellow Book of Lecan). Strachan and Bergin in *Stories from the Táin* are doubtless correct in restoring nonpalatized consonants for Old Irish in the two relative verb forms, *tongas* (MSS *toinges*) and *tongtae* (MSS *toingte*), but for the sake of simplicity I will retain the familiar manuscript reading.

The use of this "formula of asseveration" (Royal Irish Academy's *Dictionary*, s.v. *tongaid*) is widespread in the saga literature. In my original paper I had stated, "Even the most resolute antinativists have never suggested a Latin origin or model for the phrase, and we may take it at face value as a genuine and inherited form of the Irish oath."

The authenticity of the phrase has in fact now been called into question by Ruarí Ó hUiginn 1989, who studies the phrase and its variants and asserts that "Far from reflecting an inherited prechristian archaism, it has every appearance of being a contrived learned phrase . . . the creation of archaicizing christian *literati*." Now I am wholly in sympathy with the antinativists, when their cause is just; but I believe that in the present case the arguments adduced are ill-founded. Ó hUiginn acknowledges (339) that *tongu do dia toinges mo thúath* is an archaic construction, the so-called "dative" use of the relative, as elucidated by Breatnach 1980. Ó hUiginn suggests as an alternative that the construction is "mixed," for the verb can also take the accusative of the divinity sworn by, which Breatnach had earlier said (3, n. 10) might well be "the original construction." But in view of the fact that "to swear by" in both Latin and Classical Greek could take either the accusative or a prepositional phrase, it is likely that both syntactic possibilities had coexisted in Irish as well for a long time prior to our documentation. A rarer form of oath in Irish, not noted by Ó hUiginn, is that sworn by Cú Chulainn's charioteer Lóig in a *rhetoric* ('rosc', 'run') in TBC Rec. I, 1149-50,

> .r. *Lóeg dixit* in marg:
> *artung-sa déu*
> "I swear by the gods"

where the gods are in the accusative, as in Greek ὄμνυμι θεούς, ἐπόμνυμαι θεούς. The Latin verb *iurare* can take an accusative; the oldest instance is from the beginning of the fifth century B.C.: Duenos inscription, Corpus inscriptionum latinarum I² 2,

> *iouesat deiuos*
> "he swears by the gods"

"iurat deos" Leumann 1977, 6.

For Ó hUiginn "the two possible constructions [*tongu do dia toinges* . . . /*tongu dia toinges* . . .] are both rather awkward, and do nothing to solve the problem of the syntactic inbalance" (339). But because the "dative" use of the relative is as grammatical as the "accusative" use, there is no imbalance by definition. It is the prepositional relative clause that is late, as Thurneysen saw (1946, §510). Ó hUiginn would further translate *tongu do* as 'I swear to/for' rather than 'I swear by', and then curiously adduces in support archaic Old Irish *toing do dia* in *Córus aitire* with Thurneysen's translation 'schwöre bei Gott'. The reasoning is unclear; if "the swearer invokes God as his guarantor, . . . a perfectly normal thing for a christian to do," it is surely no less a perfectly normal thing for a pagan to do, too.

Ó hUiginn concludes with a most unlikely scenario. The "original version of the oath" (340) is the "extremely common" (332) type

> *tongu a toinges* [d-] *mo thúath*
> "I swear what my people swear."

Contamination with "the christian phrase" (340) yielded

> *tongu do dia a toinges* [d-] *mo thúath*
> "I swear to God what my people swear."

This type, as he admits, is "not very numerous" (339). He cites one example from *Brislech mór Maige Muirtheimni* and three from *Togail Bruidne Da Derga*; but two of the latter instances (from the

Yellow Book of Lecan) lack the pronoun *a (n-)* in the version of manuscript D (Royal Irish Academy MS D iv 2). This rare type is then to have undergone elision of the unstressed pronoun *a (n-)*, yielding

tongu do dia (a) toinges [d-] *mo thúath.*

It is not clear whether Ó hUiginn thinks that *is* the "extremely common"

tongu do dia toinges mo thúath

or whether we have a separate (and unmotivated) development of the syntactic and semantic reanalysis,

"I swear by the god my people swear by"

(presumably with [t-]), which on the evidence of the later parallels is how the phrase was taken.

The point is simply this: given that the starting point is very common, why should it undergo a series of undocumented and unmotivated changes to get to the next very common, but synchronically coexisting, change? It makes far more sense to take *tongu do dia toinges* [t-] *mo thúath* as the basic oath, the performative speech act, just like the variant cited by Ó hUiginn from the *Táin* in the Book of Leinster (O'Rahilly 1984, 44.1630)

tongu-sa na dé dá n-adraim
"I swear by the gods whom I worship."

The older common variant *tongu a toinges* [d-] *mo thúath* "I swear what my people swear" is not a performative speech act but an abbreviation, just as much as *tongu et reliqua.* "I swear what my people swear" is just not what people actually swear; but "I swear by the god my people swear by," or "I swear by the gods whom I worship," is. We may indeed take it at face value as a genuine and inherited form of the Irish oath.

Consider the following. We find semantically and syntactically exactly parallel oaths in two other Indo-European traditions. The god or gods invoked are characteristically defined and specified as "swearer's own" by a restrictive relative clause.

We may first make a comparison with the earliest Russian paganism, as elucidated by Roman Jakobson (1985, 34–35). The Old Russian Primary Chronicle cites three peace treaties with the Greeks, in 907, 945, and 971. In the first, the representatives of Rus' took their oath according to their law (*po ruskomu zakonu*) and swore "both by *Perunŭ*, their own god (*Perunŭmĭ bogŭmĭ svoimĭ*) and by *Volosŭ*, the god of cattle (*Volosŭmĭ skotĭemĭ bogŭmĭ*). The word *svojĭ* "one's own" of the purely narrative *Perunŭmĭ bogŭmĭ svoimĭ* of 905 finds its true explanation in the direct quoted speech of the oath itself in 971. In Jakobson's words, " 'The god whom we ourselves venerate,' i.e. 'our own god' (*svojĭ*)." The full phrase of the oath of 971 is

> *da iměemŭ kljatvu otŭ boga vŭ nĭže věruemŭ—[vŭ] Peruna i [vŭ] Volosa boga skotĭja*
> "may we be accursed of the god whom we worship—Perun and Volos god of cattle,"

literally, "the god in whom we believe."

In 1967, resuming an oral presentation of 1958, Reinhold Merkelbach demonstrated that the virtually identical oaths on two papyri of the first and third centuries C.E. (respectively, P[ubbl.] S[oc.] I[tal.] 1290 and 1162) represent the oath of the Isis mysteries. It begins with a dualistic litany

> I swear ([ὀμν]ύω) by the one who divided and separated earth from heaven, and darkness from light, and day from night, and sunrise from sunset, and life from death, and birth from corruption, and black from white, and dry from wet, and sea from land, and bitter from sweet, and flesh from spirit,

and continues ἐπόμνυμαι δὲ καὶ οὓς π[ροσκυνῶ θ]εούς,

> and I swear by the gods whom I worship (that I will preserve and protect the mysteries vouchsafed to me).

The uniqueness of the phrase was noted by Walter Burkert in his Harvard Jackson lectures (1987, 50). Merkelbach in a note had suggested that the phrase probably refers to the other gods of the circle of Isis and Osiris. To this Burkert responds (emphasis mine), "This approach overlooks the *tradition of oath formulaics* that have similar provisions from ancient times: each partner has to swear '*the greatest local oath*'[3] because only such an oath, by *one's own gods 'whom I revere,'* will be a serious obligation. The 'mystery oath' complies with this practice; it is built on the foundations of a previous and lasting religious attachment to 'the gods I actually worship.'"

I suggest that in the three specifications of "one's own god(s)," "the gods one's people worship,"

tongu do dia toinges mo thúath (tongu-sa na dé dá n-adraim),

iměemŭ kljatvu otŭ boga nīže věruemŭ, and

ἐπόμνυμαι οὓς προσκυνῶ θεούς,

we have not only a primary syntactic comparandum but the material for reconstructing an inherited Indo-European oath formulation, the "greatest local oath." The resemblances are such that we must assume the Indo-European way of saying that was not very different.

2

Lionel Joseph (1982) has given us the welcome etymological analysis of Old Irish *tuir* 'house-post', dat. sg., nom. pl. *tuirid*: a compound *to-rid-* with second member the root noun to Greek ἐρείδω 'prop (up)', Latin *ridica* 'stake for vines' (with the same suffix as in *pertica* 'rod, stake'), IE *$h_1r(e)id$-. Joseph notes that *tuir* shows "the usual transferred meaning 'champion, chief'," with a reference to my earlier study (1978) of OIr. *clí* with the same range of meanings, as especially clear in *Cormac* (Yellow Book of Lecan) 275. Characteristic are noun phrases like *tuirid na túath* "lords, pillars of the tribes" (*Saltair na Rann* 6261), and in Classical Modern Irish *tuir Bhreagh* "pillar of Bregia" from the Grammatical Tracts (Armstrong 1985 [1988] s.v.) The metaphor is a natural one, probably created independently many times and in many places. I noted Ṛgveda *kṛchre-śrít-* 'support in need' (: *clí*). It is also persistent with particular lexical items in Modern English: the expression "pillar of the church," still alive and well, is first attested by the *Oxford English Dictionary* in 1325. For a variant that is no longer possible note also "pillers and studds of popery" in 1603. It is therefore interesting in light of Joseph's etymology *tuir*: ἐρείδω to note alongside *tuir Bhreagh* that the Greek poet Pindar, a traditionalist in the inherited genre of praise poetry, calls his patron Theron ἔρεισμ Ἀκράγαντος "pillar of Akragas" (*Olympian* 2.6., 476 B.C.), with a derivative of the same root.

Pindar repeats the metaphor with a different lexeme later in the same ode (2.81-82) of Hector: Τροίας . . . κίονα "pillar of Troy." The traditional character of this whole passage is clear. It is a variant of the thematic pattern that I have termed elsewhere the "basic formula" (1986, 320; 1987: 277), which is the definition of the hero:

HERO   SLAY (*$g^u hen$-)   SERPENT
HERO$_1$ SLAY (*$g^u hen$-)   HERO$_2$

In *Isthmian* 5.39-41 (478 B.C.?) Pindar asks, λέγε, τίνες Κύκνον, τίνες Ἕκτορα πέφνον/ καὶ . . . / Μέμνονα "Say, who killed Kuknos, who Hektor, and . . . Memnon?" The traditional answer preexisted; here in *Olympian* 2.81-83 we find it, embedding the phrase "pillar of Troy":

ὃς Ἕκτορα σφᾶλε, Τροίας
. . . κίονα, Κύκνον τε . . .
Ἀοῦς τε παῖδ Αἰθίοπα.

(Akhilleus), who felled Hektor, pillar of Troy, and Kuknos . . . and the Ethiopian son of Dawn [= Memnon].

In the preceding century a different answer (for a different Kuknos) had been given in the *Shield of Herakles* (57), attributed to Hesiod: ὃς καὶ Κύκνον ἔπεφνεν "(Herakles), who killed Kuknos." The relative clauses underline the clear thematic link, and σφᾶλε is one of many variants of the basic verb πέφνε.

The traditional nature of *Olympian* 2.81-83 is emphasized by Pindar himself in the metaphor in the very next sentence (83-85): πολλά μοι ὑπ᾽ ἀγκῶνος ὠκέα βέλη / ἔνδον ἐντὶ φαρέτρας / φωνάεντα συνετοῖσιν "Many swift arrows I have under my arm in my quiver which speak to those who understand." The "arrows" are a traditional metaphor for the poet's formulas and themes, which he shares with the discerning audience.

The whole passage of *Olympian* 2 was analyzed in detail by the late Elroy Bundy, whose *Studia Pindarica* of 1962 (reprinted 1986) can legitimately be regarded as the foundation of modern Pindar criticism. Bundy's contribution was a proper understanding and appreciation of the rhetorical conventions of professional encomiastic poetry, the "conventional aspects of choral communication" (1962, 2). Of *Olympian* 2.83-85 just cited he says, "when Pindar speaks pridefully in the first person this is less likely to be the personal Pindar of Thebes than the Pindar privileged to praise the worthiest of men" (1962, 3).

Bundy's message, and more importantly the proper study of Pindar, is of direct relevance to the Celticist. In Ireland and Wales of the European Middle Ages just as in fifth-century Greece and the Greek Mediterranean we have "an oral, public, epideictic literature dedicated to the single purpose of eulogizing men and communities" (1962, 35). It can be beneficial to Hellenist and Celticist alike to think of Pindar and Bacchylides as Bardic poetry, *dán díreach*, or *dindsenchus*, for the challenges are the same.

In Bundy's linguistic metaphor we need "a thorough study of conventional themes, motives, and sequences in choral poetry—in short, a grammar of choral style" (1962, 32). We are looking for "systems of shared symbols" (ibid.); "in this genre the choice involved in composition is mainly a choice of formulae, motives, themes, topics, and set sequences of these . . . the thematic and motivational grammar of choral composition" (1962, 92). We can go farther; praise need not be only of "men and communities," but of gods as well, and the whole hymnic tradition of Vedic India and Iran can become part of the same universe of discourse. We are looking at "the products of poetic and rhetorical conventions whose meaning, though at present dark to us, is recoverable from comparative study" (1962, 35). Bundy's words take on new meaning in the context of comparative historical ethnosemantics, comparative historical ethnopoetics, the genetic comparative literature of the Indo-European speaking peoples.

"Pillar of *x*" in Greece and Ireland is part of just such a "system of shared symbols," as is the choice of formulas, themes, and their set sequence in Pindar's frame, "who killed Hektor, pillar of Troy, and Kuknos, and the Ethiopian son of Dawn."

Pindar uses once more the expression "pillar of *x*," with the noun ἔρεισμα cognate with Irish *tuir*. It occurs in a famous dithyramb in praise of Athens for her role in the Persian wars (fr. 76):

> Ὦ ταὶ λιπαραὶ καὶ ἰοστέφανοι καὶ ἀοίδιμοι,
> Ἑλλάδος ἔρεισμα, κλειναὶ Ἀθᾶναι, δαιμόνιον πτολίεθρον
>
>> Oh, the shining and the violet-crowned and the storied in song, pillar of Hellas, glorious Athens, divine citadel.

We need not linger on the remarkable phonetic figure that indexes, points to, and frames our expression "pillar of Hellas" while linking it to the sequencing of i-diphthongs:

- ai ∪ ∪ ai ai ∪ - ∪ ∪ oi ai ∪ oi ∪ oi
Helládos éreisma ei ai ∪ - ai ∪ ∪ - ∪ ∪ - ∪

For this single verse of praise, according to Isocrates, Pindar was rewarded by Athens with ten thousand drachmas. "All other versions of this anecdote mention one thousand drachmas; Isokrates' is undoubtedly a rhetorical exaggeration," as William H. Race points out (1987, 131), whose article drew my attention to the expression. As likely as they are to be independent creations, Irish *tuir Bhreagh* "pillar of Bregia" and Pindar's phrase Ἑλλάδος ἔρεισμα "pillar of Hellas" (together with its reward) remain together, as I have said of another phrase elsewhere (Watkins 1989), "a valid and powerful icon of the Indo-European poet, his art, and his social function."

CALVERT WATKINS
Harvard University

NOTES

1. Middle Welsh (Math uab Mathonwy) *dwyn eu heilyw e hun a oruc, a dodi eilyw arall arnunt, ual nat adnepit*; Old Hittite (Zalpa) *nu-smas* DINGIR.DIDLI-*es tamaīn karātan daīr nu* AMA-ŠUNU [*-u*]*s natta ganeszi*.
2. For example, Táin Bó Cúailnge, Recension I (O'Rahilly 1976), 736, 3629, 4018. Hereafter abbreviated TBC Rec. I.
3. Thucydides 5.189, 47.8, ὀμνύντων τὸν ἐπιχώριον ὅρκον . . . τὸν μέγιστον.

REFERENCES

Armstrong, John. 1985 [1988]. A Glossarial Index of Nouns and Adjectives in Irish Grammatical Tracts II-IV. *Proceedings of the Harvard Celtic Colloquium* 5: 187-410.
Benveniste, Emile. 1963. Saussure après un demi-siècle. *Cahiers Ferdinand de Saussure* 20: 7-21.
Breatnach, Liam. 1980. Some Remarks on the Relative in Old Irish. *Ériu* 39: 1-9.
Bundy, Elroy. 1962. (Reprinted 1986.) *Studia Pindarica*. Berkeley, Los Angeles: University of California Press.
Burkert, Walter. 1987. *Ancient Mystery Cults*. Cambridge, Mass.: Harvard University Press.
Jakobson, Roman. 1985. *Selected Writings* 7. Berlin: Mouton.
Joseph, Lionel. 1982. Old Irish *tuir* 'house-post'. *Ériu* 32: 176-77.

Leumann, Manu. 1977. *Lateinische Laut- und Formenlehre*. Munich: C. H. Beck.

Merkelbach, Reinhold. 1967. Die Eide der Isis-Mysterien. *Zeitschrift für Papyrologie und Epigraphik* 1: 55-73.

Ó hUiginn, Ruarí. 1989. Tongu do dia toinges mo thúath and Related Expressions. In *Sages, Saints and Storytellers: Celtic Studies in Honour of Professor James Carney*, Donnchadh Ó Corráin, Liam Breatnach, and Kim McCone, eds., 332-41. Maynooth Monographs 2. Maynooth: An Sagart.

O'Rahilly, Cecile. 1976. *Táin Bó Cúailnge Recension I*. Dublin: Dublin Institute for Advanced Studies.

———. 1984. *Táin Bó Cúailnge from the Book of Leinster*. Dublin: Dublin Institute for Advanced Studies.

Race, William H. 1987. Pindaric Encomium and Isokrates' *Evagoras*. *Transactions of the American Philological Association* 117: 131-55.

Thurneysen, Rudolf. 1946. *A Grammar of Old Irish*. Dublin: Dublin Institute for Advanced Studies.

Watkins, Calvert. 1978. Old Irish *clí* and *cleth* 'house-post'. *Ériu* 29: 155-60.

———. 1986. The Name of Meleager. o-o-pe-ro-si. In *Festschrift für Ernst Risch*, Annemarie Etter, ed., 320-28. Berlin: de Gruyter.

———. 1987. How to Kill a Dragon in Indo-European. In *Studies in Memory of Warren Cowgill (1929-1985)*, Calvert Watkins, ed., 270-99. Berlin: de Gruyter.

———. 1989. New Parameters in Historical Linguistics, Philology and Culture History. Linguistic Society of America presidential address, New Orleans, December 1988. *Language* 65.4.

Some Celtic Otherworld Terms

The idea that Ireland and Wales are both "Celtic" is quite recent; it is based on postmedieval perceptions of the affinities between the Gaelic and Brittonic languages on the one hand and, on the other, of the linguistic and cultural similarities between the early Britons and the continental peoples known to the ancient world as Celts. "The Irish preserved no tradition of being Celts, and neither did the Welsh. The medieval pseudo-historical theories about their origin did not connect them either with one another or with the ancient Gauls" (Byrne 1974, 144). Moreover, the Irish and Welsh languages were mutually incomprehensible, and even that early comparativist Giraldus Cambrensis failed to observe their special kinship within the European family of languages, whereas the common origin of Welsh, Cornish, and Breton was obvious to him (Coulter and Magoun 1926; Bartlett 1982, 209–10). This is not surprising, for even today there is no agreement as to how many millennia ago the Celtic languages diverged (cf. Greene 1983; Piggott 1983; Elsie 1983–84), nor whether Common Celtic was succeeded by an intermediate, mutually comprehensible dialect of "Insular Celtic" confined to Ireland and Britain, as opposed to Gaul and Spain. (It can be argued that modern impressions of an opposition between "Insular Celtic" and "Continental Celtic" may reflect the chronological disparity in the data rather than the existence of a genuine language group; see Sims-Williams 1984, 147–48). Evidence for any neo-Celtic linguistic community between medieval Ireland and Wales has to be sought in loanwords and linguistic drift rather than in long-lost common origins (see in general Meid 1986). The present state of research, however, suggests that such linguistic community was less a matter of direct commerce between the Brittonic and Gaelic vernaculars than of common membership of successive Latin, French, and (excluding the case of Breton) English speech-areas.

Because scholars agree that the concept of "Celtic" is fundamentally a matter of language, and because the distance between the medieval Celtic languages is so great, the modern tendency to treat medieval Irish and Welsh culture as fundamentally the same seems anachronistic. For example, Dillon and Chadwick described their book *The Celtic Realms* as an attempt to "present the Celts in history as one people, with a common tradition and a common character," and this aim was recently endorsed in the programme for a proposed UNESCO encyclopaedia on the "History and Culture of the Celts" (Schmidt 1986, 21). Any argument which assumes that it is legitimate to generalize about "Celts" in history, or even in prehistory, is doomed to circularity. We should need first to unpick the composite image of the Celt and Celtic culture that has been constructed over the past few centuries (see Sims-Williams 1986). Then we should need to contrast as well as compare the various Celtic-speaking cultures within a wider (and not exclusively Indo-European) framework. We should also need to assess how much intercourse there was between them. To what extent, for example, is it legitimate and useful to think about medieval Irish and Welsh culture in terms of an "Irish Sea Province" (Moore 1970)? Certainly, there was colonization across the Irish Sea, as well as political links and ecclesiastical contacts; and there was also a shared Latin and artistic culture, as we can see from manuscripts and their glosses. But were these contacts closer than with other neighbouring non-Celtic speaking peoples such as the Franks, Anglo-Saxons, Picts, or Norsemen?

My own special interest is the matter of Irish vernacular literary influence on Wales. Here, above all, there is a widespread misconception that because medieval Irish and Welsh literature were both "Celtic" they must have been closely related if not identical, whereas in fact there was scarcely any shared "Celtic" vernacular literature in the Middle Ages (Sims-Williams 1982; 1989; forthcoming). Nevertheless, there *are* definite similarities between the vernacular literatures and mythologies of Ireland and Wales which demand explanation. Where we can use philological tools, as when comparing the (*relatively* small) number of names of gods or heroes found in both Irish and Welsh literature, we find that only a handful of unimportant names are borrowed and that nearly all of the shared names are cognates rather than loans. To give a well-known example, the name of the Welsh hero *Gwyn* ap Nudd is cognate with the name of the Irish hero *Finn* mac Cumaill. Both can be derived from a Common Celtic *Windos 'The white one' (cf. Nagy 1985, 22 and

236; Ó hÓgáin 1988, 5), an adjective that Hamp (1979) has tentatively derived from the Indo-European root *sụeid(h)- 'to shine', mentioned further below. Obviously, *Finn* is unlikely to be a medieval borrowing of *Gwyn(n)* (or vice versa). We cannot, however, rule out the possibilities of medieval translation—replacing a name meaning 'white' in one language with its semantic equivalent in the other —and of "translation" from one phonological system into another; these possibilities are especially attractive when there are problems in reconstructing a Common Celtic original, as in the case of Irish *Manannán* and Welsh *Manawydan* (see Mac Cana 1966, 247; Koch 1987, 20). But these are minor exceptions or problems; most of the important heroic and divine names which are related are clearly cognates rather than borrowings. This seems to me to be the strongest proof of Proinsias Mac Cana's opinion (1966, 246) that "one can scarcely doubt that most of the similarities between Welsh and Irish literary use and content are to be ascribed to common origins."

We should, nevertheless, stress the limitations of such philological evidence for "common origins." Labelling *Finn* and *Gwyn* as "cognates" does not necessarily mean that Common Celtic speakers had a god or hero called **Windos* two or three millennia ago (or whenever Gaelic and Brittonic diverged); it simply implies that he was already talked about in both languages *no later than* the sound changes that differentiated the forms *Finn* and *Gwyn(n)*, that is to say, on Jackson's chronology, before **w-* > *f-* in Irish in the seventh century and **i* > *y* and **w-* > *gw-* in Welsh in the sixth and eighth centuries.[1] In the unlikely event of an archaeologist's coming along with proof that the cult of **Windos* was introduced into Ireland from Britain, or vice versa, earlier than these sound changes, in (say) the fourth century, linguists would not be able to disprove such early borrowing merely by stating that *Gwyn* and *Finn* had been labelled as cognates. In other words, the time depth of the linguists' concepts of "common origins" and "cognates" is elastic, depending on the dates of the sound changes relevant to the case in question. So, to say that two names are cognate is *not* proof that the reconstructed shared name, and the myth, cult, or story that it represents, are necessarily a common inheritance as old as the Celtic languages themselves (whatever that might mean), rather than the product of cultural contact in the Irish Sea Province, or over a still wider area, in, say, the first few centuries after Christ.

If it is difficult to account precisely for shared names, it is almost impossible to account for shared stories and motifs. Words and names, being generally arbitrary, are unlikely to recur with the same signification in different areas without there being some connection. Story motifs, by contrast, may well be polygenetic; and this may even be true of those elaborate story-patterns which are mimetic of universal features of human life and thought, such as the "Heroic Biography" (Taylor 1964) or which are at least mimetic of aspects of many societies, such as the "Heroic Age" (Chadwick 1912).[2] For example, Greek influence on Irish literature cannot be deduced from the facts that Achilles and Cú Chulainn are both born in supernatural circumstances (the "Heroic Biography") and that they both drag defeated opponents behind their chariots (the "Heroic Age").[3] The issue of literary influence between two stories should only arise when they are so uncommonly similar as to preclude coincidence. Even when coincidence has been ruled out, no tool like historical philology is available by which the similarities can be attributed to direct borrowing in a particular direction or to independent borrowing from a third source (see, for example, Sims-Williams 1977–78; 1978; cf. Sayers 1986).

Other similarities between Irish and Welsh narratives may be due less to coincidence or international borrowing than to "a common Celtic inheritance of mythology, belief, and social custom" (Bromwich 1965, 204). Yet, if the cultural feature in question was shared with non-Celtic speakers in northwestern Europe, we should be wary of regarding it as "Common Celtic" or "Insular Celtic" rather than Indo-European, "Old European," or simply indigenous. The idea of the Otherworld may serve as an example.

What modern scholars term "the Otherworld" appears in both medieval Irish and Welsh literature, where it has two main locations, under the ground (including beneath lakes and springs) and on an island across (or under) the sea. Before proceeding further, it is worth stressing that in early Celtic texts there seems—although Welsh *Annwfn* is a possible contender (see below)—to be no single term, embracing both types of location, equivalent to our *the Otherworld* (*l'Autre Monde*, and so on). Our useful, but probably misleading, modern term *Otherworld* seems to derive partly from unconscious analogy with the Christian dichotomy of *this world/the other world* (see below) and partly from a calque on *orbis alius* in Lucan's account of the druidic doctrine that souls survived not in Hades but *orbe alio* (*Pharsalia* 1.457; cf. Reinach 1901, 454).

Lucan's phrase probably meant not "the Otherworld" (nor even "an Otherworld"), supernatural and divorced from "this world," but simply "another region" of the earth (Reinach 1901; de Vries 1963, 256-57). This literally mundane usage was known to Irishmen in the early Middle Ages: the Antipodes were described by Virgil of Salzburg in the mid-eighth century as *alius mundus* (according to Pope Zacharias) and as *alius orbis* by a ninth-century glossator (Heiric of Auxerre?) who was probably influenced by the teachings of John Scottus Eriugena (Carey 1989, 1 n. 2 and 3 n. 8; Marenbon 1981, 134). Such an *alius mundus/orbis* could be separated from the world—our world—merely by an impassable sea. Thus Dícuil, writing in the mid-ninth century but following Solinus verbatim, says that Ceylon was long thought to be *orbis alter* until Alexander the Great's admiral managed to voyage to it (Tierney 1967, 80-81 and 117; cf. Carey 1989, 2 n. 5 and 9 n. 38). Early medieval Celtic *literati* like Virgil and Dícuil may well have been aware of affinities between such an "other world" and the realms of the supernatural beings of their native mythology (Carey 1989). Yet, if so, this awareness did not (as far as I know) lead any early vernacular writer to calque the Latin terms (with or without a definite article) to refer to the native locality. *Otherworld*, then, should be understood with tacit inverted commas in what follows.

The underground Otherworld in Irish literature is frequently located in a 'fairy mound' or *síd* (homophonous with but, according to Eric Hamp [1982], etymologically distinct from *síd* 'peace'; cf. differently Ó Cathasaigh 1978). Thurneysen (1887) compared this word, an *s*-stem, with Latin *sidus* 'star', implying an originally astral Otherworld; his comparison was incorrect, however, for *sidus* derives (as Hamp [1975] and others have recognized) from the abovementioned root *$sueid(h)$- 'shine', which in Irish would have yielded a form with s- ~ f- and the wrong vocalism. It is preferable to derive *síd* from the root *sed- 'sit' and to suppose that it originally meant 'seat, abode', was later specialized as 'abode of divinities', and was finally restricted to their abode in Ireland par excellence, the 'fairy mound' (cf. Ó Cathasaigh 1978, 149-50). According to Ó Cathasaigh *síd* is "the normal generic term which can be used without further definition to denote the Otherworld" (Ó Cathasaigh

1978, 149 and n. 44), but the evidence for this broad sense has been disputed by Carey (1982, 40 n. 20). It is indeed difficult to evaluate, for the writers of the few texts that seem to refer to overseas *síde* may still have been thinking of "fairy mounds" on islands. It may be relevant that many northwestern European megalithic chamber tombs were built on islands or on promontories that became islands when the sea level rose (Daniel 1960, 73 and 88).

In Welsh the Otherworld is generally called *Annw(f)n*; this is often located underground, but not exclusively so, for it can be overseas—and possibly also *under* the sea (see Carey 1982, 42; Haycock 1983–84, 56, 59 n. 32, 65); if so, note that the Antipodes are "under the waters" in two Irish texts cited by Carey (1989, 4–5), and that in 1632 John Davies equated *Annwfn* and *Antipodes* (*GPC* s.v.). The term *Annwfn* was doubtless understood as intensive *an-* plus *dwfn* 'deep' (cf. *anoddyn* 'abyss' < *an-* + **wo-* 'under' + *dwfn*), and this may indeed be the correct etymology, as Eric Hamp has noted (1977–78, 10; similarly Wagner 1975, 7 n. 14). Ifor Williams (1951, 100) suggested that the second element might be *dwfn* 'world' (cf. Gaulish *dubno-, dumno-*), an idea developed by Parry (1963, 449 and 470), who reinterpreted Dafydd ap Gwilym's *I Annwfn oddwfn ydd af* "I go deep down(?) to Annwfn" as *I Annwfn o ddwfn ydd af* "I go from (the) world to Annwfn." With *dwfn* 'world' as the second element, the first could be *an-* < **n̥-* 'not', hence 'Not-World', a formation comparable with the district name *Anergyng* 'area that is not Ergyng, area of Ergyng lost to the English' (see Richards 1969, 6). If so, *Annwfn* would be semantically close to *alius orbis* and English *Otherworld*. Williams preferred *an-* 'in', hence 'In(ner)-World, Under-World'. This *an-* (*an³-* in *GPC*) derives from **ande-* (Hamp 1956; 1977–78, 9–10); one might therefore compare Gaulish *andededion* (acc. sg./gen. pl.) 'infernal one(s)' (Lejeune 1985, 87; Lambert 1987, 13). A similar formation, **yr Is-ddwfn* 'the Lower-World', may survive in corrupt form in the Modern Welsh name for fairies, *Plant Rhys Ddwfn* 'the children of Rhys the Deep' (Rees and Rees 1961, 179); compare here Dafydd ap Gwilym's *pendefig, gwledig gwlad yr hud is dwfn* "prince, lord of the land of magic *below the world*" (Parry 1963, 34 and 449). There seems to be no cognate of *Annwfn* in Irish, nor in the other Celtic languages. (It is phonologically impossible to accept the view of Gaidoz 1897 that *Annw(f)n* is cognate with Breton *anao(u)n* 'souls' < *anaffo(u)n* < **anamones*; cf. Jackson 1967, 121, 592, and 600).

Although the Irish *síd* and the Welsh *Annwfn* are both basically chthonic Otherworlds, there is an important difference between them. Annwfn seems to be a single realm, which can be entered from many places on earth and sea; in the *Four Branches of the Mabinogi* (on which see Hamp 1972-73; 1974-75) we hear of "*a* king from Annwfn" (*Hafgan brenhin o Annwuyn*, MS R) making war on "*the* king of Annwfn" (*Arawn urenhin Annwuyn*), whose realm is contiguous with his (Thomson 1957, 2 and 25), just as Annwfn is itself contiguous with the terrestrial land of Dyfed. (Indeed Arawn brings the hero there by an ordinary mode of overland travel; Carozzi 1983, 453 compares the vision of Dryhthelm in Bede's *Historia ecclesiastica* 5.12.) Apparently, then, Annwfn was a single kingdom, divided into separate subkingdoms and dominated, with opposition, by a king claiming overlordship under the title "king of Annwfn"—a fair reflection of medieval Welsh politics. The Irish fairy mounds or *síde*, by contrast, are independent kingdoms, which enjoy more or less friendly relations with one another, like the mortal *tuatha* of early Irish Law. They are not entrances to a single underground kingdom. Even the two neighbouring *síde* between the Two Paps of Anu in Kerry had no subterranean communication (see Nagy 1985, 168-69 and 216). Nor is it clear that the many *síde* of early Ireland (mapped by Löffler 1983, 620) were regarded as avatars of a single Otherworld, notwithstanding the following assertion by O'Rahilly: "In pagan Ireland every district of importance tended to have its own *síd* or hill within which the Otherworld was believed to be located; nevertheless there was in Celtic belief but one Otherworld, despite the fact that so many different locations were assigned to it. In the same way the deities who presided over the different *síde* were ultimately the same everywhere, despite the variety of local names applied to them" (O'Rahilly 1946, 290; cf. Rees and Rees 1961, 342-43; Carey 1989, 6). This conception of 'but one Otherworld' looks like a modern abstraction, as far as Irish evidence is concerned. Certainly there is no Irish term so likely to mean 'the Otherworld' as *Annwfn* is; as already noted, it is doubtful whether *síd* ever meant '*the* Otherworld' rather than '*an* Otherworld'. It is in *Christian* contexts that we find the dichotomies between *í-siu* 'here' and *í-thall* 'beyond' (for example, Hull 1968, 60), and between *cenntar* 'this world, the world on this side' and *alltar* 'the other world, the world beyond' (for example, O'Keeffe 1905, 202; Smith 1928, 90; cf. *DIL* s.vv.). So, too, it is in Christian contexts that the expression "the other world" entered

English, judging by the *Oxford English Dictionary*; for example, Wyclif rendered *neque in hoc saeculo neque in futuro* (Matt. 12:32) "nether in this world, ne in the tother." This sort of dichotomy does not occur in early Celtic texts about the native mythology. (Carey 1989, 6, states that "the Otherworld was described by the Irish as the 'other side' of the world that they knew," but the citations in *DIL* s.v. *leth* (col. 125) do not support his interpretation of *Is ferr damsa techt leth n-aill* in *Serglige Con Culainn* §13 as a "terse designation of the supernatural realm as the 'other side' "; the supernatural woman is only telling Cú Chulainn "I had better go away.")

We find, then, a general, but not complete, similarity in Otherworld mythology but a divergence in terminology between Ireland and Wales. A possible terminological link across the Irish Sea has been seen in the Welsh word *gorsedd*, which derives, like *síd*, from **sed-* 'sit' and denotes both a manmade tumulus and a natural hill (not necessarily a reputedly hollow one like the Irish *síd*). The range of meaning was well illustrated in the late seventeenth century: "I hear that your Tumuli are called Orsedd in Flintshire . . . Gorsedd or Orsedd commonly used in Anglesey &c. for any riseing [*sic*] ground from whence we have a prospect" (Roberts 1971–72, 106). *Gorsedd* is a compound of *sedd* 'seat' with the preposition **wor* 'over' and possibly another preposition as well, such as **-uks-* 'up' (suggested by Hamp 1977–78, 13; cf. Lejeune 1985, 86; Russell 1988, 117–18), which would explain why **-rs-* has not been assimilated to **-rr-*. The presence of a second preposition was doubted by Loth (1915, 396), rejecting Morris-Jones's reconstruction **u̯or-en-sed-*, and Loth could be correct if we suppose that the compound was formed after the change of **rs > rr*, which was "probably very early" (Jackson 1953, 541). There is no exact cognate in Irish: *forad* 'mound', which Ó Cathasaigh aptly describes as "etymologically a near-match" for *gorsedd* (1978, 150), is unlikely to contain **wor-*, for this should not cause the lenition of **sed-* (see Russell 1985); *forad* may derive from **wo-ro-sed-*, as Pedersen (cited by Ó Cathasaigh) thought.[4]

The most famous literary *gorsedd*, *Gorssed Arberth* in the *Four Branches of the Mabinogi*, plays a clearly supernatural role, though it is not absolutely clear that supernatural beings dwelt within it, as in the Irish *síd* (cf. Koch 1987, 29). It is when Pwyll Prince of Dyfed is sitting on this *gorsedd* that he sees his future wife Rhiannon, presumably a goddess of territorial sovereignty (Koch 1987, 34), riding by on her magic horse. Again, when Rhiannon's second consort,

Manawydan, sits on it with his companions, he sees Dyfed turn into a Waste Land. Later on, Manawydan erects a gallows on it to execute one of the magic mice that have devastated his corn. Ifor Williams identified this *gorsedd* as a *síd* (1951, 101 and 121). While he did not make it clear whether he saw any etymological link between the Welsh and the Irish terms, one is explicitly made by Ó Cathasaigh, who goes on to say that "it may be assumed on the evidence of *gorsedd*, that *sedd* had Otherworld connotations" (1978, 154).

The fact that *síd* and *gorsedd* derive from different grades of the root **sed-* shows that, if they were at all related, it would be as a common inheritance, not as a borrowing from Ireland to Wales or vice versa at a late stage (cf. the comparable variation between *síd* 'peace' and Welsh *hedd* 'id.', discussed by Hamp 1982; see also Hamp 1981, 158 n. 2). But probably *síd* and *gorsedd* are independent formations based on **sed-*. Whereas the uncompounded Irish term seems to emphasize that a *síd* was the 'seat' or 'abode' within which divinities dwelt (cf. Latin *sedes*, also with *ē*-grade), the preposition(s) prefixed to the *sedd* of Welsh *gorsedd* seem rather to emphasize that the *gorsedd* was an eminence *up and upon* which ordinary mortals could sit for various purposes. These purposes included looking out, as in the early Cynddylan *englynion* (Williams 1953, 43 and 229), and holding an 'assembly', a sense for *guorsed* already found in the Old Welsh Juvencus *englynion*, in a religious context as often elsewhere in Welsh (Wiliams 1972, 112-13). Ifor Williams (1951, 120) rightly explained the semantic development of *gorsedd* to 'assembly' with reference to the Manx Tynwald and the frequent occurrence in English hundred-names of elements denoting mounds and hills, including Old English *hlāw* and *beorg* and Old Norse *haugr* 'barrow, tumulus'. These hundred-names referred to the places where folk assembled "on hill-tops or on high ground so as to afford the hundred-men an undisturbed view of the surrounding country and assure their privacy" (Anderson 1939, 157). A similar custom was also current in Ireland, where the *forad*, discussed above, was both a lookout post and associated with assemblies, normally of no particular mythological or sacral significance (see *DIL* and cf. Ó Cathasaigh 1978, 150 n. 52; Rees and Rees 1961, 171 and 183-84). In time of war assemblies might occur on a *tulach tinóil* 'hill of meeting' (O'Sullivan and Ó Riain 1987, lines 610, 650 and n.), and the administration of brehon law on hills is often condemned in English sources (Patterson 1989, 47). A more recreational custom is suggested by "*Suidhe Finn* [Fionn's Seat] as a name for an elevated spot, the idea being that the hero sat there while observing and directing the hunt" (Ó hÓgáin 1988, 306; cf. 127). In Norse texts, too, mortal kings sit on the *haugr* to assert their power, watchmen look out from it, and folk assemble on it (Ellis 1943, 105-11).

Even the *gorsedd* in the *Four Branches* was not exclusively supernatural, unlike the *síde* of Irish texts. The legal as well as the magical significance of the *gorsedd* seems to be in Manawydan's mind when he decides to execute the mouse there, and Pwyll evidently climbs it to look out, or as a recreation (compare *Goreiste ar vrynn a eruyn uym bryt* "My mind desires to sit on a hill" in the Claf Abercuawg *englynion*, Williams 1953, 23), or simply in fulfilment of the international storytelling motif "Kings have seat on hills."[5] In fact, he is at first unaware of its magical properties:

> A guedy y bwyta kyntaf, kyuodi y orymdeith a oruc Pwyll, a chyrchu penn gorssed a oed uch llaw y llys, a elwit Gorssed Arberth. "Arglwyd," heb un o'r llys, "kynnedyf yr orssed yw, pa dylyedauc bynnac a eistedo arnei, nat a odyno heb un o'r deupeth, ay kymriw neu archolleu, neu ynteu a welei rywedawt." (Williams 1951, 9)

> And after the first feasting, Pwyll arose to go for a walk, and he made for the top of a *gorsedd* which was above the court, which was called Gorsedd Arberth. "Lord," said one of the court, "the property of the *gorsedd* is that whatever noble sits on it goes not away without one of two things: either a wound or blows, or else he could see a wonder."

Gorsedd Arberth may have had magic potential because it was a mound (see Chadwick 1968, 44), not because it was a *gorsedd* in particular. We may compare Gwely Idris ('Idris the Giant's bed'), on the mountain called Cadair Idris ('Idris's Seat'); according to Siôn Dafydd Rhys, writing in the sixteenth century,

> ebh a dhywedir taw pwy bynnac o dhyn a 'orwedho ac a gysco ar y gwely hwnnw, vn o'r dhev beth a dhamchweina idhaw, nailh ai bod yn Brydydd o'r bhath 'orev, ai yntev myned yn lhwyr ynbhyd o honaw. (National Library of Wales, MS Peniarth 118, fol. 829, ed. Grooms 1988)

> it is said that whatever man lies down and sleeps on that bed, one of two things will happen to him: he will either be a poet of the finest kind, or else he will go completely mad.

Such statements about the magic properties of mounds—whether mere storytelling motifs (cf. Welsh 1988, 56) or genuine beliefs—

seem to have been widespread in medieval Europe. In the Icelandic *Helgakviða Hjörvarðssonar* Helgi, like Pwyll, sits on a mound and sees valkyries, including his future wife, while in the Icelandic *Völsunga saga* King Rerir, sitting on a mound, is given a magic apple by a maiden who appears there (Ellis 1943, 107; Sigurðsson 1988, 57 and n. 38). The "peculiarity" of "blows" incurred on Gorsedd Arberth may be compared with the "Growing Lookout" in the Middle High German *Lanzelet* of Ulrich von Zatzikhoven:

> Here let me tell you the peculiarity of this lookout. From it one saw all over England and yet further. The hill was scarcely sufficient for two fighting men, yet on occasion it grew so large that a hundred knights tourneyed on it. Whatever incentives to manly valor anybody could think of, he would be well provided with there. To a river which flowed by came a great strong army; and against it rode another. Yet not a single man was aware of more than one other even if he wished. (Webster 1951, 95)

In view of the hero and locality, one might suppose a Welsh source here, but a parallel has been noted in Catalonia, as recorded by Gervase of Tilbury about 1210 (Webster 1951, 8 and 208-9). Again, Gwely Idris is reminiscent of the Icelandic story of the shepherd Hallbjörn, who attempted to become a poet by passing the night on a poet's barrow: the barrow opened and the dead poet emerged and recited a poem to him, promising "one of two things"—either that he would become a great poet (if he remembered it) or that he would be a complete failure (Ellis 1943, 108; Chadwick 1968, 42; on initiation by lying on graves see Eliade 1964, 82).

The idea of supernatural tumuli and hills may well be indigenous in Europe and not particularly Celtic. It would seem almost inevitable that it should arise independently among peoples confronted by the wonders of Bronze Age megalithic tumuli. If we discount, as I think we should, the doubtful terminological equivalence of *síd* and *gorsedd*, the case for a peculiarly "Celtic" underworld has yet to be made. Indeed, whereas in Wales we seem to have a unitary Otherworld, *Annwfn*, in Ireland there seem to have been a multiplicity of underworlds beneath the *síde* and (despite O'Rahilly) no clear notion of a single chthonic Otherworld.

A belief in overseas Otherworlds seems to be universal among maritime peoples (Löffler 1983, 118, 326, and 375), so it is predictable that it should occur among coastal Celtic-speakers. Otherworld islands are familiar from medieval Celtic sources such as the Irish *Voyage of Bran*, the Welsh *Four Branches of the Mabinogi* (with its Otherworld on the island of *Gwales*, in English *Grassholm*), and Marie de France's *lai breton* of *Lanval*. Although some of the classical accounts of wonderful islands near Britain may be no more than *Greek* travellers' tales (Sims-Williams 1986, 90), the accounts of ritual islands off Brittany given by Posidonius (*apud* Strabo, *Geography* 4.4.6) and Pomponius Mela (*Chorographia* 3.6.48) are quite circumstantial and point to the antiquity of the medieval Celtic beliefs. The widespread and ancient practice of ship burial implies that beliefs in overseas Otherworlds are an ancient inheritance in northwestern Europe in general (see Ellis 1943, 63; Rees and Rees 1961, 318; Löffler 1983, 297 and 339). Can one affirm that there was a peculiarly *Celtic* version of the overseas Otherworld belief? An *exclusive* similarity between the various Celtic accounts seems not to have been sufficiently demonstrated, though some striking shared details have been noted. For example, Pomponius Mela's *nine* priestesses on the island of *Sena* are paralleled in Irish and Welsh (Mac Cana 1976, 112 and n. 25; Rees and Rees 1961, 193), yet in Norse, too, the sea god Ægir has nine daughters (Wagner 1981, 27), and the nine Muses dwelt on an island (Löffler 1983, 349). Is this an ancient European idea? We have also to reckon with the fact that the "Otherworld on island" is an international story-motif (Welsh 1988, 59) and that descriptive details may recur through polygenesis: Posidonius's account of the women on an island off the Loire annually reroofing their temple is paralleled not only in the Irish accounts of Otherworld thatching (Sims-Williams 1977–78, 114–15) but also as far afield as Hawaii—even down to the use of birds' feathers in the Irish and Hawaiian stories (Beckwith 1970, 91, 408, 526, 536, and 538; Löffler 1983, 368).

The view that the Insular Celts believed in an "overseas Otherworld" has been questioned by John Carey (1982; 1987; 1989, 8–9; cf. Mac Mathúna 1985, 281–82; Sims-Williams 1986, 87–88). Pursuing a suggestion by James Carney, Carey denies that the vague, unlocalized "overseas Otherworld" (as oppposed to the specific offshore-island Otherworld) is an ancient, indigenous motif in medieval Irish literature. His case is impossible to disprove, partly because any counterexample (such as the *Voyage of Bran*) can always be attributed to Christian or classical influence and partly because the distinction between the real offshore island and the overseas Otherworld is a fine one: apparently vague "overseas otherworlds" often turn out to be identified within the tradition with particular offshore islands (Carey 1982, 40 n. 21), and Atlantic islands that we regard as mythical were real enough to medieval geographers (Carey 1982, 42 n. 31; Löffler 1983, 306–25 and 622–23). Carey's acceptance of native beliefs in Otherworlds on "actual islands" off the Irish coast but rejection of the "overseas Otherworld" as an extraneous notion seems implicitly to deny the degree of abstract thinking about *"the Otherworld"* generally attributed to early Irish mythographers by modern scholars (including Carey 1989, 6); yet if *"the Otherworld"* is a modern abstraction, as I suggested above in connection with O'Rahilly's ideas on the *síde*, this is not an objection. Students of Irish mythology who follow Carey's argument to its logical conclusion should, however, cease to refer to the "location of the Otherworld" (as in the title of Carey's 1982 paper) and instead should refer to multiple Irish Otherworlds, located in specific places, both underground and on islands.

Carey's rejection of the Irish "overseas Otherworld" leads him to conclude that if the theme appears in medieval Welsh literature, this may be due to Irish literary influence (1982). The early Welsh poem *Preiddeu Annwn* (The Spoils of Annwfn) in the Book of Taliesin (Haycock 1983–84) creates an unnecessary problem here. In this poem Arthur, Taliesin, and others voyage to Annwfn on an expedition to capture a magic cauldron and to rescue a prisoner called Gwair. This looks, of course, like a vague "overseas Otherworld"; if so, Carey suggests (1982, 42) that the Welsh poem may be contaminated by (allegedly innovative) Irish material. This conclusion is unnecessary. In the first place, there is no reason why Irish and Welsh mythological concepts should not differ, as in the case of their chthonic Otherworlds. In the second place, although at first sight the Annwfn of *Preiddeu Annwn* may seem to be a vague "overseas Otherworld," the name of the prisoner *Gwair* suggests that Annwfn may here have a precise location on the Isle of Wight or on Lundy Island, both of which bore the Welsh name *Ynys Wair* (Bromwich 1978, 141 and 231–32); this name probably really meant 'Grass Island' (like *Grassholm*, mentioned above), but could be interpreted as 'Gwair's Island', because *Gwair* was a well-attested personal name (Williams 1938, 326).

Only one small piece of philological evidence, mentioned by Ó Cathasaigh (1978, 150) and Carey (1982, 42–43), points to some Irish input into the Welsh picture of the overseas Otherworld. This is the name *kaer sidi*. In *Preiddeu Annwn*, Annwfn is in one stanza called *kaer sidi*: "Bu kyweir carchar Gweir ygkaer sidi" (Well-equipped was Gwair's prison in the fortress of Sid(d)i) and, in a closely related poem in the Book of Taliesin (Sims-Williams 1982, 244) Taliesin boasts, "Ys kyweir vyg kadeir ygkaer sidi" (Well-equipped is my [bardic] chair in the fortress of Sid(d)i). As was first seen by Sir John Rhys (1901, 678), *sidi*, in *kaer sidi*, was probably borrowed from Middle Irish *sídi* (Old Irish *síde*), gen. sg. or nom./gen. pl. of *síd*, meaning 'fairy mound'—in the plural also 'fairies', probably an ellipsis for expressions such as [*áes*] *síde* 'folk of the fairy mound(s)'.[6] (The attempt by Timothy Lewis (1931, 66–68) to link *síde* and *sidi* with ON *seiðr* is implausible, as the latter is surely cognate with Welsh *hud* 'magic'.) It is unlikely that Welsh *sidi* is merely *cognate* with *síd*, because in that case the Welsh -*i* would be difficult to explain (Sims-Williams 1982, 245).

The terminological borrowing does not, however, prove that the Welsh author(s) borrowed their conception of the overseas Otherworld from the Irish; they may already have had the concept and have borrowed only the name. In an earlier paper, I stressed that *kaer sidi* is only one of a whole string of alternative names for Annwfn in *Preiddeu Annwn*, none of the rest being Irish, and I argued that the borrowing from Irish may have occurred in a learned and literary rather than an oral context, so that *kaer sidi* may have been an esoteric name, never widely understood in Wales (Sims-Williams 1982, 245–48). Two further arguments may now be added. First, although medieval Welsh literati often refer to Annwfn, they hardly ever call it *kaer sidi*: I have found only three examples, all from the fifteenth century or later, and all three clearly literary echoes of the Book of Taliesin poems quoted above. Second, in all these three sources the metre and orthography show that *sidi* was pronounced with /d/ rather than with the fricative /ð/ of early Irish pronunciation. This suggests that the Irish-derived name was always a sort of fossil in the Welsh literary tradition and never an important part of the Welsh idea of the Otherworld.

Because Rhys derived *sidi* from Irish, the ambiguous medial *d* has generally been assumed to represent /ð/, as in early Irish, rather than /d/: Modern Welsh writers always give the name as *Caer Siddi* (Mod. W. *dd* = /ð/). Rhys himself, however, expressed some uncertainty (1901, 678 n. 2), as did Ifor Williams (1951, 101). Rhys even seems to imply (1901, 678 n. 2) that if the *d* represented /d/, the word might be cognate with *síd*. That is unlikely, not only because of the problem of explaining the Welsh -*i* but also because a Common Celtic reconstruction as *sītos* would deprive *síd* of its Indo-European etymology to the root **sed*-.[7] Rather, the significance of Welsh /d/ rather than /ð/ would be to support the idea that the original borrowing from Irish occurred in a literary rather than an oral context. Now it is significant that the well-read seventeenth-century lexicographer John Davies, in his modernizing copy of the Book of Taliesin, transcribes *sidi* with *d* = /d/ rather than *dd* = /ð/ (NLW 4973, 74r and 88r). This also seems to have been the normal view of nineteenth-century scholars, including Rhys in his earlier work, where he connected *sidi* with *sidyll* 'spinning wheel' and explained *kaer sidi* as a revolving castle (Rhys 1891, 301), an idea still not buried (cf. Löffler 1983, 332-33). In this reading Rhys was surely influenced by the notorious William Owen-Pughe's invention of a nonexistent Welsh nominal root *sid* 'a wind, a round, a circling' (1793-1803), which Pughe apparently deduced from a *Hanes Taliesin* poem (discussed below), which he quoted s.v. *sidin*, and from the genuine words *sidan* 'silk' (< Old English *sīde*) and *sidell/sidyll* 'wheel' (Parry-Williams 1923, 33; Parry 1963, 547). The eighteenth- and nineteenth-century evidence for /d/ is thus of little value, but Davies' spelling remains significant.

John Davies' /d/ is supported by earlier testimony. The name *Cadair Sidi* 'the Chair of Sidi' occurs in a fifteenth-century prophetic poem (*cywydd brud*) sometimes attributed to Rhys Goch Eryri. It is probably a deliberate reminiscence of the Book of Taliesin line "Ys kyweir vyg kadeir ygkaer sidi" (see above). The fifteenth-century prophet invokes his forebears Taliesin and Myrddin (Merlin) and, instead of naming them directly, alludes to recognizable elements in their stories: thus Taliesin is one "A'i sud yng Nghadair Sidi" (with his *sud* in *Cadair Sidi*), according to the published edition (Lewis et al. 1937, 335 no. CXI v. 14, cf. pp. xlix and 397). The word *sud/sut* 'order, mode, form' is a loan from English *suit* (see Parry-Williams 1923, 173; Williams 1938, 360; Parry 1963, 453), and as *suit* comes from Old French *si(e)ute* 'succession or set of persons or things' (< **sequitu*-), the expression seems exactly to match the sense of *kyweir* 'well-equipped' in the Book of Taliesin line: in the Otherworld Taliesin perhaps has a train of attendants or splendid livery and insignia. If the reading *sud* is correct, the *cynghanedd* (internal alliteration) proves that the -*d*- in *Sidi* is a stop, rather than the fricative of early Irish *sídi*, and indicates that by the fifteenth century, if not earlier, the form was a fossil, with no living oral descent from the Irish word *síd(i)*. Admittedly, one might restore a fricative by emending to "*A'i sedd yng Nghadair Siddi" (With his seat in *Cadair Siddi*), and such an emendation is slightly supported by four of the twenty-two manuscripts, which read *sed* or *sêd* rather than *sud*; nonetheless, these are manuscripts that would normally employ *dd* for /ð/, so their scribes presumably intend *sêd* 'seat, mansion' (< English *seat*) rather than *sedd*.[8]

In the early sixteenth century, Elis Gruffudd refers to the otherworld as *Kaer Sidia* in his autograph Chronicle (National Library of Wales 5276D, 357v):

> j mae ymrauaelion oppiniw[n]s a sonn y mysc y bobyl, kanis hrai ohonnaunt twy yssydd yn dal opiniwn ac yn dywedud yn gadarn mae ysbryd ydoedd Verddin ynn hrith dyn, yr hwn a vu ynn y modd hwnw o amser Gwrtheyrn hyd yn nechreuad brenin Arthur ynn yr amser j diulanodd ef. Ac ynn ol hynn jr ymddangoses yr ysbryd hwn dracheuyn ynn amser Maelgwn Gwynnedd ynn yr amser jr henwyr ef Taliesin, yr hwn a ddywedir j vod ef ynn vyw etto mewn dinas a elwir Kaer Sidia. O'r man, jr ymddangoses ef y drydedd waith ynn amser Moruryn Vrych mab Esylld, jr neb j dywedid j vod ef [ynn vab], ac ynn yr oes hon jr henwyd y vo Merddin Wylld. Ac jr hyny j hyd heddiw j dywedir j vod ef ynn gorffowys o vewn Kaer Sidia, o'r man j mae serttain o bobyl yn koelio ynn ddiamau j kyuyd ef etto vnnwaith j vynnu kyn dydd y varn.

> There are a variety of opinions and talk among the people, for some of them hold the opinion and maintain firmly that Merlin was a spirit in human form, who was in that shape from the time of Vortigern until the beginning of King Arthur when he disappeared. After that, this spirit appeared again in the time of Maelgwn Gwynedd at which time he is called Taliesin, who is said to be alive yet in a place called Caer Sidia. Thence he appeared a third time in the days of Morfryn Frych son of Esyllt, whose son he was said to be, and in this period he was called Merlin the Mad. From that day to this, he is said to be resting in Caer Sidia, whence certain people believe firmly he will rise up once again before Doomsday. (Ford 1976, 388–90; cf. Jones 1958–59, 320–21)

Whether *Kaer Sidia*, a latinate-looking form, really appeared in popular tales is difficult to know. In any case, it probably derives ultimately from the Taliesin poems (Jones 1958–59, 322–23; Haycock

1983-84, 65). The form in *d* is again notable, for Elis uses *dd* when he intends /ð/.

A related name appears in the metrically corrupt final stanza of the poem "Prifardd cyffredin / wyf i i Elffin" in *Hanes Taliesin*, as printed in *The Myvyrian Archaiology of Wales* (London 1801) I.20 (= second edition [Denbigh 1870], p. 25). Taliesin boasts,

> Mi a fum ynghadair flin
> Uwch Caer Sidin
> A honno yn troi fydd
> Rhwng tri alfyd
> Pand rhyfedd ir byd
> Nas argenydd.

> I was in a wearisome chair above Caer Sidin, and that is wont to turn/move through three worlds/regions. Is it not a wonder for the world that it [the world, mankind] does not perceive it?[9]

The editors of the *Myvyrian Archaiology* cite the variant *Sidydd*,[10] which would leave *flin* without a rhyme, unless it rhymes with *fum*, which is quite possible in this sort of late, "popular" verse. To restore *Caer *Sid(d)i*, with a rhyme, a drastic emendation of *flin* to *fri* 'a famous chair' or even to *fry* 'a chair in high' is not absolutely impossible, but has no manuscript support. Be that as it may, because the stanza is about Taliesin, it seems most likely that its *Caer Sidin* is a direct reminiscence of the *kaer sidi* of the two Book of Taliesin poems. (Perhaps the inorganic -*n* is patterned on that of words like *cwpan* 'cup', *hosan* 'hose', *sidan* 'silk': Parry-Williams 1923, 31-33.) Moreover, the statement that the *caer* or *cadair* 'revolves' (if *troi* has that meaning here) recalls a description of *kaer sidi* in *Preiddeu Annwn* as *kaer pedryuan pedrychwelyt* 'a four-turreted, fully revolving fort', and the 'three regions' recall threefold features in Taliesin's cosmology such as the 'three springs' (see Haycock 1983-84, 69; Sims-Williams 1982, 254-55; and in general Haycock 1987, 10 and 21-22).

Fifty-four manuscript copies of this *Hanes Taliesin* poem are extant, but only four include the relevant stanza, which is presumably an addition.[11] The earliest of the four, Aberystwyth, NLW Llanstephan 124, p. 56, written about 1648 (see p. 658), is very close to the *Myvyrian* text throughout and agrees exactly with it in the relevant stanza (except in reading *Alfydd [sic]* and *argennydd*). Next in date are eighteenth-century manuscripts by Lewis Morris (British Library Add. 14934, 104v, begun in 1722: see 3r), who has a long note on the poem's supposed doctrine of metempsychosis, and by his brother Richard Morris (British Library Add. 14936, 17v); in the latter *Sidydd* appears as a pencilled marginal variant beside *Sidin*, with *flin* and *Sidin*, the words in rhyme position in adjacent lines, both underlined: perhaps this was the ultimate source of the *Myvyrian* variant. The fourth and latest manuscript of the poem is British Library Add. 15002, 10r, a collection of transcriptions from the Morris brothers' manuscripts by Owen Jones, one of the editors of the *Myvyrian* (although Add. 15002 was clearly not the main source of its text). Owen Jones puts a line (implying a corruption?) in place of *flin* and cites *Sidydd* as an alternative to the *Sidin* of his main text.

Thus the stanza may not be much older than the seventeenth century, and the variant *Sidydd* may be no older than the marginal variant (of uncertain date) in Richard Morris's copy. *Sidydd* may merely have been inspired by the following rhyme in *-ydd*. Soon afterwards, however, *sidydd* appears in Welsh as a word for 'zodiac' (replacing earlier *sodiac*? cf. Evans 1898–1910, vol. 2, on British Museum MS 31, 50v); possibly it is to be derived (if genuine) from Latin *sidus* 'star', though Owen-Pughe (1793–1803) derives it from his bogus root *sid*. Pughe has "*Sidyz* [$z = dd$] the agent of revolving; the zodiac," and adds, "*Caer Sidyz*, the circle of the zodiac, the ecliptic." Under *Sidi* 'a state of revolution' he adds, "*Caer sidi*, a zone of revolving, the zodiac; also called *caer sidin*, and *caer sidyz*." Here Pughe is obviously using the *Hanes Taliesin* stanza, which he actually quotes s.v. *sidin* 'winding, revolving'. It is harder to know whether any of these terms and usages had any preceding independent existence. They are used by later writers. Robert Roberts of Holyhead (1777–1836), in his *Daearyddiaeth* (Caerlleon 1816), frequently uses *Sidydd* for 'zodiac' (pp. 14, 18, 75), along with exotic Welsh appellations, reminiscent of the *Mabinogi*, such as *Llys Don* for Cassiopeia, *twr tewdws* for the Pleiades, and *Caer Arianrod* and *Caer Gwdion* for the Milky Way (pp. 16, 68–69, 74), and later on "Caersidydd, neu y *Zodiac*" appears in the *Poetical Works* of Tegid (i.e., John Jones, 1792–1852) (Roberts 1859, 21 n. 1). The unpublished *GPC* slips[12] lead us to a list of constellations, purporting to come from an old manuscript, printed by "Dyfedon" in *Y Brython* 5 (1862–63) 29, which includes *Caer Sidi*, alongside mythological names such as *Caer Arianrod, Telyn Arthur, Caer Gwydion, Pair Cariadwen [sic], Cadair Elffin*, and *Neuadd Olwen*. Suspiciously, the only manuscript of this list I can find is National Library of Wales 13089, p. 333, in the hand of Pughe's contemporary, the forger Iolo Morganwg. Another printed copy, in *Barddas* I (152), is presumably from Iolo's manuscripts: here *Caer Sidi* was translated 'The Circle of Sidi' and explained in a footnote as "The zodiac, or ecliptic. Mentioned in 'Hanes Taliesin' " (Williams ab Ithel 1852, 402–5). A number of the names (though not *Caer Sidi/Sidydd*, etc.) also appear in Iolo's much shorter lists of "[Some] Constellations in Glam[organ]" in National Library of Wales 13100, p. 29, and 13131, p. 46. Many of these constellation names may be bogus; nevertheless, astronomical applications of native mythological names were certainly much older than Iolo's time; for example, *kaer gwdion* for the Milky Way is at least as early as Salesbury's Dictionary of 1547 (*GPC* s.v. *caer*, Lloyd-Jones 1931–63 s.n. Gwydyon—but on Casnodyn's *carr gwydyon ay son ywch syr* see Rowlands 1958–59, 57; cf. Owen-Pughe 1793–1803 s.v. *caer*; Gruffydd 1928, 138, 198–99 and n. 76, 203 n. 90, 255), *Tŵr Tewdws* is used as a metaphor for a girl's hair by Dafydd ab Edmwnd (Roberts 1914, no. XIV) and is equated with the Pleiades by Lewis Morris (copied by Iolo in National Library of Wales 13100, p. 28), and *Sarn Badrig* 'Patrick's road', for the Milky Way, is attested from the fifteenth century down to the present day (Bachellery 1950, 105; Rowlands 1975, 391). For a similar process in Gaelic, one can compare *Slighe Chlann Uisne* "the way of Clan Uisne" for the Milky Way in nineteenth-century Uist (Carmichael 1914, 152). Attested early Celtic mythology (*pace* O'Rahilly 1946) seems to have been chiefly concerned with chthonic and terrestrial divinities, and it may be due to poor recording that we do not have such mythological names for constellations in the early Middle Ages. On balance, however, *Caer Sidi, sidydd*, and the like as astronomical terms look like eighteenth-century inventions based on the extant Taliesin poetry. The Welsh antiquaries were already accused of inventing constellation names by Ritson (1825, 60–61).

Because all of the late medieval and modern references to *sidi* in Welsh are in collocations with *caer* or *cadair*, they are probably all direct or indirect allusions to the Book of Taliesin poems, and not due to fresh influence from Ireland (or Scotland), where, in any case, the *-d(h)-* of *síd(h)e/síd(h)i* had not been sounded as a dental since the twelfth century (Jackson 1951, 83 and n. 3 and 86) and would be unlikely to yield *siddi* or *sidi* in Welsh.

I conclude that the Irish-derived term *sidi* is a minor and insignificant element in Welsh sources. To this extent, then, I would agree with Ó Cathasaigh (1978, 150) that "there can be little doubt that for the most part the Welsh conception of Annwfn derives independently from the Celtic Otherworld." At the same time, I would doubt whether it has yet been demonstrated that speakers of Common Celtic (or Insular Celtic), as distinct from speakers of other northwestern European languages, shared a peculiar conception of "the Otherworld." Certainly, it left no trace in terminology.[13]

St. John's College
Cambridge

PATRICK SIMS-WILLIAMS

NOTES

1. Jackson 1951, 80; 1953, 696-97. There is also the consideration that the assimilation of *nd* to *nn* took place by the sixth century in Welsh (Jackson 1953, 513 and 695), but in the eighth in Irish (Jackson 1951, 81), so that *if* the Welsh name were borrowed from Irish it would not have appeared as *Gwynn* with *-nn* unless borrowed before the sixth century. Ó hÓgáin (1988, 16) regards Fi(o)nn and Gwyn(n) as cognates, but suggests that "the attribution of a father called Nudd to Gwynn could be a borrowing from Ireland by a Welshman who knew that the names Fionn and Gwynn had the same meaning." This does not explain the entirely Welsh phonology of Gwyn's patronymic and is really only required by the speculation that Nuadu first became attached to Finn with Irish tradition (where he is Finn's grandfather) in the Boyne Valley (1988, 3, 16-17, 57, 68, 83, and 85).
2. The meaning of "heroic" is quite different in the two cases; "Heroic Age" epics tend not to include complete "Heroic Biographies."
3. Carney 1983, 129-30 proposes Greek influence on the chariot incident (which is not found in the *Ilias Latina*), but cf. Sims-Williams 1977-78, 84. That it had a basis in real life was already pointed out by Aristotle; see Pfeiffer 1968, 69-70.
4. For similar problems see my notes on *gormes* and *armes* (Sims-Williams 1985, 125 and 128-29). The phonology is clarified by Russell 1985.
5. Welsh 1988, 58 cites this motif for Brân on Harlech rock in the Second Branch. Compare the case of Arthur in *Vita sancti Cadoci* as noted by Borst 1983, 6. For another *gorsedd* with magic associations see *Branwen*, ed. Williams 1951, 35.
6. For *síde* 'fairies' see *DIL* s.v. 1 *síd* II, especially the quotation from Lebor na hUidre 4039. It is not clear how much older the usage is; the citation from Fiacc's Hymn, *túatha adortais síde*, could mean, pejoratively, "the peoples used to worship fairy-mounds." Kenneth Jackson (in a personal comment on Sims-Williams 1982, 246 n. 45) suggested to me that the instance of *síde* in Tírechán (cited s.v. 1 *síd* I(a)) might mean 'fairies' in the gen. pl. and be glossed by *aut deorum terrenorum* accordingly.
7. The objection that according to the normal rules (Hamp 1973) the expected Old Irish form from *$*s\bar{\imath}tos$ should be *síth* is less of a problem because in fact *síth* is attested surprisingly often, as Ó Cathasaigh (1978, 137 n. 2) notes.

8. The four copies are: Aberystwyth, National Library of Wales J. G. Evans II.1, 71v; London, British Library Add. 14970, 19v (olim 11v); Add. 14971, 194r; and Add. 31080, 22r. *A'i sud* is the reading in most of the twenty-two manuscript copies listed in the unpublished *Mynegai i Farddoniaeth Gaeth y Llawysgrifau* at the National Library of Wales. National Library of Wales 6499, p. 546 has *sadwych y nghadair sidi* and Bangor, Mostyn 2, 20r (sixteenth century) has *Asoded ynghadair sidi*. In two National Library of Wales manuscripts, Pen. 104, p. 152 and NLW 8330, p. 513, the readings are *Ai syt* and *Ai syd*, and *A syd* occurs in National Library of Wales 642, 10r and British Library Add. 14866, 253v. For information about Bangor manuscripts I am indebted to D. R. Johnston, I. C. Lovecy, and Tomos Roberts.
9. My translation assumes the readings *elfydd*, as in the citation by Owen-Pughe 1793–1803 s.v. *sidin*, and *argen[u]ydd* (cf. *argennydd* in Llanstephan 124).
10. *Sidydd* is assigned no siglum. Most of the variants are cited from 'L.M.' (Lewis Morris) or 'R.I.' (Rhys Jones?—in British Library Add. 15002 Owen Jones notes the existence of an inferior copy in "Llyfr Rhys Jones").
11. Again, I am indebted to I. C. Lovecy and Tomos Roberts for checking Bangor manuscripts.
12. I am grateful to the staff of *GPC* for allowing me to consult relevant slips some years ago.
13. In addition to the acknowledgments already made, I should like to thank Marged Haycock for comments. This article is an expansion of part of a paper delivered at UCLA in April 1988.

REFERENCES

Anderson, Olaf S. 1939. *The English Hundred-Names: the South-Eastern Counties.* Lund Universitets Årsskrift n.f. Avd. 1, 37.1.
Bachellery, E., ed. 1950. *L'oeuvre poétique de Gutun Owain.* Bibliothèque de l'École des hautes études 297. Paris: H. Champion.
Bartlett, Robert. 1982. *Gerald of Wales 1146–1223.* Oxford: Clarendon Press.
Beckwith, Martha. 1970. *Hawaiian Mythology.* Honolulu: University of Hawaii Press.
Borst, Karen Gail. 1983. A Reconsideration of the *Vita sancti Cadoci.* In Patrick K. Ford, ed., *Celtic Folklore and Christianity*, 1–15. Santa Barbara, Calif.: McNally and Loftin.
Bromwich, Rachel. 1965. The Celtic Inheritance of Medieval Literature. *Modern Language Quarterly* 26: 203–27.
―――, ed. 1978. *Trioedd Ynys Prydein.* Cardiff: University of Wales Press.
Byrne, Francis John. 1974. *Senchas*: The Nature of Gaelic Historical Tradition. *Historical Studies* 9: 137–59.
Carey, John. 1982. The Location of the Otherworld in Irish Tradition. *Éigse* 19: 36–43.
―――. 1987. *Echtrae Conlai*: A Crux Revisted. *Celtica* 19: 9–11.
―――. 1989. Ireland and the Antipodes: The Heterodoxy of Virgil of Salzburg. *Speculum* 64: 1–10.
Carmichael, Alexander. 1914. *Deirdire and the Lay of the Children of Uisne.* London: Mackenzie.

Carney, James. 1983. Early Irish Literature: The State of Research. In Mac Eoin 1983, 113-30.
Carozzi, Claude. 1983. La géographie de l'au-delà et sa signification pendant le haut moyen âge. *Settimane di studio del Centro Italiano di Studi sull'Alto Medioevo* 29: 423-81.
Chadwick, H. Munro. 1912. *The Heroic Age.* Cambridge: Cambridge University Press.
Chadwick, Nora. 1968. Dreams in Early European Literature. In James Carney and David Greene, eds., *Celtic Studies*, 33-50. London: Routledge and Kegan Paul.
Coulter, Cornelia C. and F. P. Magoun. 1926. Giraldus Cambrensis on Indo-Germanic Philology. *Speculum* 1: 104-9.
Daniel, Glyn. 1960. *The Prehistoric Chambered Tombs of France.* London: Thames and Hudson.
DIL = *Dictionary of the Irish Language.* 1913-76. Dublin: Royal Irish Academy.
Eliade, Mircea. 1964. *Shamanism: Archaic Techniques of Ecstasy*, trans. Willard R. Trask. London: Routledge and Kegan Paul.
Ellis, Hilda Roderick. 1943. *The Road to Hel: A Study of the Conception of the Dead in Old Norse Literature.* Cambridge: Cambridge University Press.
Elsie, Robert. 1983-84. Lexicostatistics and Its Application to Brittonic Celtic. *Studia celtica* 18-19: 110-27.
Evans, J. G. 1898-1910. *Report on Manuscripts in the Welsh Language.* London: Historical Manuscripts Commission.
Ford, Patrick K. 1976. The Death of Merlin in the Chronicle of Elis Gruffydd. *Viator* 7: 379-90.
Gaidoz, H. 1897. Annwn. *Zeitschrift für celtische Philologie* 1: 29-34.
GPC = *Geiriadur Prifysgol Cymru.* 1950-. Cardiff: University of Wales Press.
Greene, David. 1983. The Coming of the Celts: The Linguistic Viewpoint. In Mac Eoin 1983, 131-37.
Grooms, John Christian. 1988. *Giants in Welsh Folklore and Tradition.* Ph.D. dissertation: University College of Wales, Aberystwyth.
Gruffydd, W. J. 1928. *Math vab Mathonwy.* Cardiff: University of Wales Press.
Hamp, Eric P. 1956. anian. *Bulletin of the Board of Celtic Studies* 16: 279-80.
———. 1972-73. On Dating and Archaism in the *Pedeir Keinc. Transactions of the Honourable Society of Cymmrodorion*: 95-103.
———. 1973. On Voicing in Old Irish Final Spirants. *Ériu* 24: 171-72.
———. 1974-75. Mabinogi. *Transactions of the Honourable Society of Cymmrodorion*: 243-49.
———. 1975. Latin *sīdus, sīdera. American Journal of Philology* 96: 64-66.
———. 1977-78. Intensives in British Celtic and Gaulish. *Studia celtica* 12-13: 1-13.
———. 1979. Notulae etymologicae Cymricae 4. gwyn OIr. *find. Bulletin of the Board of Celtic Studies* 28: 214.
———. 1981. πάθος. *Glotta* 59: 157-59.
———. 1982. Irish *síd* 'tumulus' and Irish *síd* 'peace'. *Études celtiques* 19: 141.
Haycock, Marged. 1983-84. "Preiddeu Annwn" and the Figure of Taliesin. *Studia celtica* 18-19: 52-78.
———. 1987. "Some Talk of Alexander and Some of Hercules": Three Early Medieval Poems from the Book of Taliesin. *Cambridge Medieval Celtic Studies* 13: 7-38.

Hull, Vernam, ed. 1968. Apgitir Chrábaid: The Alphabet of Piety. *Celtica* 8: 44–89.
Jackson, Kenneth Hurlstone. 1951. "Common Gaelic": The Evolution of the Goedelic Languages. *Proceedings of the British Academy* 37: 71–97.
———. 1953. *Language and History in Early Britain.* Edinburgh: Edinburgh University Press.
———. 1961. *The International Popular Tale and Early Welsh Tradition.* Cardiff: University of Wales Press.
———. 1967. *A Historical Phonology of Breton.* Dublin: Dublin Institute for Advanced Studies.
Jones, Thomas. 1958–59. The Story of Myrddin and the Five Dreams of Gwenddydd in the Chronicle of Elis Gruffudd. *Études celtiques* 8: 315–45.
Koch, John T. 1987. A Welsh Window on the Iron Age: Manawydan, Mandubracios. *Cambridge Medieval Celtic Studies* 14: 17–52.
Lambert, Pierre-Yves. 1987. A Restatement on the Gaulish Tablet from Chamalières. *Bulletin of the Board of Celtic Studies* 34: 10–17.
Lejeune, M. 1985. Gaulois VXEDIOS. *Études celtiques* 22: 81–94.
Lewis, Henry, et al., eds. 1937. *Cywyddau Iolo Goch ac Eraill.* Cardiff: University of Wales Press.
Lewis, Timothy. 1931. *Mabinogi Cymru.* Aberystwyth: Gwasg y Fwynant.
Lloyd-Jones, J. 1931–63. *Geirfa Barddoniaeth Gynnar Gymraeg.* Cardiff: University of Wales Press.
Löffler, Christa Maria. 1983. *The Voyage to the Otherworld Island in Early Irish Literature.* Salzburg Studies in English Literature 103. Salzburg: Institut für Anglistik und Americanistik, Universität Salzburg.
Loth, J. 1915. Remarques et additions à la grammaire gauloise historique et comparée de John Morris-Jones. *Revue celtique* 36: 391–412.
Mac Cana, Proinsias. 1966. Review of Jackson 1961. *Celtica* 7: 242–48.
———. 1976. The Sinless Otherworld of *Immram Brain. Ériu* 27: 95–115.
Mac Eoin, Gearóid, ed. 1983. *Proceedings of the Sixth International Congress of Celtic Studies.* Dublin: Dublin Institute for Advanced Studies.
Mac Mathúna, Séamus, ed. 1985. *Immram Brain: Bran's Journey to the Land of the Women.* Tübingen: Niermeyer.
Marendon, John. 1981. *From the Circle of Alcuin to the School of Auxerre.* Cambridge: Cambridge University Press.
Meid, Wolfgang. 1986. The Celtic Languages. In Schmidt 1986, 116–22.
Moore, Donald, ed. 1970. *The Irish Sea Province in Archaeology and History.* Cardiff: Cambrian Archaeological Association.
Nagy, Joseph Falaky. 1985. *The Wisdom of the Outlaw: The Boyhood Deeds of Finn in Gaelic Narrative Tradition.* Berkeley: University of California Press.
Ó Cathasaigh, Tomás. 1978. The Semantics of 'síd'. *Éigse* 17: 137–55.
Ó hÓgáin, Dáithí. 1988. *Fionn mac Cumhaill: Images of the Gaelic Hero.* Dublin: Gill & Macmillan.
O'Keeffe, J. G., ed. 1905. Cáin Domnaig. *Ériu* 2: 189–214.
O'Rahilly, Thomas F. 1946. *Early Irish History and Mythology.* Dublin: Dublin Institute for Advanced Studies.
O'Sullivan, Anne and Pádraig Ó Riain, eds. 1987. *Poems on Marcher Lords from a Sixteenth-Century Tipperary Manuscript.* Irish Texts Society 53. London: Irish Texts Society.

Owen[-Pughe], William. 1793-1803. *A Dictionary of the Welsh Language*. London.
Parry, Thomas, ed. 1963. *Gwaith Dafydd ap Gwilym*. Cardiff: University of Wales Press.
Parry-Williams, T. H. 1923. *The English Element in Welsh*. Cymmrodorion Record Series 10. London: Honourable Society of Cymmrodorion.
Patterson, Nerys. 1989. Brehon Law in Late Medieval Ireland: "Antiquarian and Obsolete" or "Traditional and Functional"? *Cambridge Medieval Celtic Studies* 17 (Summer).
Pfeiffer, Rudolf. 1968. *History of Classical Scholarship from the Beginnings to the End of the Hellenistic Age*. Oxford: Oxford University Press.
Piggott, Stuart. 1983. The Coming of the Celts: The Archaeological Argument. In Mac Eoin 1983, 138-48.
Rees, Alwyn and Brinley Rees. 1961. *Celtic Heritage*. London: Thames and Hudson.
Reinach, Salomon. 1901. Le mot *orbis* dans le latin de l'Empire à propos de l'*orbis alius* des druides. *Revue celtique* 22: 447-57.
Rhys, John. 1891. *Studies in the Arthurian Legend*. Oxford: Oxford University Press.
―――. 1901. *Celtic Folklore, Welsh and Manx*. Oxford: Oxford University Press.
Richards, Melville. 1969. *Welsh Administrative and Territorial Units*. Cardiff: University of Wales Press.
Ritson, Joseph. 1825. *The Life of King Arthur from Ancient Historians and Authentic Documents*. London: Payne and Foss.
Roberts, Bryn, ed. 1971-72. Llythyrau John Lloyd at Edward Lhuyd. *National Library of Wales Journal* 17: 88-114, 183-206.
Roberts, Henry, ed. 1859. *Gwaith barddonol y Diweddar Barch. John Jones, Tegid*. Llanymddyfri and London: W. Rees.
Roberts, Thomas, ed. 1914. *Gwaith Dafydd ap Edmwnd*. Bangor: Jarvis and Foster.
Rowlands, Eurys I. 1958-59. Y Tri Thlws ar Ddeg. *Llên Cymru* 5: 33-69.
―――, ed. 1975. *Gwaith Lewys Môn*. Cardiff: University of Wales Press.
Russell, Paul. 1985. A Footnote to Spirantization. *Cambridge Medieval Celtic Studies* 10: 53-56.
―――. 1988. The Celtic Preverb **uss* and Related Matters. *Ériu* 39: 95-126.
Sayers, William. 1986. *Mani maidi an nem* . . . : Ringing Changes on a Cosmic Motif. *Ériu* 37: 99-117.
Schmidt, Karl Horst, ed. 1986. *Geschichte und Kultur der Kelten*. Heidelberg: Carl Winter.
Sigurðsson, Gísli. 1988. *Gaelic Influence in Iceland*. Studia Islandica 46. Reykjavík: Bókaútgáfa Menningarsjóðs.
Sims-Williams, Patrick. 1977-78. Riddling Treatment of the "Watchman Device" in *Branwen* and *Togail Bruidne Da Derga*. *Studia celtica* 12-13: 83-117.
―――. 1978. "Is it fog or smoke or warriors fighting?": Irish and Welsh Parallels to the *Finnsburg* fragment. *Bulletin of the Board of Celtic Studies* 27: 505-14.
―――. 1982. The Evidence for Vernacular Irish Literary Influence on Early Mediaeval Welsh Literature. In Dorothy Whitelock et al., eds., *Ireland in Early Mediaeval Europe*, 235-57. Cambridge: Cambridge University Press.
―――. 1984. The Double System of Verbal Inflexion in Old Irish. *Transactions of the Philological Society*: 138-201.
―――. 1985. Some Functions of Origin Stories in Early Medieval Wales. In Tore Nyberg et al., eds., *History and Heroic Tale*, 97-131. Odense: Universitetsforlag.

———. 1986. The Visionary Celt: The Construction of an Ethnic Preconception. *Cambridge Medieval Celtic Studies* 11: 71-96.
———. 1989. Fionn and Deirdre in Late Medieval Wales. *Éigse* 23: 1-15.
———. (Forthcoming). Irish Elements in Late Medieval Welsh Literature: The Problem of Cuhelyn and *Nyf. In Martin J. Ball et al., eds., *Festschrift for T. Arwyn Watkins*. Amsterdam: Benjamin.
Smith, Roland M., ed. 1928. The *Senbriathra Fithail* and Related Texts. *Revue celtique* 45: 1-92.
Taylor, Archer. 1964. The Biographical Pattern in Traditional Narrative. *Journal of the Folklore Institute* 1: 114-29.
Thomson, R. L., ed. 1957. *Pwyll Pendeuic Dyuet*. Dublin: Dublin Institute for Advanced Studies.
Thurneysen, R. 1887. Irisch *síd*. *Zeitschrift für vergleichende Sprachforschung* 28: 153-54.
Tierney, J. J., ed. 1967. *Dicuili Liber de mensura orbis terrae*. Dublin: Dublin Institute for Advanced Studies.
Vries, Jan de. 1963. *La religion des Celtes*, trad. L. Jospin. Paris: Payot.
Wagner, Heinrich. 1975. Studies in the Origins of Early Celtic Traditions. *Ériu* 26: 1-26.
———. 1981. Origins of Pagan Irish Religion. *Zeitschrift für celtische Philologie* 38: 1-28.
Webster, Kenneth G. T., trans. 1951. *Ulrich von Zatzikhoven: Lanzelet*. New York: Columbia University Press.
Welsh, Andrew. 1988. The Traditional Narrative Motifs of *The Four Branches of the Mabinogi*. *Cambridge Medieval Celtic Studies* 15: 51-62.
Williams, Ifor, ed. 1938. *Canu Aneirin*. Cardiff: University of Wales Press.
———, ed. 1951. *Pedeir Keinc y Mabinogi*. Cardiff: University of Wales Press.
———, ed. 1953. *Canu Llywarch Hen*. Cardiff: University of Wales Press.
———. 1972. *The Beginnings of Welsh Poetry*. Cardiff: University of Wales Press.
Williams ab Ithel, J., ed. 1852. *Barddas*, vol. 1. Llandovery: Welsh Manuscripts Society.

PART II

IRISH

Notes on the Diminutive Suffix -*ín* in Modern Irish

1.0. The origin of the Modern Irish diminutive suffix -*ín* is uncertain. Thurneysen (1946), in dealing with the suffix -*én* (for instance, in *cu(i)lén*) states (§272), "Later it is replaced by -*ín*, e.g. Baíthín, presumably on the model of *Áugustín* 'Augustinus' and similar forms." He adds (§274), "In Mid. Ir. the endings of (a) [-*ne*, -*ine*] and (b) [-*éne*] combine into -*íne*, e.g. dat. sg. *glainíni* LU 4883; *slegíne* (from *sleg* 'javelin'). Cp. -*ín*, 272." Gerard Murphy expresses his uncertainty thus: "Ní fios go cruinn cá dtáinig an deire úd -*ín* chúinn: -*éne* is minicí in' áit sa tSeana-Ghaolaing" (1948, 221) ["The origin of the ending -*ín* is not known for certain: -*éne* is what most commonly occurs in Old Irish in its place"].

1.1. Whatever the direct line of descent may have been, -*íne*, -*éne*, and sometimes -*én* have been replaced by -*ín* in Modern Irish. The fact that the modern suffix was common by the Early Modern Irish period (ca. A.D. 1200–1600) is borne out by mention of it (with reference to gender) in the Grammatical Tracts (McKenna 1944, §72a 30), which prescribe rules for the standard literary language to be taught in the bardic schools.

2.0. Modern Irish has many words ending in -*ín* apart from the diminutive suffix, for example, -*ín* can replace a lost fricative (such as *muirín* < *muirghin*) or can be substituted for a loosely similar ending in loanwords (such as *féirín* < *fairing*).

2.1. The diminutive suffix can also have affectionate or derogatory connotations, as in *a mhuirnín* 'my darling'; *ainniseoirín* 'a miserable wretch'.

2.2. The suffix has lost its diminutive connotation in some words in which it has become petrified and no longer is felt to be the productive suffix, for instance, *paidrín* 'rosary beads', *sabhaircín* 'primrose'. The suffix also occurs in words denoting a protective device applied to parts of the body, as in *glúinín* (< *glúin*, knee) 'kneepad'; *méirín* (< *méar*, finger) 'finger stall'; *sróinín* (< *srón*, nose) 'nose ring'; *troithín* (< *troigh*, foot) 'vampless sock'.

2.3. In contrast to English, where diminutive suffixes (-let, -ling, -ock, and the like) are no longer productive, *-ín* has remained remarkably productive in both written and spoken language. It can be added to any concrete noun. Because of this, dictionaries tend not to include these diminutives and to lack any indication of how *-ín* affects the word to which it is attached.

2.4. It is worth noting that the diminutive suffixes *-óg* and *-án* are no longer productive (except in recent learned coinings of technical terms) and that consequently *-ín* can be added to them, for example, *amadán* > *amadáinín, baothóg* > *baothóigín.*

3.0. The following brief account of the consonant and vowel changes brought about by the addition of this suffix is based on field work in the Cois Fharraige district of County Galway. Were a similar study to be made for other dialects in Connacht or in Munster, the results would be roughly similar.

3.1. A final velarized consonant or consonant group (for exceptions see 3.2) is replaced by the corresponding palatalized consonant, which constitutes a separate phoneme.[1] Examples include *béal* /b'e:l/ > *béilín* /b'e:l'i:n'/; *bodóg* /budo:g/ > *bodóigín* /budo:g'i:n'/; and *molt* /mult/ > *moiltín* /miʎt'i:n'/.

3.2. In the final groups *-cht, -rt, -rd, -rn, t, d,* and *n* are palatalized but *ch* and *r* remain velarized, for instance, *locht* /loxd/ > *loichtín* /loxd'i:n'/, *gort* /gort/ > *goirtín* /gort'i:n'/, *bord* /baurd/ > *boirdín* /baurd'i:n'/ *bearna* /b'a:rnə/ > *beairnín* /b'a:rɲi:n'/.

3.3. In disyllables ending in a vowel the medial consonant or consonant group is palatalized, for example, *ionga* /uŋgə/ *ingín* /iŋ'g'i:n'/, *siopa* /ʃupə/ > *sipín* /ʃip'i:n'/.

3.4. Final *-ch* /x/ formerly became /ç/ and later became /h/, but in contemporary speech intervocalic /h/ is silent. To compensate for the loss of /h/, the final *-ch* is now normally retained in monosyllables before *-ín*, as in *croch* /krox/ > *crochín* /kroxi:n'/, *deoch* /d'ox/ > *deochín* /d'oxi:n'/. Monosyllables with the diphthong *ua* and disyllables have two forms, one in which *ch* is palatalized > /h/ > zero, and another in which velar *-ch* is retained, such as *cruach* /kruəx/ > *cruaichín* /kruəin'/ and *cruachín* /kruəxi:n'/; *coileach* /kel'əx/ > *coilín* /kel'i:n'/ and *coileachín* /kel'əxi:n'/, *óinseach* /u:n'ʃəx/ > *óinsín* /u:n'ʃi:n'/ and *óinseachín* /u:n'ʃəxi:n'/.

3.5. Where the medial consonant is velar it is also palatalized in the forms that are reduced to disyllables, such as *bacach* /bakəx/

> *baicín* /bak'i:n'/ and *bacachín* /bakəxi:n'/; *bromach* /bruməx/
> *broimín* /brim'i:n'/ and *bromachín* /bruməxi:n'/; *ceapach*
/k'a:pəx/ > *ceaipín* /k'a:p'i:n'/ and *ceapachín* /k'apəxi:n'/.

3.6. In original monosyllables that have become disyllabic through the development of an epenthetic vowel, the medial consonant is palatalized, for example, *bolg* /boləg/ > *boilgín* /bel'ig'i:n'/; *banbh* /ba:nəw/ > *bainbhín* /ba:n'iv'i:n'/.

3.7. By analogy with such words (3.6), some original disyllables palatalized the medial consonant, for instance, *solas* /soləs/ > *soilisín* /sel'iʃi:n'/; *doras* /dorəs/ > *doirisín* /der'iʃi:n'/.

3.8. Exceptionally, the initial consonant is palatalized, as in *mac* /ma:k/ > *micín* /m'ik'i:n'/, with a more recent by-form *maicín* /ma:k'i:n'/.

4.0. Original long vowels and the diphthong *ua* are not affected phonemically by *-ín*, for example, *bád* /ba:d/ > *báidín* /ba:d'i:n'/; *méar* /m'e:r/ > *méirín* /m'e:r'i:n'/; *bóthar* /bo:r/ > *bóithrín* /bo:r'i:n'/; *múr* /mu:r/ > *múirín* /mu:r'i:n'/; *cual* /kuəl/ > *cuailín* /kuəl'i:n'/; *bó* /bo:/ > *bóín* /bo:i:n'/; *cú* /ku:/ > *cúín* /ku:i:n'/.

4.1. The diphthong *ia* /iə/ historically became *éi* /e:/ before a palatalized consonant. This development is still heard, but the modern tendency is to retain /iə/, resulting in two forms, as with *cliabh* /k'l'iəw/ > *cléibhín* /k'l'e:v'i:n'/ and *cliaibhín* /k'l'iəv'i:n'/; *mias* /m'iəs/ > *méisín* /m'e:ʃi:n'/ and *miaisín* /m'iəʃi:n'/.

4.2. The diphthong /iə/, which has developed comparatively recently from *ío* before *l* and *r*, is retained, as in *síol* /ʃiəl/ > *síoilín* /ʃiəl'i:n'/; *cíor* /k'iər/ > *cíoirín* /k'iər'i:n'/. An earlier form of the latter, *círín* /k'i:r'i:n'/, survives but means 'a cockscomb', without diminutive connotation, whereas *cíoirín* is the general word for 'a small comb'.

4.3. The diphthongs /au/ and /ai/, which have developed as a result of the loss of a fricative, are not affected phonemically, for example, *leabhar* /ʎaur/ *leabhairín* /ʎaur'i:n'/; *Tadhg* /taig/, *Taidhgín* /taig'i:n'/.

4.4. Short vowels in monosyllables (except before the groups *-cht, -rt, -rd, -rn* (for which see 3.2. above) are affected as follows:

    io /u/ > *i* /i/, e.g. *siopa* /ʃupə/ > *sipín* /ʃip'i:n'/;
    o /o/ > *ei* /e/, e.g. *sop* /sop/ > *soipín* /sep'i:n'/;
    u /u/ > *ui* /i/, e.g. *muc* /muk/ > *muicín* /mik'i:n'/.

4.5. The vowels written *ea* and *a*, which were originally short, have been lengthened in the dialect under review. This comparatively recent lengthening results in two possible forms, one in which the long vowel /a:/ is retained, and another in which the original short *a* becomes /e/ or /i/, as in *brat* /bra:t/ > *braitín* /bra:t′i:n′/, *broitín* /bret′i:n′/; *glac* /gla:k/ > *glaicín* /gla:k′i:n′/, *gloicín* /glek′i:n′/; *fear* /f′a:r/ > *feairín* /f′a:r′i:n′/, *firín* /f′ir′i:n′/; *leac* /ʎa:k/ > *leaicín* /ʎa:k′i:n′/ *leicín* /ʎek′i:n′/; *breac* /b′r′a:k/ > *breaicín* /b′r′a:k′i:n′/, *bricín* /b′r′ik′i:n′/. The current tendency is to retain the long vowel. Certain common words have only the form with the long vowel, such as *geata* /g′a:tə/, *geaitín* /g′a:t′i:n′/; *mada* /ma:də/, *maidín* /ma:d′i:n′/.

4.6. Original short stressed vowels are regularly lengthened or diphthongized before certain final consonants or consonant groups, but are retained when the consonant or group is followed immediately by a vowel, for instance, *coill* /kaiʎ/, gen. *coille* /keʎə/; *cill* /k′i:ʎ/, gen. *cille* /k′iʎə/. Formerly the short vowel was retained before *-ín*, and examples of such retention are still found; but the almost universal practice now is to retain the long vowel or diphthong, as in *poll* /paul/ > *poillín* /pauʎi:n′/ /peʎi:n′/; *aill* /a:ʎ/ > *aillín* /a:ʎi:n′/; *meall* /m′a:l/ > *meaillín* /m′a:ʎi:n′/; *greim* /g′r′i:m′/ > *greimín* /g′r′i:m′i:n′/; *coill* /kaiʎ/ > *coillín* /kaiʎi:n′/; *bonn* /bu:n/ > *boinnín* /bu:ɲi:n′/; *bord* /baurd/ > *boirdín* /baurd′i:n′/; *lann* /la:n/ > *lainnín* /La:ɲi:n′/; *carr* /ka:r/ > *cairrín* /ka:r′i:n′/.

5.0. Irish grammars rarely pay any attention to the suffix *-ín*, and when they do, they restrict its use to nouns and confine their examples to concrete nouns and personal names. But a much wider morphological use of *-ín* is evidenced in writings that aim at representing familiar conversation. The following examples give some indication of its productive range. It should be noted that the examples, though mainly from Connacht, partly due to the author's research, are not confined to that area.[2]

5.1. It may be found joined to an adverbial phrase, such as *ar ball* ('soon') > *ar baillín*; *anois b'fhéidir*! (literally, 'now perhaps!') > *anois b'fhéidirín!*; *go fóill* ('yet') > *go fóillín*; *dar ndóigh* ('of course') > *dar ndóinín* (Ó Cadhain 1949, 103); *ó chiainibh* ('a while ago') > *ó chiainibhín* (Dinneen 1927, s.v. *cian*); *nóiméad ó shoin* ('a moment ago') > *nóiméidín ó shoinín* (Ó Gaora 1943, 93).

5.2. It is also seen joined to a noun, used as an adverb to qualify an adjective, for instance, *cineál fuar* ('somewhat cold') > *cineáilín fuar*; *beagán níos fearr* ('a little better') > *beagáinín níos fearr*.

5.3. The suffix may be joined to a prepositional pronoun, in exclamatory phrases (with sympathetic undertones), such as *Dia linn!* ('God bless us!') (*linn* = with us) > *Dia linnín!* (Ó Maolchatha 1963, 132); *a chroí liom!* ('my dear') (*liom* = with me) > *a chroí liomín* (Nic Pháidín 1987, s.v. *-ín*); *chugad!* ('here comes to you!') > *chugaidín*; *nach aon drochscéilín atá agaitín* ('that you have no bad news') (*agat* = at you) (Ó Gaora 1943, 94).

5.4. It is also found joined to an adjective, for example, *a dhuine uasailín*[3] ('my fine man') (*uasal* = fine, noble); *mam móirín* ('grandmother') (*mór* = big) (Ó Cuiv 1947, 159); *leis féinín* ('by himself') (*féin* = self); *milis* ('sweet') *milsín* (Ó Cadhain 1949, 111); *sláinín* ('safe journey') (*slán* = safe) (Ó Cadhain 1968, 184).

5.5. It may be joined to an abstract noun, as in *aighneas* ('quarrelsomeness') > *aighnisín* (Ó Cadhain 1949, 294); *cantal* ('cantankerousness') > *cantailín*; *grá* ('love') > *gráín* (Ó Cadhain 1949, 184); *fearg* ('anger') > *feirgín*; *olc* ('ill-will') > *oilcín*;[4] *slócht* ('hoarseness') > *slóichtín*; *súil* ('expectation') > *súilín* (Ó Gaora 1943, 94); *suaimhneas* ('tranquility') > *suaimhnisín* (Ó Cadhain 1970, 95); *uaigneas* ('loneliness') > *uaignisín* (Ó Cadhain 1939, 82).

5.6. Finally, the suffix may be joined to an imperative second-person singular, in talking to children, for example, *tar* ('come') > *tairín*; *siúil* ('walk') > *siúilín*.[5]

6.0. Because Irish and English have been in contact for centuries, borrowings from one to the other are common.

6.1. English to Irish: There is evidence of the addition of *-ín* to loanwords from the sixteenth century, though the use of such words was probably common in speech from an earlier period. Risteard Pluincéad's unpublished Latin–Irish Dictionary[6] includes a number of such loanwords, for example, belt > *beilt* > *beiltín* (baltheolus); cap > *caipín* (capitium); clout > *clúitín* (fasciola); cratch > *craistín* (echinus); fiddle > *fidilín* (fidicula); pig > *pigín* (porcellus); pink > *pincín* (superba); stick > *sticín* (bacillum).

6.2. Many such words are in current use, both written and spoken, and are no longer felt to be loanwords, for example, *caipín, pincín*.

7.0. The prevalence of *-ín* made it readily available for replacing in loanwords with loosely similar endings such as -een, -ian, -in, -ine, -ing, -ion, -on, or -y. Examples of this substitution of ending, with no diminutive, affectionate, or derogatory connotations, are found from the sixteenth century onwards, and the process is still current.

7.1. Examples of early loanwords of this type from literature are *lóistín* 'lodging', *róistín* 'roasting iron' from the sixteenth century (Knott 1922, 117); *flaigín* 'flagon', *maistín* 'mastin' (Anglo-Norman) from the seventeenth century (Mac Erlean 1917, 6, 184). The following are from Pluincéad (1662): *báisín* (malluvia) 'basin', *bhaigín* (currus) 'waggon', *bóidicín* (cnasona) 'bodkin', *caiptín* (capitaneus) 'captain', *cúirtín* (cortina) 'curtain', *cuisín* (accubitale) 'cushion', *daimsín* (damascenus) 'damson/damsin', *féirín* (nundinalis) 'fairing', *gairdín* (floretum) 'garden', *laibhín* (fermentum) 'leaven', *naipicín* (mantelium) 'napkin', *pisín* (catulus) 'pussy', *poimpín* (zuccomarin) 'pompion', *reibín* (capital) 'ribbon', *snaoisín* (sternumentaria) 'sneezing' (= snuff).

7.2. To the preceding list, most of which are still in use, many more could be added from current speech, such as *aintín* 'aunty', *builicín* 'bulkin', *caintín* 'canteen', *cairdín* 'accordion', *duisín* 'dozen', *laisín* 'lesson', *meaisín* 'machine', *measilín* 'Vaseline', *muilscín* 'moleskin', *naigín* 'noggin', *rigín* 'rigging', *rísín* 'raisin', *ruifín* 'ruffian', *sicín* 'chicken', *svaiscín* 'swanskin', *treiscín* 'dressing', *veidhlín* 'violin'.

7.3. An exceptional use of *-ín* in a loanword may be mentioned. The word 'police' was understood by Irish speakers as a plural and 'the police' became *na* (pl. article) *póilíos* /nə po:l'i:s/. This in turn produced a singular *póilí*, which in time became *póilín* 'policeman', thus bringing the word in line with the ubiquitous *-ín* words (but without any diminutive or affectionate connotations).

8.0. Irish to English: Many diminutives are found in the works of Irish writers of English or Hiberno-English in which *-ín* becomes *-een*. Some of these hybrids found their way into standard English dictionaries. The *Oxford English Dictionary*, for example, includes the following: boreen (*bóithrín* 'small road'), carrageen (*carraigín* 'edible sea-moss'), caubeen (*cáibín* 'old hat'), colleen (*cailín* 'young girl'), dudeen (*dúidín* 'short-stemmed pipe'), gombeen-man (*gaimbín* 'usury'), kippeen (*cipín* 'small stick'), mavourneen (*mo mhuirnín* 'my darling'), shoneen (*seoinín* 'imitator of English ways'), spalpeen (*spailpín* 'hired harvester'), thraneen (*tráithnín* 'blade of grass'). *Collins* (1986) includes drisheen (*drisín*, a type of pudding).

8.1. It is worth noting that a few words in -*een* that are commonly regarded as of Irish origin are only so at one remove, having come originally from English and having been gaelicized before finding their way back into English, for example, pink > *pincín* > pinkeen; pot > *poitín* > poteen; smithers > *smidiríní* > smithereens; devotee > *vóitín* > voteen, all of which occur in the *Oxford English Dictionary*.

9.0. Hiberno-English: Speakers of Hiberno-English in many areas, particularly in Connacht and parts of Munster, can add -*ín* (> -*een*) at will to any English concrete noun or personal name. Words like "maneen," "ladeen," "girleen," "biteen," "Mikeen," "Daneen," and many others are common in speech.

9.1. Such hybrids rarely occur in twentieth-century literature, but the following are found in J. M. Synge's *The Playboy of the Western World:* "houseen," "priesteen," "supeen." Some words of this kind from nineteenth-century writings have acquired dictionary status,[7] such as "buckeen" and "squireen," both signifying a second-rate idle member of the gentry; and "jackeen," a slick, self-assertive, lower-class Dubliner.

TOMÁS DE BHALDRAITHE
Royal Irish Academy

NOTES

1. Palatalized consonants are marked with the sign /'/ according to the accepted practice in Irish studies. Unmarked consonants are velarized except for ʃ, which is palatalized, and the palatals ç, ʎ, ɲ.
2. Examples without footnotes were recorded in County Galway.
3. MS 733 p. 90 in Irish Folklore Department, University College, Dublin.
4. MS 390, p. 48, Irish Folklore Department, University College, Dublin; Wagner 1959, 47.
5. Word-List (in Royal Irish Academy) from Seosamh Ó Dálaigh, Dún Chaoin, County Kerry.
6. *Vocabularium Latinum et Hibernum*, MS Z.4.2.5 in Marsh's Library, Dublin.
7. Cf. "a buckeen, a jackeen, a squireen, or any of the intermediate classes," *Frazer's Magazine* 22 (1840): 320; in the *Oxford English Dictionary* s.v. jackeen.

WORD INDEX

agaitín < *agat* (prep. pron.), 'at you' 5.3.
aighneas 'quarrelsomeness' 5.5.
aighnisín < *aighneas* 5.5.
aill 'cliff' 4.6.
aillín < *aill* 4.6.
ainniseoirín 'small miserable person' 2.1.
aintín 'aunty' 7.2.
amadáinín < *amadán* 2.4.
amadán 'male fool' 2.4.
Áugustín (prop. name) 1.0.
bacach 'tramp' 3.5.
bacachín < *bacach* 3.5.
bád 'boat' 4.0.
baicín < *bacach* 3.5.
báidín < *bád* 4.0.
baillín < *ball* 5.1.
bainbhín < *banbh* 3.6.
báisín 'basin' 7.1.
Baíthín (prop. name) 1.0.
ball : *ar b.* 'soon' 5.1.
banbh 'piglet' 3.6.
baothóg 'foolish girl' 2.4.
baothóigín < *baothóg* 2.4.
beagáinín < *beagán* 5.2.
beagán 'somewhat' 5.2.
beairnín < *bearna* 3.2.
béal 'mouth' 3.1.
bearna 'gap' 3.2.
béilín < *béal* 3.1.
beilt 'belt' 6.1.
beiltín < *beilt* 6.1.
bhaigín 'waggon' 8.1.
biteen, 'small bit' 9.0.
bó 'cow' 4.0.
bodóg 'heifer' 3.1.
bodóigín < *bodóg* 3.1.
bóidicín 'bodkin' 7.1.
boilgín < *bolg* 3.6.
bóín < *bó* 4.0.
boinnín < *bonn* 4.6.
boirdín < *bord* 3.2, 4.6.
bóithrín < *bóthar* 4.0, 8.0.
bolg 'belly' 3.6.

bonn 'coin' 4.6.
bord 'table' 3.2, 4.6.
boreen < *bóithrín* 8.0.
bóthar 'road' 4.0.
braitín < *brat* 4.5.
brat 'cloak, covering' 4.5.
breac 'fish' 4.5.
breaicín < *breac* 4.5.
bricín < *breac* 4.5.
broimín < *bromach* 3.5.
broitín < *brat* 4.5.
bromach 'colt' 3.5.
bromachín < *bromach* 3.5
buckeen 9.1.
builicín 'bulkin' 7.2.
cáibín 'old hat' 8.0.
cailín 'young girl' 8.0.
caintín < canteen 'a can' 7.2.
caipín 'cap' 6.1, 6.2.
caiptín 'captain' 7.1.
cairdín 'accordion' 7.2.
cairrín < *carr* 4.6.
cantailín < *cantal* 5.5.
cantal 'cantankerousness' 5.5.
carr 'car' 4.6.
carrageen < *carraigín* 8.0.
carraigín 'type of edible sea-moss' 8.0.
caubeen < *cáibín* 8.0.
ceaipín < *ceapach* 3.5.
ceapach 'plant bed' 3.5.
ceapachín < *ceapach* 3.5.
chugad (prep. pron.) 'towards you (sg.)' 5.3.
chugaidín < *chugad* 5.3.
chiainibh : *ó ch.* 'a while ago' 5.1.
chiainibhín < *chiainibh* 5.1.
cill (gen. *cille*) 'churchyard' 4.6.
cineáilín < *cineál* 5.2.
cineál 'somewhat' 5.2.
cíoirín < *cíor* 4.2.
cíor 'comb' 4.2.
cipín 'small stick' 8.0.
círín 'cockscomb' < *cíor* 4.2.
cléibhín < *cliabh* 4.1.
cliabh 'pannier basket' 4.1.

cliaibhín < cliabh 4.1.
clúitín 'rag' 6.1.
coileach 'cock' 3.4.
coileachín < coileach 3.4.
coilín < coileach 3.4.
coill (gen. coille) 'forest' 4.6.
coillín < coill 4.6.
colleen < cailín 8.0
craistín 'cratch' 6.1.
croch 'pot hanger' 3.4.
crochín < croch 3.4.
cruach 'turf stack' 3.4.
cruachín < cruach 3.4.
cruaichín < cruach 3.4.
cú 'hound' 4.0.
cuailín < cual 4.0.
cual 'heap' 4.0.
cúín < cú 4.0.
cúirtín 'curtain' 7.1.
cuisín 'cushion' 7.1.
daimsín 'damson' 7.1.
Daneen (personal first name) 9.0.
deoch 'drink' 3.4.
deochín < deoch 3.4.
dóigh : dar ndóigh 'of course' 5.1.
dóinín : dar ndóinín < dar ndóigh 5.1.
doirisín < doras 3.7.
doras 'door' 3.7.
drisheen < drisín 8.0.
drisín 'type of pudding' 8.0.
dudeen < dúidín 8.0.
dúidín 'short-stemmed pipe' 8.0.
duisín 'dozen' 7.2.
feairín < fear 4.5.
fear 'man' 4.5.
fearg 'anger' 5.5.
féidir : anois b'fhéidir (lit.) 'now perhaps!' = 'here goes!' 5.1.
féidirín : anois b'fh. < anois b'fhéidir 5.1.
féin 'self' 5.4.
féinín < féin 5.4.
feirgín < fearg 5.5.
féirín 'fairing' 2.0, 7.1.
fidilín 'small fiddle' 6.1.
firín < fear 4.5.
flaigín 'flagon' 7.1.
fóill : go f. 'yet' 5.1.

fóillín : go f. < go fóill 5.1.
gaimbín 'usury' 8.0.
gairdín 'garden' 7.1.
geaitín < geata 4.6.
geata 'gate' 4.6.
girleen 'small girl' 9.0.
glac 'handful' 4.5.
glaicín < glac 4.5.
gloicín < glac 4.5.
glúin 'knee' 2.2.
glúinín 'kneepad' 2.2.
goirtín < gort 3.2.
gombeen(-man) < gaimbín 8.0.
gort 'cultivated field' 3.2.
grá 'love' 5.5.
gráin < grá 5.5.
graim 'bite' 4.6.
greimín < greim 4.6.
houseen 'small house' 9.1.
ingín < ionga 3.3.
ionga 'fingernail' 3.3.
jackeen 9.1.
kippeen 'small stick' 8.0.
ladeen 'small lad' 9.0.
laibhín 'leaven' 7.1.
láinnín < lann 4.6.
laisín 'lesson' 7.2.
lann 'blade' 4.6.
leabhairín < leabhar 4.3.
leabhar 'book' 4.3.
leac 'flagstone' 4.5.
leaicín < leac 4.5.
leicín < leac 4.5.
linn (prep. pron.) 'with us'; Dia linn! 'God Bless us!' 5.3.
linnín : Dia linnín < Dia linn 5.3.
liom (prep. pron.) 'with me'; A chroí liom! 'My darling' 5.3.
liomín, A chroí liomín < a chroí liom 5.3.
locht 'blame' 3.2.
loichtín < locht 3.2.
lóistín 'lodging' 7.1.
mac 'son' 3.8.
mada 'dog' 4.6.
maicín < mac 3.8.
maidín < mada 4.6.
maistín 'mastin' (= 'mastiff') 7.1.

mam, see *mór*.
maneen 'small man' 9.0.
mavourneen < *mo mhuirnín* 8.0.
meaillín < *meall* 4.6.
meaisín 'machine' 7.2.
meall 'lump' 4.6.
méar 'finger' 2.2, 4.0.
measailín 'Vaseline' 7.2.
méirín (< *méar*), 'finger stall' 2.2, 4.0.
méisín < *mias* 4.1.
miaisín < *mias* 4.1.
mias 'dish' 4.1.
micín < *mac* 3.8.
Mikeen (personal first name) 9.0.
milis (adj.) 'sweet' 5.4.
milsín < *milis* 5.4.
moiltín < *molt* 3.1.
móirín : *mam mhóirín* < *mam mhór* 5.4.
molt 'wether' 3.1.
mór (adj.) : *Mam mhór* 'grandmother' 5.4.
muc 'pig' 4.4.
muicín < *muc* 4.4.
muilscín 'moleskin' 7.2.
muirín, muirghin 'family' 2.0.
múirín < *múr* 4.0
múirnín 'darling' 2.1; *mo mhuirnín* 'my darling' 8.0.
múr 'shower' 4.0.
naigín 'noggin' 7.2.
naipicín 'napkin' 7.1.
oilcín < *olc* 5.5.
olc 'ill-will' 5.5.
óinseach 'female fool' 3.4.
óinseachín < *óinseach* 3.4.
óinsín < *óinseach* 3.4.
paidrín 'rosary beads' 2.2.
pigín 'piglet' 6.1.
pincín 'gillyflower' 6.1, 6.2.
pincín 'minnow' 8.1.
pink 'gillyflower' 6.1, 6.2.
pink 'minnow' 8.1.
pinkeen < *pincín* 8.1.
pisín 'pussy' 7.1.
póilí (pl. *póilíos*) 'policeman' 7.3.
póilín 'policeman' 7.3.
poillín < *poll* 4.6.

poimpín 'pompion' 7.1.
poitín 'homemade whiskey' 8.1.
poll 'hole' 4.6.
poteen < *poitín* 8.1.
priesteen 'little priest' 9.1.
reibín 'ribbon' 7.1.
rigín 'rigging' 7.2.
rísín 'raisin' 7.2.
róistín 'roasting iron' 7.1.
ruifín 'ruffian' 7.2.
sabhaircín 'primrose' 2.2.
seoinín 'obsequious Irishman aping English ways' 8.0.
shoin : *ó shoin* 'ago' 5.1
shoinín : *ó shoinín* < *ó shoin* 5.1.
shoneen < *seoinín* 8.0.
sicín 'chicken' 7.2.
síoilín < *síol* 4.2.
síol 'seed' 4.2.
siopa 'shop' 3.3, 4.4.
sipín < *siopa* 3.3, 4.4.
siúil (imperf.) 'walk' 5.6.
siúilín (imperf.) < *siúil* 5.6.
sláinín < *slán* 5.4.
slán 'safe (journey to you)' 5.4.
slóichtín < *slócht* 5.5.
slócht 'hoarseness' 5.5.
smidiríní 'broken fragments' 8.1.
smithereens < *smidiríní* 8.1.
snaoisín 'sneezing' (= 'snuff') 7.1.
soilisín < *solas* 3.7.
soipín < *sop* 4.4.
solas 'light' 3.7.
sop 'straw' 4.4.
spailpín 'itinerant harvester' 8.0.
spalpeen < *spailpín* 8.0.
squireen 9.1.
sróinín 'nose ring' 2.2.
srón 'nose' 2.2.
sticín 'stick' 6.1.
suaimhneas 'tranquility' 5.5.
suaimhnisín < *suaimhneas* 5.5.
súil 'expectation' 5.5.
súilín < *súil* 5.5.
supeen 'small sup' 9.1.
svaiscín 'swanskin' 7.2.
Tadhg (a personal first name) 4.3.
Taidhgín < *Tadhg* 4.3.

tairín (imperf.) < *tar* 5.6.
tar (imperf.) 'come' 5.6.
thráithnín 'blade of grass' 8.0.
thraneen < *thráithnín* 8.0
treiscín 'dressing (in cloth)' 7.2.
troigh 'foot' 2.2.
troithín (< *troigh*) 'vampless sock' 2.2.

uaigneas 'loneliness' 5.5.
uaignisín < *uaigneas* 5.5.
uasailín < *uasal* 5.4.
uasal 'gentle' 5.4.
veidhlín 'violin' 7.2.
vóitín 'sanctimonious person' 8.1.
voteen < *vóitín* 8.1.

REFERENCES

Collins 1986. *Collins Dictionary of the English Language*. London and Glasgow: Collins.
Dinneen, P. S. 1927. *Foclóir Gaedhilge agus Béarla*. Dublin: Irish Texts Society.
Knott, E. 1922. *The Bardic Poems of Tadhg Dall Ó Huiginn, I*. London: Simpkin, Marshall, Kent.
Mac Erlean, J. C. 1917. *Duanaire Dháibhidh Uí Bhruadair, III*. London: David Nutt.
McKenna, L. 1944. *Bardic Syntactical Tracts*. Dublin: Dublin Institute for Advanced Studies.
Murphy, G. 1948. *Éigse* 5. Dublin: Colm O Lochlainn.
Nic Pháidín, C. 1987. *Cnuasach Focal ó Uíbh Ráthach*. Dublin: Royal Irish Academy.
Ó Cadhain, M. 1939. *Idir Shúgradh is Dáiríre*. Dublin: Oifig an tSoláthair.
———. 1949. *Cré na Cille*. Dublin: Sáirséal agus Dill.
———. 1968. *An Braon Broghach*. Dublin: Oifig an tSoláthair.
———. 1970. *An tSraith dhá Tógáil*. Dublin: Sáirséal agus Dill.
Ó Cuív, B. 1947. *Cnósach Focal ó Bhaile Bhúirne*. Dublin: Dublin Institute for Advanced Studies.
Ó Gaora, C. 1943. *Mise*. Dublin: Oifig an tSoláthair.
Ó Maolchatha, S. 1963. *An Gleann is a raibh ann*. Dublin: An Clóchomhar.
Thurneysen, R. 1946. *A Grammar of Old Irish*. Dublin: Dublin Institute for Advanced Studies.
Wagner, H. 1959. *Gaeilge Theilinn*. Dublin: Dublin Institute for Advanced Studies.

Vowel Hiatus in Early Modern Irish

My main purpose in this paper is to discuss evidence relating to vowel hiatus[1] in the Irish language in the period from about 1200 to 1650, during which time the professional poets of Ireland and Scotland shared a common literary language which had been evolved towards the end of the twelfth century.[2] Nonetheless, it may not be out of place to set down by way of introduction some observations on hiatus in Old and Middle Irish.

Vowels in juxtaposition (hiatus vowels) are not uncommon in Old Irish. Typical examples among nouns, adjectives, numerals, prepositional pronouns, and verbs are: *biäd, bruäch, diäs; coïr, oäc; deäc, teöir; diïb, doäib, leü, riäm; a-taäm, biïd, con-diëig*. Vowel hiatus may arise from the loss of intervocalic *j, p, s,* or *u* (*v*) before the historical period. Examples are: *sciän* < **skijēna, teë* (later *té, te*) < **tepent, iärn* < **isarno, oäc* < **ieuanc*. Hiatus is also seen in such forms as *fo-ruär* and *do-ruïch*, perf. indic. of *fo-fera* and *do-fich*, respectively, in composition forms in which the first element ends in a vowel and the second begins with a vowel, such as *soäs* (< *so* + *fis*), *duäilche*, and *nuiadnisse* (< *nuae* + *fiadnaisse*), and in borrowed names such as *Beniämin, Eöin,* and *Iäcob*.

To judge from extant Old Irish verse, hiatus forms such as those already cited were maintained fully down to the end of the seventh century, but there are signs of a tendency towards contraction, resulting in a long vowel or diphthong, in the course of the eighth century.[3] Early examples include *ích, líc,* and possibly *ól* (for *iïch, liïc,* and *ool*) in "Immram Brain" (possibly ca. 700)[4]; *díb, dóib,* and *ích* in the Blathmac poems (ca. 750–70);[5] and *boí, cóir,* and *trír* in "Félire Oengusso" (ca. 800).[6]

In the metrical monastic rule known as the "Rule of Mo Chutu," which I would date to the ninth century, contracted forms *cóir, díad, dóib,* and *do-gníam* occur, but there are also regular hiatus forms including *biäit, diüite, treó,* and *tuüs*.[7] Particularly noteworthy is the line *as-beir "Diä lib"* where the metre requires an unhistoric disyllabic form (showing hiatus) in place of monosyllabic *Día* 'God'. This phenomenon, described as "false hiatus" by Carney,[8] reflects the transitional stage when historically disyllabic *diä* 'day' might be pronounced as a monosyllable or as a disyllable.

Texts of the Middle Irish period show a growing tendency on the part of poets to use contracted forms, so that by the middle of the eleventh century there is comparatively little evidence of hiatus forms except in personal names and place-names.[9] In this case extant literary texts do not seem to reflect fully the phonological realities in all of the Gaelic-speaking areas, for the existence of hiatus in such words as *bruäch* (spelled *bruthach*), *diis* (spelled *dithis*), dat. sg. of *diäs*, and *fiäch* (spelled *fitheach*) in later Scottish Gaelic is clear evidence of the maintenance of this phonological phenomenon in speech in the northeastern zone. Nevertheless, the fact that apart from a few exceptions the contracted forms of such words were established as the only acceptable ones in bardic usage in Early Modern Irish suggests that when the prescriptive standard language was being evolved in the latter half of the twelfth century the use of hiatus forms in speech was confined to areas that were either remote or limited in extent or that lacked a strong literary "voice."[10]

The most satisfactory evidence of hiatus forms in Early Modern Irish, as in the earlier periods, is to be found in syllabic verse. Less satisfactory, though useful, is the occurrence of word-forms that contain vowel clusters that do not have a recognised place in the phonological system as simple vowels or diphthongs. Such are *aeiea, aíea, ée, éei, eóa, óa, óo,* and the like.[11] In addition there are comments made by medieval grammarians that are relevant.

While contracted forms are the norm in nouns, adjectives, and verbs in classical Early Modern Irish, there are exceptions. In his discussion of hiatus in Scottish Gaelic, T. F. O'Rahilly cited *aér* (*aiéar*), *cáóg*, and *príóir* as nouns showing hiatus in bardic verse (O'Rahilly 1932, 143, 268–69). To these we may add *dreéan*[12] and *iärn*.[13] Hiatus is far from rare in borrowed proper names, thus *Iób, Puéar, Roälbh, Saül, Seaán* or *Seoán,* and *Sión*. Furthermore, vowel clusters occur regularly in internal position in words formed with prefixed elements such as *dí, do, mí, ro* (*ra*), and *so,* for instance, *di-airm, do-fhaisnéise, mí-onóir, ro-éisd, so-óil,* as well as in other compound words. In the following couplets, which are taken from the bardic tract on noun declension (Bergin 1916–28), the words in boldface type are riming disyllables showing hiatus.

ex. 373, Mad Gall tí fa tuighi n-**iairn** . do-ní duine **diairm** de.

ex. 917, Ní féd mé maitheamh in **aieór** . ná caitheadh sé **raieól** rium.

ex. 932, Sgél do théigh grúaidh re **ngleoágh** . Seoán féin úair ón **aiér**.

ex. 1310, An **príóir** sul do ligh léi . do-bhir sé na **míoóigh** mhnáoi.

An instance of disyllabic *iairn* (gen. sg.) as part of a compound proper name is seen in a fourteenth-century poem (Carney 1943, 43, line 1161): *Fuair Ó Glóiairn, gég Mhis*.[14]

A well-known development within the Old Irish period was the use in absolute position of verbal forms such as *tic, tuc* in place of *do-ic, do-uc*. It is noteworthy that forms of the latter type, with hiatus between the pretonic vowel and the stressed vowel in compound verbs, were part of the morphological system of the Early Modern Irish poets. Examples are *do-egmhaim* (more normally *teagmhaim*) and *do-igim* (more normally *tigim*). On the analogy of such forms the bardic grammarians produced a new paradigm for the verb *téid* with forms such as *do-éighim, do-iaghmaid* (Bergin 1946, §8), from *téighim* (Old Irish *tíagu*), *tiaghmaid* (Old Irish *tíagmai*).

It may be noted that in bardic usage the vowel of *do* was not elided before a vowel when that element was used as a preverb with a finite verbal form,[15] thus *do innis, do fhás*, whereas the preposition *do* was reduced to *d'* before the corresponding verbal nouns, thus *d'innisin, d'fhás*. Elision is the norm with finite forms as well as with the verbal noun in the later language, and there is evidence that such was the case outside of bardic usage in the Early Modern Irish period. Occasionally the nonclassical usage was imposed on a text by a scribe, as can be seen in the opening couplet of a poem found in the fourteenth-century Leabhar Breac:

> Cumhthach labhras an Ionsa,
> an t-olc do fhuair d'fheadarsa.

Scholars who have published this poem[16] have not pointed out that according to bardic usage the last word should be *do-fheadarsa*.[17] I have little doubt that the poet used the correct form and achieved the required heptasyllabic line by using the monosyllabic form *uair* (without the preverb *do*)[18] as he did elsewhere in the poem (viz. line 5), that is, his second line was *an t-olc uair do-fheadarsa*.

Apart from hiatus in words such as I have instanced already, there are indications of hiatus within the inflexional system. Some of these indications are inconclusive as they may be merely orthographic irregularities, but in a small number of instances the hiatus forms are established by metrical criteria. In the case of nouns and adjectives whose radical form ended in a vowel, it seems that the bardic grammarians recognised a possible structure VV, where the second V was a short unstressed vowel *e*, *a*, or *o* that could be final, as in *lóa*, *lóo*, acc. pl. of *lá* (Bergin 1916–28, §82), *crúa*, acc. pl. of *cró* (§87), *cnúa*, nom. pl. and acc. pl. of *cnú* (§98), *rée*, nom. pl. and acc. pl. of *ré* (§99), *annróa*, nom. pl. and acc. pl. of *annró* (§108), *bíe*, gen. sg. fem., and *beóa*, nom. pl., of *beó* (§139), and *tée*, gen. sg. fem. and nom. pl. of *té* (§82); or medial, as in gen. pl. forms *craíeadh* (§87) and *réeadh* (§99), and dat. pl. *cnúaibh* (§98) and *réeibh* (§99). It must be pointed out that forms with *ua* and *ie* are ambiguous, as they could be forms with diphthongal pronunciation: hence the importance of determining metrical examples.

A comment by the bardic grammarian on gen. pl. forms such as *réeadh* is worth noting. It comes at the end of a list of words with inflexions similar to that of *ré*: *inann ghabhaid ₇ cnú chumhdaigh acht silla d'imarcaidh ar tháoibhréim illraidhe na n-anmann gcáol* "they are declined in the same way as *cnú chumhdaigh* but the slender nouns have an extra syllable in the genitive plural." Here the comment makes sense if we consider the plural forms of *ré* and of the first word of the phrase *cnú chumhdaigh*, the inflexion of which is given in the preceding paragraph of the tract.

	NOM.	ACC.	GEN.	DAT.
ré:	rée	rée	réeadh	réeibh
cnú:	cnúa	cnúa	cnú	cnúaibh

It is only in the gen. pl. that there is a structural difference. We may conclude, I think, that the bardic grammarian accepted that the consecutive *é* (of *ré*) and *e* (of the termination *-eadh*) were in separate syllables. It follows that the other forms (that is, for nom., acc., and dat.) were also disyllabic.

Despite the large number of forms cited in the tract on declension that apparently indicate hiatus,[19] I have found only one metrical example (1782) that establishes hiatus in an inflected form:

Cnúa cumhdaigh roinntir rú . ughdair is tú a ccoiltibh cnó.

Here *cnúa* must be pronounced as a disyllable to give a heptasyllabic line. In example 1810 we find

> Tairrngi chrúa ní fhill fa eoch . ó Chill Da Lua go Luimneach.

Here *crúa* (: *Lua*) is monosyllabic, but it is not an inflexional form of *crú* but the gen. (either sg. or pl.) of *crúa* that is listed in §108 as a variant form of *crú*.

Turning to extant poems I have noted three examples of final short vowels in hiatus in seventeenth-century compositions:

> dea séite na síonghaoth (Bergin 1970, 31, §4);
> is ní trī Dēe iad soin (Mhág Craith 1967, 60, §17); and
> Trí gnée mar léughthar linn (Carney 1950, 129, line 3001).

When we examine the bardic tract on verbs we find further indications of the recognition, at least in theory, of hiatus forms. These might be expected where a morpheme with vowel initial is added to a stem ending in a vowel. For instance, the regular endings of fut. 1. sg. are *-f(e)ad* (independent) and *-(e)abh* (dependent), thus *buailfead, ní bhuaileabh*. Typical forms cited for verbs with stem ending in a vowel are *cífead : ní chíeabh* (Bergin 1946, §33 *caei*), *gnífead : ní ghníeabh* (§37 *gním*), and *sgéifead : ní sgéieabh* (§38 *sgeith*). Further relevant material will be found in §39 (*gleódh, leódh*) and §42 (*snámh*). What appear to be hiatus forms cited for other tenses and persons include pres. ind. 1. sg. *gníim* (§37), *snaeiim* (§42); past ind. 1. sg. *do ghníeas* (§37),[20] *do shnaeieas* (§42).

As in the case of the noun tract there is a dearth of evidence among the accompanying metrical citations to confirm the use of hiatus forms. The only ones I have noted are

> ex. 364, Fer hé gan glésheadh 'na goin . **gléeadh** sé ris na slúagaibh; and
> ex. 377, **Snaeiid** sgoth Eanuig gu hard . Loch Feabail ó burd go burd.

The first of these is particularly interesting for the rime between *glésheadh* (a compound noun composed of *glé* 'clear' and *seadh* 'heed') and *gléeadh* (impv. 3. sg. of *gleó*) shows that intervocalic *sh* could be balanced for riming purposes by whatever phonetic element acted as boundary between two vowels in hiatus.

I have noted in a late sixteenth-century poem (Knott 1922, 244, §7) this example of a finite form where internal rime and syllable count establish that it features hiatus:

fáth róaithfir dod ghné ghloin,
ní gnóaighthir é ar h'éachdoibh.

Here the editor failed to point out that because the intensive prefix *ro-* normally has a short vowel, it is likely that the verbal form as used by the poet was *gnoaighthir*. The related verbal noun is listed in Bergin (1946, §106) as *gnoachadh*, together with a variant *gnodhuchadh*.[21] A seventeenth-century example of this verb showing hiatus is in the heptasyllabic line *bíodh nár ghnoaoigheas orra* (Mhág Craith 1967, 224, §194).

An instance from a seventeenth-century poem of a verbal noun showing hiatus is in the line *Ar ttaithbheóadh suil tí dhi* (Bergin 1970, 135, §16).

Against the fact that metrical examples proving the use of hiatus forms by poets are so few we may set the fact that what appear to be hiatus forms, in both nouns and verbs, are far from uncommon in prose texts written at various times within the Early Modern Irish period. I give here a small selection of examples found in texts dating from the fifteenth and sixteenth centuries:

ceó:	gen. sg. *ceoa*[22] (Wulff 1929, 280, line 11); gen. pl. *ceoand* Wulff 1929, 50, line 8); dat. pl. *ceouib* (O'Grady 1926, 254, line 24)
cló:	gen. pl. *cloo* (Ó Maonaigh 1944, line 3980); *cloe* (Ó Maonaigh 1944, line 5633); *cloadh* (Oxford MS Rawl. B 513, fol. 3rb 3); dat. pl. *clóaibh* (Ó Maonaigh 1944, line 4001)
gné:	gen. sg. *gnee*[22] (Ó Ceithearnaigh 1942, line 307)
ré:	gen. sg. *réé*[22] (Plummer 1922, 1.80, §157) *ree* (Plummer 1922, 1.83, §165)
clódh:	past ind. 3. pl. *do clóadar* (O'Grady 1929, 91, line 36)
faoíeachtain:	pres. ind. 3. sg. *faíidh* (Stokes 1897, §23) *faienn* (Stokes 1897, §67)
gnoachadh:	past. ind. 2. sg. *do gnoaighes-sa* (O'Kelleher and Schoepperle 1918, 404, lines 24–25)

In discussing vowel quantity in Old Irish, Thurneysen (1946, 33) said that there are indications that stressed long vowels were shortened in hiatus, and he instanced *-taam* (1. pl. of *at-tá*), *biid*, and *deu, deo* (acc. pl. of *día* 'God'). He went on to discuss the use in the Wurzburg glosses of a length mark over vowels that were originally short, and he concluded, "Within our period, therefore, hiatus-vowels have been lengthened under the accent, though whether they have the full quantity of other long vowels is doubtful."

There are indications that long vowels in hiatus might be shortened in Early Modern Irish. In this connection two passages in the tract on noun declension deserve attention. The first is §87:

> gach inadh a teagaimh dá ghuthaidhe dá chéile and gu gearr as .c. é.

The comment "in every place where two vowels come together in it, it is short that it is according to correct usage" refers to the word *cró*. I take *and* 'in it' to refer to the declension of *cró* and *é* 'it' to refer to the first vowel of two. The forms in the paradigm in which two vowels appear to come together are *crúa* and *craíeadh*. The comment suggests that we should interpret the acc. pl. form as *cru-a*. In the case of gen. pl. *craíeadh*, which might be spelled *craoieadh*, the rule would suggest shortening to *cra-eadh*. While I have no example from Early Modern Irish to confirm the latter suggestion, there is support for it in the rime *ro-fhial* : *Tro-fhian* found in a poem composed about 1165 (Byrne 1964, 61, §1) wherein *Tro-* is a reduced form of Middle Irish *Troí* (later *Traoi*).

The second passage is §108:

> ANNRÓ, don annró, med an annró, na hannróa, dona hannróaibh, méd na n-annró, féch annróa gu gearr is .c. a deiredh ón táoibhréim úathaidh anúas.

The comment "it is short that its ending is according to correct usage from the genitive singular on" may be taken as referring to the quantity of the *ó* of the radical form; that is, it is long in absolute final position but it is shortened when followed by another vowel, namely, in *annro-a* and *annro-aibh*.

Vowel shortening in hiatus is also discussed in a rather puzzling passage[23] in the bardic tract described by Bergin as "Introductory" (Bergin 1916, §91):

> An tan teagmhuid dá ghuthaidhe re cneas a chéile gan chonnsuine eatarra, gearr as cóir an cédghuthaidhe dhíobh mas guthaidhi do bhí gearr ríamh é mur so: an **la úd** $_7$ an **ga úd**, cóir do chomhardadh; an **día úd** $_7$ an **t-úa úd**, lochdach d'úaithne riú, ó nach rabhadar gearr ríamh.
>
> Bean shídh go ngrúaidh ngnéfháoilidh,
>   ar chígh chúain dá cháoifhéchuin—(cóir)

Bean shídh go ngrúaidh ngnééidigh—(lochdach)
Beanfaidh mé siobhal a Seaán
   mun Mac nDé úd.
   mun Día úd—(lochdach)

I would take *úd* to be enclitic in the phrases cited and I would translate, "When two vowels come together with no vowel between them, the first of these vowels is short according to correct usage if it is a vowel that was short formerly (or 'ever'); thus *an la-úd* and *an ga-úd* are correct to rime, but *an día-úd* and *an t-úa-úd* are faulty as consonance with them because they [that is, the 'vowels' *ía* and *úa*] were not formerly (or 'ever') short."

Old Irish *laa* (disyllabic form with hiatus) or *lá* 'day' is normally *lá* in Early Modern Irish (Bergin 1916-28, §82), but Old Irish *gaí/gaé* 'spear' is *ga* as well as *gaoi/gae* (Bergin 1916-28, §81). The implication of the comment seems to be that in hiatus position the vowel in *lá* can be shortened to provide full rime with *ga*. The commentator, however, rejects the possibility of shortening of the diphthongs *ia* and *ua*. Unfortunately, the metrical examples are unsatisfactory. The second one would appear to be intended to be relevant to the comment on *an la-úd*, insofar as in *Seaán* we have a hiatus word in which a long vowel is preceded by a short one; but even if we allow for shortening of *é* to *e* in *nDe-úd*, we do not have correct consonance for *Seaán*. In the first example the eclipsis after *ngrúaidh* is irregular, and neither the *l* of *ngnéfháoilidh* nor the *d* of *ngnééidigh* correctly balances the *ch* of *cháoifhéchuin* for full consonance.

A matter that is relevant to this general discussion is the treatment of unstressed final vowels in words that form the first element of a compound. The bardic language allowed elision of such a vowel before a vowel initial in the following word, thus *usguisge* (< *uisge* + *uisge*), *budhuaine* (< *buidhe* + *uaine*),[24] *coirceórna* (< *corca* + *eórna*), *iarlfhuil* (< *iarla* + *fuil*), and the like (Bergin 1916, §94).

This paper would not be complete without some discussion, however brief, of the process of hiatus filling. Evidence of this phenomenon is found at many stages of the language. We may instance, for example, the appearance in Donegal Irish of unhistorical hiatus-filling *h* discussed in O'Rahilly 1932, 174-75, where *scé* + *óg* > *scihag* 'hawthorn', corresponding to Scottish Gaelic *sgitheag*, is cited.

Mention has been made already of the occurrence of vowel clusters in words formed with a prefix ending in a vowel, as in *di-*

airm. But contraction could take place, as is clear from the word *suaithnidh*,[25] which is disyllabic in bardic verse, that is, orthographic *uai* represents the diphthong. In contrast we may note that *suáilc(h)e*, the compound formed from *so* + *áilc(h)e*, appears commonly in Early Modern Irish with a hiatus-filling *bh*, for example, *subhailce* (Ó Maonaigh 1944, line 419). It may be noted here that the loanword corresponding to Middle English *towaille* appears in Early Modern Irish texts in forms with and without *bh*, thus *tubhaille, túaille*. The pronunciation in the modern dialect of West Cork is /tu:ˈaːlˈə/.

Mention has also been made (in n. 7) of scribal *treothu* in late manuscript copies of a ninth-century text where the expected form would be *treö*. In this case the scribal spelling reflects the contemporary form, for forms with hiatus-filling *th* are found in the inflexional system of the prepositional pronouns in Early Modern Irish,[26] thus *fó* has 3. sg. fem. *fúithe, fóithe, faoithe*, and 3. pl. *fútha, fúthaibh, faoithibh*, corresponding to Old Irish 3. sg. fem. *foae*, 3. pl. *foïb*; and *tré* (*trí*) has 3. sg. fem. *tríthe* and 3. pl. *tríotha*, corresponding to Old Irish 3. sg. fem. *treë*, 3. pl. *treü, treö*.

The occurrence of -*th*- plural forms in some of the nouns already discussed, such as *cró*, is recorded in the bardic declensional tract (Bergin 1916–28). Thus *craíthe* and the like, which are given for *cró* (§87), are described as *do chanamhain*, that is, unhistorical. The same term is used of plurals such as *dlaoithe* and *gnéithe* (§98) and *crúaithe* (§108).

Probably the most extensively used hiatus filler from the Middle Irish period on is *dh* (*gh*). Thus in the noun tract (§57) we find *ladharg* side by side with *lárag*. O'Rahilly (1942, 123) derived both forms from Old Irish *loärg*. Forms with -*dh*- are very common in the verbal system,[27] and it seems that a scribe found nothing incongruous in putting such a form alongside a hiatus form, as is shown by the sentence *na caiidh orm-sa, acht caidhigh oraibh fein* "do not weep for me, but weep for yourselves" (Ó Maonaigh 1944, line 3943). Of the many late spellings with intrusive *gh*, mention may be made of *Seaghán* for *Seaán*, normally contracted to *Seán*, and *doighearraideach* (Ó Súilleabháin 1962, line 5344) for *do-earráideach*.

BRIAN Ó CUÍV
Dublin Institute for Advanced Studies

NOTES

1. The discussion here is confined to hiatus within the word. Hiatus was common within phrases in the earlier language, but there was a growing tendency towards elision of unstressed short vowels at word junction. Contrast *crochais, nípu i cinta* (Greene and O'Connor 1967, 20) with *Robadh maith damhsa, a Mheic Dé* (ibid., 197), both heptasyllabic lines but the first showing hiatus, the second elision. In strict metres of the Early Modern Irish period such elision was obligatory in certain circumstances.
2. In this connection see Ó Cuív 1980a.
3. Osborn Bergin and several other scholars used to include loss of hiatus among signs of Middle Irish, that is, the language from about 900 on, but the presence of a contracted form in a text does not preclude the possibility that it was composed in the Old Irish period.
4. See Carney 1983, 194; Mac Mathúna 1985, 398. Carney would date the verse in "Immram Brain" to about 700; Mac Mathúna would put the date much later.
5. See Carney 1964, xxvii. He has pointed out that for every one contracted form in the Blathmac poems there are seven hiatus forms.
6. See Carney 1983, 195. Hiatus forms are normal in this work.
7. This text is extant only in late manuscripts in which the orthography frequently obscures the original form. Thus *treö* is spelled *treothu*, and all of the manuscripts have *tus* where the metre requires *tuüs*. The development of *-th-* forms of the prepositional pronouns is discussed later.
8. Carney 1983, 195. Earlier examples of disyllabic *Diä* occur in the "Irish Gospel of St. Thomas" (Carney 1964, 100, §31), the Blathmac poems (ibid. 30, §85) and "Félire Oengusso," Ep. 153.
9. Hiatus and contracted forms of the word *laa* (*lá*) appear in this quatrain in one of the poems in "Buile Shuibhne" (see O'Keeffe 1931, 17), which probably dates from the eleventh or twelfth century:

> Beg mo chuid ó thig laa,
> ní thǽt ar scáth lá noa,
> barr biorair Chluana Cille
> la gleorán Chille Cua.

The last word in each line is a disyllable; *noa* in line 2 is probably scribal for *nua* (: *Cua*).
10. Cf. "fully stressed disyllabic words with hiatus had contraction in Irish early in the tenth century, but in Scottish Gaelic they have mostly remained uncontracted to the present day. . . . This preservation of hiatus is not found in Manx, though it may well be that contraction there is comparatively late" (Jackson 1951, 86).
11. To be contrasted with these are digraphs and trigraphs, such as *ai, ea, ei, io, iai, oi*, and *ui*, which represent simple vowels or diphthongs and in which one of the letters is a glide indicating consonant quality.
12. For examples, see Ó Cuív 1977, 16–17; for the form, see Ó Cuív 1980b, 57–58.
13. Besides this form bardic poets used *iarann* and monosyllabic *iarn*.
14. The form *Glóiairn* is trisyllabic. A late scribe emended to *Gloithiarainn*, using *th* as a hiatus filler and substituting the recognised variant form for *iairn*.

15. The preverb *do* commonly replaced *no* and *ro* of the earlier language.
16. Knott 1928, 29; Greene and O'Connor 1967, 154.
17. In Old Irish the preverb was *ro*, as in *ro-fitir*.
18. For such forms see Bergin 1946, §22.
19. The word *dia* (*dé*) 'day' is found in §108 (where the paradigmatic headword is *annró* with nom. pl. *annróa*) in the phrase *Dé Lúain, Dia Lúain*. It is also found in another grammatical text (McKenna 1944, 18) where *na Díaa céadáoine* and *na Dée céadáoine* are given as pl. forms of *Día céadáoin* and *Dé céadáoin*.
20. An example of this form is found in the phrase *do ghníeas m'eocha* in Bergin 1916, §78.
21. For a discussion of this and related forms, see O'Rahilly 1950.
22. According to the bardic tract on declension *ceó*, *gné*, and *ré* were undeclined in the singular.
23. This passage is echoed by seventeenth-century grammarians (Mac Aogáin 1968, 88 and 139), but the sense is made no clearer by them.
24. But cf. Bergin 1955, §137, where this form with elision is described as faulty.
25. Thurneysen (1946, 81) cites the Old Irish form *súaichnid* as 'for *su-aith-gnid*'.
26. Noteworthy in this connection is the early form *lethu* (for more usual *leu, leo*), for which see Thurneysen 1946, 273.
27. For examples see the Royal Irish Academy *Dictionary of the Irish Language*, s.vv. *foaid, gnóaigid, sceïd,* and *snáid*.

REFERENCES

Bergin, O. 1916. Irish Grammatical Tracts. I. Introductory. Supplement to *Ériu* 8.
———. 1916–28. Irish Grammatical Tracts. II. Declension. Supplements to *Ériu* 8–10.
———. 1946. Irish Grammatical Tracts. III. Irregular Verbs. Supplement to *Ériu* 14.
———. 1955. Irish Grammatical Tracts. V. Metrical Faults. Supplement to *Ériu* 17.
———. 1970. *Irish Bardic Poetry*. Dublin: Dublin Institute for Advanced Studies.
Byrne, F. J. 1964. Clann Ollaman Uaisle Emna. *Studia Hibernica* 4: 54–94.
Carney, J. 1943. *Topographical Poems*. Dublin: Dublin Institute for Advanced Studies.
———. 1950. *Poems on the O'Reillys*. Dublin: Dublin Institute for Advanced Studies.
———. 1964. *The Poems of Blathmac son of Cú Brettan*. Dublin: Educational Company of Ireland for the Irish Texts Society.
———. 1983. The Dating of Early Irish Verse Texts, 500–1100. *Éigse* 19.2: 177–216.
Greene, D., and O'Connor, F. 1967. *A Golden Treasury of Irish Poetry*. London: Macmillan.
Jackson, K. 1951. "Common Gaelic": The Evolution of the Goidelic Languages. *Proceedings of the British Academy* 37: 71–97.
Knott, E. 1922. *The Bardic Poems of Tadhg Dall Ó Huiginn*, 1. Lúndain: Simpkin, Marshall, Hamilton, Kent ar son Chumainn na Sgríbheann Gaedhilge.
———. 1928. *An Introduction to Irish Syllabic Poetry of the Period 1200–1600*. Cork: Cork University Press.
Mac Aogáin, P. 1968. *Graiméir Ghaeilge na mBráthar Mionúr*. Baile Átha Cliath: Institiúid Árd-léinn Bhaile Átha Cliath.

Mac Mathúna, S. 1985. *Immram Brain*. Tübingen: Max Niemeyer Verlag.
McKenna, L. 1944. *Bardic Syntactical Tracts*. Dublin: Dublin Institute for Advanced Studies.
Mhág Craith, C. 1967. *Dán na mBráthar Mionúr*. Baile Átha Cliath: Institiúid Árd-léinn Bhaile Átha Cliath.
Ó Ceithearnaigh, S. 1942. *Regimen na Sláinte*, iml. 1. Baile Átha Cliath: Oifig an tSoláthair.
Ó Cuív, B. 1977. Donnchadh Mór's Poem on the Wren. *Éigse* 17: 13–18.
———. 1980a. A Mediaeval Exercise in Language Planning. In *Progress in Linguistic Historiography: Papers from the International Conference on the History of the Language Sciences (Ottawa, 28-31 August 1978)*. Amsterdam: John Benjamins B.V.
———. 1980b. Some Gaelic Traditions about the Wren. *Éigse* 18: 43–66.
O'Grady, S. H. 1926. *Catalogue of Irish Manuscripts in the British Museum*, 1. London: Trustees of the British Museum.
———. 1929. *Caithréim Thoirdhealbhaigh*. London: Simpkin, Marshall for the Irish Texts Society.
O'Keeffe, J. G. 1931. *Buile Śuibhne*. Dublin: Stationery Office.
O'Kelleher, A., and Schoepperle, G. 1918. *Betha Colaim Chille*. Urbana, Ill.: University of Illinois.
Ó Maonaigh, C. 1944. *Smaointe Beatha Chríost*. Baile Átha Cliath: Institiúid Árd-léighin Bhaile Átha Cliath.
O'Rahilly, T. F. 1932. *Irish Dialects Past and Present*. Dublin: Browne and Nolan.
———. 1942. *Iarann, Lárag*, etc. *Ériu* 13.2: 119–27.
———. 1950. *Gnó, Gnóaigh, Gnóughadh*. *Celtica* 1.2: 322–27.
Ó Súilleabháin, P. 1962. *Lucerna Fidelium*. Baile Átha Cliath: Institiúid Árd-léinn Bhaile Átha Cliath.
Plummer, C. 1922. *Bethada Náem nÉrenn*, 1. Oxford: Clarendon Press.
Stokes, W. 1897. The Gaelic Abridgment of the Book of Ser Marco Polo. *Zeitschrift für celtische Philologie* 1: 245–73, 362–438.
Thurneysen, R. 1946. *A Grammar of Old Irish*. Dublin: Dublin Institute for Advanced Studies.
Wulff, W. 1929. *Rosa Anglica*. London: Simpkin, Marshall for the Irish Texts Society.

Another Look at Old Irish *imbúaruch* 'this morning', *imbárach* 'tomorrow morning'

Some years ago, I published a note (1977) in which I argued that *imbúaruch* and *imbárach* derive from absolute constructions of the same type as the Latin ablative absolute. Positing different cases, namely, dative and accusative, to underlie the alternation *-úa-/-á-*, I assumed[1] that both adverbs were ultimately derived from a base consisting of a preposition,[2] a noun 'cow', and a deverbal adjective 'bound'.

Since then, two colleagues[3] have provided interesting comments on my proposals, so that a few further remarks now seem possible, especially in view of the fact that one of these commentators happens to be the recipient of this Festschrift himself. Therefore, I shall begin with his comments, most of which in fact represent signal improvements on my original proposals. First, he points out (Hamp 1983, 53) that the root behind *-ruch* and *-rach* must be '*$rigā$-' instead of my '*reg' (Ahlqvist 1977, 110); I accept his reasoning. He then suggests that *-$bān$-$rigān$ is preferable to my *$bān$-$regon$ on the grounds of gender. This may well be so, even if I prefer to consider the possibility that, like certain Greek adjectives (cf. Kastner 1967), *$rigo$- had remained an *o*-stem in the feminine too.

Regarding *-búaruch*, Hamp (1983, 54) adopts my tentative suggestion (Ahlqvist 1977, 110) of a compound, rather than a dative absolute, which is the solution I still favour. Lastly, Hamp briefly discusses the different cases of *-bárach* and *-búaruch*. His formulation is elegant and therefore worth repeating here: "the expression for 'this morning', like 'today', is a simple locative, for location at a point in time. The expression for 'tomorrow' is an accusative of goal *'until (into) such-and-such a future time'." It is much more to the point than my original formulation (1977, 111), according to which "the dative would have been interpreted as denoting a point in time 'now' and the accusative a point in time 'not now'."

This formulation is the target of the main criticism made by Mac Mathúna (1978, 222–23) of my original proposals. Certainly, he is right in insisting that my invoking a parallel with *indiu* 'today' and *indé* 'yesterday' is semantically rather difficult. Instead, he suggests that "*Imbúaruch* can be satisfactorily interpreted as '(at the time) when the cow is bound, i.e., at milking-time' (dat. of rest), and *imbárach* as 'to the (time of the) state of being bound' referring to the driving in for milking (acc. of motion)." This reading has points in common with Hamp's formulation and is on the whole fairly satisfactory, with the possible exception that there does not seem to be a need to take the accusative as referring to something quite as concrete as "the driving in for milking"; Hamp's accusative of goal is more suitable, as it currently seems to me.

To sum up, in the light of the very helpful and constructive criticism my original proposals have received, I should like to modify them as follows: *(en) + $g^w owi$ + $rigōi$ (loc. + dat.)[4] > *(in) + bou^4 + $rigū^4$ > *(im)bōruy > imbúaruch 'when the cow (is) bound' and *(en) + $g^w ōm$ + rigom > *(in) + bān + rigon > *(im)bārray. > *imbárach 'until the cow (is) bound'.

ANDERS AHLQVIST
University College Galway

NOTES

1. Just as mediaeval Irish scholars did; see the references in my original article (108[3]).
2. Cp. my original article (111[23]) for some suggestions about the date of its introduction into this construction.
3. I.e., Hamp (1983) and Mac Mathúna (1978). Bachellery (1979, 314) offers a succinct and useful summary, but no criticism or improvements.
4. With locative meaning: see McCone (1978, 35) for the syncretism of the dative and locative cases in early Celtic.

REFERENCES

Ahlqvist, A. 1977. Old Irish *imbúaruch* 'this morning', *imbárach* 'tomorrow morning'. *Celtica* 12: 108–12.
Bachellery, E. 1979. Review of *Celtica* 12. *Études celtiques* 16: 314–16.
Hamp, E. 1983. *Imbúaruch, imbárach. Celtica* 15: 53–54.
Kastner, W. 1967. *Die griechischen Adjektive zweier Endungen auf -ΟΣ.* Heidelberg: Winter.
McCone, K. 1978. The Dative Singular of Old Irish Consonant Stems. *Ériu* 29: 26–38.
Mac Mathúna, L. 1978. Review of *Celtica* 12. *Studia Hibernica* 17–18: 220–24.

Old Irish *cú*: A Naïve Reinterpretation

In his many important studies of Indo-European nouns, Eric Hamp has often given us provocative and yet convincing reappraisals of the Celtic evidence.[1] His goal has always been to account for all of the attested forms, including those which are too often slighted by scholars who do not share Hamp's command of the primary sources and the modern dialects. As he reminds us,

> the aim of an etymology is to unite observations and make them mutually explanatory, not to dissociate possible connexions unless there is very strong reason. The latter principle is bound up with the fact that we prefer to be able to show that in a given development there has been no replacement, and that all change has been purely superficial; this is because the fundamental nature of language (and of culture) is continuity. (1974, 275)

I hope to show here that this is true of the paradigm of OIr. *cú* 'dog, hound', which has always been assumed to reflect several morphological innovations.

On the contrary, I believe that the archaic character of this paradigm has never been sufficiently appreciated. Nom. sg. *cú*, W. *ci*, Co. Br. *ki* continue the old nom. sg., Celt. **kū* < PIE. **ku̯ō*.[2] The gen. sg. *con* continues **kunos* = Skt. *śúnas*, Gk. κυνός. The Welsh pl. *cwn* has always been interpreted as continuing **kunes*, with the same generalization of the zero grade as Gk. κύνες and Lith. *šùnes*. The Irish gen. pl. *con* continues **kunōn*, the dat. pl. *conaib* **kunobis*, and the acc. pl. *cona* **kunās*. All of this is in the handbooks, and (except for the assertion about W. *cwn*) I am sure that it is correct.

It is the dat. acc. sg. and nom. pl. forms *coin* that cause trouble: Thurneysen (*GOI* 46–47) suggested that the unexpected *o* was taken over from the gen. pl. *con* and from the first compound member *con-* < **kuno-* (cf. Brit. *Cunobelinos*, etc.). Pedersen (*VKG* 1.35, 41, 361–66; *CCCG* 2, 4, 103–5), by contrast, believed that forms like nom. pl. *coin*, which he derived from **kones*, continuing **kunes*, arose by rule. The representation of his views given in Thurneysen's *Grammar* (loc. cit.) is misleading. Thurneysen says, "Pedersen . . . holds that *i* and *u* in almost every position had fallen together with *e* and *o*, being retained only in those positions where original *e* and *o* have become *i* and *u* . . . ; in particular, *i* and *u* do not remain before *e* in the following syllable." It is the phrase "in almost every position" that is confusing. What Pedersen actually said is, "Im Irischen erscheint in der Regel *o*; *u* nur unter dem Einfluß eines *u* oder *i* der folgenden Silbe" (*VKG* 1.35; same wording with respect to *i*, 41), or, in the English version, "Irish as a rule has *o*, and *u* only before *u* or *i* in the following syllable" (*CCCG* 2; so also for *i*, 4). What he is talking about, evidently, is the surface representation of **u* and **i* in initial syllables; Pedersen was too clear a thinker to have envisaged a time (e.g., in Prim. Ir.) when the high vowels had all become mid-vowels, but would be raised again by high vowels that had mysteriously survived only in noninitial syllables. That this was not his intent is shown by his careful wording of the conditions for the retention of **u* and the raising of **o* (*VKG* 1.362): in addition to the *u* that results from retention/raising before final high vowels, whether retained after apocope or not, we also find *u* "vor einem gebliebenen alten -*u*- (gleichviel in welcher Gestalt dies *u* in historischer Zeit erscheint) . . . Dagegen bewirkt ein sekundäres (durch Umlaut entstandenes) *u* keine Hebung." There is no confusion here; any that has arisen since may be attributed to the (unfortunate) use of the single term *Hebung* to cover both the retention of **u* and the raising (*Hebung* proper) of original **o*.

Pedersen's view, then, was that unless it was followed by a high vowel, **u* or **i* in the initial syllable of a stressed word would be written *o* or *e* in Irish. That is, he would introduce another rule into the well-established sequence in which the raising and lowering of vowels in stressed syllables precedes the *a/o* affection of high vowels in unstressed syllables.[3] After the raising of stressed **o* and **e* before a following high vowel, etymological **u* and **i* would have merged with **o* and **e* unless supported by a high vowel in the following syllable. Pedersen's would thus be a kind of height harmony rule; this makes more sense than a stage at which only stressed **u* and **i* would have merged with **o* and **e before* raising (and lowering), but unstressed **u* and **i* would have remained distinct from them. It is of course in stressed syllables that we expect the greatest number of distinctions to be maintained, and in unstressed syllables that we expect to find merger, weakening, and syncope.[4]

Thurneysen and Pedersen attempted to solve the problem of

the paradigm of *cú* because they assumed, as a result of their intimate knowledge of the Irish noun, that there was a problem there to solve. Only one noun in all of Irish unambiguously shows apophany in its oblique cases: this is of course *ben* 'woman, wife' (*GOI* 184):

	singular	*dual*	*plural*
N	ben < *benā	mnaí < *bnai	mná < *bnās
G	mná < *bnās	ban < (= masc.)	ban < *banon
D	mnaí < *bnai	mnáib < *bnābin	mnáib < *bnābis
A	arch. bein < *benæn	mnaí (= nom.)	mná < *bnās[5]

Because we know that the gen. sg. and pl. and the dat. and acc. pl. of *cú* contain the stem **kun-* with zero grade, it is only logical to assume that, except for the nom. voc. sg., the rest of the paradigm does too. The frequent generalization of the zero grade in Celtic is well known; and McCone (1986, 234 etc.) has begun referring to it as "Watkins's rule."

These facts (that we find zero grade of the stem where we expect to, in the weak cases of the paradigm, and that zero grade is frequently generalized in Celtic, both in the noun and in the verb), have led to the following reconstruction for the paradigm of *cú*, a reconstruction that has never been challenged (problematical forms in boldface):

	singular	*dual*	*plural*
N	cú < *k(w)ū < *k̂u̯ō	**coin < *kune**	**coin < *kunes**
G	con < *kunos	con (= pl.)	con < *kunon
D	**coin < *kun(e)i**	conaib (= pl.)	conaib < *kunobis
A	**coin < *kunen < *kunm̥**	coin (= nom.)	cona < *kunās < *k̂unn̥s

But if we reconstruct these forms mechanically, without preconceived ideas about what their ablaut must have been, we will get a very different result:

	singular	*dual*	*plural*
N	cú < *k(w)ū	**coin < *k(w)one**	**coin < *k(w)ones**
G	con < *kunos	con (= pl.)	con < *kunon
D	**coin (= acc.)**	conaib (= pl.)	conaib < *kunobis
A	**coin < *k(w)onæn**	coin (= nom.)	cona < *kunās[6]

When this word appears in compounds, we find zero grade in the first compound member **kuno-*, for example, CUNOMAGLI (*CIIC* 125), CUNAGUSOS (139); Late Brit. CUNIGNI (362) (= W. *Cynin*, *LHEB* 174), CUNATAMI (449) (= W. *Cyndaf*, *LHEB* 183).

We may compare the exclusive use of the weak stem *ban-* as a first member in compounds. But it is certain that in Brittonic, when 'dog' was used as a second compound member, at least nom. sg. **kī* and gen. sg. **kunos* were distinguished, for we have them in the Welsh proper names *Meilyg* < **maglokī* and *Maelgwn* < **maglokunos* (Ogam MAGLICUNAS (*CIIC* 446; *LHEB* 182). Some evidence for short o-grade in the nom. pl. comes from the British tribal name Ουενικωνες, recorded in the Ptolemaic itinerary and equated by John Koch with early W. *Gwynngwn* (1980, 87–89).⁷ The fact that this is Ουενικωνες, not *Ουενιπωνες, also suggests that the labial component of the initial consonant had already been analogically eliminated in the full grade forms in Common Celtic, and that the word began with a simple velar throughout its paradigm. All of this leads me to suggest that *cú* is the second noun in Old Irish that has root apophony and to set up the following revised paradigm for Proto-Celtic:

	singular	*dual*	*plural*
N	*kū	*kone	*kones
G	*kunos	(= pl.)	*kunom
D	*kun(e)i	(= pl.)	*kunobis
A	*konam	(= nom.)	*kunās/konās

Now let us compare the familiar paradigm of Skt. *śvā́* 'dog':

	singular	*dual*	*plural*
N	śvā́ < *k̑uō	śvā́nā < *k̑u̯onō	śvā́nas < *k̑u̯ones
G	śúnas < *k̑unos		śúnām < *k̑unōm
D	(I śúnā < *k̑unē)		śvábhyas < *k̑un̥bhi̯es
A	śvā́nam < *k̑u̯onm̥	(= nom.)	śúnas < *k̑unn̥s

The ablaut in the two paradigms is identical in every detail. Even the Welsh plural *cwn* can be derived with perfect regularity from **kones*, because **o* is raised to *u*, ModW. *w*, before a single nasal in Welsh (first half of the sixth century; *LHEB* 272–73). It is only our assumption that Celtic must have innovated by generalizing the zero grade that has kept us from recognizing that it preserves the Indo-European paradigm of this word with complete fidelity, as we would expect of 'dog'.⁸

But this new interpretation of the paradigm of *cú* will remain only an alternative to the received wisdom unless we can show that Pedersen's hypothetical lowering of high vowels in Primitive Irish is wrong. Now Pedersen was well aware that there are problems with his account. He himself pointed out (*VKG* 1.366; *CCCG* 65) that the voc. sg. *a fir* of *fer* 'man' requires a special explanation in his system; he would expect *wire to become *were by his rule, giving OIr. *a feir. In *CCCG* he suggests that absolute final *-*e* became *-*i*, but remained *e before final obstruents (to account for, e.g., pres. indic. 3. sg. conj. -*beir* < **beret'*).[9] The history of voc. *a fir* would therefore have to be *wire > *wiri, with subsequent lowering blocked by the new final high vowel; the simpler explanation that *a fir* continues *wire directly seems at least as attractive.

Fil 'there is', which continues ipv. *wele 'see!' (*GOI* 479), might seem to support the idea that *-*e* was raised in absolute auslaut; but the variants *feil*, *fel* (and *fail*) are well attested in the glosses, as is *do-feil* 'is coming, approaches' beside *do-fil*. The vocalism of the (synchronic) ipv. *beir* 'carry!' (never **bir) < *bere could be attributed to paradigm leveling, but it is simpler to assume that it is *lautgesetzlich*.

Nevertheless, Pedersen found support for his theory in the *o* of the B III nasal presents, such as *as-boind* 'refuses' and *fo-loing* 'supports', for which we reconstruct Celtic *-*bunde*- and *-*lunge*- on the strength of their subjunctive and preterite stems:

present	*subjunctive*	*preterite*
ad-boind 'proclaims'	ad-bo	
as-boind 'refuses'	ma's-bo	at-bobuid
bongid 'breaks'	rel. bóus	-bobig; buich
con-boing 'breaks'	con-bó	con-buig, -buich
do-boing 'plucks; exacts'	do-bo	
dingid 'presses down'		dedaig
for-ding 'crushes, oppresses'	3. pl. for-díassat	for-dedig
dlongid 'splits'		ros-dedlaig
fo-loing 'supports'	fo-lo	
in-loing 'puts together; imposes; claims'	nad ella	in-lolaig
roindid		
tongid	tó	do-cuitig
as-toing 'swears away, refuses'	as-to	at-cuitig

This is the Classical Old Irish situation, and we will have to take it seriously. For the moment, however, I would like to turn to several different morphological classes that provide evidence—in my opinion compelling evidence—against Pedersen's proposed sound law.

There are really only two contexts that can yield potential counterexamples to it: fully stressed, originally monosyllabic zero-grade forms (as opposed to preverbs and prepositions) that still contain *u* or *i* in Old Irish; and words in which **u* or **i* in the initial syllable is followed by **e* in the second syllable (whether final or not), for **e* is the only phonemic vowel[10] that neither raises nor lowers a preceding vowel. Both types of counterexamples can be found; they are not plentiful, or Pedersen would have taken note of them, but they are there, and they cannot readily be explained away.

We find etymologically short high vowels preserved in case forms of root nouns and other monosyllabic consonant stems: *brí* 'hill' < **brig-s*, not **bré*; even more telling is acc. *brig* O'Dav. 61 < **brigœn*, instead of **breg*, because this is an exact counterexample to the putative lowering in acc. *coin*. A "short dat." *brí* < **brig'* is also attested.

    clí 'housepost' < **kli-t-s*, not **clé*[11]
    clú 'fame' < **klu-t-s*, not **cló* (the word is a t-stem, not an s-stem, *pace* Thurneysen, *GOI* 216)
    crí 'body, flesh' < **krixs* < **k^{u}r̥p-s*, not **cré*
    rú 'red dye (plant)' < **rud-s*, not **ró*[12]
    trú 'doomed person' < **truk-s*, not **tró*

There are also isolated words, which provide the strongest counterexamples, for there is no possibility that they have adopted a given inflectional pattern secondarily, as one might try to argue for the preceding group of words. One of the most convincing of these is *Brigit* < **brigœntī* = Skt. *br̥hatī́* (*GOI* 187).

There are also the Irish *tudáti*-presents, whose existence has been demonstrated by Cowgill (1983, 998) and McCone (1982, 12–13; 1986, 228): *rigid* 'reaches out, rules' < **rigeti* and its compounds, incl. *con-rig*.[13] At least by the Prim. Ir. period, this class also included the rhyming verbs *mligid* 'milks' and *sligid* 'cuts down' and their compounds. For *ligid* 'licks' and *snigid* 'drips' there are no decisive forms, but I suspect that they also belong here. For *dligid* 'is entitled to', we find old forms that belong to both B I and B II.[14] *Nigid* 'washes' was originally a B II verb, as, apparently, was *-icc* 'comes' (*GOI* 354); *figid* 'weaves' still is.[15] *Fichid* 'fights' exhibits B I flexion, so it too is a *tudáti*-present, continuing **wiketi*.[16]

Here also belong the three rhyming (and semantically close) thematic presents *cingid* 'steps, strides', *dringid* 'climbs', and *lingid* 'leaps', which originally had e-grade of the root and owe their radical *i* to a Common Celtic sound change, or at least to a very strong tendency for **eng* to become **ing*, rather than to raising before an **i* (from **i̯e*) in the present stem.[17] In Prim. Ir. terms, these verbs continue:

cingid < **kingeti*
dringid < **dringeti*
lingid < **ling^weti*

Any one of these verbs *could* have had an *i̯e/i̯o*-present right up to the period of primary raising (mid-fifth century),[18] and then have adopted simple thematic flexion just in time to pass for B I in our earliest records; that *all* of them did so seems very unlikely. Still, *nigid* rather than **nibid* < **nig^u*- is almost certainly to be explained by the early loss of the labial component before **i̯* (*GOI* 115; Osthoff, *IF* 27 [1910]: 177); we find the same phonetic development in Gk. νίζω 'wash' < **nig^u-i̯ō*. But another early Celtic change, that of interconsonantal **i̯e* to **i*, would have eliminated the conditioning **i̯* at most points in the paradigm of the *i̯e/i̯o*-present, so it seems best to order the loss of labiality before this; and as this change of **i̯e* to **i* is shared with Italic,[19] **nigiti* < **nig^ui̯eti* could have been replaced by **nigeti* at any time during the Celtic period.

Of course we notice that most of these verbs have the shape (C)Cig- or (C)Cing-, but this is not an obligatory feature of this class, for in addition to *fichid* 'fights' it includes *ibid* 'drinks' < Prim. Ir. **ibeti*, and we know on comparative grounds that this was never an *i̯e/i̯o*-present.

Elsewhere in the verbal system, valuable because they are isolated, we have *luid* 'went' < **ludet* and *-buig* 'broke' < **buget*; the system would have been happy with ***lod lod loid, bog bog boig*. If one were determined to vindicate Pedersen at all cost, one could argue that the aorist endings had been replaced early enough by the modified perfect endings **-a*, **-os* (or the like), and **-e* for the **-e* to be raised to **-i*, as Pedersen claimed it was in the thematic voc. sg. But this would clearly be special pleading, because the same thing did not happen in *do-cer* 'fell' < **kerat*, not ***do-cir* < **keri* < **kere* (in his system).

This leaves us with the genuine problem of the vocalism of the singular of the B III nasal presents. But one of the first things we notice about these verbs is that although only one of them has radical *i, that i is not lowered to e in dingid < *dhingheti = L. fingō. Now because the change of *eng to *ing had already taken place in Common Celtic, whereas Pedersen's supposed lowering was restricted to Irish, the retention of i in dingid and its compounds shows that the problem of the B III presents really has to do with the treatment or the representation of *u specifically, and not of high vowels generally, in these verbs in Irish.

It will be objected that not all of the B III present stems contain etymological *u, and it is at this point that we must begin our analysis. Not all of the B III presents have secure etymologies, but I have given below the ones that are in the handbooks.

Root etymologies of B III nasal presents

-boind ad- 'proclaims' as- 'refuses'	*bheudh-	Gk. πυνθάνομαι 'hear, learn', Lith. bundù 'awaken' (*IEW* 151)
bongid 'breaks'	*bheg-	Skt. *bhanákti* 'breaks', Arm. *bekanem* 'break' (*IEW* 114)
dingid 'presses'	*dheiĝh-	Gk. θιγγάνω 'touch', L. *fingō* 'shape', Arm. *dizanem* 'heap up' (*IEW* 244)
dlongid 'splits'	*delgh-	ON. *telgja* 'hew, cut' (*IEW* 196)
-loing fo- 'supports' in- 'imposes'	*leug-	Gk λυγίζω 'bend', L. *lūctor* 'wrestle', Go. *galūkan* 'shut in' (*IEW* 685)
roindid 'reddens'	*h₁reudh-	Gk. ἐρεύθω 'redden' (*IEW* 872)
tongid 'swears'	*teg-	Hom. τεταγών 'having seized', OL. *tagō*, L. *tangō* 'touch' (*IEW* 1055; Vendr. *Lex.* T-108)
	*teng-	ON. *þing* 'assembly', OCS. *tęža* 'lawsuit' (*VKG* 1.106)

The traditional etymology of *bongid* is beset with difficulties. As always, when one approaches problems like this one, one has the sense that Thurneysen has been there first. In *KZ* 48 (1979): 65ff. he suggested that *bongid* contains not the root *bheg- but rather the *bheug- of Skt. *bhujáti* 'bends'.[20] I am very sympathetic to this proposal, for it has the advantage of being based on the Irish facts themselves. Thurneysen went on to offer a solution for the puzzling

1. sg. *do-aithbiuch* with no nasal, which glosses *abrogo* at Sg. 22b2, which he took to be back-formed from the vn. *taithbech*. While it is clear from his wording that he thought that *do-aithbiuch* is based on a secondary stem **beg-*, we should remember that *to-ate-bugū will also give the correct output, so the only *necessary* analogy is the elimination of the nasal, which is after all found only in the present indicative system. Others (e.g., Watkins in *Celt. Verb* 117 n. 8) have sought to explain such *n*-less forms as causatives, but these inflect as A II verbs in Irish (*GOI* 336):

fo-lugi 'conceals' < **logīt'*
ad-suidi 'holds fast' < **sodīt'*

Tongid, like *bongid*, offers nothing but problems. Still, we can probably rule out Pedersen's etymology, because the preterite *do-cuitig* shows no sign of a radical nasal. Also, *ping* is more usually assigned to the root **tenk-* 'curdle' (*IEW* 1068) and *tęža*, to **tengh-* 'pull, drag' (*IEW* 1067). Thurneysen (*GOI* 425) is cautious about a possible connection between *tongid* and *con-tethaig* 'holds in common with', especially because the root of the latter must be **tag-*. I think it much more likely that *tongid* and *con-tethaig*, which after all mean completely different things, are not etymologically related. I would rather assign *con-tethaig* to the root **tag-* 'hold' of OL. *tagō*, Lat. *tangō*, and so on, and see a word equation between *con-tethaig* and *contigit*.

All of these B III verbs make s-subjunctives (which have full grade of the root), but only in CEUC-roots will the subjunctive regularly have a long vowel (from an *i*- or *u*-diphthong). Sj. 3. pl. *fordíassat* < **dēss-* (to *for-ding*), 3. sg. *-bó* < *bōst (to *-boind*), *-ló* < *lōst (to *-loing*) (*-ró** is not attested) are all regular.[21]

Preterites are not attested for all of these verbs, but when they are, they are always reduplicated in the older language. I have tried to show elsewhere (following *Celt. Verb* 162ff.) that contrary to appearances, the Irish preterite system was highly regular, and that whichever preterite a given verb made was absolutely determined by its root shape, specifically by its Celtic root shape. Roots with the structure *C_1EUC_2- invariably made reduplicated preterites *$C_1UC_1oUC_2$-, but CET-roots made long vowel preterites unless their root vowel was *a. *-Bobig* 'broke' is a problem for this analysis, for it patterns with the *CEUC-roots, whereas most scholars believe on etymological grounds that the root of *bongid* is **bheg-*.

But sufficient attention has not been paid to the importance of the subjunctive, in this instance *bó* < **bọ̄xt* < *beugst. In the Irish verbal system, there is no special synchronic relation between the subjunctive and the preterite, such as there is between the subjunctive and the present indicative, or between the present indicative and the preterite, which can influence each other. This means that if the subjunctive and the preterite share an unexpected feature, we must look for that feature elsewhere in the verbal system as well.

Because we know on independent grounds that both the preterites *-bobig* and *-buig* and the subjunctive *-bó* point to an Irish root **beug-*, this is what the root of *bongid* must have been in Primitive Irish. The final piece of evidence in favor of this view is the vn. *búain* < **bọ̄nā* < *bugnā or *bougnā, with the regular outcome of a **u-* or *u-*diphthong. It is intuitively less obvious, but no less true, that all of the vns. of the compounds of *bong-* can also continue **bugo-* or **bougo-* (*GOI* 355). *Bongid* itself must therefore continue Prim. Ir. *bungeti, irrespective of whether it has replaced **bn̥egti* or the like in Indo-European or in the dialectal period.

We may note that a *bangeti would probably not have been replaced by *bongeti on the purely phonological level, because Irish tolerates *a* after labials. There are even a few examples of *a* between labials and *ng*, though at least one of the words that contain this sequence belongs to the so-called (and poorly delimited) "Ivernic" stratum, namely, *fang* 'raven' : W. *gwanc* 'voracity'. In addition to *fang*, there are no fewer than three rare words *bang*, and a word *mang* 'young deer'. But none of them sits anywhere near the core of the Irish lexicon, so one could make a case for the very early replacement of *bangeti by *bongeti or *bungeti, if one believed that **bang-* was significantly less stable than, say, **band-* (in *band* 'effort; distance') or **mand-* (in *mand* 'measure of weight; ingot'). The subjunctive, preterite, and vn. stems would all have to be secondary formations based on this new present stem, on the model of B III verbs with etymological *u. The most that can be said for this scenario is that it would enable us to keep the ultimate connection among *bongid* and *bhanákti* and *bekanem*.

What it will not do, however, is help us to account for *tongid*, if we wish to assign this verb to a root with the shape **teg-* or **tag-*, for here there is no initial labial to trigger rounding. So I think we must work with a Primitive Irish preform *tungeti for the present indicative, on the strength of the sj. *tó* < Prim. Ir. **tọ̄xt* < *teugst.

I think there is even some slight evidence that the original vn. of *tongid* also contained **u*. In Old Irish, the simplex is suppletive, the vn. being supplied by the old word *luge* 'oath', which also occurs in Brittonic (and in Germanic, *IEW* 687). But the compounds of *tong-* all have the cognate vn.: *aurthuch, airthech* 'guarantee', *cotach* 'covenant', *díthech* 'denial', *etech* 'refusal', *éthech* 'perjury', *fretech* 'renunciation', and so on, all originally neuter o-stems (*GOI* 355; *VKG* 2.652–53). I believe that *luge* was pressed into service as the vn. of the simplex because the old vn. was **tuge* < **tugiā* (an *i̯ā*- stem like *fortige* 'oppression' to *for-ding*), and that *tuge* was replaced because it was homonymous with *tuge* 'covering' < **togiā*.

But the second compound member *-tech, -tach* has traditionally been taken as evidence that this root had a variant **teg-*, and Co. *ty* 'oath' has figured importantly in the discussion. Pedersen (*VKG* 2.653) asserted that "Corn. ty entspricht dem ir. -tech aus **tego-m*." Thurneysen (loc. cit.) more cautiously called the source of the *e* in the Irish vns. "obscure" but noted that it is phonologically regular at least in *taithbech* 'dissolving; releasing' < **t'aθ'β'oγ* < **to-ate-bugon*. But Co. *ty* tells us almost nothing about the vocalism of this root and definitely does not commit us to reconstructing **teg-* beside **tug-*. In fact, we see a different treatment of **-eg-* in W.Co.Br. *bre* 'hill' < **breya* < **brigā* (*LHEB* 445). Contrast OW.OBr. *tig*, OCo. *ti*, MW. *ty*, Mod.Co. *chy* 'house', apparently from Late Brit. **tiyos* < **tegos* (446). But Cornish also has *my*, pl. *myow* 'field' = MW. *ma*, OBR. *ma*, pl. *maou* < **magos*. Finally, the Cornish cognate of OIr. *luge*, W. *llw*, Br. *le* 'oath' is *ly*. The treatment of intervocalic *g* in Brittonic is one of the least understood areas in Celtic phonology, and that of **gi̯* is even more problematical, so all we can say is that these words either continue **lugio-* like Ir. *luge*, or **lugo-*, as Baudiš has suggested (*Gr.* 94; *LHEB* 451). So in Cornish we actually find the homophonous pair *ty* : *ly*, like the **tuge* : *luge* which we guessed had existed in early Old Irish.

Because Co. *ty* 'oath' can and almost certainly does continue **tugo-* or **tugio-/ā*, the Irish vns. like *fretech* 'renunciation' are the only forms anywhere in Celtic that may be incompatible with the reconstruction of a root **tug-* for *tongid*. As in *taithbech* < **to-ate-bugon*, *-tech* beside *-tach* must have spread from compound verbs with the disyllabic preverbs **are-* and **ate-*. I think we actually have such a verb in *ar-toing* 'guarantees'. What is reconstructed for this verb in the handbooks is **air-fo-tong-* (Marstrander, *Lochlann* 2

(1962): 213), because of spellings like *aurthuch* and *urthach* for the vn. These certainly point to *are-wo-tugon, but the important variant *airthech*, which occurs both in the legal tracts and in the *dindśenchas*, has been overlooked: *airrthech* (H 3.18 646a); *airthech* (*Met. Dinds.* 3.14.168). The finite verb itself is always *ar-toing*, never **ar-fothaing; contrast *ar-fogni* 'serves', *ar-foichlea* 'prepares' (vs. *ar-cíallathar* 'cares for'), *ar-fuirig* 'restrains' (vs. *ar-rig*), and the like. *Fo-* is not an optional particle; it is never present in the forms of the finite verb; therefore Old Irish had a verb **are-tong-* whose vn. was *are-tugon, and this is what we have in *airthech*. The spread of *-tech* to *díthech, etech, éthech* (with unidentified preverb), and *fretech* would seem to have been caused by the presence of *i* or *e* in the preverbs of these compounds.

But does this not still leave the *o* of the B III presents unaccounted for? In order to understand their vocalism, we must reexamine the attestation and distribution of these forms with *o* in the texts themselves. What seems to have happened is that the authors of the handbooks, along with most of the editors of Irish texts, have faithfully reported (and in some instances restored) *bongid* and the other B III presents in their *Classical* Old Irish form, with *o* as their root vowel throughout their paradigms. But they have ignored, or edited away, variants, including some forms from very early texts, that have *u* as their root vowel instead. It is only the scrupulousness of the compilers of the Royal Irish Academy's *Dictionary* that has kept these forms from being consigned altogether to the limbo of *variae lectiones*.

as-boind
    ni innarban nad **apunn** co n-athc[h]ur (*ZCP* 14 [1923]: 378 §41 [*Cain Aigillne*])
    ni innarban nad **apuinn** co nathcur (*CIH* 1797.5 [H 3.17])
    ni indarban nad **apainn** co nathchur (1005.7 [H 3.18] = 2235.18-19 [Copenhagen 261B])
    ni annarband nad **naband** co nathcur (492.34-35 [H 2.15A])

bongid
    tobuing dlai dam (*Fing. R.* 907-9 [Rawl. 502])
    toboing dlai lat dam (Hy Maine)

This example is especially instructive because the editor does not include *tobuing* in his otherwise complete apparatus, even though he points out that this is one of the very few passages in which *do-boing* preserves its original meaning 'plucks'.

> ni **tobuing** nech forna **tobun[g]ar** (*CIH* 358.24)
> ni **tobaing** nech forna **tobongar** (887.1)

The original line is almost surely to be restored as *ní tobuing nech forna tobongar*.

> **tongid**
>> fer midboth **im[m]athuing** smachtu **imtoing** ó (t)snáthait co dairt (*Críth G.* 23-24)
>> as e **fortuing** cach n-imresain bius eturradh imin airbiad (*CIH* 1909.11 [main text])
>> as e **fortoing** gac imresain bis etaru 7 a c.ii. iman airbiadh (1923.29)
>
> **fo-loing**
>> huaitne: **fonluing** 7 frisellaghar in fer .i. friseillget troigh 7 aidheilgen; fer **foloing** einechgresa cin imluad fine (*CIH* 585.32-33)
>> proferebam .i. **fulungáin** (Ml. 86c13 [equiv. to *-lungainn*])[22]

It is not hard to see from what the Classical Old Irish *o* in these verbs spread. There are descriptively two types of simple thematic flexion in Irish, that of *berid* 'carries' and that of *ibid* 'drinks'. Their paradigms differ at only two points, the 3. sg. and the 2. pl. In the *berid* type, which we may call B I 1, the root has a mid-vowel in these forms; whereas in the *ibid* type, which we may call B I 2, the root has a high vowel. One consequence is that in the B I 2 type, the 2. sg. and 3. sg. conjunct are identical. For the sake of brevity I have left out the relative forms in the following paradigms:

B I 1

	absolute		conjunct	
1.	biruṫ	bermai	-biurṫ	-beram
2.	biriṫ	**beirthe**	-birṫ	**-berid**
3.	**berid**	berait	**-beir**	-berat
pass.	berair		-berar	

B I 2

1. ibu	ebmai↓	-iub	-ebam↓
2. ibi	**ibthe**	-ib	**-ibid**
3. **ibid**	ebait↓	**-ib**	-ebat↓
pass.	ebair↓		-ebar↓

Of course in diachronic terms this close similarity is the result of two opposite processes: raising of *e* in the 1. and 2. sg. in the B I 1 verbs, and lowering of *i* (or *u*) in the 1. and 3. pl. active and the passive in the B I 2 verbs. But what we are concerned with here is the synchronic pattern after vowel affection had taken place.

Only a few verbs belong to the B I 2 type; it is clearly the category on its way out. In addition to *ibid* itself, there are *fichid* 'fights'; the three verbs of motion with what is in Celtic terms a radical *n*, *cingid* 'steps', *dringid* 'climbs', and *lingid* 'leaps'; and the rhyming *tudáti*-presents already discussed.

What I believe has happened to the B III nasal presents, which originally inflected like B I 2 verbs, is that those with *u* as their original root vowel adopted the more common B I 1 inflectional pattern secondarily during the Early Old Irish period.[23] In practical evidentiary terms, because our texts give us 2. pl. forms only rarely, this means that 3. sg. *bungid -buing* was replaced by *bongid -boing* within the historical period. In fact, the older forms survive right down into Early Modern Irish, for example:

a cnúas ni **buing** dalta dó (*KM Misc.* 174 §31).

In fact, in the native Grammatical Tracts, which set the standard for bardic usage, the section in which the inflectional pattern for these verbs is given (§76), is headed *buing, boing*.

Composite Paradigm for *bong-, long-, tong-*
(attested OIr. forms only)

1. tungu	tongmai	-bung,	-lung,	-longam
tongu		-tung		
2.				-fulngid-si
3. toingth-i		**-buing,**	**-luing,**	-bongat, -longat,
		-tuing		-tongat
		-boing,	-loing,	
		-toing		
pass. tonga[i]r				-bongar, -longar, -tongar

One index of the fact that it is the *o* that has spread is that we usually find 1. sg. absol. *tongu* in the famous oath: *tongu do día tonges mo thúath*, in the sagas. Of course, only *tungu* is the regular form, both synchronically and historically.

My point is not that the 3. sg. forms in *o* are bad Old Irish, or that texts that have the variants in *u* are necessarily older than those which have *o*; it is, rather, that always choosing to print the variants in *o*, instead of the equally well attested variants in *u*, reflects an unexamined assumption on the part of the editors of our texts. And when these texts are early enough that they can give us clues about the pre-Classical Old Irish situation, this editorial assumption has interfered with our attempts to arrive at a satisfactory interpretation of the B III verbs.

Finally, what is the value of this interpretation, given that it is almost trivial to infer it from the texts themselves if one approaches them without prejudice? In part, this question contains its own answer, for even such an original thinker as Cowgill was still inclined to work with Pedersen's idea that high vowels were lowered before a following **e*. Whatever we may think of the merits of this hypothesis in terms of phonological probability, we have seen that it is false on the evidence. This leads us to another principle, that of coherence, and it is this, I believe, that lends weight both to the shallow interpretation of *bongid* and *tongid* as continuing *bungid* and *tungid* and to the historically somewhat deeper interpretation of the paradigm of *cú* with which we started. Whether they are correct or not, they at least have the advantage over other interpretations of being structured, and as such they simultaneously satisfy one of our most fundamental tests of truth, that of consistency, and one of our equally fundamental desires, the desire for a new interpretation of familiar facts that surprises us by making sense.

LIONEL JOSEPH

Cambridge, Massachusetts

NOTES

1. A partial list of recent studies which are of special interest to Celticists would include:

axle	"Indo-European *$H_a eks$- 'axle'," *KZ* 95 (1981): 81-83.
bee	"Varia III 2. The 'bee' in Irish, Indo-European, and Uralic," *Ériu* 22 (1971): 184-87.
bone	"On the Stem Forms of IE 'bone'," *Ricerche linguistiche* 6 (1974): 231-35. See also *KZ* 97.2 (1984): 197-201.
breast	"OIr. *ucht*, γένος," *IF* 88 (1983): 92.
chief	"Varia XXV. Notes on Word Formation 5. **brigantīnos*," *Études celtiques* 23 (1986): 50-51.
daughter	"**DhugHtēr* in Irish," *MSS* 33 (1975): 39-40.
day	"**DIEU*- 'day' in Celtic," *Études celtiques* 14 (1974): 472-77.
face	"Varia 2. *enech*, ἐνιπή," *Ériu* 25 (1974): 261-68.
footprint	"Some Italic and Celtic Correspondences 6. Irish *és* 'footprint'," *KZ* 91 (1977): 243-44. See also *Ériu* 32 (1981): 159.
four	"Varia I 9. *teüir*," *Ériu* 24 (1973): 177-78.
groin	"Celtic and Indo-European Words in *MVL- 1. OIr. *mlén*," *Celtica* 10 (1973): 150. See also *Živa Antika* 20 (1970): 6-7.
hearth	"Varia 1. On the Fundamental IE Orientation," *Ériu* 25 (1974): 253-61.
heel	"Varia XI. OIr. *seir*, Welsh *ffer*, IR. *sírid*; OIr. *seirig*," *Études celtiques* 19 (1982): 141-42.
house	"Celtic **dām*- and *vṛddhi* and δᾶμος," *ZCP* 36 (1978): 5-12.
ivy	"'Ivy' in Italic and Celtic," *Journal of Indo-European Studies* 2 (1974): 87-93.
lifetime	"Some Italic and Celtic Correspondences. II 9. Lat. *saec(u)lum*, Welsh *hoedl*," *KZ* (1982-83): 95-97.
near/and	"Varia III 3. *acus/ocuis*," *Ériu* 32 (1981): 159-61.
nose	"Varia 6. Lith. *nasraĩ*, Slav. *nozd(ĭ)ri*, OIr. *srón*, Gk. ῥίς," *Ériu* 25 (1974): 275-78.
quern	"IE *$g^w r e H_a u o n$-," *MSS* 33 (1975): 41-43. See also *BBCS* 26 (1975): 97-98.
rain	"IE. **ures*- 'moisten' and Its Traces in Celtic," *IF* 86 (1981): 191-93.
request	"Some Italic and Celtic Correspondences 5. Welsh *rheg*," *KZ* 91 (1977): 242-43.
river	"Palaic *ha-a-ap-na-aš* 'river'," *MSS* 30 (1972): 35-37.
sinew	"Bret. *gwazh*, *goah*, *goéh*, OIr. *féith*," *Études celtiques* 14 (1974): 201-4.
spit	"Some Italic and Celtic Correspondences. II 8. **g^w eru*," *KZ* 96 (1982-83): 95.
sun	"Indo-European **āu* Before Consonant in British and Indo-European 'sun'," *BBCS* 26 (1975): 97-102.
sweat	"Old Irish *allas*, Hittite *allaniya*-," *IF* 87 (1982): 124-26.

tabu	"Varia III 4. *geis*," *Ériu* 32 (1981): 161–62.
tear	"Varia III 1. The Keltic Words for 'tear'," *Ériu* 22 (1971): 181–84.
tomorrow	"Imbúaruch, imbárach," *Celtica* 15 (1983): 53–54.
wild	"Welsh *gŵydd* 'wild' and IE *guna*," *Studia celtica* 18–19 (1983–84): 128–32.
woman	"Indo-European *$g^w en$-H_a*," *KZ* 93 (1979): 1–7.
worth(y)	"Varia 3. *fíu*, *feb*, ἦῦς, *vásu*-," *Ériu* 25 (1974): 270–73.

2. The lenition of the initial of dependent genitives like *Chulainn* is of course etymologically justified.
3. Greene (1973, 129–32); *LHEB* 131ff.; Mc Manus (1983, 30ff.).
4. Merger (of *i, *e and what I write as *$æ$) in unstressed syllables is precisely what we find in those palatalizations caused by these vowels (for details see Greene 1973, 132–35).
5. For the very important evidence of the Gaulish Larzac inscription see M. Lejeune et al. (*Études celtiques* 22 [1985]: 88–90). I do not accept D. Testen's explanation (*ZCP* [1986]: 272–79) of the ā-stems as reflecting the replacement of nominal with pronominal endings, and hope to return to the problem in a future study.
6. Or possibly *$k(w)onās$, as Mark Hale points out to me.
7. Because Koch is trying to derive -κωνες from *-$kunes$, he is troubled by the *o*. Of the forms he cites that contain the element *con*, I take it that the Pictish royal names *Congust* and (archaic) *Meilochon* are indeed "Gaelicized" (1980, 88) and simply show the regular Irish treatment of *$kuno$-. On the spelling of Late OW. *Guincon* (87 n. 9) I have no view. Ifor Williams (*CA* 94) already compared it with *Gwynngwn*.
8. It has long been seen that the two synchronically indeclinable words *dú* 'place' and *don* 'place, ground' were once case forms of the same word (*GOI* 212), cognate with Gk. χθών 'ground, earth', etc. (*IEW* 415). As in Greek, final -n < *-m has been generalized to word-internal position, so we have, e.g., gen. sg. *alladon* 'of another place' < *$donos$ (*Misc. Hib.* 28), like Gk. χθονός. This would seem to have taken place already in Common Celtic, given the Gaul. compound TEUOXTONI[O]N 'of gods and humans', cf. Gk. χθόνιος 'chthonic'.

So besides *cú con*, the earliest Irish may still have had the single paradigm *dú don*. But the levelings that followed the splitting of this paradigm have made it impossible for us to determine whether there were ever dat. acc. sg. forms *$doin$.
9. In *VKG* he follows Meillet, *MSL* 14 (1906): 413, who seems to have believed that only *i*, rather than *i* or *e*, could occur before palatal consonants in the paradigm of *fer*.
10. As opposed to the vowel I represent as *$æ$, the conditioned variant of *a before nasals, Hamp, who also recognizes the need for a six-vowel system for Prim. Ir. (1965, 225, esp. n. 2) prefers the symbol ъ, but we are both talking about the same sound in the same environments. It is worth noting that this vowel shares with *e the feature that it does not palatalize where it survives into OIr., but does palatalize in those environments in which it is lost through apocope or, later, syncope. The palatalization of the final consonants of the acc. sg. of ā-stems and the nom. acc. sg. of neuter n-stems is an example of the former; that of the predesinen-

tial consonants of the dat. acc. pl. of nt-stems (where these are subject to palatalization) is an instance of the latter (I will justify these assertions in a future study).
11. Calvert Watkins (1978, 157) has argued persuasively that we have dat. sg. *clith* in *Audacht Morainn*: "ate-midiur-sa ar mo chenéuil clith" *AM* 18, 163 ("I estimate them by the house-post of my kin").
12. I am convinced by Watkins's explanation (1978, 156) of dat. sg. *roid* rather than **ruid* as the result of paradigm leveling.
13. Thurneysen (*GOI* 47) is thus wrong that "for *i* there is no evidence"; he does not appear to have regarded these verbs as *tudáti*-presents. Even so, it is difficult to understand why he did not see that *ibid* does offer such evidence of the nonlowering of **i* before **e*.
14. To Bergin's classic study (*Journal of Celtic Studies* 1.2 [1950]: 183–89) we may add the following B I forms from the *Bechbr.* (mid-seventh century): pass. sg. *dlegair* 23, 25; *-dlegar* 25; 3. pl. act. *dlegait* 4, 5, 9; *-dlegat* 6, 23; and B II forms from *Audacht Morainn* (seventh century, archaic style): pass. sg. rel. *dligther* 16, 78. For convenience, I will give the expected B I and B II paradigms in full, with actually attested Old Irish forms in bold type:

B I 2

	singular	
1.	dligu	-dliug
2.	dligi	-dlig
3.	dligid	-dlig
rel.	dliges	
pass.	**dlegair**	-dlegar
rel.	dlegar	

	plural	
1.	dlegmai	-dlegam
rel.	dlegmae	
2.	dligthe	-dligid
3.	**dlegait**	**-dlegat**
rel.	**dlegtae**	
pass.	**dlegtair**	-dlegtar
rel.	dlegtar	

B II

	singular	
1.	**dligiu**	-dligiu
	dligim	
2.	dligi	**-dligi**
3.	dligid	-dlig
rel.	dliges	
pass.	**dligthir**	**-dligther**
rel.	**dligther**	

	plural	
1.	dligmi	-dligem
rel.	dligme	
2.	dligthe	-dligid
3.	**dligit**	-dliget
rel.	dligte	
pass.	dligtir	-dligter
rel.	dligter	

15. This verb is important because, though it continues **wegiti*, it has not adopted the mixed flexion of *laigid* 'lies', *saidid* 'sits', and *saigid* 'pursues' (*GOI* 354). This might lead us to conclude that mixed flexion arises only where **a* was the original vowel of the root, but this is directly contradicted by nouns like *aig* 'ice', *daig* 'fire', and *fraig* 'wall', where the external cognates show that **e* was the original vowel in all three words.
16. McCone (1982, 12–13) has argued that a number of what are in Irish terms hiatus verbs also went through a stage of being *tudáti*-presents. Calvert Watkins points out to me that McCone should probably not have added *ad-ci* 'sees' to the list, given Gaul. PISSIUMI.

17. (*GOI* 49; *VKG* 1.37; *LHEB* 278; Ellis Evans 177 n. 9, 392–93). Even if we were to assert (against the evidence) that *cingid* must have been a B II verb **kingiti* originally, this would still leave us with *cing cinged* 'hero' < **kingets *kingetos*. The history of *lingid* and *dringid* is exactly parallel to that of *cingid*: *lingid* continues Prim. Ir. **ling^weti* < **h₁leng^uheti* (that the Ir. **i* is not original is shown by the vn. *léimm* = W.Br. *lamm* [*VKG* 1.47], and by the external cognates, esp. Skt. *ramhate* 'hurries' [*IEW* 660–61]).
   Despite early Welsh *drigyaw* 'climbing' (Book of Taliesin 71.26, etc.), Ir. *dringid* is unambiguously B I (e.g., archaic OIr. pres. indic. pass. sg. rel. *drengar*, *Ériu* 32.70.88 ('Cauldron of Poesy'); for the artificiality of *dringthiar*, ACC §68, see Cowgill (1983, 97–99).
18. For the relative chronology of developments within Prim. Ir. see Mc Manus's admirable study (1983, 21–71, esp. 30ff.).
19. Ringe, *Diachronica* 3.1 (1986): 110–11, reviewing Collinge 283–86. For the Osco-Umbrian situation see Buck 165–66.
20. And, with final voiced aspirate, if one allows for the existence of such pairs, the **bheugh-* of Go. *biugan*, Gm. *biegen*.
21. Elsewhere I have offered additional evidence to support Thurneysen's insight (*GOI* 414) that the root vocalism of the s-future was originally different from that of the s-subjunctive; the original situation was R(z) + *s* in the future vs. R(e) + *s* in the sj. The B III futures fit this pattern perfectly, because, for example, 3. pl. *bibsat*, Lebor na hUidre 6194, is regular from **bibuss-* but not from **bibōss-*, which should have given **bebsat*. Future forms are not attested for all of the verbs listed above, but where they are attested, we can set up the following:

-boind	-bibuss-,	replacing Thurneysen's -bib. .s-, etc.
bongid	bibuss-	
dingid	didiss-	
dlongid	didliss-	
-loing	-liluss-	(so already *GOI*, loc. cit.)
tongid	tithuss-	

   There are, of course, forms in which the long vowel of the sj. stem has been analogically extended to the future, but even in these, the vowel of reduplication is never lowered in Old Irish, even when the sj. stem contains *o*.
22. *GOI* 371; the absence of palatalization of *-ng-* is regular, for the form continues **lungenn +* . *-áin* and *-ainn* are of course alternative ways of representing "middle quantity" (Greene 1952, 212–18).
23. Jay Jasanoff kindly informs me that the Bengali verbal system shows an almost identical development. There is also a parallel from Irish itself, in the treatment of the Latin loanword *croch* 'cross':

   N croch = cloch *GOI* 575 Wb. 24a28
   G cruche 8a5
   D croich 28b4
   A cruich *Thes.* ii 245.5 (Cambrai), croich Wb. 8a14

   Here Early Old Irish preserves the regular outcome of **krukœn* (assuming that the word was borrowed as an ā-stem into Prim. Ir.; so Mc Manus (1983, 56 n.

91) or (less likely) of L. *crucem* directly). Acc. sg. *croich* already in Wb. is the consequence of paradigm levelling *within* the Old Irish period (*GOI* 46). Contrast acc. sgs. *cloich* 'stone', Early OIr. *bein* 'woman', etc.; the acc. sg. of ā-stems is not a raising environment, so *cruich* must be the older form.

W. *crog* 'cross' < *crucem shows the lowering of high vowels that is characteristic of feminine nouns (Lewis, *EL* 35).

REFERENCES

ACC	Amra Choluimib Chille, ed. W. Stokes, *Revue celtique* 20-21 (1899).
AM	F. Kelly, *Audacht Morainn*, Dublin (1976).
Bechbr.	T. Charles-Edwards and F. Kelly, *Bechbretha*, Dublin (1983).
Baudiš, *Gr.*	J. Baudiš, *Grammar of Early Welsh*, part 1, Oxford (1924).
BBCS	*Bulletin of the Board of Celtic Studies*.
Buck	C. D. Buck, *A Grammar of Oscan and Umbrian*, Munich (1974), a reprint of Boston (1928).
CA	*Canu Aneirin*, ed. I. Williams, Cardiff (1978).
Celt. Verb	C. Watkins, *Indo-European Origins of the Celtic Verb*, 1: *The Sigmatic Aorist*, Dublin (1969).
CCCG	H. Lewis and H. Pedersen, *A Concise Comparative Celtic Grammar*, 3d ed., Göttingen (1974).
CIIC	R. A. S. Macalister, *Corpus Inscriptionum Insularum Celticarum*, Dublin (1945, 49).
CIH	D. A. Binchy, *Corpus iuris hibernici*, Dublin (1979).
Collinge	N. E. Collinge, *The Law of Indo-European*, Amsterdam (1985).
Cowgill (1983)	W. Cowgill, "On the Prehistory of Celtic Passive and Deponent Inflection," *Ériu* 34 (1983): 73-111.
Críth G.	*Críth Gablach*, ed. D. Binchy, Dublin (1979).
DIL	Royal Irish Academy, *Dictionary of the Irish Language*, compact ed., Dublin (1983).
Ellis Evans	D. Ellis Evans, *Gaulish Personal Names*, Oxford (1967).
Fing. R.	*Fingal Rónáin*, ed. D. Greene, Dublin (1975).
GIB	Roparz Hemon, *Geriadur Istorel ar Brezhoneg*, Paris (1958-79).
GOI	R. Thurneysen, *A Grammar of Old Irish*, Dublin (1946).
GPC	University of Wales, *Geiriadur Prifysgol Cymru*, Cardiff (1950-).
Greene (1952)	D. Greene, "Middle Quantity in Irish," *Ériu* 16 (1952): 212-18.
Greene (1973)	———, "The Growth of Palatalization in Irish," *Transactions of the Philological Society* (1973): 127-36.
H	Trinity College, Dublin, MS H.
Hamp (1965)	E. Hamp, "Evidence in Keltic," in *Evidence for Laryngeals*, ed. W. Winter, The Hague (1965), 224-35.

Hamp (1974)	———, "Varia 6. Lith. *nasraĩ*, Slav. *nozd(ĭ)ri*, OIr. *srón*, Gk. ῥίς," *Ériu* 25 (1974): 275-78.
IEW	J. Pokorny, *Indogermanisches etymologisches Wörterbuch*, Bern (1959).
IF	*Indogermanische Forschungen*.
KM Misc.	*Miscellany Presented to Kuno Meyer*, ed. O. Bergin and C. Marstrander, Halle (1912).
Koch (1980)	J. Koch, "The Stone of the *Weni-kones*," *BBCS* 29.5 (1980): 87-89.
KZ	*Zeitschrift für vergleichende Sprachforschung* ("Kuhn's Zeitschrift")
Lewis, *EL*	H. Lewis, *Yr Elfen Ladin yn yr Iaith Gymraeg*, Cardiff (1943).
LHEB	K. Jackson, *Language and History in Early Britain*, Edinburgh (1953).
McCone (1982)	K. McCone, "Further to Absolute and Conjunct," *Ériu* 33 (1982): 1-30.
McCone (1986)	———, "From Indo-European to Old Irish: Conservation and Innovation in the Verbal System," in *Proceedings of the Seventh International Congress of Celtic Studies, Oxford, 10-15 July 1983*, ed. D. Ellis Evans et al., Oxford (1986), 222-66.
Mc Manus (1983)	D. Mc Manus, "A Chronology of the Latin Loanwords in Early Irish," *Ériu* 34 (1983): 21-71.
Met. Dinds.	*The Metrical Dindshenchas*, ed. E. Gwynn, Todd Lecture Series 8-12 (1903-35).
Misc. Hib.	*Miscellanea Hibernica*, ed. K. Meyer, Urbana, Ill. (1917).
MSL	*Mémoires de la Société de Linguistique de Paris*.
MSS	*Münchener Studien zur Sprachwissenschaft*.
O'Dav.	O'Davoren's Glossary, ed. W. Stokes, *Archiv für celtische Lexicographie* 2 (1904).
Rawl.	Bodleian Library MS Rawlinson B 502.
Thes.	*Thesaurus Palaeohibernicus*, ed. W. Stokes and J. Strachan, Dublin (1975).
Vendr. *Lex.*	J. Vendryes, E. Bachellery, and P.-Y. Lambert, *Lexique étymologique de l'irlandais ancien*, Dublin (1959-).
VKG	H. Pedersen, *Vergleichende Grammatik der keltischen Sprachen,* Göttingen (1909).
Watkins (1978)	C. Watkins, "OIr. *clí* and *cleth* 'house-post'," *Ériu* 29 (1978): 155-60.
ZCP	*Zeitschrift für celtische Philologie*.

Sword as *Audacht*

Among Eric Hamp's innumerable contributions to our understanding of the Indo-European roots of Irish vocabulary is a note (1978) in which he refines the etymology of Old Irish *audacht/udacht* offered by Alan Ward (1973). Until relatively recent times, scholars have explained this word (albeit uneasily) as a borrowing from Latin *ēdictum* (Pederson 1909, 209; Vendryes 1959, 26) or *adoptare* (Marstrander 1962, 206). In fact, *audacht* 'testament' is native to Irish, deriving from the Indo-European root *$\mathit{uek^w}$*- (Hamp 1978, 154) and originally meaning "the saying of something to someone" (Ward 1973, 185). This sense is still very much apparent in the various legal and literary contexts in which we find the word. As Fergus Kelly in his edition of the Old-Irish "speculum regale" *Audacht Morainn* has pointed out, this so-called *audacht* is clearly framed as the utterance of the expiring sage Morann, addressed to his regal charge Feradach Find Fechtnach: *Finda búana (mo bretha no) / mo bríathra rem bás* (1976, 2.13-14), "Bright and lasting are [my judgments or] words before my death."[1] Furthermore, this concept of *audacht* as a deathbed speech, the force of which lasts beyond the death of the speaker, is also attested in medieval and modern Irish in the idiom *fri audacht (báis)* 'at the point of death' (Royal Irish Academy, *Dictionary*, s.v. *aidacht*) or *i n-udhacht bháis* (Dinneen 1927, s.v. *udhacht*).

In what way does the *audacht* live beyond the actual speech-act that produced it? Is it purely an aural or memorial phenomenon, or can it have a physical or textual dimension? In a passage from the *Additamenta* in the Book of Armagh, reference is made to an *edoct* being passed on, apparently in the form of a written document, by the seventh-century abbot Áed of Sletty to his ecclesiastical colleague Segéne, bishop of Armagh, and Áed's own successor in the abbacy, Conchad (Bieler, 1979, 178.7-11). Commenting on the reference here to an *audacht* as a physical, transferable object, Thomas Charles-Edwards and Fergus Kelly have stated: "The *audacht*, then, is a solemn declaration, occasionally written down, by a man in authority which prescribes the conduct of affairs, within a sphere considered subject to that authority, after his death or retirement. It is a device which prolongs authority beyond its natural span and thus secures a continuity of arrangements over a generation or more" (1983, 160).

No doubt the understanding of *audacht*, as both legal mechanism and literary device—the utterance that has a permanence and fixity independent of the particular speaker—must have changed considerably during the cultural transition from an overwhelmingly oral mode of transmission to a semiliterary mode, a process that occurred in Ireland during the period of Christianization. For the medieval Irish scribal community, we might ask, did it matter whether the *audacht* survived in traditional memory or in textual form? Was the power of the spoken word deemed fully containable and communicable in a written form? Did the text strengthen or weaken its force?

An exceptional usage of *audacht* in a Middle-Irish text (preserved in the fourteenth-century Book of Ballymote and the Yellow Book of Lecan) provides us with intriguing evidence that these questions were in fact pondered by the bearers of the literary tradition themselves. In this passage, from an account of the various magical devices for determining the truth that were among the hallmarks of the reign of the semimythological king Cormac mac Airt, the fabulous sword of one of the hostages in Cormac's court, Socht, son of the poet-sage Fíthel, is described as an *audacht*: *Atbert-som be hesin in Cruaidin Coidticheann .i. claideb Conculainn. Audacht ceneoil 7 aitri 7 seanaitri leosom in claideb sin* (Stokes 1891, 199). This is the only instance cited in the RIA *Dictionary* where *audacht* appears to have the meaning "heirloom."[2] Given, however, the cultural implications of the story in which the sword plays a role, it is possible that what we have here is not a unique or innovative usage of *audacht* but a specialized and pointed usage of the word in its primary sense. (It is worth noting that the sword is described as an *audacht* only once in the text, in this passage which introduces it and its owner into the story; elsewhere, the sword is called a *sét* 'treasure').

The owner of this sword—which glows in the dark, evinces remarkable elasticity, and cuts with unerring precision—is the son of Fíthel the *fili*, one of Cormac's advisers, and, according to our text, one of the authors of the *Saltair Cormaic*, a compendium of *senchas* supposedly (and anachronistically) put together during the king's reign. Despite his seeming literary pedigree, Socht is nearly undone by the force of the written word. Cormac's steward Dubdrenn desires Socht's sword and makes him lavish offers for it, but Socht refuses to strike a deal, claiming that he has no right to give away what (originally) belonged to his father, as long as his father is still alive (*Nídam tualaing reca sed mo athar cen beous beo*, ibid., 200). Frustrated in his attempts to obtain the coveted treasure, Dubdrenn plies Socht with drink until he falls asleep, takes his sword to a smith, and has his own name inscribed inside the hilt. He then presents his dispute with Socht to Cormac and declares his opponent a liar for swearing that the sword is a family possession (*sed fine*, ibid., 201). When Cormac asks for proof of the accusation, Dubdrenn responds: *Masa limsa in claideb ata m'ainm scribhta and* . . . (ibid.), "If the sword is mine, my name is written on it." Dubdrenn has the hilt opened and the writing revealed, and thus he apparently wins his case. The author then makes the curious and suggestive comment: *Is andsin rodgella marbh for bíu inagar log don scribadh* (ibid.), "Thus did the dead bear witness against the living, in that value was [ascribed] to the writing."[3]

Of this incident, its interpretation within the text, and its implications for the culture of medieval Ireland, Georges Dumézil has said, "L'écriture peut servir au mal comme bien: en mainte occasion elle trahit et se retourne contre le 'vivant' qui ne peut lutter contre elle. Ce texte vénérable exprime-t-il le regret d'un poète le temps heureux où le Juge ne s'embarrassait pas de témoignages écrits,— de cette écriture gravée sur les instances de l'Intendant, par l'Artisan, rival naturel de l'Inspiré?" (1981, 329).

The matter, however, is even more complex. In their discussion of the tale of Socht and Dubdrenn, Françoise Le Roux and Christian-J. Guyonvarc'h, following in Dumézil's footsteps, point out that the story does not end with the victory of Dubdrenn, and that the continuation in effect reverses what had happened before in the narrative (1986, 263–69). After the revelation of the writing on the hilt, Socht swiftly changes his strategy and publicly declares that he recognizes Dubdrenn to be the owner of the sword and, as such, responsible for its liabilities (which Dubdrenn accepts). Then, the former owner, cagily belying his name (*socht* 'silence'), reveals that his grandfather had been slain with this sword, and that he, Socht, had never known who had done the deed—but now he knows, at least, who owes him restitution. Cormac, in his capacity as judge, orders the discomfited Dubdrenn to return the sword as well as pay a hefty sum to Socht. This turn of events proves too much for the steward, who, along with the smith, confesses to the ruse. But the quick-moving story does not settle for the sword's being restored to Socht: in a final plot twist, the wily Cormac reveals that his grandfather too was slain by this sword, which then by right falls into his hands. Thus, contrary to Dumézil's perception of what happens in this story, public testimony and utterance do ultimately prevail over the inert and false authority of the written word. The sword proves less effective as bearer of a "dead" inscription than as a mnemonic device that triggers the recall of memories—and, even more important, the articulation of memories—about death and the dead (the grandfathers who both fell victim to the sword's wielders). The sword is indeed a testament to the past, but it lies dormant, even helpless, as it experiences a distortion of its testimonial power at the hands of the literate smith: the sword and its authority as a token of past truth await reactivation through an act of speech.

Given the final outcome and gist of the story, the description of the sword as an *audacht cenéoil* takes on special meaning. It is a seemingly tangible *audacht* that is associated with death and actually becomes a text. But its value as an *audacht* is realized only when it evokes speech—albeit speech that is not at the point of death, but about death.

The notion of a sword as intimately connected with the speech-act, and with the validity of what is said, is in fact to be found elsewhere in medieval Irish literature. In the description of the ritualized boasting of the Ulstermen during their Samain assembly in the *Serglige Con Culainn*, we are told, *Ocus is amlaid dognítis sin ₇ a claidib for slíastaib in tan dognítis in comram. Ar imsoítis a claidib fríu in tan dognítis gúchomram. Deithbir ón, ar no labraitis demna fríu dia n-armaib conid de batir comarchi forro a n-airm* (Dillon 1953, 1), "It is thus they would do it [the boasting], with their swords placed upon their thighs, for their swords would turn against them when they would contest falsely. This was fitting, for demons would speak to them from out of their weapons, so that their weapons functioned as their guarantors."

Furthermore, in the *Cath Maige Tuired*, we read of a marvelous sword found by Ogma, the champion of the Túatha Dé Danann: *Is and sin roindis an claideb nach ndernad de, ar [ba] béss do claidbib an tan-sin dotorsilcitis doadhbadis na gnímha dogníthea díb in tan-sin. . . . Is aire immorro nolabraidis demna d'armaib isan aimsir-sin ar noadraddis airm ó daínib isin ré-sin ₇ ba do comaircib na haimsire-sin na hairm*, "Then the sword told what had been done by it, because it was the habit of swords at that time to recount the deeds that had been done by them whenever they were unsheathed. . . . Now the reason why demons used to speak from weapons then is that weapons used to be worshipped by men and were among the sureties of that time" (Gray 1982, 68–69).

Socht's sword, then, while it does not speak itself, resembles other mythical swords that act as guarantors for the word of their owners—although in this case, thanks to the complication of writing, the sword's testimonial function is nearly subverted. Specifically, these swords verify or elicit true statements about killings performed with them: they testify both to death and to the truth of speech. In both of these respects, such a sword is indeed an *audacht* in a specialized sense: not quite a true saying itself, but a metalinguistic sign of what has already been said truthfully and a catalyst for the future utterance of truth. Significantly, this *audacht* resists the appropriation and distortion of its function by writing: that is, it resists textuality.

This study is dedicated to Professor Hamp, a scholar whose memorable publications and public "utterances" together form a testament as imposing as any *audacht* that proclaims the truth for generations to come.

JOSEPH FALAKY NAGY
University of California, Los Angeles

NOTES

1. "Morann is also accredited with authorship of the lost *Ti[u]g-anál Morainn*. . . . It is noteworthy that both *Audacht Morainn* . . . and *Tiug-anál Morainn* ('the last breath of Morann') seem to be death-bed compositions" (Kelly 1976, 23, n. on *Morainn*).
2. Compare the designation of St. Patrick's bell, found in his tomb, as the *Clocc in Aidhechta* in the entry for A.D. 553 in the Annals of Ulster (Mac Airt and Mac Niocaill 1983, 78) and elsewhere, and the name of the brooch Columba obtained from Pope Gregory, *Delg Aidechta* (Reeves 1874, lxxxix–xc, 289). In neither of these cases, however, does the word *audacht* actually refer to the inherited object itself.
3. There is an allusion to this conceit in the so-called *Bretha Nemed* text: *Ann consich marbh for bheo i bfoirgheall oghaim ógh airibh* (Gwynn 1942, 34; on the "version" of the story of the sword alluded to in this text, see ibid., 226, and Henry 1976, 83–85).

REFERENCES

Bieler, Ludwig, ed. and trans. 1979. *The Patrician Texts in the Book of Armagh.* Scriptores Latini Hiberniae 10. Dublin: Dublin Institute for Advanced Studies.
Charles-Edwards, Thomas, and Fergus Kelly, eds. and trans. 1983. *Bechbretha.* Early Irish Law Series 1. Dublin: Dublin Institute for Advanced Studies.
Dillon, Myles, ed. 1953. *Serglige Con Culainn.* Mediaeval and Modern Irish Series 14. Dublin: Dublin Institute for Advanced Studies.
Dinneen, Patrick S., ed. 1927. *Foclóir Gaedhilge agus Béarla: An Irish-English Dictionary.* Dublin: Irish Texts Society.
Dumézil, Georges. 1981. "La tradition druidique et l'écriture: le vivant et le mort." *Pour un temps/Georges Dumézil.* Paris: Centre Georges Pompidou/Pandora Editions. 325-38. (Orig. pub. in *Revue de l'histoire des religions* 122 [1940]: 125-33.)
Gray, Elizabeth A., ed. and trans. 1982. *Cath Maige Tuired: The Second Battle of Mag Tuired.* Irish Texts Society 52. Naas: Irish Texts Society.
Gwynn, E. J., ed. 1942. "An Old-Irish Tract on the Privileges and Responsibilities of Poets." *Ériu* 13: 1-60, 220-32.
Hamp, Eric P. 1978. "Varia II.3. *iomna* and *udhacht.*" *Ériu* 29: 153-54.
Henry, P. L. 1976. *Saoithiúlacht na Sean-Ghaeilge. Bunú an Traidisiúin.* Dublin: Oifig an tSoláthair.
Kelly, Fergus, ed. and trans. 1976. *Audacht Morainn.* Dublin: Dublin Institute for Advanced Studies.
Le Roux, Françoise, and Christian-J. Guyonvarc'h. 1986. *Les druides.* 2d ed. Rennes: Ouest-France.
Mac Airt, Seán, and Gearóid Mac Niocaill, eds. and trans. 1983. *The Annals of Ulster (to A.D. 1131).* Dublin: Dublin Institute for Advanced Studies.
Marstrander, Carl. 1962. Review of Vendryes 1959. *Lochlann* 2: 196-226.
Pedersen, Holger. 1909-13. *Vergleichende Grammatik der keltischen Sprachen.* 2 vols. Göttingen: Vandenhoeck and Ruprecht.
Reeves, William, ed. and trans. 1874. *Life of Saint Columba, founder of Hy, written by Adamnan.* Edinburgh: Edmonston and Douglas.
Stokes, Whitley, ed. and trans. 1891. "The Irish Ordeals, Cormac's Adventure in the Land of Promise, and the Decision as to Cormac's Sword." *Irische Texte* 3d ser. 1, edited by W. Stokes and E. Windisch. Leipzig: S. Hirzel. 183-229.
Vendryes, Joseph. 1959. *Lexique étymologique de l'irlandais ancien. A.* Dublin and Paris: Dublin Institute for Advanced Studies, and Centre National de la Recherche Scientifique.
Ward, Alan. 1973. "Varia II. 'Will' and 'testament' in Irish." *Ériu* 24: 183-85.

Noínden: Its Semantic Range

The Royal Irish Academy's *Dictionary* cites the form *noínden* twice. The first word is etymologized as a compound of *noí* 'nine' and a suffix from the same root as shown in *denus* 'space of a day'. It is far more likely to be *noí* plus the neuter noun/adjective suffix *-de(n)*, as suggested by Tomás Ó Broin, meaning a ninefold period or group, an *ennead* (Ó Broin 1970, 167). Nonetheless, the word is not used to denote nineness specifically, but refers to the debility that the Ulstermen periodically suffer and which prevents them from defending the Donn Cuailgne in the *Táin*. In this context it is usually coupled with the word *cess*.

The second citation of the form *noínden* is translated as "warlike gathering, melée, fray." Attention to the various examples cited for this form reveals two applications. The first refers to an assembly of some kind, a gathering. Indeed, in O'Davoren's Glossary *noínden* is glossed by *tinól, ut est, ardnoendin sluaigh .i. tinol sluaigh mhor*, "a collection, ut est 'the high gathering of a host', i.e., the collection of a great host" (Stokes 1903-4, 426) with the suggestion of some more extensive size involved. The second application refers to a kind of heroic deed, martial accomplishment, or adventure. The RIA *Dictionary* proposes with a question mark that the second *noínden* may be the same word as the first but concludes that "the connection of meaning is not clear."

There is no reason to think that these are different words. In fact, considering the range of meaning just in the second form cited, we might as well conclude that there were three separate words, not two. But such is not the case. The task of this paper, one undertaken to honor Eric Hamp and his contributions to our understanding of Celtic linguistics, is to account for *noínden*'s entire range of meaning. The nature of this investigation, however, is not strictly linguistic but rather cultural in a broad sense. Because there is no reason to question that inherently the word carried the sense of 'nineness,' the genuine problem is to understand how 'nineness' became extended in the three attested directions I have cited. In turn, the key to *this* problem is to understand the nature of the Ulster debility in which context the word is most often found.

1.

Zimmer (Meyer 1913, 100–101), Vendryes (1934), Thurneysen (1921), Sjoestedt (1940), Ó Broin (1963, 1967, 1970), and most recently Killeen (1974) have all offered interpretations of the *cess noínden Ulad*, and all but Killeen have felt that the debility refers to or reflects a specifically Ulidian ritual of an archaic nature. But opinions diverge when attempts are made to characterize this ritual. Sjoestedt's views are the culmination of her immediate predecessors' and the most clearly articulated (Sjoestedt 1940, 40–41). She like most of them identifies the debility with a couvade, a childbirth ritual in which the husband through sympathetic magic assists his wife's labor by simulating the symptoms of labor and, in some cultures, by undergoing traditional ritual seclusion.[1] Sjoestedt quite rightly points out that while the couvade is generally an individual performance, the Ulster debility would have to reflect a seasonal, group activity and could not, therefore, have attended an actual birth.

Subsequently, Ó Broin has vigorously rejected this interpretation in the three articles cited above. His alternative explanation relies heavily on his reading of the *Táin*, which he sees as an Irish reflection of the vegetation-god myth first defined by Sir James Frazer in *The Golden Bough*. Ó Broin develops parallels between the Irish saga and Graeco-Semitic ritual drama as filtered through the Frazerians (Harrison 1927, Cornford 1961, and Gaster 1950). These parallels might be convincing if Frazer's hypotheses had not been eroded by modern anthropology. Ó Broin's interpretation of the Ulidian debility as the attendant myth of a ritual in which the vegetation god is symbolically killed, to be resurrected in the spring, is based on an invalid comparison, and I shall not take up space here to work through the false assumptions of the ritual theory of myth, which are adequately addressed in the literature (see Leach 1961 and Fontenrose 1971).

If Ó Broin's vegetation ritual theory of the *cess noínden Ulad* is a false hypothesis, however, his criticism of the couvade theory has never been adequately answered. He, along with Killeen, points out that a couvade is a rite of passage involving individuals, while the accounts of the *cess noínden* make it clear that the debility affected the entire group of Ulster warriors, excluding Cú Chulainn. Ó Broin goes farther in suggesting that the *cess* is inherent to and originated from the *Táin*, where nothing explicitly mentioning a couvade occurs; the couvadelike material appears in tales he considers subsequent etiological accounts developed to explain in some way the *Táin* motif. Killeen's position is somewhat similar in that he too sees the *cess noínden* as a function of the *Táin*, in his case as a simple function of a narrative motif, "magic paralysis as a curse" (Killeen 1974, 84). He cites many multiform motifs from a wide range of traditional literature.

Let us address Killeen's solution first. In some ways it is simple to deal with. There can be no question that in the *Táin* the Ulster debility operates as the narrative function he suggests. But to explain how a motif or theme functions is not to tell us what it means. The *Táin* narrator(s) might have employed any number of less elaborate and less mysterious narrative devices to keep the Ulaid from the battlefield. Neither would we expect to find other narratives specifically designed to explain the debility if the debility were not meaningful in its own right. So Killeen's suggestion that the narrative function of the debility is its only significance simply ignores the nature of meaning, linguistic and narrative. Moreover, it tells us nothing at all about *noínden*. Nonetheless, Killeen does have a point, to which we must return later.

Part of the difficulty in coming to terms with the debility as a meaningful construct in the Ulster Cycle is that two distinct traditions are involved in the accounts of its origin, only one of which involves the word *noínden*. The first is preserved only in one very short, linguistically muddled anecdote that involves Cú Chulainn, Fedelm, and Fedelm's husband Elcmaire (Hull 1962–64). Ó Broin shows that this story is closely related to the *Táin*. But the phrase *cess Ulad* is used exclusively in this story; the word *noínden* does not appear. Indeed, in the *Táin* the word meaning 'debility' occurs in only one place, in a small passage of the *Macgnímrada* (O'Rahilly 1976, 17, lines 524–39). In her edition O'Rahilly points out that the opening phrase of this passage "would seem to be a direct quotation from the tale Noínden Ulad" (250). This tale is not the one identified by Ó Broin as related to the *Táin* obviously. If O'Rahilly is correct, however, the *Táin* as we have it cannot have been prior to this other, more coherent tradition because, obviously, it is quoting from it in this one instance.

The tradition in which the word *noínden* appears is preserved in a number of forms. In several redactions and manuscripts we find a tale entitled *Noínden Ulad* (NU), and the same story is told in the prose and metrical *dindsenchas* on Ard Macha.[2] According to Hull, the language of the earlier version of this story suggests a mid-ninth-century date (Hull 1968, 23), and there is no reason to believe that the tradition is any later or more artificial than the Cú Chulainn tradition.

The story, reduced to a common summary, runs thus: a wealthy peasant (*aithech*) is widowed. One day a beautiful woman walks into his house, takes over his housekeeping, and shares his bed. The peasant becomes even more wealthy, and it is clear by implication that his wife is an otherworld being. This otherworld wife is soon pregnant. The Ulstermen hold an *óenach*, an assembly or fair, and the peasant despite his wife's warnings attends it. All sorts of games are played at the *óenach*. The king of the Ulaid wins the chariot race. The peasant boasts that his wife is faster than the king's horses. The incensed king demands that the boast be tested on pain of the peasant's death. In order to save his life, the wife returns with the messenger sent to fetch her, even though she is in labor. She begs the king that she be allowed to give birth before racing, but he denies this request. She wins the race, giving birth to twins (*emain*) after crossing the finish line. She then reveals herself as the goddess Macha. She curses the Ulaid: "When things shall be most difficult for you, all those of you who guard this province shall have only the strength of a woman in childbirth; and as long as a woman is in childbirth, so long shall you [likewise] be, namely to the end of five days and four nights, and, moreover, it shall be on you unto the ninth [generation], that is to say, for the lifespan of nine persons" (Hull 1968, 38).

This place-name myth, it must be said, mentions the word *noínden* only in the title. If the *Táin* is quoting from it, it must be a different recension, for where NU has *cess Ulad* the *Táin* has *noenden Ulad*. In fact, except for the brief passage in the *Táin* the word seems to be chiefly a learned one, the sort of word that a scribe might use but not a storyteller. Nonetheless, the concept of an *ennead* is clearly brought out in the myth. It refers implicitly to the term of pregnancy, explicitly to the nine half-days of labor, and is extended to include nine generations. The story explains the place-name Emain Macha, suggesting thereby a time at the founding of the Ulster tribe. The nature of the debility is made very specific: the warriors—and only the warriors it seems—will resemble women in labor. The annual nature of the *noínden* is not specified; on the contrary, the myth itself suggests that the debility will occur in response to external threats. Elsewhere, as in the *Táin*, the annual nature of the debility is specified; and the *dindšenchas* texts make it abundantly clear that the Óenach nEmna is a yearly celebration in honor of her death and that her curse specifically puts the Ulstermen *fo cess óited*, "under feebleness of childbed" (Stokes 1895, 45-46). Note that the major events take place at an *óenach*, certainly the Óenach nEmna, which, as Daniel Binchy has suggested, was similar to the Óenach Tailten of the Uí Néill and must have been the most important ritual gathering of the Ulidian year (1958, 128, 135). Indeed, the myth is about both an *óenach* and the founding of *the* Óenach nEmna. In other words, the tradition reflected in NU and its associated texts suggests that the Ulster warriors annually underwent an affliction similar to labor pains and that this attack was directly connected with the Ulster sovereignty goddess Macha.

Is this a couvade? In fact, what is a couvade? Ethnologists have shown a tendency to call any ritual performed by a male to accompany childbirth a couvade, a tendency criticized by Frazer three-quarters of a century ago without much effect.[3] A couvade proper is the simulation of labor by a husband while the wife is actually in labor. Other kinds of restrictions, taboos, or seclusions that must be undergone by a new father in some societies may or may not cluster about a couvade proper but surely represent somewhat different rituals, though all may be classed as childbirth rituals. But the *noínden* tradition *looks* as if it supports the idea of a real couvade. Of course, one of Ó Broin's objections to the couvade theory, and Killeen's also, is that the sources describe a communal ritual while the couvade proper is a rite of passage. This objection is not insuperable. It is in the nature of rites of passage, according to Van Gennep, that they can be replicated to a seasonal rite level (1960, 178ff.). Indeed, the very nature of the word *noínden* suggests replication, nine-foldedness replicated to a set of nine at the diurnal, monthly, and generational levels.

Vendryes (1934) and later Dumézil (1946, 1978) have attempted to demonstrate parallels with certain Scythian rituals described by Herodotus. Dumézil in particular has tried to reveal a basic similarity between NU and an Ossetic legend. Both of these comparisons are shaky. Plutarch, however, in the *Theseus* quotes a Cypriot authority to the effect that an annual couvade was performed on that island in honor of Ariadne, who died there in childbirth: "at the sacrifice in her honour on the second day of the month of Gorpiaeus, one of their young men lies down and imitates the cries and gestures of women in travail" (Plutarch 1914, 43). Here is a seasonal couvade, albeit with only one person acting out the labor. The couvade as part of a seasonal festival is not a unique occurrence. Moreover, we might expect a festival consecrated to Ἀριάδνη Ἀφροδίτη to be directed toward fertility, improving fertility in general and human fertility in particular. Interestingly, Ó Broin himself makes a powerful case for the *cess noínden Ulad* being a fertility festival; and what else would a seasonal couvade be but a fertility festival?

More suggestive is a set of parallel Roman concepts. In a note in his edition of O'Davoren's Glossary, Stokes remarked that *noínden* "seems cognate with Latin *nundinae* 'market-day'," from *novum dies* (Stokes 1904, 426). While not etymologically cognate, these two words (*noínden* and *nundinae*) may be conceptually cognate. The Roman ninth day was the period in which the countryside came into town to sell or exchange its goods, a holiday marked by special religious observances as well as commerce. The wife of the priest of Jupiter sacrificed a ram to that god, an interesting inversion of sex roles in our context (Macrobius 1969, 1.16, 30). The Roman *nundinae* reflects an urban society periodically incorporating the rural community and sanctifying its relations with it. Celtic society was exclusively rural; and if *noínden* is a concept parallel to the *nundinae*, we must expect it to take a different form, greater periodicity for instance. Where the 'ninefoldedness' in Rome has to do with the recurrence of observance and performance, in the Irish context it seems related to the content of the performance.

Macrobius in the *Saturnalia* also provides a connecting link between periodic observance and the notion of fertility or childbearing. "There is, . . . ," he wrote, "a Roman goddess called Nundina, and she takes her name from the ninth day after the birth of a child. This day is called the 'day of purification' [*dies lustricus*] because on it an infant is purified and given a name: the day being for boys the ninth day after birth and for girls the eighth" (1969, 1.16, 36). Nundina was apparently a goddess presiding over a widespread rite of passage, protecting the child during the transitional period between birth and the achievement of social identity and incorporation. The relationship of the market day and the goddess is implicit in Macrobius because his mention of the goddess follows directly after his discussion of *nundinae*. It is hard to imagine how any ordinary Roman could have failed to make some connection. Certainly each replicates the pattern isolated by Van Gennep: separation, transition, and incorporation. Moreover, to some extent the *nundinae* must replicate the offices of Nundina on the communal level. In Rome both the incorporation of the child into the community and the integration of (ideally) fruitful rural and wealthy urban communities are associated with an *ennead*. In Ireland the NU myth and its traditions suggest that a single *ennead* concept covered both fertility and community cohesion, again symbolically rather than periodically. The Irish *noínden* is a more condensed ritual symbol,[4] and it is just this condensation which accounts for the range of meaning *noínden* develops. Still, it might be instructive to add that Irish tradition supports *noínden* as a proper name too. In *Togail Bruidne Da Derga* the giantess Cailb chants for Conaire a list of her various names, which seem to cover a wide range of Irish goddesses including the river goddess Sinand, the new year Samhain, the war goddess Bodb, and Noenden (Knott 1936, 17). Cailb seems to be an embodiment of female divinity, and it is highly suggestive that a goddess once existed whose name was identical to the *ennead* concept.

The Irish and Roman evidence together indicates a set of shared concepts centering about an *ennead*. It is hard to see the *ennead* itself as having any basic root other than the term of pregnancy, but the notion in both cultures has been replicated in several ways. For both the notion of *communitas* achieved in periodic celebration of vegetable, animal, and human fertility along with a certain economic dimension (always present in seasonal festivals[5]) is apparently coded into the *ennead*. Hence we have no reason not to think of the Ulster debility as anything other than the kind of couvade ritual the tradition supports—or, rather, that the tradition or one tradition about this debility saw it as a kind of ritual observance in which Ulster warriors went into laborlike seclusion to honor the tribal goddess Macha.

Putting the situation in this way, we may ask if *noínden* was a learned word connected to a genuine seasonal couvade ritual. And the fact is that we do not know. Killeen's perspective here has some value because, although he does not point this out, it is highly suspect to use the materials of myth as the basis for making ethnographic statements about ritual, not to mention everyday life.[6] One line of thought in the Ulster Cycle reflects an Ulidian seasonal couvade ritual; but while this ritual has *sense* in a set of myths considerably removed from their pre-Christian context, it does not necessarily have *reference* to actual practice. Without some external evidence it becomes impossible to know for certain whether the Ulaid engaged in such a ritual. Nevertheless, there are two indications in favor of supposing that they did: first, the oblique nature of NU is such that it resembles a charter for ritual. Indeed, the consistent references in the Ulster Cycle to a *cess* 'sickness, suffering, prostration' (Ó Broin 1967) are to some actual, not ritual debility. This fact led Killeen to dismiss any significance to the debility outside of its narrative function, but it is typical enough for myths that provide charters for ritual to relate as actual that which in ritual will be mimetic. Mimesis, indeed, is their common method.

Perhaps more telling are the "traces" of actual couvade practice in Ireland reported from the nineteenth century on (Ó Súilleabháin n.d., 43). The earliest reference from the field that I know of was reported in an 1887 paper by James Mooney, a Connemara Irish speaker who did some of his collecting first hand. He reported,

> There is also a way by which the pains of maternity can be transferred from the woman to the husband. This secret is so jealously guarded that a correspondent in the west of Ireland, who had been asked to investigate the matter was at last obliged to report: "In regard to putting the sickness on the father of a child, that is a well-known thing in this country, but after making every inquiry I could not make out how it was done. It is strictly private." It came out, however, in a chance conversation with a woman who, when a child, had once been selected to wait upon a nurse on such an occasion. At a critical moment the nurse "hunted her out of the room," and then, taking the husband's vest, she put it on the sick woman. The child had hid behind the door in the next room and saw the whole operation, but was too far off to hear the words which were probably repeated at the same time. It is asserted by some that the husband's consent must first be obtained, but the general opinion is that he feels all the pain, and even cries out with the agony, without being aware of the cause. (Mooney 1887, 146)

The practice described here is not unique. The following items were provided to A. C. Haddon by various informants:

> Woman, before childbirth, *occasionally* wears coat of father of expected child, with the idea that he should share in the pains of childbirth. (1893, 357)
>
> On Lettermore Island, which also is in South Connemara, immediately after the birth of a child—which, by the way, is al-

> ways delivered with the mother in a kneeling position—the father throws (counting as he does so) *nine* articles of clothing over the mother: the number never varies. (358)
>
> In the counties mentioned [Connemara], women in childbirth often wear the trousers of the father of child round the neck, the effect of which is supposed to be the lightening of the pains of labour. I have myself seen a case of this in Dublin, about two years ago. (359)[7]

These customs are not examples of a couvade proper, not to mention a seasonal couvade, but they do suggest a general relation to the notion of fathers undergoing labor pains. The second item, involving the nine articles of clothing and the insistence on the number, is certainly suggestive. They offer no proof that the *cess noínden Ulad* referred to an actual Ulidian group couvade but do indicate that the general concepts of a couvade were operating in parts of Gaelic Ireland in relatively recent times.

2.

Continuing with the idea that *noínden* referred to an actual ritual assembly associated with human fertility and group integration, I should like to comment briefly on the word *tinól*, which serves to gloss our word. *Tinól* is found in the Law Tracts meaning "a collection for the young people made amongst friends at the marriage of a daughter" (Laws 2.346; 5.723-24). Apparently it also meant an assembly of friends for the purpose of such a collection. Moreover, Thurneysen has suggested that the word in its earliest use meant a collection of cattle as part of the dowry (1936, 125-28). Discussing the word, he quotes from a seventeenth-century *Description of the County of West Meath* by Sir Henry Piers:

> In their marriages, especially in those countries where cattle abound, the parents and friends on each side meet on the side of a hill . . . about midway between both dwellings; if agreement ensue, they drink the agreement bottle . . . which is a bottle of good usquebaugh . . . and this goes merrily round; for payment of the portion, which generally is a determinate number of cows, little care is taken; only the father and next to kin of the bride, sends to his neighbors and friends *sub mutuae vicissitudinis obtentu*, and everybody gives his cow or heifer; . . . nevertheless, caution is taken from the bridegroom on the

day of delivery for restitution of the cattle, in case the bride die childless within a certain day limited by agreement, and in this case every man's own beast is restored; . . . on the day of bringing home, the bridegroom and his friends ride out and meet the bride and her friends at the place of the treaty, being come near each other the custom was of old to cast short darts at the company that attended the bride, but at such a distance that seldom any hurt ensued. (126–27)

Here are a set of customs for a rite of passage closely connected with fertility, which involves assembly and exchange, as well as martial athletic activity. The latter appears to be a symbolic expression of the "otherness" inherent in exogamous marriage, an "otherness" that the various other exchanges are designed in part to overcome. In this perspective, a *noínden* was a grander *tinól*, indeed a *tinól* raised to the tribal level. The word does not occur in the Laws presumably because it governed not so much legal behavior as technical ritual behavior, behavior that was probably no longer properly valid in a post-Christian world. Again, *noínden* in this context appears to be a technical word, a metonymic extension from the *óenach* of which it was thought originally to be a part or actually a part. The particularly interesting aspects of the *tinól* described by Piers is the communal nature of Irish marriages (indeed most marriages), the economic aspect governing social behavior, and in particular the ritualistic "dart"-throwing contest.

3.

Yet a third attested meaning of *noínden* was 'heroic activity' or 'adventure'. There are few really good, clear uses of the word with this meaning, partly because editors and translators are never quite sure if the word should not be taken as 'assembly' or 'debility' in its particular context. A sentence from the *Táin* will illustrate this confusion:

Táin I: Nícon tíagait a noíndin itir nach erdalta gona duine bís leó-som (lines 3224–25)
   "They never go to an assembly but that they are sure to kill someone" (O'Rahilly 1976, 210–11)
Táin II: Ní thecat-sain i nnóenden acht ra hirdalta gona duine do grés (lines 3691–92)

"They never go into battle that they are not assured of wounding a man" (O'Rahilly 1967, 237)

In her note on this sentence in the edition of the LL *Táin*, O'Rahilly tries to clarify:

> Lit. 'They come into battle only with the assurance of always killing a man'. . . . *Ní teaccait-sin i ccath na i comlonn nach ba demin leó neach do ghuin do ghrés* (ST 3617-8). . . . Gordon Quin translates the TBC² sentence: "They do not undergo *noínden* at all; whatever man-slaying has been decided on by them (i.e., Ailill and Medb), it is they (Oll and Oichni) who carry it out." This implies that Oll and Oichni are of the Ulaid. The meaning 'warlike gathering, fray' is given in the Contributions s.v. 2 *noínden*, but the word is doubtful. I have translated the Stowe meaning. (O'Rahilly 1967, 329)

It seems indisputable, however, that we must translate the word as 'adventure, warlike fray, heroic activity' in the saga *Fled Bricrenn ocus Longes mac nDuil Dermait*. The Ulster warriors are about to begin a feast at the beginning of the story when Bricriu stops them. "Ní bo choir mo fled-sa . . . do thomailt cen noínden Ulad impe," he says ("it would not be proper to consume my feast without a *noínden Ulad* along with it"; Windisch 1884, 174). The word *coir* here has a legal coloring of "lawful" attached to it. But we cannot here translate *noínden Ulad* as 'debility of the Ulstermen' or 'assembly, gathering'. In fact, what we get immediately following this statement is an occasion for a heroic adventure. In the context of *coir* there is a general sense of right social order to having an adventure before having a feast, a sense that on the face of it makes no sense. Nevertheless, we find the same narrative theme in French and English Arthurian romance: Arthur and his knights are about to have a feast, usually one associated with a seasonal festival (Christmas, Whitsuntide, Easter), when an adventure is thrust upon them. *Sir Gawain and the Green Knight* is a notable example, and one that suggests that the theme may be borrowed from Celtic narrative.

The Irish example fits into this complex if we recall that a *noínden* is associated with an *óenach* or *feis*, an annual tribal assembly held to mark the separation of the seasons. One would expect it to conclude with a communal meal, an incorporation rite. During the transitional period, which in the case of the Óenach nEmna was probably five days and four nights, warriors participated in various competitive games and athletic contests. At least that would be perfectly in line with what we know of the early Irish *óenach* and seasonal festivals in general (Van Gennep 1960, 19). There may have been storytelling as well. And in a particular self-reflexive sense, I think, we should interpret *noínden*. *Noínden* here means "adventure as in a story told at a communal meal perhaps associated with a seasonal festival." Or perhaps "heroic activity like mimetic heroic activity," here also really mimetic heroic activity because we are in the bounds of a story. I rather think that the denotation or connotation of adventure or heroic action in the use of *noínden* occurs always in contexts in which the adventure or activity is mimetic, as in a story or as in a *tinól*. In turn, these senses derive from a real or fancied seasonal activity in which the replication of "nineness" served to denote a special kind of heroism—taking on the pains of women in labor. It is in the pattern of seasonal festivals that the range of the word's meaning is clarified. Underlying the concept of *noínden*, therefore, is the important notion that childbearing is a fundamental activity for society as a whole and that women are the real heroes. Warriors can only imitate this kind of courage.

EDGAR M. SLOTKIN
University of Cincinnati

NOTES

1. This definition will not be to the liking of all anthropologists though it is the simplest and most useful one to offer here. See at n. 3 below.
2. See Thurneysen 1921, 360–63; Hull 1968; Gwynn 1903–35, 4.124–31; and Stokes 1895, 44–46.
3. See Frazer 1910, 1.244–55 and Rivière 1974. Dawson 1929, the only monograph on the subject, is out of date and naïve but contains a useful if uncritical bibliography.
4. For the notion of condensed ritual symbolism, see Turner 1967, 280–98; also Turner 1969 for the use of *communitas* below.
5. See Binchy 1958, especially 124–25, on the character of the *óenach*. He tends to play down a bit the economic aspects of these fairs or assemblies and also underplays Keating's suggestion (1902–14, 2.248) as to the importance of matchmaking at the Fair of Tailtiu. But the evidence of this paper would suggest that marriage arrangements were very much a part of these annual meetings.
6. See especially the introduction to Benedict 1935 on this point.
7. The first item came from the doctor of Kilkeiran and Carna, April 1892. The second came from a T. V. Costello of Bealadangan; the third from C. R. Browne, May 1892, who presumably worked on the Aran Islands. The general geographical proximity of all these reports is of interest.

REFERENCES

Benedict, Ruth. 1935. *Zuni Mythology*. 2 vols. Columbia University Contributions of Anthropology 21.
Binchy, Daniel. 1958. The Fair of Tailtiu and the Feast of Tara. *Ériu* 18: 113-38.
Cornford, Francis Macdonald. 1961. *The Origin of Attic Comedy*, ed. Theodor Gaster. Garden City, N.Y.: Doubleday.
Dawson, Warren R. 1929. *The Custom of Couvade*. Manchester: Manchester University Press.
Dumézil, Georges. 1946. Les *énarées* scythiques et la grossesse du Narte Xaemyc. *Latomus* 5: 249-55.
———. 1978. *Romans de Scythie et d'alentour*. Paris: Payot.
Fontenrose, Joseph. 1971. *The Ritual Theory of Myth*. Berkeley, Los Angeles, London: University of California Press.
Frazer, Sir James G. 1907-15. *The Golden Bough: A Study in Magic and Religion*. 3d ed. 12 vols. London: Macmillan.
———. 1910. *Totemism and Exogamy: A Treatise on Certain Early Forms of Superstition and Society*. 4 vols. London: Macmillan.
Gaster, Theodor H. 1950. *Thespis: Ritual, Myth, and Drama in the Ancient Near East*. New York: Schuman.
Gwynn, Edward. 1903-35. *The Metrical Dindshenchas*. Todd Lecture Series 8-12. 5 vols. Dublin: Hodges, Figgis.
Haddon, A. C. 1893. A Batch of Irish Folk-lore. *Folk-Lore* 4: 349-64.
Harrison, Jane E. 1927. *Themis: A Study of the Social Origins of Greek Religion*. 2d ed. Cambridge: Cambridge University Press.
Hull, Vernam. 1962-64. Ces Ulad: The Affliction of the Ulstermen. *Zeitschrift für celtische Philologie* 29: 305-14.
———. 1968. Noínden Ulad: The Debility of the Ulidians. *Celtica* 8: 1-42.
Keating, Geoffrey. 1902-14. *Foras Feasa ar Éirinn. The History of Ireland*, ed. P. S. Dinneen. 4 vols. London: Irish Texts Society.
Killeen, J. F. 1974. The Debility of the Ulstermen—A Suggestion. *Zeitschrift für celtische Philologie* 33: 81-86.
Knott, Eleanor, ed. 1936. *Togail Bruidne Da Derga*. Dublin: Dublin Institute for Advanced Studies.
Laws. 1865-1901. *Ancient Laws of Ireland*, ed. W. N. Hancock, T. O'Mahoney, A. G. Richey, W. M. Hennessy, R. Atkinson. 6 vols. Dublin: A. Thom.
Leach, Edmund R. 1961. Golden Bough or Gilded Twig? *Daedalus* 90.2: 371-87.
Macrobius. 1969. *The Saturnalia*, trans. Percival Vaughan Davies. New York and London: Columbia University Press.
Meyer, Kuno. 1913. Aus dem Nachlass Heinrich Zimmers. *Zeitschrift für celtische Philologie* 9: 87-120.
Mooney, James. 1887. The Medical Mythology of Ireland. *Proceedings of the American Philosophical Society* 24: 136-66.
Ó Broin, Tomás. 1963. What Is "The Debility of the Ulstermen"? *Éigse* 10.4: 286-99.
———. 1967. The Word *cess*. *Éigse* 12.2: 109-14.
———. 1970. The Word *noínden*. *Éigse* 13.3: 165-76.
O'Rahilly, Cecile. 1967. *Táin Bó Cúalnge from the Book of Leinster*. Dublin: Dublin Institute for Advanced Studies.

———. 1976. *Táin Bó Cúailnge: Recension I*. Dublin: Dublin Institute for Advanced Studies.

Ó Súilleabháin, Seán. n.d. *Irish Folk Custom and Belief*. Dublin: At the Three Candles.

Plutarch. 1914. *Plutarch's Lives*. Vol. 1, ed. and trans. Bernadotte Perrin. London: W. Heinemann; New York: G. P. Putnam.

RIA *Dictionary*. 1913-76. *Dictionary of the Irish Lanuage*. Dublin: Royal Irish Academy.

Rivière, P. G. 1974. The Couvade: A Problem Reborn. *Man* n.s. 9: 423-35.

Sjoestedt, Marie-Louise. 1940. *Gods and Heroes of the Celts*, trans. Myles Dillon. Berkeley: Turtle Island Foundation, 1982.

Stokes, Whitley. 1894-95. The Prose Tales in the *Rennes Dindshenchas*. *Revue celtique* 15: 272-336, 418-84; 16: 31-83, 135-67, 269-312.

———. 1903-4. O'Davoren's Glossary. *Archiv für celtische Lexikographie* 2: 197-504.

Thurneysen, Rudolf. 1921. *Die irische Helden- und Königsage bis zum siebzehnten Jahrhundert*. Halle: Max Niemeyer.

———, Nancy Power, Myles Dillon, Kathleen Mulchrone, D. A. Binchy, August Knoch, and John Ryan. 1936. *Studies in Early Irish Law*. Dublin: Hodges Figgis; London: Williams and Norgate.

Turner, Victor. 1967. *The Forest of Symbols: Aspects of Ndembu Ritual*. Ithaca, N.Y.: Cornell University Press.

———. 1969. *The Ritual Process*. Chicago: Aldine Publishing.

Van Gennep, Arnold. 1960. *The Rites of Passage*, trans. Monika B. Vizedom and Gabrielle L. Caffee. Chicago: University of Chicago Press.

Vendryes, J. 1934. La couvade chez les Scythes. *Comptes rendus de l'Académie des Inscriptions*: 329-39.

Windisch, Ernst, ed. 1884. Das Fest des Bricriu und die Verbannung der Mac Duil Dermait mit Übersetzung. *Irische Texte* 2.1: 164-217.

The Semantic Fields of Early Irish Terms for Black Birds and Their Implications for Species Taxonomy

In earlier work on Celtic nature imagery I have attempted to fill out the cultural and historical background of various references to nature and natural kinds, and a central concern has been to illuminate the symbolic, mythological, and native religious significance of elements we tend to view as naturalistic and scientific. Here I explore the semantic fields of terms for ravens, crows, blackbirds, and other species of black birds in early Irish to underscore the mythological and religious dimension of the linguistic usage. Because the object field of this study involves natural kinds, it presents a limiting case of the way in which cultural salience impinges on the biologically determined hierarchy of perceptual and conceptual distinctions (cf. Lyons 1977, 1.248). The method to be followed is fourfold: a survey of the object field is followed by a consideration of the designations for the object field, including a consideration of such features as collocations, thus providing both a paradigmatic and a syntagmatic overview of the semantic fields of the lexemes in question; in order to avoid drawing inferences about world view solely on the basis of linguistic structures (cf. Lyons 1977, 1.250), the paper then turns to an independent assessment of Celtic myth and Celtic cosmology, concluding with a correlation of the linguistic and the cultural evidence.

The birds to be investigated in this study are those defined by the semantic range of the Irish term *dub*, not of the English *black*.[1] *Dub* is the word used, for example, to describe the black bird to which the Morrígan metamorphoses in *Táin Bó Cúailnge* and *Táin Bó Regamna*, and it is equally the adjective used to describe the blackbird in, for example, hermit poetry. *Dub*, 'black, dark, swarthy', has a broader semantic range than English *black*; consequently it defines a broader field of birds than the English term does. It is this broader field defined by the Irish term that determines the birds to be considered in this essay. Black birds fall into two principal families, the Corvidae (crows) and the Turdidae (thrushes), though there are dark birds in other families as well, as we will see.[2] A brief survey of the birds in question follows, beginning with the Corvidae.

> *Corvus corax.* The raven at twenty-six inches is the largest of the Corvidae in Ireland; it is all black and has a black beak. Generally living year round in one location and nesting on rock ledges, it is one of the earliest birds to nest, often in February or even January in Ireland. Ravens feed on all sorts of animal matter, including dead animals and fish; they may feed on the seashore. They tend to be solitary or to gather in small flocks, with the largest recorded flock being fifty-six (Ruttledge 1966, 145); and they may range considerable distances, particularly during the autumn and the winter. They are woodland and forest birds more than birds of the open field; though ravens are currently widespread in Ireland, they would have been even more common in the Middle Ages when Ireland was heavily wooded, and their distribution would have been more extensive.
>
> *Corvus corone.* There are two types of crow in Ireland—the all-black carrion crow, *Corvus corone corone*, and the black-and-gray hooded crow, *Corvus corone cornix*, also called the scald crow or the royston crow. These crows have complementary ranges, with the hooded crow breeding all over Ireland; nonetheless the carrion crow is also seen, most frequently in the northeast. They have identical habits, including their propensity to nest in high trees and to form large flocks. In recent years crows have been known to arrive in Ireland as migrants (Moriarty 1967, 126). Smaller than ravens, about nineteen inches in length, crows are principally birds of the open field. To some extent their range is complementary to that of ravens, and in earlier times when Ireland was wooded they may have been less common than they are currently. They are scavengers, though they also take young or weak birds and animals.

There are several other black members of the Corvidae in Ireland:

> *Corvus frugilegus.* The rook, about the same size as the crows, is similar in appearance to the carrion crow, being all black with, however, a gray, bare beak. Its habits differ, for rooks feed mainly on insects and grubs and their breeding cycle is tied to the insect cycle. Rooks are scavengers, commonly seen eating carrion along the motorways in Ireland today, but they are less predatory and less apt to be carrion eaters than crows or ravens.

> Gregarious in their nesting sites, rooks form huge flocks after the breeding season. They are mainly resident in Ireland, though in the autumn migrants arrive in large numbers from Britain and from the Continent (Moriarty 1967, 127).
>
> *Corvus monedula.* At thirteen inches the jackdaw is the smallest of the group and is similar in coloring to the hooded crow, with gray on its shoulders and underbelly. Melanistic examples occur on which the markings are very faint.[3] Jackdaws, like the larger Corvidae, are omnivorous, though they eat animal matter primarily, usually insects. Birds of the open field, they frequently perch on the backs of domestic animals, collecting ticks and other parasites for food and hair for nests (Moriarty 1967, 128). The birds are sociable and usually feed in groups. They are known for their noise and their loud, chuckling calls.
>
> *Pyrrhocorax pyrrhocorax.* The chough is a small black member of the Corvidae resident in Ireland, principally on sea cliffs along the western coast. It has a restricted range, being found only in rocky wild areas. The chough is about fifteen inches long and is distinguished by its bright red curved bill and its reddish feet.

Of the Corvidae the magpie, *Pica pica*, is also found in Ireland currently, but because it was unknown in Ireland until near the end of the seventeenth century (Moriarty 1967, 128), it does not figure in a discussion of early Irish bird terms.

Aside from members of the Corvidae, the most common dark birds in Ireland are the blackbird proper, the starling, the cormorant and shag, and the buzzard.[4]

> *Turdus merula.* The blackbird is much smaller than most of the Corvidae, generally about ten inches long. The male is distinctive in the species as being the only black bird; the young and females are brown, the female being darker than most thrushes but not black. The *merulus* stands out as "the only jet-black bird of the [British Isles] that has a bright orange-yellow bill" (Heinzel, Fitter, and Parslow 1972, 256). One of the most common birds in Ireland, the blackbird is a member of the bird family boasting some of the world's best singers, including the nightingale and the hermit thrush. Not surprisingly, the blackbird is known for its pleasant song; it sings with slow, melodious, cadenced, whistling phrases, but also has shrieking alarm calls and a harsh chacking. In Ireland blackbirds are principally resident, but in addition there are many immigrants in the winter

(Moriarty 1967, 136). They inhabit all parts of the country. Rather solitary, blackbirds are rarely seen in flocks.

Sturnus vulgaris. The starling is eight and one-half inches long, blackish with green and purple iridescence in the summer and pale spots in the winter; it has a yellow bill. It differs from the blackbird in having a shorter tail, a bustling gait, and triangular wings in flight. It makes a variety of sounds, including chattering and whistling. It inhabits open woods and cultivated areas, roosting communally. It both breeds and winters in Ireland, with thousands of immigrants arriving per day in the southeast during the autumn.[5]

Phalacrocorax carbo and *Phalacrocorax aristotelis*—respectively, the cormorant, black with white markings on head and thigh and brown on the back, and the smaller all-black shag. Both are sea birds, nesting in large colonies along sea cliffs and primarily restricted to the shore environments. The cormorant, however, occasionally comes inland in Ireland, at times nesting in trees or steeples. Both are resident, but also partially migratory. The shag is known for its harsh, croaking call.[6]

Buteo buteo. The buzzard, a member of the family Accipitridae, has a variable coloration; though it can be very light in color, it is occasionally quite dark and seems to be included in the semantic field of at least one of the early Irish terms for dark birds, as will be seen. The buzzard, also called "vulture" in Ireland, inhabits open forest and woodland, farmland with scattered woods, and moorlands; it is the most common of the European raptors, taking live prey as large as rabbits, but also scavenging. The bird is twenty to twenty-two inches and has a shrill, whistling call.

Let us turn now to a brief survey of terms for these dark birds in Old and Middle Irish. What is immediately obvious and at first frustrating is that the Irish terms cannot be neatly matched up with the natural species of dark birds to be found in Ireland. One finds that virtually every word for black birds is used for several different species or in a generalized or generic way, and the semantic fields of the Irish words for black birds overlap one another in multiple ways.[7]

Old Irish *bodb*, later *badb*, 'scald crow' refers primarily to the hooded crow in early Irish, the dominant resident crow of Ireland. The term is cognate with one of the earliest attested Celtic words for the Corvidae, Gaulish *Cathubodva* 'battle-crow', appearing in an inscription in Haute-Savoie (Ross 1967, 282). Julius Pokorny derives the word from the Indo-European root *bhedh- 'to cut, to dig' and analyzes the Celto-Germanic root *bod̯u̯o- as meaning 'fight, battle' (Pokorny 1951-69, 1.113). We may note that the resident western European crow is the carrion crow, an appropriate "cutter" and "digger," particularly on the battlefield.[8] In Old Irish Badb is the name of one of the war goddesses, and the plural badba is the term for a triad of war goddesses or for the war goddesses collectively, who may take the shape of Corvidae. The term is also used as a name for male figures, including one male deity, Bodb Derg 'the bloody crow', as well as for human chieftains such as Badb Chrúachain, a chieftain of Connacht (*DIL* s.v.). As an attributive genitive *badb* means 'deadly, fatal, ill-fated' in the early language and 'martial' in modern Irish. Compounds attested in the early language include *badbfíach*, where *badb* seems to be compounded with a term used to refer to other species of black birds (*DIL* s.v., cf. *badbraind*?).

A second term for the Corvidae in Old Irish is *bran*, normally 'raven'; the compound *brandub* is explained as *fíachdub* in *Cormac's Glossary* (*DIL* s.v., but see also the discussion of *fíach dubh* below). In early Welsh the simplex *bran* was used for both 'crow' and 'raven', Mod. W. *brân* and *cigfran*, respectively. The term was used as a male name in Ireland.[9] The term *bran* seems to have been used of more than one type of black bird. *Muirbran* (literally 'sea-raven') is used to gloss *mergus* 'cormorant' in the St. Gall glosses on Priscian (Stokes and Strachan 1901-3, 2.109). Moreover, a compound of *bran*, *cocbran*, is a Modern Irish word for the small jackdaw (Dinneen 1927, s.v.); and, as we have seen, the specific term in Modern Welsh for 'raven' is also a compound of *bran*, *cigfran* (literally 'flesh-raven'). The Irish and Welsh evidence combined suggests that *bran* served as a generic for the Corvidae and as a species term for the raven in particular.

A third Old Irish term for black birds is *fíach* 'raven', which is used to gloss both *corvus* 'raven' and *corvinus* 'raven' (*DIL* s.v.). Pokorny derives *fíach* from the Indo-European root *u̯es 'to feast, to be in good spirits' (Pokorny 1951-69, 1.1171). While the simplex is used for the species *Corvus corax*, with defining adjectives and attributive genitives *fíach* is used to distinguish several other species of black birds. *Fíach mara* and *fíach fairge* (both literally 'raven of the sea') translate 'cormorant' in Isaiah 34:11 and Deuteronomy 14:17, respectively, in Bedell's 1685 translation of the Old Testament (*DIL* s.v.), and the terms probably included *Phalacrocorax aristotelis*, the shag, as well as *Phalacrocorax carbo*, the cormorant proper.[10] Bedell translates 'vulture' as *fíach garb* (literally 'rough raven') in Leviticus 11:14, where it is given as a synonym of *badb* (*DIL* s.v.).[11] With reference to the same biblical passage, however, *fíach garb* is explained as *préachan ingneach* (literally 'taloned bird of prey') in the 1690 glossary appended to the second edition of Bedell's Irish Bible (*DIL* s.v.); apparently the glossator takes *fíach garb* as a reference to the buzzard, *Buteo buteo*. Finally, in modern Irish, *fíach dubh* 'black raven' denotes both the carrion crow and the raven (Dinneen 1927, s.v.).[12] Thus *fíach*, like *bran*, operates as a generic, referring to a number of species of dark birds, which are differentiated by defining adjectives and attributive genitives.

The term *fennóc*, attested in Leabhar Breac, is still another early Irish term for black birds, the Corvidae in particular. The term may be a hypochoristic formation, cognate with Old Irish *fennaid* 'flays, skins; strips, plunders'; it is an adequate descriptor representing the carrion-eating activities of the Corvidae. In modern Irish the term refers to the hooded crow in particular, replacing the earlier *badb*; rooks are also usually called *feannóg*, and the carrion crow is referred to as *feannóg dubh* (Moriarty 1967, 126-27). *Feannóg* is given as a synonym for *badhbh* and *badhbh catha* by O'Clery, and in a gloss in Dublin, Trinity College MS H.3.18 we find *fennoga no bansigaidhe*, where they are identified as demons of hell (Lottner 1870-72, 36). Hence this term, like *badb* and *bran*, has mythological associations, though they are more muted than those associated with the other terms.

Caóc, later *các* (Modern Irish *cág, caog, cabhag*), is an early term referring specifically to the jackdaw. Parallel in formation to *fennóc*, the initial element is probably an example of onomatopoesis, imitating the characteristic cry of the Corvidae in general and the cry of the jackdaw in particular, a species that is, as we have seen, known for its racket. Instances of the word *caóc* occur in contexts stressing the cry of the birds in question; *caóc* also occurs in phrases that have a proverbial ring, such as *ben...canaid scél .i....amuil cabhoig oc innisin scel ngua* 'a woman tells a story like a jackdaw telling a lying tale' and *amail coic oc indisin cach ruin* 'like a jackdaw telling every secret' (*DIL* s.v.). These proverbial associations of the jackdaw with lies and telling secrets relate the bird in folk culture to (hidden) knowledge and to the inauspicious revelation of knowledge, aspects of lore associated with dark birds to be discussed below. *Caóc*, like the other terms already discussed, is also used as a formative with a defining adjective to further differentiate the field of dark birds. In Modern Irish the chough is called *cág dhergchosach*, literally 'red-footed jackdaw' (Moriarty 1967, 129), suggesting that in the early language *caóc* was more than a species-specific term.

The term for the blackbird proper is *lon*, and it explains *merula* in the Carlsruhe glosses to Augustine (Stokes and Strachan 1901-3, 2.5), clearly identifying it as a species term for *Turdus merula*. Yet this term, like the others already discussed, seems at times to be used as a generic. Thus, for example, it seems by metonymy to represent black birds in general as contrasted to white birds in a phrase *luin hic elaib* 'as blackbirds to swans', which occurs in a quatrain attributed to Colmán mac Lénine in the preface to *Amra Choluim Chille* (Stokes 1899, 40-41):

> Luin hic helaib, uingge oc dirnai
> crotha banathech ic crothaib rígnai
> rig oc Domnall, dord ic aidbse,
> adann oc [c]aindill, colgg oc mo choilggse.
>
> (As) blackbirds to swans, an ounce to a pound,
> forms of peasant-women to forms of queens,
> kings to Domnall, a murmur to a chorus,
> a taper to a torch, (is) a sword to *my* sword!

The phrase has a proverbial ring to it, and the succeeding comparisons indicate that size, beauty, and value are elements in the contrast. The contrast of blackbirds to swans brings to mind the iconography of the fork found at Dunaverney, on which are opposed figures of swans and ravens, figures that may have been used in divination because the birds can be moved along the shaft of the fork (Ross 1967, 311, 327).

The term *lon* also seems to be used as a higher-order classifier, or at least to refer to black birds other than *Turdus merula*, in the phrase *lon gaile*, which is given as a gloss to the phrase *enblaith* in a passage of *rosc* in the Book of Leinster *Aided Con Culainn*.[13] *Lon* has other heroic associations, for it like *bran* and *badb* is used as a man's name and as a term to refer to chieftains (*DIL* s.v.). Such heroic associations for the term are anomalous if its semantic field is limited to *Turdus merula*; the paradox is resolved if the term in some contexts can refer to a wider range of black birds, to the Corvidae in particular. In Modern Irish the term *lon* refers to the ring ouzel, *Turdus torquatus*, as well as to the blackbird; they are differentiated as *lon creige* and *lon dubh*, respectively (Dinneen 1927, s.v.).[14] In early Irish the term *lon uisci* 'water ouzel' is attested; it continues to be used in Modern Irish along with the analogous *lon abhann*, literally 'river ouzel' (Dinneen 1927, s.v.; *DIL* s.v.).[15]

Terms for the female blackbird introduce yet another set of associations to the term *lon*, for the term *cearc luin* 'female blackbird' in Modern Irish also means 'tapeworm; gluttony, voracity; a demon' (Dinneen 1927, s.v. *lon*). It is significant that in the Middle Irish *Aislinge Meic Conglinne* the beast exorcised from the throat of Cathal mac Finguini is called *lon craís*. This term is translated by Meyer as "demon of gluttony," but the editors of the *DIL* suggest that *lon* in this phrase may be the same term as that for the blackbird (s.v.). Clearly related to these associations is the Modern Irish *lonach* 'full of blackbirds' or 'voracious' (Dinneen 1927, s.v.). These negative and "ravenous" associations are much more appropriate for the Corvidae than for the Turdidae, and indicate again an overlap in the semantic fields of the word *lon* and terms for the Corvidae.

Finally, the Old Irish term for the starling is *druit, truit*. Many of the early attestations refer to flocks of starlings, and there are references to their speed. In one case the flocking behavior of starlings is a proverbial figure for timidity (*DIL* s.v. *druit*), thus providing a paradigm for unheroic behavior. In this case, despite the dark color of these birds, the semantic field of the term for starling is distinct from those of the terms for the other species of black birds, and we find neither that the bird is included in any of the terms considered earlier, nor that *druit* is used for black species other than the starling. The starling, therefore, seems to stand apart from the rest of the birds under consideration.

To summarize, most of the terms for black birds refer to more than one species. In compounds or with defining modifiers *bran* is used for the raven, the daw, and the cormorant; *fíach* is used for the raven, the cormorant (and probably the shag), the carrion crow, and the buzzard; *fennóc* is used for the hooded crow, the carrion crow, and the rook; *caóc* is used for the jackdaw and the chough; and *lon* is used for the blackbird, for various types of ouzel, and perhaps for gallinules and dippers as well, and as a generic for black birds universally, possibly referring to the Corvidae in some examples. At the same time we may note that several of the species are not distinguished by specific terms at all, notably the rook. At least one dark bird, the starling, stands apart from the others semantically. To a great extent the overlappings in the semantic fields of the terms for the species of the Corvidae are not surprising, for the birds themselves are similar in a number of ways and it can be difficult to distinguish some of the species from afar. Ravens, carrion crows, and rooks are similar in appearance: large, black birds with the typical beak of the Corvidae. In fact, ravens and carrion crows are hard to tell apart even for trained observers. The markings of jackdaws and hooded crows give them a similar appearance. Similar qualities and habits—particularly their intelligence, their scavenging and predation—also make the various species of Corvidae similar in their environmental position, while partially complementary distributions underscore the functional roles they play. What is more surprising is to find an overlap between terms for the Corvidae and terminology for black birds in other families, in particular the marine birds, where the radically different physical characteristics, the different ecological matrices, and the divergent habits make the similarities in terminology notable. It is most striking of all to discover similarities in the semantic fields of terms for the Corvidae and the blackbird, for here appearance, size, song, habits, and ecological position differ markedly and are immediately apparent to the most casual observer.

Even this brief examination demonstrates that the semantic fields of the early Irish terms for black birds in most cases, if not all, overlap species boundaries and even family boundaries. Although these redundancies in linguistic mapping may be partially attributable to scientific or naturalistic features, such as certain observational similarities in the birds, the linguistic phenomena are best illumined by the matrix of religious belief, cosmology, and myth related to black birds that link the various species in early Irish culture. It is to an exploration of the mythological background that we now turn, an exploration that will perforce be abbreviated.

Birds in general had important religious functions for the Celts, as for other early peoples. Birds were associated with the soul; various types, including geese, swans, and ravens, were emblematic of attributes of divine figures; they were central to augury and omens. Thus it is in the larger context of bird lore that the mythic material about black birds is situated.[16] In addition, the Celts were heroic peoples; birds associated with war had particular symbolic values, and the scavengers of the battlefield, the Corvidae, are important elements in Gaulish iconography and in the earliest literary documents from Britain and Ireland.[17]

In the Gaulish evidence, ravens or crows are associated with a series of mother goddesses, goddesses who may be figured simultaneously with fertility symbols and the Corvidae. Such goddesses seemingly have ambivalent natures: they are associated with life and death, with fertility and dissolution. The Gaulish goddesses may also have had a role related to war; there is a Gaulish inscription to *Cathubodva* 'battle-crow' found in Haute-Savoie (Ross 1967, 282) which is suggestive when considered in conjunction with the Corvidae attributes of Gaulish goddesses and the nature of the Irish goddesses of war to be discussed below.[18] Gaulish raven and crow symbolism is predominantly but not exclusively associated with female figures, for there are also Gaulish gods who have the Corvidae as attributes, including Lugus in the region of Lyons (Ross 1967, 318ff.). In early Welsh literature there are parallels to the Gaulish deities with the Corvidae as attributes,[19] and the Corvidae also figure in the earliest heroic poetry of Britain. In these poems, as in early Celtic heroic literature as a whole, the imagery related to crows and ravens is ambivalent: glorious if you provide the birds with carrion; fateful, hideous, and pathetic if you become the prey yourself.

In the early vernacular literature of Ireland there are analogues to these Gaulish and British types. In Irish tradition we have already noted that there is one male deity illustrating the iconographic connection between the Corvidae and warlike or heroic activity: Bodb Derg 'the bloody scald crow' who, in *Aislinge Oenguso* (The Dream of Oengus), is consulted because his knowledge is celebrated throughout Ireland; he does indeed discover and reveal the identity of the woman Oengus has seen in a dream (cf. Rees and Rees 1961, 278).[20]

Most striking of the Irish mythic figures associated with black birds are the Irish war goddesses such as the Morrígan, Nemain, and the Badb. These goddesses may singly or collectively take the form of black birds, presumably crows or ravens. One of the group, the Badb, is named 'the scald crow', and as a triad the war goddesses are referred to as *badba* 'scald crows' as noted above; these goddesses are, thus, counterparts to the Gaulish *Cathubodva*. In some texts the Irish war goddesses metamorphose to their bird shapes as part of the action. In *Táin Bó Cúailnge* (The Cattle Raid of Cúailnge), the Morrígan speaks to the Donn Cúailnge *i ndeilb eúin* 'in the form of a bird', revealing to him "a secret," namely, the fact that Medb and her army have invaded Ulster to seek him (O'Rahilly 1976, 30, 152). In *Táin Bó Regamna* (The Cattle Raid of Regamna), the Morrígan disappears in her human form and Cú Chulainn sees her as a black bird, *én dub*, on a branch near him (Windisch 1887, 245). The war goddesses rarely fight per se; rather, they triumph through magical means and supernatural powers, through spreading confusion and panic, and through deception (cf. Mac Cana 1970, 86ff.; O'Rahilly 1976, lines 3877ff.). Although these Irish goddesses are primarily associated with war, they are also connected in some texts with fertility, motherhood, and the land; thus, they are ambivalent figures, and in this ambivalence reminiscent of the Gaulish mother goddesses who have ravens as attributes.[21] The Irish war goddesses, particularly the Morrígan, are also fateful figures; they are associated with prophecy, especially the ability to foretell disaster and death.[22] These mythological qualities resonate with the symbolism of the Corvidae, for the Celts like many other peoples of the world attribute to crows and ravens the possession of special knowledge and special powers, perhaps because of the extraordinary intelligence of these birds. Thus the raven or crow as a divine attribute may be, among other things, emblematic of the supernatural knowledge and magical powers possessed by otherworld figures, especially supernatural knowledge and power related to fate and death.

Still another mythic association of black birds is suggested by the Middle Irish tale *Aislinge Meic Conglinne* (The Vision of Mac Conglinne), in which the king of Munster, Cathal mac Finguine, is possessed by a *lon craís*, translated by Meyer as 'demon of gluttony'.[23] We may note that after the *lon craís* is enticed out of Cathal, it shows its avian nature by leaping to the hearth where it is trapped under a pot, thence escaping to the roof beam of the next house, and ultimately flying (*folúamnigis* < *folúaimnigid* 'flutters, flies') into the air among the people of hell (Meyer 1892, 101-7). These behaviors suggest a literal translation of 'blackbird of gluttony'. The emergence of a bird from the mouth is related to the motifs of the soul as bird and the separable soul emerging from the body through the mouth.[24] But in this case the bird is demonic—as it were the evil alter ego of Cathal's soul. The *lon craís* in this text bears comparison with the identification of *fennóca* as *bansigaidhe*, identified in turn as demons of hell (Lottner 1870-72, 36); it causes hunger, devastation, and social destruction. It may therefore be compared with the female figure who is identified with famine or blight in Modern Irish folklore.[25] The avian *lon craís*, the figure of the woman as famine or blight, the *fennóc* as banshee who can prophesy death of an individual or defeat of a tribe, the war goddesses who prophesy disaster and gorge themselves on the defeated of the battlefield—all of these together form a significant mythological complex in Irish tradition of voracious consumption and devastation.

These early Celtic mythological associations for black birds are supported by the position of black birds in modern Celtic folklore, in which ravens in particular figure saliently.[26] In Ireland ravens have been prominent in bird lore down to the present century, particularly in prognostication from bird flight or bird calls. Ravens and other black birds were often considered harbingers of defeat or death; and in contemporary Ireland a crow or other black bird calling outside a window is still considered a sign of bad luck or death, and may accordingly be driven away. The folklore about ravens relates both to the early Irish proverbial phrases regarding the daw's revelation of secrets, discussed above, and to the special knowledge, prophetic powers, and fateful utterances associated with deities having the Corvidae as attributes.

In the folklore and mythological evidence we have considered, thus, black birds and mythic figures associated with them are characterized by such features as their predatory or consuming capacities, their heroic virtue and warlike natures, their sinister connection with evil or demonic power, and their possession and revelation of hidden knowledge, often ambiguously or deceptively. Behind these mythological and folkloric materials there are also deeper cosmological conceptions that bear examination, as they influence the native grouping and taxonomy of black birds.[27] The birds are related by a salient visible characteristic, darkness, that in Irish is a conceptual category as well as a color category. Although *dub* is primarily a color word meaning 'black, swarthy, dark', it has by extension the moral sense 'dark, dire, gloomy, melancholy'; the latter in turn results in the meaning 'great', in the sense of 'momentous', expressing intensity (*DIL* s.v.). *Dub* has as antonyms (1) *finn* 'white; fair, light-hued; fair, handsome; bright, blessed; fair, just, true'; (2) *bán* 'white, fair, bright; pure, holy, blessed'; and (3) *gel* 'fair, white, bright, shining' (*DIL* s.v.). As an opposite to these words, *dub* has the connotations of 'ugly, dull' as well as perhaps 'unjust; impure; cursed, damned'. The former certainly are implicit in the poem contrasting blackbirds and swans, considered above, wherein beauty is clearly indicated as one of the aspects of comparison. In view of these semantic associations of *dub* it is not surprising that almost all of the black birds are seen as related, even the *merulus* and the dark sea birds, and that mythological figures associated with the dark birds may be figured at times as deceptive and ominous.

Cosmological elements are, of course, implicit in the semiotics of 'black' as opposed to 'white' outlined above, but black birds are associated with more specific aspects of Celtic cosmology. A notable feature of Celtic mythology and religion is the ambivalent nature of the mother goddesses, goddesses encompassing the elements of creation and dissolution in the life cycle, nurture and destruction, as we have seen. As divine attributes, black birds, particularly the large Corvidae, embody one aspect of that ambivalence, figuring dissolution and destruction (Tymoczko 1985). Time too, in Celtic cosmology, was bifurcated into fortunate and unfortunate periods, a temporal scheme reflected in the Calendar of Coligny. The Gaulish calendar is lunar, and there is a fundamental distinction of *mat/ anmat* 'good/not good' or 'lucky/unlucky' that characterizes the months. Months in turn are divided in half, and the half-months are designated as auspicious or inauspicious. Although the system is only partially understood, we may note that the half-months are characterized as the light half and the dark half of the month, lucky and unlucky, respectively, the division of time corresponding roughly with the waxing and waning of the moon, and thus with the changing balance of light and dark. This cosmological outlook, which marks Gaulish thought about time, has left traces in Irish tradition as well, particularly vestigially in the Irish hero tales. We may note that in bird augury, black birds generally are associated with inauspicious rather than auspicious prognostication; thus the birds take their place collectively on one side of the *mat/anmat* distinction that marks Celtic thought about time, views that are in turn related to Celtic attitudes regarding light and darkness.[28] The Celtic cosmology of space is also relevant to the Irish taxonomy of black birds. James Doan (1980, 34ff.) has argued that in Celtic thought there is a primal division between sea and land. In early Irish tradition the two are separate realms, mirroring each other in their organization, alien yet alike; there are functional equivalents for the sea dweller and the land dweller. Thus, insofar as black birds have a cosmological aspect and important semiotic functions, it is natural that functional equivalents of the black land birds should be found on the sea. The Celtic cosmological view of land and sea elucidates the equation of cormorants as equivalents of the raven in the domain of the sea, and their consequent designation as *fíach mara* and *fíach fairrge*.

The linguistic evidence considered in the last section fits with the mythological and folkloric contexts in which black birds appear in early Irish literature and later Irish tradition. Heroic figures and war goddesses associated with black birds are indeed cutting (*badb* < I.E. **bhedh*) in their effects; they are deadly and fatal (O. Ir. *badbae*). The feasting and rapacity of the scavengers of the battlefield (*fíach* < I.E. **ues*) as well as the consumption associated with the *lon* (Mod. Ir. *cearc luin* 'gluttony' and *lonach* 'voracious') can be connected with the consumption of the body by death and by the worms of the earth after death; these qualities fit with the chthonic nature of early Irish Sovereignty goddesses and the war goddesses and with their consuming and overwhelming magical powers. Such consuming qualities are linked in turn to the female figure of the famine and the blackbird of gluttony that consumes Munster in *Aislinge Meic Conglinne*. Thus the birds strip and plunder (cf. *fennóc*) not only bodies but, through famine and gluttony, the natural and social orders. Finally, black birds are seers and prophets, possessors and revealers of special knowledge and fateful information, as are the mythic figures who take their shapes or who bear their names. As in many cultures of the world, in the early Irish ritual practice of divination, vision emerged after feasting/consuming; this same complex of feasting/consuming/prophecy and knowledge is projected onto the birds' natures and is reflected in the mythos about figures associated with black birds. The raven, *fíach*, is paradigmatically both consumer and knower.

This evidence from both branches of Celtic tradition, spanning more than two millennia, indicates that black-bird imagery is a major symbolic node in Celtic thought. We see that the imagery is tied to central structures and values of Celtic society. Black birds, particularly the Corvidae, represent the ambivalent Celtic attitude about battle and are symbols of different aspects of the heroic ethic. In the affiliation of the Corvidae with goddesses of war and also with warriors and heroic gods, there is a nexus of heroic potential, death, fate, prophecy, and special knowledge. The imagery of the Corvidae contributes to the linkage of life and death, generation and dissolution, in the iconography of the mother goddesses. Even small black birds—particularly the thrush *Turdus merula*—are figures for the demonic powers of the world: demonic possession of individuals, as well as the demonic forces that can result in natural disaster and social dissolution. The black birds bring together the symbolism of consumption and feasting with prophecy and knowledge, important in early Celtic ritual patterns; and black birds are implicated in the cosmological meaning of light and dark, as well as in the organization of time and space. Thus, these birds figure in fundamental patterns of native Celtic thought; they were a central image expressing elements of the Celtic world view, intimately involved with the elaboration of Celtic mythology and religious belief.

The mythological and literary evidence about black birds serves as a guide to the mappings of the early Irish terms for black birds and the consequent classification of the species themselves; in turn these mappings have implications for the theory of taxonomy. It is clear that the scientific taxonomy of black birds governing current classifications of these species does not match the semantic range of early Irish terms classifying black birds. As with all such ethnobiological examples, this evidence, thus, has implications for the current debate about whether there is a "natural" basis for species identification. Here the question appears in a very dramatic form, for not only are different species grouped in the same semantic fields, but there are also crossovers between families of birds. The early Irish evidence does not support the contention that scientific taxonomy is "natural"—that the species distinctions presupposed in modern ornithological study, for example, are a matter of simple observation and recognition that will be duplicated worldwide.

Rather, the Irish linguistic evidence suggests an alternate taxonomy quite different from the scientific one. A hierarchical categorization can be discerned: (1) large, black or dark birds are related as types of *fíach* (including the raven, the carrion crow, the cormorant and shag, and the buzzard, *Buteo buteo*); (2) crows and rooks are considered types of *fennóc* (formerly perhaps *badb*, including the hooded crow, the carrion crow, and the rook); (3) small Corvidae are grouped as types of *caóc* (the jackdaw, the chough); and (4) small dark birds are classified as types of *lon* (including the blackbird and types of ouzel). These subgroups form a "family" of birds related primarily by their dark coloration and their predatory nature, but differing very widely in shape of bill and claw, diet, and nesting and flocking habits. Virtually all of the dark birds of Ireland are included in this family, except the starling. Not only is the native Irish taxonomy for black birds different from the modern scientific taxonomy in its tree structure and its construction of a "family" for these species, it is noteworthy that some of the birds—specifically the rook and the shag—are not distinguished as species at all, but are subsumed within terms for other species.[29] There are both overlappings and gaps in the semantic fields of the bird terms.

As was observed earlier, part of the overlap in the semantic fields of terms for black birds in Irish may be explained by the fact that in a vertical ordering of the object field, some of the terms seem to serve both as higher-order generic or category terms and as species terms. Terms from several of the subgroupings in the tree structure are used as general referents or higher-order classifiers for many of the species within the entire "family" of black birds, including birds from other subgroupings. Eugene Nida (1964, 73–82) notes that one problem in performing hierarchical analyses of languages and in determining hierarchical classifications in other cultures is that specific words may occur in more than one locus in a hierarchical ordering; that is, a lower-order word may also serve as a generic or category term. This is the case for some of the early Irish terms for black birds, particularly the terms *fíach, bran, fennóc, caóc,* and *lon,* as we have seen. Nonetheless, such usages of species terms for higher-order classifiers cannot explain the entire taxonomic puzzle at hand.

It is not lack of observational skill or analytical capability that leads to the early Irish taxonomic patterns for black birds; instead there are conceptual constructs that join and relate the various species of birds and render certain differences of physiology and habit of secondary importance. The cosmological outlook on time and space, on the life cycle, on light and dark, causes black birds of all types, from the small blackbird to the raven, to be linked in a tree structure in Irish taxonomy, forming a family of birds associated with consumption, destruction, dissolution and death, intelligence and knowledge, heroism and aggression. These conceptual categories underlie both the native mythology associated with black birds and the native taxonomy of black birds. Black birds are central images expressing the Celtic world view; the semiotic values and the cosmological significance of the birds are the basis of the taxonomic grouping and classification together of birds with extremely different physical and naturalistic characteristics. To make this point another way, cosmology determined taxonomy in the case of black birds in early Irish culture. We see the tangible result in the overlapping semantic fields of the early Irish black-bird terms discussed above. In this process of conceptual association and likening of the various types of black birds, observational characteristics may have had some part. Nonetheless, it is primarily the conceptual significance of *dub* 'dark, black' and its role in relation to time, space, and the process of life that led to the association of the various birds regardless of their physical structure.

The Irish taxonomy of black birds is determined by an observation of external signs, *visibilia*. But what is seen is conditioned by what is believed and what is valued. The Irish taxonomy is not determined by the same signs and external characteristics used by contemporary naturalists. Color instead of shape of bill and foot, diet, or nesting habits is paramount, for color was of primary significance in early Irish culture, and attention to distinguishing characteristics in any observational exercise depends on cultural priorities, an antecedent decision about which characteristics are significant.[30] The case of black-bird terminology is a reminder of the ways in which native Celtic cosmology and mythology determined the bases of thought and the linguistic fabric in Ireland, even determining elements of language that we see as primarily referential and scientific.

MARIA TYMOCZKO
The University of Massachusetts, Amherst

NOTES

1. Here we must make explicit some scientific assumptions. We do not have firm data on the ornithological repertory of Ireland five hundred years ago, much less a millennium ago. The distributions of natural species shift over time; species shifts have been documented in Ireland's recent history, though overall the repertory of birds in Ireland has remained stable during the past several centuries. The magpie, for example, has only been resident in Ireland since the end of the seventeenth century (Moriarty 1967, 128). We cannot therefore merely inventory the current repertory of black birds in Ireland and conclude that it is identical to that of Ireland a thousand years ago. At best we can assume that in the absence of specific evidence to the contrary, the repertory of birds currently found in Ireland is an index to the repertory during the Middle Ages.
2. Sources for the ornithological material are Moriarty 1967; Ruttledge 1966; Heinzel, Fitter, and Parslow 1972; Peterson, Mountford, and Hollom 1983; Keith and Gooders 1980; as well as personal study of specimens and documentation in the British Bird Pavilion of the Natural History Museum in London.
3. See, for example, the exhibit in Case 17 of the British Bird Pavilion in the Natural History Museum, London.
4. The survey of dark birds in this paper is presented in a somewhat schematized fashion; the focus is on the principal dark birds with which early Irish bird terms

can be correlated. A more systematic survey of dark birds in Ireland would include, among others, the swift, the coot, the moorhen, and the dipper.
5. The range in Ireland has been variable in recent history, with the birds currently inhabiting every county, while before 1800 their range was more restricted.
6. Still another black marine bird is the common scoter, *Melanitta nigra*, a sea duck. The scoter is rarely seen on land except when breeding, at which time it may inhabit lakes and slow-moving rivers in moorlands; it also inhabits Lough Neagh. It is resident, but also a winter migrant and passage migrant. Large rafts of these birds often ride the waves offshore.
7. One should note that in an investigation of this sort one cannot rely with confidence on translators, for there are frequently vagaries in translations with respect to vocabulary for natural species. Thus one must proceed somewhat cautiously in attempting to delineate semantic fields and to do a hierarchical analysis of species and family terms. Cf. Ó Ruadháin 1954, 669.
8. If the current European and insular ranges of the carrion crow and the scald crow reflect those during the Celtic settlement of Europe, they suggest that the common Celtic term referred to the hooded crow of eastern and central Europe, that it was transferred to the carrion crow as the Celts moved to western Europe, and perhaps thence from the carrion crow to the scald crow as the Celts spread to Ireland.
9. For example, it is the name of the Old Irish hero Bran mac Febail who sails to the Otherworld, and it is compounded in the name Brandub mac Echach (*DIL* s.v.; cf. Bran the hound of Finn). The same name was given to the Welsh hero, Bran fab Llyr.
10. In contemporary Irish the locutions persist, but the cormorant is called *broigheall* and *amplóir*, the latter literally 'glutton', as well.
11. The hooded crow is perhaps intended as a dynamic-equivalence translation, indicating less ignorance of the biblical species than the designation of the bird with the same local ecological function as an equivalent.
12. Moriarty 1967, 125–26, lists *fiach dubh* only for the raven, giving *feannóg dubh* for the carrion crow; cf. *DIL* s.v.
13. Book of Leinster 120a45. The *DIL* lists the phrase with a question mark under 2. *lúan*, but as the phrase both glosses a bird term and makes sense as *lon*, there is no need to construe it in this manner. Cf. also the phrase *én gaile*, which occurs in the texts with similar usage, as a heroic attribute (*DIL* s.v. *én*). See also Tymoczko 1981, 52, 98. Here the warrior's "blackbird of valor" suggests comparison with the iconography of Gaulish friezes and coins in which a warrior in a chariot seems to be accompanied overhead by a large bird in flight, perhaps a raven.
14. The ring ouzel is a brown thrush closely related to the blackbird and somewhat resembling the female of *Turdus merula*. Clearly the similarity in coloration between the ouzels and the female and young of the blackbird contributed to the linguistic grouping of these birds.
15. *Lon uisci* may refer to the moorhen or the coot (cf. Connellan 1860, 54 n. 1). Moriarty 1967, 133, gives *lon abhann* as a term for the dipper.
16. For a more extensive discussion of Celtic beliefs related to birds see Ross 1967, chap. 6; cf. Piggott 1968, 15. See also Ó Ruadháin 1954 and the important references he cites on the larger context of bird lore.

17. The extensive documentation of terminology for black birds in early Irish as well as in the early Brythonic languages occurs largely because of their importance in mythological and heroic contexts.
18. For a more extensive discussion of the Gaulish goddesses see Ross 1967, chap. 5 and chap. 6, pp. 311ff., and Mac Cana 1970, chaps. 2 and 5, as well as sources cited by these authors.
19. Most notable is Bran of the *Mabinogi*, whose name means 'raven' and whose immense size and incorruptible protective head indicate a divine origin, as discussed above. It is significant that when Bran is mortally wounded, he tells his surviving people how they must proceed, prophesying the events to come. A second figure in Welsh tradition, the hero Owein fab Urien in *Breudwyt Ronabwy* (The Dream of Rhonabwy), also has Corvidae as attributes; Owein is master of a flock of dangerous and heroic ravens, his *branhes* 'raven-flock'. See Bromwich 1961, 284ff. and 479ff., for a more extensive discussion of these two figures.
20. In *Aislinge Oenguso* (The Dream of Oengus) and *De Chophur in dá Muccida* (The Tale of the Two Swineherds), Bodb Derg also figures as the king of the *síd* of Munster, the Irish province most celebrated for its occult powers (Rees and Rees 1961, 139).
21. A full discussion of this aspect of the war goddesses is not possible in this context; see Tymoczko 1985 and references cited there for a more detailed consideration of the evidence.
22. In *The Cattle Raid of Regamna* the Morrígan in bird shape prophesies the cattle raid of Cúailnge and claims to foresee and control Cú Chulainn's fate and his life span (Windisch 1887, 245), while, as we have seen, the Morrígan in bird shape alerts the Donn Cúailnge to the disaster of the invasion of Ulster. In *Cath Maige Tuired* (The Second Battle of Mag Tuired), the Morrígan prophesies "the end of the world, . . . foretelling every evil that would be therein, and every disease and every vengeance" (Stokes 1891, 110–11).
23. The *lon craís* has possessed Cathal for three half-years, "to the ruin of Munster and the Southern Half [of Ireland] besides" (Meyer 1892, 104). The twelfth-century *Vision of Mac Conglinne* is structured around a version of AT 285B*, "Snake Enticed out of Man's Stomach," an international tale-type that continues to be productive (see Antti Aarne and Stith Thompson, *The Types of the Folktale* [Helsinki, 1961]). Normally in European folklore the invasive agent is a tapeworm or a snake, but in Ireland, where there are no resident snakes, the snake is replaced by a native concept.
24. See, for example, motifs E 715.1ff., Separable soul in bird; E 722.1.4, Soul leaves the body in form of bird; E 732ff., Soul in form of bird (see Stith Thompson, *Motif-Index of Folk-Literature*, rev. ed., 6 vols. [Copenhagen and Bloomington, Ind., 1955–58]).
25. See MacNeill 1962, 411ff. and passim, for examples and a discussion of this material.
26. See Ó Ruadháin 1954 along with the references he cites for a more extensive discussion of the folklore about these birds, particularly the raven; he also notes, at 670ff., evidence for the similarity between early bird lore and folklore about birds and, hence, the importance of both in investigations of this sort.
27. We must note here that a reconstruction of Celtic cosmological views can only be tentative, because the native Celtic cosmogony and eschatology have been

almost entirely eradicated and replaced by Christian views (cf. Mac Cana 1970, 131ff.). Nonetheless there are certain conceptual categories pertaining to cosmology that can be noted in a discussion of black-bird terms.
28. On the Calendar of Coligny see Mac Cana 1970, 93; Dillon and Chadwick 1967, 15, and references cited there.
29. Even in Modern Irish the rook is called *feannóg*, the same term used for the crow, or *preachán*, literally 'a bird of prey', a late term that is both a higher-order generic and an inappropriate species term for rooks, which are less predatory than the crows (Moriarty 1967, 127). Dinneen 1927, s.v., indicates that in Modern Irish *preachán* with a variety of defining adjectives is used for the crow, raven, rook, magpie, osprey, chough, kite, buzzard, and vulture; he gives *preachán dubh* for 'rook'. Our evidence for other species distinctions, such as *cág dhergchosach* for the chough, is late; and the magpie, which became part of the avian repertory in Ireland in the seventeenth century, is called *snag breac*, terminology that indicates taxonomic assimilation to the family of woodpeckers rather than to the Corvidae. Moriarty 1967, 128, also gives *cabaire breac, magaide*, and *snagaide* as terms for the magpie.
30. In many ways this paper is a standard example of ethnobiology. It is interesting, nonetheless, to demonstrate differences in taxonomic categories with European cultural data instead of with evidence from cultures farther afield from Western scientific thought. Ó Ruadháin 1954, 670, outlines some of the reasons that Irish culture can offer apt examples in investigations of this sort. We may note in passing that much of the native and archaic early Irish taxonomy persisted to the present, to be reflected in Modern Irish black-bird terminology, thus demonstrating once again the archaism of Irish tradition and the tenacity of native patterns of thought. Because for many decades most Irish speakers have been bilingual, the persistence of the native taxonomy in the modern Irish classifiers of black birds shows that archaic groupings can be maintained within a modern scientific cultural context or in the context of an alternate taxonomy. The archaic cultural salience is in this case preserved in linguistic features for a notable length of time (cf. Lyons 1977, 1.248).

REFERENCES

Bromwich, Rachel. 1961. *Trioedd Ynys Prydein, The Welsh Triads*. Cardiff: University of Wales Press.
Connellan, Owen. 1860. *Imtheacht na Tromdhaimhe; or, The Proceedings of the Great Bardic Institution*. Dublin: Ossianic Society.
DIL = *Dictionary of the Irish Language*. 1983. (Compact edition.) Dublin: Royal Irish Academy.
Dillon, Myles and Nora K. Chadwick. 1967. *The Celtic Realms*. London: Weidenfeld and Nicolson.
Dinneen, Patrick S. 1927. *Foclóir Gaedhilge agus Béarla, An Irish–English Dictionary*. Dublin: Irish Texts Society.
Doan, James. 1980. Five Breton *Cantiques* from *Pardons. Folklore* 91: 27–40.

Heinzel, Hermann, Richard Fitter, and John Parslow. 1972. *The Birds of Britain and Europe*. Philadelphia and New York: J. B. Lippincott.
Keith, Stuart and John Gooders. 1980. *Collins Bird Guide*. London: Collins.
Lottner, Carl. 1870-72. The Ancient Irish Goddess of War. *Revue celtique* 1: 32-57.
Lyons, John. 1977. *Semantics*. 2 vols. Cambridge and New York: Cambridge University Press.
Mac Cana, Proinsias. 1970. *Celtic Mythology*. London, New York, Sydney, Toronto: Hamlyn.
MacNeill, Máire. 1962. *The Festival of Lughnasa*. London: Oxford University Press.
Meyer, Kuno. 1892. *Aislinge Meic Conglinne, The Vision of MacConglinne*. London: David Nutt.
Moriarty, Christopher. 1967. *A Guide to Irish Birds*. Cork: Mercier.
Nida, Eugene A. 1964. *Toward a Science of Translating*. Leiden: E. J. Brill.
O'Rahilly, Cecile. 1976. *Táin Bó Cúailnge, Recension I*. Dublin: Dublin Institute for Advanced Studies.
Ó Ruadháin, Micheál. 1954. Birds in Irish Folklore. *Acta XI Congressus Internationalis Ornithologici*, pp. 669-76. Basel: Birkhauser.
Peterson, Roger Tory, Guy Mountford, and P. A. D. Hollom. 1983. *Field Guide to the Birds of Britain and Europe*. Boston: Houghton Mifflin.
Piggott, Stuart. 1968. *The Druids*. Repr. Harmondsworth: Penguin, 1974.
Pokorny, Julius. 1951-69. *Indogermanisches etymologisches Wörterbuch*. 2 vols. Bern and Munich: Francke Verlag.
Rees, Alwyn and Brinley Rees. 1961. *Celtic Heritage*. Repr. London: Thames and Hudson, 1973.
Ross, Anne. 1967. *Pagan Celtic Britain*. Repr. London: Cardinal, 1974.
Ruttledge, Robert F. 1966. *Ireland's Birds*. London: H. F. and G. Witherby.
Stokes, Whitley. 1891. The Second Battle of Moytura. *Revue celtique* 12: 52-130.
———. 1899. The Bodleian Amra Choluimb Chille. *Revue celtique* 20: 31-55, 132-83, 248-89, 400-437.
Stokes, Whitley and John Strachan. 1901-3. *Thesaurus Paleohibernicus*. 2 vols. Repr. Dublin: Dublin Institute for Advanced Studies, 1975.
Tymoczko, Maria. 1981. *Two Death Tales from the Ulster Cycle: "The Death of Cu Roi" and "The Death of CuChulainn."* Dublin: Dolmen.
———. 1983a. "Cétamon": Vision in Early Irish Seasonal Poetry. *Éire-Ireland* 18.4: 17-39.
———. 1983b. Knowledge and Vision in Early Welsh Gnomic Poetry. *Proceedings of the Harvard Celtic Colloquium* 3: 1-19.
———. 1985. Unity and Duality: A Theoretical Perspective on the Ambivalence of Celtic Goddesses. *Proceedings of the Harvard Celtic Colloquium* 5: 22-37.
———. 1985-86. Animal Imagery in *Loinges Mac nUislenn*. *Studia celtica* 20-21: 145-66.
Windisch, Ernst. 1887. Táin Bó Regamna. In *Irische Texte mit Ubersetzungen und Wörterbuch*, ed. Whitley Stokes and Ernst Windisch, 2d ser. 2, pp. 239-54. Leipzig: S. Hirzel.

"Men Will Die": Poets, Harpers, and Women in Early Irish Literature

This essay calls attention to two Irish stories about the origins of the noble arts of poetry and harp music. Origin myths cast into the form of allegorical birth-tales, these stories carry messages central to Irish culture. Although neither tale can be shown to be very ancient—their recensions date perhaps from the early Middle Irish period—both illustrate the ways in which sustenance and danger were associated with the noblest arts in Ireland from the first documentation onward. They focus discussion of the paradoxical nature of poetry and harp music, and of the unique links between them, in early Irish tradition. And they suggest, finally, that these arts formed part of a semiotic system connected with female sexuality—one of the most important and least studied tropes in Celtic culture.

Poetry, that best known of the noble Irish arts, is the starting point. The story I want to highlight, the story of the birth of poetry, is from a group of three Middle Irish tales in the Book of Leinster and the Yellow Book of Lecan which are introduced by the question, *Cia tréide cétna-labratar iarna genemain fo chétóir 7 cid ro-labraiset?* "Who were the three who first spoke immediately after birth, and what did they say?" (Thurneysen 1918, 272). The first precocious speaker in this triad is Aí son of Ollam (Poetic Inspiration, son of the Greatest); the second in Morann son of Moen, the legendary judge and lawgiver; the third is the much more shadowy Noidiu (or Noinniu) Nóibrethach (Infant of Nine Judgments), who delivers nine maxims about the proper responsibilities of mothers to their infant sons.

The story of Aí is short, allegorical, and didactic; it reads almost like a bare paradigm of a certain sort of birth tale.

> Baí Fiachu mac Delboeith rí Hérenn for cuairt ríg 7 a bráthair 'na fharrad .i. Ollom mac Delboeith. Bátar laa and ic tomailt i n-Inis Tige i n-iarthur Hérenn .i. in rí Fiachu 7 a bráthair Ollom. Leth in tige oc cechtar de. A drúi dana for bélaib ind ríg

.i. Fiachach. O ro-bátar oc tomailt a fessi, do-thaet athach gaethe móre tarsin tech. Conos-tarat uile i socht mór mét in delma. "Cid forcanas ind athach?" ar Fiachu frisin druid. —"Is sed fhorcanas," or in drúi, "dán ingnad do thurcbáil i n-Hérinn." —"Cinnas dána ón?" or in rí, "₇ cia ó-ngenend ₇ cia bale i-ngenfe?" —"Dán bas chomgráid frit grád so," ol in drúi, "et bid is tig seo genfes ₇ bid ón mnai út tall do bráthar genfes. Is torrach ₇ béraid mac innossa bid comgráid frit so. Et ticfa grád amra aile and bas uasliu, dia-fogénat for ngráda si .i. grád ecalsi." —Ra fírad trá uili anísin. Ra-génair in mac fo chétóir ₇ ro-thriall in rí a marbad in meic, coro-thairmisc a athair .i. Ollom; ar níba lia in rí is taig andáside. In tan ro-bás ocond imrádud imme, co-cualatar in mac oca rád: "Dom-urcbaid súas coro-acilliur in ríg." Turgabair suas iar sin. "Ní dam sa dot inchaib, a Fhiachrai," orse. —"Cid do-bér duit?" ar in rí. —"Ni hannsa. Mo bruig mo lánamuin lónchore co ndabaig dándlugae tucthar óm ríg mucra escra [126b] cuach carpat calg tricha bó bró fiann. Fiach ó Fhiachna dam sa in sin uile," ar in mac. —"Do-bérthar," ar Fiachu. "Cia ainm regas arin mac sa i fect sa?" —"Tabar Aí fair," ar in drui. Conid assain trá ro-ainmniged ái airchetail .i. ó Aí mac Olloman. Et is sí sein aí ceta-érbairt Aí mac Olloman. (Thurneysen 1918, 272–73)

Fiacha son of Delbaeth, king of Ireland, was on a royal visitation, accompanied by his brother, Ollam, son of Delbaeth. One day they were eating in Inis Tige in the west of Ireland, that is, the king, Fiacha, and his brother Ollam. Each had half the house. His druid sat in front of the king.

While they were eating at the feast a great gust of wind passed over the house. The greatness of the noise cast them all into silence.

"What does the gust of wind forebode?" Fiacha asked of his druid.

"This is what it forebodes," said the druid, "that a wonderful art will arise in Ireland."

"What kind of art?" asked the king. "From whom is it born, and in what place?"

"It will be an art of a dignity equal to your own," said the druid. "It will be born in this house, from the woman yonder, your brother's wife. She is pregnant, and she will bear a son now and he will have an order equal to your own. And there will come another wonderful order that will be nobler, which your orders will serve, the order of the Church."

All this came about. The child was born forthwith, and

the king sought to slay him. But the boy's father Ollam prevented this, for the king's folk were no more numerous in the house than his. As they were discussing this they heard the child say: "Lift me up, so that I may speak to the king."

He is lifted up then. "Grant me something by your honour, Fiacha," said he.

"What shall I give you?" asked Fiacha.

"Not difficult:
My land, my coupling,
a full cauldron with a vat,
be given by the king . . .
a vessel, a goblet,
a chariot, a tusk-hilted sword,
thirty cows, a quern,
a band of warriors.
All this is a debt (*fiach*)
to me from Fiacha."

"It will be given," said Fiacha. "What name will be given to the boy now?"

"Let him be called Aí (Poetic Art)," said the druid. It was from this that poetic craft (*aí airchetail*) was so called, that is, from Aí son of Ollam. And that was the first poetical composition spoken by Aí, son of Ollam. (Carney 1969, 169-70)

Appropriately, the story is set in mythic time, among the old gods, the Túatha Dé Danann. It is a spare, didactic tale, which sets down the charter for the legal status and economic rights of poets. The point of this allegory is underlined by the name given to Aí's father, Ollam (Greatest): in the oldest Irish sources the title of the highest grade of every hierarchy, but later restricted to the highest degree among poets, those with the most rigorous training (Binchy 1958, 48-50). Early legal tracts (specifically the *Uraicecht Becc*, compiled by the eighth century) set forth the honor price of an *ollam* as the equal of that of a tribal king (Binchy 1979, 6.1603). So the "prophecy" in this story is an established fact, announced with twenty-twenty hindsight: poetry *is* an "art of a dignity equal to [the king's] own." (Aí's equality in status to Fiacha is indicated, further, by the fact that his father's forces in the house equal in number the king's own.) And this high status of the best-trained poets of course reflects their social function in the essentially preliterate culture of the early Irish: it was the *filid*, the court poets, who were the custodians of that knowledge—of genealogies, of contracts, of history—without which government and social and intertribal order would founder (Williams 1972).

The infant Aí, whose name might most literally be translated "inspired poetic composition," embodies those supernatural gifts unique to poets.[1] The powers of *aí* are succinctly summarized in the Middle Irish manual of poetry *Auraicept na n-Éces: itat coic ae and: .i. ae ailes ⁊ ae chanas ⁊ ae aiges ⁊ ae mides ⁊ ae suides* (Calder 1917, 30), "There are five crafts of poetry: poetry that nourishes and poetry that sings and poetry that impels and poetry that judges and poetry that establishes." Poetry thus carries on the major functions that support society. First comes nourishment: poetry actually sustains life as food does, and nurtures as would a nurse or foster parent. In *Lebor Gabála Érenn*, when a druidic wind keeps the sons of Míl away from the shore of Ireland, it is their poet Amorgen's celebration of the fruitfulness of the country that enables them to land:

> A[i]liu íath nÉrenn,
> hÉrmach muir mothach,
> Mothach sliab srethach,
> Srethach caill cíthach,
> Cíthach aub essach,
> Essach loch lindmar,
> Lindmar tór tipra,
> Tipra túa[i]th óenach,
> Oenach ríg Temrach.
>
> I seek the land of Ireland,
> Coursed be the fruitful sea,
> Fruitful the ranked highland,
> Ranked the showery wood,
> Showery the river of cataracts,
> Of cataracts the lake of pools,
> Of pools the hill of a well,
> Of a well of a people of assemblies,
> Of assemblies of the King of Temair.
> (Macalister 1956, 114–17)

Second, poetry *sings*, or chants—activities suggesting two other aspects of its function: its employment in spells and magical acts and its connection with teaching. The principal verb representing the activity of teachers is a compound of *canaid* 'sings', *for-cain*, literally 'sings/chants *over*', connoting chanting from a superior position to students who are in a deferential relationship to the teacher.[2] Such teaching was the function of the sacral class of wise men that included not only the *filid*, but also druids.

Third, poetry *impels*; it is capable of irresistible compulsion, not only in overtly magical forms such as charms and invocations, but also in the ordinary activities of the Irish aristocracy. Poets incited chieftains and troops to battle; and their effectiveness was attested, even by their enemies, as long as native Irish chieftainships continued to exist. In 1561 the English apothecary Thomas Smyth wrote from Dublin complaining that Irish poets through their praise poems were "very hurtfull to the comonwhealle, for they chifflie mayntayne the rebells; and, further, they do cause them that would be true, to be rebelious theves, extorcioners, murtherers, ravners, yea and worse if it were possible" (Kenney 1929 [1966], 30).

Fourth, poetry *judges*: in prehistoric times *filidecht* and *breithemnas*, poetry and law, were probably parts of the same profession (Binchy 1955). Certainly poets were believed to have extraordinary powers to perceive the truth, extending, for instance, to their mastery of spells for divining the identities of thieves (Chadwick 1935).

And fifth, poetry *establishes*: it creates and maintains things as they are. In royal inaugurations the poet recited the history, versified king-lists, and genealogy that chartered and legitimized the new ruler's reign, and officiated with ritual instructions proclaiming the king's duties and taboos (Dillon 1973a, 1973b; Williams 1972, 40–51).

Much of this seems to have more to do with sustenance than with danger. But the birth tale of Aí reflects some ambivalence. Coming from a society that esteemed poets highly and depended on their gifts for its very survival, this tale is oddly disquieting, not altogether positive. The arrival of poetic inspiration is heralded by a blast of wind that terrifies the feasting company into silence. This dangerous gust acts like a poet or druid: *Cid forcanas ind athach?* asks Fiacha; "What does this gust *teach*?"—using the verb *for-cain*. Although his druid explains the nature of the marvelous art that is about to be born, King Fiacha does not greet the infant gladly, but rather tries to murder it; and when this attempt is frustrated (by the efforts of an *ollam*), he is forced by the infant's own poem (poetry is an art that *impels*) to agree to an outrageously generous gift to the newborn. He has no choice but to ratify the new being—doubly—at first by promising gifts and then by calling for the child's name.

Threats to newborn infants are common, of course, in the

Birth of the Hero story pattern (Rees and Rees 1961, 238–40). But there is a special irony in the variant of that pattern selected for the story of the birth of Aí. The near-to-hand model for this tale's opening motifs—the feasting company, the terrifying noise interpreted by a king's druid as a prognostication of birth—was that most famous of early Irish birth tales in *Loinges mac nUislenn* (Hull 1949). That story's opening augurs destruction for King Conchobor and his war band, the end of the social order; Aí Airchetail, the allegorical representation of the art of poetry, occupies the same position in his story as the lethally attractive Deirdriu in *Loinges mac nUislenn*. To select this particular pattern, which would have had such inevitable connotations for its medieval Irish audience, for the story of the arrival of professional poetry is charged with irony. The message to the audience is danger—and in the story of Aí, King Fiacha's immediate murderous impulse shows his own awareness of the threat, the complexity added to the situation by his jealousy of the poet figure who will rival his own status, who will simultaneously support and (by his innate powers) potentially challenge his royal authority.

The story thus accurately reflects the ambivalence of attitude about poets that pervades early Irish literature, as well as the paradoxical nature of the poets' powers. the *filid* were indeed dangerous. If their words could heal, could sustain prosperity, could create and maintain effective government, their words could also destroy through satire. Poetry could blight the fruits of crops and domestic animals, as it does in *Cath Maige Tuired* in the mouth of Cairpre son of Étaín, *fili* of the Túatha Dé Danann, after whose satire on Bres *ní boí acht meth foair-sim ónd úair sin*, "there was only blight on him from that hour" (Gray 1982, 34–35). Treated as a lethal weapon in the laws, poetic satire appears as a sanction of last resort for the enforcement of contracts, and as a cause of death in the annals (Robinson 1912; Meroney 1950, 1953; Elliott 1960). The etymology in the tenth-century *Sanas Cormaic* for the word *fili* 'poet' sums up the situation: *Fili .i. fí a n-aoras ৴ lí a mmolas ৴ brecht a fúacras in file* (Meyer 1912, 49), "*fili*, that is, *fí* 'poison' in satire, and *lí* 'splendor' in praise, and it is variously that the poet proclaims."

Poets made up a closed, secretive group. It is instructive to note the contrast between the first speech of the infant Aí—an obscure, archaized, and difficult poem asserting that Fiacha owes him compensation—and the first speech of the next figure in the triad of tales, the judge Morann, whose initial experiences of the world lead him to utter three gnomic statements: *Garg bé tond* 'The wave is rough'; *úar bé gáeth* 'Wind is cold'; *Solus bé caindell* 'A candle is bright'. Morann's speeches reflect the proper sphere of the judge: absolute truth, perceptions about the universe that ratify his human judgments; but Aí's first utterance is not about truth, but about privilege and status, and reflects the contentious arrogance of poets, as his entire story reflects medieval Irish society's nervousness about dependence on a powerful and to some extent uncontrollable caste of artists. D. A. Binchy has suggested that there may be a grain of historical fact in the tradition that the *filid*, because of the obscurity of their language, were deprived of their juridical powers during the reign of Conchobor mac Nessa (Binchy 1955, 5; Stokes 1891, 186–87, 204–5). Perhaps, given the famous obscurity of their professional language, it was feared that they were wielding the law for the sake of personal power. In any case, Irish literature again and again—but usually with humor—presents the theme of the excessive demands of the *filid*: in the stories of Senchán in *Scéla Cano meic Gartnáin*, for instance, and in the later *Imthecht na Tromdhaimhe* (Binchy 1963, 9–11; Connellan 1860; Joynt 1931).

Early Irish literature tends to foreground *filid* (who were often, after all, its authors); harpers receive less attention. But their profession shared important attributes with *filidecht*. The noblest artists were in Celtic society given sacral legal status, *neimed*, comparable to that of the highest nobility. The *áes dána*—literally, the 'gifted people'—are subdivided in *Uraicecht Becc* into *sáernemed* and *dáernemed*, 'free-sacral' and 'unfree-sacral,' and it is in the higher category, along with clerics, chieftains, and nobles, that the *filid*, the court poets, are listed. All other artists and artisans (*áes gacha dána olchena*) are relegated to *dáernemed* status, with the sole and specific exception of harpers: *Cruit, is e aendan ciuil indsein dliges sairi ceni 'mteid la h-ordain* (Binchy 1979, 5.1616), "The harper, his is the one musical gift that is entitled to free legal status, as long as it accompanies nobility."

Thus harpers and *filid* are socially and legally akin, and the literature shows them conjoined in several ways. *Trí ségainni hÉrenn*, runs triad 89: *fáthrann, adbann a cruit, berrad aigthe* (Meyer 1906, 10), "Three things for which Ireland is preeminent: a witty quatrain, a tune on the harp, shaving a face." Here (if we sidestep barbers) harpers and poets are linked together as quintessentially *Irish*. Other well-known triads suggest further connections in the ways poets and harpers were perceived. Both kinds of artist, for instance, were characterized by the mastery of three kinds of art. According to the triads, *Tréde neimthigedar filid: immas forosna, teinm laeda, dichetal di chennaib* (Meyer 1906, 16), "There are three things that confer professional status on a *fili*: *imbas forosna, teinm laida, dichetal di chennaib*"—citing three divinatory poetic spells (Chadwick 1935; O'Rahilly 1946, 323, 339–40; Thurneysen 1933). And the preceding triad concerns harpers: *Tréde neimthigedar cruitire: golltraige, gentraige, súantraige*, "There are three things that confer professional status on a harper: music to cause weeping, music to cause laughter, music to cause sleep."

In the early literature, these three types of magical, compelling music are inevitably mentioned in connection with famous harpers. So important are they to the definition of a qualified harper that there is a myth—again, like the myth of Aí, a birth tale, and strongly allegorical—about their origin. It is inserted into *Táin Bó Fraích* at the point at which Froech's marvelous harpers are playing before Ailill and Medb:

> Ba cáin ⁊ ba bind in triar sa ⁊ batar caíni Uaithni insein. Is hé in triar irdaircc: tri derbráthir .i. Goltraiges ⁊ Gentraiges ⁊ Súantraiges. Boind a ssídib a mmáthair a triur. Is din chéol sephainn Uaithne cruitt in Dagdai ainmnigther a triur. In tan bóe in ben oc lámnad ba gol mairgg lee la gúri na n-idan i tossuch. Ba gen ⁊ fáilte arabeiti ar medón ar imtholtain in dá mac. Ba súan álgine arabeitte in mac dédenach ar thrumme inna brithe, conid de ro ainmniged trian in chíuil.
>
> Dofíussig íarum assint súan in Boind. "Aurfhoímsiu," ol si, "do thrí maccu, a Uathni lánbrotha, fo bíth file súantride ⁊ gentride ⁊ goltride ar búaib sceo mnáib dosoifet la Meidb ⁊ Ailill. Atbélat fir la clúaiss ngléssa dóib." (Meid 1967, 4–5)

> Fair and melodious were these three, and they were the playthings of Uaithne. This famous three are three brothers: Goltraiges, Gentraiges and Suantraiges. Boand from the Otherworld was the mother of the three. It is from the music played by Uaithne, the Dagda's harper, that the three are named. When the woman was in travail it seemed to be like weeping and sorrow at first with the sharpness of the pangs; then, in the middle, it was laughter and gladness that he played on account of eagerness for the two sons; it was sleep and gentleness for the last son on account of the heaviness of the birth, so that from it a third of the music was named.

> Thereupon Boand awoke from her sleep. "Accept," said she, "your three sons, O passionate Uaithne, for there, for cattle and for women who shall bring forth under Ailill and Medb, are Music of Sleeping, Music of Smiling and Music of Weeping. Men will die on hearing them being played." (Carney 1955, 4)

The story is hardly elaborate, but it is richly suggestive. Like the story of Aí Airchetail, it is set in mythic time among the Túatha Dé Danann; the three types of harp music are born from the goddess Boand, divine eponym of the sacred Boyne River. And like the story of Aí, this harp-music myth reflects ambivalence about the newborn—and, by extension, about the art that they represent. On the one hand, skilled harp music—like poetry—functions to support wealth, fertility, and the continuation of society: Boand presents her triplets for the sake of cattle, the standard of wealth and exchange in the pastoral Celtic world, and for women who will give birth during the reign of Ailill and Medb. On the other hand, harp music is destructive, as Boand's last comment about the tunes indicates: "Men will die on hearing them being played." And the birth allegory seems to have been inserted into *Táin Bó Fraích* at this point as a kind of gloss on what has just occurred in the story: Froech's harpers have played before Ailill and Medb's court, and the culmination of their excellence is that "they played to them so that twelve men of their household died of weeping and sadness."

In Irish literature vitality and death, sustenance and danger commonly coexist in connection with harp music as well as with poetry. In *Orgain Denna Ríg*, for instance, the harper Craiphtine uses his music twice, once to cast the court of the Fir Morca into what is described as *súanbás* 'deathlike sleep', so that his master can consummate a tryst with a princess whose watchful and wakeful mother has been an obstacle; and once to put to sleep all of the warriors inside Cobthach's fortress with *súantraige*, so that his master's war band can slaughter the immobilized garrison and sack the fort. A quatrain ascribed to Flann mac Lonáin emphasizes the connection between the destruction of the fortress and Craiphtine's harp playing:

> Feib con-attail Moriath múad
>   fiad sluag Morcae, mó cach séol,
> dia n-ort Dind Ríg, réim cen tréis,
>   dia sephaind céis cendtoll céol.
>   (Greene 1955, 21)

> As proud Moriath slept
> before the host of Morca—greater than every strain—
> when Dind Ríg was destroyed—course without treachery—
> when the harp with the pierced head (?) played music.

In *Cath Maige Tuired*, it is the test of the three kinds of harp playing that culminates Lug's demonstrations of his skills, finally convincing Núadu that he is qualified to lead the Túatha Dé Danann into battle against the Fomorians. And toward the end of the narrative, the Dagda's magical harp itself becomes a weapon, leaping from its hook on the wall and killing nine Fomorians on its way back to its rightful owner; once in the Dagda's hands, it plays the three kinds of music:

> Doluid an crot assan froig íerum, ⁊ marbais nonbór ⁊ tánuicc docum an Daghda; ⁊ sepainn-sie a trédhi fora nem[th]i[g]thir cruitiri dóib .i. súantraigi ⁊ genntraigi ⁊ golltraigi. Sephainn golltraigi dóib co ngolsad a mná déracha. Sephainn genntraigi dóib co tibsiot a mná ⁊ a macraith. Sephainn súantraigi dóib contuilset ant slúaigh. Is de sen diérlatar a triur slán úaidib— cíamadh áil a ngoin. (Gray 1982, 70)

> Then the harp came away from the wall, and it killed nine men and came to the Dagda; and he played for them the three things by which a harper is known: sleep music, joyful music, and sorrowful music. He played sorrowful music for them so that their tearful women wept. He played joyful music for them so that their women and boys laughed. He played sleep music for them so that the armies slept. So [they] escaped from them unharmed —although [the Fomorians] wanted to kill them. (Gray 1982, 71)

Like the art of noble poets, then, the art of noble harpers is both wonderful and dangerous, nurturing and deadly. It seems particularly appropriate that the creation of just these two highest arts should have been portrayed allegorically as birth tales. The connection to birth is not simply through the idea of *beginnings*. What is involved here, I would guess, is a much larger trope in Irish culture relating to female sexuality.

In early Irish culture birth is often imaged as a woman's gift to this world, a miraculous mediation of new life. After the birth of the musical triplets in *Táin Bó Fraích*, Boand turns and explicitly *presents* them to her husband, Uaithne, with a speech about their natures and destiny. The triads state the idea gnomically: *Trí aithgine in domuin: brú mná, uth bó, ness gobann* (Meyer 1906, 20), "Three renewals of the world: a woman's womb, a cow's udder, a smith's molding-block."

But at the same time, this gift of life carries with it the threat of death, even in the seemingly innocuous idea of the succession of generations. The birth of a child presages the death of its parents; this reality is embodied in many of the commonest and most ancient folk motifs: a child is destined to kill its father, or a parent attempts to destroy an infant. Both of these patterns occur, significantly, in the story of Noidiu Nóibrethach, the third legendary baby to speak immediately after birth (Thurneysen 1936). It has been prophesied that Noidiu's mother's father will die if she bears a son; this prophecy is fulfilled at Noidiu's birth, and, moreover, his mother immediately attempts to put her infant to death. His eponymous nine judgments are traditional maxims and proverbs through which Noidiu not only prevents his mother from murdering him, but, in fact, brings about *her* death. Murder and motherhood are brought deliberately together here. Intergenerational rivalries are expressed starkly; and birth symbolizes a complex truth. According to the myth of the origin of harp music, for instance, the natures of the three types of music are determined by the actual and plausible feelings of the mother during her delivery of the triplets: pain, joy, and then exhaustion; and finally, in the presence of the newborn infants, their own mother announces triumphantly that by their very natures they will bring death to others: *Atbélat fir la clúaiss ngléssa dóib*, "Men will die on hearing them being played."

As far as I know, only the origins of *aí* and harp music, of all the arts in Irish tradition, are depicted as births. (Allegory is also not very common.) Through their presentation in the form of mythic birth tales, these noble arts—noble *male* arts—were represented as the gifts of women. And as women's gifts, they were imaged as naturally partaking in the nature of women, and they were regarded with the same ambivalence with which Irish society regarded the female. As kings depended on the skills of *filid* and harpers for their own continuance, so were all men seen to depend on the skills of women. Triad 75: *Trí cóil ata ferr folongat in mbith: cóil srithide hi folldeirb, cóil foichne for tuinn, cóil snáithe dar dorn dagmná* (Meyer 1906, 10), "Three slender things that best support the world: the slender stream of milk from the cow's dug into the pail, the slender blade of green corn upon the ground, the slender thread over the hand of a fine woman.''

But, again like poets and harpers, women were seen as passionate, selfish, and potentially immoderate, ultimately beyond the control of—and threatening *to* control—even a king. Daniel F. Melia has pointed out that the hero's sexual liaison with a woman is an invariable component of the story patterns of the early Irish death-tales (Melia 1977–78). As sexual beings, women are often classed with wild and savage forces, with nature rather than culture, as in triad 238: *Trí luchra ata mesa: luchra tuinde, luchra mná bóithe, luchra con foléimnige* (Meyer 1906, 32), "Three worst smiles: the smile of a wave, the smile of a lewd woman, the smile of a dog ready to leap.'' So it is the female body as both maternal and sexual that figures the image of the paradoxical powers of poets and harpers: the sustaining power of the mother coexists with the dangerous and destructive power of female sexuality.

One final, essential connection links poets and harpers and the Irish cultural idea of the female. The harper, like the *fili*, shares key power belonging to the pagan Celtic Otherworld and its Christian Irish reflex, the realm of the *síd*. And this Otherworld is symbolically a female realm. Its geography is suggestively female: access is through a passageway into a mound, or down a well, or under or across water (Carey 1982). And sometimes it is portrayed as *Tír na mBan*, the Land of Women. The fairy woman in *Echtrae Connlae* lures Connla to

> . . . a tír subathar
> menmain cáich do-d-imchela
> ní-fil cenél and nammá
> acht mná ocus ingena.
> (Pokorny 1928, 201)
>
> . . . the land that makes joyful
> the minds of all who go about it.
> There is no race there at all
> except women and maidens.

Fittingly, the Irish Otherworld stands in an equivocal relation to humankind, inimical and destructive at one moment (as in the campaign of the *síd* of Cruachan to destroy Connacht in *Echtrae Nerai*), and beneficial and supportive the next (as in the *síd*'s gifts to Nera himself in the same tale). And it is from the Otherworld that poets and harpers derive their decisive powers—those unique aspects of their art which associate them with kings, which lift them into *sáernemed* status, and which render them to some degree ungovernable by human institutions.

These noble artists have special links to the supernatural; they function as liminal figures, powerful because they exist in the in-between, through their inspiration mediating knowledge and power from the Otherworld to this. The Otherworld connections of Celtic poets, particularly in regard to their powers of divination, have been too frequently documented to be repeated here;[3] but harpers have received less attention. Perhaps the most vivid evidence of the affinity of harpers and the Otherworld is their ability to play *súantraige*, the music that causes sleep. Old Irish distinguishes two types of sleep: *súan* and *cotlud*. *Cotlud*, the verbal noun of *con-tuili*, names sleep in general, including that which is in human control, a matter of personal decision. (Even drunkenness is regarded as a matter of volition, and thus leads to *cotlud*.) The term *súan*, by contrast, is usually restricted to designating magically overpowering sleep. In literature *súan* is induced principally by potions or a spell (*bricht súain*) and by the music or actions of Otherworld beings ranging from birds, mermaids, and angels to supernatural warriors shaking silver fairy branches. Cú Chulainn's magical coma in *Serglige Con Culainn* (The Sickbed of Cú Chulainn) is *súan serglige* or *súan síthbroga* 'the sleep of fairyland' (Dillon 1953, 11, 13); in *Echtra Cormaic i Tír Tairngiri* (Cormac's Adventure in the Promised Land) an Otherworld warrior sings Cormac into *súan*: *Canais in t-oglach dord dho cor' cuir a suan* (Stokes 1891, 197). Only one *human* figure, however—the harper—is principally associated with music that brings on *súan*.

Such are the powers of harpers and *filid* in early Irish tradition that they seem to share certain kinds of symbolic liminality and to have been regarded with similar sorts of ambivalence. They belong to this world *and* the other; they serve the king but cannot be controlled by him; they uphold law and order at the same time that their supernatural professional powers threaten to introduce chaos; and the same powers by which they promote fertility, health, and wealth can also be deadly. Such paradoxes of sustenance and danger set apart poets and harpers and link them with women into a single semiotic system that is particularly obvious, in medieval Irish tradition, in these unusual allegorical birth-tales about the origins of poetry and harp music. Representing their powers symbolically as the gifts of women as well as of the Otherworld foregrounds the extent to which the sustaining and threatening female is symbolically the source of the unique qualities of these arts.

JOAN N. RADNER

The American University

NOTES

1. See especially the fascinating (but unfortunately obscure) treatise on *aí* imbedded in the tract in Trinity College Dublin MS H.2.15B, pp. 135-56 (Gwynn 1942, 35-40).
2. Hearing an earlier version of this paper, Eric Hamp commented on the cognate idea embodied in the Sanskrit *upanishad*.
3. See the summary in Williams 1972, 22-26; also Chadwick 1935; Elliott 1960; Rees and Rees 1961; Robinson 1912.

REFERENCES

Binchy, D. A. 1955. *Bretha Nemed*. Ériu 17: 4-6.
———. 1958. The Date and Provenance of Uraicecht Becc. *Ériu* 18: 44-54.
———, ed. 1963. *Scéla Cano meic Gartnáin*. Mediaeval and Modern Irish Series 18. Dublin: Dublin Institute for Advanced Studies.
———, ed. 1979. Corpus Iuris Hibernici. 6 vols. Dublin: Dublin Institute for Advanced Studies.
Calder, George. 1917. *Auraicept na n-Éces: The Scholars' Primer*. Edinburgh: John Grant.
Carey, John. 1982. The Location of the Otherworld in Irish Tradition. *Éigse* 19.1: 36-43.
Carney, James. 1955. (Reprinted 1979.) *Studies in Irish Literature and History*. Dublin: Dublin Institute for Advanced Studies.
———. 1969. The Deeper Level of Early Irish Literature. *The Capuchin Annual*: 160-71.
Chadwick, N. K. 1935. *Imbas Forosnai*. Scottish Gaelic Studies 4: 97-135.
Connellan, Owen. 1860. *Imtheacht na Tromdaimhe; or, The Proceedings of the Great Bardic Institution*. Transactions of the Ossianic Society 5.
Dillon, Myles, ed. 1953. *Serglige Con Culainn*. Mediaeval and Modern Irish Series 14. Dublin: Dublin Institute for Advanced Studies.
———. 1973a. The Consecration of Irish Kings. *Celtica* 10: 1-8.
———. 1973b. A Poem on the Kings of the Eóganachta. *Celtica* 10: 9-14.

Elliott, Robert C. 1960. *The Power of Satire: Magic, Ritual, Art*. Princeton: Princeton University Press.
Gray, Elizabeth A., ed. 1982. *Cath Maige Tuired, The Second Battle of Mag Tuired*. Irish Texts Series 52. Kildare: Irish Texts Society.
Greene, David, ed. 1955. *Fingal Rónáin and Other Stories*. Mediaeval and Modern Irish Series 16. Dublin: Dublin Institute for Advanced Studies.
Gwynn, E. J. 1942. An Old-Irish Tract on the Privileges and Responsibilities of Poets. *Ériu* 13: 1–60, 220–36.
Hull, Vernam. 1949. *Longes mac n-Uislenn, The Exile of the Sons of Uisliu*. New York: Modern Language Association of America.
Joynt, Maud, ed. 1931. *Tromdámh Guaire*. Mediaeval and Modern Irish Series 2. Dublin: Dublin Institute for Advanced Studies.
Kenney, James F. 1929. (Reprinted 1966.) *The Sources for the Early History of Ireland: Ecclesiastical*. Original, New York: Columbia University Press; reprint, New York: Octagon Books.
Macalister, R. A. Stewart. 1956. *Lebor Gabála Érenn, The Book of the Taking of Ireland*. Irish Texts Series, part V. Dublin: Irish Texts Society.
Meid, Wolfgang, ed. 1967. *Táin Bó Fraích*. Mediaeval and Modern Irish Series 22. Dublin: Dublin Institute for Advanced Studies.
Melia, Daniel F. 1977–78. Remarks on the Structure and Composition of the Ulster Death Tales. *Studia hibernica* 17–18: 36–57.
Meroney, Howard. 1950; 1953. Studies in Early Irish Satire. *Journal of Celtic Studies* 1: 199–226; 2: 59–130.
Meyer, Kuno. 1906. *The Triads of Ireland*. Royal Irish Academy Todd Lecture Series 13. Dublin: Hodges, Figgis.
———. 1912. *Sanas Cormaic, An Old-Irish Glossary*. Anecdota from Irish Manuscripts, ed. O. J. Bergin, R. I. Best, Kuno Meyer, and J. G. O'Keefe. Halle: Max Niemeyer; Dublin: Hodges, Figgis.
O'Rahilly, T. F. 1946. *Early Irish History and Mythology*. Dublin: Dublin Institute for Advanced Studies.
Pokorny, Julius. 1928. Conle's Abenteuerliche Fahrt. *Zeitschrift für celtische Philologie* 17: 193–205.
Rees, Alwyn and Brinley Rees. 1961. *Celtic Heritage: Ancient Tradition in Ireland and Wales*. London: Thames and Hudson.
Robinson, Fred Norris. 1912. Satirist and Enchanters in Early Irish Literature. In *Studies in the History of Religions Presented to Crawford Howell Toy*, ed. D. G. Lyon and G. F. Moore, 95–130. New York: Macmillan.
Stokes, Whitley. 1891. The Irish Ordeals, Cormac's Adventure in the Land of Promise, and the Decision as to Cormac's Sword. *Irische Texte* 3.1, ed. Whitley Stokes and Ernst Windisch: 183–229. Leipzig: S. Hirzel.
Thurneysen, Rudolf. 1918. Zur keltischen Literatur und Grammatik. *Zeitschrift für celtische Philologie* 12: 271–78. (From LL 126a30ff.)
———. 1933. Imbas For-osndai. *Zeitschrift für celtische Philologie* 19: 163–64.
———. 1936. Die drei Kinder, die Gleich nach ihrer Geburt Sprachen. *Zeitschrift für celtische Philologie* 20: 192–200. (From Yellow Book of Lecan cols. 808–10.)
Williams, J. E. Caerwyn. 1972 [1971]. The Court Poet in Medieval Ireland. Sir John Rhŷs Memorial Lecture. *Proceedings of the British Academy* 58: 1–51.

A Poetic Klein Bottle

Domfarcai fidbaidae fál · fomchain lóid luin lúad nad cél.
huas mo lebrán indlínech · fomchain trírech innanén.
Fom*m*chain cói menn medair mass · hiṁbrot glass de dindgnaib doss.
debrath nomchoim*m*diu cóima · cáinscríbaim*m* foróida r(oss).
(Stokes and Strachan 1903, 2.290)

A hedge of trees overlooks me; a blackbird's lay sings to me (an announcement which I shall not conceal); above my lined book the birds' chanting sings to me.
A clear-voiced cuckoo sings to me (goodly utterance) in a grey cloak from bush fortresses. The Lord is indeed good to me: well do I write beneath a forest of woodland. (Murphy 1962, 5)

Because of its seemingly transparent, even Wordsworthian, message of rural literary pleasure expressed in highly personal terms, this short poem in Old Irish has been particularly appealing to twentieth-century readers. Because nothing in the poem, which appears in the lower margin of pages 203–4 of the ninth-century St. Gall glosses on Priscian's Latin grammar, would seem to contradict a ninth-century date for its composition it appears to serve as a kind of aesthetic link between the twentieth century and the ninth.

Gerard Murphy (1962, 4) normalizes the text as follows (alliteration is shown by italics, consonance by boldface italics, full rhyme by boldface type, *aicill* rhyme by underlining, anaphora by asterisks [*], and independent prepositions by reverse slashes [\\]):

1.
   a. Dom-*fh*arcai *f*idbaide f*ál*
      over-me-looks of-trees hedge
   b. *fom-chain   *l*oíd *l*uin,   *l*úad   nād   c*él*;
      under-me-sings lay of blackbird, speaking I-shall-not hide
      [accompanies (music)]   [cheville]
   c. \hūas\   mo *l*ebrán, ind *l*ín<u>ech</u>,
      above my booklet, the lined-one
         [hypocor. -án]

    d. *fom-chain   trírech inna n-**én**.
       under-me-sings trilling of-the birds
       [song/poem]

2.
    a. *Fomm-*c*hain *c*oí *m*enn,   *m*edair *m*ass,
       under-me-sings cuckoo clear, discourse fine
                                         [cheville]
    b. \hi\ mbrot glass \de\ *d*ingnaib *d*oss.
       in   cloak grey from hill-forts of bushes
    c. Débrath! nom-*C*hoimmdiu-*c*oíma:
       God's-doom!   X-me-Lord-cherishes
       [Patrick's oath]   [tmesis]
    d. *c*áin-scríbaimm \fo\ *r*oída *r*oss.
       well-I-write   under of woods woodland
                                  [ro-fid] [promontory?]

(The interlinear translation and glosses are mine, and I have added the accent in *Débrath*. For definitions of the prosodic terms, see my appendix.) Murphy's note on the poem reads in part, "The metre is *rannaigecht* ($7^1\ 7^1\ 7^2\ 7^1$), with rhyme between the final words of lines *b* and *d*, consonance between the final of *a* and the finals of *b* and *d*, and *aicill*-rhyme between the final of *c* and a word in the interior of *d* (and in quatrain 2 between the final of *a* and a word in the interior of *b* as well). Alliteration is frequent" (Murphy 1962, 173).

There is, of course, nothing wrong with Murphy's translation and brief note on the poem, which represent, I think, the mainstream of twentieth-century reactions to it. I hope to demonstrate here, however, that there is far more to the poem than is revealed in the translatable semantic equivalents of the words, which can only scratch the surface of the density of internal linkages in the poem. For the exploitation of the phonological, morphological, syntactic, and semantic resources of the language in these two quatrains allows the poet to take the slightest of themes (two birds sing to the speaker as he writes outdoors) and extremely formal prosodic restrictions and turn all to a brilliantly interwoven artifact which serves as an emblem itself of what it purports to describe. Paradoxically, the poet is able to turn the poem's very limitations and restrictions in form and substance from the appearance of intense self-reference to a microcosmic metaphor for the author's place in the universe. What to a twentieth-century reader might seem to be a postromantic lyric statement of a rather banal kind reveals itself, when looked at with sufficient attention, rather as a more substantial statement and illustration of personal belief.

A close reading of the poem, and especially of its formal prosodic and linguistic features, gives a far more complex picture than one would imagine from taking Murphy's English translation as a reflection of the poem's content. At issue here is "poetic" information, that is, intentionally coded information residing in the language, syntax, and prosody. It is, as I hope to show in what follows, not enough to look to the simplest level of semantic extraction to understand how this poem functions; to do so is fundamentally to misread it.

The reading I propose here is an explicitly rhetorical one in that I am trying to reconstruct via the evidence in the text (and what we can divine of the context) what the implied author intended his contemporary audience to be able to understand of the poem's signification. I am speaking here of intention in the technical and not the fallacious sense. That is, when I speak of intention, I am speaking not of the possible private motives that might have animated the actual author of the poem, but of those coherent significations discoverable in the text itself, which hearers of the poem take to be the "point" or "meaning" embodied in it. The "author" who has these intentions is the authorial voice that a reader or auditor is almost certain to discover in a text. Likewise, the audience I am concerned with is the audience discoverable in the text itself, the audience whom the implied author expects to recognize and respond to certain strategies he uses in the text.

However charming we may judge this poem to be from our own aesthetic viewpoint, if we look at it strictly in terms of what seems to be its surface meaning, it is pretty thin. The speaker depicts himself as being surrounded by a hedge of trees; he hears the song of a blackbird; he is writing in a small lined book; birds sing; a cuckoo of the usual color sings to him from the bushes; he exclaims that he is favored by God and writes well in a woodland setting. To add to the apparent slenderness of content, two phrases in the poem, *lúad nād cél* and *medair mass*, are stock phrases, chevilles, which seem merely to serve to eke out the lines in which they appear while adding nothing to the poem's overall semantic content.

I am not alleging here that the information I have just extracted —the translatable semantic information—is not actually in the poem; it is. In that sense Murphy's choice of title, "The Scribe in the Woods," is both highly descriptive and justified. At one level the poem presents just that picture: a scribe sitting in a glade writing as birds sing from the bushes. But encoded in this poem there is a good deal more information that such an interpretation ignores, and it is information that vastly enlarges the poem's scope.

First of all, a glance at the poem itself, as printed above, shows an almost obsessive concentration on linkages amongst the lines. Every line in the poem is linked to at least one other by one or more of a number of prosodic or rhetorical means. Line 1a is linked to 1b and 1d by the assonance of the final syllables of each line. Line 1b is linked to 1a by assonance and to 1d by full rhyme in the final syllables. Line 1b is linked to 1c by shared (though not continuous) alliteration in *l* and, again, to 1d by the anaphora of *fom-chain*. Line 1c is linked to 1b by the *l* alliteration and to 1d by the *aicill* rhyme of *línech/trírech*. The internal stanzaic links of 1d have already been noted; it is also linked to 2a by the *fom-chain* anaphora.

In stanza 2, 2a is linked to 2b and 2d by final-word assonance and to 1b and 1d by anaphora. It is also linked to 2b by the *aicill* rhyme *mass/glass*. Line 2b is linked to 2a by final assonance (as well as by the *aicill* rhyme just mentioned), and to 2d by full rhyme. Furthermore, 2b's alliteration in *d* carries over to the first word of 2c, and the pattern is repeated when the *c* alliteration in 2c carries over to the first word of 2d. Lines 2c and 2d also share the *aicill* rhyme of *coíma/roída*, and 2d rhymes fully with 2b and assonates with 2a.

Some of the links outlined above are, of course, required of the verse form (*rannaigecht*), but they go far beyond the minimum here. Is this just ornament for its own sake, as Murphy's comment quoted above seems to imply? I think not. First of all, our twentieth-century feeling that ornament is extraneous is probably anachronistic in the case of a poem composed, after all, by someone who lived in a world aesthetically characterized by the intricate "Celtic" interlacing of the Ardagh Chalice, Insular manuscript illumination, and the decoration of the great High Crosses. Second, the existence in medieval Irish (though, admittedly, not attested as early as this poem) of technical terms that indicate approval of such intricate linkages argues that the poet was striving for a recognizable effect with his "ornament." This poem qualifies both as *trebraide* 'woven' (Murphy 1961, 29), in that "all lines of a stanza are inextricably linked to one another in a pattern of rime or assonance," and as *cetharcubaid* 'quadrirhymed', in that each line-ending word either rhymes or assonates with another word (Murphy 1961, 35).

It is not, however, merely that ninth-century Irish people liked intricacy in their art. The elaborate system of "weaving," to borrow the Irish figure, is particularly appropriate to a poem that concerns itself both with part singing and with poetry writing. Throughout, the poet exploits the ambiguity of semantic reference in all the terms connected with producing poetry and singing (*-cain, laíd, trírech*). While it is perfectly clear that *fo-cain* can signify just plain 'sing' or 'chant', most of the citations of its use in the early period in the Royal Irish Academy's *Dictionary* are to the musical extension of the fundamental sense of "sing under": "accompany" or "sing the burden"; and it seems clear enough that it is with this use that our poet is playing in this poem. The birds are over him physically, but sing "under" him in his poetry composition. The blackbird sings a *laíd* and the other birds *trírech*. While it is impossible to know what the full semantic range of these terms may have been in ninth-century Irish, their ambiguous use here appears to answer to some degree to an English sentence such as, "the birds were singing their sonnets and lyrics to me." The early introduction of the musical terms implies that the author may be referring to himself writing this poem (song) itself which, then, forms the melody or tune of the performance to the birds' continuo. Like the ornaments of his song itself, the birds' songs are intertwined with his song as music is intertwined in parts, and as the words and lines of this poem are with each other.

In addition to the prosodic and phonological linkages outlined above, there is an awful lot of positional specification in this poem. Things are over and under a lot of other things here. There are four independent prepositions in the poem: *hūas* (1c); *in, de* (2b); and *fo* (2d); 'over', 'in', '(out) from', and 'under'. The blackbird is "above" the speaker's little book (though singing "under" him); the speaker writes "under" the impending wood in 2d, and the cuckoo who is "in" his *glass* cloak sings (again "sings under") "from" a high fort of bushes. It may, of course, be pure chance that the positional prepositions have been distributed as they are in this poem, but it is harder to make the same argument from fortuity about the compound verbs. *Fo-cain*, literally, 'sings under' ('accompanies') occurs thrice at the beginning of lines, and the poem opens with *do-farcai* 'looks over' (< *to-for-ad-ci* = 'toward-over-at-see' or something of the sort), which is itself paired and contrasted with the *fo* in the final line of stanza 2. These notions are semantically woven into the poem itself. The first four lines begin with words indicating the notions over, under, over, under. This play with locative notions, physically and musically, is so systematically exploited in this poem that even if the unmarked meanings of *do-farcai* and *fo-cain* had lost much of the underlying sense of their positional preverbs, *for* and *fo*, their use here would recall the sense of the preverbs forcibly to mind.

We have no way of knowing what the unmarked "feel" of compound verbs was for speakers of ninth-century Irish, but we can infer with some confidence that in this case the *repetitio* of verbs with the "over" and "under" preverbs, coupled with the *ūas, in, de, fo* set, gives us strong reasons to read the poem as being intended to bring those meanings forward and to call attention to their prepositional meanings in combination with the verbal roots to which they are attached. We ordinarily do not notice the systematic "time equals money" metaphor in English ("he saved a lot of time taking the bus,") but the money element can be brought to the surface if pursued systematically or in a strange context (for example, "he spent his time as if there were no tomorrow but hoarded the handful of precious moments he spent with his beloved.")

And let us not forget the trees. In the first line the over–under relationship is expressed from the point of view of the trees, as it were, with the hedge (*fál*) looking over the speaker, while in the final line the same relationship is expressed—quite forcibly, with the only first-person verb in the poem (*scríbaimm*)—from the perspective of the speaker, who is under the overhanging (*ross*) trees. This final word itself, *ross*, signifies a 'high or projecting wooded place' and rhymes with *doss* (2b), which modifies and alliterates with *dingnaib* 'fortress on a high place'. Like the repetitive suggestion of "enclosure" discussed below, these words serve to reinforce the complex of over–under interplay already discussed with reference to the prepositions and preverbs.

The birds also seem to function in a comparative and representative way and to reinforce the pictorial balance. The blackbird (stanza 1) is the color of ink and sings over the speaker's book, while the cuckoo in stanza 2 sings from the bushes in which he is camouflaged by his organic gray-green (*glass*) color. I will here pass by a Levi-Straussian "nature versus culture" reading of the poem, as I am sure that readers can supply it for themselves if required.

The verbs in this poem represent a special category of interweaving and contrast. For instance, the verbs in the middle of the poem are connected phonologically to one another or to other elements in the poem, the *fom-chain*s in a chain of anaphora and *coíma* (2c) by *aicill* rhyme to *roída* (2d). The verbs in the first and last lines (*do-farcai* and *scríbaimm*), however, form a sharp contrast between repose and action, the speaker as observed and the speaker as actor.

Additionally, the structure of infixation is echoed in the final prepositional phrase of the poem in which the woods (*roída*) are contained by the preposition *fo* and its object, the overhanging or projecting branches, *ross*; not an unusual construction, but not obligatory either.

Another notable repetitive feature of this poem is the fact that with one exception, the *scríbaimm* of the final line, all the verbs have the same form. They are all third-person singular present indicative active, and all have the infixed first-person pronoun *m*. Now it is, indeed, true that this is the unmarked form of saying "*X* does-something-to me" in Old Irish. Nevertheless, the insistent repetition can hardly be without some effect. Furthermore, the repetition itself is marked when the turn is made in the last line to the speaker as subject (of *scríbaimm*) instead of infixed object, as well as by the switch in the penultimate line from compound verbs with semantically charged preverbs (*do-farcai, fo-cain*) to the same construction with a semantically empty preverb (*no-*) attached to a simple verb (*cáemaid*) and serving to create a highly marked tmesis (*nom-Choimmdiu-coíma*) in addition to infixing the speaker.

The tmesis *nom-Choimmdiu-coíma* is one of the best-known examples of this figure in Old Irish. It is composed of the semantically empty prefixing preverb *no-*, followed by the infixed first-person object pronoun, the subject of the sentence, and the verb itself. It may be translated "the Lord cherishes me" (or "may the Lord cherish me," as it is impossible to distinguish formally here between the present indicative 3. sg. conjunct and present subj. 3. sg. conjunct of *cáemaid*, both of which are realized as *-cáema* [spelled *-coíma* in this scribe's orthography]. Thurneysen cites it as an example of the poetic use of tmesis in his *Grammar of Old Irish* (Thurneysen 1946, §513), and Calvert Watkins points out that it matches both phonologically and syntactically a Classical Hittite inscription *nu-mu ^{d}IŠTAR . . . kaniššan ḫarta*, "Ishtar held me in favor," arguing that the tmesis here is an inherited Indo-European device (Watkins 1963, 13).

It is, of course, interesting in itself that such a parallel can be drawn between tmesis in Classical Hittite and in Classical Old Irish, separated as they are by better than two millennia, but my chief interest here is to examine the way in which the author of this Old Irish poem was able to exploit the possibilities of the morphological system of Irish verbs in such a way as to augment, or even determine, the signification of his two brief and repetitive quatrains. *Cáemaid* could take (especially in poetry) a suffixed first-person object pronoun (*coimtium?*), but the tmesis—especially after the hammering of the anaphora of *fom-chain*—emphasizes the notion of enclosure that is at the center of the figuration in this poem. The speaker's syntactic position in the sentence *nom-Choimmdiu-coíma* is made congruent with his physical and metaphysical position in the poem.

Nom-Choimmdiu-coíma is a particularly marked sentence because the combination of the tmesis and the infixed pronoun creates an OSV sentence, a most unusual shape for an Irish sentence, ordinarily VSO, or in the relatively normal case of an infixed pronoun, OVS. In this it is, though, merely the most marked of a whole series of infixes of the speaker as object. He is surrounded by the verbs themselves, by a hedge (*fál*), by birdsong (*laíd, trírech*), by high fortresses (*dingnaib*) of bushes (*doss*), by overhanging woods (*roída, ross*), and here, finally and most notably, by the cherishing of God, who is packed into the middle of the same verb with him. And this, I think, is the point, the preferred subject of the poem, that the embrace of words, of trees, of music, of language, and of nature is ultimately the embrace of the Lord himself, just as every element in the poem is representation of His embrace. And if the tmesis does not call sufficient attention to itself, the apostrophe *Débrath*, the oath most frequently put into St. Patrick's mouth by his biographers, ought to wake up even the most somnolent reader or listener.

Two further theoretical questions arise from the sort of reading I am presenting here. The first is the question of whether one is not "overreading"—putting in signification that was not intended to be there. It may, of course, be true that one or another of the features I have assigned significance to here may be my own invention in some way. At the same time, the density and consistency of the marked devices of all kinds must serve as evidence that they were meant to have some effect on their intended audience, even if we do not understand properly what that effect was meant to be.

The second question arises from the paradoxical fact that to analyze a poem as I have done, looking at it globally, fundamentally falsifies the experience of hearing the poem for the first time. And it is inescapable that having read a poem is not the same thing as reading a poem for the first time. It is all very well in retrospect to say that a word is linked with some word in the next line, but in hearing the poem for the first time one could not know that it would be. Although this state of affairs is true of all text analysis, the difficulty is somewhat less with respect to a traditional poetic form such as we have here. Just as in a modern limerick or sonnet, the presumed audience for this poem would have had certain phonological and structural expectations, which would have served as a kind of template against which the features I have discussed above could have been laid out. The poem is so short as to be apprehensible almost at one gulp, and I think an audience with the proper form in its ears and eyes would have had little trouble with this apparent paradox inherent in linear text analysis.

The interwoven complexity of this little poem and the intense overdetermination of the notion of the speaker embraced by God and God's nature eliminate, I think, the possibility of a postromantic reading of the poem as a simple paean of rustic praise in plain words for al-fresco writing. It must be read, rather, as a prime example of how traditional poetic materials, seeming barriers to communication of emotional states or stances, can be put to ends of great expressiveness. If we can understand what the poet has accomplished in this poem it must be because we have taken the trouble to pay attention to the means by which he attempted to accomplish it.

A constant thread in Eric Hamp's scholarly work has been his insistence that the people who wrote things down long ago *knew what they were doing*, and that we must begin any inquiry into what it was they did by respecting their intelligence, seriousness, and ability to interpret their own world sensibly. This is not merely an inflated way to justify the doctrine of *lectio difficilior*, nor a simple warning to avoid overvaluing our own capacity to internalize dead languages and orthographic systems, but an injunction to remember that whatever the temptation to schematize data may be, schematizing actual human beings or imposing our own values and assumptions on them leads inevitably into a variety of fatal errors, intellectual and moral. By contrast, close attention to what people actually said (wrote) can pay rich dividends in understanding more of their own world, how they lived in it, and what they may have to say to us in our world.

APPENDIX

The features of medieval Irish prosody relevant to this poem are: (1) Alliteration. Consonants alliterate with themselves in word-initial position in successive stressed syllables only. Vowels all alliterate with one another under the same circumstances. Enclitic preverbs (e.g., *do-m-*) do not count in verbs; the initial sound of the verb's stressed syllable counts in alliteration. Alliteration is morphophonemic: mutated forms of most consonants alliterate with one another. For instance, *b*, *bh*, and *mb* alliterate perfectly.

(2) Rhyme. Rhyme "begins with the first stressed vowel of the riming word. From then on, every vowel must normally be identical (the identity including identity of quantity) and every consonant (when the consonants are single and not in groups) must normally be balanced by a consonant belonging to the same phonetic class and having the same quality [palatal or velar]" (Murphy 1961, 30). The classes of consonants (phonetic, not orthographic classes) are: Voiced Stops (*b, d, g*); Voiceless Stops (*p, t, k*); Voiceless Spirants (*f, th, ch*); Voiced Spirants and Weakly Pronounced Voiced Liquids (bilabial spirants *bh, mh*, voiced *th, gh, l, n, r*); Strongly Pronounced Liquids and Resonants (*mm, ll, nn, ng, rr*; following a long vowel, these may rhyme with the Voice Spirants class); $s = s$ (Murphy 1961, 30–31).

(3) Consonance ("Irish Rhyme"). Rules are the same as for exact rhyme except that corresponding stressed vowels need be of the same quantity only and corresponding interior consonants need not be of the same quality. Final consonants and corresponding unstressed vowels in final syllables must be identical. Consonance is used only in conjunction with exact rhyme.

(4) *Aicill* ('client') rhyme. A rhyme between the last word of one line and an internal stressed word of the following line.

DANIEL FREDERICK MELIA
University of California, Berkeley

REFERENCES

Murphy, Gerard. 1961. *Early Irish Metrics*. Dublin: Royal Irish Academy.
———. 1962. *Early Irish Lyrics*. Oxford: Clarendon Press.
Dictionary of the Irish Language. 1983. (Compact Edition.) Dublin: Royal Irish Academy.
Stokes, W. and Strachan, J. 1903. (Reprinted 1975.) *Thesaurus Palaeohibernicus*. Vol. 2. Reprint, Dublin: Dublin Institute for Advanced Studies.
Thurneysen, R. 1946. *Grammar of Old Irish*. Dublin: Dublin Institute for Advanced Studies.
Watkins, Calvert. 1963. Preliminaries to a Historical and Comparative Analysis of the Syntax of the Old Irish Verb. *Celtica* 6: 1–49.

PART III

SCOTTISH GAELIC

A Brief Historiography of
Scottish Gaelic Dialect Studies*

The fields of Celtic studies and descriptive linguistics find common ground in the area of Scottish Gaelic dialect studies. These two disciplines offer differing perspectives on the goals of recording spoken language, but a close reading of several Scottish Gaelic dialect investigations will point up both historical continuity and methodological change in the general body of dialect literature, due to a continuing intersection of the two fields. This essay is not intended to be a comprehensive survey, but rather gives the outlines of the various theoretical approaches applied to Scottish Gaelic dialectology. Eric Hamp's work on Scottish Gaelic illustrates the broad spectrum of concerns, uniting the goals of historical comparison with the methods of systematic and principled description. A historiography of the field of Scottish Gaelic dialect studies will illustrate the conflicts and the compromises that he has so well resolved, and which inevitably confront any student of a living, spoken language.

Although E. C. Quiggin and A. Sommerfelt did not write on Scottish Gaelic, their works represent examples of opposing directions in the study of Celtic dialects. Both Quiggin's description of the speech of Meenawannia and Sommerfelt's works, on the dialect of Torr (1922) and on the Breton spoken in St. Pol-de-Léon (1921), served as models for later Scottish Gaelic dialect studies. As their titles and subtitles suggest, both considered it important to convey an emphasis on the spoken language of a particular area—at that point still a relatively recent topic of interest. Sommerfelt's work is synchronic and descriptive, and grounded in the methodological concern proper to advances in theory. Quiggin's description, in contrast, is exclusively historical or comparative in orientation and refers back to the general philological interest of Celtic studies. He writes:

> Phonetic decay seems to have set in all over the Gaelic-speaking area; and consequently it is imperative that . . . every effort

should be made to obtain scientific records of the speech of persons born before the famine who still have a firm grip on the vernacular. As a general rule the speech of the younger people is of little or no value to those who are trying to unravel the mysteries of Old and Middle Irish orthography. (Quiggin 1906, v)

This prefatory statement to Quiggin's *Dialect of Donegal* is indicative of early approaches to dialect studies: the preface itself is less a statement of purpose than an exhortation to other scholars to pursue the scientific study of the Irish vernacular. The study of Scottish Gaelic dialects owes its origins to the works of scholars such as Quiggin, who pushed back the boundaries of their field to include the living, spoken language, side by side with the written sources of philological study, and who widened the horizons of the Celtic scholar to include "herding cows, or chatting at night by the side of a peat fire" (1906, 3), as well as consulting manuscripts in a library.

For Quiggin, the driving cause for the investigation of a spoken language could not be a love of the vernacular, as such, but was rather a philological purpose, a hope for clues to "the mysteries" of Old Irish orthography. This concern is played out in the structure of the work itself: the bulk of his text takes up individual phones, describes each in articulatory terms, and then presents each as a reflex of a historical form. In addition to this phonetic and philological information, Quiggin presents a chapter on "synthesis," which deals with internal sandhi phenomena or surface phonotactics. Again, emphasis is placed on reference to earlier forms, pointing out sound change rather than synchronic alternation. Correspondences with forms in other dialects are included sporadically. Quiggin's study is a wholly phonological one, and any verb or noun alternations that may be found in this work appear by accident, mere illustrations of phonological events.

Although Sommerfelt's study is similarly heavily weighted toward the phonology of the Breton of St. Pol-de-Léon, we see here the inception of a structuralist approach to dialect studies—the St. Pol-de-Léon dialect is explored as a closed system and includes self-consciously limited references to historical sources. In contrast to Quiggin's work, Sommerfelt's study is not strictly limited to phonology, but includes a brief exposé of phrase-level syntactic organization, "M. Meillet m'ayant fait voir l'intérêt et l'utilité qu'il y avait à y joindre la grammaire" (Sommerfelt 1921, 5). More concerned with synchronic description than was Quiggin, Sommerfelt outlines his policy: "je me suis tenu strictement à la description, sans examiner l'histoire de la langue, sauf sur un ou deux points où c'était indispensable" (ibid.). Here the organization of Breton phonology approaches the "item and arrangement" template, as Sommerfelt lists various series of vowels, for example, and for each states the usual environment of its occurrence. The phonological description introduced in this study is elegantly precise, the environments succinct, and it is only in confronting the question of long and short vowels that Sommerfelt feels forced to bring in historical evidence. A short vowel "ne se présente que suivi d'un consonne qui était double en moyen breton, ou bien suivi d'une groupe de consonnes, ou encore en hiatus," while a long vowel "se trouve généralement en syllabe accentué suivi d'une consonne simple" (1921, 24). Sommerfelt also refrains from any cross-dialectal remarks, referring his readers instead to the forthcoming *Atlas Linguistique de la Basse Bretagne*, which he did not intend to preempt.

Works and authors cited by Sommerfelt can teach us much about the purpose and direction of his text. He presents a brief bibliography embracing other major Breton dialect studies while affirming two points. First, no historical works are included, and we are not to expect any such references in a work on a living dialect. Second, dialect studies are listed as reference materials, but they will not be cited in the body of the text, as he focuses attention on the Breton of St. Pol-de-Léon.

Significantly, Sommerfelt cites both Jespersen and Saussure in his Breton study, which leads us to inquire what influence these linguists may have had on his work. Jespersen, notably, emphasized the value of a study of "the living language" in his *Philosophy of Grammar* (1924), thus setting out the importance of spoken, rather than written, language for the development of a science of grammar. For both Jespersen and Saussure, a language must be analyzed in and for itself, and Sommerfelt aptly illustrates the structuralist tradition as he avoids historical or comparative evidence and presents the St. Pol-de-Léon dialect in systematic arrangement. Thus he illustrates paradigmatic relationships of singular–plural alternations, "conjugated" prepositions, and verb forms in the latter half of the study.

C. Borgstrøm's close study of the dialect of Barra (1937) and subsequent sketches of the dialects of the Outer Hebrides (1940) were preceded by various dictionaries and "pronouncing dictionaries" of Scottish Gaelic, but his work stands alone to announce the advent of modern linguistics to specifically Scottish Gaelic dialectology. Borgstrøm combines scientific accuracy of description with a diachronic perspective of language change, taking note of predecessors such as Quiggin and Sommerfelt. The organization of the section on vowels in the *Dialects of the Outer Hebrides*, for example, includes two subheadings: the phonological system, and the phonetic and historical description. The first section lays out in schematic form the nine vowels "with independent phonological value" (1940, 11) and introduces sets of minimal pairs "to prove the phonological independence of the nine vocalic timbres" (ibid.). A phonetic and historical description illustrates the vowel sounds in articulatory terms and presents correspondences between these vowel occurrences and historical O.Ir. and O.N. sources. This latter section is strongly reminiscent of Quiggin's work; a comparable concern for the philological usefulness of his text prompts Borgstrøm to include the historical orthography of each form, while rarely showing the contemporary Gaelic spelling.

Within the scope of Borgstrøm's work in dialectology, it is possible to interpret an awareness of the European model of phonological theory. The notion of distinctiveness is applied in his discussion of dependent versus independent nasality, where the dependent element of nasality in vowels is predictable from the environment, such as contact with a nasal segment, and need not be marked in transcription, while independent nasality must be so noted. The phoneme is seen as the minimal unit of the speech stream, a principle illustrated in a later discussion of the palatal consonants: these "are single phonemes, and not groups of the type *kj*" (1940, 18). In this he treats palatalization as a part of the stop and as somehow indivisible from it. Borgstrøm attests to this with evidence from articulatory and acoustic impressions, indicating that for a palatal k "there is only one movement of the tongue towards the palate," and the short glide following the stop can easily be distinguished from the "fully pronounced consonant i (j)" (ibid.), which is an independent unit, or phoneme. In addition to drawing a phonetic distinction between a single palatal consonant and a sequence of two segments, Borgstrøm directs our attention to the phonological importance of this distinction and to the "systematic opposition" of palatal and nonpalatal forms.

The theoretical importance of this systematic opposition is pointed up by a discussion of the "palatal" quality of the labials, where no such distinctive opposition applies. Again Borgstrøm appeals, on the one hand, to phonetics; on the other, to phonology. Acoustic correlates present only "indistinct and varying" palatalization of labials, while the systematic, phonological organization of the "correlation of palatality" here "depends entirely on surrounding phonemes, so that the opposition between non-palatal and palatal labials, even if it could be distinctly perceived, would have no phonological function" (1940, 18–19). That is, the occurrence of a palatal labial is predictable according to the environment, and therefore neither distinctive nor phonologically relevant.

From this discussion of palatal and nonpalatal segments, we approach something like the Prague school's notion of a feature of palatalization, as Borgstrøm specifies the behavior of the "correlation of palatality" that "pervades the whole system except the labials and h" (1940, 17).

Borgstrøm recognizes, then, an essential distinction between phonetic description and phonological organization, and in his dialect studies of Barra and the Outer Hebrides employs both methods to present the reader with an accurate picture of the spoken language. While phonological information is included, it is not the driving principle of Borgstrøm's studies, and we are warned early that the transcription throughout will be phonetic and not phonological. Unlike Sommerfelt's Breton study, Borgstrøm's *Dialects of the Outer Hebrides* offers a full diet of cross-dialectal comparisons and adds considerably to our corpus of Scottish Gaelic dialect data.

N. M. Holmer's studies of Kintyre (1962) and Arran Gaelic (1957) were originally composed in the late thirties, and thus belong to a prephonemic style of presentation. He shows an awareness of the phonemic principle without ever applying this method to his own work, warning that "it is sometimes difficult to know from the frequent modification of the different sounds in different environments what is an independent sound (a phoneme) and what is merely a variant, so the transcription will never be quite consistent" (1957, 5). Sections on "phonology" then are rather impressionistic phonetic descriptions, and little attempt is made to distinguish predictable variants from significant alternations. The sounds he describes "are to be considered as normal basic sounds," while certain variants, "although existing in the pronunciation of individual speakers, are nevertheless extraneous to the dialect" (1962, 38). As we have seen elsewhere, sections on historical correspondences and morphology (or "accidence") follow, but little syntactic information is included.

Magne Oftedal opens his study of Leurbost Gaelic with an acknowledgment to his teachers Marstrander, Sommerfelt, and Borgstrøm. Although a debt to the latter two is particularly evident from numerous references to the earlier dialect works, this investigation is the first of Scottish Gaelic dialect studies to situate itself firmly within a theoretical framework. L. Bloomfield's *Language* (1933) is the only general linguistic text to be included in the references, and we see the influence of this work in the body of Oftedal's study. A section on "Principles of Description" gives an outline of the goals of Bloomfieldian phonemics, and from the outset Oftedal warns his readers that "historical considerations will not be allowed to interfere with the synchronic analysis" (Oftedal 1956, 19–20). This is a far distance from Quiggin's philological approach to Meenawannia speech, where we saw the synchronic description of a dialect subsumed to the overarching importance of historical study. Instead, most forms in Oftedal's work are cited in phonemic transcription, while a more narrow phonetic transcription may be included in square brackets when the discussion warrants more detail. Oftedal will not disappoint readers interested in historical correspondences, however, for these too are included in separate sections reminiscent of Quiggin's format. Like his predecessors in Scottish Gaelic dialectology, Oftedal devotes the bulk of his study to the sound system of Leurbost Gaelic; later sections on morphophonemics and morphology are thorough, but for syntactic information we are referred to Borgstrøm. The section on morphophonemics develops the system of mutations so cherished by Celtic scholars, and here too Oftedal sees value in adopting a theoretical position on the representation of initial mutation. He breaks with the previous philological tradition in Celtic studies, implementing Hamp's (1951) proposal. This entails the use of a superscript symbol in phonemic transcription (for example, ^{L} for lenition), because "a morpheme which demands an initial mutation in the next word is not exhaustively described unless we provide it with a symbol for this quality" (1956, 164).

Indeed, the strength of Oftedal's dialect work lies in his ability to perceive the theoretical implications for the representation of a spoken language; his phonemic analysis is buttressed by the inclusion of prosodemes such as stress, intonation, and nasality, which are "superimposed on the succession of phonemes" and recognized as phonologically as well as phonetically significant.

Dialect studies of Scottish Gaelic (Dorian 1978; Ternes 1973) since Oftedal's writing have placed more emphasis on a consistent synchronic analysis and have played up the value of a theoretical framework. Ternes clearly delineates his concern for a strictly phonemic approach to dialect study, specifying that "what is needed for the synchronic description of individual dialects is the phonemic interpretation of those [specific] phenomena within the phonemic framework of every single dialect" (1973, 101). Thus we see the application of informed phonemics as a tool for the exploration of a spoken dialect.

Although Ternes includes detailed discussions of historical interest, it is always with a view to emphasizing the systematic coherence of a synchronic study. He maintains the strong position that historical evidence brings no explanatory power to a dialect study. A probing investigation of vowel sequences, including a discussion of svarabhakti and hiatus phenomena, illustrates his commitment to the phonemic principle. With *The Phonemic Analysis of Scottish Gaelic* we realize the value of bringing evidence from Scottish Gaelic dialects to bear on linguistic theory.

Although this paper has specifically focused on various theoretical approaches to Scottish Gaelic dialect studies, there is another side, equally important. Current linguistic theories will be challenged and moved forward with the inclusion of evidence from the Celtic languages. We hold out a hope that the Gaelic section of the Linguistic Survey of Scotland, now in motion at the University of Edinburgh, will serve as a magnet to this cause, drawing linguists and Celtic scholars to fathom together the mysteries of Scottish Gaelic dialects. Although the twin goals of synchronic description and historical comparison have typically been seen as conflicting, a respect for the specific principles and methods of each brings both depth and breadth to Scottish Gaelic dialectology.

ANNA BOSCH

University of Chicago

NOTE

* I wish to thank Professor Bill Darden for his helpful comments on an earlier version of this paper.

REFERENCES

Bloomfield, L. 1933. *Language*. New York: Holt.
Borgstrøm, C. 1937. *The Dialect of Barra in the Outer Hebrides*. Norsk Tidsskrift for Sprogvidenskap [NTS] 7.
———. 1940. *The Dialects of the Outer Hebrides*. NTS supplementary volume 1. Oslo.
———. 1941. *The Dialects of Skye and Ross-shire*. NTS supplementary volume 2. Oslo.
Dorian, N. 1978. *East Sutherland Gaelic*. Dublin: Dublin Institute for Advanced Studies.
Hamp, E. P. 1951. Morphophonemes of the Keltic Mutations. *Language* 27: 230–47.
Holmer, N. M. 1957. *The Gaelic of Arran*. Dublin: Dublin Institute for Advanced Studies.
———. 1962. *The Gaelic of Kintyre*. Dublin: Dublin Institute for Advanced Studies.
Jespersen, O. 1924. *The Philosophy of Grammar*. New York: Holt.
Le Roux, P. 1924–63. *Atlas linguistique de la Basse Bretagne*. Rennes: Plihon et Hommay.
Oftedal, M. 1956. *The Gaelic of Leurbost, Isle of Lewis*. NTS supplementary volume 4. Oslo.
Quiggin, E. C. 1906. *A Dialect of Donegal*. Cambridge: Cambridge University Press.
Saussure, F. de. 1949. *Cours de linguistique générale*. Paris: Payot.
Sommerfelt, A. 1921. *Le Breton parlé à Saint Pol-de-Léon*. Paris: Edouard Champion.
———. 1922. *The Dialect of Torr, Co. Donegal*. Oslo: J. Dybwad.
Ternes, E. 1973. *The Phonemic Analysis of Scottish Gaelic*. Forum Phonetikum 1. Hamburg: Helmut Buske Verlag.

An Impersonal Usage in Scottish Gaelic

I wish to draw attention to a Scottish Gaelic construction that is of fairly widespread occurrence in the literature but has not received much notice hitherto. It is perhaps most noticeable in poetry, where concision and precision are at a premium; but the examples to be cited from the *òrain luaidh* ('waulking songs') should warn us against thinking of it as a "literary" construction; and it is not absent from traditional prose narrative.[1]

The construction in question involves the use of *(a) bhith* (verbal noun/infinitive of the substantive verb *tha*) as an auxiliary to the verbal noun of another verb. Its effect is to give the action described an impersonal meaning—the nuance attained in the finite tenses and moods of the verb by the addition of the endings *-ar/-tar* (primary tenses), *-te/-teadh* (secondary tenses), and *-adh/-as* (preterite). The general context is that of subordinate noun clauses and explicative phrases dependent on nouns or nominal phrases, of the sort that is rendered in Gaelic by means of a verbal noun (intransitive verbs) or the so-called "accusative and infinitive" construction (transitive verbs; see Stewart 1876, 108; Fraser 1912, 219): Typical examples of this construction would be:

1. Thòisich mi air *taigh a thogail.*
   I began *to build a house* (literally, *a house to build/for building*).[2]
2. Feumaidh tu *coiseachd.*
   You must *walk* (literally, *a walking*).
3. Se *Iain a bhith tinn* a thug orm *tighinn dhachaidh.*
   It was *John's being ill* that forced me *to come home* (literally, *John to be/for being ill . . . to come/a coming*).
4. Dh'iarr mi orra sin a dhèanamh
   I asked them *to do that* (literally, *that to do/for doing*).

I now give some examples of the use of *(a) bhith* to express impersonal agency in sentences of this type:

5. Chunnaic mi *bhith gabhail* umad.
   I saw *people dressing* (literally, *taking about*) you.³
6. Nam faicinn . . . *bhith 'd chàradh* fo'n chrùn.
   If I could see *people placing you* under the Crown (in other words, placing you on the throne).⁴
7. Dh'fhairich mi fear làimhe fuaire
   's gliogadaich nan crios 'gam fuasgladh,
   's *bhith cur* nan arm an taobh shuas dhiom.
   I became aware of a cold-handed man, and of the clinking of belts being loosened, and of *somebody placing (his) weapons* alongside me.⁵

The actions described in the italicized portions of examples 5–7 are expressed, in Gaelic terms, as noun-equivalent phrases functioning as objects to the main verbs. The clause beginning *bhith cur* (7) is grammatically parallel to *fear làimhe fuaire* and *gliogadaich nan crios*.

In the next examples the equivalence is one of apposition to, or explication of, an expressed subject or object:

8. B'e sin an *sealladh* éibhinn
   bhith 'g imeachd air na sléibhtean.
   That was the pleasant *sight—people moving* on the hillsides.⁶
9. Dh'innsinn *sgeula* . . .
   nam faighinn éisdeachd . . .
   bhith marbhadh chéile . . .
   I would tell *a tale*, if I were given a hearing, (of) *people killing each other*.⁷
10. O 's truagh *an car,*
    bhith d' ar n-éileadh 's d' ar n-ar
    d' ar armaibh *'gar faileadh 's gar rùsgadh.*
    It is a sad *turn* (of events) for *people to be fleecing (?) us and stripping us* of our Highland dress, our land and our weaponry.⁸
11. Dh'aithnghinn *do long mhór* an caladh,
    a bhith togail a siùil gheala,
    fuaim an t-sìoda r' a cuid chrannaibh.
    I would recognise *your great ship* in a harbour; *people*

hoisting her white sails, the sound of the silk against her masts.[9]

In 11 the "recognising" extends to the bustle of activity suggested by the visual image of the ship. Again, the clause beginning *a bhith togail* is grammatically parallel to the noun *fuaim*.[10]

12. 'S *uaibhreach* dhuibh-se *bhith fiamhach*
     an taobh shìos de Bhun Abha.
     It *is a matter of pride* for you *that people* down beyond Bonawe *are fearful*.[11]

Here the "matter of pride" is equated with the *bhith* clause in a copula construction. In the next example the verb *leig* 'let', which is standardly followed by a verbal noun (intransitive verbs) or "accusative and infinitive" (transitive verbs), plays host to our construction:

13. Cuir do threud fo lann,
     's *na leig a bhith* dar geur-leanmhainn.
     Put your flock into the fold, and *do not let people* persecute us.[12]

The next example is particularly interesting, for it shows the speaker qualifying the impersonal—to a certain extent—by offering a gloss on the unspecified "person or persons" of the initial statement:

14. Chuala' mi *a bhi leughadh*,
     bharr air Reumair ioma fàigh,
     gu bheil curainean aig Séumas.
     I have heard (of) *men presaging*—not just the Rhymer, but many prophets—that James has heroes.[13]

If, as I suggest, each of the examples 5–14 bears a meaning that in a finite clause would require an impersonal form of the verb *bi* (*thathar* or similar), then it is obvious that each contains the agentive element that is integral (even though the agent in question is "unspecified" or "unidentified") to the latter. If we wished to translate 13 accurately and at the same time use an English passive verb we should have to say, "Don't let us be persecuted *by people*." The distinction between this and "Don't let us be persecuted" *tout court* is obvious in Gaelic. Thus, in 6, the Gaelic for 'you being placed' would be *thu (bhith) 'd charadh*; in 7, 'weapons being placed' would be *na h-airm (a bhith) 'gan cur*; in 8, 'people being killed by each other' would be *daoine (a bhith) 'gam marbhadh le 'chéile*; in 10, 'for us to be . . . stripped' would be *sinn (a bhith) . . . 'gar rùsgadh*; in 11, 'her white sails being hoisted' would be *a siùil gheala (a bhith) 'gan togail*; and in 13, "Do not let us be persecuted" would require the addition of *sinn* 'us'.[14]

The following example might seem to go against this principle:

15. Nach truagh leat fhéin mar thachras,
     na saoidhean a bh'agad am Preston,
     a bhith toirt diubh an airm 's am breacan
     le prasgan a' Bhùidseir.[15]

As one hears the statement develop, one anticipates an outcome similar to the previous examples:

> Do you yourself not regret the way things turn out: the heroes who followed you at Preston, that people should be stripping them of their weapons and plaids. . . .

But the verse is then brought to a conclusion by the addition (or so it would appear) of a specified personal agent—"by the Butcher's rabble"—which immediately suggests a reinterpretation of the preceding phrase as "(the heroes) . . . being stripped of their weapons." But there are other ways in which we can take 15, and I see no grounds for doubting our identification and interpretation of the construction.[16]

The next example I wish to cite also introduces an instructive ambiguity:

16. Dh'innsinn-sa beus an tighearn' òig dhùibh,
     taigh mór farsainn, ùrlar còmhnard,
     a bhith cur shaighdearan an òrdugh,
     le ghunna fo sgéith an dòblait.[17]

The passage is a traditional one—conceptually formulaic in the usual Gaelic manner elucidated by Ross (1959). It involves an image-building exercise designed to convey the atmosphere of the chief's house; and it is one that makes good use of our construction.[18] It begins:

> I would tell you the young laird's custom:
> a great spacious house, a level floor . . .

We start by taking the next line as

men arraying soldiers in rank;

but what follows gives us pause:

with *his* gun protected by the doublet;

for this most naturally suggests that the singer took the intervening line also to refer to the *tighearna òg*. That is, she probably took the line to mean "him (the young laird) arraying soldiers in rank." Our provisional expectation of *le 'n gunna* 'with their gun(s)' proved unfounded.

It is not necessary, however, to count this example as an exception to our interpretation of *(a) bhith* + verbal noun either. If we accept that the singer took the activity to be that of the 'young laird', we may suggest that *a bhith cur* stands for e (a) bhith cur, 'him arraying'.[19] On that hypothesis, 16 would be an example, not of the impersonal construction, but of the type exemplified by 1-4. Compare the following:

17. Làmh stiùradh nan stuadh
    i bhith deas no bhith tuath
    A hand capable of negotiating the billows, whether the wind (literally, 'it' [fem.], sc. *a' ghaoth*) were southerly or northerly.[20]

If the foregoing analysis is well-founded we may conclude that the role of the *(a) bhith* construction is straightforward enough: within the framework of verbal-noun usage adumbrated by examples 1-4 it enables the simple statement *Thathar ag òl* to be subordinated in various types of complex sentence in the same way that *iad/daoine a bhith ag òl* does duty for *Tha iad/daoine ag òl*. Such sentences are semantically close to sentences of a quite different syntactic shape, in which subordination takes the form of noun clauses with finite verbs introduced by *gu(n)*, for example, *gu bheilear ag òl* and *gu bheil iad/daoine ag òl*. The fact that the *(a) bhith* construction is not a particularly common type in contemporary Gaelic is to be ascribed to the incipient decline of the impersonal (that is to say, *tha iad/daoine* is beginning to oust *thathar*), and to the well-established tendency for the more distinctive and versatile *gu(n)* clauses to encroach upon verbal-noun constructions in most if not all the sorts of environment illustrated above.[21] Nevertheless, the construction still has its contribution to make to the language, as can be seen from the following recently noted example:

> Ciamar a tha thu a' faireachadh mu dhéidhinn *a bhith a' dùnadh* an àite?
>
> How do you feel about *the fact that they are closing* the place?

It is obviously advantageous to be able to focus on the fact that there are (nameless) people who are closing the place, as well as on the fact that a closure is taking place (*dùnadh an àite*), or on the fact that there is a place that is getting closed (*an t-àite bhith 'ga dhùnadh*), and so forth.

The fact that these *(a) bhith* impersonals occur as they do in Scottish Gaelic raises a number of questions, when one recalls that Scottish Gaelic has inherited what is essentially the verbal-noun syntax of Middle and Early Modern Irish, but that impersonality marked by the presence of *beith* is not a feature of that earlier system.[22]

In the first place, it may be asked whether we are dealing with a relatively recent Scottish Gaelic phenomenon—an idiosyncratic extension of the Common Gaelic usage of *beith* + *ag* + verbal noun ('being/to be engaged in'). Can it be motivated in Scottish Gaelic terms—for example, as an impulse to create an impersonal correlative to *mi (a) bhith* and the like, in order to enable statements like *thathar ag òl* to be subordinated using the verbal-noun construction during the period in which the periphrastic "progressive present" with *tha* was consolidating its stake in the language? Can we explain the mechanics of the development by clarifying the synchronic status of *(a) bhith*, which could be taken *prima facie* as (1) 'for being' (that is, continuing earlier *do bh(e)ith*), which might suggest the usual syntagm *X do bheith* with deleted or "zero" subject; or (2) as 'his/its being', which might suggest an embryonic impersonal possessive "one's" based on the unmarked third-person singular masculine; or (3) as 'being' (in other words, with meaningless or at least irrelevant *a* imported analogically from other environments), which might suggest the development of *bith* itself as an impersonal marker? I believe that in principle each of these alternatives could be supported.

Second, one cannot overlook the fact that Welsh seems to show a rather striking parallel to this construction, in the impersonal use of *bod* discussed by Richards (1938, 57–58); for example:

> A holl bobloedd y ddaear a welant *fod yn dy alw di* ar enw yr Arglwydd, ac a ofnant rhagot. (Deut. 28:10)
>
> And all the people of the earth shall see *that thou art called* by the name of the Lord, and they shall be afraid of thee.[23]

But what are we to make of the correspondence? May we add this category (which, as far as I am aware, is not paralleled in Cornish or Breton) to the list of Scottish Gaelic-Welsh parallels previously identified, which already numbers several items from the area of verb syntax, and which led Greene to state (1983, 107) that "the argument for the influence of the [British] substratum [on Scottish Gaelic] seems very strong"?[24] Or should we recall that such apparently neat correspondences as the Welsh and Scottish Gaelic "recent perfects" *mae John wedi newydd mynd* and *tha Iain air ùr thighinn* ('John has just gone/come') tend to be balanced by such equally neat correspondences as Manx *lurg* and Cornish *(war) lyrgh* (both used to perfectivize verbal nouns), where no theory of unique relationship has so far been adduced, and proceed with a more widely based model of Insular Celtic constraints and departure points for verbal-noun syntax and the usage of the verbal noun of 'to be'?[25] And, in either case, how will the perceptions gained outside Scottish Gaelic, whether gleaned from Welsh *bod* or from Old Irish *buith*, colour our thinking with regard to the origins and development of Scottish Gaelic *(a) bhith*?

To tackle these questions adequately would take us well beyond the limits and purposes of this note, which have been to establish the existence and credentials of the impersonal usage in Scottish Gaelic. If I have ended up with more questions than I started with, I hope that will be received with indulgence by Eric Hamp, to whom this experience is neither new nor daunting, but a perpetual stimulus from which so many branches of linguistic study derive benefit. Long may it so continue!

WILLIAM GILLIES

University of Edinburgh

NOTES

1. See note 10 below.
2. This, at least, is the conventional explanation; I believe that there are in fact grounds for supposing that it came to be understood as 'the house its building' (and similarly with 3 and 4 at some stage in the history of Scottish Gaelic.
3. Campbell and Collinson 1969-81, 1, line 226. In the numbered examples that follow, texts are given as printed in the sources quoted. Translations, however, are my own. Note that in translating examples 5-15, and the examples of the imper-

sonal construction cited in the notes, I have deliberately generalized the English active voice with "people" or "somebody" as subject. In some cases the passive voice could equally well have been used and might even have made a more felicitous English statement; though not without loss of nuance: see below. But in other cases (i.e., where intransitive verbs are concerned) the possibility of translating the Gaelic as an English "passive" does not arise.

4. MacLeod (1952, lines 841-43) translates "if I were to see thee . . . invested with the crown."
5. Campbell and Collinson (1969-81, 2, lines 447-49) translate "and of weapons being put beside me."
6. MacLeod (1952, lines 5516-17) translates "this was a happy picture—to be tramping on the hillsides." But "tramping" is an activity; the "picture" (which Donnchadh Bàn is concerned with) is of others bestirring themselves to go out hunting (or similar), where now all is deserted (cf. lines 5584-91).
7. Ó Baoill (1972, lines 454-56) translates "I would tell . . . a story if I were given a hearing . . . : that people were killing each other."
8. Campbell (1984, 141) translates "sad is our state, deprived of our land, and stripped of our arms and our clothing"; MacDonald and MacDonald (1924, 127) had given "how sad to be stripped . . . robbed. . . ." The text is difficult: I have provisionally assumed that *['s] dar [n-]armaibh* is intended, and that Campbell has correctly substituted *d'ar* for the *d'ur* of earlier editions. (One could equally read *ur* throughout; it is the change from one person to the other that is hard to accommodate.)
9. Campbell and Collinson (1969-81, 3, lines 1844-45) translate "I would recognise your galley . . . , when her white sails are being hoisted." Cf. *'S truagh nach cluinninn . . . bhith dol seachad* (2, lines 1387-89) translated ". . . when they're passing," with which I would agree if "they" includes the "host" (1387) and could be paraphrased as "(the sound of) men on the march" or similarly.
10. Compare the versions of the following phrase in successive tellings of the tale *Fear na h-Eabaid* recorded from Duncan MacDonald (Peninerine):

    D2 an àit anns na dh'fhairich e *a' bhuille*
    D3 an àit anns na dh'airich e *a bhith a' bualadh na buille*
    D4 an àit as an cual' e *bhith toirt seachad na buille*
    D5 an àite 'n cual e *bhith toirt na buille*

    Here 'the blow' gives way to 'someone striking/dealing/giving the blow', which in its turn reverts to 'the blow' in the version recorded from Duncan's son Neil (Bruford 1978, 30).
11. Mackenzie (1964, lines 2189-90) translates "it is a matter of pride with you that you are feared."
12. Campbell (1984, 103) translates "allow no more our harrying"; MacDonald and MacDonald (1924, 125) had given "let us not be hounded." Cf., with *feumaidh* 'needs, must', Campbell and Collinson 1969-81, 2, lines 836-39: *Dh'fheumadh e bhith làidir fearail . . . 'S a bhith 'g iarraidh sìdh dh'a anam*, "He would need to be strong and manly . . . people/someone to seek peace for his soul," where the editors translate ". . . and peace for his soul to be prayed for."
13. Turner 1813, 282; *a bhi* is, of course, for *a bhith*.
14. The relevant Gaelic distinctions, using *'gan cur* (literally, 'at their putting') are:

i. Active (definite): *tha iad 'gan cur* 'they [identified] are putting them [different from 'they']'
ii. Active (indefinite): *thathar 'gan cur* 'they [i.e., 'people'] are putting them [different from 'they']'
iii. Passive (definite): *tha iad 'gan cur* 'they [identified] are being put'
iv. Passive (indefinite): *thathar 'gan cur* 'they [i.e., 'people'] are being put'

Actual speech context usually clarifies topic and resolves ambiguity (cf., however, note 21 below). In subordinated infinitive phrases of our sort the above specimens seem to come out as follows: i or iii, *iad (a bhith) 'gan cur*; ii or iv, *(a) bhith 'gan cur*.

15. Campbell (1984, 123) translates "thy heroes . . . being of arms and plaid deprived by the Butcher's rabble." MacDonald and MacDonald (1924, 133) had given "the heroes . . . of all their arms and of their plaids stripped by the Butcher's rebel cattle [*sic*]."

16. It is a perfectly normal feature of uncontrolled natural speech for the speaker's viewpoint to be revised in the course of an utterance, with asyntactic results. This may be thought less likely to occur within the constraints of verse; but such spontaneous effects are not rare in the conceptually unruly poetry of Mac Mhaighstir Alasdair. In that case it would seem that the situational given of "their deprivation" underwent a shift of focus from "people depriving them" to "them being deprived." Alternatively, we may recall the wider use of *le* 'by the agency of' (e.g., *thuit X le Y* 'X fell by [the hand of] Y'), which raises two further possibilities. First, this could be a standard example of the impersonal construction followed by partial explication of the indefinite "subject," as in example 14: "that people [sc. the Hanoverian authorities etc.] should be stripping them . . . by the agency of the Butcher's rabble [sc. Cumberland's soldiers]." Second, we could take *toirt diubh* as 'taking off, divesting oneself of' and construe it with *na saoidhean* (i.e., as in example 3 above): "that the heroes should be divesting themselves . . . under compulsion from the Butcher's rabble."

17. Campbell and Collinson (1969-81, 3, lines 1851-54) translate:

> I would tell you the young laird's custom,
> A great spacious house, with level flooring,
> *Putting soldiers* into order,
> His gun protected by his doublet.

18. See Campbell and Collinson (1969-81, 3, line 25), and compare "Oran Mór Sgorabreac" (MacInnes 1962), lines 20-25:

> 'S gheibhte sud an taigh an uasail,
> *bhith 'g òl fion* á pìosan fuara. . . .
>
> 'S gheibhte sud an taigh mo leannain
> *muc 'ga sgrìobadh* 's *mart 'ga feannadh*.

(Note here the clear syntactic distinction between the impersonal construction "people drinking wine" and the passive "a hog being scoured and a beef being flayed"; "wine being drunk" would be *fion 'ga òl*.)

19. One should perhaps state that *a bhith* cannot simply be taken as 'his being' in Modern Scottish Gaelic. Although one can cite examples like *do chur chiùil 's mo ghabhail dhàn-sa*, "your musical accompaniment and my singing of song-texts"

(Ó Baoill 1972, line 1304), the use of possessives with verbal nouns is in general restricted, and in particular does not nowadays occur with *bith* 'being'. In example 16 we of course leave open the possibility of reinterpretation of a text that once contained the impersonal construction, e.g., in association with *le 'n gunna* 'with their gun(s)'.
20. Campbell and Collinson 1969-81, 1, lines 395-96 and 1355-56; and cf. 1, lines 1339-40: *Mac mo mhàthar rinn mo leòn / e bhith 'san fheamainn gun deò*, "My mother's son has occasioned my distress, (by) his being [literally, 'him to be'] in the seaweed lifeless."
21. 'More distinctive': cf. the ambiguity of examples like *fuil rìoghail nam buadh / bhith 'ga dìobradh san uair* (Watson 1959, lines 2436-37), which can mean "that the royal blood . . . should be rejected" or "the royal blood . . . —that people should be rejecting it," beside the nonambiguity of *gu bheil (i)* and *gu bheilear*. (Note that the version printed by Campbell (1984, 176) has eliminated the difficulty by another means.) 'More versatile': finite-verb noun-clauses give access to the full range of tense-aspect variation, which is not easily covered by the verbal-noun phrase. (For example, Gaelic lacks a perfectivizing usage like Middle Welsh *ry-* + verbal noun and has to resort to stratagems like *an dèidh na saoir a bhith 'ga dubhadh* (Campbell and Collinson 1969-81, 2, lines 141-42 and 514-15).
22. For the earlier system (and for Modern Irish) see O'Rahilly 1941, 262-71, and especially Gagnepain 1963, pts. 2-3.
23. More literally, or at least in keeping with the convention estabished (see note 3) for translating the Scottish Gaelic examples, ". . . shall see people calling you"— distinct both from "your being called" *(dy fod . . .)* and "their calling you" *(eu bod . . .)*. For this usage in Middle Welsh see Evans 1964, 164.
24. Cf. also Greene 1979-80.
25. For Welsh *newydd* see, e.g., Richards 1938, 19; Jones and Thomas 1977, 121 and 152. For Manx *lurg* see Kneen 1931, 142; Thomson 1952, 286; Broderick 1984, 108. For Cornish *(war) lyrgh* see Lewis 1946, 54.

REFERENCES

Broderick, G. 1984. *A Handbook of Late Spoken Manx*. 2 vols. Tübingen: Niemeyer.
Bruford, A. J. 1978. Recitation or Re-Creation? Examples from South Uist Story-Telling. *Scottish Studies* 22: 27-44.
Campbell, J. L. 1984. *Highland Songs of the Forty-Five*. 2d ed. Edinburgh: Scottish Academic Press.
——— and F. Collinson. 1969-81. *Hebridean Folksongs*. 3 vols. Oxford: Oxford University Press.
Evans, S. 1964. *A Grammar of Middle Welsh*. Dublin: Dublin Institute for Advanced Studies.
Fraser, J. 1912. A Use of the Verbal Noun in Irish. In O. Bergin and C. Marstrander, eds., *Miscellany Presented to Kuno Meyer*, 216-26. Halle: Niemeyer.
Gagnepain, J. 1963. *La syntaxe du nom verbal dans les langues celtiques*, 1: *Irlandais*. Paris: Klinksieck.

Greene, D. 1979-80. Perfect and Passive in Eastern and Western Gaelic. *Studia celtica* 14-15: 87-94.
———. 1983. Gaelic: Syntax, Similarities with British Syntax. In D. S. Thomson, ed., *The Companion to Gaelic Scotland*, 107-8. Oxford: Blackwell.
Jones, M. and A. R. Thomas. 1977. *The Welsh Language*. Cardiff: University of Wales Press.
Kneen, J. J. 1931. *A Grammar of the Manx Language*. Oxford: Oxford University Press.
Lewis, H. 1946. *Llawlyfr Cernyweg Canol*. 2d ed. Cardiff: University of Wales Press.
MacDonald, A. and A. MacDonald. 1924. *The Poems of Alexander MacDonald*. Inverness: Northern Counties Newspaper and Printing and Publishing.
MacInnes, J. 1962. Personal Names in a Gaelic Song. *Scottish Studies* 6: 235-43.
Mackenzie, A. M. 1964. *Òrain Iain Luim*. Edinburgh: Oliver and Boyd.
MacLeod, A. 1952. *The Songs of Duncan Ban Macintyre*. Edinburgh: Oliver and Boyd.
Ó Baoill, C. 1972. *Bàrdachd Shìlis na Ceapaich*. Edinburgh: Scottish Academic Press.
O'Rahilly, T. F. 1941. *Desiderius*. Dublin: Dublin Institute for Advanced Studies.
Richards, M. 1938. *Cystrawen y Frawddeg Gymraeg*. Cardiff: University of Wales Press.
Ross, J. 1959. Formulaic Composition in Gaelic Oral Literature. *Modern Philology* 57: 1-12.
Stewart, A. 1876. *Elements of Gaelic Grammar*. 3d ed. Edinburgh: MacLachlan and Stewart.
Thomson, R. L. 1952. The Syntax of the Verb in Manx Gaelic. *Études celtiques* 5: 260-92.
Turner, P. [Pàruig Mac-an-Tuairneir]. 1813. *Comhchruinneacha do dh'òrain taghta Ghàidhealach*. Edinburgh: T. Stewart.
Watson, W. J. 1959. *Bàrdachd Ghàidhlig*. 3d ed. Stirling: A. Learmonth and Son.

Writing Without Reading: An Illiterate Imperfect Speaker's Adventures in Writing Gaelic

In the spring of 1974, a young (in her early thirties) imperfect speaker of East Sutherland Gaelic (ESG) whom I had first met and begun working with in 1967 reacted to the news that I was about to make another visit by exuberantly writing the salutation of her answering letter, and its opening sentences, in Gaelic. There were three remarkable things about that. She was not literate in Gaelic, for one. For another, her Gaelic was neither fully fluent nor fully grammatical. And finally, most remarkable of all given the other two facts, it was perfectly clear to me what she was saying.

This young woman had spent the war years of her early childhood in her grandmother's household in the village of Embo, in East Sutherland. But at the age of about six or seven she joined her Embo born-and-bred parents in London, where they had lived before the war. Although her parents spoke Gaelic to each other automatically and regularly, they did not speak it to their daughters. My friend, the elder of the two daughters, had heard Gaelic all her life and was of a gregarious and curious temperament. The social life in her parents' London home was almost entirely Gaelic, as Embo exiles living in that city or its near vicinity gathered there regularly, especially on weekends. This particular group of exiles numbered about thirty in the early 1970s, but had been larger still a decade or two before. Except for special occasions (weddings, funerals), the full group was probably rarely together; but all of them were kin in one degree or another (plus affines), and my friend's mother kept the "*ceilidh* house" for that group by reason of her own vivacity, strength of personality, and ready hospitality. EI, my friend, liked people and liked language; by her own account she wanted to be on the social and linguistic inside, and she pressed her parents, especially her mother, to speak Gaelic to her, to teach her words, to include her in the lively

Gaelic interactions: "They [her parents] weren't paying [any] attention [to] what I was speaking. . . . It was me, I'm thinking. I was always saying to them, 'What's that you're saying?' It was my nose [i.e., curiosity, nosiness]!"[1] Through her own interest and effort, EI became the youngest "semi-speaker"[2] of East Sutherland Gaelic, with her mother her most regular conversation partner. Living in London but valuing her Highland village background to a particularly high degree, she consciously preserved and extended her knowledge of Gaelic until her mother's death in 1978 deprived her of her daily opportunities to use the language. She still makes an effort to keep up her Gaelic, though the deaths and changes of residence of older relatives continue to reduce the number of opportunities for her to speak Gaelic.

In the summer of 1974, after I had visited (and worked with both generations in the family) in London and gone north to Sutherland for four or five weeks, EI surprised me by writing part of another letter in Gaelic; and two more still, each with a slightly longer section in Gaelic, after I was back in the United States. At the time these Gaelic letters presented me with a major challenge: to forget what I knew of Gaelic orthographic conventions, figure out EI's method of writing the dialect we both spoke, and use it to write back to her so that she could understand me roughly as well as I understood her. For once it was advantageous to me that I had never studied Gaelic formally, spoke only an unusual and unwritten dialect, read standard Gaelic only with effort, and barely made shift to write the standard language.

Belatedly, a few years later, I realized that in EI's letters I had a unique document: a record of an illiterate and imperfect (but intelligent and intelligible) ESG speaker's ingeniously improvised system for writing her unwritten dialect. I asked for permission to use the letters I had kept for research purposes and it was gladly given. I had not done much beyond transcribing the letters into an approximation of normal Gaelic orthography, however, when—a full thirteen years later—I got a further boon: EI herself, on a visit to me this time. Practically at the front door EI found herself the proud possessor of a variety of highly local-patriotic items from the Bryn Mawr College bookshop, several decorative folders, pads, and writing implements conspicuous among them—and would she please keep a daily journal in Gaelic? The journal lasted all of four days, after which we were too busy doing other things; but it doubled the corpus on which this paper is based and so served its purpose.

The total number of Gaelic words in EI's letters and journal entries is only 794, but this is reckoning by EI's own word divisions. As she collapses a great many traditional words in her writings, whereas she only very, very rarely writes a single traditional word as more than one, the total word count would be quite a bit higher if her texts were converted into the closest possible traditional equivalent—even without supplying any of the particles and conjunctions that she quite frequently leaves out.[3] As there are four letters and four journal entries, they will be identified as L1 through L4 and J1 through J4, respectively. The letters were spaced about a month apart (April 9, May 22, June 24, and July 29, 1974). Because each was sent (without a copy being kept) and not available when the next was written, EI could not check back to see what spellings she had used before. She refers to this problem herself in L4: *Ha me cho sheesh how tigal me . . . ach ha nail me "sure," bail a "spelling" am new roods fad a cheam!* "I'm so pleased you're understanding me, but I'm not sure my spelling is the same way all the time!" The journal entries were written on four consecutive days, and I did not take away each entry as it was written. EI could turn back to an earlier day, if she liked, to see how she had spelled a word previously. Although the variations in her spellings offer convincing proof that she did not do this regularly, she may have done it here and there.

In writing from London, it is possible that EI sometimes asked her parents how to say something she wanted to write. But because they did not read and write Gaelic themselves, they certainly did not affect her orthographic choices. In Bryn Mawr, EI once asked me to remind her of a Gaelic word, namely the word for "Saturday." Although I gave the normal ESG pronunciation, /či'sɔːrn/, she wrote it in what was obviously her own normal pronunciation, because her journal rendering after hearing my version matched a rendering from L4 and was aberrant in both cases in substituting /š/ for /s/ in the second syllable of the word (*dishorn* was the L4 writing, *diishorn* the J1 writing). It seems quite certain that EI followed her own genius and wrote what was natural for her; certainly this is true of the grammar of her letters, which is that of a semi-speaker and does not approach the grammatical norms for even the youngest of the fluent speakers.

In her efforts to write letters and journal entries in a language she had never really seen in writing (apart from the odd greeting-card phrase, gravestone memorial inscription, or biblical quotation, possibly), EI had necessarily to operate in terms of the orthographic system she knew well, that of English. As a model, English orthography has certain advantages, in spite of its etymological bias and its corresponding—and notorious—disregard for phonological regularity (in the sense of using one symbol reliably to represent a particular sound). The common practice of combining two letters to represent a sound different from the value of either one separately offers a way of handling a relatively large number of sound distinctions, for example. And even the lack of phonological consistency offers a certain freedom, of which EI took full advantage. For a simple example that combines these two features, she freely uses the letter combination *ch* both to represent [č], as in English *which*, and to represent [x] and [ç], as in Scottish English *loch* and *dreich*.

Still, there are obvious obstacles to a sensible writing of Gaelic via an English model. If EI were a fully fluent speaker of ESG, for example, she would be faced with the need to represent distinctive vowel and consonant length and to represent such features as distinctively nasalized vowels, vowel qualities not matched by anything in English (most especially among the multiple-vowel sequences), palatalized consonants (lateral and nasal), and a velarized consonant (lateral). Like many other semi-speakers, however, she does not "have" distinctive vowel length or nasalization; she substitutes a consonant cluster (/rl/) for the velarized lateral, and more often than not she substitutes a nonpalatalized for a palatalized consonant in the position most "exotic" for English speakers, namely, word-finally. The vowel sequences that remain in her imperfect ESG are far fewer than those of a fully fluent speaker; though they will not be treated in the present limited study, they are among the more ingeniously handled of her challenges.

Although EI's ESG phonological inventory is reduced and her phonotactics slightly simplified (most notably by deletion of final consonants), her speech rhythms are surprisingly good. On the one hand this causes her difficulties in guessing at word boundaries, and because of the prominent liaison phenomenon of Gaelic, whereby the final consonants of unstressed or lightly stressed words fall under the stress of any following stressed vowel-initial word,[4] her difficulties are perfectly understandable. On the other hand, if the pacing and flow of her Gaelic is comfortable, as in familiar phrases, short and simple clauses, or strings of high-frequency conversational responses, she occasionally displays a conservative feature to a degree she can not reliably or consciously maintain. She does not "control" vowel or consonant length; because of the collapse of these phonological distinctions, semantic distinctions also collapse for her, and she has lost all plural marking in the rather large class of /n/-final ESG nouns that form their plural by doubling (in other words, lengthening) the /n/. Yet in a tape-recorded Gaelic interview with me in 1974, during which EI said of her parents' speech habits when she was a child *Bha aideas bruidhinn Gàidhlig, bha aid bruidhinn Beurl' riumas*,[5] "*They* were speaking Gaelic, they were speaking English to *me*," none of the traditionally long vowels is fully long, but *aideas* and the first instance of *bruidhinn* have half-long vowels, and the emphatic prepositional pronoun *riumas* has a very clear rendition of the geminate /m/ that is traditional for monosyllabic prepositional pronouns in final /-k/ and final /-m/ before the emphatic suffix /-əs/ in ESG.[6]

Initially I had thought to present here an overall analysis of the handling of phonological (as opposed to grammatical) features in EI's texts. Once launched on the analysis, however, and dealing for a start just with her vowel writings, I found evidence of a pattern that was—as far as I was concerned—quite unexpected and remarkably pervasive, affecting not only most vowel writings, as it turned out, but even consonant writings. Following its trail became more alluring even than investigating word division or vowel sequences in EI's Gaelic orthography, and the tracing of that trail occupies the remainder of this study.

Vowels and Stress

The Embo Gaelic of older fluent speakers has a vowel system with the following short-vowel distinctions:

i		u
e	ə	o
ɛ	a	ɔ

All of these may have distinctive nasalization for older fluent speakers, and all but /ɛ/ and /ɔ/ distinctive length. As already noted, however, neither nasalization nor length is distinctive for EI.

The most striking feature of EI's handling of vowels in her written Gaelic appears in connection with the four vowels that can occur both in stressed syllables and in unstressed syllables within a single word as well as within the general clause or sentence structure: /i u ə a/. Of these, the vowel that appears most commonly in unstressed syllables is /i/, and it was in tabulating the spellings of /i/ in EI's texts that it became apparent to me how marked a role stress played in the writings she chose for that vowel.[7] I will treat it here particularly fully for that reason.

In the simplest sort of counting exercise, the nicety of EI's distinctions is not fully evident. If one looks solely at spellings of stressed versus unstressed /i/, for example, the results appear as in table 1. Obscured in this tabulation is the fact that the spelling with the greatest overlap, *ee*, shows overlap primarily because EI spells the two personal pronouns /šĩn'/ 'we/us' and /i/ 'she/her' with *ee*, uniformly (eighteen occurrences) for *sheen* and two out of three times for *ee ~ e*. Because EI lacks distinctive nasalization and (in common with some others among the semi-speakers of ESG) often converts word-final /n'/ to [n] or [ŋ], there is little difference in pronunciation between English *sheen* 'luster, brightness' and EI's Gaelic *sheen* 'we/us'; the English spelling is most likely adopted for a quasi-homophonous Gaelic word. This explanation becomes quite persuasive if one looks at the way EI otherwise handles stressed versus unstressed /i/ when they occur next to each other or within one to three syllables of each other within a single clause.

There are twenty-four clauses in EI's texts that have stressed

Table 1. Spellings of Stressed and Unstressed /i/

Spellings	Stressed /i/ Number	Percent	Spellings	Unstressed /i/ Number	Percent
ee	36	56	e	56	48
i	19	30	i	35	30
ei	5	8	ee	23	20
ea	1	1.5	y	1	1
eea	1	1.5	ii	1	1
ui	1	1.5		116	100
e	1	1.5			
	64	100			

and unstressed /i/ in that sort of proximity. Some examples (here and subsequently given when between slashes in the traditional older fluent speaker's phonological—but not necessarily grammatical—form):

1. /ˈskriː mi/ *scree mi* (L2), *scree me* (L4) 'I wrote';
2. /va/ha mi ˈtʰigal/ *va me teegal* (L2), *ha me tigal* (L4) 'I was/am understanding';
3. /ɔrn ˈmiš ri ˈskriː rɛtʰ/ *orn meesh re scree ret* (L3) 'for me [emphatic] to write to you';
4. /ˈvi mi ˈširu ˈšəuɫ/ *vee me sheero sheourl* (J1) 'I'll be wanting to walk'.

Note that traditional vowel length is not a factor. In the third example stressed /miš/ is a short-vowel word and stressed /skriː/ a long-vowel word, traditionally; EI writes both with *ee*, as opposed to /ri/ in that same example written with *e*, and she likewise writes *me* in the unstressed fourth example's nonemphatic counterpart to stressed emphatic *meesh* of the third example.

Of the twenty-four clauses in which a stressed and an unstressed /i/ occur close by each other, only three fail to make a distinction in spelling between the two sorts of /i/ vowel. Two of the three exceptions involve *sheen* 'we/us' as an unstressed-/i/ spelling, which suggests that the attraction of the quasi-homophone's English spelling overcomes the avoidance of identical spellings for stressed and unstressed instances of the same vowel. The third exception is a genuine lapse: EI normally writes the future of the verb 'to be' in some fashion congruent with her stressed-/i/ spellings generally (*vees ad* [L2] 'you'll have to'; *bees am* [L4] 'I'll have to'; *vee me* [J1] 'I'll be'); but in J2 there is an instance of *ve me* 'I'll be'.

For a more revealing picture of the pattern of EI's /i/ spellings, a table that shows the various syllable types in which stressed and unstressed /i/ appears is necessary. Table 2 breaks down the stressed-/i/ occurrences into monosyllabic environments on the one hand and into bisyllabic environments in which /i/ is in either the first or the second syllable on the other. The percentages become more striking in such a breakdown: the *ee* writing is more clearly dominant in monosyllables, while the *i* writing becomes slightly more prevalent than *ee* writings in bisyllabic environments with /i/ in the first syllable; where stressed /i/ falls in the second syllable of bisyllabic words, the *ei* writing—only 8 percent of *all* stressed-/i/ writings—emerges as the favored spelling. For unstressed occurrences of /i/, the patterns are particularly systematic for the four most frequently occurring syllable types; only with the three least common syllable types is there no strongly favored spelling.

Viewed from a chronological perspective, EI's handling of the commoner unstressed-/i/ syllable types is actually still more systematic than table 2 shows. All five of the *i* writings for /Ci/ monosyllables appear in L1 and L2; the fifty-three subsequent appearances are consistently written *e*. With /i/ as the second-syllable nucleus of bisyllabic /'CVCiC/words (type 2), the only *ee* spelling appears in L1; the eighteen other appearances are consistently written *i*.

A still more obvious picture of differentiation between stressed and unstressed instances of the same vowel in EI's invented writing system is to be found in her treatment of /ə/. This vowel is phonetically least like any English vowel, among the range of ESG vocalic qualities, though some of its unstressed manifestations do have a schwa-like character more or less resembling the rather backed vowel of an English word such as *ugly*. In traditional ESG the long stressed form of /ə:/ is phonetically [ɯ:]; it has an exotic, unfamiliar sound to English-accustomed ears. Under stress, even the short form of this vowel is typically higher and more backed than the closest English parallels, the ESG value being closer to [ɣ] than to [ə].

EI is as wholly consistent as it is possible for her as a writer trained in English to be in her rendering of stressed /ə/: she uses the spelling *u*, again quite regardless of traditional length distinctions, except in the two lone cases (of nineteen) in which the initial consonant is /w/. English orthography does not allow the word-initial sequence *wu*- (except in a few dialect words carried over into the written language and in loanwords). In the two cases of /wə-/, both before an /s/, EI writes *wi*-, but in no other cases at all, stressed or unstressed; in view of English words such as *wistful* and *wisteria*, which in at least American English allegro speech can have [ɨ] as the first vowel, her choice of a *wi*- spelling is not a bad one. Examples of the dominant *u*-spelling for the vowel /ə/: traditionally long, /(ə)n ə:š am/ *nush am* (L3) 'my age'; traditionally short, /(an ə) šən/ *shun* (L3) 'here'.

The simplest charting of stressed and unstressed /ə/ writings in EI's texts shows the distributions indicated in table 3. Although the *u* so prevalent in the writing of /ə/ in stressed occurrences is also

Table 2. Spellings of Stressed and Unstressed /i/ According to Syllable Type

Stressed /i/ Spellings	Number	Percent	Unstressed /i/ Spellings	Number	Percent
Monosyllabic Words			**Monosyllabic and Bisyllabic Words**		
1. (C)(C)Ci(C)(C)			1. C i		
ee	29	67.5	e	53	91
i	9	21	i	5	8.5
ei	2	4.5		58	99.5
e	1	2	2. '—CiC		
eea	1	2	i	18	95
ui	1	2	ee	1	5
	43	99[a]		19	100
			3. CiC		
Bisyllabic Words			ee	18	100
2. (C)(C)iCV(C)(C)[b]			4. 'CVCiCVC		
i	8	53	i	9	100
ee	7	46.5	5. 'CVCC(VC)i		
	15	99.5	i	2	40
3. (C)V'CiC			ee	2	40
ei	3	50	y	1	20
i(—e)	2	33		5	100
ea	1	16.5	6. Ci'CVC		
	6	99.5	e	2	50
			i	1	25
			ii	1	25
				4	100
			7. i		
			ee	2	66.5
			e	1	33
				3	99.5

[a] Percentage columns in this and other tables may not add up to 100 percent because of rounding.

[b] The vast majority of all Gaelic words have first-syllable stress; but because EI writes as one word a number of phrases that are two in standard Gaelic orthography, more syllable types in her writing system are bisyllabic than is typical of Gaelic overall. Unless a tick (') indicating stress onset appears within the canonical-shape representation, stress should be assumed to fall on the first syllable.

Table 3. Spellings of Stressed and Unstressed /ə/

Spellings	Stressed /ə/ Number	Percent	Spellings	Unstressed /ə/ Number	Percent
u	17	89.5	e	54	52
i	2	10.5	a	23	22
	19	100	ø	5	5
			ue[a]	2	2
			o[a]	1	1
				103	100.5

[a] This spelling appears only in an orthographic variant of a word which otherwise has one of the spellings listed above the dotted line.

used for unstressed /ə/, it is less common than *e* or *a* in that position. Once again a syllable-specific tabulation of the unstressed-/ə/ writings shows that there are patterns of preference within the variety of representations (table 4).

There is one very marked reversal in the patterning of table 4 as compared with that of table 2: the highest-frequency syllable type shows the greatest variety of writings. The explanation is an interesting one: most of the variation is produced by repetitions of a single phonological form, velar stop plus /ə/, with (twice) or without (all other instances) final sibilant. The form /kə(s)/ accounts by itself for six of the eight *u* writings, both of the *ue* writings, and three of the four ø-writings (consonant *k* standing alone, no vowel written). The other two *u* writings occurred after /m/ in the first two letters; *u* was not used for the two later instances of /mə/. The other unaccompanied-consonant writing was also a stop, namely, *t*; and the lone *o* writing likewise occurred with a *t-*. There is phonetic logic, perhaps, to the choice of *u* to represent the vowel /ə/ in an unstressed vowel-final monosyllable after an initial velar; and the writing *que* as a variant of *qu* may well be influence from EI's school French. It is not accidental that the only two of the five unstressed /Cə(C)/ monosyllables that begin with stops show far the greatest variation in writings; but the discussion relevant to that matter belongs properly under consonants and not under vowels (see the next section). The aberrance of the two stop-initial monosyllables of this type can be summed up for the present purpose by noting that sibilant + /ə/

Table 4. Spellings of Unstressed /ə/ According to Syllable Type

Monosyllabic Words

Spellings	Number	Percent
1. Cə(C)		
e	23	55
u	10	24
ø	5	12
ue	2	5
a	1	2
o	1	2
	42	100
2. ə		
a	16	59
e	8	30
u	3	11
	27	100

Bisyllabic Words

3. (C)VəC		
e	12	52
a	6	26
u	5	22
	23	100
4. (C)ə'CV(V)(C)		
e	11	100

(eight instances) has no variants; dental nasal + /ə/ (six instances) appears five times as *ne* and just once as *na*; and bilabial nasal + /ə/ (four instances) appears twice as *mu* in the first two letters and then twice as *me* in adjacent journal entries, J2 and J3. By contrast, velar stop + /ə/ appears four times as *qu(s)*, twice as *que*, twice as *c(h)us*, and three times as *k* alone, attaining a settled spelling in none of the three texts in which it appears more than once. Similarly, dental stop + /ə/ shows the variants *te* (five instances), *de* (three instances), *t* alone (one instance), and *to* (one instance); and different variants appear in two of the three texts that contain more than one instance of the form.

For the vowel /u/, EI's writings continue to treat stressed and unstressed occurrences differently. The pattern of stressed-/u/ writings resembles that of stressed /i/, in that a variety of different spellings occur; but it resembles the pattern of stressed-/ə/ writings in that one spelling is greatly favored. The pattern of unstressed-/u/ writings is novel, as compared with those of unstressed /i/ and unstressed /ə/, in the sense that two spellings are equally prominent; but again there are patterns of preference according to syllable type among the unstressed-/u/ writings, despite the parity in number of occurrences overall for *u* and *oo*. Table 5 presents the stressed versus unstressed writings overall, and table 6, the seemingly more balanced unstressed writings sorted according to syllable type.

The vowel /a/, the last of the four vowels that can occur in both stressed and unstressed syllables within a single word, was relatively uncomplicated for EI.[8] The vast majority of the time she wrote *a* for all occurrences, stressed and unstressed alike. What little variation appears is confined to stressed-/a/ writings; and as there is *no* variation in unstressed-/a/ writings, even though they are fairly plentiful (sixty-six instances), there remains even in this unusually uniform case some difference in the way EI handles stressed versus unstressed occurrences of the vowel.

The only repeated deviation from simple *a* writings is one that is very noticeable, as it is not really a spelling characteristic of English writing. If English writers make any attempt to write stressed and/or lengthened [a], they resort most often to *ah* spellings: for example, *hah!; ah!; blah, blah, blah;* or *bah, humbug!*; exceptional is *baa-baa* for the sound made by sheep. In just ten instances out of eighty stressed-/a/ writings, EI doubled the vowel to write *aa*. This

Table 5. Spellings of Stressed and Unstressed /u/

Spellings	Stressed /u/ Number	Percent	Spellings	Unstressed /u/ Number	Percent
oo	38	79	oo	7	35
u	5	10	u	7	35
ou	2	4	ou	2	10
ew	2	4	o	2	10
eoo	1	2	ow	1	5
	48	99	e	1	5
				20	100

Table 6. Spellings of Unstressed /u/ According to Syllable Type

Bisyllabic Words

Spellings	Number	Percent

1. Postconsonantal word-final unstressed /u/

u	7	54
o	2	15.5
oo	2	15.5
ow	1	7.5
e	1	7.5
	13	100

2. Postvocalic word-final unstressed /u/

ou	1	100

Monosyllabic Words

3. (C)u(C)

oo	5	83
ou	1	16.5
	6	99.5

happened for the first time in L2, where she wrote *Naa cheam's hig oo k Looming, vees ad fourichal grush nas fad*, "Next time you come to London, you'll have to stay a little longer." Because the phrase /(ə)n a:/ 'next' has a long vowel in traditional ESG, I immediately supposed that she was doubling the written vowel out of some faint subliminal sense of the traditional length. There were no other traditionally long stressed-/a:/ vowels in the brief Gaelic text of that letter, but in the opening of the next letter a month later the word *gar* 'laughing' appeared with a single *a*, despite its traditional long vowel: /ka:r/. The irrelevance of traditional length became perfectly clear in the first line of the second paragraph of that same letter (L3), where a traditionally short and a traditionally long stressed /a/ appeared side by side, both written with the doubled vowel: *Neesh, draw fees ad k bael [personal name] se Vaal, draas?* "Now, did you know that *X* is in the village [Embo] just now?"—where *Vaal* represents traditional /val/ and *draas* represents traditional /(ən) dra:st^h/. Once again syllable type plays a certain role: double-vowel writings appear exclusively (though not by any means regularly) in monosyllabic /Ca(C)/ words. The particularly telltale instance is the phrase *qu daan sheen* 'until we arrived' in J1.

In traditional ESG, the irregular verb in that phrase, "arrive," has both bisyllabic (/hã:nig/, independent past, and /tã:nig/, dependent past) and monosyllabic (/ha:n/, /ta:n/) forms, the latter usually without nasalization and appearing only in casual speech. EI uses monosyllabic forms only twice, both times in J1. As the quoted phrase at the end of the last paragraph indicates, one of the short forms shows the *aa* writing that EI reserves for stressed monosyllables. The fact that she reserves the *aa* writing for that environment is highlighted by comparison with her handling of the bisyllabic forms of the same verb. There are five occurrences of bisyllabic forms of the verb "arrive" in her texts, but not one of them deviates from the single-*a* writing.

Naa is a nonce form in EI's texts, as are two others of the words with *aa* writings. Of those which have more than one occurrence, *draas* 'just now' has the double *aa* writing invariably (three instances), while *Vaal* 'village' shows variability (like *daan:dan*); it appears as *Vaal* three times in L3 and L4, but as *Val* once in L2. Table 7 sets out the writings of stressed and unstressed /a/ generally. The sole spelling not yet discussed (also not accounted for by variation within a particular stressed-vowel syllable type) is the writing of /čax/ 'went' (dependent) as *diach*, where the *i* before the *a* is most likely prompted by consonantal rather than vocalic considerations, that is, by the palatal sound of the preceding consonant.[9]

While the vowels /e o ɛ ɔ/ cannot occur outside the stressed syllable in a single word, they *can* occur with different levels of stress over the course of a sentence or a clause. And in plotting the distributions of various spellings according to stressed versus unstressed

Table 7. Spellings of Stressed and Unstressed /a/

Spellings	Stressed /a/		Spellings	Unstressed /a/	
	Number	Percent		Number	Percent
a	69	86	a	66	100
aa	10	12.5			
ia	1	1			
	80	99.5			

(or very lightly stressed) sentence/clause position, certain distinctive patterns again appear.

Of these four vowels, /ɔ/ has the highest frequency in EI's texts: fifty-five occurrences (in twenty different words). Sixteen of those fifty-five appear in elements that, by reason of their function in the sentence or clause in question, do not fall under stress (monosyllabic prepositions, one prepositional pronoun, and adverbs). There is no variation at all across those sixteen instances: all have the spelling *o* (examples: *vo* 'from', *orn* 'for', *to* 'to me', *cho* 'so'). Nouns, adjectives, verbs, the adverbial 'here', and a bisyllabic prepositional pronoun account for the remaining thirty-nine instances of /ɔ/: spelling variation appears only in stressed monosyllables, all other writings being again *o*. Table 8 sets out the various sorts of /ɔ/ occurrences that do and do not show variation in EI's writings. In this one case, the rendering of /ɔ/, it is fairly easy to understand how EI arrives at her writings. All fifteen /(C)Cɔ/ monosyllables written with *-aw* coincide with English quasi-homophones spelled the same

Table 8. Spellings of Stressed and Unstressed /ɔ/ According to Syllable Type

Stressed /ɔ/ Monosyllabic Words			Unstressed /ɔ/ Monosyllabic Words		
Spellings	Number	Percent	Spellings	Number	Percent
1. (C)Cɔ			(C)ɔ(C)(C)		
aw	15	83	o	16	100
o	2	11			
oaw	1	5.5			
	18	99.5			
2. (C)CɔC(C)					
o	5	71.5			
io	1	14			
eo	1	14			
	7	99.5			

Bisyllabic Words

3. /ɔ/ necessarily in the first syllable ('(C)(C)ɔ(C)(C)____)
    o   14   100

way (*draw* [for *d' robh*] 'was/were' (dependent), *shaw* 'here', *law* 'day'). Apart from the very earliest instances of 'here' and 'was/were' in L2, where they were written with *o* rather than with *aw*, no stressed or unstressed monosyllable written with *o* has an English quasi-homophone with *-aw*. The one /(C)Cɔ/ monosyllable written with neither, but rather with *-oaw*, appears relatively late (J1), when EI was no longer using the writing *o* for stressed vowel-final monosyllables; it lacked an English quasi-homophone. For this one word, *bloaw* 'warm', a curious hybrid with both writings combined appears.

Although the vowel /e/ is next most frequent in occurrence of the four vowels under review now, it is orthographically out of line with the others and will be discussed last for that reason.

The vowel /ɛ/ occurs twenty-two times; just seven words account for all of those instances, and of those /rɛtʰ/ 'to you' (sg.) accounts for eight and /fɛkən ~ y ɛkən/ 'seeing' accounts for another eight. (Four words have single occurrences.) In stress there is also very little variation: only the two occurrences of the prepositional pronoun /ekʰ/ 'at-her' and the one occurrence of the preposition /l'ɛ/ 'with'[10] are without sentence or clause stress. English does not provide the enticement of many variant spellings for its own /ɛ/ vowel, and EI writes this vowel as *e* with complete consistency. Nonetheless one minor effect from English orthography does appear, though for once it has no connection with stress or with syllable type. Where /ɛ/ appears before a voiceless velar consonant, EI goes over, in the journal entries, to writing *ck* (and twice, quite aberrantly, *ch*) for the consonant, using this device presumably to emphasize the short, lax character of the vowel. In the letters she had not done this (four instances of *yekan* or *yeken*); but in the journal all four instances of that word and its variant with initial *f-* have *ck* or (once) *ch*. Both instances of /ɛkʰ/ 'at-her' are journal occurrences; they also have *-ck/-ch*. Because syllable type *has* had an effect so frequently, it should be noted that two very distinct syllable types occur with /ɛ/, namely, /(C)ɛ(C)/ and /ˈCɛCVC/, without effect on the writing of /ɛ/.

The vowel /o/ is poorly represented in EI's texts. There are only twelve instances, six of them in the recurrent word /(ə)n oːrd/ 'up' and the other six each nonce forms for these texts. All twelve instances of /o/ appear in stressed syllables.[11] The word that accounts for half of all /o/ occurrences, /(ə)n oːrd/, is spelled with *oo* five out of six times; the sixth spelling is a single *o*. Single *o* is also the spelling of most other /o/ vowels, whether in monosyllabic or in bisyllabic words; but again there is a variant that almost certainly represents the influence of English quasi-homophones. The words /(ən) doːs/ *dose* 'first' (adv.; J4) and /lˈoːr/ *lŏre* "book" (L4) are written with final "silent *e*" as in the English words *dose* and *lore*. By contrast, EI writes *lōōr fad* (an imperfect-speaker rendition of /fad ə lˈoːr/ 'long enough') in L2 for the genuinely homophonous /lˈoːr/ *leòir* 'enough' (versus /lˈoːr/ *leabhar* 'book'); that is, with no silent final -*e*, though both /o/ words appear with diacritics. Diacritics are rare for EI (only nine in her eight texts); they are too rare, and too various, in fact, to be readily interpretable. Here and in one other instance they may be intended to represent a palatalized consonant, but the same diacritic is also used elsewhere in environments in which it is either unlikely to indicate a palatalized consonant (word-finally, where EI has mostly replaced palatalized with unpalatalized consonants) or would be incorrect as a palatalized consonant (though not impossible by analogy to a semantically related word). Generally speaking, EI's diacritics appear to be ad hoc; they serve best perhaps as reminders of the difficulty of the orthographic challenge she was undertaking.

For /o/ as for /ɛ/ there are two syllable types: monosyllabic /ˈCoC(C)/ and bisyllabic /ˈCoCV(C)/. Syllable type per se does not seem to have an effect, unless by chance the final /-CC/ has some bearing on the prevalence of *oo* writings in *noord*, the only one of five monosyllabic words to end in a consonant cluster rather than in a single consonant.

Finally we come to /e/, with thirty-one occurrences in EI's texts. This vowel has no close rivals for the variousness of its renditions proportionate to its occurrences. The vowel /i/ is written nine different ways, but it occurs 180 times. The vowel /u/ has eight written variants and sixty-eight occurrences. The vowel /e/, with just thirty-one occurrences, enjoys twelve different writings. This profusion has more to do with the lack of a settled or dominant writing for the nearest English counterpart than with stress (or its absence) or with syllable type. Tables 9 and 10 present displays for /e/ that can be compared to the tabular displays for more freely occurring vowels that likewise have many spellings, such as /i/ and /u/. The spellings for the syllable type /(C)Ce/ can be said to be distinctive, as they exclude the otherwise commonest spelling, *ai*, while themselves appearing in no other syllable type. Otherwise there is both great diversity and a wide distribution of the diverse spellings.

Table 9. Spellings of Stressed and Unstressed /e/

Spellings	Stressed /e/ Number	Percent	Spellings	Unstressed /e/ Number	Percent
ai	9	33	e—e	4	80
e	6	22	ai	1	20
ae	3	11		5	100
ay	2	7.5			
a—e	2	7.5			
ey	1	3.5			
é	1	3.5			
aa	1	3.5			
ea	1	3.5			
ee	1	3.5			
	27	98.5			

While the variability in writing /e/ is not strongly linked to any phonological feature, it is fairly strongly linked to EI's English literacy. Her dominant rendition (ten instances) is *ai*; five of the ten are quasi-homophones of English words (*nail* [*'n eil*] 'not', three instances; *bail* [*(am) beil*] 'is/are [dependent]' and *air* 'on', one instance each); the other five are candidates for orthographic analogy. The three *ae* writings (all in forms of the verb 'to be') might seem unusual but for the salience of the words *Gael* and *Gaelic* for EI. The three *ere* writings (for /er/ 'on') and the *care* writing (for /k^{h}e:r/ 'four') are transparent Anglicisms, in view of the final "silent *e*." The nonce writings *nay, glay,* and *shey* (for two different forms of the so-called "consuetudinal 'be'" and for the adverb /kle:/ 'very') follow English analogues (*say, hey, gray/grey,* and the like), though only the first has a common English quasi-homophone. Of the remaining six writings, one perhaps shows French influence, for an acute accent is used: *résh* (for /re:šč^h/ 'then'). Four are nonce writings for nonce forms, three of the four distinctly on the odd side compared with EI's other writings; the fourth, *yean* for /y ẽ:n/ (complementizer + lenited gerund 'getting'), has a solid model in the universal Scottish English pronunciation of the common clan surname MacLean with /e/ in the second syllable. Only one writing without clear English parallel repeats: /e/ is represented six times by the vowel *e* alone in vowel-final monosyllables. Five of the six are instances of the question-word /te:/ 'what?' which never takes any

Table 10. Spellings of Stressed and Unstressed /e/ According to Syllable Type

Stressed /e/ Monosyllabic Words			Unstressed /e/ Monosyllabic Words		
Spellings	Number	Percent	Spellings	Number	Percent
1. (C)Ce			eC		
e	6	66.5	e—e	4	80
ay	2	22	ai	1	20
ey	1	11		5	100
	9	99.5			
2. (C)CeC					
ai	6	46			
ae	3	23			
é	1	7.5			
a—e	1	7.5			
aa	1	7.5			
ea	1	7.5			
	13	99			

Bisyllabic Words

3. /e/ necessarily in the first syllable ('(C)eCV(C))

ai	3	60
ee	1	20
a—e	1	20
	5	100

other form in EI's texts; the other is the only journal instance of the word written as *shey* in L4. (The question-word *te* appears three times in letters and twice in the journal entries without variation; it is in fact the only truly stable /e/ writing for EI, because four other recurrent words have variant writings, and otherwise only *ainan* /e:nan/ 'birdie' retains its spelling—in two adjacent sentences in the same journal entry.

To sum up the situation with vowels, then, variation in EI's written representations is high for three of the four vowels that have the greatest freedom of occurrence (/i/, /ə/, /u/) and can be linked to differences in stress and in syllable type. In the fourth case, /a/, where the stability of English writings of the Scottish counterpart vowel[12] presumably plays a role in restraining variability in EI's Gaelic writings, what little variation appears nonetheless shows a link with stress and syllable type.

By contrast, variation in EI's written representations is low for three of the four vowels that have lesser freedom of occurrence (/o/, /ɛ/, /ɔ/); what variation there is seems linked to English spelling practices above all, rather than to stress or syllable type. In the fourth case, /e/, where there is a relative lack of constancy in the spellings of English counterpart vowels (whether American, Scottish, or English in pronunciation), six of twelve writings have English analogues and one has a French analogue; there is no notable link with stress, but one set of writings has a link to syllable type (/Ce/-final monosyllables).

Consonants and Stress

In connection with the variability in spellings of the unstressed /ə/ vowel in /Cə/ monosyllables, I noted above that among the five unstressed /Cə/ monosyllables that occurred in EI's texts, the two that begin with the stops /k-/ and /t-/ account for most of the variant writings. Those which have /s-/, /n-/, and /m-/ as initial consonants show little variation by comparison.

Fascinatingly, the connection of stop consonants with variant spellings does not end there. At the beginning of this paper I stated that EI does not control the initial consonant mutation known as nasalization. This means, for a speaker of ESG, that she does not have the three-way contrast in initial stops and affricates that arises via nasalization, for example: (1) /'pʰɛ̃n/ 'a pen', (2) /pɛ̃n/ 'a woman', (3) /(ə) bɛ̃n/ 'the pen' (with any vocalic representation of the definite article in the third example normally omitted after a vowel-final word, as in /xəi:l' mi bɛ̃n/ 'I lost the pen'). Because EI's first and dominant language is English, one might expect that she would use the voiced unaspirated stops/affricate /b d ǰ g/ in environments that call for either /b/ or /p/, /d/ or /t/, /ǰ/ or /č/, and /g/ or /k/; the latter are not distinctive in English and are in fact notoriously difficult for English mother-tongue learners of Gaelic (or French, for that matter) to learn to hear and produce. As it happens, EI does the opposite: she generalizes the voiceless *un*aspirated /p t č k/ series, only very rarely using the symbol for a voiced variant (and that haphazardly, not necessarily in environments that would call for nasalization).[13]

Because /p/ versus /b/, /t/ versus /d/, /č/ versus /ǰ/, and /k/ versus /g/ are not kept as distinctive contrasts for her, she might choose one writing and use it in all settings that call for either member of those pairs. And this is indeed what she does if two conditions prevail: (1) the consonants in question appear initially only (or almost so) in stressed syllables, and (2) English has a single accepted writing for the consonant in question. Both of these conditions apply in the case of /p/ and /b/. Among twenty-nine occurrences, all but one are clearly under stress (with that one potentially under secondary stress if the speech rhythm is slow). The few /p^h/-initial words that occur are also all in stressed syllables (five instances only); all are English loanwords, and EI follows English in writing them with *p*. She then writes the twenty-nine /p/- or /b/-initial words (of which in fact eight would be nasalized /b/-initial nouns or verbs in traditional ESG) uniformly with *b*-.

For /č/ and /ǰ/, neither of the conditions applies, though the first is a near miss. Most words with (traditionally) either of those consonants fall under stress—as do *all* words in initial /$č^h$/; but four weekday names with unstressed prefix in initial /č-/ do occur. Where the second condition is concerned, English of course has no single convention for the [dž] sound, and EI uses spellings in initial *d*-, *g*-, and *j*-.

Although there are only eighteen words in initial /č-/ or /ǰ-/ in EI's texts, and only four of them occur in unstressed syllables, a pattern of spelling variation emerges that is similar to the ones that appeared for writings of the more freely occurring vowels, as seen later in table 11. Most significantly, the dominant *stressed*-syllable writing (*g*-) is unique to stressed position, while one of the two *unstressed* writings (*j*-) is unique to that environment. EI's writings of initial (and always stressed) /c^h/ are without variation: eleven occurrences, 100 percent written as *ch*-.

Environments that would traditionally require nasalization are again not a factor. There are five nouns that would have to appear with /ǰ/ traditionally because of nasalization; of the five, EI writes two with initial *g*- and three with initial *d*- (the latter all instances of /(ən) ǰu/ 'today'); but *g*- initial and *d*-initial writings also both occur where nasalization traditionally would not be called for.

The situation is similar but not identical with the series /t^h/,

/t/, /d/. There are only ten occurrences of initial /tʰ/; all appear in stressed positions and all are written as *t-*. Although the writing *d-* is very heavily favored for stressed-syllable initial traditional /t/ and /d/, the writing *t-* is favored for *unstressed* initial /t/ or /d/, only a few of the latter appearing with initial *d-*. The fact that EI writes 93 percent of the stressed initial /t, d/ instances as *d-* certainly suggests that she hears the intermediate position of Gaelic unaspirated voiceless /t/ relative to English [d] (voiced, unaspirated) and English [tʰ] (voiceless, unaspirated). It seems downright odd that EI as an English speaker and writer does *not* respond to the fully voiced /d/ that traditionally results from the nasalization of /tʰ/—for example, for traditional /kəs (n) dɛ/ *cus an taigh* 'to the house', she both says [tʰ] and writes *t-* (*qus e te*, J1). Yet at the same time she has enough aural sensitivity to respond to the intermediate position of Gaelic unaspirated voiceless /t/ by writing the stressed occurrences largely differently from the unstressed occurrences.

Odd as this may seem, she repeats the same pattern in her handling of the series /kʰ/, /k/, /g/. The data are more complex for two reasons: (1) English offers several writings for the [kʰ] sound, and (2) a relatively large number of words in initial /k/ (though not /g/) can occur in unstressed position. The second of these factors is true of /t/ as well, but there are no spelling variations for initial [tʰ] and [d] in English to muddy the waters for a Gaelic speaker literate only in English.

There is total overlap in the letters used by EI to spell Gaelic initial /kʰ/ on the one hand and Gaelic initial /k, g/ on the other, but the complementarity of the distribution is striking, as table 11 shows. For initial /kʰ/, almost all occurrences are in stressed syllables; the dominant writing is *c-*. The sole unstressed occurrence of initial /kʰ/ is written with *g-*, a writing otherwise never used for initial /kʰ/. For initial /k, g/, by contrast, all stressed occurrences are written with *g-*, which never represents stressed /kʰ/. Among the unstressed occurrences (which outnumber the stressed occurrences only for b of series 3), the dominant writing is *q-*, a spelling that occurs for stressed initial /kʰ/ only if the next element is /-w-/, as is the case in three instances. (None of the unstressed *q-* writings for a /k, g/ is followed by /-w-/.) The second most common writing, *k-*, is also rare for stressed initial /kʰ/. Rarest of all for unstressed initial /k, g/ is the writing that is *commonest* for stressed initial /kʰ/, namely *c-*.

EI has repeated her unusual pattern: she responds sufficiently well to the intermediate phonetic position of voiceless unaspirated Gaelic /k/ to write it one way in stressed syllables and another in unstressed syllables, but she pays no attention to the distinction between fully voiced traditionally nasalized /g/ and voiceless nonnasalized /k/. Thus she writes /kʰɔriš/ 'along with him' with initial *c*-, but both traditional /kɔrštʰ/ 'sore' and /(ən) goːni/ 'always' with initial *g*-. She may be making an odd choice for an English speaker/writer, but she makes it with dazzling consistency.

Conclusion

The ingenious writing system devised by EI for her imperfect East Sutherland Gaelic was "invented" twice over: once when writing spontaneously in 1974, and once when writing on request in 1987. Across the thirteen-year interval, the feature discussed here remained a basic one in her writing system: all four vowels with greatest freedom of occurrence, along with all three stop-and-affricate series that occur with some frequency in both stressed and unstressed syllables, display a pattern with spelling variations according to stressed versus unstressed environment; and for the vowels (and even more so for the four vowels with lesser freedom of occurrence), variation according to syllable type is also notable, especially so in most cases for their renderings in unstressed environments (the vowel /a/ being the chief exception).

Because EI reads and writes English but had never previously read or written Gaelic, one looks of course to English for a prompting factor. And, within limits, one finds it.

The English vowels that have near equivalents in Gaelic and occur very widely in both stressed and unstressed syllables are /iy/, /ow/, and /ə/. It is possible to find English words that use the same spelling for these vowels regardless of the stress:

teepee, tipi   solo   what : Clara
key : monkey   so : also   bus : syllabus
fee : coffee   bow : elbow   Monday : sermon

But more often than not, the commonest unstressed-syllable spellings are different from the stressed-syllable spellings:

Table 11. Spellings of Initial Stop-Plus-Affricate Series in Stressed Versus Unstressed Syllables

	Stressed Syllable			Unstressed Syllable		
Spellings		Number	Percent	Spellings	Number	Percent
1. Series /čʰ, č, ǰ/						
a. /čʰ/	ch-	11	100	[nonoccurrent]	—	—
b. /č, ǰ/	g-	8	57	g-	0	0
	d-	6	43	d-	2	50
	j-	0	0	j-	2	50
		14	100		4	100
2. Series /tʰ, t, d/						
a. /tʰ/	t-	10	100	[nonoccurrent]	—	—
b. /t, d/	d-	41	93	d-	3	21.5
	t-	3	7	t-	11	78.5
		44	100		14	100
3. Series /kʰ, k, g/						
a. /kʰ/	c-	13	72	c-	0	0
	q-	(3)ᵃ	16.5	q-	0	0
	k-	(2)ᵇ	11	k-	0	0
	g-	0	0	g-	1	100
		18	99.5		1	100
b. /k, g/	g-	11	100	g-	2	10
	q-	0	0	q-	11	55
	k-	0	0	k-	6	30
	c-	0	0	c-	1	5
		11	100		20	100

ᵃ All three instances of initial /kʰ/ written as *q*- appear before an immediately following /-w-/. EI writes all three with initial *qu*-.

ᵇ One of the instances of initial /kʰ/ written as *k*- without doubt represents an initial [kʰ] (*kudgach* 'also'). The other appears in a word that has the initial cluster /kʰy/ in traditional ESG; it is spelled *kh*- by EI. Two other instances of words spelled *kh*- occur, both again initial /kʰy/ words; but because these other two occurrences are in positions that would permit lenition, producing [ç], it is impossible to determine whether EI intends initial *kh*- spellings to represent the cluster /kʰy/; the two additional occurrences of *k*- spellings in stressed syllables are discounted for purposes of this table (because they might represent [ç] or [kʰy] equally well).

key : shaky	hoe : Soho	rough : Clara
she : banshee	low : halo	bus : bulbous
bees : babies	doughnut : window	Monday : human
tease : cities	row : thorough	color : mocha
scene : casein		

The dominant English spelling for unstressed word-final /-iy/ is undoubtedly -*y* (*pony, grassy, idly*); it is almost never the spelling for stressed /iy/. The dominant English spelling for unstressed word-final /-ə/ is probably -*a* (*sofa, bandana, China*); it is rarely the spelling for stressed /ə/, where *u* (*cup, suffer, bluster*) and *o* (*come, love, mother*) and even *ou* (*double, tough, country*) are commoner. The dominant English spellings for unstressed word-final /-ow/ are probably -*ow* (*borrow, pillow, tomorrow*) and -*o* (*zero, ghetto, soprano*). Both do occur as common stressed-syllable spellings as well (*row, low, show; old, over, omen*); but there are several others that rarely or never occur outside the stressed syllable, such as *oa* (*boast, toad, foam*), *ou* (*soul, boulder*), and *oe* (*toe, foe, woe*).[14]

There is a model in English for EI's choice of different spellings for stressed versus unstressed versions of the same vowel, then. But to my thinking it is not by any means to be taken for granted that she would adopt that model and carry it to the extremes that she did. In her general aversion to using the same spelling for any stressed and unstressed /i/ vowels that appear near each other in a single clause; in her occasional use of double *aa* spellings for stressed—but never unstressed—/a/; and perhaps especially in her handling of the consonant series with stops and affricate (the voiceless aspirated elements mainly stressed and highly consistent in spelling; the voiceless unaspirated and voiced unaspirated elements differentiated above all according to stress patterns and not at all according to the voicing differences), EI seems to have followed with a remarkable degree of consistency an orthographic principle that she must have arrived at quite unconsciously. She did indeed go adventuring when she began to write in Gaelic, and she blazed a trail very much her own.

NANCY C. DORIAN

Bryn Mawr College

AN ILLITERATE IMPERFECT SPEAKER'S ADVENTURES IN WRITING GAELIC   243

NOTES

1. The English quotation is a translation from a Gaelic interview which EI undertook with me in her home in London in 1974.
2. Semi-speakers of ESG are characterized by the presence of forms in their speech that are explicitly recognized and labeled as "mistakes" by fluent speakers. The younger fluent speakers can also be shown to deviate from the traditional ESG norms represented by the speech of the older fluent speakers, but their deviations are less frequent and of a somewhat different type and are very rarely recognized as or called "mistakes." Even so, semi-speakers are able to manipulate ESG words well enough to produce intelligible phrases and sentences (beyond memorized strings), and they demonstrate excellent knowledge of the sociolinguistic norms of the ESG-speaking community generally. Within any particular village, semi-speakers are younger than the fluent speakers. Despite her London residence, EI is clearly an Embo semi-speaker by reason of her kin network, her age in reference to the age range for Gaelic speakers in that village, and her local dialect features.
3. To take one example, the third of EI's four letters has 132 Gaelic words, reckoning by her word divisions, but 148 reckoning by traditional word divisions.
4. I found that even the most fluent speakers did not know, in the case of etymologically opaque place-name elements, whether they were vowel- or consonant-initial in these circumstances: /skiˈrəːrd/ 'Rogart' [a village in East Sutherland] has /skiːr/ 'parish' as a recognizable first element, but even highly competent speakers were unable to say whether the name was 'parish of /rəːrd/' or 'parish of /əːrd/'.
5. The spellings used are chosen to render ESG dialect patterns.
6. See Dorian 1978, 114.
7. For purposes of analysis and tabulation, the clause environment of any particular word was taken into consideration in determining whether a syllable or word should be reckoned as stressed or unstressed. In this matter it was critically important that I had been a hearer/speaker of ESG for twelve years before EI began writing to me in Gaelic and that I had by then also worked seriously with her and with other ESG semi-speakers over a two- to four-year period. (Helpful too, of course, are certain features of Gaelic generally: the root-syllable stress pattern of native Gaelic words and the existence of special emphatic forms for personal pronouns in stressed position.) The chief ambiguities in EI's texts arose in connection with some instances of *ha* 'is/are' and *(c)ha* 'not'. Both typically occur sentence- or clause-initially, and how the rest of the sentence or clause proceeds sometimes, but not always, makes the stress value of *ha/(c)ha* clear. The following are examples of two clear-cut cases: *law ha sheen chean dachi* 'the day we're coming home' (where *law* and *dach-* have primary stress but *ha* in the relative clause is certainly unstressed in the absence of the [omitted] relative particle); *ha nail a parentan am ra* 'my parents aren't saying' (where *pa-* and *ra-* are most strongly stressed, but *nail* also falls under stress, while *ha* is unstressed). An example of an uncertain case is *Ha me tigal oos kudgach* 'I'm understanding you, too' (where *oos* and *ku-* have primary stress; *ha* 'am' is most likely unstressed, but could take secondary stress in a lento speech style). The instances that were uncertain in this fashion were left out in counts and tabulations.

8. In reckoning instances of the vowel /a/, the very high-frequency word *agus* was deliberately discarded. This is the one word all ESG speakers know how to spell and will bring up when discussing reading and writing Gaelic. It begins a great many Bible verses, and even speakers who know absolutely nothing else about Gaelic writing are familiar with it.
9. It is fortuitous that EI's spelling here is more or less in line with standard orthography. Of eighteen /ǰ/-initial words in EI's texts, only five appear with *di-* or *de-*, and of nine words with medial or final /ǰ/, none are written with *d* + front vowel.
10. This preposition does occur three times in the slightly different form it takes before the definite article. The ESG norm for this other form is /l'eš/; EI consistently writes *lish*. It may be that she is writing *i* because of the influence of the initial palatal consonant (especially because the final consonant is slightly palatalized, too) while still pronouncing an /ɛ/; but because I cannot be sure of this, I have left the three instances of *lish* out of account in all vowel counts and tables.
11. There is one possible instance of unstressed /o/, namely, in the preposition /ro/ 'before'. It would be a lone unstressed environment, if it does in fact have that vowel, as it would for an Embo fluent speaker. But as it has a very low incidence for EI generally and *would* be unusual precisely in having an /o/ in unstressed position, I am reluctant to tabulate it—especially as I have never heard her speak it spontaneously.
12. A great many words spelled with *o* but pronounced as [a] in most American English, such as *hot, common*, and the like, would not have an [a] vowel in Scottish English or in most varieties of English in England; many *a* writings with other values in American English *would* have [a] pronunciations in the Scottish English spoken by EI's parents, such as *family, dance, bat, rag*, and so on.
13. In another reported case in which overgeneralization appears in the weaker language of a feature not characteristic of the speaker's (and the wider society's) dominant language (Campbell and Muntzel 1989, 189-90), Woolard suggests (1989, 363) that the overgeneralization is motivated precisely by the uniqueness of the overgeneralized feature. It thus has a differentiating function for the speaker of the two languages.
14. Stressed-syllable spellings, especially in monosyllabic words, can of course become unstressed or lightly stressed spellings via compounding in English: *toe* : *tiptoe*; *cup* : *teacup*; and the like. Because they derive their spelling patterns from the noncompounded occurrences, they should be interpreted as stressed-syllable spellings displaced to unstressed position.

REFERENCES

Campbell, Lyle and Martha C. Muntzel. 1989. The Structural Consequences of Language Death. In N. C. Dorian, ed., *Investigating Obsolescence: Studies in Language Contraction and Death*, 181-96. Cambridge: Cambridge University Press.

Dorian, Nancy C. 1978. *East Sutherland Gaelic*. Dublin: Dublin Institute for Advanced Studies.

Woolard, Kathryn A. 1989. Language Convergence and Language Death as Social Processes. In N. C. Dorian, ed., *Investigating Obsolescence: Studies in Language Contraction and Death*, 355-67. Cambridge: Cambridge University Press.

PART IV

WELSH

Constituent Order in the Negative Declarative Sentence in the White Book Version of *Kulhwch ac Olwen*

The positive declarative sentence in the White Book version of *Kulhwch ac Olwen* is discussed in detail in T. A. Watkins, "Constituent Order . . . in *Kulhwch ac Olwen*," *Innsbrucker Beiträge zur Sprachwissenschaft* (1988): 5–24. Disregarding reporting phrases (e.g., *amkawd y urenhines* . . . "said the queen . . ." 453.28, where the verb is always in initial position), and all except the first example of recurring phrases (e.g., *kyt keffych hynny yssyd ny cheffych* "though thou may get that there is [that which] thou wilt not get" 480.10, and the like), there are 245 positive sentences. Adopting a similar basis of assessment, there are 56 negative declarative sentences in the text; their constituent order distribution is as follows.

Verb-initial

nyd oes plant itaw 453.33; *Ny chwyuei* ulaen blewyn arnaw rac yscawnhet tuth y gorwyd . . . 455.36; *ny wnaf* i dim o hynny 456.39; *ny weleis* i eirmoet dyn kymryt . . . 458.7; ny dothwyf i yma yr frawdunyaw . . . 459.18; *ny chauas* eiroet ae kyfrettei . . . 463.14; *ny allwys* mil pedwar troedawc eiroet y ganhymdeith . . . 463.17; *ny feit* neb dwuyr a than yn gystal . . . 465.7; *ny byd* gwasanythur na swydvr mal ef 465.10; *Ny cheffit* gwyn gwen arnaw . . . namyn tra uei lawn 467.14; *ny rygiglef* i eirmoet y uorwyn a dywedy di . . . 470.18; *nyt arswydwys* bedwyr y neges yd elhei gei idi 471.15; *nyt oed* neb kymryt ac ef yn yr ynys honn namyn arthur . . . 471.17; *ny chollet* oen eiroet ganthaw . . . 472.23; *Nyd athoed* kyweithyd hebdaw eiroet . . . 472.25; *nyt edeweis* uynet namyn hyt yd elhut titheu 472.33; *nyd oes* anaf ym llygru namyn uym priawt 473.5; *ny dodyw* neb y erchi yr arch honno . . . 473.19; . . . *ac nyd ai* idaw 473.26;

ny weleis i eirmoyt gelein gymryt a hi 473.37; *nyd oes* ouenic imi o hwnn . . . 475.8; *ac nyn lladawr* namyn y gyd 475.11; *ny thwyllaf* ui am crettwy 475.30; *ny daw* ef oe uod genhyt ti 480.14; *ny elly* ditheu treis arnaw ef 480.15; *ny wna* ef weith oe uod namyn y urenhin . . . 480.21; *ny elly* ditheu treis arnaw ef 480.23; *nys ryd* ef oe uod 480.28; *ny elly* ditheu treis arnaw 480.29; *ny cheffy* ti hi oe uod ef 481.24; *ny elly* titheu treis arnaw 481.24; *nys ryd* ef oe uod y neb 481.33; *ny elly* titheu y dreissaw ef 481.34; *nys ryd* ef oe uod 481.37; *ny elly* titheu y treissaw ef 481.37; *nys ryd* ef oe uod 482.5; *ny elly* titheu treis arnaw ef 482.5; *Nyt oes* yn y byt ae tynho . . . namyn odgar . . . 482.19; *Nyt ymdiredaf* y neb o gadw yr yskithyr namyn y kadw . . . 482.22; *ny daw* ef oe uod oe teyrnas 482.25; *ny ellir* treis arnaw ynteu 482.26; *nyt estwg* uyth ony cheffir . . . 482.29; *Ny mwynha* y gwaet onyt . . . 482.33; *nyt oes* lestyr yn y byt a gattwo . . . namyn botheu . . . 482.34; *ny ryd* ef oe vod 483.3; *ny elly* titheu y treissaw 483.3; *nyt aruaeth* [MS *arllaeth*] kaffel lleurith y bawb nes kaffel botheu . . . 483.5; *nys ryd* ef oe uod y neb 483.9; *ny ellir* treis arnaw 483.9; *Nyt oes* yn y byt crib a guelleu . . . namyn . . . 483.11; *nys ryd* ef oe uod 483.16; *Ny helir* twrch . . . hyny gaffer . . . 483.17; *Nyt oes* yn y byt gynllyuan a dalhyo . . . namyn . . . 483.20; *Nyt oes* torch . . . a dalhyo y gynllyuan namyn . . . 483.23; *Nyt oes* yn y byt kynyd a digonho . . . onyt mabon . . . 483.28; *ny wys* py tu y mae . . . 483.32; *nys [ryd]* ef oe uod . . . 483.37; *Ny cheffir* mabon vyth 483.38; *ny wys* py tu y mae nes kaffel . . . 484.1; *ny helir* twrch trwyth uyth hebdaw 484.6; *ac ny ellir* mwynyant a hi onyt ac ef yn vyw y tynnir oe varyf 484.10; *Ny at* neb oe vywyt gwneuthyr hynny idaw 484.13; *ny mwynha* hitheu yn uarw canys breu vyd 484.14; *Nyt oes* kynyd yn y byt a dalhyo y deu geneu hynny namyn . . . 484.16; *ny cheffy* ti ef byth 484.21; *Ny heli* twrch . . . nes kaffel . . . 484.23; *ny hebcorir* ef odyno 484.27; *Nyt oes* uarch a tyckyo y wynn y hela . . . namyn . . . 484.28; *ac ny daw* uyth yma 484.35; *Ny helir* twrch . . . vyth heb caffel . . . 484.36; *Ny helir* twrch . . . uyth nes kaffel . . . 484.38; *ny ellwngwyt* eiroet ar mil nys lladwynt 485.3; *ac ny daw* genhyt 485.6; *Ny ellir* hela twrch . . . vyth nes kaffel . . . 485.9; *nys ryd* ef y neb nac ar werth nac . . . 485.29; *ny elly* titheu treis arnaw ef 485.30; *ac nys keffy* 485.33; *ny oruyd* arnat na bwyt na dillat . . . 486.1; *nyt oes* yn y byt ny wyppo pieu . . . 486.14; *ny dodyw* neb guestei eiroet oheni ae uyw ganthaw 486.18; *ny edir* neb idi namyn a dyccwy . . . 486.20; *nys rygeueis* 487.10.

Non-verb-initial

Fronted subject. a mineu nys kelaf 454.7; *nac hi nae chennad* ny daw byth amdanunt 475.26; *na du na gwynn* ny doeth ohonaw etwa 481.8.

Fronted object. Namyn mab brenhin . . . ny atter y mywn 456.17; *ac a goryw pawb* . . . nys goruc ef 458.32; . . . *mi* ny cheffy . . . 476.35; *a[m] merch inheu* nys keffy 485.34.

Fronted adverbial. Py diaspettych ti bynhac am gyfreitheu . . . nyth atter y mywn hyny elwyf ui . . . 457.17; *bei gwnelhit uyg kyghor i* ny thorrit kyfreitheu . . . 458.23; *pan uei yn hwyl* [MS *wynhywl*] *kerdet yndaw* . . . ny cheisswys ford eiroet am gwypei . . . 463.22; *ac yn hyt y oes* ny flygwys konyn dan y draet anoethach . . . 463.29; *yr pan deuth ymma* ny thrigwys carn arnei uyth 463.38; *(osit rann imi oth uab . . .)* ac ny byd gwres yn y dwylaw 464.36; *pan dycco beich* . . . ny welir uyth na rac vyneb . . . 465.3; *or bei eisseu dim arnaw* ny adei ef hun uyth ar legat dyn tra uei yndi 465.15; *Pan elhynt y west* nyd edewynt wy na thew na thenau . . . 467.5; *hyd pan dywettych ti nat oes hi yn y byt* . . . nyn hyscarhawr a thi 470.33; *kyt bei unllofyawc* nyt anwaydwys tri aeruawc kyn noc ef . . . 471.21; *Pan debygynt vy eu bot yn gyuagos yr gaer* nyt oydynt nes no chynt 472.12; *pei mi rywascut uelly* ny oruydei ar arall uyth rodi serch im 474.30; *Rac eirychu pechawd iti ac i minheu* ny allaf ui dim o hynny 476.24; *ac ot amheu dim* mi ny cheffy 476.34; *namyn y gerdawr a dyccwy y gerd* nyt agorir 486.29.

Fronted object of verb-noun. Cleuydawd kei ny allei uedyc y waret 471.2.

The most obvious difference between constituent order of positive and negative declaratives in *Kulhwch ac Olwen* (as in all medieval prose texts) is in the frequency with which inflected verb occurs in initial position. In the positive sentence only 21 of the 245 examples are verb-initial, half with the verb in absolute initial (e.g., *Tyghaf tyghet* . . . "I swear an oath . . ." 454.16) and half with declarative particle *y(d)* preceding the verb (e.g., *ac y dyuu glewlwyt yr porth* "and Glewlwyd came to the gate" 458.31). The great majority have a non-verb constituent (in the following proportions) preceding the verb: (i) noun-subject (40) (e.g., *kilyd . . . a uynnei wreic* "Cilydd . . . wanted a wife . . ." 452.1); (ii) pronoun-subject (30) (e.g., *a thi ae keffy* "and thou wilt have it" 460.14); (iii) noun/pronoun-object (31) (e.g., *a gwreic arall a uynny ditheu* "and another wife wilt thou want" 452.30); (iv) verb-noun constituent of periphrastic verb (67) (e.g., *a chymryt y mab a oruc y meichat . . .* "and the swineherd took the boy . . ." 452.17); (v) adverbial (64) (e.g., *Dytgweith . . . y deuth y dy henwrach . . .* "One day . . . she came to an old crone's house . . ." 453.24; (vi) object of verb-noun (5) (e.g., *a hynny ol[l] a uynaf y wneuthur* "and all that, I shall want it done" 480.6). The figures suggest strongly that there was in the writing of MW prose a grammatical rule prohibiting the occurrence of verb in initial position of the positive declarative sentence. Of the 21 exceptions in the White Book version, some have been restructured in the later (and more careful) Red Book text so that the verb is no longer in initial position (e.g., *Tyghaf tyghet . . .* 454.16, *Mi a tynghaf dynghet . . .* Red Book 102.2; *Gorucpwyt hyny* "That was done" 477.16, *Hynny a wnaethpwyt* Red Book 118.21). By contrast, in the negative declarative sentence, verb-initial is the norm; it occurs in 32 of the 56 examples. The distribution of the 24 remaining sentences is: fronted noun-subject (3), fronted noun/pronoun-object (4), fronted adverbial (16), fronted verb-noun object (1).

In OW non–verb-initial declaratives, fronting could be either cleft or non-cleft, the formal distinction between them being presence (cleft) versus absence (non-cleft) of initial copula. When the fronted constituent was subject or object of inflected verb, there were two other formal differences, subordination of verb (cleft), and anaphoric reference to the fronted constituent (non-cleft). In the case of fronted adverbial, anaphora does not apply, and (with the exception of the occurrence of the interrogative adverbial conjunction *pan* 'where' in very limited circumstances) there was no oblique subordinating particle.

By the beginning of the MW period initial copula had, except for vestiges, disappeared, and there are no examples among the non–verb-initial negative sentences of *Kulhwch ac Olwen*. There was no inherited negative relative particle, and subordination is consequently not a distinguishing feature of either subject/object (or adverbial/verb-noun object) preposing. (The adoption of *na(d)* as a negative relative particle came about later.) In the case of subject/object fronting, however, anaphora does apply, and its presence in *a mineu nys kelaf* "and for myself, I shall not hide him" 454.7 (subject-fronted), as well as in *ac a goryw pawb* . . . *nys goruc ef* "and what everyone did, he did not do it" 458.32 and *a[m] merch inheu nys keffy* "and my daughter, thou shalt not have her" 485.34 (object-fronted), makes these sentences overtly non-cleft. The other two subject-fronted sentences are formally inconclusive because the subject is in each case a 3. sing. unit. The object-fronted sentence *Namyn mab brenhin . . . ny atter y mywn* "except for a king's son . . . (no one) is let in" 456.17 is also inconclusive despite the absence of anaphoric infixed accusative pronoun. The form reflects the 3. passive origin of Welsh impersonal verbs (cf. *pan dycco beich . . . ny welir uyth . . .* "when he carries a burden . . . it is never seen . . ." 465.3). (This passive meaning was later lost when accusative pronoun was introduced by analogy with 1. and 2. forms such as *ni'm gwelir* "I am not seen.") In all three formally inconclusive sentences the meaning is indicative of non-cleft fronting.

The remaining object-fronted sentence, *ac ot amheu dim my ny cheffy* "and if he doubts anything, (it's) I that thou wilt not get" 476.34, is, by absence of anaphoric pronoun, overtly marked as cleft. The cleft structure echoes contrastively the structure of the immediately preceding sentence, *adef ditheu y gaffel a minheu a geffy* "promise to get it and it's I too that thou shalt have." The Red Book, however, seems to have preferred a meaning associated with non-cleft fronting, as is indicated by its insertion of an anaphoric pronoun: *ac ot amheu ef dim mi nys keffy* "and if he doubts anything, me, thou will not get it" Red Book 118.9.

When adverbial (including verb-noun object) is fronted, there is no overt feature to distinguish cleft from non-cleft fronting. As in the case of subject/object fronting, the adoption of *na(d)* as subordinating negative particle was a later development, and whereas in the positive adverbial-fronted sentence, pronoun + *a* was gradually being adopted as a non-cleft marker (e.g., *onys agory mi a dygaf anglot yth arglwyd* "if thou dost not open it, I shall bring dishonour to your Lord" 457.2), this did not happen in corresponding negative sentences. But the meaning of all of the listed adverbial-fronted sentences is non-cleft—a judgement borne out by the relevant translations in G. Jones and T. Jones, *The Mabinogion*, Everyman's Library 97 (London, 1949).

Suggesting possible reasons for non-cleft fronting of adverbials is outside the scope of this article. It is noticeable, however, that all "scene-setting" adverbial clauses (both verb and verb-noun) are fronted, cf. 457.17 (manner), 458.23 (condition), 463.22 (time), 471.21 (concession), and 476.24 (purpose), whereas verb complements are not, cf. 459.18, 465.7, 472.33, 473.19, and 483.16.

T. ARWYN WATKINS

University College, Dublin

Word-Order in Old Irish and Middle Welsh: An Analogy

The normal word-order in Old Irish, as in Modern Irish, is VSO. As I have endeavoured to show elsewhere, however (Mac Cana 1973, 94ff.), this may be replaced in appropriate contexts by a noun-initial sentence (S/OV) belonging to one or other of several different types. The fronted *nominativus pendens* has a high frequency at all periods of Irish. Also relatively frequent is the use of subject or object followed by a nonrelative verb to convey emphasis, assertion, blessing, or imprecation: Mod.Ir. *Toil Dé go rabh déanta* "May God's will be done" (cf. the Middle Irish *Lucás dom leth roib* "May Luke be at my side" [Carney 1977-79, 434], or followed by a relative verb to indicate an explanation or response: *"Mícheál Rua a bhuail mé," ars an mac* " 'Mícheál Rua gave me a beating,' said the son." The latter occurs also in various other stylistically controlled contexts (Mac Cana 1973, 106ff.), while verb-final order with nonrelative verb is quite a common feature of syllabic verse in both Old Irish and Classical Modern Irish (Mac Cana 1973, 94-95; Greene 1977, 21). The inversion of the normal order of VSO in these types of sentence thus functions as a marker of various kinds of emphasis and as a stylistic and metrical variant in verse. To these types one may add the two familiar categories which I did not discuss directly in the article referred to: tmesis and sentences with noninitial verb, both of which were discussed by O. Bergin in his famous article in *Ériu* 12 (Bergin 1938).

The inference I drew from those types surveyed in my earlier article was that VSO was the norm in Archaic Old Irish as well as in Old Irish and that where S/OV occurs in Archaic Old Irish texts, it does so as a marked variant of the norm. This assumption is endorsed by David Greene (1977, 22). More recently, however, this might seem to have been obliquely queried by John T. Koch (Koch 1987, 169ff.), who believes that "the VSO pattern in Old Irish and Old Welsh prose was, relatively speaking, a recent occurrence." Noting the instances of verb-second sentences in the Welsh *hengerdd* and the Leinster poems, he proceeds from his analysis of the Gaulish evidence to the conclusion that this word-order was the norm in Old Celtic, more precisely that the verb-initial syntagm was the marked alternative to the neutral verb-second order. From this he goes on to suggest that instances of absolute verb-initial in the Welsh *hengerdd* are still marked for verbal emphasis. The argument (presented in his 1987 article and elsewhere) by which he arrives at his conclusion is impressive but leaves some problems unanswered; for the moment, however, I would merely reiterate a point made earlier (1973, 94), namely, that one cannot without considerable reserve and qualification use the evidence of verse to establish the patterns of word-order in normal contemporary prose, oral or written. Virtually all the types of S/OV that I cited in 1973, with the obvious exception of verb-final in syllabic verse, are found in the written prose of various periods as well as in modern spoken Irish. For tmesis and the noninitial verb sentence, the so-called "Bergin's Law," the position is quite different, however. These belong characteristically to verse or to otherwise artistically stylized language, and Heinrich Wagner has suggested that they and other examples of "unregelmässigen Wortstellungstypen" which he discussed are the artistic creation of the learned poets (*filid*) and jurists and therefore cannot be taken to reflect the normal speech usage of any period (1967, 304, 314). Certainly one cannot lightly accept them as a guide to general prose syntax, contemporary or antecedent.

In the present context I am concerned only with some variants of the tmesis-type sentence (excluding the "Bergin's Law" category with its noninitial verb but without a particle at the head of the sentence). This type has been discussed in some detail by a number of scholars, most recently by Greene (1977) and Fergus Kelly (1986). Greene distinguishes three subdivisions of the tmesis group: (1) the tmesis of deuterotonic compound verbs with one or more stressed words inserted between the unstressed preverb at the head of the sentence and the following stressed element: *Ath- cathu fri crícha comnámat -cuirethar* "he dispatches battalions to the borders of hostile neighbours" (Kelly 1976, 6, §15); (2) (which he regards as a development of 1) tmesis in which the encompassing elements are a negative particle (*ní, nád, nách*) and a conjunct or prototonic verb: *Ní mmo guin immgabaim* "I do not shun my death" (Bergin 1938, 211); and (3) tmesis similar to 2 except that the syntagm is headed by a particle other than *ní, nád, nách*, which is compounded with a form of the copula: *ceso femmuin mbolgaig mbung* "though I reap blistered seaweed" (Bergin 1938, 197), *manip fri fasach fuirmider sceo fur-*

santar fír Féine "unless the truth of Irish law be fixed and illuminated by precedent" (Bergin 1938, 199). Kelly (1986, 3) has pointed out that the criteria by which Greene distinguishes between 2 and 3 do not cover all of the relevant instances, for example: *naba fia thuaith taisilbe* (read *-taisilbea*) "who may not expound [?] before the people" (ibid.), which has both the negative particle (Greene's tmesis 2) and the copula (his tmesis 3). However precisely we classify them, it is specifically with those instances which combine particle and copula that I am concerned here.

Bergin (1938, 211-12) had surmised that the "meaningless copula" in sentences like *ceso femmuim mbolgaig mbung* derived from the dual role of *ní* (as well as *nád* and *nách*) as simple particle and as copula. He allows that by the Archaic Old Irish period a sentence like *ni mmo guin immgabaim* (Greene's tmesis 2) might well have been felt to contain a copula, which, if it were the case, would nullify the clear distinction that Greene observed between his tmesis 2 and tmesis 3; if the ambiguous forms of the negative particle were sometimes understood to contain the copula, as Bergin suggests, then one would not be surprised to find occasional examples, such as are noted by Kelly, of the negative particles combined with distinctive forms of the copula. Greene for his part (1977, 25) agrees with Bergin that it was this ambiguity in the negative particles that gave rise to the coupling of particle and copula which he designates as tmesis 3. Both of them observe that in general early Irish usage the particles *ce, ma, mani, dia n-*, and *co n-* occur only when followed directly by a verb or combined with the copula, and Greene adds that we cannot decide on the available evidence whether it had at one time been permissible to open a sentence with the bare particle; since then, however, Kelly (1986, 4-6) has cited instances from extant texts of *ma, mani*, and *co n-* used in this position without the copula.

The essential difference between Wagner's view of the evidence and that of Bergin and Greene is that he invests the copula with more significance than they do. The copula, he insists, is not "meaningless" in the tmesis construction, as is borne out by the fact it changes tense, mode, and aspect according to context; and he places considerable stress on the optional suppression of the copula, particularly in *roscad* and poetry, and, consequently, on the "kopulahaltig" or "kopulaartig" character of the several particles used at the head of the sentence. This leads him (Wagner 1967, 302-3) to see the cleft sentence as the source or model of the category of verb-final sentences introduced by the combined particle-copula. As Greene has shown (1977, 25-26), the evidence on which Wagner bases this argument is spurious, though he does agree that the influence of the cleft sentence may have led to the generalization of particle-copula in initial position. (Incidentally, Greene's statement that "the patterns of Tmesis III and of cleft sentences are identical, with the important exception of the verbal forms appropriate to each" is phrased a little loosely: it holds true for his cited example *manip fri fasach fuirmider sceo fursantar fír Féine* beside the cleft sentence **Manip fri fasach fo-ruimedar sceo for-osnathar fír Féine*, where the copula is followed by an adverbial phrase, but obviously not for instances such as *ceso femmuin mbolgaig mbung*, in which, as Bergin had long since remarked, the cleft sentence would have *femmun bolgach* in the nom. as well as a relative verb.)

What emerges from the contributions on the topic surveyed in this brief commentary is that the ambivalent negative particles *ní, nád*, and *nách* probably had an influence on the spread of the pattern particle-copula . . . conj./protot. verb, but that some doubt remains regarding its earlier evolution. For that reason it may be useful to take note of a somewhat analogous development in the syntax of the Middle Welsh sentence. As is well known, the normal independent sentence in (written) Middle Welsh is not VSO as in Modern Welsh, but rather S/OV, thus: *Deu uarchauc a doeth i waret i wisc hela y amdanaw* "Two knights came to relieve him of his hunting garb," *Pedeir Keinc y Mabinogi* 4.10; *Ef a'y hebryghaud yny welas y llys a'r kyuanned* "He accompanied him to where he saw the court and the dwellings," 4.1; *Ef a geif hynny yn llawen* "He will get that gladly," 17.24. When, however, the sentence opens with a preverbal particle or conjunction, this is followed by VSO: *ny chymerwn ninheu y gan y tayogeu hynny* "We will not take that from the churls," 53.28; *yny welynt y uarchoges yn dyuot yr vn ford* "until they could see the rider coming by the same road," 11.24; *yny want y mab yn wysc y benn yn y gynneu* "(and) he thrust the boy headlong into the blazing fire," 43.25; *A fan welas Uranwen y mab yn boeth yn y tan* "And when Branwen saw her son burning in the fire," 43.26; *Digawn yw gennyf i . . . ual y llunnyawd Riannon* "I am satisfied with the way Rhiannon has arranged it," 18.7; *O gwnaeth hitheu gam* "If she has done wrong," 21.17; *ony wdosti dim y wrth hynny* "if you have not some knowledge of that," 35.9. Naturally such cases account for a high proportion of the sentences with finite verb occurring in Middle Welsh prose texts.

I have noted a few instances, however, in which the preverb/conjunction is not followed directly by the verb, but instead is compounded with the copula and followed by the S/OV or "abnormal" order (and in which a cleft sentence is not indicated by the context):

1. *Mynet a orugant hyd pan deuuant y uaestir mawr hyny uyd kaer a welynt mwyhaf ar keyryt y byt* "Off they went till they came to a great wide plain and saw a fort, the greatest of forts in the world," *The White Book Mabinogi* 472.10 (*Kulhwch ac Olwen*).

2. *Mal y deuant eisswys ar un maes a hi, han ny* [= *yny*, The Red Book of Hergest 114.29] *vyd dauates uawr a welynt* "However, as they came to the same plain as it, they could see a great flock of sheep," *The White Book Mabinogi* 472.16 (*Kulhwch ac Olwen*).

3. *Kerdet a orugant wy y dyd hwnnw educher. hyny vyd kaer uaen gymrwt a welasit uwyhaf ar keyryd y byt* "They travelled that day till evening, until there was seen a fort of mortared stone, the greatest of forts in the world," *The White Book Mabinogi* 486.6 (*Kulhwch ac Olwen*).

4. *Ac y kerdassant hyt pann deuthant am y uagwyr ar karcharawr, yny uyd kwynuan a griduan a glywynt am y uagwyr ac wy* "and they travelled until they came to the other side of the wall from the prisoner, and they could hear wailing and lamentation on the other side of the wall from them," *The White Book Mabinogi* 492.32 (*Kulhwch ac Olwen*).

5. *onyt ef a wyr peth or hynn a geisswch chwi, ny wnn i neb ae gwypo* "Unless he knows something about what you are seeking, I know no one who will," *The White Book Mabinogi* 492.11 (*Kulhwch ac Olwen*).

6. *Ac nys mynnaf etwa, onyt ti a'm gwrthyt* "nor will I have him even now unless thou reject me," *Pedeir Keinc y Mabinogi* 12.25–26.

7. *Os ynteu a uyd, iawnach yw idaw dy gynnhal nogyt y mi* "And if he live, it is more fitting that he should support you than that I should," *Pedeir Keinc y Mabinogi* 26.28.

8. *"A uyn ef dyuot y'r tir?" "Na uynn, Arglwyd," heb wynt, "negessawl yw wrthyt ti, onyt y neges a geif."* " 'Does he wish to come ashore?' 'No, Lord,' said they, '—he has come on an errand to you—unless he succeeds in his errand,' " *Pedeir Keinc y Mabinogi* 30.17.

9. *Ac yn yr oes honno Math uab Mathonwy ny bydei uyw, namyn tra uei y deudroet ymlyc croth morwyn, onyt kynwryf ryuel a'y llesteirei* "And at that time Math son of Mathonwy could not live except while his two feet were in the fold of a maiden's lap, unless the turmoil of war prevented him," *Pedeir Keinc y Mabinogi* 67.7.

10. *". . . ac os gouut a daw, o gallaf les, mi a'e gwnaf. Afles ny wnaf inheu"* " 'and if trouble comes, if I can do good, that I will. Harm, however, I will not do,' " *The White Book Mabinogi* 139.171 *(Peredur).*

I have not sought out examples in verse for the reason that word-order can all too easily be influenced by metrical requirements, but the following instance from Gruffudd Llwyd ap Dafydd ab Einion may have the same structure:

11. *Da ydyw'r swydd, daed â'r sâl, / os Duw ni ddengys dial* "Good is the office, as good as the gift, if God does not show vengeance" (Rowlands 1976, 9.4).

Examples 1–4 have *(h)yny* (Old Welsh *hit ni*), which as a conjunction normally means 'until', but which is also used in narrative as a connective 'and' in the same way as Irish *co n-* (for the latter see Watkins 1963, 10; Thurneysen 1980, 555), and sometimes, as in 2, becomes almost as semantically weak as *co n-* in the narrative forms *co n-accae* and *co cuala*; like *co n-*, however, it may convey a suggestion of something new or unexpected when used with sense-verbs (cf. Evans 1976, 245). In 1–4 *(h)yny* is combined with *byd*, the form of the copula used in the sense of the historic present, and, given that *Kulhwch ac Olwen* contains many lexical and stylistic features not found in later prose texts, it is possible that *(h)yny uyd* was a familiar combination in early (oral) prose narrative that fell into disuse in the Middle Welsh period. This might explain the curious syntagm reproduced in the two following instances:

12. *Hwnnw hagen a darogannwys y corr ar gorres it a uu drwc Kei wrthunt. A thitheu ae dieleist." Ac ar hynny*

hyny vyd y vrenhines ae llawuorynyon yn dyfot " 'Yet the dwarf and she-dwarf, to whom Cei did injury, foretold it of you, and them you have avenged.' And with that the queen and her handmaidens came," *The White Book Mabinogi* 145.2-4 (*Peredur*).

13. *A phan yttoedynt uelly yn digrifaf gantunt eu gware uch yr wydbwyll, nachaf y gwelynt o pebyll gwynn penngoch . . . yny vyd mackwy ieuanc pengrych melyn llygatlas yn glassu baryf yn dyuot . . . yn dyuot tu ar lle yd oed yr amherawdyr ac Owein yn gware gwydbwyl* "And just when they were thus most preoccupied with their play over the *gwyddbwyll*, they could see coming from a white, red-topped pavilion . . . a young squire, with yellow, curly hair and blue eyes . . . coming towards the place where the emperor and Owein were playing *gwyddbwyll*," *The Red Book of Hergest* 153.8-21 (*Breudwyt Ronabwy*).

In 12 *(h)yny vyd* functions as a virtual synonym and syntactic equivalent of *llyma* 'voici, voilà' (cf. *nachaf* in 13), a usage that could have come about as a secondary development from the syntagm reflected in 1-4. In 13 *(h)yny uyd* is one of several stylistic devices exploited in a long and elaborate sentence in which the author is intent on displaying his narrative and descriptive virtuosity, and it gives the impression of a traditional formula not fully integrated into the syntactic sequence.

Since the S/O of the "abnormal" sentence is regularly followed by a relative verb, it becomes formally, if not semantically, indistinguishable from the cleft sentence when preceded by the composite particle-copula (in this regard it differs from Irish tmesis sentences with initial particle-copula). Normally this ambiguity does not arise, since the particle is followed by VSO. The only way it could be avoided while maintaining the subject or object in preverbal position would be to have the particle immediately before the verb—thus **y neges ony cheif* for 8 *onyt y neges a geif*—which, as far as I can recall, is unattested, at least in a subordinate clause; but where the order S/OV is maintained, the preceding particle cannot stand alone before noun or pronoun and must be conjoined with the copula. Bergin explained the union of particle and copula in Irish tmesis by the dual function of the negatives *ní, nád,* and *nách,* but this will hardly do for Welsh, where the simple particles *ny(t), na(t)* and the copula compounds coincide in form only when the former occur before vowels.

The main question with regard to the pattern particle-copula + subject/object + rel. verb is whether it is a relatively late and infrequent development or whether it is an older syntagm which is already obsolescent in early Middle Welsh. The instances in *Kulhwch ac Olwen* may suggest the latter, but a more definite answer must await further research and perhaps further evidence.

PROINSIAS MAC CANA
Dublin Institute for Advanced Studies

REFERENCES

Bergin, O. 1938. On the Syntax of the Verb in Old Irish. *Ériu* 12: 197-214.
Carney, J. 1977-79. Aspects of Archaic Irish. *Éigse* 17: 417-35.
Evans, D. S. 1964. (Reprinted 1976.) *A Grammar of Middle Welsh*. Dublin: Dublin Institute for Advanced Studies.
Evans, J. Gwenogvryn, ed. 1907. *The White Book Mabinogi*. Pwllheli: J. G. Evans.
Greene, D. 1977. Archaic Irish. *Indogermanisch und Keltisch: Kolloquium der Indogermanischen Gesellschaft . . . 1976 in Bonn*, hrsg. Karl Horst Schmidt. Wiesbaden: Dr. Ludwig Reichert Verlag.
Kelly, F., ed. 1976. *Audacht Morainn*. Dublin: Dublin Institute for Advanced Studies.
———. 1986. Two Notes on Final-Verb Constructions. *Celtica* 18: 1-12.
Koch, J. T. 1987. Prosody and the Old Celtic Verbal Complex. *Ériu* 38: 143-76.
Mac Cana, P. 1973. On Celtic Word-Order and the Welsh "Abnormal" Sentence. *Ériu* 24: 90-120.
Rhŷs, John and J. Gwenogvryn Evans, eds. 1887. *The Text of the Mabinogion . . . from the Red Book of Hergest*. Oxford: J. G. Evans.
Rowlands, E. I., ed. 1976. *Poems of the Cywyddwyr*. Dublin: Dublin Institute for Advanced Studies.
Thurneysen, R. 1946. (Reprinted 1980.) *A Grammar of Old Irish*. Dublin: Dublin Institute for Advanced Studies.
Wagner, H. 1967. Zur unregelmässig Wortstellung in der altirischen Alliterationsdichtung. *Beiträge zur Indogermanistik und Keltologie, Julius Pokorny . . . gewidmet*, hrsg. Wolfgang Meid. Innsbruck: Sprachwissenschaftliche Institut der Universität Innsbruck.
Watkins, C. 1963. Preliminaries to a Historical and Comparative Analysis of the Syntax of the Old Irish Verb. *Celtica* 6: 1-49.

Where Was *Rhaeadr Derwennydd* (*Canu Aneirin*, Line 1114)?*

Because nothing Celtic (nor, indeed, anything Indo-European) is alien to Eric Hamp, anyone honoured by an invitation to contribute to a *Festschrift* for him is faced with an *embarras de choix* when considering possible topics. But because he has written so learnedly, perceptively, and elegantly on problems relating to early Welsh poetics and poetry, including *Y Gododdin* (Ford 1983, 50-57), a brief note within that field may be thought not inappropriate. Such a note will hardly advance learning in the way that any one of Eric Hamp's numerous and varied publications is wont to do, but it is here dedicated to him as a small token of respect and affection for a scholar of towering stature.

Lines 1101-17 in the *Book of Aneirin*, as edited by Sir Ifor Williams (Williams 1938, 44; cf. Jackson 1969, 151) have generally been interpreted as an early Welsh cradle-song ostensibly sung by his mother to a little boy named Dinogad: even R. L. Thomson's darker reading (Bromwich and Jones 1978, 207) does not change this picture fundamentally. It has therefore been seen as an interpolation in the heroic poem *Y Gododdin*, which chiefly fills the manuscript; another such interpolation is the six-line fragment of a eulogy celebrating the victory of Owain ap Beli of Strathclyde over Domnall Brecc of Dalriada at the Battle of Strathcarron about 642 (Williams 1938, 39; Jackson 1969, 147). It is not proposed to challenge the received interpretation of either poem here, but merely to ask the question whether the cradle-song (which we shall call by its traditional title "Pais Dinogad") can be located and dated more precisely than hitherto.

All turns on the place-name *Rayadyr Derwennyd* "The Waterfall of *Derwennydd*" (line 1114, capitals supplied). As demonstrated by Eilert Ekwall (1928, 113-15, 121-23), and more precisely by Professor Kenneth Jackson (1953, 282, 351-53), Brit. *$Der\underline{u}éntiū$ 'oak river, river flowing through an oak wood' gave rise to numerous river names in England and one (through a by-form *$Der\underline{u}entíjū$) in

Wales; the Rom.-Brit. reflection is DERVENTIO (Rivet and Smith 1979, 333–36). The English names are as follows (pre-1974 county names are given in brackets):

>Darent (Kent)
>Dart[1] (Devon)
>Dart[2] (Devon)
>Little Dart (Devon)
>Darwen (Lancashire)
>Derwent[1] (Cumberland)
>Derwent[2] (Derbyshire)
>Derwent[3] (Durham, Northumberland)
>Derwent[4] (Yorkshire: North Riding and East Riding)

The sole surviving Welsh example is *Derwennydd* (Caernarvonshire), though there may once have been others (Thomas 1938, 137–38; cf. Lloyd-Jones 1928, 94); all occurrences of the name in Welsh seem to assume this form.

The question is, has any of these rivers a waterfall upon it striking enough to demand for itself the creation of a place-name Mod.W. *Rhaeadr Derwennydd* 'the waterfall on the Derwent' (or whatever other form the river's name took)? To answer this question with a fair degree of certainty each of the rivers named above would have to be surveyed from effluence or confluence to source, either on foot or from the air. In my case, however, lack of time precluded the one course, lack of money the other. Instead, recourse was had to the singularly unheroic expedient of writing to all of the English water authorities to ask them, if they had any appropriately named river within their area, whether that river had any significant waterfall(s). All water authorities replied, and all of their replies were uniformly negative. Severn Trent Water, however, sounded a note of caution about the Derbyshire Derwent because it has been heavily reservoired, and indeed a scrutiny of early maps has revealed a small waterfall (shown on the O.S. 6-inch map only) at SK 134980, some half-mile from the source; but this is of little account. The Welsh *Derwennydd* also has several waterfalls along its brief course (SH 692521, 694517), but the stream itself and the waterfalls are so puny as to make it highly unlikely that an established place-name would have come into being to mark them.

This leaves only one credible candidate for indentification as the *Rhaeadr Derwennydd* of "Pais Dinogad," and that is the Lodore Cascade at the southeastern end of Derwentwater in Cumbria (NY

265188) through which the Cumberland Derwent passes. The Lodore Cascade is not itself on the Derwent, but rather on Watendlath Beck; however, the fact that it falls into Derwentwater would clearly justify naming it *Rhaeadr Derwennydd*. It is a striking landmark, especially after heavy rain, and was celebrated as such by those who discovered the Lake District from the mid-eighteenth century onward (*Discovery* 1984, passim). Samuel Lewis called it "a stupendous cataract" (1831, 2.497) and Robert Southey, who lived nearby, immortalized it in a delightful poem—also, incidentally, written for a child (Grigson 1970, 105-8).

If *Rhaeadr Derwennydd* is in fact to be equated with the Lodore Cascade, the presumption must be that the place so designated lay within the borders of the North British kingdom of Rheged. While historians have disagreed about the true extent of that kingdom, there is probably a majority view that its centre was Carlisle, and Derwentwater lies not much more than twenty miles to the south of Carlisle (Williams and Williams 1968, xxxvi-xlii; contrast MacQueen 1961, 55-64). The poem is likely to have been the product of the household of, at the least, a local magnate: note the crucial reference to *wythgeith* 'eight slaves' (line 1104). Such a household is most unlikely to have remained in existence after the Northumbrian occupation of Rheged. Historians have disagreed also about the date of this occupation, but few would place it much later than the middle of the seventh century (Duncan 1978, 65; O'Sullivan 1980, 56; contrast Smyth 1984, 23-25). As it happens, we have what practically amounts to proof that the country around Derwentwater was in Northumbrian hands before 685 because the hermit Herebehrt, who lived on St. Herbert's Island in the lake, visited St. Cuthbert at Carlisle that year (Colgrave 1940, 124-25, 248-49). It would seem therefore that the cradle-song must have been composed toward the middle of the seventh century or earlier.

Granted that "Pais Dinogad" is a Rheged poem of about 650 or earlier, how did it get among the heroic *awdlau* of *Y Gododdin*? Both Sir Ifor Williams and Kenneth Jackson agree that it must have been through scribal error: an "early" scribe jotted it down on the margin of his copy of *Y Gododdin* and a "later," somewhat dim-witted, scribe incorporated it by mistake into the text. Both authorities also agree that the fragment of a Strathclyde eulogy celebrating the victory at Strathcarron about 642 was incorporated into the text of *Y Gododdin* in the same way (Williams 1938, l-li; Bromwich 1972, 62-63, 78-80; Jackson 1969, 46-48). The fact that we now seemingly have two seventh-century North British poems included by accident in the text of *Y Gododdin* very strongly suggests that the accidents happened as a result of scribal activity in North Britain itself, probably before the end of the seventh century. Because the kingdom of Gododdin is thought to have succumbed to Northumbrian pressure before the middle of the seventh century, and Rheged followed not long after, the only remaining North British kingdom was Strathclyde, which survived for a further two and a half centuries, with a notable ecclesiastical centre at Glasgow (Duncan 1978, 90–100; Smyth 1984, 215–18). It seems increasingly likely that the texts we now have of *Y Gododdin* had their genesis in a Strathclyde scriptorium sometime in the latter half of the seventh century.

I need only add that this tentative conclusion agrees remarkably well with that reached, by quite another route, by Thomas Charles-Edwards in his masterly chapter in *Astudiaethau ar yr Hengerdd* (Bromwich and Jones 1978, 44–72), and with the more general argument for early writing in Welsh recently advanced, most persuasively, by John T. Koch (1985–86, 43–66). The conclusion, however, merely replaces the earlier model for *Y Gododdin* of three centuries of oral tradition followed by another three and a half centuries of manuscript transmission, with a model positing a full six centuries of manuscript transmission. Such a change of model does not, of course, do away with the need to identify textual corruption and accretion, to the extent that this can be done; but it does render untenable the notion that the poem has its origin in a ninth- or tenth-century forgery (Greene 1971, 11).

As a postscript, one might note that A. A. M. Duncan has recently argued that Bede's Battle of Degsastan was in fact a British (not a Dalriadan) defeat at the hands of the Northumbrians (Davis and Wallace-Hadrill 1981, 16–19). Perhaps we should look again at the evidence for the wars between the Britons and the Angles in North Britain during the later sixth and earlier seventh centuries, in case a more convincing historical context than has hitherto been suggested for the Battle of Catraeth may not yet emerge (cf. Alcock 1987, 241–54).

R. GERAINT GRUFFYDD
Centre for Advanced Welsh and Celtic Studies
The University College of Wales
Aberystwyth, Dyfed

NOTE

* I wish to thank V. J. Adlard (South West Water), G. Amy (Southern Water), D. Badcock (Wessex Water), Ms. J. Belcher (Thames Water), L. Crowther (North West Water), J. Dodd (Anglian Water), R. Harland (Yorkshire Water), D. A. D. Reeve (Severn Trent Water), and N. J. Ruffle (Northumbrian Water) for their prompt and full replies to my letters of enquiry; also to my son R. Pyrs Gruffudd of the Department of Geography, Loughborough University, for investigating the upper reaches of the Derbyshire Derwent on my behalf.

REFERENCES

Alcock, L. 1987. *Economy, Society and Warfare Among the Britons and Saxons*. Cardiff: University of Wales Press.
Bromwich, R., ed. 1972. *The Beginnings of Welsh Poetry: Studies by Sir Ifor Williams*. Cardiff: University of Wales Press.
—— and R. B. Jones, eds. 1978. *Astudiaethau ar yr Hengerdd*. Caerdydd: Gwasg Prifysgol Cymru.
Colgrave, B., ed. 1940. *Two Lives of Saint Cuthbert*. Cambridge: Cambridge University Press.
Davis, R. H. C. and J. M. Wallace-Hadrill, eds. 1981. *The Writing of History in the Middle Ages*. Oxford: Clarendon Press.
The Discovery of the Lake District. 1984. London: Victoria & Albert Museum.
Duncan, A. A. M. 1978. *Scotland: The Making of the Kingdom*. Edinburgh: Oliver & Boyd.
Ekwall, E. 1928. *English River-Names*. Oxford: Clarendon Press.
Ford, P. K., ed. 1983. *Celtic Folklore and Christianity*. Santa Barbara and Los Angeles: McNally & Loftin.
Greene, D. 1971. Linguistic Considerations in the Dating of Early Welsh Verse. *Studia celtica* 6: 1–11.
Grigson, G., ed. 1970. *A Choice of Robert Southey's Verse*. London: Faber.
Jackson, K. H. 1953. *Language and History in Early Britain*. Edinburgh: Edinburgh University Press.
——. 1969. *The Gododdin: The Oldest Scottish Poem*. Edinburgh: Edinburgh University Press.
Koch, J. T. 1985–86. When Was Welsh Literature First Written Down? *Studia celtica* 20–21: 43–66.
Lewis, S. 1831. *A Topographical Dictionary of England*. London: S. Lewis & Co.
Lloyd-Jones, J. 1928. *Enwau Lleoedd Sir Gaernarfon*. Caerdydd: Gwasg Prifysgol Cymru.
MacQueen, J. 1961. *St Nynia*. Edinburgh: Oliver & Boyd.
O'Sullivan, D. M. 1980. *A Reassessment of the Early Christian Archaeology of Cumbria*. Unpublished University of Durham M.Phil. dissertation. (I have to thank Professor Leslie Alcock for drawing my attention to Miss O'Sullivan's work.)
Rivet, A. L. F. and C. Smith. 1979. *The Place-Names of Roman Britain*. London: Batsford.

Smyth, A. P. 1984. *Warlords and Holy Men: Scotland 80–1000*. London: Edward Arnold.

Thomas, R. J. 1938. *Enwau Afonydd a Nentydd Cymru*. Caerdydd: Gwasg Prifysgol Cymru.

Williams, I. 1938. *Canu Aneirin gyda Rhagymadrodd a Nodiadau*. Caerdydd: Gwasg Prifysgol Cymru.

——— and J. E. C. Williams, eds. 1968. *The Poems of Taliesin*. Dublin: Dublin Institute for Advanced Studies.

The study of the earliest Welsh poetry is likely to be significantly advanced by two recent publications from the National Library of Wales: *Early Welsh Poetry: Studies in the Book of Aneirin*, ed. Brynley F. Roberts (1989); and (with the South Glamorgan County Council), *Llyfr Aneirin: A Facsimile*, ed. with an introduction by Daniel Huws (1989).

Twin Mystery Verbs of the *Canu i Gadfan*

The *Canu i Gadfan*, a Welsh poem dating from the second or third quarter of the twelfth century and preserved in the early fourteenth-century Hendregadredd manuscript, contains two anomalous and perplexing verb forms in a text that is otherwise fairly clear, as *Gogynfeirdd* poems go—in syntax and semantics, at least, if not always in its frame of reference.[1] The first occurs in line 26, in the context of a list of three miraculous altars to be found in St. Cadfan's church at Tywyn in Meirionydd:

	teir allawr gwyrthuawr gwyrtheu glywed. yssy[t]
24	rwg mor a gorwyt a gwrt lanwed.
	allawr ueir or peir hygreir hygred.
26	allawr bedyr yw uedyr y **dyruolhed**.
	ar drydet allawr a anlloued o nef.
	Gwynn y uyd y thref gan y thrwyted.

The second of the problematic verbs occurs in line 36. The poet continues to occupy himself, in this passage, with praise of the physical splendors of the church:

	eglwys gadyr gaduann gann gynweled.
34	eglwys wenn wyngalch wynhaed.
	eglwys fyt a chreuyt a chred. a chymun
36	ual wrth duw eu hun y **dyrlunhyed**.

The forms in boldface type appear to be impersonal verbs in the imperfect subjunctive or preterite indicative (Evans 1964, 126, 129) preceded by the simple affirmative particle *y(d)* (Evans 1964, 171–72). Read as such, however, they pose challenging lexical questions, presenting us as they do with the otherwise unknown roots *dyruol-* and *dyrlun-*.

Henry Lewis (1931, 234) regroups characters in line 26 to arrive at the form *yd yruolhed*. He then reads the verb's initial *y-* as an error for or variant of *a-*, interpreting *yruolhed* as *arfolled*, the impersonal preterite of *arfoll*, 'receive, accept, welcome', which makes good enough sense in semantic context. Similarly, he takes the *dyrlunhyed* of line 36 as an orthographical variant of *darlunied*, the impersonal preterite of *darlunio* 'form, fashion, represent, depict', which also makes good semantic sense.

One difficulty with Lewis's emendations is that, while alternation of the vowels *a* and *y* is common before nasals (for example, *amherawdyr/ymerawdyr*; Evans 1964, 2), this is not true in other environments (Morris-Jones 1913, 16–17). More specifically, we do not typically find *yr*- as a variant of the prefix *ar*- (< Brit. *are- < Celt. *ari-), though the variant *er*- is common enough (in the third-person present indicative of *arfoll*, for example, that is, *erfyll*) and the tendency toward confusion of *y* and *e* could account for the remainder of the transformation. Nor does *dar*- (< Celt. *do-are) normally alternate with *dyr*-, a distinct prefix (< Celt. *do-(p)ro-), though a confusion of the two cannot be ruled out. Lewis's analysis of the form in line 36 poses an additional problem in that the verb *darlunio* is not attested before the late sixteenth century (*GPC*, 894a).

Lewis's readings of the two verbs are sufficiently uncertain, then, that it may be permissible at this point to suggest an alternative analysis, particularly because John Lloyd-Jones (1931–63) offers no assistance with these difficult forms. I should like to propose that we consider reading *y dyruolhed* (line 26) as *yd(d) yr folhed*, and *y dyrlunhyed* (line 36) as *yd(d) yr lunihed*, with both forms exhibiting the same unusual collocation of two introductory affirmative particles, the second with a perfective function. The verbs themselves, according to this interpretation, are impersonal imperfect subjunctive forms of the verbs *moli* 'praise, extol' and *llunio* 'shape, fashion', respectively.

The particle *y/yd* (with *y* before a consonant and *yd* (= *yð*) before a vowel, is, of course, the standard preverbal affirmative particle in Middle Welsh, and occurs regularly "with an adverb or adverbial expression preceding" (Evans 1964, 171), which would appear to be the syntactic context of both verbs in question here. The difficulty is that in the orthography of α, the main hand of the Hendregadredd manuscript, and the hand responsible for this poem (Huws 1981, 3), *d* ordinarily represents *d*, while *ð* is represented by *t*, so that my analysis of the forms under discussion appears to involve a different preverbal particle *yd* (= *yd*). There are several ways of addressing this difficulty.

One possibility is that the particle is not *y/yd* (= *yð*) but *yt* (= *yd*). Such a particle occurs in early Middle Welsh (Evans 1964, 171–

72; Williams 1935, 67–68, 112; Williams 1938, 136), normally before a verb beginning with a consonant (but cf. Morris-Jones 1913, 286) and sometimes supporting an infixed pronoun (Evans 1964, 56). Most cited instances of this particle are found in the *Gododdin* and in the *englynion*.

Another possibility is that *yd* is a scribal error for the expected *yt* (= *yð*). If the scribe understood a *-d-* in his exemplar to be the initial letter of a verb, he would naturally have represented that initial consonant by *d-*, whether or not he understood it to have undergone lenition. Such is the orthographical convention of α: initial *d-* and initial *ð-* are both represented by *d-*. It might be appropriate, then, in the reanalysis of these verbs, to read *ydd* as the original introductory particle.

As for the particle *yr*, which has become in Modern Welsh the simple affirmative particle before a vowel, it originated as a variant of the perfective *ry*. Examples of its use as an affirmative particle occur from the mid-fourteenth century, but in the twelfth century it would seem to have been still very much related to *ry* (Evans 1964, 169; Williams 1951, 170–71; Williams 1938, 251, 366).

What is unusual, of course, is the collocation of *yd(d)* and *yr*: normally, only one of these particles is attached to a given verb. Evans (1964, 63), however, cites instances of *y ry* and *yr ry* (mostly in relative clauses), and Strachan points out that in prose, at least, "*yd* is sometimes found before *ry*, even when there is no infixed pronoun" (1909, 56). The *Hirlas* of Owain Cyfeiliog, poet-prince of Powys, affords a possible example in the poetic record, though *yt* here might be *ŷd* 'grain': *llys ywein ar preid yt ry borthet eiryoet* (Evans 1911, 1432.24–25).

Despite evidence for the possibility of particle doubling in Middle Welsh, the precise collocation *yd(d) yr* (as opposed to *y/yd(d) ry*) is somewhat anomalous. The only other instance I have been able to find occurs in the Book of Taliesin, also in conjunction with an impersonal verb: *ac ar wyneb gwyn yd yr gaffat* (Evans 1910, 39.21). Nevertheless, it appears to have been a possible construction.

Moreover, analyzing *yr* as a variant of *ry* that retains perfective force (which has not, that is, come to be felt as a simple affirmative particle, utterly redundant after *yd(d)*) accounts satisfactorily for the lenition of the initial *m-* of *moli* in line 26 and perhaps for the apparent lenition of the initial *ll-* of *llunio* in line 36 as well. Joseph Loth pointed out nearly eighty years ago that the perfective *yr* might be distinguished from the simple affirmative particle *yr* by its lenition of a following consonant (1910, 349). In the case of *llunio*, devoicing of initial *l-* after *-r* might be expected (Evans 1964, 20); but that rule is not strictly observed in Middle Welsh, and perhaps the identification of the two forms of the perfective particle permitted lenition to operate after *yr* as if the particle were in fact *ry*.

The verb ending *-ed* is characteristic of the third-person singular imperative (Evans 1964, 115), sometimes of the preterite impersonal (Evans 1964, 126), and occasionally of the impersonal imperfect subjunctive (Evans 1964, 129). The imperative appears to make no sense in the context of either of the two lines in question. Reading the verbs as impersonal preterite indicative forms (as Henry Lewis did) makes good sense but fails to account for the *-h-* in each. Lewis seems to have taken the *-lh-* of *dyruolhed* in line 26 as an alternative digraph for *-ll-*, but that usage seems generally to have been unknown until the sixteenth century (Morris-Jones 1913, 10, 22). Such an *-h-* in a verb ending is most readily taken as a sign of the subjunctive. In line 36, a subjunctive verb is entirely appropriate, because a contrary-to-fact situation is being described: "as if it had been fashioned by God Himself." The orthographical preservation of the *-h-* would appear to be something of an archaism, but it is at least sometimes written in subjunctive forms (Evans 1964, 128). *Lunyhed* might be expected rather than *lunhyed*, but basically nothing stands in the way of reading this verb as an impersonal imperfect subjunctive given pluperfect meaning by *yr* (< *ry*).

In the case of the verb of line 26, *yd(d) yr uolhed*, the subjunctive verb appears to express the desirability of *moliant*: in other words, the line might be translated "Peter's altar—for its authority it should be praised." The function of the particle *yr* (< *ry*), if this interpretation is correct, is not perfective, but rather optative, a usage found frequently enough with the present subjunctive (Evans 1964, 168) and presumably not impossible with the imperfect.

This analysis, it may be noted, accentuates a parallelism between the two forms which also marks both the Lewis emendations and the manuscript forms. It might be argued on the one hand that the manuscript parallelism is merely a function of the scribe's attempt to make sense of one form by reference to another, so that preserving it only perpetuates error and confusion. On the other hand, the occurrence in a single poem (and in relatively close proximity) of *two* obscure verbs apparently beginning with *dyr-* seems unlikely to be a sheer coincidence. More readily credible, in my view, is the notion that, having hit upon *yd(d) yr folhed* as a phrase well suited to the metrical/syntactic/semantic requirements of line 26, it came naturally to the poet to repeat the construction in a similar environment at the end of the first section of his poem, that is to say, in line 36.

That line is the last with *prifodl -ed* before the commencement of the second section, or *awdl* (lines 37–66), with *prifodl -ydd*. Thus, the poet's constraints here included the need to effect *cymeriad* (linking) with the first line of the following *awdl*. The verb affords one very practical means of executing the *cymeriad*: one conjugated form can be used in the first line of the pair of linked lines and another in the second. In this case, as I read it, the poet employed two forms of the verb *llunio* 'shape, fashion': the impersonal imperfect subjunctive in line 36 and the third-person singular preterite in line 37 (Evans 1964, 123). The result, in the orthography of the manuscript, is

> ual wrth duw eu hun y dyrlunhyed.
> Llunywys y dews dewisedryd itaw,

or, according to my analysis,

> ual wrth duw eu hun yd yr lunyhed.
> Llunywys y dews dewis edryd itaw.

In support of this contention that the coincidence of two similar anomalous forms at close quarters within a single text is the consequence of self-imitation by the poet, it may be pointed out that he employs not a single impersonal verb to carry the *prifodl* in the first twenty-five lines of the thirty-six-line *-ed awdl* of the poem (with the possible exception of *weled* in line 13), while there are five or six in the final eleven lines, most of them preterite indicatives (*yd yr uolhed*, line 26; *anlloued* 'was bestowed', line 27; *uawrhaed < mawrhaed* 'was exalted', line 31; *digoned* 'was made', line 32; *yd yr lunhyed*, line 36; and possibly *wynhaed < gwynhaed* 'was whitened', line 34). Having moved into a passage of his poem in which he found the impersonal verb to be a useful way of sustaining his *-ed prifodl*, it is hardly surprising to find him making use of such a form to effect the first term of the *cymeriad* with a new *prifodl*, and certainly conceivable that he might solve metrical difficulties by recourse to an innovation devised for an earlier line in the section.

The resourcefulness implied by this analysis of the two anomalous verbs in *Canu i Gadfan* is not out of keeping with the literary technique of Llywelyn Fardd. The poem in question includes several words—*dyhuted* (line 15), *ednywed* (line 30), and *kynnwad* (line 89), for instance—that occur not at all or only once or twice elsewhere in the extant records of Middle Welsh. Like others of the *Gogynfeirdd*, Llywelyn Fardd was a poet able to use all of the resources of his language—archaisms, neologisms, and constructions that stretched the rules of syntax to their limits—in the service of a metrically demanding verse of cultivated obscurity.

CATHERINE A. McKENNA
Queens College of the City University of New York

NOTE

1. For the text of the poem, see Morris-Jones and Parry-Williams 1933, 42-48, or Lewis 1931, 84-89. On the date of the poem see Lewis 1931, 235, and R. R. Davies, *Conquest, Coexistence and Change: Wales 1063-1415* (Oxford: Oxford University Press, 1987), 176. On the date of the manuscript, see Huws 1981, 12-13.

REFERENCES

Evans, D. Simon. 1964. *A Grammar of Middle Welsh*. Dublin: Dublin Institute for Advanced Studies.
Evans, J. Gwenogvryn, ed. 1910. *Facsimile and Text of the Book of Taliesin*. Llanbedrog: n.p.
———, ed. 1911. *The Poetry in the Red Book of Hergest*. Llanbedrog: n.p.
GPC. 1950–. *Geiriadur Prifysgol Cymru: A Dictionary of the Welsh Language*. Cardiff: University of Wales Press.
Huws, Daniel. 1981. Llawysgrif Hendregadredd. *National Library of Wales Journal* 22:1-26.
Lewis, Henry, ed. 1931. *Hen Gerddi Crefyddol*. Cardiff: University of Wales Press.
Lloyd-Jones, John. 1931-63. *Geirfa Barddoniaeth Gynnar Gymraeg*. Cardiff: University of Wales Press.
Loth, Joseph. 1910. Questions de grammaire et de linguistique brittonique. *Revue celtique* 31: 23-48, 333-67.
Morris-Jones, John. 1913. *A Welsh Grammar*. Cardiff: University of Wales Press.
——— and T. H. Parry-Williams, eds. 1933. *Llawysgrif Hendregadredd*. Cardiff: University of Wales Press.
Strachan, John. 1909. *Introduction to Early Welsh*. Manchester: Manchester University Press.
Williams, Ifor, ed. 1935. *Canu Llywarch Hen*. Cardiff: University of Wales Press.
———. 1938. *Canu Aneirin*. Cardiff: University of Wales Press.
———. 1951. *Pedeir Keinc y Mabinogi*. 2d ed. Cardiff: University of Wales Press.

Problems Relating to the Composition of the Welsh Bardic Grammars

Notable among the achievements of medieval Celtic cultures are the vernacular grammars of Irish and Welsh.[1] Both are closely dependent upon Latin models, but both introduce remarkably independent efforts to grapple with peculiarities of the Celtic linguistic and metrical systems for which there were no analogies in their Latin models. If in this respect alone, the Celtic grammars are extraordinary and represent an advance in linguistic sophistication beyond that which we find, for example, in Aelfric or the Middle English grammars (Zupitza 1880, Thomson 1984).[2] With a few notable exceptions (Bergin 1938; Ó Cuív 1965–66, 1973; Parry 1961), neither the Welsh nor the Irish tracts have occasioned a great deal of commentary or general interest, a condition that applies generally to medieval grammatical texts, which are largely understudied and underedited.[3] There are some seventy-eight extant texts of the Welsh bardic grammar, the four earliest appearing in manuscripts traditionally dated as ranging from c1400 to c1450 and the latest, a paper copy belonging to 1832. Most of the texts belong to the later sixteenth and seventeenth centuries. Among the fullest and most interesting of these is the *Pum Llyfr Kerddwriaeth* in the hand of Simwnt Fychan (c1575), which increases the parts of speech to eight, expands the triads with additional bardic material, and "updates" the medieval text to a Renaissance standard by adding commentary that pointedly draws the Welsh grammar into the tradition of classical and late medieval grammatical and rhetorical study. Other notable texts of the late sixteenth century are those marked by a determined effort to Cymricize the technical vocabulary, substituting where possible a Welsh terminology for the Latin loans used in the Middle Welsh texts.[4] In general, however, these grammars agree with the Middle Welsh texts in major content and organization.

Scholarship on the Welsh grammars dates from the early part of this century when Ifor Williams called attention to their affinities with the Latin grammars associated with Donatus and Priscian, and pursued the identity of Einion Offeiriad (Williams 1913-14, 1916). In his lengthy introduction to *Gramadegau'r Penceirddiaid*, G. J. Williams supplied what remains the most comprehensive survey of the grammars—their content, manuscripts, attribution, the major stages in their historical transmission and development—and, believing them to have been bardic texts, he includes a sizable unit on bardic education as well. Since these few early works, scholarly attention has been sporadic and consists of the following: Sir Thomas Parry's British Academy lecture, which questions the bardic authority of the grammar (Parry 1961); J. Beverly Smith's historical research on the identity of Einion Offeiriad (Smith 1962-64); Saunders Lewis's lecture on the grammars, which concentrates on Peniarth 20 and which attempts to place it within the context of medieval grammatical study, especially that of the speculative grammarians (Lewis 1967); and my own analysis of the grammatical unit, which is greatly indebted to Eric Hamp, particularly in the description of the syllables and diphthongs (Matonis 1981). There is, in addition, a general survey by Ceri Lewis in the second volume of Jarman's literary history (Lewis 1979).

Beyond this very little has been written about the Welsh bardic grammars. Because just enough has been said and repeated about them, and because interest in these vernacular grammars is likely to grow among historical linguists as well as among those with an interest in the Welsh bardic tradition, a review of what we know, what remains uncertain, and what might be reasonably conjectured bears setting forth. In fact, we know remarkably little outside of what the texts themselves divulge. Nonetheless, they tell us a great deal.

1. There are four extant copies of the grammar belonging to the Middle Welsh period; they are located in the Llyfr Coch Hergest, Llanstephan 3, Peniarth 20, and Bangor 1. My remarks in this paper are based on the first three grammars and exclude Bangor 1.

2. The grammatical tract divides into two major units: (a) the grammar proper, or *ars grammatica*, which is thoroughly normative and based on a Latin model; and (b) a far larger unit on *cerdd dafod*, based on native bardic tradition. The *cerdd dafod* (or *ars versificatoria*, to place it within its medieval context) comprises several subsec-

tions: an *ars metrica* on Welsh meter; the metrical faults to be avoided; a *prydlyfr*; a brief passage on *prydyddiaeth* (found in Peniarth 20 and Llanstephan 3 but lacking in Llyfr Coch Hergest); and the *trioedd cerdd*.

3. The grammars agree in content, organization, and style.

4. The grammars are throughout pedagogic, prescriptive, and proscriptive, so unmistakably so that they look like primers and have, in fact, been taken for manuals of instruction.

5. The treatise as a whole represents an amalgam of three distinct traditions: the late Latin grammatical tradition, the native bardic tradition, and the ideological system of Roman Christianity. The grammar proper derives from a Latin model, which accounts for the peculiarities and shortcomings of the description of Welsh, the compiler's frequent presentation of language as a written system, and the linguistic terminology made up of unassimilated Latin terms (for example, *berf, bogal, dipton, ffutur, perffeith, sillaf*) and calques (such as *archedig, enw, cytsein, lluossawg*). It also contains interpolated material on the Welsh syllables and diphthongs in a discussion that not only departs from the Latin source but is on the whole a remarkably intelligent classification by a compiler alert to what he evidently regarded as inconsistencies between the written and spoken character of Welsh syllables. Native bardic tradition accounts for the discussion of the Welsh syllables and the larger account of the principles of bardic composition. In their different ways, both the *prydlyfr* and the passage on *prydyddiaeth* owe much to Roman Christian thought, as any cursory glance will reveal.

Against this we might reexamine those areas in which uncertainty still exists. The immediate questions surrounding the Welsh grammars are long-standing: the dating and provenance of the manuscripts in which the grammars are located; the date and circumstances of the grammar's composition; the genealogical relationship of the early texts; and attribution. There are in addition questions of the grammar's bardic authority, first raised by Parry in 1961.

Manuscripts and Dates

The four earliest texts appear in what were thought until fairly recently to be roughly contemporaneous manuscripts. Following the manuscript dating suggested by John Morris-Jones and Gwenogvryn Evans, and believing the chronological sequence of the grammars to correspond to the chronology of the manuscripts that housed them, G. J. Williams and E. J. Jones dated the texts as follows: Llyfr Coch Hergest (c1400), Llanstephan 3 (c1400), Peniarth 20 (c1440), and Bangor 1 (c1450).[5] The Llyfr Coch Hergest is now more firmly identified as largely the work of Hywel Fychan ap Hywel Goch of Builth and assigned to the years c1382–c1410 (Charles-Edwards 1979–80),[6] a dating that is not incompatible with the date accepted by G. J. Williams. Peniarth 20 is now placed in the first half of the fourteenth century and assigned to Valle Crucis.[7] Although largely on nonpalaeographical grounds, Saunders Lewis argued for a date closer to 1350 for Peniarth 20 (Lewis 1967). As far as I am aware, nothing further has been said or published on either Llanstephan 3 or Bangor 1, but the dates supplied for them cannot be regarded as firm.

Date, Place, and Circumstances of the Grammar's Composition

There have been few attempts at dating the grammar itself. The redating of Peniarth 20, however, now establishes it as the earliest of the manuscripts containing a grammatical text. Although such a redating does not of itself necessarily affect the dating, chronological order, or stemma of the grammatical texts, it underlines a number of uncertainties that continue to surround the grammar, not least of which are their genealogical relationship, textual affiliations, and date of original compilation.

When Ifor Williams first tackled the problem of dating, he did so believing the grammar in Llyfr Coch Hergest to represent the earliest text. Working from the metrical portion of the tract and in particular upon the metrical examples drawn from poets whose floruits are known, Sir Ifor used an example of the *toddaid* measure from an ode composed by Gwilym Ddu o Arfon (fl. c1280–1320) in praise of Sir Gruffudd Llwyd of Tregarnedd to argue that the grammar cannot predate the composition of the ode. He concluded from this and other historical material that the likely period of the grammar's compilation was sometime after 1335 ("Dosbarth," Williams 1915–16). Saunders Lewis, unlike Morris-Jones, G. J. Williams, and Ifor Williams, however, believed that the earliest text of the Welsh grammar appears in Peniarth 20, which he dated no later than 1350,[8] though he believed that blocks of it were composed earlier (such as the *prydlyfr*), and that, in fact, the tract as we have it represents the final stage of an evolutionary process which began in the twelfth century. His arguments are based on historical circumstances stretching from the appointment of one Adam, a Parisian-educated Welshman, to the bishopric of Llanelwy in 1175 (whom Lewis believed to have been influential in introducing the dialectic cast to the grammar), to the reforms affecting monastic education enacted by the Cistercian Pope Bennet, reforms that Lewis takes to have been the impetus behind the final compilation of the grammar. This compilation he thought to have been produced by a cleric either at Aberconwy or at Dinas Basing sometime between 1336 and 1350 (Lewis 1967).

Within the treatise itself there are inconsistencies that complicate the dating.[9] For instance, some material in the *ars metrica* suggests a stage of composition much earlier than the fourteenth century, such as metrical rules that must have been formulated before certain historical changes took place in the language (for instance, rules prohibiting final rhyme between heavy [*trwm*] and light [*ysgafn*] syllables, a distinction no longer made by fourteenth-century bards). And while, on the one hand, the metrical unit concentrates on the classical native meters (including two *englyn* measures typical of the *hengerdd* but out of use by the late fourteenth century), on the other, it includes a measure borrowed from medieval Latin (the *cywydd llosgyrnog*) for which we lack examples before the middle of the fifteenth century. Moreover, curiously absent is an adequate treatment of *cynghanedd* and *cymeriad llythrennol*, both conspicuous features of fourteenth-century poetry. Although *cynghanedd* is mentioned, it is described as limited to the middle of the line, a description applicable to its earliest developmental stages but inaccurate when applied to 1350, and inaccurate as a description of the *cynghanedd* found in the verse of Einion Offeiriad. There is a similarly inadequate account of the *cywydd*, including a verse example that does not represent the *cywydd* forms used by Dafydd ap Gwilym but rather "suggests an archaic type of verse which the higher grades of bards must have practised at a fairly early period'' (Parry 1961, 188). It is, of course, possible that these anachronisms reflect historical stages of the compilation and represent the accretion of material over an indeterminate period. It is equally possible that the bardic material (as distinct from the grammatical unit) was brought together by the final compiler.

The possibility of accretion is high and has, as far as I am aware, yet to be examined. Interpolation is certainly present in the introduced native material on syllables and diphthongs in the grammar proper. Conflation may be present as well, for the tract as we have it gives every appearance of having been composed of at least two once independent blocks of material (namely, the grammar proper and the *ars versificatoria*), at least one of which (the grammar) was a written text. Indeed, the two blocks appear to have been recognized by a compiler at some stage as once separate tracts, for they are deliberately bridged by a transitional paragraph on *mydr*, which reads as though it were introduced to provide coherence, and may therefore be an interpolation. But when it was added and by whom is less scrutable. The number and sources of accretion in the *cerdd dafod* and the following units are harder to locate, as is the stage (or stages) when they were introduced. A glance through the divisions and subdivisions of the tract will give some idea of how the final compilation was stitched together, and provide some indication of which passages or compositional blocks may be the result of accretion.

1. The tract begins with a Latin-derived grammar in which, as has already been mentioned, interpolation appears in the discussion of the Welsh syllables and diphthongs, introduced from a native source. (a) The grammar proper concludes with a paragraph on permitted faults or solecisms, called *lliweu*, a direct translation for the Latin *colores* (rhetorical figures of speech).

2. A bridge passage between the *ars grammatica*, or grammar proper, and the *ars metrica* marks a major division of content and was presumably inserted by one who saw the division as such. The passage opens with a sentence which draws upon the subject matter of the penultimate paragraph of the grammar (*yr ymadrodyon perffeithyon kyfyawnyon,* Llyfr Coch Hergest 6) and applies it to

mydr a phrytyat, which is then defined. The definition of *mydr* leads naturally to a series of bardic classifications, ending with a classification of the *englyn*.

3. An *ars metrica* concentrates on technical composition and forms the largest block of material in the tract. It draws on, or shares, material found in the grammar proper, notably the distinctions among syllables and diphthongs that matter in verse composition.

4. The section on faults to be avoided also concentrates on formal principles, and to that extent shares material with the grammar proper and the preceding *cerdd dafod*. In addition, faults are said also to be avoided in *yr ystyr, a'r synnwyr, a'r dechymic*, although the first two are given short shrift and *dechymic* is ignored altogether.

5. The *prydlyfr* seems to represent another compartition. In addressing the broader topic of poetry (as opposed to verse or meter), it departs from the concerns of the preceding units, which are entirely devoted to the formal, technical components of verbal expression. Moreover, unlike the earlier units, the *prydlyfr* is abruptly introduced and lacks both transitional remarks and the internal organizational strategy that provided coherence among the earlier blocks of material. Concluded equally abruptly, the *prydlyfr* is essentially self-contained, self-explanatory, and detachable, and may have been drawn from a once discrete block of material, possibly from a source independent of the preceding and following units. However, since all three texts include the *prydlyfr*, it was probably attached to the bardic grammar at an early stage of its manuscript history.

6. Following the *prydlyfr* and preceding the *trioedd cerdd* in Llanstephan 3 and Peniarth 20 is a notable passage on *prydyddiaeth*, exceptional among medieval grammars and rhetorical manuals in addressing topics such as *awen, dechymig, ethrylithr, arfer*, and *celfydydd*.[10] It, too, looks like a discrete unit, possibly interpolated, though like the *prydlyfr* it attends to the notional topic of poetry and is conceptual rather than technical in nature.

7. The *trioedd cerdd* conclude the tract. These are essentially a pedagogic set of mnemonics identifying what a bard needed to master. They introduce various items of bardic lore not previously touched upon, or briefly touched upon in the bridge passage and the passage on *prydyddiaeth*. But they also summarize the principal points made in the grammatical and metrical sections (notably the different kinds of syllables, diphthongs, faults), and therefore look as though they were intended to serve as the concluding unit. It is worth noting, however, that they do not incorporate material from the *prydlyfr*, and what material they share with the immediately preceding passage on *prydyddiaeth* may have existed or been present in the tract before the passage was incorporated. This may explain why Llyfr Coch Hergest, which lacks item 6, nonetheless contains in its *trioedd cerdd* topics pertaining to *dechymig, ethrylithr, arfer*, and *awen*, which are elsewhere not represented in its text. The *trioedd cerdd* are additionally suggestive as regards the textual history of this unit, for whereas the three early texts mostly agree closely and throughout, they are widely variant in the *trioedd cerdd*.

Given the intrusion of independent material into the grammar proper and considering the blocks of material in the *ars versificatoria* (that is, from the *cerdd dafod* on), it is not altogether improbable that the second part of the treatise was built up from several originally discrete units, any one or two or three of which may have been attached to the treatise either at the point of the original compilation or at any subsequent stage of transmission. The dating of the tract is thus not only complicated by the traditional problems attendant upon medieval texts, but also by the presence of blocks of material in the bardic unit which may have been introduced and combined by the original compiler or the final compiler—if there were two such hands at work. It is also possible that any single piece of material may be an accretion added at an intermediate stage. Thus answers to questions of date, authorship, and circumstances of the grammar's composition may not apply to the bardic units.

Whatever the motivation behind the final tract and whoever the compiler, the interest in the bardic system is unmistakable, and it seems likely that the unknown compiler was as much interested in it as he was in the grammar, if not more so. It is also safe to assume that he was an educated man and therefore presumably a cleric of some sort. The bardic authority of the grammars is yet another question, and one that will be examined later.

Genealogical Relationship of the Texts

Equally unsettled is the genealogical relationship of the four earliest texts. This is not, however, an impossibly recalcitrant area, although Ceri Lewis not so long ago expressed what presumably remains current opinion:

> There are, to begin with, some tantalizing obscurities in the manuscript stemma. . . . For these four copies, it must be emphasized, are not identical in every respect. Although there is not, on the whole, any great divergence in the subject-matter, there are nevertheless some significant differences in places in the phraseology and terminology, in the precise order in which various items are occasionally arranged, and, more particularly, in the examples of the different metres quoted in the important section on prosody, so that it is difficult to believe that any three of these early sources are direct transcriptions of the fourth or, indeed, that all four are transcriptions of a common original that is now lost. (1979, 64–65)

This summary calls attention to how little has been added since 1934 to our knowledge of the grammar's currency and textual history. It also identifies as problematic, textual differences that may well be accounted for. If the "common original now lost" refers to a common immediate exemplar, Lewis's statement may well be correct. It becomes questionable, however, if it refers to the archetype, or original, *ur*-ancestor. Here we might look to W. W. Greg, who opened his hallmark work on textual criticism with this sentence: "If we exclude the possibility of memorial transmission, all manuscripts of a given work are derived (by transcription) [*sic*] from a single original" (1927). That related texts will also include variant readings is equally predictable.

Because they are more alike than different and preserve what is recognizably the same text, the grammars in Llyfr Coch Hergest,

Llanstephan 3, and Peniarth 20 may be assumed to share a common original, though not necessarily the same immediate ancestor or exemplar. The variants among the three early texts are typical of medieval manuscripts: simple variants, such as addition, omission, substitution, transposition; complex variants, in which any combination of simple variations may occur; peculiar errors, such as conscious or unconscious deviations introduced by the copyist. While no two manuscripts are in complete agreement, Peniarth 20 contains a large number of readings (including substantive variations and inflations) that depart from the readings shared by Llyfr Coch Hergest and Llanstephan 3. On the other hand, although Llyfr Coch Hergest and Llanstephan 3 appear closely enough related to suppose that they belong to the same branch, or line of descent, they may not share the same exemplar; Peniarth 20, for example, shares many readings with Llanstephan 3, most notably the passage on *prydyddiaeth*, which is lacking in Llyfr Coch Hergest. In any case, the agreement among all three is sufficiently pervasive to accept the three as states of the same text and to discount any one as being an independent composition or stemming from a different original ancestor. But of all of the variants, it is the differences in the verse examples that have most intrigued scholars, who have used them to argue that Peniarth 20 belongs to a different textual tradition.

The problem in attempts to date a text by identifying and dating verse examples is that the illustrative verses could quite easily be later interpolations or substitutions. In fact, their very nature and textual separation allows them to be discarded and substituted without disturbing the text. Pedagogic examples found in such texts are therefore not in themselves reliable as evidence of independent manuscript tradition or as clues in dating. Indeed, the substitution of independently generated examples into an established pedagogic text by a teacher or student copyist is a practice documented from classical antiquity on. Not only is it a relatively easy task to substitute illustrative material, but it is a predictable source of textual variants among genealogically related copies. We should therefore not be surprised to find the practice represented in the various texts of the Welsh grammar. This is not to discount or diminish the value of the verse examples, for they can tell us a great deal, and when combined with other historical and textual data their value increases.

ATTRIBUTION

In the matter of authorship the evidence is conjectural and rests upon attributions made some two and a half centuries after the compilation of the tract—*if* we take c1350 to be the terminus ad quem for the grammar's composition. As is not unusual for medieval texts, the early manuscripts give no attribution. In 1609, however, Sir Thomas Wiliems, a noted antiquarian, produced an anthology of Welsh prose (Mostyn MS 110) in which he included two copies of the Welsh grammatical treatise. We lack the exemplars from which Sir Thomas made his transcriptions, but he presents the two as if they were two distinct texts. One he attributed to "Dafydd Ddu Athro o Degeingl" and the other to "Einion Offeiriad o Wynedd." At the end of his transcription of the grammar he attributes to Einion Offeiriad, Thomas Wiliems adds the following: *Ac felly y terfyna y llyfr kerddwriaeth a wnaeth Einion Effeiriad o Wynnedd i Syr Rys ap Gruff. ap Howel ap Gruff. ap Ednyfed Vychan yr ynrrydedd a moliant iddo ef* ("And thus ends the book of poetic song which Einion Offeiriad of Gwynedd made in honor of Sir Rhys ap Gruffydd ap Howel ap Gruffydd ap Ednyfed Vychan"; Williams and Jones 1934, xvii). At the end of the copy attributed to Dafydd Ddu, he adds, *Ac felly y terfyna llyfr celfydyt y gerdwryaeth o awdurdawd Dauyd du athro o Degeingyl a Hiradur* (sic). *Allan o hen Dext ar vemrwn* ("And thus ends the book of poetic art authored by Dafydd Ddu, teacher, of Tegeingl [i.e., Englefield] and Hiraddug. From an old parchment [here, "skin"] text"; ibid.). The testimony from later copyists of the grammar reflects the same dual attribution. Some claim the work to have been by Einion Offeiriad, others make the same claim for Dafydd Ddu.

A fair amount of scholarly activity on the grammar(s) has been spent pursuing the identities of the two putative authors. Possibly because research has turned up more by way of reference to Einion Offeiriad (or several roughly contemporaneous Einions) than to Dafydd Ddu, it is Einion's name that has been most persistently associated with the grammar in modern scholarship. The following summarizes the arguments that have credited Einion Offeiriad with the grammar.[11]

1. In 1609 Sir Thomas Wiliems attributes a copy of the grammar to Einion Offeiriad, stating that it was composed in honor of Sir Rhys ap Gruffudd.

2. There is an undated, incomplete Middle Welsh *awdl* to Sir Rhys ap Gruffudd (d. 1356) attributed to one Einion Offeiriad. Historical circumstances and documents, as interpreted by Ifor Williams, place the composition of the *awdl* c1314–22.

3. The metrical features of Einion's incomplete ode to Rhys ap Gruffudd connect it to a verse example of the *awdl tawddgyrch cadwynog* that appears in the Llyfr Coch Hergest and Llanstephan 3, where it is said to have been the invention of Einion Offeiriad (Williams and Jones 1934, 12, 31).

4. The name Rhys ap Gruffudd appears in the final line of the *awdl* in both the Llyfr Coch Hergest and Llanstephan 3. Sir Ifor took the metrical similarity between the incomplete ode and the ode found in the grammars, plus the presence of Rhys's name in the final line of the verse example contained in the grammars, as sufficiently persuasive to credit Einion with the composition of the grammar.

5. The personal names Rhys and Einion appear as compound subjects in a grammatical example illustrating subject–verb correspondence. Sir Ifor saw in this further evidence of Einion's authorship.

6. The name Einion Offeiriad appears in Llyfr Coch Hergest and Llanstephan 3 as the man responsible for inventing several measures included in the metrical unit. G. J. Williams, following Ifor Williams and Morris-Jones, accepted the testimony of these two manuscripts because two of the three measures appear in the *awdl* Einion composed for Rhys ap Gruffudd (Williams and Jones 1934, xxi).

7. Though scanty, there are four references to an Einion Offeiriad (or several Einions) in official documents dating from 1344–54/55, associating Einion variously with Ceredigion, Carmarthen, Caernarfon, and Gwynedd. The dates are not incompatible with past and current thinking on the probable time of the grammar's compilation. Although Thomas Wiliems associated Einion

Offeiriad with Gwynedd, it has been suggested that Einion might have had affiliations in several territories, especially those in which Sir Rhys ap Gruffudd held land.

8. All four historical documents place the date of death of their Einion as occurring between 1349 and 1354. It is therefore thought that Einion Offeiriad lived in the first half of the fourteenth century and composed the grammar sometime before—perhaps only slightly before—1350.

9. None of the historical testimony is inconsistent with the dates of the putative original compiler of the grammar. In the words of Ceri Lewis, "It seems probable . . . that the poet who composed the *awdl*, the inventor of the [meters attributed to Einion Offeiriad in the Llyfr Coch and Llanstephan 3], . . . and the author of the grammar were really one and the same person" (1979, 70).

The evidence is circumstantial. In addition, the same problems connected with the textual authority of verse examples as reliable guides to authorship also attach to the use of personal names in grammatical examples. Moreover, because neither the name Einion nor the epithet Offeiriad was unusual, the historical documents may not all pertain to the same Einion Offeiriad.

The testimony regarding Dafydd Ddu is even thinner. He is first credited with the composition of the grammar, or a grammar (which is in fact indistinguishable from Einion's), by Thomas Wiliems. Peniarth 20 claims that Dafydd Ddu devised the three new measures attributed to Einion Offeiriad in the Llyfr Coch Hergest and Llanstephan 3. It was Dafydd Ddu *Athro*, not Einion Offeiriad, who from the second half of the fifteenth century was the more highly acknowledged by leading bards as the authority on bardic tradition. He was also considered the compiler of the bardic grammar by a large number of copyists from the early seventeenth century on, though many of these copied from one another and therefore inherited the attribution.[12]

The dual attribution raises complications more serious than the unresolved historical identities of Einion Offeiriad and Dafydd Ddu, for it implies that there were two grammars rather than two copies of one grammar. The grammatical tracts found in the earliest extant manuscripts, however, reflect a common archetype. Even though the exemplars from which Thomas Wiliems copied have not survived, it is hard to believe that they represented two independent grammars. On the basis of Thomas Wiliems's identification, Morris-Jones suggested that Einion Offeiriad composed the grammar and Dafydd Ddu augmented it.[13] Some such process would explain the interpolations that distinguish one manuscript branch from another.

Whether Einion Offeiriad or Dafydd Ddu or both are solely responsible for the original compilation, or two redactions, may finally be beyond proof. But whoever the compiler(s) or redactor(s) of the grammar may have been, it is fairly safe to assume that they were educated clerical men with more than a passing interest in the Welsh bardic tradition. It is not just the familiarity with the Latin grammatical tradition that suggests an educated compiler, but the presence of the transitional paragraph on *mydr*, which can best be explained as the effort of someone who was acquainted with the principles of compositional organization (*dispositio*) and who would therefore have been motivated to supply coherence between two otherwise disparate parts. It might even be said that the transitional paragraph clarifies the relation (or establishes it) of the grammar proper to the rest of the tract, a relationship that at first is not obvious, even though metrics and grammar were combined by long tradition in classical texts. Certainly, the interpolated material on Welsh syllables in the grammar proper facilitated the transition. Moreover, the elaborate description of syllables and diphthongs critical in the composition of Welsh verse indicates that the compiler (or *a* compiler) had a profound interest in and knowledge of the bardic system. But if, as Thomas Parry and others have reasoned, the treatment of language in the grammar would have been of little or no value to a bardic pupil, then it is also difficult to see why the grammar was appended to the metrical tract—or vice versa—for the discussion of Welsh meters, despite the curious lapses that appear, has as its specific and exclusive audience the bardic pupil or practitioner.

Bardic Authority and the Motivation Behind the Grammatical Tract

There can be little doubt that the subject matter that most interested the compiler was Welsh poetry and not grammar per se (except insofar as a command of the syllables and diphthongs was essential in the composition of verse), and that the motivation behind the treatise was pedagogical. Given both the substantial amount of material pertaining to Welsh poetry and the pedagogical nature of the treatise, it is not surprising that the grammars are assumed to be either manuals of bardic instruction or representative of such manuals. The inconsistencies in the technical account of the verse, which led Thomas Parry to question the grammar's bardic authority, have not yet been explained and raise questions about the nature of the original compiler's access to and intimacy with fourteenth-century bardic practice. If the treatise originated in the fourteenth century, it is difficult to account for the inadequate treatment of fourteenth-century bardic techniques, the failure to include *cymeriad*, and the inaccurate characterization of *cynghanedd* and the *cywydd deuair hirion* as versus the many archaisms uncharacteristic of fourteenth-century practice, which are presented as essential. Curious too is the concentration on the *englyn*, its forms and faults, and that, of the twenty-four meters identified in the grammar, only twelve were used by the court poets.

Although we lack hard evidence for the existence of bardic schools or their curricula, the orthodoxy of the poetry itself (as reflected in technical composition, subject matter, and conventional treatment) from the early to the late *Gogynfeirdd* implies a stable, exacting standard, the consistency of which is most likely to have been promoted through training. With the loss of independence in 1282, however, the patronage that supported bardic institutions disappeared or was dramatically transformed. Who, then, in the middle of the fourteenth century would have been the audience for a bardic grammatical tract seriously deficient in its description of fourteenth-century Welsh poetry? Perhaps the tract as we have it represents a staying effort, an attempt to codify and preserve the bardic tradition; if so, all then practicing and future bards will have constituted the intended audience. Because tradition is a potent force, there is much fourteenth-century poetry written in the older, conservative style. The bards committed to perpetuating the older tradition (for instance, Casnodyn, Gruffudd ap Maredudd, Rhisierdyn) constitute one likely audience. Whether they needed, sought, or used the instruction the treatise provides has to remain an unsettled question until closer formal analysis of their work, both against the practice of the earlier *Gogynfeirdd* and against the injunctions set down in the grammar, is undertaken.[14] There can be little doubt that all Welsh bards respected the legacy of their native tradition. Further away from the events of 1282 and heirs to its consequences was the next generation of bards, and they indeed formed an audience receptive to the grammar, for testimony from the mid-fifteenth century on indicates that these bards were not only familiar with the grammar but regarded it as authoritative.

Conclusion

When we consider the rate of detrition of most medieval manuscripts, the presence of four extant fourteenth-century texts suggests that the grammar was widely circulated, copied, and therefore esteemed. This does not, of course, answer the question of how or by whom it was used, but common sense would indicate that the four transcriptions were not idle exercises. Why it was esteemed would of course have to do with its content. If a period of active copying and circulation took place in the latter half of the fourteenth century and/or the early part of the fifteenth (as the dates of the extant copies and the inclusion of the *cywydd llosgyrnog* suggest), it may have been during this period and process of copying and circulation that the grammar acquired or grew in authority. It was in the fourteenth century that the classical, conservative tradition showed signs of an inevitable erosion initiated by the Conquest and the collapse of the bardic orders. The conflict between conservatives, such as Casnodyn and Gruffudd ap Maredudd, and the practitioners of the "new" poetry, such as Dafydd ap Gwilym, is reflected not only in the new subject matter (hence the inclusion of the canonical and prescriptive *prydlyfr*?) and the new verse form, the *cywydd*, which usurped the classical meters (hence the concentration on the *englyn*?), but in the open debate within the bardic community itself, notably in the many *ymrysonau*. In these debates (between Dafydd ap Gwilym and Gruffudd Gryg, and Rhys Goch Eryri and Llywelyn ap y Moel), questions of orthodoxy, canon, *awen*, and respect for tradition are central. When read together with the grammatical tract, and when both are placed in their historical context, they yield a picture of literary tradition resisting cultural threat.

At the same time, there is also the possibility that the original compiler (supposing him to be the final compiler who put together the aggregate of material that constitutes the existing text) selected those features of the metrical tradition which he judged to be classical, worthy of and needing preservation. The conservative impulse is unmistakable and, aside from having medieval and classical precedent, was locally justifiable in light of the threat of Welsh culture and nationalism. We might, therefore, envision a compiler who was not himself a bard, nor even intimately associated with bardism, but rather a learned antiquarian sensitive to the very real threat to Welsh bardic tradition. In that case, the compiler's response was in every way dictated by a conservative impulse, and in that, whether knowingly or not, his document continued a tradition of cultural preservation established centuries earlier in the history of western civilization.

A. T. E. MATONIS
Temple University

NOTES

1. For the Irish texts, see Bergin 1913-16, 1921-23, 1946, 1952-55; Calder 1917; McKenna 1944; for the Welsh, Williams and Jones 1934.
2. The comparison with Aelfric's grammar, however, needs to be qualified because it was intended to describe Latin, and provides English forms alongside the Latin primarily to illustrate the Latin system.
3. There have been a number of recent studies that merit attention, most notably the work of Vivien Law, for which see the references. A new edition of Donatus with an extensive introductory essay and full textual apparatus has recently been provided by Holtz 1982.
4. Efforts in this direction appear from the late sixteenth century on, in the copies of the *gwyr bonheddig*, for which see the commentary in Williams and Jones 1934, xlii-lxii.
5. The first three of these grammars were edited by Williams and Jones (1934). All subsequent references to the texts will be from this edition. Bangor MS 1, incomplete at the beginning and end, was edited by Jones (1922-23).
6. For further references see Huws 1981-82, especially n. 1.
7. Thomas Jones, in his introductory commentary to his *Brut y Tywysogion, Peniarth MS 20 Version*, argues for placing Peniarth 20 early in the second half of the fourteenth century (1941). For further discussion of the dating and provenance of Peniarth 20, see the important review by Sir Goronwy Edwards of Jones's *Brut* in *English Historical Review* 57: 370-75.
8. S. Lewis relies on the dating of Peniarth 20 supplied by Thomas Jones in his edition to *Brut y Tywysogion*.
9. All three early texts printed in Williams and Jones 1934 contain the inconsistencies outlined here. See Parry 1961 for a fuller discussion of the problematic material.

10. For a fuller discussion of this passage, see my remarks in "The Concept of Poetry in the Middle Ages: The Welsh Evidence from the Bardic Grammars," forthcoming in *Bulletin of the Board of Celtic Studies*.
11. The arguments are those of J. Beverley Smith and the three papers of Ifor Williams cited in the references. G. J. Williams reviewed the associations of both men with the grammars in Williams and Jones 1934, xvii–xxiv, while Ceri Lewis provides a survey in his chapter (1979).
12. British Museum MS 15,046 in the hand of Roger Morris and dated by G. J. Williams "yn hanner olaf yr 16g" (xiv) appears as one of the earliest texts attributed to Dafydd Ddu and belongs to the same manuscript family as Wiliems's transcription of Dafydd's text. In 1605 John Jones produced a grammar, which he attributes to Dayfydd Ddu and which he claims to have copied from a *hen dext* in Dafydd's own hand. Hafod 24 shares the same manuscript tradition with BM 15,046 and text *a* of the Mostyn 110 grammars.
13. This judgment made in the *Transactions of the Honourable Society of Cymmrodorion* (1923–24) is reported by G. J. Williams in Williams and Jones 1934, xxiii.
14. Rachel Bromwich, who is expert in the poetry of this period and whose opinion is to be respected, believes that fourteenth-century bards, including Dafydd ap Gwilym, were heavily guided by the grammar.

REFERENCES

Adams, G. Brendan. 1970. Grammatical Analysis and Terminology in the Irish Bardic Schools. *Folia linguistica* 4: 157–66.
Ahlqvist, Anders. 1979–80. The Three Parts of Speech of Bardic Grammar. *Studia celtica* 14–15: 12–17.
Bergin, Osborn. 1913–16. *Irish Grammatical Tracts*, 1: *Introductory*; 2: *Declension*. *Ériu* 9 supplement.
———. 1921–23. *Irish Grammatical Tracts*, 3: *Irregular Verbs*. *Ériu* 9 supplement.
———. 1938. The Native Irish Grammarians. *Proceedings of the British Academy* 24: 204–35.
———. 1946. *Irish Grammatical Tracts*, 4: *Abstract Nouns*. *Ériu* 14 supplement.
———. 1952–55. *Irish Grammatical Tracts*, 5: *Metrical Faults*. *Ériu* 17 supplement.
Calder, George, ed. 1917. *Auraicept na n-Eces: The Scholars' Primer*. Edinburgh: J. Grant.
Charles-Edwards, G. 1979–80. The Scribes of the Red Book. *Cylchgrawn Llyfrgell Genedlaethol Cymru* 20: 246–56.
Greg, W. W. 1927. *The Calculus of Variants*. Oxford: Clarendon Press.
Holtz, Louis. 1982. *Donat et la tradition de l'enseignement grammatical*. Paris: Centre National de la Recherche Scientifique.
Huws, Daniel. 1981–82. Llawysgrif Hendregadredd. *Cylchgrawn Llyfrgell Genedlaethol Cymru* 22: 1–23.
Jones, J. T. 1922–23. Gramadeg Einion Offeiriad. *Bulletin of the Board of Celtic Studies* 2: 184–200. Jones here supplies the fragmentary text of Bangor 1.
Jones, Thomas. 1941. *Brut y Tywysogion, Peniarth MS 20 Version*. Caerdydd: Gwasg Prifysgol Cymru.

Law, Vivien. 1982a. *The Insular Latin Grammarians*. Woodbridge, Suffolk: Boydell.
———. 1982b. Notes on the Dating and Attribution of Anonymous Latin Grammars of the Early Middle Ages. *Peritia* 1: 250–67.
———. 1983. The Study of Latin Grammar in Eighth-Century Southumbria. *Anglo-Saxon England* 12: 43–71.
Lewis, Ceri. 1979. Einion Offeiriad and the Bardic Grammar. *A Guide to Welsh Literature*, 2, A. O. H. Jarman and G. R. Hughes, eds., 58–87. Llandybie, Dyfed: Christopher Davies.
Lewis, Saunders. 1967. *Gramadegau'r Penceirddiaid*. Caerdydd: Gwasg Prifysgol Cymru.
McKenna, Lambert, ed. 1944. *Bardic Syntactical Tracts*. Dublin: Dublin Institute for Advanced Studies.
Matonis, A. T. E. 1981. The Welsh Bardic Grammars and the Western Grammatical Tradition. *Modern Philology* 79: 121–45.
Morris-Jones, J. 1925. *Cerdd Dafod*. Oxford: Clarendon Press.
Ó Cuív, Brian. 1965–66. Linguistic Terminology in the Medieval Irish Bardic Tracts. *Transactions of the Philological Society*: 141–64.
———. 1973. The Linguistic Training of the Mediaeval Irish Poet. *Celtica* 10: 114–40.
Parry, Thomas. 1961. The Welsh Metrical Treatise Attributed to Einion Offeiriad. *Proceedings of the British Academy* 47: 177–95.
Smith, J. Beverley. 1962–64. Einion Offeiriad. *Bulletin of the Board of Celtic Studies* 20: 339–47.
Thomson, David. 1979. *A Descriptive Catalogue of Middle English Grammatical Texts*. New York: Garland Publishing.
———. 1984. *An Edition of the Middle English Grammatical Texts*. New York: Garland Publishing.
Williams, G. J. and E. J. Jones, eds. 1934. *Gramadegau'r Penceirddiaid*. Caerdydd: Gwasg Prifysgol Cymru.
Williams, Ifor. 1913–14. Rhys ap Gruffudd. *Transactions of the Honourable Society of Cymmrodorion*: 193–203.
———. 1915–16. Dosbarth Einion Offeiriad. *Y Beirniad* 5: 129–34.
———. 1916. Awdl i Rys ap Gruffudd gan Einion Offeiriad ar Ramadeg a'i Ddyled i Ddonatus. *Y Cymmrodor* 26: 115–46.
Zupitza, Julius. 1880. *Aelfrics Grammatik und Glossar*. Berlin: Weidmann.

A Highly Important Pig

Recently, Eric Hamp asserted that Culhwch, arguably the hero-protagonist of the early Welsh tale *Culhwch ac Olwen*, "was originally a highly important pig" (Hamp 1986a). This may come as startling news to the less well-informed general reader of early Welsh narrative, or to the antimythological school of scholars and critics ("Euhemerists and Others"; O'Rahilly 1946), of which there are still a few "votaries." But Hamp insists, with the unabashed directness that characterizes his scholarly writing, "It is clear Culhwch literally was a pig" (1986a, 257). Note the use of the past tense in both statements. Hamp does not claim that in the eleventh century, say, audiences of the tale of *Culhwch ac Olwen* imagined they were hearing a tale about a pig who mounted a horse and rode off to Arthur's court to have his hair (bristles) cut. But in offering us a brilliant explanation of the name Culhwch, he is reminding us all that in the onomastics of medieval Irish and Welsh narratives the mythological element is usually expressed overtly: names such as Cú Chulainn 'Hound of (?)Caulann', Énchenn 'Birdhead', Medb (?)'Intoxication', Fer Diad 'Man of the Pair' (Hamp 1982), Pwyll 'Discretion', Bran(wen) 'Raven- ', Gwydion 'Windy',[1] or Blodeu(w)edd 'Flowers; Owl' all bear witness to the process despite their dissimilarities. It is clear that embedded in the tale of Culhwch is the kernel of a myth about a (the) pig divinity of the British Celts. Hamp has illuminated our understanding of that myth by offering an etymology of the name of the hero that makes it more certain than ever before that he is indeed 'Mr. Pig'.[2] It is the purpose of this brief paper to extend Hamp's argument and, I hope, to reinforce it by showing how *Culhwch ac Olwen* is a traditional Celtic narrative in several important ways and therefore likely indeed to carry traditional and inherited notions about an important Celtic divinity.

In Hamp's analysis of the name, *Cul-hwch* contains a gloss, *hwch*, on a 'pig' word, the etymon of which derives from "a North (or Central) European pre-IE substratum such as the one that contributed the North European word for the 'apple' attested in Celtic,

Germanic, Baltic and Slavic" (Hamp 1987). Specifically, *Cul-* is analyzed as **keulV-* and so equated with Lith. *kiaũlé* 'pig' < **keuliā.* He then compares the Lith. word for 'boar' *kuilỹs,* gen. *kuilĩo* and suggests that perhaps the name of Culhwch's father Cilydd derives from the same preform **kūlios* (1986a, 1987). Hamp supports his linguistic analysis with an argument at the cultural level, suggesting that the importance of the pig in the (Greek) Eleusinian mysteries may be traced to pre-Hellenic settlers whose origins are to be sought in north Europe, or at least as far north of the Aegean as central Europe. Among these peoples, as among the Celts, the pig had a special value. The cultural and linguistic relation of these peoples to the Celts is further demonstrated in Hamp's analysis of four other problematic pig words: "Thus it may be that we have recovered, besides **keul-* and **kuili-*, four North European substratum terms **mokku-* [Ir. *mucc,* W. *moch*], **suku-* [W. *hob*; cf. **sukko-* in Ir. *socc-*, W. *hwch*], **banu-* (or **gu̯anu-*) [Ir. *banb,* W. *banw*], and **turko-* [Ir. *torc,* W. *twrch*]" (1987, 188). *Banba,* of course, was one of the three best-known names for Ireland, along with *Fodla* and *Ériu,* and as M. A. O'Brien noted long ago, whatever its proper etymology "the name would very likely become assimilated to the native word *banb* 'young pig' at an early period" (O'Brien 1932; Hamp 1973).

With respect to the names, then, Hamp has taken care of Culhwch and probably his father Cilydd: Pig son of Boar (no doubt Cilydd's father Celyddon belongs here too). But what about Olwen? Mr. Pig ought to be married to Mrs. Pig. The story says that she was called *Olwen* 'white track' because *Pedeir meillonen gwynnyon a dyuei yn y hol myn yd elhei* (Evans 1907, 476.15–16), "Four white clovers would spring up in her track [or after her] wherever she went" (Ford 1977, 135). One could easily get the impression that Olwen was a quadruped, but the explanation is by no means clear, and we are left to wonder whether four clovers appeared in each footprint, or one in each hoofprint, or what. In any case, the element *ol-* is connected to pigs elsewhere in the same narrative. It is said of Ol son of Olwydd: "seven years before he was born his father's pigs were stolen; when he had grown into manhood, he traced the pigs, and brought them home in seven herds" (Evans 1907, 469.17–23; Ford 1977, 131). Thus Ol is the mythical tracer of lost pigs. Finally, it should be noted in this connection that the name Olwen matches in morphology Henwen, the celebrated 'ancient white one (sow)' of the Triads (Bromwich 1978), as well as Branwen 'white raven' (Ford

1987-88), in which the second element *-(g)wen* carries the more specialized meaning of 'holy' or 'blessed', signifying otherworldly connections (Ford 1983).³ Thus do the names of the principal characters reinforce our view of the tale as a mythological narrative concerned with supernatural swine.

Despite its identification with the International Tale Type "The Giant's Daughter" (Foster 1959; Jackson 1961), *Culhwch ac Olwen* is a thoroughly native tale: it is the earliest Arthurian tale that has survived (Roberts 1976) and reflects two native storytelling genres: the "wooing" tale (cf. Irish *tochmarc*) and the "birth" tale (cf. Irish *compert*) (Mac Cana 1980; Rees and Rees 1961). As such, it is a fitting vehicle for handing on native traditions of the swine god.

The unwary might argue that the narrator of *Culhwch* loses sight of his protagonist and concentrates on the hero Arthur. It is a fact that Culhwch is not in evidence in the last third of the story except for his appearance at its very end. Indeed, if one subtracts the list of Arthur's retinue and the list of tasks that Ysbaddaden imposes on Arthur's men, then Culhwch is around for less than one-third of the tale. But before we think of Arthur as an interloper into the account of Culhwch's quest for Olwen, let us bear in mind the real identity of Culhwch as revealed by Hamp and remember that the heart of the Arthurian section, indeed the longset episode and the climax of the "impossible tasks" section, is Arthur's quest for the great boar, Twrch Trwyth. The antiquity of Culhwch's association with Arthur has been emphasized by Hamp, who called Culhwch's salutation to Arthur upon entering his hall "The Oldest Welsh Poem."⁴

Boar hunts are almost a hallmark of Celtic culture, and the hero's pursuit of the divine or supernatural boar is a common literary motif. Arthur's hunt for the supernatural swine Twrch Trwyth is paralleled in early Irish tradition by Finn's celebrated pig-hunts (Nagy 1985, 56f.; Meyer 1910, esp. 65-67), as well as those recounted in the *dindsenchas* and elsewhere (Ní Chatháin 1979-80). It is this common motif, among other things, that led A. G. van Hamel to insist that "Finn's counterpart in Britain is, of course, King Arthur" (Hamel 1934). He meant that the two heroes are reflexes of a common Celtic heroic tradition: "They are both based on the same notions, and the resemblances of their constitutive elements [boar hunting, releasing of prisoners, attacks on the Otherworld, fights with monsters, protecting the land] is too strong to be accidental"

(221). In other words, pigs and heroes are complementary, and it is clear that the early Arthur is as much at home on the trail of the supernatural swine as is his Irish counterpart Finn.

There are several interesting things about Twrch Trwyth. The first is that, in characteristic Celtic mythological fashion, he is both man and animal.[5] This is very neatly accounted for in Christian terms by Arthur's comment that Twrch Trwyth "had been a king, but God changed him into a swine for his sins" (Ford 1977, 153). Although the battle between them is ostensibly a boar hunt, it is hard to imagine a more worthy human opponent for Arthur than Twrch Trwyth, as he and his retinue of boars, piglets, and sows defend themselves against the pursuing hero.

Another significant thing is that Twrch Trwyth is a *hwch*. The general word for pig in *Culhwch ac Olwen* is *moch*; *hwch* is used but three times in the text: once for Culhwch in etymologizing his name (Evans 1907, 452.21) and twice for Twrch Trwyth (Evans 1907, 499.38; 500.02). The latter two instances are especially revealing, for Arthur's men virtually ask for a definition: *peth oed ystyr yr hwch hwnnw* (Evans 1907, 499.37-38), "what was the meaning of that *hwch*?" Arthur replies, *brenhin uu. ac am y bechawt y rithwys Duw ef yn hwch* (Evans 1907, 500.01-02) "he was a king, but for his sin God transformed him into a *hwch*." Thus, Culhwch and Twrch Trwyth have a shared identity: both are *hwch* in contradistinction to the other porcines of the narrative, and one is literally a 'pig' while the other actually is one. In Twrch Trwyth's entourage are two other boars, Ysgithrwyn Pen Beidd and Grugyn Gwrych Ereint. I have suggested elsewhere (Ford 1977) that these were perhaps doublets of Twrch Trwyth or alternative names for him.[6] Certainly *pen beidd* 'chief boar' ought to be Twrch's title, and *ysgithrwyn* 'white or shining tusks' would be an appropriate epithet for him. *Gwrych ereint* 'silver bristles' is a similar epithet, and both conjure the image of Henwen 'the ancient white or shining one' already mentioned. When Arthur's messenger is sent to speak to Twrch Trwyth to seek a parley, it is Grugyn Gwrych Ereint who answers, not Twrch Trwyth (Evans 1907, 500.12-13; Ford 1977, 153). Twice the narrator calls him *gwallt ereint* 'silver hair' and twice *gwrych ereint* 'silver bristle' (Evans 1907, 502.24; 503.10; Ford 1977, 155). While this fact may be interpreted variously, one possible interpretation is that the human and animal natures of the divinity are confused or given equal weight.

The connection between the sublime Henwen and Twrch Trwyth is tantalizingly reinforced by the tradition of *Henwinus dux Cornubiae*, whose story is recounted by Geoffrey of Monmouth in *Historia regum Britanniae* 2.12, 15-16. Rachel Bromwich suggests that Henwinus too might have been a prince-turned-pig (Bromwich 1978, 406). Henwinus, the duke of Cornwall, was defeated by his father-in-law King Lear, who returned to Britain with the aid of his daughter Cordelia and her husband. Later, when Cordelia assumed the sovereignty of Britain, Henwinus's son Cunedagius laid waste to the land and finally deposed Cordelia. Cornwall is the site of the confrontation between Arthur and Twrch Trwyth in *Culhwch ac Olwen*: " 'Twrch Trwyth has killed many of my men,' said Arthur to the warriors of the Island, 'and by the might of my men he shall not go into Cornwall while I am alive!' " (Ford 1977, 155). Twrch Trwyth is driven into the Severn, where the battle rages. "From there, Arthur and his hosts went forth until they overtook him in Cornwall. . . . Thereupon he was chased out of Cornwall, and they drove him to the sea. No one ever knew after that where he went" (Ford 1977, 156). Arthur himself was begot on Ygerna wife of Gorlois, Duke of Cornwall, by Uther Pendragon, even as Uther's men were killing the duke and scattering his army. In Geoffrey's *Prophetiae Merlini*, Arthur is called *aper cornubiae* 'the boar of Cornwall'.

In the last analysis, then, it would perhaps be more accurate to say that *Culhwch ac Olwen* merges several traditions (with strong Cornish connections) about the pig god and his heroic hunter than that the story has been overcome by Arthuriana.

The importance of the pig among the Celts, both socially and culturally,[7] hardly needs emphasizing; with respect to the latter, the pig's significance has been well documented recently in the work of Anne Ross (1967) and Próinséas Ní Chatháin (1979-80).[8] Ní Chatháin quotes Ross's conclusion, that in Celtic religion the boar "is the most typical Celtic animal and in insular tradition the most important cult animal" (Ní Chatháin 1979-80, 201). The meat for the Otherworld Feast was pork, and one of the shapes assumed by the Lord of that feast was a man carrying a pig. This, of course, is O'Rahilly's argument, as Ní Chatháin acknowledges, though the conclusion that the Lord of the Otherworld Feast is, therefore, "in effect a swineherd" is hers alone (Ní Chatháin 1979-80, 201).

O'Rahilly's point is that Fer Caille, the man carrying the pig in the early Irish tale *Togail Bruidne Dá Derga* (The Destruction of Dá Derga's Hostel) is a psychopomp, a supernatural being (in the shape of either a man or a beast) who guides or lures the hero to the Otherworld. A Welsh example of a porcine psychopomp can be found in the fourth branch of the Mabinogi, "Math son of Mathonwy": the sow that leads Gwydion to the Otherworld plain of Lleu's torment. Of the sow, the swineherd tells Gwydion, "When the pen is opened each day, she goes out. She isn't observed closely and we don't know where she goes, any more than if she went into the earth" (Evans 1907, 106.36–107.04; Ford 1977, 106). Gwydion follows her, and she leads him to Lleu. Even St. Patrick has a boar for a guide: "the angel said to him, 'Mind thou the herd to-day, and thou wilt see a boar [*torcc*] uprooting the earth, and he will bring a mass of gold thereout" (Stokes 1887, 2.442). And that gold is the means whereby Patrick is able to ransom himself from his master Miliucc.

That swineherds were something more than prosaic overseers of the herd is well attested in insular tradition, as Ní Chatháin amply shows. There is the famous Welsh triad of the "Three Powerful Swineherds of the Isle of Britain." The triad recounts the adventures of Henwen the 'Ancient White' sow, whose keeper was Coll son of Collfrewy. Like Culhwch's mother, her pregnancy made her run; she fled her native Cornwall, entered the Severn, and came to land in Wales with Coll holding fast to her bristles (a variant says that Arthur assembled the army of the Island of Britain to seek to destroy her, for it had been prophesied that Britain would be the worse for the "womb-burden" (Bromwich 1978, 45–48). The second Powerful Swineherd is Drystan, swineherd of King Mark of Cornwall. The third Powerful Swineherd is Pryderi, whose story is told in the first and fourth branches of the Mabinogi, wherein pigs are seen to have been a gift from the Otherworld to Dyfed in exchange for Pwyll's friendship with Arawn, Chief of Annwfn (the Otherworld). When Pwyll prince of Dyfed died, his son Pryderi assumed the responsibility of safekeeping the swine; hence Pryderi was known as one of the three Powerful Swineherds. Belying his name, Pryderi is careless with the pigs and as a result loses his life.[9]

The two most famous swineherds in early Irish narrative are no doubt those whose enmity is prosecuted across time and in various shapes until they end up as the two bulls, the Findbennech and the

Donn of Cuailnge, whose epic struggle is told in the *Táin Bó Cuailnge*, and who may, therefore, be viewed as avatars of the provinces of Connaught and Ulster (see below).

The extended association of swineherds with sovereignty as indicated in the stories of Pwyll and Pryderi is attested in early Ireland too and is well rehearsed by Ní Chatháin. As she shows, swineherds play an important part in the origin legends attached to Cashel, for it is the swineherd who presages the supremacy of that seat of Munster. In so doing, Ní Chatháin claims, "the swineherd has the function of the druid and his successor the *fili*: he blesses the king, he receives his garment" (Ní Chatháin 1979-80, 207). Ní Chatháin takes the name of the swineherd of the king of Múscraige, Cuirirán, Cuilirán to be identical with *cularán, culuran* (OI *curar-*), which might be translated 'little pig-nut'.[10] She concludes that, therefore, "his function as a seer goes back to a time when swineherds were sacred and engaged in important specialized activity in a primitive society where settlement near or in forests was the order of the day. Thus the pig and his keeper could eat the same food, which would be associated with their tutelary deity, a Celtic swine-god" (Ní Chatháin 1979-80, 209-10). She remarks further on the connection between pigs and the oak tree, whose fruit they eat. That the oak was sacred to the Celts (cf. *Drunemeton*) is well known, and its leaves or acorns may have been associated with seers' visions if not downright hallucinogenic.

It appears that Christianity in Ireland acknowledged the premier position of swineherd: the patron saint of Ireland was no shepherd, he was *Succet* 'swineherd', *porcarius* in both Muirchú and Tírechan (Bieler 1979).[11] And when Patrick returns to Ireland to begin his mission there, it is a swineherd (*porcinarius*) who first espies him in the land and who leads his master Díchu to Patrick; the man brought by the swineherd becomes Patrick's first convert (Bieler 1979, 79). Eoin MacNeill (1964) contended that the name Succet was representative of the "obloquy which was cast upon Patrick," Magunios 'slaveling' being another. But it is abundantly clear that 'swineherd' was anything but a term of opprobrium—at the cultural level, at least. In the tale *De Chophur in Dá Muccida* (Book of Leinster 246[a]18-247[a]36), the two swineherds of the kings of the fairy mounds (*sídhe*) of Munster and Connaught were masters of wizardry (*suithe ngentlechta*) and could change themselves into any shape (*nos delbtais in cech richt*). After competing with each other in various shapes, they are swallowed in the shape of worms by two cows and reborn as the bulls Findbennech and Donn of Cuailnge, whence they become epitomical adversaries in the great *Táin Bó Cúailnge*. Surely the name 'swineherd' cannot be labeled obloquy. When Christianity sought an equivalent to the parabolic shepherd of the Old Testament it naturally hit upon 'swineherd', as it was he who had the custodial function in early Ireland.

The pig was accorded an extraordinary and supernatural position among the Celts. In the *interpretatio romana* of Caesar, the continental Celts worshiped Mercury above all others; the Lingones called him *Moccus*—"a highly important pig" to be sure. The weight of all of the evidence surveyed briefly here lends strong support to the etymologies offered by Hamp and to my view that *Culhwch ac Olwen* preserves traditions about the pig god, traditions preserved onomastically, thematically, and generically. For whatever the contributions of the literary redactor of the tale may have been, and whatever international motifs and tale types may be discovered in the version that has been recorded for us, *Culhwch ac Olwen* is demonstrably a traditional Celtic tale.

We might say that *Culhwch ac Olwen* begins with a birth tale. It is perhaps the briefest birth tale of those which have survived from medieval Irish and Welsh literature, and will not take much space to quote in full here:

> Cilydd son of Celyddon Wledig desired a woman as well-born as himself. The woman he wanted was Goleuddydd daughter of Anlawdd Wledig. After his wedding feast with her, the country went to prayer to see whether they would have an heir. And through the country's prayers, they got a son. From the time she became pregnant she went mad and avoided civilized places. When her time came her senses returned to her. Where they did so was in a place where a swineherd was watching a herd of pigs, and the queen gave birth from fright of the swine. The swineherd took the boy and brought him to court. They baptized him and named him Culhwch, because he was found in a pig run. The boy was noble, however, and a cousin to Arthur. He was put out to fosterage. (Ford 1977, 121)

In their durable study of *Celtic Heritage*, Alwyn Rees and Brinley Rees enumerated the characteristics of the Celtic birth tales (1961, 223ff.); their discussion remains the starting point for anyone interested in studying the subject, and I lean on their analyses in the present discussion. The first thing we notice about the birth of Culhwch is that the country went to prayer to see whether Cilydd and his bride would have an heir; furthermore, it was through the country's prayers that "they got a son." That is clearly a Christian interpretation of the events leading to Culhwch's conception, events that are closely paralleled elsewhere in early Irish and Welsh birth tales. In one version of the Irish tale of the birth of Conchobor (Rees and Rees 1961, 216), Nes conceives the child as a result of a prophecy by Cathbad the druid; that is, Cathbad identifies the day as "good" for conceiving a king on a queen, and Nes, trusting in the efficacy of the prophecy, takes Cathbad to her and she conceives. In another version (ibid.), Cathbad compels Nes to drink water from the river Conchobor; the cup from which she drinks contains two worms, and as a result of swallowing them with the water she conceives.

The several tales of the birth of Cú Chulainn present us with an almost bewildering array of conceptions: Dechtine (Dechtire) conceives by a mysterious nocturnal visitor (Lugh), or by swallowing a worm with a draught of liquor, or by Lugh in an otherworldly setting to which she fled in the shape of a bird. It is clear from these and other narratives of the births of heroes that conception is the result of outside (supernatural) interference of some sort. This is exactly the case in *Culhwch ac Olwen*, the only difference being that an interpretation quite consistent with Christian practice is offered: "more things are wrought by prayer than this world dreams of." Note that a more or less rational approach is taken in *Pwyll*, too, where again conception has become a problem. Pwyll and Rhiannon have been married for more than two years and there are no children as yet. This is a matter of great concern to Pwyll's councillors, who suggest that he try another wife. Pwyll puts them off—for a year, at least—saying (rather prophetically), "much may happen yet"! (We shall return to *Pwyll*.)

Notice how the narrative of *Culhwch ac Olwen* wastes no time in getting to the next feature common to Celtic birth tales: "From the time she became pregnant she went mad and avoided civilized places." This represents a feature I would label "alienation": the birth is not destined to take place within the bounds of human society. In the several versions of the birth of Cú Chulainn, Dechtine either flees Emain Macha in the shape of a bird or she joins her brother (or father) Conchobor in a bird hunt, which brings them and the Ulstermen to an otherworldly venue where the epiphany of the future hero will occur. In the story of *Pwyll*, a remarkable device is employed to "alienate" the mother: upon the disappearance of her newly born child, she is accused of killing him and is driven from the court and compelled to act like a horse. At the same time, the narrative switches to an account of Lord Teyrnon and his wonderful mare (I have examined the structure of this part of the tale in Ford 1981-82). At this point, *Culhwch ac Olwen* is remarkably similar to *Pwyll*. I have argued (1981-82) that in the latter tale, the narrative is at pains to account for both the anthropomorphic and the zoomorphic aspects of the horse goddess (Epona) with whom Rhiannon has so often and rightly been identified. Rhiannon must, as it were, dissolve into both woman and mare at the point that her child appears. The child of the woman disappears as the mare foals successfully for the first time. The human child appears simultaneously alongside the foal. Later, the mare's lord, Teyrnon, restores the child to his proper place at court. In *Culhwch ac Olwen*, the text says simply that Goleuddydd's "senses" returned to her (that is, she became *herself* again) "in a place where a swineherd was watching a herd of pigs, and the queen gave birth from fright of the swine. The swineherd took the boy and brought him to court." The presence of animals at the birth of a hero is known from other Celtic birth tales and is not unique to the Celts. But in *Culhwch ac Olwen* and *Pwyll* the animals are not simply "helpers," rather they are meant to signify the hero's divine paternity. In *Pwyll* this is managed efficiently by the Teyrnon episode, where Teyrnon and his wife (read 'mare') pretend that the child is theirs. In *Culhwch ac Olwen* it is less explicit, but we note that the boy is baptized into human society only after he is returned to the court by the swineherd, the characteristic persona of both sovereign and lord of the Otherworld, as we have seen.

In short, I would argue that as a birth tale, *Culhwch ac Olwen* is characteristically Celtic with respect to the significant features of the supernatural interference in conception, the alienation of the mother, the questionable (or dual) paternity, and the presence of animals: surely the case could be prosecuted even more vigorously.

As a "wooing" tale, *Culhwch ac Olwen* compares interestingly with the Irish *Tochmarc Emire* (The Wooing of Emer), though there are of course many differences between the two narratives. In *Tochmarc Emire*, the men of Ulster want Cú Chulainn to take a wife because their women are too attracted to him and because they wish him to leave an heir. In *Culhwch ac Olwen*, Culhwch seeks Olwen because of his stepmother's curse. In both narratives the first search for the maiden ends in failure, and only then does the hero take up the search—in the case of Culhwch, accompanied by superhuman helpers from Arthur's court. In both instances, the maiden's home is in the Otherworld. Both Cú Chulainn and Culhwch have obstacles placed in their way by the maidens' fathers, who fear death upon the marriage of their respective daughters; additionally, Cú Chulainn has further tasks imposed by the maiden herself. Along the way, the hero is assisted by one or more women: in Cú Chulainn's case first by a foster-sister, then by the Amazon Scáthach's daughter, Uathach; Culhwch is abetted by his mother's sister. The tasks are accomplished, the hero gets the maiden, her father is killed. We know too little of the storytelling tradition of medieval Wales (or of Ireland for that matter) to speculate on the reasons that *Culhwch ac Olwen* differs so much from *Tochmarc Emire* if both are traditional wooing tales, but it is clear that the storyteller or redactor of the former tale was more interested in catalogs (of heroes, tasks) than in developing the narrative along the lines of the latter.[12]

Other traditional elements of *Culhwch ac Olwen* include the "Raid on the Otherworld," an exploit that has individual expressions in *Branwen, Preiddeu Annwn* (Haycock 1983-84), and *Culhwch ac Olwen*. I refrain from discussing these elements further, for surely enough has been said to suggest the traditional character of the story, even though we have but one version of it. Perhaps any doubts that may have lingered that "Culhwch literally was a pig" and "originally a highly important pig" have been laid to rest by Hamp's important contribution to the discussion . . . *gratias agamus, O Vagister!*

PATRICK K. FORD

University of California, Los Angeles

NOTES

1. Eric Hamp once suggested to me that this name may be cognate with OI *gaíth*, ModI *gaoth* 'wind', and therefore belong to a set of cultural notions about poets and poetry well exemplified by OI *aí* 'poetic inspiration' and W *awen/awel* 'poetic inspiration/wind, breeze'.
2. Other examples of Hamp's penchant for porcine particulars will be found in Hamp 1973, 1976, and 1986a.

3. Hamp discussed the color white in its association with the Otherworld in a paper, "The Otherworld in Celtic and the Rigveda," read in February 1980. As far as I know, the paper has not been published.
4. Evans 1907, 458-59: *Henpych gwell penn teyrned yr ynys honn* . . . ; Hamp's unpublished paper was read in April 1979.
5. An excellent account of the zoomorphic element in Celtic mythology may be found in Ross 1967.
6. Cf. Idris Foster's comment, "It is probable that the two boar hunts in which Arthur and his hound participated are local variants of the same original tradition" (1959, 37), and references given there.
7. That pigs were an important part of the domestic economy of the Celts is a fact of Celtic society, for pork was a dietary staple; but at the cultural level, in their myths and rituals, the pig was a cult animal. On the distinction being made here, see further Ford 1988, esp. 418-19.
8. Hamp confesses (1987) that he "overlooked the rich article" by Ní Chatháin when he wrote "*Culhwch*, the Swine" (1986a); the first section of his 1987 article is therefore devoted to a critique of several of Ní Chatháin's arguments.
9. I follow Brinley Rees (1982), and take the rule of *Pwyll* 'wisdom, discretion' and his son *Pryderi* 'care, concern' to represent a Welsh version of Irish *cíallfhlaith*.
10. The derivation of the personal name from *curar* "looks dubious" to Hamp (1987, 185), though the cultural context outlined here might well have suggested a connection (through folk etymology), spurious or not, to the early Irish.
11. Patrick says of himself in his *Confessio, pecora pascebam*, and Bieler says that this wording suggests that Patrick was a shepherd. *Pecus*, however, may mean a herd of smaller animals without specifying the breed.
12. It is clear, however, that *Tochmarc Emire* has plenty of digressions of its own. It is of course a mark of our own ignorance of the aesthetics of early Irish and Welsh storytelling that we speak of "digressions" and a narrative development that betrays an Aristotelian standard.

REFERENCES

Bieler, Ludwig. 1979. *The Patrician Texts in the Book of Armagh*. Scriptores Latini Hiberniae 10. Dublin: Dublin Institute for Advanced Studies.
Bromwich, Rachel. 1978. *Trioedd Ynys Prydein: The Welsh Triads*. Cardiff: University of Wales Press.
Evans, J. Gwenogvryn. 1907. *The White Book Mabinogion*. Pwllheli: n.p.
Ford, Patrick K. 1977. *The Mabinogi and Other Medieval Welsh Tales*. Los Angeles, Berkeley, London: University of California Press.
———. 1981-82. Structural Approaches to the Mabinogi: *Pwyll* and *Manawydan*. *Studia celtica* 16-17: 110-25.
———. 1983. On the Significance of Some Arthurian Names in Welsh. *Bulletin of the Board of Celtic Studies* 30: 268-73.
———. 1987-88. Branwen: A Study of the Irish Affinities. *Studia celtica* 22-23: 29-41.
———. 1988. Celtic Women: The Opposing Sex. *Viator* 19: 417-38.

Foster, Idris Llewelyn. 1959. *Culhwch and Olwen* and *Rhonabwy's Dream*. In Roger Sherman Loomis, ed., *Arthurian Literature in the Middle Ages*. Oxford: Clarendon Press.
Hamel, A. G. van. 1934. Aspects of Celtic Myth. *Proceedings of the British Academy* 20: 207-48.
Hamp, Eric P. 1973. Banba Again. *Ériu* 24: 169-71.
———. 1976. Celtic *banuo-*. *Bulletin of the Board of Celtic Studies* 27: 214.
———. 1982. *Fer Diad*. *Ériu* 33: 178.
———. 1986a. *Culhwch*, the Swine. *Zeitschrift für celtische Philologie* 41: 257-58.
———. 1986b. *Orc* in Irish. *Etudes celtiques* 23: 49-50.
———. 1987. The Pig in Ancient Northern Europe. In *Proto-Indo-European: The Archaeology of a Linguistic Problem. Studies in Honor of Marija Gimbutas*, ed. Susan Nacev Skomal and Edgar C. Polomé. Washington: Institute for the Study of Man.
Haycock, Marged. 1983-84. "Preiddeu Annwn" and the Figure of Taliesin. *Studia celtica* 18-19. 52-78.
Jackson, Kenneth H. 1961. *The International Popular Tale and Early Welsh Tradition*. Cardiff: University of Wales Press.
Mac Cana, Proinsias. 1980. *The Learned Tales of Medieval Ireland*. Dublin: Dublin Institute for Advanced Studies.
MacNeill, Eoin. 1964. *Saint Patrick*, ed. John Ryan. Dublin: Clonmore and Reynolds.
Meyer, Kuno. 1910. *Fianaigecht* RIA Todd Lecture Series 16. Dublin: Royal Irish Academy. Corrigenda and addenda: *Zeitschrift für celtische Philologie* 8 (1911-12): 599.
Nagy, Joseph Falaky. 1985. *The Wisdom of the Outlaw*. Los Angeles, Berkeley, London: University of California Press.
Ní Chatháin, Próinséas. 1979-80. Swineherds, Seers, and Druids. *Studia celtica* 14-15: 200-211.
O'Brien, M. A. 1932. *Banba*. *Ériu* 11: 168.
O'Rahilly, Thomas F. 1946. *Early Irish History and Mythology*. Dublin: Dublin Institute for Advanced Studies.
Rees, Alwyn and Brinley Rees. 1961. *Celtic Heritage: Ancient Tradition in Ireland and Wales*. London: Thames and Hudson.
Rees, Brinley. 1982. Apair fris, ní fil inge cethri flathema and. . . . *Bulletin of the Board of Celtic Studies* 29: 686-89.
Roberts, Brynley F. 1976. Tales and Romances. In A. O. H. Jarman and Gwilym Rees Hughes, eds., *A Guide to Welsh Literature*, 1. Swansea: Christopher Davies.
Ross, Anne. 1967. *Pagan Celtic Britain: Studies in Iconography and Tradition*. London: Routledge and Kegan Paul.
Stokes, Whitley. 1987. *The Tripartite Life of Patrick*. 2 vols. London: Eyre and Spottiswoode.

A Note on a Possible Anglo-Saxon Pun in *Branwen*

In a well-known episode in *Branwen Uerch Lyr*, Branwen's brother Bendigeiduran, acting on a message he has received (via trained starling) from the degraded Branwen, wades across the Irish sea to attempt his sister's rescue. Neither the swineherds who first sight this bigger-than-life chieftain nor the Irish messengers nor Matholwch's courtiers can explain the wondrous vision; they decide therefore to ask Branwen about it. The manner in which they address her—and her reply—are intriguing:

> "*Arglwydes*," heb wy, "*beth dybygy di yw hynny?*"
> "Lady," they said, "what do you suppose that is?"
> "*Kyn ny bwyf arglwydes, mi a wnn beth yw hynny.*"
> "Though I be no lady, I know what that is." (Williams 1964, 40, lines 2-4)

The title *arglwydes* (modern spelling *arglwyddes*) is always rendered from Welsh into English as "lady," parallel to *arglwyd* (modern *arglwydd*) "lord." Branwen's reply has occasioned little published comment,[1] but even beginning students of Medieval Welsh rarely fail to appreciate the delicately humorous irony of it, considering Branwen's condition. Her nobility is certainly not removed by her degradation, and the statement works well as irony. Lady Charlotte Guest, the Victorian translator of the Mabinogi, left it out,[2] perhaps finding something offensive or incongruous in it. I believe that it is a pun; not a Welsh one (if so, one of the many scholars who have examined the text would have pointed it out). Rather, it is in its ultimate origins an Anglo-Saxon wordplay, the meaning of which has been lost in the course of its being either translated directly (unlikely) or merely transmitted in situ as part of a somewhat larger piece of material from the Anglo-Saxon to the Celtic (Welsh) milieu.

Branwen's punishment consists of two parts: first, to cook for the court (and she is specifically portrayed as being at a kneading trough); second, to have her ears boxed daily by the butcher. Only the first part is of concern here.

To rephrase the passage quoted above: the messengers address her as *Hlǽfdíge*—that is, "Lady, *Domina*"—as she presumably sits at her kneading trough. She replies, "Though I be no *hlǽfdíge* . . ." —in other words, no "loaf kneader," though in fact that is precisely what the "Lady" has become.[3] I cannot see how this wordplay could be in origin Welsh or Irish. The etymologies of *arglwyd* and *arglwydes* are not entirely clear, but "loaf kneaders" and "loaf wardens" they are not.[4]

The possibility of an Anglo-Saxon pun in this Welsh text raises questions of timing and geography that to my knowledge cannot currently be answered. The usage in Anglo-Saxon must date from a time in which both meanings of *hlǽfdíge* could be comprehended and enjoyed by an Anglo-Saxon audience. I think that there is a hint of social stratification here too. Among the nobility, *hlǽfdíge* could have come to mean strictly "lady, *domina*," while at the same time, among the lower classes (having no fine ladies but plenty of bread to bake), it may have retained its earlier meaning well after its meaning had become quite changed among the nobility. Nor can we discount the possibility of late dialect retention of the two meanings. One can imagine a widely known joke among servants in the halls of the Anglo-Saxon nobility; the one who eats the bread is no less a "loaf kneader" than the one who makes it, and vice-versa. Such a tale would have been broadly appealing, I suspect. On these points, perhaps an Anglo-Saxon or a Middle English scholar can shed light.

However ancient the Anglo-Saxon origin of this proposed wordplay, there is no reason to suppose that a Welsh storyteller— pre- or post-Conquest, early or late—would of necessity have had any idea whatever that this little story of the "loaf-kneading lady" had ever been a pun at all. It was simply, in its small way, a good yarn, a wonderful episode he could incorporate into his larger tale of the wronged queen. The episode itself may well have hung around as an element in an Old English or Middle English tale long after it had lost its punning flavor completely, and it may have circulated widely among English, Welsh, and even Irish storytellers, some of whom must have been bilingual, before settling into the written record in *Branwen* (its only attestation as far as I have been able to ascertain). How much more than the kneading trough and associated pun on *hlǽfdíge* could have come from the same source is well-nigh impossible to determine.

The piece of evidence that argues most strongly for an external source of some kind for this episode is that *arglwydes* as a form of address or description occurs nowhere in *Branwen* outside of this passage. It is used frequently in the other three Branches. The ultimate source, Anglo-Saxon or something else, is separate from any of the other elements in the tale; but this should not surprise us considering the wide-ranging affinities the tale has with other non-Welsh (specifically Irish) tales. Its use is but another example of the masterful way in which storytellers attempt to weave together many different yarns into a seamless garment.

KATHRYN A. KLAR
University of California, Berkeley

NOTES

1. See, for example, Thomson 1961, xlv.
2. "Messengers then went unto Branwen. 'Lady,' said they, 'what thinkest thou that this is?' 'The men of the Island of the Mighty' " (Guest 1902, 35).
3. I use here only the Old English form, *hlǽfdíge*, as it is the most etymologically transparent, historically speaking. For the etymology "loaf kneader," see the *Oxford English Dictionary* s.v. "lady."
4. See *Geiriadur Prifysgol Cymru* for a suggested etymology, s.v. *arglwydd* (*ar-* + *glyw* 'chieftain, lord, leader, ruler, governor' + *-ydd*) and its derivative feminine form *arglwyddes*.

REFERENCES

Geiriadur Prifysgol Cymru. 1950. Caerdydd: Gwasg Prifysgol Cymru.
Guest, Lady Charlotte. 1902. *The Mabinogion*, with notes by Alfred Nutt. Longacre: David Nutt.
Thomson, Derick. 1961. *Branwen Uerch Lyr*. Dublin: Dublin Institute for Advanced Studies.
Williams, Ifor. 1964. *Pedeir Keinc y Mabinogi*. Caerdydd: Gwasg Prifysgol Cymru.

An Early Work on Irish Folklore and Dylan Thomas's "A Grief Ago"

The question of whether Dylan Thomas was "*really* Welsh" (as a friend of mine, a native Welsh speaker, once phrased it) is now rarely heard. Gwyn Jones has recently placed Thomas at the pinnacle of modern Anglo-Welsh literature for reasons including "his power of words and mastery of poetic form," "his nurture in Swansea and Dyfed," the "Antaean nature of his essential and life-giving contacts there," and his choosing "in his moments of exultation to attempt . . . themes timeless and universal—love, birth, death, joy and grief and the heart's affections; our kinship with all living things; the wonder and blessing of life" (Jones 1988, 192). One need only add his debt to Welsh bardic techniques, which, as I have shown, cannot be uniquely dependent on the influence of Gerard Manley Hopkins (Loesch 1983), to make the image of Thomas as a Welshman, specifically an Anglo-Welshman because he spoke in English, irrefutable.

My purpose here is to add to the evidence a probable source suggesting that Thomas, while Welsh to the core and universal in his themes, also identified himself more broadly as an insular Celt. When he sought in his environment the things that would answer what was within that he wanted to express, he surely included consultation of the libraries.

It is true that the creative process is such that it is often not possible to know with precise assurance where this or that detail in a literary work came from. I am persuaded, however, that two poems by Dylan Thomas, "Altarwise by Owl-Light" (Thomas 1957, 80) and "A Grief Ago" (1957, 63-64) were influenced by W. G. Wood-Martin's *Traces of the Elder Faiths of Ireland* (1902): the first on the basis of a three-part configuration not found elsewhere, and the second on the basis of a comparable general discussion with comparable embedded details, together with scattered details throughout Wood-Martin's text, which are more likely than the others to have come from elsewhere, but which are also comparable. I should add that the sheer number of comparable items is a further positive consideration. Both ideas and verbal likenesses are involved.

In considering Thomas's "Altarwise by Owl-Light" sonnet, which begins his ten-sonnet series of the same title, and "A Grief Ago," I shall start with a short discussion of the opening six lines of "Altarwise." I shall give a structured[1] reading of the whole of "A Grief Ago," because all five of its stanzas are affected. These are the first six lines of "Altarwise by Owl-Light":

Sonnet I

Altarwise by owl-light in the half-way house
The gentleman lay graveward with his furies;
Abaddon in the hangnail cracked from Adam,
And, from his fork, a dog among the fairies,
The atlas-eater with a jaw for news,
Bit out the mandrake with to-morrow's scream.
(Thomas 1957, 80)

Altarwise, that is, as if stretched on an altar, in the dusk that is the half-light before death,[2] the *gentleman* presented here in largely Christian terms probably stands for all gods who are wounded, die, and then are resurrected. He is now lying halfway or hovering between life and death. The halfway house may come from Yeats's poem "Lapis Lazuli." The *furies* are probably related to the Greek Furies, who "arose from the drops of blood soaked up by the earth (Gaia) when Kronos mutilated (castrated) his father (Uranos, another dying god)" (Lurker 1987, 111–12). I have also, in other sources, seen sperm and tears given the role of the drops of blood. The *mandrake* has eerie qualities because its roots resemble a human being without a head.[3]

The third line has occasioned considerable discussion, including its grammatical status, which I have fully discussed elsewhere (Loesch 1980, 174–76). I take the line to be a *nominal* sentence cast into the poem as a *sangiad*, a Welsh bardic syntactic device (see Loesch 1980, 163–66 and 200–202 for definition of these terms), and that Abaddon, which is death, or who is the destroying angel, resides in the hangnail, that is, the gentleman, here given the image of Christ who is descended from Adam, and that it is in apposition with the preceding line. *Hangnail* also suggests the male organ and the castration referred to in the next three lines. Death lay in the gentleman and in his organ. The next three lines contain the crux. A *dog*, accompanied by *fairies*, bites out the *mandrake* (here a metaphor for the male organ) with a scream because of the symbolic meaning of the seed it contains, heralding those to be born far into the future. *Atlas-eater* may contain a resonance of man-eater; again, those humans yet to be born all over the world.

Thomas's own reading of lines five and six should be included here. He wrote in answer to Edith Sitwell,

> A jaw for news is an obvious variation of a "nose for news," and means that the mouth of the creature can taste already the horror that has not yet come, or can sense its coming, can thrust its tongue into news that has not yet been made, can savor the enormity of the progeny before the seed stirs, can realize the crumbling of dead flesh before the opening of the womb that delivers that flesh to tomorrow. What is this creature? It's the dog among the fairies, the rip and cur among the myths, the snapper at demons, the scarer of ghosts, the wizard's heel-chaser. (Treece 1949, 149–50; Thomas 1985, 301)

The textual problem here concerns mandrake lore, which goes back into antiquity, Greek and Hebraic antiquity especially, and in other lands around the Mediterranean. Hugo Rahner (1963) and James G. Frazer (1917–18) give the most thorough and scholarly treatment of the Christian and Judaic traditions, which are, of course, not mutually exclusive. H. H. Kleinman (1963, 16–20) gives the most extended application of mandrake lore to the "Altarwise" sonnet. In none of these discussions, nor in any of the others I have scanned, is the configuration *mandrake-dog-fairies* to be found. Typically, though not invariably, we find the *mandrake* coupled with the *dog*.

Let us look at Marie Trevelyan's account of Welsh lore about the mandrake, a source Thomas may well have known:

> In many parts of Wales the black bryony . . . was known as the mysterious and uncanny mandrake. The leaves and fruit were called "charnel food," and formerly it was supposed only to grow beside the gallows-tree or near crossroads. . . . When uprooted it shrieked and groaned like a sensible human being, and its agony was dreadful to hear. From its stalk a sweat-like blood oozed, and with each drop a faint scream was heard. There was an old saying that people who uprooted the mandrake would die within a year. They would die groaning as the mandrake died, or approach their death raving, or uttering penitent

prayers for having uprooted the unholy plant. . . . A process for uprooting the mandrake was described as follows: The person who wished to do so had to put cotton or wax in his ears, and go before sunrise on a Friday. With him he had to take a black dog that had not a white hair on him. After making the sign of the cross thrice over the mandrake, the man or witch, as the case might be, had to dig around the plant till the root held by thin fibres only. Then he had to tie the roots with a string to the dog's tail, hold a piece of bread before him, and move away. The dog would rush after the bread, and thus wrench up the root of the mandrake. Then, pierced by the agonizing groans of the mandrake, the dog would fall dead at the man's feet. (1909, 92-93)[4]

Concerning the dog and his death, Rahner tells us that "the most important feature of all this mandrake magic, . . . is that the root must be taken out of the earth with the help of a black dog" and that "the magic of the mandrake and the black dog . . . was at one time spread all over western Christendom," and he mentions its role in Graeco-Roman and Byzantine times as well, also citing Pseudo-Apuleius as saying, "It was said that this root has so divine a character that it kills the dog in the moment when the latter tears it up" (237).

Although I have found no triad—mandrake, dog, fairies—outside of Wood-Martin (1902), I have found in Sir John Rhŷs Manx fairy dogs and fairies who had like "Welsh fairies . . . horses to ride; they had also dogs, just as the Welsh ones had" (1901, 1.292).

T. Gwynn Jones tells us of the Cwn Annwn (Dogs of the Otherworld), which are "death omens," of "ghost dogs" (1930, 46), and of dogs that are "spectral apparitions" (56). But the dog in the sonnet is not a ghost, rather a scarer of ghosts.

Why does Thomas put the dog among the *fairies*? Kleinman, explicating just the sonnets, called the fairies "puzzling creatures," asking, among other things, whether they are "the sexless angels of Abaddon's retinue," creatures "abroad this magic night charged with announcing an important event," and whether they are "the fairies transformed into a half-rhyme with the poet as conjurer?" (1963, 18). Such clang associations belong to what Freudians call primary process thinking; rime based on consonant framing is a kind of rime Thomas uses. Not irrelevant here are these delicious words from a letter of July 27, 1944 from Thomas to Vernon Watkins:

> The Sussex months were beastly. When it wasn't soaking wet, I was. Aeroplanes grazed the roofs, bombs came by night, police by day, there were *furies at the bottom of my garden* [italics mine], with bayonets, and a floating dock like a kidney outside the window, and Canadians in the bushes, and Americans in the hair; it was a damned banned area altogether. (Thomas 1985, 517)

When Thomas wrote, doubtless many more people were aware of the absurd opening lyric line, "There are fairies at the bottom of my garden." (As presumably a digression, we should not fail to note that in London, Dylan Thomas belonged to the Mandrake Club [Watkins 1983, 99].)

At last we come to Wood-Martin and the full triad, mandrake–dog–fairies. He explains the relationship as part of Irish mandrake lore.

> The fairies do not unresistingly resign their power over herbs to mortals, since they may, in some instances, be used against themselves, and they therefore vigorously punish those who lay unhallowed hands on them. Thus the mandragora or mandrake, supposed to possess animal life and to shriek when uprooted, must be drawn from the soil in which it grows, by means of a dog, as the fairies visit their displeasure on the creatures actually abstracting this plant. (1902, 2.197–98)

Here the fairies belong to the mandrake connection, and because they do in "Altarwise by Owl-Light" as well, this would seem to be the most likely source, unless there is a similar source available to Thomas that I have simply not encountered.

As to the furies, they, too are found in Wood-Martin, but much further on in his work. He speaks of three important " 'hags,' Aine or Aynia, Bav, the Goddess of War and Bheartha (Vera)" (Wood-Martin 1902, 1.354). And a bit further on, he tells us that "the term Badb (pronounced Bav), signifying rage, fury or violence, ultimately came to be applied to a witch, *fairy* [italics mine] or goddess. . . . Ancient Irish tracts, romances, and battle pieces teem with details respecting this goddess and her sisters, Neman, Macha and Morigan or Morigau *furies* [italics mine] witches and sorceresses able to confound whole armies" (Wood-Martin 1902, 1.359). Thus we have another fury–fairy linkage to add to the rhyme one.

When we come to "A Grief Ago," we come to a condensed

narrative of one of the timeless and universal themes of which Gwyn Jones spoke—"love, birth, death," or the human life-cycle. This, to my mind, is Thomas's overriding theme, seen in a religious or holy light. This was recognized early by a few critics, the poet W. S. Merwin among others. Merwin sees the religious aspect of the theme more clearly, and that the function of the religious artist is to be a celebrator, "A celebrator in the ritual sense: a maker and performer of a rite. And also a celebrator of one who participates in the rite, and whom the rite makes joyful" (1953, 73). And he sees the full life-cycle—including the act of procreation.

> For he will see himself, man, as a metaphor or analogy of the world.... In both man and the world he will perceive a force of love or creation which is more divine than either man or the world, and a force of death or destruction which is more terrible than man or the world. Although his ultimate vision is the tragic one of creation through suffering, his ultimate sense will be of joy. For in the act of love, the central act of creation, he will see the force of love in man and the world merge inextricably and mysteriously with the force of death, and yet from this union new creation born through suffering. (ibid.)

Let us look now at "A Grief Ago" (Thomas 1957, 63-64):

> A grief ago,
> She who was who I hold, [the fats and flower],
> Or, water-lammed, from the scythe-sided thorn,
> [Hell wind and sea],
> [A stem cementing], wrestled up the tower,
> Rose maid and male,
> Or, [masted venus], through the paddler's bowl
> Sailed up the sun;
>
> Who is my grief,
> [A chrysalis unwrinkling on the iron],
> [Wrenched by my fingerman, the leaden bud
> Shot through the leaf],
> Was who was folded on the rod the aaron
> Rose cast to plague,
> [The horn and ball of water on the frog
> Housed in the side].
>
> And she who lies,
> [Like exodus a chapter from the garden],

[Brand of the lily's anger on her ring],
Tugged through the days
Her ropes of heritage, [the wars of pardon],
[On field and sand
The twelve triangles of the cherub wind
Engraving going].

Who then is she,
She holding me? The people's sea drives on her,
Drives out the father from the caesared camp;
The dens of shape
Shape all her whelps with the long voice of water,
That she I have,
[The country-handed grave boxed into love],
Rise before dark.

The night is near,
[A nitric shape that leaps her], [time and acid];
I tell her this: before the suncock cast
Her bone to fire,
Let her inhale her dead, through seed and solid
Draw in their seas,
So cross her hand with their grave gipsy eyes,
And close her fist.

(The brackets in the above poem enclose *sangiadau*.)

It is possible that the resemblances in the poems under discussion to ideas and images in Wood-Martin may stem from what Jungians call archetypes, and as a source for Thomas's often archaic writing, especially in his early writing, something of this kind cannot be dismissed. I believe that images stemming from these archaic things were nearer the surface of Thomas's mind than they are in most of us. He both drew images from within and recognized and seized upon images from without, in the service of what he was trying to say.

"A Grief Ago," as it begins the poem, sets the word *grief* into the fixed collocation for *time* (an *hour* ago, a *while* ago) meaning at the most literal level, "a time of love-making ago," with its semantic spectrum containing the Elizabethan notion of "to die" for orgasm and the clang association "grave." Thus, a time of love-making ago, she who was the person I am making love with now, joined with me in sexual union. For an excellent early discussion of this poem see Maud 1963, 81–94.

Let us look now at the first *sangiad*, "the fats and flower," which refer to "she who was who I hold." The latter phrase has a universalizing effect, as Maud points out. *Flower* is a well-known symbol for the female and her sexual organ. *Fats*, meaning flesh or body, may have been suggested by the following from Wood-Martin: "Adipocere is a soft, unctuous, or waxy substance, of a light brown colour, into which the fat and muscular fibre of bodies are converted by burial in soil of a peculiar nature . . . fat, like blood, is regarded as a seat of life" (1902, 1.298-99). The following passage concerning Irish wake games[5] is drawn upon by Wood-Martin (1902, 1.314-15), but cited here from John G. A. Prim:

> The "game" usually first performed was termed "Bout," and was joined in by men and women who all acted a very obscene part which cannot be described. The next scene generally was termed "Making the Ship," with its several parts of "laying the keel," forming the "stem and stern," and erecting "the mast," the latter of which was done by a female using a gesture and expression, proving beyond doubt that it was a relic of Pagan rites. (1853, 333-34 n. 2)

This wake passage is concerned with two things, (1) fighting and (2) the notion of a ship, both in the expression of sexual union. In fact, there are echoes of fighting through the fourth stanza, and of water and seas in all but stanza three. The poem, however, unfolds not only the aftermath of their union, but its consequences in the future—birth and death.

Lam, the word in "water-lammed," is an old transitive verb meaning 'to beat soundly; to thrash; to thwack', now colloquial or vulgar, and can be found in the *Oxford English Dictionary*.[6] The fighting metaphor with a sexual meaning is clear. The "scythe-sided thorn," a metaphor for the male organ, is given added religious overtones by the following quotation from Wood-Martin:

> The white-thorn, according to Aryan tradition, sprang originally from the lightning: hence it acquired a wide reverence, and became invested with many supernatural properties. It was amongst other things, associated with marriage rites. The Grecian bride was, and still is, decked with its blossoms, and the torch which lighted the Roman bridal couple to their nuptial chamber on the wedding-eve was formed of its wool. It is evident, therefore, that the white-thorn was considered a sacred tree long before Christian tradition identified it as forming the Crown of Thorns. (1902, 1.156)

"Hell wind and sea" has a relevant phrase in Partridge (1970), "shot between wind and water," glossed as "to coit with woman," listed as colloquial. This phrase may have been mixed with "between hell and high water," glossed by Partridge as "in great difficulty." I have heard in America "come hell or high water," meaning "no matter what comes."

"A stem cementing" is related to Prim's passage, as is "masted venus." "Wrestled up the tower" is clearly a fighting image. "Rose maid and male" might also be interpreted as a *nominal sangiad* rather than as a full sentence. "Through the paddler's bowl" says that, by means of the amniotic fluid of fetal growth, the woman "sailed up the sun." She sailed clockwise or sunwise—*desiul* (Wood-Martin 1902, 1.51), the opposite of widdershins, into the holy midday or high noon of her life. The "paddler" may come from Yeats's "Among School Children," where it stands for a child.

In stanza two, "A chrysalis unwrinkling on the iron" surely refers to the embryo's unfolding. Metals or minerals in Thomas always refer to the material aspect of the world, including the flesh—here, the womb.

"Wrenched by my fingerman, the leaden bud shot through the leaf" means ejaculation by the male organ into the female. Note especially that the *leaf* recalls Adam and Eve in the garden, where their sin brought death into the world and, importantly, progeny. *Bud* in this context refers to the male organ and its opening.

The next phrase is "was who was folded on the rod the aaron rose cast to plague." Put simply, she was made pregnant. *Plague* and *plagued* are used six times in Thomas 1953 with the meaning of pregnancy. *Cast* has an enormous listing of meanings in the *Oxford English Dictionary*. Three are especially relevant here: to cause to fall or happen, to bear young, *obs.* or *dial.*, and, also *obs.*, to ejaculate.

The final *sangiad* in this stanza, "The horn and ball of water on the frog housed in the side" I would suggest is a *nominal* exclamation. The *horn* may be a metaphor for the male member, or may stand for sexual excitement and power in both sexes; the *frog*, a metaphor for the *fetus*, is the embryo housed in the amniotic fluid.

It is in the third stanza, in the after phase of love-making, that we learn clearly that the woman protagonist is moving toward actual death. She now lies, in the words of the first *sangiad*, "Like exodus a chapter from the garden." As Exodus is the chapter following Genesis, in this chapter of her life she is expelled from Eden after love-making. For "Brand of the lily's anger on her ring" I suggest that the fire of the pure virgin now ignites and marks the woman's sexual organs with the fire of mortality, causing the expulsion from paradise of the mated pair.

"Her ropes of heritage," presumably the placentas of her children, she has "tugged through the days" suggests a passage dealing with another wake game, "the game of ropes," from Wood-Martin (1902, 1.317), taken from Lady Wilde (1890, 128), where she gives a more extended treatment.

The next *sangiad*, "the wars of pardon," again suggests the fighting, except that the wars are peacegiving. The final three lines are a long adverbial phrase. "On field and sand / The twelve triangles of the cherub wind / Engraving going" says that the cherub wind, coming in the form of the full-cheeked cherub portrayed on maps, represents weather and, hence, time. *Engraving* is a pun on the way the map was produced, meaning time carrying everything in the direction of the grave, even as she brings children to term. *The twelve triangles* may also refer to the twelve divisions of the zodiac circle or the twelve months of the year.

The question that opens the fourth stanza has a universalizing character, as well as an individualizing one. The next two clauses, separated by a semicolon, can be separated for analysis. First, "The people's sea" represents the sacred liquid carrying his half of the ancestral heritage from the past. Then he prays that the ancestral wombs that have carried the genes of the past give her children life and form and shape, in order that she gain immortality. Her resurrection is to come mainly or entirely through her children, though there is left open the possibility of personal resurrection.[7]

In the *sangiad* beginning the last stanza he asserts that death/night is near, and that death *leaps her* as he does. Wood-Martin describes another wake game in which a man is bent in the center "as in leap frog" (1902, 1.321–22).

The *sangiad* "time and acid" refers to the destructive, corrosive power of time; "night-trick acid" is a serious pun. Cf. Partridge (1970) *do the trick*, 'to get a woman with child'. He prays that before she dies in *time*, seen as a *suncock*, which is related to sundial, the weathercock, and the rooster who crows mornings awake, that her generations past by means inherited (*seed*) and her own flesh (*solid*) make possible children for her to bear before she dies. Then let her hand/palm be crossed with their grave gipsy eyes, their eyes that see their dead past, her living inheritance, her death, and her legacy for the future. Let their eyes, like coins, be legal tender for the ferryman who will ferry her over the river of death.

This last bit of folklore is well known, and most of us think of it as a Greek context. But it also reached Ireland. Wood-Martin's discussion of the coins include an old saying:

> The following quaint Irish proverb is a relic of paganism, analogous to the Roman custom of placing a small coin with the corpse to pay Charon his toll: "No man ever went to hell without sixpence at the time of his death." A humorous and mock imprecation, the employment of which is generally confined to the fair sex, appears to be derived from this ancient custom, when a country lass exclaims: "May the devil go with you and sixpence, and then you will want neither money nor company." (1902, 1.240)

Coins for the ferryman in Wood-Martin and Thomas may be coincidence, or Wood-Martin may have been merely a supporting source in this case. But what of the mandrake–dog–fairy triad? What of the wake customs? What of the other comparisons? Most, if not all, of the images and ideas we have discussed are archetypal. Some may have arisen independently from the same underlying archetypes. But the sheer number of closely matching ideas, images, and words make Wood-Martin an important direct source for Dylan Thomas virtually impossible to exclude.

KATHARINE T. LOESCH
Chicago, Illinois

ACKNOWLEDGMENTS

The basic material of this article was presented by the author at two University of California Celtic Studies Conferences held in conjunction with the Celtic Studies Association of North America Annual Meetings: "Celtic Sources Beyond Wales for Imagery in Dylan Thomas's Poetry," Berkeley, March 23, 1985; and "An Irish Antiquarian and a Dylan Thomas Poem," Los Angeles, April 9, 1988.

The author wishes to thank The Newberry Library and its staff for the use of its collections and for providing a haven for work. She also wishes to thank Professor J. E. Caerwyn Williams for his kind permission to quote from his letter to her of October 6, 1981.

NOTES

1. By a structured reading, I mean here an explication that will show the narrative movement to which Thomas somewhere refers as an aspect of his poems. I have also elucidated as many details along the way as time and space allowed. For comparison an excellent early discussion of "A Grief Ago" is to be found in Maud 1963, 81-84 and 90-94.
2. George Ferguson tells us also that "the owl is an attribute of Christ who sacrificed himself to serve mankind, 'To give light to them that sit in darkness and in the shadow of death . . .' (Luke I:79). This explains the presence of the owl in scenes of the Crucifixion" (1979, 22).
3. It is traditionally said to have aphrodisiac and soporific qualities. Both male and female mandrakes are included in traditional lore.
4. Parts from this passage are paraphrased and credited to Trevelyan by C. J. S. Thompson (1934), who is in turn cited by Kleinman (1963, 19). Thompson is another source Thomas may well have seen. Kleinman cites conveniently all of the Shakespeare and Donne references to mandrakes (1963, 32 n. 7). Thomas knew both well.
5. I first came across the Irish wake games in an article by J. E. Caerwyn Williams (1979-80, 338-39), where he quotes the Prim footnote I cite immediately below, but at greater length, and makes some other observations. I corresponded with him regarding the relation I saw between "A Grief Ago" and the wake games and received the following interesting reply from Aberystwyth in a letter dated October 6, 1981. I quote the relevant paragraph:

> The poem you cite seems to be connected with the Irish game [sic] not in the sense of showing the influence of the Irish (or of Welsh) but in the sense that they both show a primitive (in the Jungian psychological sense) imagery. I speak of course as an ignoramus on the work of Dylan Thomas [I doubt this] but I can see why the lines of the poem were evoked by what you read in the article. Unfortunately I don't think there are any parallel Welsh wake-games. The Methodist Revival in the 18th century effectively disposed of the Welsh Wake and its games.

Williams's remarks have influenced my thinking regarding sources generally, and especially in Dylan Thomas, even though we do not agree concerning the role of wake games in this particular poem. He did not consider, nor did I at that time, the influence of Wood-Martin, whom he cites in his article only with respect to marriage lore (Williams 1979-80, 334). He cites also Seán Ó Súilleabháin (1967 and 1962), the most complete discussion of Irish wake games (Williams 1979-80, 334). Though too late for Thomas to have seen, some of the information may have come to him by other routes. Ó Súilleabháin lists Wood-Martin (1902) in his bibliography. Another important discussion of wake games cited by Williams (1979-80, 338-39) is to be found in Mercier 1962, 49-53. See especially his discussion of mock marriages, drawn from John O'Donovan, which differs from the descriptions I have seen elsewhere. I came across Wood-Martin while looking up Lady Wilde (1890), if I remember correctly.

6. Maud (1960) was the first to put in print the importance of obsolete and dialect words in reading Dylan Thomas. A serious student of Thomas's poetry will realize early on the importance of using many dictionaries, and that any kind of word book would be important to him. As he said in more than one place, he always worked from words, not toward them. Thus the scandalized attitude taken by David Holbrook (1972, 182–85) on discovering proof of extensive use of Roget's *Thesaurus* seems utterly misplaced. It seems probable that Welsh medieval bards would have understood.

7. The *sangiad* "The country-handed grave boxed into love" has been interpreted by Thomas, again in answer to Edith Sitwell: "My image, principally, did not make the grave a gentle cultivator, but a tough possessor, a warring and complicated raper rather than a simple nurse, or an innocent gardener. . . . I meant that the grave had a country for each hand, that it raised those hands up and boxed the hero of my poem into love. 'Boxed' has the coffin and the pug-glove in it" (Treece 1949, 149; Thomas 1985, 300–301). Note that the fighting continues in the poem from *grief* to *grave*, and that he refers to the *hero* of the poem. Both hero and heroine are involved, and I believe *hero* condenses the two. *Love* is their passion, and provides a suggestion of lovemaking, death, resurrection, and immortality.

REFERENCES

Ferguson, George. 1979. *Signs and Symbols in Christian Art: With Illustrations from Paintings of the Renaissance.* Reprint. New York: Oxford University Press. [First published 1954. New York: Oxford University Press.]

Frazer, James G. 1917–18. Jacob and the Mandrakes. *Proceedings of the British Academy* 8: 58–79.

Holbrook, David. 1972. The Code of Night: The "Schizoid Diagnosis" and Dylan Thomas. *Dylan Thomas: New Critical Essays*, ed. Walford Davies, 166–97. London: J. M. Dent & Sons.

Jones, Gwyn. 1988. Anglo-Welsh Literature, 1934–46: A Personal View. *Transactions of the Honourable Society of Cymmrodorion 1987*: 177–92.

Jones, T. Gwynn. 1930. *Welsh Folklore and Folk-Custom.* London: Methuen.

Kleinman, H. H. 1963. *The Religious Sonnets of Dylan Thomas: A Study of Imagery and Meaning.* Berkeley: University of California Press.

Loesch, Katharine T. 1980. Welsh Poetic Syntax and the Poetry of Dylan Thomas. *Transactions of the Honourable Society of Cymmrodorion 1979*: 159–202.

———. 1983. Welsh Poetic Stanza Form and Dylan Thomas's "I Dreamed My Genesis." *Transactions of the Honourable Society of Cymmrodorion 1982*: 29–52.

Lurker, Manfred. 1987. *Dictionary of Gods and Goddesses, Devils and Demons.* London: Routledge and Kegan Paul.

Maud, Ralph. 1960. Obsolete and Dialect Words as Serious Puns in Dylan Thomas. *English Studies* 41: 28–30.

———. 1963. *Entrances to Dylan Thomas's Poetry.* Pittsburgh: University of Pittsburgh Press.

Mercier, Vivian. 1962. *The Irish Comic Tradition*. London: Oxford University Press.
Merwin, W. S. 1953. The Religious Poet. *Adam International Review: Our Dylan Thomas Memorial Number* 238: 73–78.
Ó Súillebháin, Seán. 1967. *Irish Wake Amusements*, trans. S. Ó Súillebháin. Dublin: Mercier Press. [Originally published in 1962 as *Caitheamh Aimsire ar Thórraimh*.]
Partridge, Eric. 1970. *A Dictionary of Slang and Unconventional English*. 7th ed. New York: Macmillan. [Originally published in 2 vols. Vol. 1: *The Dictionary*; vol. 2: *The Supplement*.]
Prim, John A. 1853. Olden Popular Pastimes in Kilkenny. *Transactions of the Kilkenny Archaeological Society* 2: 319–35.
Rahner, Hugo S., S.J. 1963. *Greek Myths and Christian Mystery*, trans. Brian Battershaw. London: Burns and Oates.
Rhŷs, Sir John. 1901. *Celtic Folklore: Welsh and Manx*. 2 vols. Oxford: Clarendon Press.
Thomas, Dylan. 1957. *The Collected Poems of Dylan Thomas*. New York: New Directions.
———. 1985. *Dylan Thomas: The Collected Letters*, ed. Paul Ferris. New York: Macmillan.
Thompson, C. J. S. 1934. *The Mystic Mandrake*. London: Rider.
Treece, Henry. 1949. *Dylan Thomas: "Dog Among the Fairies."* London: Lindsay Drummond.
Trevelyan, Marie. 1909. *Folk-lore and Folk Stories of Wales*, intro. E. Sidney, Hartland. London: Elliott Stock.
Watkins, Gwen. 1983. *Dylan Thomas: Portrait of a Friendship*. Seattle: Washington Reprint. [Originally published as *Portrait of a Friend*. Llandysul, Dyfed: Gomer Press, 1983.]
Wilde, Lady. 1890. *Ancient Cures, Charms and Usages of Ireland: Contributions to Irish Lore*. London: Ward and Downey.
Williams, J. E. Caerwyn. 1979–80. Posidonius's Celtic Parasites. *Studia celtica* 14–15: 313–43.
Wood-Martin, W. G. 1902. *Traces of the Elder Faiths of Ireland*. London: Longmans, Green.

PART V

BRETON

Welsh *ar bwys* : Breton *war-bouez**

Welsh *ar bwys* 'near, nearby' is used as an adverb and as a preposition in many if not all of the southern dialects of Welsh. Several studies of these dialects refer to it. One of the earliest, *An essay on the ancient and present state of the Welsh language with particular reference to its dialects, being the subject proposed by the Cambrian Society for the year 1822* (Hughes 1823), 34, contrasts "S.W. *ar bwys*" with "N.W. *ar agos.*" Of the dialect descriptions that I have consulted, the following contain specific references to *ar bwys* 'near': Davies 1934, Davies 1955, Evans 1930, Jones 1929–31, and Lewis 1960. The following do not instance it: Awbery 1986, Morris 1910, Phillips 1933, and Thomas 1988. The fact that these do not mention *ar bwys* specifically as a feature of the dialect they set out to describe does not necessarily mean that it does not occur, because they vary in their design, some ignoring the lexical or morphological aspect to concentrate on the phonological. Unfortunately for my purpose, the distribution of *ar bwys* is not mapped in Thomas 1973.

There seems to be general agreement that *ar bwys* is a feature of the southern rather than the northern dialects of Welsh, and although many Middle Welsh texts seem to be of southern rather than of northern Welsh provenance, *ar bwys* does not seem to be attested in Middle Welsh, and its grammars are silent regarding it. Thus D. S. Evans (1951, 1964) and Strachan (1909) do not present any instances of it. J. Morris Jones's standard grammar (1913) ignores it, but the South-Walian grammarians of Modern Welsh, J. J. Evans (1946) and S. J. Williams (1959), naturally give it honourable mention.

Our standard lexicographers are equally reticent regarding *ar bwys*. Davies 1632, Jones 1688, Lhuyd 1707, Richards 1753, Walters 1815, and Edwards 1850 omit all reference to it. W. O. Pughe (1803) does not register it with such phrases as *ar uchaf, ar warthaf*, and the like, but under *pwys* he gives the adage *Myned trwy yr avon a font ar bwys*, "To go through the river with a bridge on the spot." (Here a caveat would seem to be in order: I have consulted these dictionaries only at the entries where I would expect to find *ar bwys*, e.g., the Welsh–Latin/English dictionaries s.vv. *ar* and *pwys*, the Latin/English–Welsh dictionaries s.vv. *prope, beside, by, near, nearby*. Evans 1887 omits *ar bwys* from his entries under *ar*, but his 1852 gives *ar bwys* among other Welsh equivalents for 'hard by', 'close by'; it is not, however, found among the Welsh equivalents for 'near, nearby'.)

More recent dictionaries have been equally reluctant to admit *ar bwys* to the community of Welsh phrases. Among the most popular in the first half of the twentieth century were those of Spurrell's, edited by J. Bodvan Anwyl. *Spurrell's Welsh-English Dictionary* (1925) does not mention it under *ar*, but under *pwys* gives *ar bwys* 'upon, near', and of these two meanings, 'upon', if it suggests that *ar bwys y bwrdd* can mean 'upon the table' as well as 'near the table', seems rather peculiar to me. *Spurrell's English-Welsh Dictionary* (1937) omits all reference to *ar bwys* under 'beside', 'by', 'near'. There has been a spate of English–Welsh and Welsh–English dictionaries since the Second World War, and they have reflected the erosion and mixing of dialects owing to the increased mobility of the population and the influence exerted upon it by the mass media. I have not consulted all of these post-1945 dictionaries, but it is probably significant that the most popular and authoritative among them, *Y Geiriadur Mawr* (1958) by two South Walians, E. M. Evans and W. O. Thomas, in consultation with another, S. J. Williams, reproduces under *ar* almost the same list of phrases as Anwyl [Spurrell] 1925, omitting *ar bwys* there but including it under *pwys*.

Somewhat surprisingly, the University of Wales's Welsh dictionary, *Geiriadur Prifysgol Cymru* (1950–, henceforward *GPC*) does not include *ar bwys* s.v. *ar*[1], though it will certainly include it under *pwys*. By contrast, Lloyd-Jones 1988, s.v. *ar* confirms the conclusion that Middle Welsh texts provide no examples of *ar bwys* 'near, nearby'.

Modern Welsh texts provide a fair number:

> (Sawdwyr . . .) ar bwys y clawdd yn gwilied (Evans 1740 [1902], 308)
> Mae rhai'n yn gorwedd ar bwys eu gilydd (Williams 1784, 251)
> Ar bwys tŷ arglwydd y faenor (Evans 1808, 156)
> Sefyll ar bwys a dala'r ganwyll iddo (Thomas 1810, 43)

i'r pwlpud diaddurn ar bwys y mur (Mathews and Jones 1886, 359)
Cymmydogion agos, ar bwys y cyffiniau (Daniel 1892, 16)
ar bwys y ffenestr (Williams 1897, 7; 1945, 12)
y llwyn a oedd ar bwys y tŷ (Davies 1923, 207)
Dyma ni bron a bod ar ei phwys yn awr (Davies 1929, 38)
Y mae'r eglwys reit ar bwys (Anwyl 1933, 117)

Of course, these examples are only a selection of the examples that could be collected and cited, but they suffice to show that W. *ar bwys* is used as an adverb: *y mae'r tŷ ar bwys*, "the house is nearby" (cf. supra, *Myned trwy yr afon a phont ar bwys*, quoted from Pughe 1803); and as a preposition: *y mae'r tŷ ar bwys yr eglwys*, "the house is near the church," and, when used as a preposition with a pronoun, the pronoun takes the form of the possessive, with or without an (emphasizing) affixed pronoun: *ar fy mhwys* (i) 'near me'.

There seems to be complete correspondence in form between Welsh *ar bwys* and Breton *war-bouez*. Breton *pouez* corresponds in meaning to the basic meaning of Welsh *pwys* 'weight'. Both words are derived from Brit.-Lat. *pēsum* (Latin *pensum*) (Jackson 1967, §§292, 297, 534 n., 286). Breton *war* corresponds to Welsh *ar* derived from *war, gwar, guor*, Old Irish *for* 'on, upon'. See *GPC*, s.v. *ar¹*. It should be noted, however, that three prepositions fell together to give Middle Welsh *ar*, namely (1) *war*; (2) *ar* < **are* 'in front of, before'; (3) *ar* < *add* 'to'. See *GPC* s.vv. *add, ar¹, ar²*. But if *add, ar*, and *war* fell together to give Welsh *ar*, there is reason to believe that Breton *war* represents more than one preposition, and it should be noted that *ar* is used instead of *war* in the dialect of Vannes (see Hemon 1975, §62.12). It would, indeed, be rather surprising if the three prepositions represented in Welsh *ar* did not exist in the Brittonic language from which Welsh, Cornish, and Breton developed. According to Jackson (1953, 5), "From the middle of the sixth century we can speak of these as separating languages and from the end of the century as separate."

It is, unfortunately, impossible to determine whether the formations W. *ar bwys*, Br. *war-bouez* derive from the preseparation or the postseparation period. In the latter case they would have been formed independently of each other despite the correspondence between the formal units. If they are from the preseparation period, the presence of *ar bwys* in southern Welsh dialects would fit in with other correspondences between South Welsh on the one hand and Cornish and Breton on the other hand, or, as Léon Fleuriot would have said, between one variety of " 'Western Brittonic', the ancestor of Welsh," and " 'Southwestern Brittonic', the ancestor of Cornish and Breton" (Evans and Fleuriot 1985, 2). See also Hamp 1953.

But if Br. *war-bouez* is derived from a formation already to be found in "Southwestern Brittonic," we should expect to find its equivalent in Cornish. But I have searched in vain for such an equivalent in Lhuyd 1707, Pryce 1790, Williams 1865, and Nance 1938 and must conclude that if it did exist at one time, it must have become obsolete or gone unrecorded. Its absence from Cornish suggests that W. *ar bwys* and Br. *war-bouez* are parallel but independent formations. Any stemma we assume for their development is complicated by the fact that we cannot take into account the effects of the Brittonic emigrations to Brittany and the localities of their departure.

The fact that there is no early attestation for Br. *war-bouez* is not surprising in view of the general paucity of Old and Middle Breton texts, and the fact that there is no early attestation of W. *ar bwys* cannot be taken as evidence that it did not exist from early times. (There are examples of *llwrw* 'track, trail, direction', and the like, used as a substantive, a preposition, and a conjunction in early texts; but the word in the forms *llwrw, llwr'*, and *llwyr*, according to *GPC*, seems to have survived only in [South Welsh] dialects and mainly if not only as a preposition.)

I should like to think that W. *ar bwys* and Br. *war-bouez* are derived from the preseparation period of the Brittonic languages and that they are derived ultimately from *ad pensum*, just as Fr. *après* is derived from Gallo-Roman *ad pressum*, which seems to have supplanted the classical *post* and to have been used first with local and then with temporal meaning. Indeed, it is instructive to compare the development of Fr. *près*, believed to represent either *presse* or a modified form *presso*, and the development of *après* 'after', believed to be from *ad pressum*, and *au près* 'close to, hard by', *auprès de* 'close to, (hard) by, beside, near' (where *au* is a development of *al* < *a le*; see Bloch 1932 and Pope 1973), all derived ultimately from *pressum : pressus : premo*.

The form *ad pensum* could conceivably be regarded as a sort of calque on *ad pressum*, not so much an *Übersetzungslehnwort* nor a *Lehnübersetzung* as a *Bedeutungslehnwort*, if British Latin and

Gaulish Latin could be considered as two different languages. Both *ad pressum* and *ad pensum* would express originally (close) proximity, irrespective of direction (front, side, back).

Welsh *ar bwys*, as we have seen, means 'near, nearby'. If Br. *war-bouez* ever meant 'near', it has lost that meaning and has been replaced by other expressions. French–Breton dictionaries seem to follow Le Gonidec (1847) fairly closely in translating *auprès* by *ékichen, tôst, harz, é-harz . . . ekeñver, étâl*, depending on the context (see Troude 1886; Vallée 1931, 1980; and Hemon 1950). By contrast, the Breton–French dictionaries—Le Gonidec 1850; Ernault 1921, 1927; Hemon 1948, 1973; Gros 1966; Williams 1984; Kervella 1976; Trépos 1980—agree with Hemon 1979, "*war-bouez*, prép. (1) au moyen (de), par, (2) dans la direction de, (3) à force de"; and with Hemon 1975, §66 Mn. Br. *war-bouez* 'about, concerning' (cf. *diwar-bouez* 'about, concerning': on *di-* see Williams 1948–50; §208 *war-bouez* 'by means of, by dint of, relating to, towards'. It should be noted that Br. *war-bouez*, unlike W. *ar bwys*, is not used adverbially but as a preposition only, and, like W. *ar bwys*, when it is used with a pronoun, the pronoun takes the form of the possessive: *war ho pouez* = W. *ar eich pwys*, morphologically but not semantically.

Both Hemon 1975 and Hemon 1979 give a local meaning to *war-bouez* 'towards, in the direction of', but this local meaning seems to be all but lost. The predominant meaning of W. *ar bwys* is local, 'near, nearby'. One occasionally comes across another meaning, 'on account of, depending on', but this meaning seems to be derived from a more literal interpretation of its elements: for example, 'from the weight/strength of, on account of', *Ond rhaid i mi gydnabod . . . ar bwys fy mhrofiad, fod mwy o dosturi ym mronnau rhai o'r hen uchelwyr* (Edwards 1963, 129); *ond caiff asyn dair a hanner (tudalen) ar bwys cysylltiadau Beiblaidd* (Y Gwyddonydd 1978, 5–6); *Cefais hwn ar bwys bywyd Endaf Lewis* (Owen 1920, 53). Examples of a similar reversion to the literal meaning of Br. *war-bouez* are found, especially in lexicographical explanations. Especially noteworthy in this connexion is the example given in Ernault 1927 of *war-bouez ma*, that is to say, of *war-bouez* as a conjunction (not cited in Hemon 1975): *war-bouez ma teuot*, 'à condition, pourvu'.

If we consult Pelletier 1716 (1978), we see under *poës*: "*Ghervel a poës e ben*, crier ou appeller en criant à pleine tette, de toute sa voix, cequi voudroit dire, mot à mot crier du poids de sa tette; *a poës e diou brec'h*, de poids de ses deux bras, c'est à dire de toute ses forces."

More to the point, as far as we are concerned, is that Pelletier also gives *"vöar poës traöun*, vers le bas," and *"vöar poës crec'h*, vers le haut"* Compare Le Gonidec 1850, s.v. *poéz, pouéz:* "*war boéz traoñ*, vers le bas; à la lettre, sur le poids du bas; *war boéz kreac'h*, vers le haut; à la lettre, sur le poids du haut." Le Gonidec seems to be following Pelletier slavishly here, for in his *Dictionnaire français–breton* (1847) he had translated *vers le bas* by "*ouc'h* ou *diouc'h ann traoñ.*"

Although Br. *war-bouez* seems to have lost almost all traces of its original meaning, there can be little doubt that its original meaning was local. In Celtic languages, most prepositions started on their semantic development from a basically local meaning, such as location or direction, and then proceeded to adopt a variety of specialized meanings falling into one or more of the categories of relation, agency, means, cause, association, purpose, and so on. As far as I am aware, it is Ernault 1927, s.v. *poez, pouez* who illustrates best the various senses in which Br. *war-bouez* is used:

> *war-bouez*, au bout (*eur gorden*, d'une corde); à force (*poanial* de travailler)
> *war-bouez an dourn*, par la main
> *war-bouez nebeut*, à peu près
> *war-bouez dek litrad dre zevez-arat*, (semer) à raison de dix litres par demi-hectare
> *ar bouiz é vlèu*, V. (suspendu) par les cheveux
> *war-bouez-se*, sous ce prétexte; qqf. en même temps que cela
> *o c'has emeaz diwar-bouez o baro*, les mettre dehors en les tirant par la barbe
> *diwar-bouez di(w)vrec'h al labourer-douar ema an holl o veva*, ce sont les bras du laboureur qui font vivre tout le mond
> *mont war-bouez traon*, aller en descendant

Particularly interesting to a Welshman are two of Ernault's examples: *mont war ar pouez*, "aller lentement Ouess.," and *kerzout a ra war e bouez (ig)*," il marche (tout) doucement, sans se presser"; cf. Welsh *cerdded wrth ei bwys(-au)* 'to walk leisurely' (Fynes-Clinton 1913, 449). Ernault gives also *pouez-traon, pouez-krec'h a zo gand an hent*, "le chemin est en pente, déscend ou monte."

Is this an example of *war-bouez* being abbreviated to *pouez*? Probably not, for *pouez* is unmutated. But compare W. *i bwys*, used by a modern Welsh author, probably under the influence of his dialect: *a cherdded i bwys y tŷ* (Williams 1954), where one could say that *pwys* has become synonymous with W. *ymyl* 'side, edge, brink'. There are examples in Welsh and other languages of the first element in a compound preposition being replaced by another: see the examples of *ar llwrw* and *yn llwrw* given in *GPC*. But here *pwys* seems to have adopted a meaning independent of its meaning in *ar bwys*—or perhaps one should say that *ar bwys* has been interpreted as synonymous with *ar ymyl*, and, as one can say *i ymyl*, it has been assumed that one can say *i bwys*, with the result that *pwys* has taken on the meaning of *ymyl*, at least in this context. I should also mention that I have heard *wrth bwys* and *ger bwys (y tŷ)* used in conversation with the same meaning as *ar bwys* 'near'.

This prompts the question, whether there is any relationship between Br. *pouez*, more especially in the context of *war-bouez*, with Br. *peuz-, peus-*. In his *Dictionary of Old Breton*, pt. 1 (1985, 287) Fleuriot discusses *pois chefel*, gl. 'mannus .i. equs breuis' in "ergo non aliter quam tellus mannus *proferri* debuit." After explaining *mannus* as 'poney, petit cheval', he goes on: "*Pois* est difficile: serait-ce la forme ancienne du bret. *peus-* (comparer *ois ous eus*)? Ex.: *peus*, 'presque, à demi, à moitié', *peus-foll* 'folâtre', *peuz-varo* 'moribond'." In pt. 2 *pois chefel* is translated 'cheval de somme', 'pack horse'; in other words, *pois* seems to be taken as 'poids', W. *pwys*. In view of our discussion of *pouez* in *war-bouez*, it may be worthwhile to look more carefully at *peus-, peuz-*, especially as Ernault (1885, 353) has suggested that the irregularity in the phonology of *peur-* (for *pur-*) 'very' is due to confusion with Fr. *per-, par-* and Lat. *per-*. See Jackson 1967, 142–43, and for *pus = puis* 'weight', ibid., 207.

According to Pelletier 1716 (1978), "*Peus* est une espece d'adverbe fort singulier et rare signifiant . . . Presque. Je ne l'ai jamais entendu tout seul; mais seulement en ces rencontres: *Disul-ar-peus*, Dimanche troisième avant les jours gras. *Disul-ar-peus-dibeus*, le Dimanche second, qui fut le troisième. C'est à dire trois ou deux Dimanches avant le Carnaval. *Disul-ar-peuslard*, le Dimanche qui précède immédiatement le Dimanche gras." Ernault in *Revue celtique* 27 (1906): 68–69 refers to Pelletier's comments as well as to Grégoire de Rostrenen, *Dictionnaire françoise celtique* (1738), where this *peus* is connected with *peus* in *peus-foll*, 'près fou'. I do not know how much attention should be given to Pelletier's "fort singulier et rare,'' for *peus-, peuz-* may not have been so peculiar as he thought; but if it was, it seems to have been a productive adverbial prefix in modern times. Ernault 1927 gives us the following examples: *peus-alies* 'assez souvent'; *peus-holl* 'presque tous'; *peus c'houek* 'doucereux'; *peusfoll* 'folâtre'; *peusklanv* 'indisposé'; *peustost* 'un peu près'; *peuzdu* 'noirâtre'; *peuzvelen* 'jaunâtre'; *peuzvad* 'passable'; *peuzvaro* 'moribond'; *peuzvras* 'assez beau' (cf. Hemon 1948). A Welshman is reminded of the productive use made of the adverbial prefix *lled* in Welsh as illustrated in *GPC*, where it is given the meanings 'half, part(ly), partially, to a certain extent, in some degree, not complete(ly); fairly, moderately, tolerably, pretty, quite, somewhat, rather; half-, semi-', and where it is said that it is possibly in origin the same word as *lled*[1] 'breadth, width' and, used as a preposition, 'throughout'. I hesitate to say that *peus-, peuz-* has any connection with *pouez* in *war-bouez*, but if it had, I would find it easy to explain the transition from its usage as a preposition to its usage as an adverbial prefix.

Perhaps I should have the same hesitation in connecting the *pwys* in Welsh *ar bwys* with the expressions *gŵr pwys* and *gwraig bwys*. In Morris Jones and Rhŷs 1894 there are several examples of *pwys* attached to *gŵr* and *gwraig*: 49.31–50.1, *Megys ydaw gwr pwys ac anneiryf luossogrwyd varchogyonn gantaw yn erbyn ywreic pwys* (= Sicut sponsus cum multitudine militum ad suscipiendam sponsam venit); 62.2, *Crist aseif yymlad dros ywreic bowys* (= Christus dicitur nunc stare, et pro sponsa sua pugnare); 64.21, *A christ ae wreic bwys*; 88.7, *yrhonn ysyd wreic bwys briawt y vnmab duw dat*. Morris Jones explains *pwys* as seemingly "derived from *sponsus*; but it is difficult to account for the omission of *s*." That *s* before *p* disappears in French we know from such examples as *époux, épouse*; but the disappearance of *s* is only one of the difficulties in deriving *pwys* from *sponsus*, and the presence of *gwraig bwys* in the Laws seems to exclude any inherent semantic connexion between the two words. In *Llyfr Iorwerth* (ed. Wiliam 1960) §25.10 we have *ni dele gureyc en e byt caffael ran o'r yt onyt gureyc pves*, "no wife in the world is to have a share of the corn but a gwraig bwys." In his note on *gureyc pves* in *Llyfr Iorwerth*, the editor explains *gwraig bwys* as 'a pregnant woman', supporting his explanation with the point made in the same law text that a man must provide a woman who is pregnant by him with provisions for rearing the child. Hence, literally a *gwraig bwys* is a 'woman of weight'. Compare *gwraig amdrom*

(: *amdrwm* 'heavy') and *gwraig feichiog* (: *baich* 'burden'), literally, 'a woman with a burden', hence 'pregnant'. This explanation, however, fails to explain why *pwys* qualifies *gŵr* as well as *gwraig*. If we return to the possibility that Brit.-Latin **pēsum* (Lat. *pensum*) was somehow confused with Brit.-Latin *pressum* and that **pesus* was confused with *pressus*, and if we remember the likelihood that *ar bwys* is ultimately derived from **ad pesum = ad pressum*, we can perhaps envisage the possibility that *gwraig bwys* meant originally the woman 'near' (and comparatively, 'nearest') to the husband, just as the *gŵr pwys* was the man 'near' (comparatively, 'nearest') to the wife. We also have, of course, the other expressions *gŵr priod* and *gwraig briod*, with *priod* derived from *privat-us, -a privatus = familiaris, amicus*, 'close friend, confidant' (see Du Cange 1890, Baxter and Johnson 1934, and Latham 1965).

J. E. CAERWYN WILLIAMS
Aberystwyth

NOTE

* I should like to thank the staff of the University of Wales Welsh Dictionary, Miss Morfydd Owen, and Professor Glanville Price for their valuable assistance to me in the preparation of this paper.

REFERENCES

Anwyl, J. Bodvan. 1925. *Spurrell's Welsh-English Dictionary*.
———. 1933. *Fy hanes i fy hunan*.
———. 1937. *Spurrell's English-Welsh Dictionary*.
Awbery, G. M. 1986. *Pembrokeshire Welsh: A Phonological Study*.
Baxter, J. H. and C. Johnson. 1934. *Medieval Latin Word-List*.
Bloch, O. 1932. *Dictionnaire étymologique de la langue française*, vol. 2.
——— and Walther von Wartburg. 1975. *Dictionnaire étymologique de la langue française*.
Cawrdaf (Jones, W. E.). 1830. *Y bardd*.
Daniel, J. 1892. *Archaeologia Lleynensis, sef hynafiaethau penaf Lleyn*.
Davies, E. J. 1955. *Astudiaeth gymharol o dafodieithoedd Llandygwydd a Dihewyd*. Traethawd M.A. Cymru Aberystwyth.
Davies, E. Tegla. 1923. *Gŵr Pen y Bryn*.
Davies, J. 1632. *Dictionarium Duplex*.

Davies, J. J. G. 1934. *Astudiaeth o Gymraeg llafar ardal Ceinewydd*. Traethawd Ph.D. Cymru Aberystwyth.
Davies, L. 1929. *Y Geilwad Bach*.
DuCange, C. D. et al. 1890. *Lexicon manuale ad scriptores mediae et infimae Latinitatis*.
Edwards, H. T. 1963. *Troi'r Drol*.
Edwards, Thomas (Caerfallwch). 1850. *An English and Welsh Dictionary*.
Ernault, E. 1885. *Dictionnaire étymologique du breton moyen* (following the text of *Le mystère de Sainte Barbe*).
———. 1895. *Glossaire moyen-breton*.
———. 1921. *Dictionnaire breton–français du dialecte de Vannes*.
———. 1927. *Gériadurig brezonek–gallek*.
Evans, C. and L. Fleuriot. 1985. *A Dictionary of Old Breton. Dictionnaire du vieux-breton*, pt. 2.
Evans, D. Gwynnallt. 1930. *Tafodiaith Cwmtawe*. Traethawd M.A. Cymru Abertawe.
Evans, D. Silvan. 1852. *An English and Welsh Dictionary*.
———. 1887. *Dictionary of the Welsh Language*.
Evans, D. Simon. 1951. *Gramadeg Cymraeg Canol*.
———. 1964. *A Grammar of Middle Welsh*.
Evans, E. M. and W. O. Thomas. 1958. *Y Geiriadur Mawr*.
Evans, J. 1808. *Hanes pleidiau y byd Crist'nogol*.
Evans, Theophilus. 1974. (Reprinted 1902.) *Drych y prif oesoedd*.
Fleuriot, L. 1985. *A Dictionary of Old Breton/Dictionnaire du vieux breton*, pt. 1.
Fynes-Clinton, O. H. 1913. *The Welsh Vocabulary of the Bangor District*.
GPC. 1950–. *Geiriadur Prifysgol Cymru: A Dictionary of the Welsh Language*.
Gros, J. 1966. *Le trésor du breton parlé*.
Hamp, E. 1953. Morphological Correspondences in Cornish and Breton. *Journal of Celtic Studies* 2: 15–24.
Hemon, R. 1947. (Reprinted 1950.) *Dictionnaire français–breton*.
———. 1948. (Reprinted 1973.) *Dictionnaire breton–français*.
———. 1975. *A Historical Morphology and Syntax of Breton*.
———. 1979. *Geriadur historel ar Brezhoneg*/Dictionnaire historique du breton.
Hughes, J. 1823. *An essay on the ancient and present state of the Welsh language with particular reference to its dialects, being the subject proposed by the Cambrian Society for the year 1822*.
Jackson, Kenneth H. 1953. *Language and History of Early Britain*.
———. 1967. *A Historical Phonology of Breton*.
Jones, T. Gwynn. 1929–31. Cagliad o eiriau llafar Dyffryn Aman. *Bulletin of the Board of Celtic Studies* 5: 327–37.
Jones, Thomas. 1688. *Y Gymraeg yn ei disgleirdeb*.
Kervella, F. 1976. *Yezhadur bras ar Brezhoneg*.
Latham, R. E. 1965. *Revised Medieval Latin Word-List*.
Le Gonidec, J.-F.-M.-M.-A. 1847. *Dictionnaire français–breton*.
———. 1850. Dictionnaire breton–français.
Lewis, D. Gerwin. 1960. *Astudiaeth o iaith lafar gogledd-orllewin Ceredigion*. Traethawd M.A. Cymru Aberystwyth.
Lewis, T. 1913. *A glossary of Medieval Welsh Law*.

Lhuyd, E. 1707. *Archaeologia Britannica.*
Lloyd-Jones, J. 1931–63. (Reprinted 1988.) *Geirfa Barddoniaeth Gynnar Gymraeg.*
Mathews, E. and J. C. Jones. 1886. *Cofiant J. Harris Jones.*
Morris, M. 1910. *A Glossary of the Demetian Dialect.*
Morris Jones, J. 1913. *A Welsh Grammar: Historical and Comparative.*
———. and J. Rhŷs. 1894. *The Elucidarium and Other Tracts in Welsh from Llyvyr Agkyr Llanddewivrevi.*
Nance, R. Morton. 1938. *A New Cornish–English Dictionary.*
Owen, R. D. 1920. *Endaf y gwladgarwr.*
Pelletier, Louis le. 1716. (Reprinted 1978.) *Dictionnaire de la langue bretonne.*
Philips, T. I. 1933. *The Spoken Dialect of the Ogwr Basin, Glamorgan.* M.A. University of Wales, Aberystwyth.
Pope, M. K. 1973. *From Latin to Modern French.*
Pryce, William. 1790. *Archaeologia Cornu-Britannica.*
Pughe, W. O. 1803. *A Welsh–English Dictionary.*
Rees, R. O. 1936. *Gramadeg tafodiaith Dyffryn Aman.* Traethawd M.A. Cymru Aberystwyth.
Richards, T. 1753. *Antiquae linguae Britannicae thesaurus.*
Strachan, J. 1909. *An Introduction to Early Welsh.*
Thomas, A. R. 1973. *The Linguistic Geography of Wales.*
Thomas, Ceinwen. 1988. *Astudiaeth o dafodiaith Nantgarw yng Nghwn Taf.* Manuscript.
Thomas, J. 1810. *Rhad Ras.*
Trépos, P. 1980. *Grammaire breton.*
Troude, A. 1886. *Nouveau dictionnaire pratique français et breton du dialecte de Léon.*
Vallée, F. 1931, 1980. *Grande dictionnaire français-breton.*
Walters, J. 1815. *An English and Welsh Dictionary.*
Wiliam, A. R. 1960. *Llyfr Iorwerth.*
Williams, Islwyn. 1954. *Storïau a Phortreadau.*
Williams, J. E. C. 1948–50. **De yn y Gymraeg. Bulletin of the Board of Celtic Studies* 13: 1–40.
Williams, M. 1784. *Speculum terrarum et coelorum.*
Williams, Rita. 1984. *Geiriadur bach Llydaweg-Cymraeg.*
Williams, Robert. 1865. *Lexicon Cornu-Britannicum.*
Williams, S. J. 1959. *Elfennau Gramadeg Cymraeg.*
Williams, W. Ll. 1897. (Reprinted 1945.) *Gwilym a Benni Bach.*
Y Gwyddonydd 16 (1978).

The Semantics of the Simple Tenses of the Verb at Plougrescant

It remains a matter of surprise and of pride to Bretons to see scholars from various parts of the world sharing their efforts to gain a better understanding of their language. Eric Hamp is a member of that international legion: may this paper be a token of gratitude for his contribution to the study of Breton.

Though long seen as a poor relation—a mere offshoot of British Celtic on the Continent—Breton has always been used by comparatists. It has also been in the past thirty years a favorite ground for fieldworkers in dialectology, phonemics, and sociolinguistics. For various reasons, however, the syntactical aspects of the language have been largely neglected, in spite of the number of Breton normative grammars (for instance, Hemon 1975) that have been published over the years. There are now encouraging signs of a growing interest in Breton syntax: suffice it to mention Urien 1987 and, concerning the verb, an excellent paper on the progressive, Hewitt 1986.

The present article follows the guideline of J. Gagnepain's "Pour une description structurale du breton" (1960). It will endeavor to analyze the structural meaning of the simple tenses of the verb in one dialect; the lack of a real norm in the language does not allow us to extend our conclusions to Breton as a whole. What is true here does not necessarily hold for another dialect, as "la valeur d'une forme ne peut être inféré de son emploi mais de sa position dans le cadre déterminant le nombre et la nature des oppositions qui les constituent" (Gagnepain 1961).

The phonology (Jackson 1961) and the morphology of the verbs (Jackson 1972) at Plougrescant have been thoroughly studied. The present author, whose mother is a native of the place—a village on the Channel near Tréguier, Côtes-du-Nord—has also written an unpublished thesis on the same dialect (Le Dû 1978). As scholars will have access more readily to K. H. Jackson's articles, it might be useful to complete and sometimes to correct some minor errors.

The word "tense" is used hereafter as a morphological term in the sense of "verb root + suffix." The preterite (*passé défini*) is rightly ignored, as it survives in only a few sayings. There remain five simple tenses, with the following endings (I.P.A.):

Present (pres.)	sg. 1. -ã		2. -əz		3. -O	
	pl. 1. -õm		2. -ət		3. -ãɲ	
	impersonal -ɛr					
Future (fut.)	sg. 1. -ĩ		2. -i		3. -o	
	pl. 1. -fõm		2. -fət		3. -õɲ	

There is no fut. impersonal. Pl. 3. is never *-fõɲ*, though this form is widely used elsewhere in Trégor. Sg. 2. and pl. 2., when stressed before neg. *ked* become, respectively, *-ęz and -ęt*.

Imperfect (imp.), present conditional (pres. cond.), and past conditional (past cond.) all have the same suffixes, with infixed *-f-* for pres. cond. and *-ʒ-* for past cond.

sg. 1. -ęn	2. -ɛs		3. -ę
pl. 1. -ęm	2. -ɛx		3. -ęn

The impersonal *-ɛd* has by now completely disappeared from the imp. It is *-fɛr* and *-ʒɛr* for pres. and past. cond. Jackson's *-ęt* for pl. 2. never occurs; he also made a mistake in the vowels: sg. and pl. 1. and 3. have the same close *ę*, and sg. and pl. 3. have the same open ɛ. The system has five phonemic apertures, with three phonemic /ę/, /e/, and /ɛ/, as shown by the oppositions /mę:z/ 'shame' versus /me:z/ 'outside', /le:r/ 'leather' versus /lɛ:r/ 'thief'. The same mistake made him come to the conclusion that the habitual pres. of *bezañ* 'to be' was "properly speaking a pres cond" (Jackson 1961, 76), where in fact the habitual pres. sg. 2. is *vęs* and pres. cond. sg. 2. is *vɛs*.

The dialect has kept to this five-tense system in the indicative, unlike that of Léon, in which pres. and past cond. seem to survive as mere allomorphs. The imperative has three persons, sg. 2., pl. 1., and pl. 2. It is morphologically identical to pres., except for sg. 2. in the affirmative. Example: *dibiñ* (rad. *deb-*) 'to eat' (from now on I shall use ordinary spelling).

	sg. 2.	pl. 1.	pl. 2.
aff.	deb	debom	debet
neg.	debéz-ked	debom-ked	debét-ked

Traces of an optative mood are found in a stock of fixed phrases. It is made up of a particle *da, d'*, followed by fut. pl. 3:

Doue d'e bardono! "May God forgive him!" (of a deceased)
Doue d'o 'frezervo! "May God preserve them!" (when admiring someone else's cattle)

The dialect distinguishes perfective and imperfective aspects, expressed, respectively, by simple and compound tenses. The opposition between progressive and nonprogressive is very similar to that of English (Hewitt 1986).

The formal organization of the system may be figured as follows (using sg. 1. of *lar-ed* 'to say'):

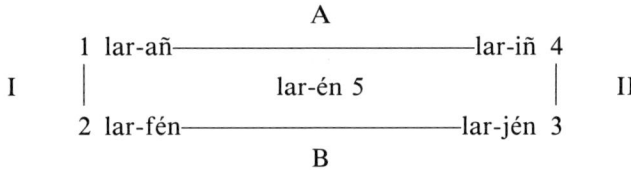

The imp. (5) stands between A and B: like A (pres. and fut.) it consists of the verb root followed by a simple suffix; its endings are identical to those of B (pres. and past cond.).

On the semantic side I shall distinguish the following oppositions: (1) A versus B: I shall call A "real" as opposed to B, "unreal." Actions or facts are or will certainly be realized for A, but are only potential or hypothetical for B. The imperfect (5) partakes of both according to context. (2) I versus II: The opposition is between "descriptive" (something that actually happens or should happen) and "projective" (something that will or might happen). Examples:

A1 vs. A4 Hennez ah ev vel e dad, "He drinks like his father"
           Hennez ah evo vel e dad, "He will drink like his father"
B2 vs. B3 Hennez a rafe, "He'd do it" (and he will)
           Lared neus e raje, "He said he'd do it" (he might)
I1 vs. I2 Me lenn kalz, "I read much"
           Me lennfe kalz, "I'd read much" (e.g., if I had books)
II4 vs. II3 Nim zavo abred, "We'll get up early"
           Nim zavje abred, "We'd get up early" (we meant to, but we didn't)
5A vs. 5B Eno tebéint o hoanio, "That's where they ate their supper"

Penever dit lahé e vreur, "But for you he'd have killed (he killed) his brother"

It can be verified indirectly that imp. is descriptive. The dialect has three adverbs covering the semantic field of English 'never': *biskoaz*, *biken*, and *jamez*. The first one does not come into account, for it is solely used with perfectives (compound verbs), as in *Meus kreded biskoaz trêo vel se*, "I've never believed such things." For simple tenses, the opposition lies between *biken* 'never in the future' and *jamez* 'never habitually'. Note that *jamez* may optionally replace both *biskoaz* and *biken*. Only A4 and B3 can take *biken*, for instance:

Biken gozeiñ outañ, "I'll never speak to him"
N'aje biken d'an overenn, "(He said, had decided) he'd never go to mass"

A1, B2 and 5 (imp.) only take *jamez*:

N'evañ jamez a gafe, "I never drink coffee"
Deufe jamez en ti! "He'd never come in!"
Ree jamez a drouz, "He never made any noise"

It is then clear that imp. is descriptive, like pres. and pres. cond. The semantic oppositions may be summed up as follows:

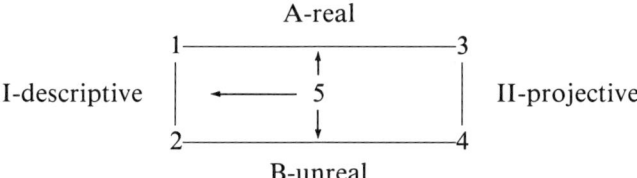

Let us now study the different shades of meaning each individual tense can take according to context:

A1 (pres.) is descriptive and real. It may convey a general truth:
Ar Vretoned blij patatez de, "Bretons like potatoes"
a repeated action:
Bemde 'h a da Landreger, "He (she) goes every day to Tréguier"
a condition that is bound to be fulfilled:
Ma teu en dro klewo gañiñ, "If he comes back I'll give him a piece of my mind" (he'll hear from me)

A3 (fut.) is projective and real. It conveys an indefinite future:
Hoaz weli anei, "You'll see her again"
a near future:
Bremazom kwei! "You are going to fall!" (soon you'll fall)
a habitual, repetitive action:
Pa vo dispaked ar journal 'h ei ar haz warni, "When the paper is (will be) unfolded, the cat goes (will go) and lie on it"
The pres. could also be used in that case:
Pa ve dispaked ar journal 'h a ar haz warni
but the projective (fut.) adds a notion of inevitability to the repetition.

5 (imp.) may be real and descriptive, expressing a habit in the past:
D'ar houlz se labourén bah menajo, "At that time I used to work (I worked) on farms" (I was a farm hand)
It can also be descriptive and unreal, expressing a condition that has not been fulfilled:
Ma oas ked bed ahe 'h én rog, "If you hadn't been (weren't) there I'd have left" (I left)
a polite request:
Me moa eom da weled ahanoh, "I need (I had need) to see you"

B2 is descriptive and unreal (pres. cond.). It conveys a meaning of probability, which presupposes a condition that can be fulfilled:
Hi larfé dah, "She would tell you" (She knows everything about it)
When the condition is expressed, it must then be in the pres. (real):
Gredañ ked teufé, "I don't believe he'll (he'd) come"
It may replace the pres. (real) in some cases, when a moral judgment is passed. The sentence
Skrwivfé jamez d'e dud! "He never writes (he'd never write) to his parents!"
is much stronger than *Skrwiv jamez d'e dud!* (id), as the

use of the unreal insists on the lack of realization of an action that is expected from a good son.

B4 is projective and unreal, thus conveying an absence of realization. It presupposes a condition that is not likely to be fulfilled:

Ma karjé oa pinvig, "If he'd wanted, he'd be rich" (should he have wanted)

or a condition that is out of our reach:

Ma ouijèr en avañs pera ve d'arioud! "If one could know in advance what is to happen!"

It also expresses a future in the past:

Me ouie teujé meudeusin, "I knew the doctor would come"

The opposition between descriptive and projective for B is quite clear in the following examples:

Mond a rafé d'an ôt, "He'd go fishing" (e.g., if there were no food left)

Mond a rajé d'an ôt, meañ, "He said he'd have gone fishing."

JEAN LE DÛ

Université de Bretagne Occidentale,
Brest

REFERENCES

Gagnepain, J. 1960. Pour une description structurale du breton. *Annales de Bretagne* 67: 377–88.
———. 1961. A propos du verbe celtique. *Études celtiques* 9: 309–26.
Hemon, R. 1975. *A Historical Morphology and Syntax of Breton.* Dublin: Dublin Institute for Advanced Studies.
Hewitt, S. 1986. Le progressif en breton à la lumière du progressif anglais. *La Bretagne linguistique* 2: 132–48.
Jackson, K. H. 1961. The Phonology of the Breton Dialect of Plougrescant. *Études celtiques* 9: 327–404.
———. 1972. The Regular and Irregular Verb at Plougrescant. *Indo-Celtica*: 73–88.
Le Dû, J. 1978. Le parler breton de la presqu'île de Plougrescant. Unpublished thesis.
Urien, J. Y. 1987. *La trame d'une langue: Le breton.* Lesneven: Hor Yezh.

BIBLIOGRAPHY

Bibliography: Autumn 1951–
Eric P. Hamp

The bibliography printed here is that kept by Professor Hamp himself. The numbering is his own; the lack of absolute numerical sequence reflects the division into articles and reviews, as well as the fact that items were not published in the order in which they were written. The editors and the publishers are indebted to Professor Victor A. Friedman of the University of North Carolina at Chapel Hill for assistance in the preparation of the bibliography.

ABBREVIATIONS

AA	American Anthropologist
AION	Annali (Istituto Orientale di Napoli)
AJP	American Journal of Philology
AL	Archivum Linguisticum
AO	Archiv Orientální
BBCS	Bulletin of the Board of Celtic Studies (Cardiff: University of Wales)
BCLC	Bulletin du Cercle Linguistique de Copenhague
BGDSL	Beiträge zur Geschichte der Deutschen Sprache und Literatur (=PBB, Paul und Braunes Beiträge, Tübingen)
BSLP	Bulletin de la Société de Linguistique de Paris
BSOAS	Bulletin of the School of Oriental and African Studies
CA	Current Anthropology
CJL/RLJ	Canadian Journal of Linguistics
CLS	Papers from the Nth Regional Meeting, Chicago Linguistic Society
CP	Classical Philology
EC	Etudes Celtiques

FL	Foundations of Language
FLH	Folia Linguistica Historica
GL	General Linguistics
IF	Indogermanische Forschungen
IJAL	International Journal of American Linguistics
IJSLP	International Journal of Slavic Linguistics and Poetics
JAOS	Journal of the American Oriental Society
JASA	The Journal of the Acoustical Society of America
JEGP	Journal of English and Germanic Philology
JIES	Journal of Indo-European Studies
JKF	Jahrbuch für Kleinasiatische Forschung
JNES	Journal of Near Eastern Studies
KZ	Kuhns Zeitschrift (= Zeitschrift für vergleichende Sprachforschung auf dem Gebiete der Indogermanischen Sprachen)
LB	Linguistique Balkanique (Bŭlgarska Akademija na Naukite: Otdelenie za ezikoznanie, literaturoznanie, i izkustvoznanie)
Lg.	Language
LR	The Linguistic Reporter
MLN	Modern Language Notes
MP	Modern Philology
REA	Revue des Etudes Arméniennes
RHA	Revue Hittite et Asianique
RP	Romance Philology
RRL	Revue Romaine de Linguistique
SIL	Studies in Linguistics
TPS	Transactions of the Philological Society
ŽA	Živa Antika
ZCP	Zeitschrift für Celtische Philologie
ZS	Zeitschrift für Slawistik
ZSP	Zeitschrift für Slavische Philologie

1951

Articles
1. "Language in a Few Words." *The Journal of General Education*, 5:286-302 (1951). (Reprinted with revisions, John P. De Cecco, *The Psychology of Language, Thought, and Instruction: Readings*. New York: Holt, Rinehart, and Winston (1967). Pp. 5-23.) Reprinted in part as 321 (1972).
2. "Morphophonemes of the Keltic Mutations." *Lg.* 27:230-47 (1951). Cf. 556 (1978)

1952

Articles
3. "*Bachgen.*" *BBCS* 14:295-6 (1952). Cf. 113 (1959); 293 (1971); 517 (1976)
4. "En quel sens et à quel point la grammaire descriptive a-t-elle une valeur pour la linguistique comparée?" *Preliminary Reports*, Section B.3, Seventh International Congress of Linguists, 1952. (Reprinted together with contributions in Sections C.1, C.2, and B.1 in *Proceedings of the VII International Congress of Linguists*, 2.377-8; 469-72 (1956).)
5. "The Anomaly of Germanic '7'." *Word* 8:136-9 (1952). Cf. 494 (1976)
6. "Non-syllabic Phonemes of Avestan." *SIL* 10:77-82 (1952).

1953

Articles
8. "Hittite Evidence for the "laryngeals"—An Addendum." *TPS* 1952 (1953) 110-13. Cf. 39 (1955)
9. "Morphological Correspondences in Cornish and Breton." *Journal of Celtic Studies* 2:5-24 (1953). Cf. 101 (1959); 889 (1984)
10. "OWelsh *guar*, Welsh *gor-*, Bret. *gour-*, OIr. *for*, Gaulish *ver-*; Welsh *wrth*, OIr. *frith*, etc." *BBCS* 15:124-5 (1953). Cf. 333 (1972); 356 (1972)
12. "Cypriote υϝαις ζαν." *CP* 48:240-2 (1953).
13. "Indo-European Nouns with Laryngeal Suffix." *Word* 9:135-41 (1953). Cf. 272 (1970); 353 (1974); 403 (1974); 587 (1979)

Reviews
7. Review of Tom Peete Cross, *Motif-Index of Early Irish Literature*. *MP* 50:274-5.
11. Review of R. Levy, *The Persian Language*. *CP* 48:213-4 (1953).
14. Review of Wacław Cimochowski, *Le Dialecte de Dushmani*. *Lg*. 29:500-12 (1953). Cf. 87 (1958)
15. Review of Brian Ó Cuív, *Irish Dialects and Irish Speaking Districts*. *Lg*. 29:512-17 (1953).
16. Reviews of Brian Ó Cuív, *The Irish of West Muskerry, Co. Cork*; Thomás de Bhaldraithe, *The Irish of Cois Fhairrge, Co. Galway*; Risteard Breatnach, *The Irish of Ring, Co. Waterford*. *Lg*. 29:517-28 (1953).

1954

Articles
17. "Gothic *iup* 'ἄνω'." *MLN* January 1954, 39-41.
18. "Final Vowels in Old Persian." *JNES* 13:115-7 (1954). Cf. 72 (1958)
19. "The Relationship of Venetic within Italic." *AJP* 75:183-6 (1954). Cf. 96 (1959)
20. "Latin *poples* 'back of the knee'." *AJP* 75:186-9 (1954). Cf. 337 (1971)
21. "Componential Restatement of Syllable Structure in Trique." *IJAL* 20:206-9 (1954).
24. "Old Irish *gaib-*, Welsh *gafael, caffael, cael, cahel*." *ZCP* 24:229-33 (1954).
25. "Les labio-vélaires indo-européennes." *BSLP* 50:44-6 (1954). Cf. 46 (1956)
27. "A Note on Structural Complexity." *SIL* 12:1-7 (1954). Cf. 70 (1958)
28. "*Viviane* or *Niniane*—A Comment from the Keltic Side." *RP* 8:91 (1954). Cf. 38 (1955)
29. "A Rejoinder on *p*-Italic and Cornish *ns*." *AJP* 75:401-2 (1954).

Reviews
22. Review of Brian Ó Cuív, *Párliament na mBan*. *ZCP* 24:312-14 (1954).

23. Review of I. J. Gelb, *A Study of Writing*. *ZCP* 24:308-12 (1954). Cf. 676 (1981)
26. Review of Bruno Snell, *Der Aufbau der Sprache*. *CP* 49:216-7 (1954).

1955

Articles
30. "Armenian *hariwr*." *KZ* 72:244-5 (1955). Cf. 525 (1976)
32. "Iota after upsilon." *CP* 50:126 (1955).
34. "Primitive Irish Intervocalic **w*." *EC* 6:281-8 (1955).
35. "Negau *harigasti*." *Lg.* 31:1-3 (1955). Cf. 108 (1959)
36. "Hieroglyphic Hittite *laīnuḫa*." *JKF* 3:93-5 (1955).
37. "La noche como unidad de tiempo." *Emérita* 23:262-4 (1955).
38. "St. Ninian/Ronyan again." *Celtica* 3:290-4 (1955). Cf. 28 (1954); 242 (1969); 426 (1974)
39. "Italic perfects in $*/-x^{W}-/$ and IE $*A^{W}$." *Word* 11:399-403 (1955).

Reviews
31. Review of J. Hubschmid, Sardische Studien. *Lg.* 30:488-94 (1954).
33. Review article: "Recent Scholarship in Ireland." *MP* 52:265-8 (1955). Cf. 53 (1956); 64 (1957)
40. Review article: "Bibliographie de la statistique linguistique." *CP* 50:289-90 (1955).
41. Review of Ammon, *-ΙΚΟΣ bei Platon*. *CP* 50:294-5 (1955).

1956

Articles
44. "Gothic *ai* and *au*." *MLN* 71:265-9 (1956). Cf. 83 (1958)
45. "Russian /e/." *AL* 7:57-8 (1956).
46. (with H. G. Güterbock) "Hittite *šuwaya-*." *RHA* 58:22-4 (1956). Cf. 25 (1954)
47. "Old Prussian *soye* 'rain'." *KZ* 74:127-8 (1956). Cf. 131 (1960)
48. "Proto-British **-eg-*; *anian*; Old Irish *indile*, Welsh *ennill*; Middle Welsh *py* 'to', *bwy-gilydd*; The allophones of Medieval Welsh /x/ and /ü/." *BBCS* 16:277-85 (1956). Cf. 205 (1966), 428 (1975); 517 (1976), 557 (1978); 700 (1982); 954 (1987)

49. "IE enclitic *-k." *KZ* 74-236-8 (1956). Cf. 632 (1980); 683 (1981)
50. "Mycenean *i-je-re-ja*." *Glotta* 35:290-1 (1956). Cf. 266 (1970)
51. "The Development of Modern Welsh Syllabic Structure." *BBCS* 17:30-6 (1956).
53. "Recent Keltic Linguistic Publications." *Kratylos* 1:104-18 (1956). Cf. 33 (1955); 64 (1957)

Reviews
42. Review of Paul Falk, *Pir- + suff. *'fuseau' à la lumière du celtique*. *RP* 9:468-9 (1956).
43. Review of E. Pulgram, *Theory of Names*. *RP* 9:346-50 (1956).
52. Review of H. Barić, *Rečnik srpskoga ili hrvatskoga i arbanaskoga jezika*. *Kratylos* 1:183 (1956).

1957

Articles
54. "Stylistically Modified Allophones in Huichol." *Lg.* 33:139-42 (1957).
57. "Albanian and Messapic." *Studies Presented to Joshua Whatmough*, ed. Ernst Pulgram. 's-Gravenhage: Mouton, 1957. Pp. 73-89. Cf. 189 (1966)
58. "Albanian *pas*, *mbas* 'behind, after'." *KZ* 75:23 (1957).
59. "Nasal plus consonant in Lettish." *KZ* 75:122 (1957).
60. "Pashto vowels." *SIL* 12:74-7 (1957).
61. "Hamites and Kelts and Substratum." *GL* 2:43-7 (1957).
62. Obituary of Carl Darling Buck, ΠΛΑΤΩΝ (1957).
63. "Note on 'four' in Hittite and Luwian." *RHA* 15:60:7-8 (1957). Cf. 264 (1969); 91 (1958)
66. "Two Notes on Albanian." *Lg.* 33:530-2 (1957). Cf. 176 (1963); 732 (1982)
65. "British Keltic *peθ*." *BBCS* 17:158-61 (1957).
71. "Jui Syllabics." *BIHP(AS)* 29:323-6 (1957).

Reviews
55. Review of E. Adelaide Hahn, *Subjunctive and Optative*. *CP* 52:37-9 (1957).
56. Review of W. Luther, *Weltansicht und Geistesleben*. *CP* 52:128-30 (1957).

64. Reviews of V. Pisani, *Allgemeine und vergleichende Sprachwissenschaft—Indogermanistik*; and J. Pokorny, *Keltologie*. *Lg.* 33:435-9 (1957). Cf. 53 (1956)
80. Review of Herbert H. Paper, *Elamite Phonology and Morphology*. *Word* 13:499-513 (1957).

1958

Articles
67. "Protopopoloca Internal Relationships." *IJAL* 24:150-3 (1958). Cf. 110 (1960)
68. "Stress Continuity in Iranian." *JAOS* 78:115-8 (1958). Cf. 18 (1954)
69. "Russian /j/." *Journal of the Canadian Linguistic Association* 4:34 (1958).
70. "The Calculation of Parameters of Morphological Complexity." *Proceedings of the VIII International Congress of Linguists* (Oslo, 1957; pub. 1958), 134-42. Cf. 27 (1954)
72. "Old Persian *avā*." *KZ* 75:239 (1958). Cf. 18 (1954)
73. "Albanian *arë*." *KZ* 75:237-8 (1958).
74. "Vedic *ī́mahe*." *Indo-Iranian Journal* 2:229-30 (1958).
78. "A Question on Ocaina Syllables." *IJAL* 24:239-40 (1958).
79. "Karok Syllables." *IJAL* 24:240-1 (1958).
81. "Prosodic Notes." *IJAL* 24:321-2 (1958).
82. "Wahgi (New Guinea) Prosodic Phonemes." *Oceania* 29:62-4 (1958).
83. "Gothic *ai* and *au* Again." *Lg.* 34:359-63 (1958). Cf. 44 (1956)
84. "Gender Shift in Albanian Plurals." *RP* 12:147-55 (1958).
85. "Consonant Allophones in Proto-Keltic." *Lochlann* 1:209-17 (1958).
89. "The Phonemic Structure of Lettish Syllables." *Die Welt der Slaven* 3:248-52 (1958).
90. "The Accentuation of Baltic Substantives." *IF* 64:39-65 (1958).
91. "Etruscan *max* '4'?" *Glotta* 37:311-2 (1958). Cf. 63 (1957)
92. Notulae Celtibericae." *The Journal of Celtic Studies* 2:147-51 (1958).
93. "Vowel Harmony in Classical Mongolian." *Word* 14:291-4 (1958). Cf. 646 (1980)

Reviews
75. Review of G. Serra, *La tradizione latina e greco-latina nell' onomastica medioevale italiana*. *RP* 11:393-4 (1958).
76. Review of G. Petrotta, *Svolgimento storico della cultura e della letteratura albanese*. *Kratylos* 3:80 (1958). Cf. 98 (1959)
77. Review article: *Fjalor Rusisht-Shqip*. *Kratylos* 3:79-80 (1958).
86. Review of S. E. Mann, *An English-Albanian Dictionary*. *The American Slavic and East European Review* 17:573-4 (1958). Cf. 340 (1972)
87. Review of L. Newmark, *Structural Grammar of Albanian*. *The Slavic and East European Journal* 16:363-6 (1958). Cf. 14 (1953)
88. Review of Z. Sako, *Folklori shqiptar*. *Kratylos* 3:188 (1958).

1959

Articles
94. "Zuara Berber Personals." *BSOAS* 22:140-1 (1959). Cf. 106 (1959); 152 (1961)
95. "Proper Names in Scottish Gaelic." *Names* 7:57-9 (1959).
96. "Venetic Isoglosses." *AJP* 80:179-84 (1959). Cf. 19 (1954)
97. "Final -*s* in Latin." *CP* 54:165-172 (1959). Cf. 397 (1974)
99. "Albanian *pres* 'I wait'." *KZ* 76:135 (1959). Cf. 855 (1985)
100. "Comment: Russian-English Transliteration." *Science* 130: 3374 (28 Aug. 1959).
101. "Middle Welsh, Cornish, and Breton Personal Pronominal Forms." *EC* 8:394-401 (1959). Cf. 9 (1953)
102. "Welsh *heb*, Irish *sech*." *EC* 8:402-3 (1959).
103. "Buividze Lithuanian Phonemes." *IJSLP* 1/2:195-202 (1959).
104. "Graphemics and Paragraphemics." *SIL* 14:1-5 (1959).
105. "An Overlappling Allograph." *SIL* 14:6 (1959).
106. "The Personal Morphemes of Classical Arabic," *SIL* 14:21-2 (1959). Cf. 94 (1959)
107. "Probabilistic Structuring." *GL* 4:41-2 (1959).
108. "Final Syllables in Germanic and the Scandinavian Accent System." *Studia Linguistica* 13:29-48 (1959). Cf. 498 (1976)
113. "*bachgen*." *BBCS* 18:274 (1959). Cf. 3 (1952)
120. "Lushai Syllables." *Indian Linguistics* (Turner Jubilee Vol. II) 1959. Pp. 238-40.

124. "Consoanele Romîneşti şi Metodologia Fonologică." *Cercetări de Lingvistică* 4:171-5 (1959). Cf. 240 (1968)

Reviews

98. Review of S. E. Mann, *Albanian Literature*. *Kratylos* 4:92 (1959). Cf. 76 (1958); 619 (1980)

1960

Articles

110. "Chocho-Popoloca Innovations." *IJAL* (Notes and Reviews) 26:62 (1960). Cf. 67 (1958); 177 (1963)
111. "O dolgote glasnyx v vengerskom jazyke." Akademija nauk SSSR, *Voprosy Jazykoznanija*, No. 1 (1960).
112. "The Germanic Words for 'tear'." *BGDSL* 81:263-6 (1960). Cf. 200 (1967); 285 (1970); 304 (1971); 344 (1972)
114. "*Varuṇa* and the Suffix *-una*." *Indo-Iranian Journal* 4:64-6 (1960).
115. "Pre-Romance *Alpēs* and **kurro-*." *RP* 13:387-90 (1960).
117. "Notes on Early Greek Phonology." *Glotta* 38:187-203 (1960). Cf. 499 (1976); 587 (1979)
118. "Irish *srón*, Greek ῥίς, ῥῑνός." *Glotta* 38:209-11 (1960). Cf. 405, 418 (1974) which supersede
119. "Florentine Stops." *Italica* 37:126-8 (1960).
121. "American English Phonemes." *JASA* 32:1079-80 (1960).
125. "Selected Summary Bibliography of Language Classifications." *SIL* 15:29-45 (1960). Cf. 186 (1965); 211 (1967)
130. "Avestan *fštāna*." *KZ* 76:273-5 (1960). Cf. 568 (1978); 798 (1983)
131. "Palatal Before Resonant in Albanian." *KZ* 76:275-80 (1960). Cf. 47 (1956); 548 (1978); 857 (1985)
132. "Der Vokalismus im älteren Tschechisch," *ZS* 5:462-4 (1960).
133. "Notes on Ket Phonemics." *Ural-Altaische Jahrbücher* 32:129-32 (1960). Cf. 583 (1979)
137. "La suffissazione dei 'nomi del centone'." *AION* 2:155-7 (1960).
138. "Mythical Prothetic Vowels in Albanian." *AION* 2:185-90 (1960). Cf. 122 (1965); 159 (1962); 819 (1984)
139. "Sur la traduction des catégories." *Latomus* 19:700 (1960).
140. "Notulae." *EC* 9:139-40 (1960). Cf. 653 (1979)

141. "O. Ir. *fecht n-aill*, Bret *guechall*." *EC* 9:475-7 (1960). Cf. 628 (1980)
150. "Buddhist Hybrid Sanskrit Syllables." *Indian Linguistics* 21:89 (1960).

Reviews
109. Review of Alfred Ernout, *Philologica II*. *CP* 55:58-61 (1960). Cf. 636 (1980)
116. Review of John Chadwick, *The Decipherment of Linear B* (Cambridge University Press, 1958). *Journal of Religion* 40:130 (1960).
126. Review of *Y Geiriadur Mawr, The Complete Welsh-English English-Welsh Dictionary*, eds. H. Meurig Evans and W. O. Thomas. *Kratylos* 5:99 (1960).
127. Review of *Gavril Darë i Riu, Kënka e sprasme e Balës*, ed. Ziaudin Kodra. *Kratylos* 5:104-5 (1960).
128. Review of *Përparimi: Revistë kulturore, Prishtinë*. *Kratylos* 5:106 (1960).
129. Review of *English-Irish Dictionary*, ed. T. de Bhaldraithe. *Kratylos* 5:214 (1960).
135. Review of Karl Wydler, *Zur Stellung des attributiven Adjektivs vom Latein bis zum Neufranzösischen*. *RP* 14:166-9 (1960).
136. Review of Holger Steen Sørensen, *Word-Classes in Modern English with Special Reference to Proper Names: With an Introductory Theory of Grammar, Meaning, and Reference*. *Studia Neophilologica* 32:349-54 (1960).

1961

Articles
142. "Marginalia to Pokorny's *Indogermanisches Etymologisches Wörterbuch*." *IF* 66:21-8 (1961). Cf. 618 (1980); 656 (1981)
143. "Loss of **t* and **n* before **s* in Illyrian." *IF* 66:51-2 (1961). Cf. 568 (1978)
144. "Albanian *dimën, dimër*." *IF* 66:52-5 (1961).
146. "The Science of Linguistics and Language Teaching." *Teachers College Record* 62:550-61 (1961).
149. "A Footnote on 'Point Betsie'." *Leelanau* (Michigan) *Enterprise-Tribune*, October 12, 1961. Pp. 10-11.
151. (with Norman N. Markel) "Connotative Meanings of Certain Phoneme Sequences." *SIL* 15:47-61 (1961).

152. "Tuareg Berber Personals." *SIL* 15:75-8 (1960-61). Cf. 94 (1959)
153. "Vidrovgrad, Vidrovac." *ZSP* 29:356-7 (1961). (Republished in error in *Zbornik za filologiju i lingvistiku* (Novi Sad, 1969), p. 225.)
154. "On the Arvanitika Dialects of Attica and the Megarid." Vol. III: *LB* pp. 101-6 (1961).
155. "An Albanian Alphabet of Demetrio Camarda." *AION* 3:105-8 (1961).
156. "On So-called Gemination in Greek." *Glotta* 39:265-8 (1960-61).
158. Τὸ ῥῆμα ἐν τῇ σημερινῇ ὁμιλουμένῃ Ἑλληνικῇ γλώσσῃ. ᾿Αθηνᾶ 65:101-28 (1961).
167. "Albanian *be, besë* 'oath'." *KZ* 77:252-3 (1961). Cf. 429 (1974); 855, 895 (1985)
168. "IE **bhendh-* in Albanian." *KZ* 77:253 (1961). Cf. 167
169. "Albanian *natë* 'night'." *KZ* 77:254-5 (1961). Cf. 260 (1970); 447 (1974); 855 (1985)
170. "Albanian *pishk* 'fish'." *KZ* 77:256 (1961). Cf. 386 (1973)

Reviews
134. Review of *American Studies in Uralic Linguistics*, ed. Thomas A. Sebeok. *AA* 63:165-8 (1961).
145. Review of Alan S. C. Ross, *Etymology; With Especial Reference to English* (1958). *Word* 17:91-103 (1961). Cf. 536 (1977)

1962

Articles
159. "About the Bronze Tables of Iguvium." *Latomus* 21:124-33 (1962).
160. "Vieil-irlandais *sétig*, Breton *ozac'h*." *Ogam* 14:376 (1962).
161. "Greco ἕλμινς, latino 'vermis'." *AION* 4:53-7 (1962).
165. "A Point of Sandawe Law." *Journal of African Languages* 1:181 (1962).
166. "Albanian Corrigenda to Pokorny's *Indogermanisches Etymologisches Wörterbuch*." *IF* 67:142-50 (1962).
171. "Fourth International Congress of Phonetic Sciences." *LR* 4:4 (1962).
172. "The Interconnection of Sound Production, Perception, and Phonemic Typology." *Proceedings of the Fourth International*

Congress of Phonetic Sciences (Helsinki 1961; pub. 1962). Pp. 639-42.

Reviews

157. Review of Karl J. Grebanier, *Audio-Lingual Techniques for Foreign Language Teaching* (1961). *Teachers College Record* 63:401 (1962).

1963

Articles

147. "The Albanian Diffusion of Slavic Toponyms in Greece." *Atti e Memorie del VII Congresso Internazionale di Scienze Onomastiche*, Vol. II (Toponomastica): 137-44 (1963).
163. "Einige slavische Toponyme in Griechenland aus dem 17. Jahrhundert." *ZSP* 31:143-5 (1963).
174. "Old Irish *scál*, Gothic *skohsl*." *Celtica* 6:118 (1963).
175. "Old Irish *esséirge* 'rising'." *Celtica* 6:66 (1963). Cf. 537 (1977); 644 (1980)
176. "An Irregular-Regularized Albanian Noun." *AION* 5:61-2 (1963). Cf. 66 (1957)
177. "On Aboriginal Languages of Latin America." *CA* 4:317 (1963). Cf. 110 (1960); 178 (1964)
327. "Notes on Eastern Armenian Phonemics." *AO* 31:398-400 (1963).

Reviews

162. Review of John P. Hughes, *The Science of Language: An Introduction to Linguistics* (1962). *AA* 65:479-81 (1963).

1964

Articles

148. "General Linguistics—The United States in the Fifties." *Trends in European and American Linguistics*, Utrecht 1964. Pp. 165-95.
164. "*Urslavisch čeršja*." *ZSP* 31:298-300 (1964).
173. "*Pa-* as a Calque on German." *IJSLP* 8:124-5 (1964).
178. "Toward the Refinement of Chiapanec-Mangue Comparative Phonology." *Actas y Memorias, XXXV Congreso Interna-*

cional de Americanistas (Mexico City, 1962; pub. 1964.) Pp. 387–402. Cf. 177 (1963)
180. " 'Chicken' in Ecuadorian Quichua." *IJAL* 30:298–9 (1964).
181. "Retrospect and Prospect on the Neglected Languages." Mimeographed (1964); distributed by Office of Education. Cf. 182 (1965)

Reviews
179. Review of André Martinet, *A Functional View of Language* (1962). *Harvard Educational Review* 34:355–7 (1964).

1965

Articles
122. "Evidence for the Laryngeals in Albanian." (Pp. 54–92 of the preprint edition 1959) *Evidence for Laryngeals*, ed. Werner Winter. The Hague: Mouton and Co., 1965. Pp. 123–141. Cf. 138 (1960); 272 (1970); 262 (1968); 337 (1971); 667 (1981); 731 (1982)
123. "Evidence for Laryngeals in Keltic." (Pp. 199–221 of the preprint edition 1959) *Evidence for Laryngeals*, ed. Werner Winter. The Hague: Mouton and Co., 1965. Pp. 224–35.
182. "The Making of Dictionaries." *LR* 7:5:6–7 (1965). Cf. 181 (1964)
183. "On Melanesian and the Origin of Austronesian." *CA* 6:220–1 (1965).
184. "Welsh *chwarddaf*, *chwerthin*, and *gwên*." *Franciplegius* (Magoun Festschrift), eds. Jess B. Bessinger, Jr. and Robert P. Creed. New York: New York University Press, 1965. Pp. 240–3.
185. (with Harry Hoijer and William G. Moulton) "Survey of the State and Future of the Linguistic Institute." *Lg.* 41:3:39–91 (1965).
186. (with Harry Hoijer and William Bright) "Contributions to a Bibliography of Comparative Amerindian." *IJAL* 31:346–53 (1965). Cf. 125 (1960)
187. "Second International Congress of Dialectologists." *LR* 7:6: 2–3 (1965).
190. "The Albanian Dialect of Mándres." *Die Sprache* 11:137–54 (1965). Cf. 280 (1970); 823 (1983)

204. "Armenian *gišer*, Latin *uesper*." *Anadolu-Araştırmaları* 2:257-9 (1965). Superseded by 203 (1966)
207. "Joshua Whatmough." *Onoma* 11:326 (1964-5). Cf. 208 (1966); full account 209 (1967)

1966

Articles
188. "Upper Chehalis q̓ał ~ q̓es-." *IJAL* 32:84-6 (1966).
189. "The Position of Albanian." *Ancient Indo-European Dialects*, eds. Henrik Birnbaum and Jaan Puhvel. Berkeley and Los Angeles: The University of California Press, 1966. Pp. 97-121. Cf. 627 (1980); 837 (1984)
191. "Vietnamuong Labials Again." *Studies in Comparative Austroasiatic Linguistics*, ed. Norman H. Zide. The Hague: Mouton and Co., 1966. Pp. 41-3.
192. "On Two Californian Grammars." *IJAL* 32:176-88 (1966). Cf. 195
193. "A Note on the Fishes of San Nicola Dell'Alto." *Bollettino dell'Atlante Linguistico Mediterraneo*, 8:61-4 (1966).
194. (with D. G. Moutsos) "Linguistic and Cultural Categories in the Toponyms of a Greek-Albanian Township (Deme)." *Proceedings of the Eighth International Congress of Onomastic Sciences*. The Hague: Mouton and Co., 1966. Pp. 310-22. Cf. 883 (1985)
195. "Studies in Sierra Miwok." *IJAL* 32:236-41 (1966). Cf. 192
196. "Notes on Kafir Phonology." *Shahidullah Presentation Volume*, ed. Anwar S. Dil. Pakistani Linguistics Series No. VII (1966). Pp. 89-100. Cf. 217 (1968); 263 (1970)
203. "Three Armenian Etymologies." *REA* (N.S.) 3:11-5 (1966). Cf. 260 (1970); 263 (1970); 285 (1970)
205. "Medieval Welsh *uch*." *BBCS* 22 (Part I):46-7 (1966). Cf. 48 (1956); 428 (1975)
206. "**Nissia—Niš*." *LB* 11:119 (1966).
208. "Joshua Whatmough." *Lg.* 42:620-31 (1966). Cf. 207 (1965); 209 (1967); 315 (1971)
210. "Ad DAG Note lviii." *Die Sprache* 12:98 (1966). Cf. 315 (1971)

1967

Articles

197. "On IE *s after *i, u* in Baltic." *Baltistica* 3:7-11 (1967). Cf. 360 (1973); 618 (1980)
198. "Lithuanian *šáukštas*." *Baltistica* 3:107-8 (1967). Cf. 647 (1980); 838 (1984)
199. "Two Albanian and Indo-Iranian Problems." *Languages and Areas: Studies Presented to George V. Bobrinskoy.* Chicago: The University of Chicago Press, 1967. Pp. 65-9. Cf. 562 (1977); 856 (1985)
200. "On Some Troublesome Indo-European Initials." *Studies in Honor of George Sherman Lane: Historical Linguistics.* Chapel Hill: University of North Carolina Press, 1967. Pp. 146-53. Cf. 252 (1969); 342 (1972); 344 (1972); 358 (1972)
201. "Assimilation and Rule Application." *Lg.* 43:179-84 (1967). Cf. 577 (1979)
209. "Joshua Whatmough: His Life and Scientific Career." *Onoma* 12:225-237 (1966-67). Cf. 208 (1966)
211. "Languages of the World." *Chambers's Encyclopaedia.* Oxford and New York: Pergamon Press, 1967. Pp. 357-67. Cf. 125 (1960)
212. "On Maya-Chipayan." *IJAL* 33:74-6 (1967). Cf. 259 (1970); 317 (1971)
213. "On the notions of 'stone' and 'mountain' in Indo-European." *Journal of Linguistics* 3:83-90 (1967). Cf. 215 (1967); 217 (1968); 431 (1974); 435 (1974); 532 (1976)
214. "Roman British *Rutupiae*, Gaulish *Rutuba*." *EC* 11:413 (1967). Cf. 371 (1973); 478 (1976)
215. "Two Armenian Etymologies." *REA* (N.S.) 4:15-7 (1967). Cf. 213 (1967); 469 (1975); 904 (1985)
221. " 'Zmeură'." *RRL* 12:523-4 (1967). Cf. 222 (1968); 388 (1973); 570 (1979); 916 (1986)

Reviews

202. Review of W. Sidney Allen, *Vox Latina: A Guide to the Pronunciation of Classical Latin* (1965). *CP* 62:44-6 (1967).

1968

Articles

216. "A Comment on Some Constraints in Southern Ivatan." *GL* 8:1-4 (1968).
217. "On *R in Kafir." *Studies in Indian Linguistics* (Emeneau Festschrift), 1968. Pp. 124-37. Cf. 196 (1966)
218. "Albanian *pidh*, Slavic **peizd'ă*. *IJSLP* 11:25-6 (1968). Cf. 637 (1979)
219. "What a Contrastive Grammar Is Not, If It Is." Monograph Series on Languages and Linguistics: *19th Annual Round Table*, No. 21 (Georgetown University School of Languages and Linguistics, 1968). Pp. 137-47.
220. "δέχομαι, δοκέω, διδάσκω, *decet, dignus, doctus, docēre, discō*." *CP* 63:285-7 (1968). Cf. 336 (1971)
222. "Addendum to " 'Zmeură' "." *RRL* 13:367 (1968). Cf. 221 (1967)
223. "Albanian *jetë* 'life'." *Essays in Romance Philology from the University of Chicago*, 1968. Pp. 41-7.
224. "Albanian *viç* 'calf', *vit* 'year'." *Gjurmine Albanologjike* 1:27-30 (1968). Cf. 589 (1979) s.v. *gwŷs*
225. "IE **Hu̯ed(h)-*." *Die Sprache* 14:156-9 (1968). Cf. 226 (1969); 302 (1970); 338 (1972); 564 (1978)
227. "Lithuanian *pa-* and *põ* Again." *Baltistica* 4:255-7 (1968). Cf. 552 (1978)
228. "Clisis and H in Latin Medieval Greek." *GL* 8:92-4 (1968). Cf. 246 (1969)
230. "La Langue albanaise et ses voisins." *Actes du Premier Congrès International des Études Balkaniques et Sud-Est Européennes* 6:663-8 (1968). Cf. 574 (1978)
233. "*mīlle*." *Glotta* 46:274-8 (1968). Cf. 331 (1972)
238. "Some Nominalizations of 'Eat'." *TPS* 1968, p. 106. Cf. 381 (1974)
240. "Unele concluzii de fonologie generativă în legătură cu palatalizarea consoanelor." *Studii şi Cercetări Lingvistice* 19:493-6 (1968).
250. "Underlying Forms versus Historical Reconstruction." *BCLC* 1968; published in *Acta Linguistica Hafniensia* 11:239-42 (1968). Cf. 241 (1969)

262. "Dy Etimologji nga Fusha e Gjuhës Shqipe." *Studime Filologjike* 3:119-22 (1968). = 261 (1969)
267. "The Name of Demeter." *Minos* (N.S.) 9:198-204 (1968). Cf. 268 (1969)
321. "Acculturation as a late rule." *CLS* IV:103-10 (1968).

Reviews

323. Review of Al. Graur, *Nume de persoane* (București, 1965). *Names* 16:59-60 (1968).

1969

Articles

226. "Addendum (to "IE *$H\underset{\smile}{u}ed(h)$-")." *Die Sprache* 15:63 (1969). Cf. 225 (1968)
229. "Two IE Lexical Notes." *Münchener Studien zur Sprachwissenschaft* 25:57-8 (1969). Cf. 553 (1977)
231. "On Proto-Ainu Numerals." *CLS* V:337-42 (1969). Cf. 269 (1970)
232. "On Maxakalí, Karaja, and Macro-Jê." *IJAL* 35:268-70 (1969).
234. "Hierarchy in Semantic Representation." *Kivung* 2:67-8 (1969).
235. "Early Welsh Names, Suffixes, and Phonology." *Proceedings of the Ninth International Congress of Onomastic Sciences* (London, 1966; pub. Louvain, 1969). Pp. 266-72. Cf. 535 (1977); 802 (1983)
236. "Notes on *Słownik etymologiczny języka polskiego* III,2." *Rocznik Slawistyczny* 30:43-5 (1969). Cf. 306 (1971); 546 (1976); 878 (1985)
239. "Fred Norris Robinson." *Lochlann* 4:309-12 (1969).
241. "Underlying Forms, Basic Forms, and Reconstructions." *Actes du Xe Congrès International des Linguistes* I:253-6 (1969). Cf. 250 (1968); 481 (1976)
242. "Varia I: (1) *uisce*, (2) *to-aithib ~ do-aithim*." *Ériu* 21:87-8 (1969). Cf. 38 (1955); 312 (1971); 342 (1972); 426 (1974); 814 (1984)
243. "Etymological Notes on DLR VI Fasc. 9." *RRL* 14:13-5 (1969).

246. "Notes on Mediaeval Inscriptions of Bosnia and Hercegovina." *Zbornik za filologiju i lingvistiku* 12:83-91 (Novi Sad, 1969). Cf. 228 (1968)
247. "Hittite *utne-*, Greek οὖδας." *Studia Classica et Orientalia (Antonino Pagliaro Oblata)* 3:7-16 (1969). Cf. 276 (1970)
248. "Ánthrōk^wos." *Atti e Memorie del 1° Congresso Internazionale di Micenologia* (Rome, 1967; pub. Rome, 1969) 786-90. Cf. 266 (1970); 697 (1981)
249. "A Phrygian and Albanian Preverb?" *Norsk Tidsskrift for Sprogvidenskap* 23:13-4 (1969). Cf. 851 (1984)
251. "Latin *īnsula*; *hedera* is not 'ivy'." *AJP* 90:463-4 (1969). Cf. 382 (1974); 430 (1974)
252. "Two Prasun Notes." *Indo-Iranian Journal* 12:24-6 (1969).
253. "Romanian *unt* 'butter'." *RRL* 14:489 (1969).
256. "On the Problem of Ainu and Indo-European." *Eighth Congress of Anthropological and Ethnological Sciences* (Tokyo, 1968; pub. Tokyo, 1969) 100-102.
261. "Two Brief Studies of Albanian Etymology." *Studia Albanica* 1:125-8 (1969). = 262 (1968)
264. "Some Remarks on Gaulish Phonology." *IF* 74:147-54 (1969). Cf. 63 (1957); 521 (1977)
268. "Postscript on Demeter and Poseidon." *Minos* (N.S.) 10:93-5 (1969). Cf. 267 (1968)
273. "Armenian *harb, hars, harc^c*." *REA* (N.S.) 6:15-7 (1969). Cf. 464 (1974)
274. "'Yesterday' in Eastern Oceanic Today." *Kivung* 2:3:12-5 (1969).
282. "*$\d{u}es$ in Indo-European." *Acta Linguistica Hafniensia* 12:151-69 (1969). Cf. 324 (1971); 477 (1976); 502 (1977); 538 (1976); 928 (1987)
286. "Albanian *ngjalë* 'eel'." *Gjurmime Albanologjike* 2:63-4 (1969). Cf. 293 (1971)
289. "Luwian *nanun* 'now'." *RHA* 27:132-3 (1969).
295. "More on Sogdian '*rdyw-*." *AO* 37:339-40 (1969).
328. "On Mountains among the Kwakiutl." *Disputationes ad montium vocabula aliorumque nominum significationes pertinentes*, Vol. II (10th International Congress of Onomastic Sciences) Wien, 1969. Pp. 131-5.

Reviews
237. Review of Gerhard Nickel, *Die Expanded Form im Altenglischen: Vorkommen, Funktion, und Herkunft der Umschreibung 'beon/wesan'* + *Partizip Präsens* (1966). *FL* 5:297-300 (1969).
244. Review of Coriolan Suciu, *Dicţionar istoric al localităţilor din Transilvania*, Vol. I (1967). *Names* 17:237-8 (1969). Republished in error as 301 (1971).

1970

Articles
245. "On Nasalization in Narragansett." *IJAL* 36:58-9 (1970).
254. "Two Semantic Convergence Phenomena." *FL* 6:19-21 (1970).
255. "Lithuanian *ugnìs*, Slavic *ognь*." *Baltic Linguistics*, eds. Magner and Schmalstieg. University Park and London: The Pennsylvania State University Press, 1970. Pp. 75-9. Cf. 847 (1985)
257. "Systems of Lateral Sounds and Perception." *Proceedings of the Sixth International Congress of Phonetic Sciences* (Prague, 1967; pub. 1970) 415-8.
258. "On Contrastive Grammar." *The Yugoslav Serbo-Croatian-English Contrastive Project, B. Studies* 2:1-13. Zagreb: Institute of Linguistics (Zagreb) and Center for Applied Linguistics (Washington, D.C.), 1970.
259. "Maya-Chipaya and Typology of Labials." *CLS* VI:20-2 (1970). Cf. 212 (1967); 904 (1985)
260. "Morpho-Syntax as Proof in Etymology." *CLS* VI:482-8 (1970). Cf. 169 (1961); 203 (1966); 276 (1970); 307 (1971); 275 (1970); 314 (1971). Reprinted as 958 (1988).
263. "Sanskrit *duhitā́*, Armenian *dustr*, and IE Internal Schwa. *JAOS* 90:228-31 (1970). Cf. 203 (1966); 442 (1975); 621 (1980); 817 (1983); 936 (1987)
265. "Wiyot and Yurok Correspondences." *Languages and Cultures of Western North America* (Sven Liljeblad Festschrift.) Pocatello, Idaho: Idaho State University Press, 1970. Pp. 107-10.
266. "Two Mycenean Notes." *Studi Micenei ed Egeo-Anatolici* 11:60-2 (1970). Cf. 248 (1969); 890 (1985)
269. "On the Altaic Numerals." *Studies in General and Oriental Linguistics* (Hattori Festschrift), eds. Roman Jakobson and

Shigeo Kawamoto. Tokyo: TEC Company, Ltd., 1970. Pp. 188-97. Cf. 231 (1969); 410 (1974)
270. "On the Frequency of Lexical Finals in Modern Greek." *Neo-Hellenika* 1:179-82 (1970).
271. "Indo-European 'young'." *KZ* 84:1 (1970). Cf. 326 (1972); 406 (1974)
272. "Albanian *djathë* 'cheese'." *KZ* 84:140-1 (1970). Cf. 13 (1953); 293 (1971); 637 (1979)
275. "On the paradigm of 'knee'." *Glotta* 48:72-5 (1970). Cf. 260 (1970); 548 (1978); 816 (1983)
276. "Lat. *über* Again." *Glotta* 48:141-5 (1970). Cf. 260 (1970); 314 (1971); 247 (1969); 351 (1972); 358 (1972); 589 (1979)
277. "Fijian-Polynesian Embedded Subject Personals." *Kivung* 2:1:26-34 (1970).
278. "*Cercetări de Lingvistică* XIII 2 (July-Dec. 1968)." *Names* 18:223-4 (1970).
279. "Early Slavic Influence on Albanian." *LB* 14:2:11-7 (1970). Cf. 294 (1971); 574 (1978)
280. "The Diphthongs of Mandrica." *LB* 14:2:21-5 (1970). Cf. 190 (1965); 574 (1978)
281. "Βοστίτσα ~ βοστίτζα." *LB* 14:2:19 (1970).
283. "On Bantu and Comparison." *IJAL* 36:273-87 (1970).
285. "Productive Suffix Ablaut in Baltic." *Baltistica* 6:27-32 (1970). Cf. 203 (1966); 286 (1969); 306 (1971); 548 (1978); 598 (1979)
287. "Thracian (?) ΑΖΑΡΑΤΗΣ (?) Again." *Beiträge zur Namenforschung* (N.F.) 5:3:301 (1970). Cf. 843 (1984)
288. "Kiekrz." *Beiträge zur Namenforschung* (N.F.) 5:3:302 (1970).
290. "A Further Note on 'Dempwolff's Law'." *Oceania* 41:50-1 (1970).
291. "*Priemenẽ* 'entrance (building), lobby'." *Donum Balticum* (Stang Festschrift), ed. Velta Rūķe-Draviņa. Stockholm, 1970. Pp. 173-7. Cf. 307 (1971)
299. "Greek and Indo-European Words in **mVl-*." *ŽA* 20:5-10 (1970). Cf. 296 (1971); 376 (1973); 799 (1983), 803
302. "*véno, vijèno*." *Zbornik za filologiju i lingvistiku* (Novi Sad) 13:255-6 (1970). Cf. 225 (1968)
309. "Locative Singular in -ει." *IF* 75:105-6 (1970). Cf. 446 (1975); 472 (1976); 783 (1983); 867, 832 (1984); 912 (1986)
334. "*pęstъ*." *Zbornik za filologiju i lingvistiku* (Novi Sad) 13:292-3 (1970). Cf. 305 (1971)

1971

Articles

292. "Ob indoevropejskix oborotax tipa pol'sk. *samoczwart*, čes. *sám čtvrt*." *Voprosy jazykoznanija* 1:91-3 (1971).
293. "'Fils' et 'fille' en italique." *BSLP* 66:213-227 (1971). Cf. 3 (1952); 832 (1984); 928 (1987)
294. "*gîtlej*." *Actele celui de-al XII-lea Congres internaţional de lingvistică şi filologie romanică II* (Bucureşti, 1968; pub. 1971), Pp. 1041-3. Cf. 279 (1970)
296. "Some Colour Words in *-no-*." *IJSLP* 14:1-4 (1971). Cf. 550 (1976); 562 (1977); 589 (1979); 636 (1980); 745 (1982)
298. "Some Phonetic Rules for Mainland Comox Vowels." *Studies in Northwest Indian Languages*, eds. James E. Hoard and Thomas M. Hess. Sacramento Anthropological Society Paper 11 (April 1971) 32-42.
304. "Varia III: (1) The Keltic Words for 'tear' (2) The 'Bee' in Irish, IE, and Uralic." *Ériu* 22:181-7 (1971). Cf. 344 (1972)
305. "Disambiguation in Reconstruction." *Kivung* 4:2:75-8 (1971). Cf. 334 (1970); 353 (1972); 375 (1973)
306. "Notes on *Słownik etymologiczny języka polskiego* III, 3." *Revue Slavistique* 32 (Part I):67-72 (1971). Cf. 236 (1969); 285 (1970)
307. "πρύμνη, πρυμνός and the rounding of **o*." *Münchener Studien zur Sprachwissenschaft* 29:71-4 (1971). Cf. 260 (1970); 310 (1971); 291 (1970); 696 (1981)
308. "Latin *uerpa*." *AJP* 92:86-8 (1971). Cf. 739 (1981)
310. "The Variants of 'Αγαμέμνων." *Glotta* 49:121-4 (1971). Cf. 307 (1971); 829 (1984); 835 (1985); 853, 897
311. "Diachronic and Synchronic Rules in Welsh." *Generative Studies in Historical Linguistics*, ed. Maria Tsiapera. Papers in Linguistics Monograph. Edmonton and Champaign: Linguistic Research, Inc., 1971. Pp. 1-8.
312. "'Water' in Italic and Keltic." *EC* 12:547-50 (1970-71). Cf. 326 (1972); 342 (1972)
314. "Tocharian 'one' and Paradigmatic Reconstruction." *CLS* 7:437-44 (1971). Cf. 260 (1970); 233 (1968); 534 (1976)
317. "On Mayan-Araucanian Comparative Phonology." *IJAL* 37:156-9 (1971). Cf. 212 (1967)
324. "Deux Fantômes de l'ethnogénèse balkanique." *Studia Balcanica V. L'ethnogénèse des peuples balkaniques.* Sofia: Acadé-

mie Bulgare des Sciences (Institut d'études balkaniques), 1971. Pp. 243-6. Cf. 282 (1969); 477 (1976)
325. "*Akóma* 'still, yet'." *Balkan Studies* 12:141 (1971).
329. "Old Prussian *seggē, seggīt*." *Baltistica* 7:43-5 (1971). Cf. 415 (1974)
335. "Russ. Slovene *oméla*, OCS. S-Cr. *imela*." *Zbornik za filologiju i lingvistiku* (Novi Sad) 14:253-5 (1971).
336. "The Meaning of IE. *dek̑-*." *IF* 76:22-3 (1971). Cf. 220 (1968)
337. "I. *ha* = IE **ed-*; II. *veshtull* 'viscum album'." *Studime Filologjike* 26 (1):81-3 (1972) = *Studia Albanica* 8(2):153-5 (1971). Cf. 20 (1954); 122 (1965); 470 (1975); 569 (1979)
398. "*Pár-ta-u-wa-ar* 'wing'." *RHA* 29:112 (1971).

Reviews

300. Review of Iorgu Iordan, *Toponimia romînească* (București, 1963). *GL* 11:133-8 (1971).
301. Review of Coriolan Suciu, *Dicționar istoric al localităților din Transilvania*, Vol. I (București, 1967). *GL* 11:138 (1971). Republication by oversight of 244 (1969).
303. Review of *Donum Balticum* (Stang Festschrift). *Names* 19:284-5 (1971).
313. Review of *Universiteti Shtetëror i Tiranës 1957-1967*. *Lg.* 47:488-9 (1971).
315. Review of Joshua Whatmough, *The Dialectics of Ancient Gaul* (Cambridge, 1970). *GL* 11:56-9 (1971). Cf. 208 (1966); 210 (1966); 264 (1969); 905 (1986)
316. Review of N. A. Constantinescu, *Dicționar onomastic romînesc* (București, 1963). *GL* 11:61-3 (1971).
318. "Brief Mention." *IJAL* (1971-). [Separately listed; see after item 960]

1972

Articles

297. "Comments on Ralph Gardner White." *CA* 13:117-9 (1972).
319. "*diod*, 'a drink'; *ny vall*." *BBCS* 24:481-3 (1972). Cf. 578 (1977)
320. "Occam's Razor and Explanation in Etymology." *CLS* 8: 470-2 (1972). Cf. 351 (1972); 385 (1974); 464 (1974)
321. "Morphemes." *Language Arts Concepts for Elementary School*

Teachers, eds. Paul C. Burns, J. Estill Alexander, Arnold B. Davis. Itasca, Illinois: F. E. Peacock Publishers, Inc., 1972. Pp. 220–5. = part of 1 (1951)

322. "The Semantics of Armenian Plurals." *From Soundstream to Discourse* (Papers from the 1971 Mid-America Linguistics Conference), eds. Daniel G. Hays, Donald M. Lance. Columbia, Missouri: The University of Missouri, 1972. Pp. 66–71. Cf. 798 (1983)
326. "Palaic *ha-a-ap-na-as* 'river'." *Münchener Studien zur Sprachwissenschaft* 30-35-8 (1972). Cf. 271 (1970); 312 (1971); 579 (1977); 612 (1979); 955 (1987)
330. "*elein, alaned; celein, calaned.*" *BBCS* 25:71–2 (1972). Cf. 404 (1974)
331. "Lith. *liekas.*" *Baltistica* 8:55–6 (1972). Cf. 233 (1968); 536 (1977)
332. "παρθένος and its cognates." *Homenaje a Antonio Tovar ofrecido por sus discípulos, colegas y amigos*. Madrid: Editorial Gredos, 1972. Pp. 177–80. Cf. 438 (1975); 617 (1979); 855 (1985); 885 (1986)
333. "Dutch *paard*, German *Pferd.*" *CJL/RCL* (Studies for Martin Joos) 17:128–31 (1972). Cf. 10 (1953); 356 (1972); 374 (1973)
338. "Varia II: Seṭ and Aniṭ verbal nouns in *-n-* in Celtic." *Ériu* 23:230–1 (1972). Cf. 225 (1968); 396 (1974); 468 (1975); 471 (1976); 530 (1977); 644 (1980)
339. "L'importance du breton dans la grammaire comparée." *EC* 13(I): (1972).
341. "On some semantic aspects of gender." *AO* 40:344–6 (1972).
342. "Keltic *dubro-* 'water': The Story of a Lexeme." *Studies in Linguistics in Honor of George L. Trager*, ed. M. Estellie Smith. The Hague: Mouton, 1972. Pp. 233–7. Cf. 242 (1969); 276 (1970); 312 (1971); 200 (1967)
343. "On Medial *s* in Italic." *Glotta* 50:290–1 (1972). Cf. 911 (1986)
344. "Latin *dacrima, lacruma* and Indo-European 'tear'." *Glotta* 50:291–9 (1972). Cf. 112 (1960); 200 (1967); 285 (1970); 304 (1971); 383 (1974); 550 (1978); 759 (1981); 821 (1984); 853 (1985)
345. "Albanian." *Current Trends in Linguistics* (Vol. 9: Linguistics in Western Europe), ed. Thomas A. Sebeok. The Hague/Paris: Mouton, 1972. Pp. 1626–92. Cf. MLA Bibliography; Horecky 1969; 378 (1974)

346. "Κριμπάτσι, Κουρμπάτσι, Γκέρμπεσι." *LB* 16(1):39 (1972).
347. "Lith. *javaĩ, javienà*." *Baltistica* 8:169-70 (1972). Cf. 545 (1976)
348. "Mažvydas Catechism 31.22-23." *Baltistica* 8:171 (1972).
350. "Bilingual contact phenomena between Greenlandic Eskimo and Danish." Report on Grant No. 886, *American Philosophical Society Year Book 1972.* 610-12.
351. "Slav. **vymę.*" *Ètimologija 1970.* Moskva: Izdatel'stvo 'Nauka', 1972. Pp. 263-8. Cf. 276 (1970); 320 (1972); 342 (1972); 411 (1974)
352. "O nekotoryx složnyx momentax albanskogo konsonantizma: 1. Alb. *kohë*, Slav. *časъ*; 2. Alb. *h(j)edh* 'brosat'; 3. Alb. *kashtë* 'soloma' i gruppa **1st.*" *Ètimologija 1970.* Moskva: Izdatel'stvo 'Nauka', 1972. Pp. 268-71. Cf. 408 (1973)
353. "*dúodo, dedù.*" *Lingua Posnaniensis* 16:83-5 (1972). Cf. 305 (1971)
354. "*doom* and *do.*" *Lingua Posnaniensis* 16:87-90 (1972). Cf. 353 (1972); 471 (1976) [Addendum: *LP* 27:11, 1984]
356. "British *u̯ar* and *u̯or-*, **u̯a* and *u̯o-.*" *Studia Celtica* 7:155-6 (1972). Cf. 10 (1953); 333 (1972); 364 (1972); 556 (1978), 557
357. "On final apicals in Cornish." *Studia Celtica* 7:157 (1972). See corrigendum 481 (1976) pp. 57-8
362. "On the reconstruction of earlier syntax from morphology." *Mid-America Linguistics Conference Papers*, 1972:207-14. Cf. 769 (1983); 882 (1985)
363. "*slȕh, slûh.*" *Zbornik za filologiju i lingvistiku* (Novi Sad) 15:242 (1972).
364. "Notes linguistiques bretonnes." *Annales de Bretagne* 4:939-47 (1972). Cf. 356 (1972); 418 (1974); 372 (1973); 556 (1978), 559; 578 (1977); 625 (1980); 802 (1983)
370. "Albanian *vrap.*" *Makedonski jazik* 23:285 (1972).
392. "On Indo-European Nouns in *e*-Reduplication." *IF* 77:159-70 (1972). Cf. 731 (1982); 928 (1987); 929 (1987)

Reviews
340. Review of Gasper Kiçi and Hysni Aliko, *Fjalor Anglisht-Shqip* (1969). *Slavic and East European Journal* 16:383-5 (1972). Cf. 86 (1958)

1973

Articles
349. "Language and prehistory." Letter to *Science* 179:1279-80 (30 March 1973).
355. "The Albanian words for 'liver'." *Issues in Linguistics: Papers in Honor of Henry and Renée Kahane*, eds. Braj B. Kachru, Robert B. Lees, Yakov Malkiel, Angelina Pietrangeli and Sol Saporta. Urbana: University of Illinois Press, 1973. Pp. 311-18. Cf. 400 (1974); 606 (1979)
358. "A semantic archaism." *Linguistic Inquiry* 4:246-51 (1973). Cf. 200 (1967); 276 (1970); 872 (1984)
359. "Inordinate clauses in Celtic." *You Take the High Node and I'll Take the Low Node; Papers from the Comparative Syntax Festival*, eds. Claudia Corum, T. Cedric Smith-Stark, and Ann Weiser. Chicago: Chicago Linguistic Society, 1973. Pp. 229-51. Cf. 400 (1974); 493 (1975); 661 (1981); 836 (1984)
360. "North European 1000." *Papers from the Ninth Regional Meeting of the Chicago Linguistic Society, 13-15 April, 1973*, eds. Claudia Corum, T. Cedric Smith-Stark, and Ann Weiser. Chicago: Chicago Linguistic Society, 1973. Pp. 172-78. Cf. 197 (1967); 436 (1974)
361. "Crimean Gothic *fers*." *JEGP* 72:60-1 (1973).
366. "More light on PA 'sun'." *IJAL* 39:205-6 (1973). Cf. 577 (1979)
367. "(For Roman, who is always) Number one." *IJSLP* 16:1-6 (1973). Cf. 430 (1974); 536 (1977)
368. "Religion and law from Iguvium." *JIES* 1:318-323 (1973). Cf. 605 (1980); 721 (1982); 754 (1983); 876 (1985)
369. "*căpșun* and [grave] clusters." *Miorița* (Bulletin of the New Zealand Romanian Cultural Association) 1:27-9 (December, 1973). Cf. 435 (1974); 576 (1979); 688 (1981)
371. "Formations Indoeuropéennes à second element *-$(H_o)k^w$-*." *BSLP* 68:77-92 (1973). Cf. 214 (1967); 418 (1974); 478 (1976); 700 (1982); 811 (1984)
372. "*Pesna* (Festus)." *Studii Clasice* 15:151-52 (1973). Cf. 364 (1972)
373. "Another lesson from 'frost'." *JIES* 1:215-23 (1973). Cf. 400 (1974); 449 (1974); 481 (1976); 733 (1982); 910 (1986)
374. "*gwaudd*; *eniwet* 'niwed, colled, harm'." *BBCS* 25:293-97 (1973). Cf. 333 (1972); 356 (1972); 557 (1978); 605 (1980)

375. "Varia I: (1) Underlying and Reapplied Lautgesetze in Germanic and Keltic (2) Notes on some Indo-European preverbs (3) *airlicud* (4) *Banba* again (5) On voicing in Old Irish final spirants (6) An ancient Indo-European idiom (7) *sechtarét* Sg. 67ᵇ21 (8) Some compounds of *téit* (9) *teüir* (10) *at·bail(l)*, *(gaé) bulga*." *Ériu* 24:160-82 (1973). Cf. 305 (1971); 419 (1974); 426 (1974); 448 (1975); 456 (1975); 476 (1976); 521 (1977); 530 (1977); 537 (1977); 557, 567, 555 (1978); 636 (1980); 790 (1982); 831 (1984); 880 (1986)
376. "Celtic and Indo-European Words in **mVl-*." *Celtica* 10:151-56 (1973). Cf. 299 (1970); 799 (1983)
377. "Some *ā*-preterites." *Celtica* 10:156-59 (1973). Cf. 468 (1975)
380. "Albanian *gat*, Slavic *gotóvъ*, and Balkan Adverbials." *RRL* 18:333-45 (1973). Cf. 475 (1976); 476 (1976); 502 (1977)
386. "Fish." *JIES* 1:507-11 (1973). Cf. 425 (1974)
388. "*mōrum*." *AJP* 94:167-9 (1973). Cf. 221 (1967)
389. "On the phonology and morphology of Lat. *cunctus*." *AJP* 94:169-70 (1973).
390. "**-wont-* and Latin *-ōsus*." *AJP* 94:170-1 (1973).
391. "On Baltic, Luwian and Albanian Participles in **-m-*." *Baltistica* 9:45-50 (1973). Cf. 531 (1977); 588 (1979); 794 (1983)
394. "*lykill ~ nykill*." *Acta Philologica Scandinavica* 29:163 (1973). Cf. 491 (1976)
395. "The Diphthongization of Long Mid Vowels." *Baltic Literature and Linguistics*, eds. A. Ziedonis, Jr., J. Puhvel, R. Šilbajoris, M. Valgemäe. Columbus, Ohio: Association for the Advancement of Baltic Studies, Inc., 1973. Pp. 167-72.
401. "Two Notes on Italic and Celtic: **meH$_a$-* in Italic and Celtic; Umbrian *tapistenu*." *Archivio Glottologico Italiano* 58:137-41 (1973). Cf. 500 (1976); 517 (1976)
402. "Lith. *sidãbras*, OCS *srěbro*." *Baltistica* 9:57-8 (1973).
404. "Miscellanea: *elein* again; Some difficult Welsh forms in *oe*." *Studia Celtica* 8-9:268-70 (1973-4). Cf. 330 (1972); 732 (1982); 867 (1984)
408. "On some etymologies of Albanian: *ble*, *bleva*; A Singular-Plural Inversion; On Some Complex Albanian Consonantisms (Albanian *kohë*, Slavic *časъ*; Albanian *h(j)edh* 'throw'; Albanian *kashtë* 'straw' and **lst*)." *Studia Albanica* 2:83-88 (1973). Cf. 352 (1972)

423. "Solutions and Problems from Speyer; Speyer *ainlibim*; Speyer *farwa* 'form'." *IF* 78:141-3 (1973). Cf. 331 (1972); 536 (1977); 830 (1984)
427. "Phonetic and semantic metrics." *Meaning: A Common Ground of Linguistics and Literature (In Honor of Norman A. Stageberg), Proceedings of a University of Northern Iowa Conference held April 27-28, 1973*, ed. Don L. F. Nilsen. Pp. 146-52.

Reviews
365. Review of Paul Friedrich, *Proto-Indo-European Trees* (Chicago: University of Chicago Press, 1970). *AA* 75:1093-96 (1973). Cf. 448 (1975); 548 (1978); 606, 613 (1979); 649 (1981), 684; 753 (1982); 805 (1984)

1974

Articles
378. "Albanian Language." *Encyclopaedia Britannica* 1.422-3 (1974). Cf. 345 (1972); 551 (1978)
381. "Once again Iranian *$\bar{a}du$-*." *TPS* 1973:137 (1974). Cf. 238 (1968)
382. " 'Ivy' in Italic and Celtic." *JIES* 2:87-93 (1974). Cf. 251 (1969)
383. "On the Stem Forms of IE 'Bone'." *Ricerche Linguistiche* 6: 231-5 (1974). Cf. 13 (1953); 344 (1972); 834 (1984)
384. "Greek τέλι, Albanian *tel*." *Schriften zur Geschichte und Kultur des Alten Orients 5: Sprache, Geschichte und Kultur der Altaischen Völker*. (Protokollband der XII. Tagung der Permanent International Altaistic Conference 1969 in Berlin.) Eds. Georg Hazai and Peter Zieme. Berlin: Akademie-Verlag, 1974.
385. "Hispanic *Peremusta*." *ZCP* 33:15-18 (1974). Cf. 320 (1972); 555 (1978); 736 (1982)
387. "Welsh *achan* and Related Words." *Norwegian Journal of Linguistics* 28:1-7 (1974). Cf. 396 (1974); 523 (1977); 557 (1978); 627 (1980)
393. " 'Pygmalion'; letter on 'foot jade'." *Verbatim* 1, 1:5-6 (1974).
396. "On **org-nV-*; *cogiaf, cogaf*; *eirioes*." *BBCS* 25:388-92 (1974). Cf. 338 (1972); 404 (1973); 387, 413 (1974), 418 (1974)

397. "On the conditioned loss and restitution of Latin -s." *Linguistic Studies in Romance Languages: Proceedings of the Third Linguistic Symposium on Romance Languages*, eds. R. Campbell, M. Goldin, M. Wang. Washington, D.C.: Georgetown University Press, 1974. Pp. 1–7. Cf. 97 (1959); 435 (1974)
399. "Grammar." *Encyclopaedia Britannica* 8.265-74 (1974).
400. "The Major Focus in Reconstruction and Change." *Historical Linguistics II: Theory and Description in Phonology* (Proceedings of the First International Conference on Historical Linguistics, 1973), eds. J. M. Anderson and C. Jones. Oxford: North-Holland Publishing Company, 1974. Pp. 141-67. Cf. 373 (1973); 355 (1973); 537 (1977); 836 (1984)
403. "Two Germanic Verb Inventions." *Lingua* 34:229-34 (1974). Cf. 13 (1953); 553 (1977); 620 (1980); 904 (1985)
405. "Lith. *nasraĩ*, Slav. *nozd( )ri*, OIr. *srón*, Gk. ῥίς." *Baltistica* 10:69-72 (1974). (Republished in 418.) Cf. 118 (1960)
406. "Vannetais *iouank*, *iaouank*, *ievank*." *Lochlann* 6:118-21 (1974). Cf. 271 (1970)
407. "*Áru, Áirne*." *Lochlann* 6:122-23 (1974).
409. "The Altaic non-obstruents." *BSOAS* 37:672-4 (1974). (Republished in error in *Researches in Altaic Languages*. Budapest: Akadémiai Kiadó, 1974.
410. "Turkic 5, 6, 7, 60, and 70." *BSOAS* 37:675-7 (1974). Pp. 67-70. Cf. 269 (1970); 465 (1975)
411. "Dopolnenija k statje o slove **vymę*." *Ètimologija* 1972. Moskva: Izdatel'stvo 'Nauka', 1974. P. 176. Cf. 351 (1972)
412. "Some Regularities in Swedish Strong Verbs." *Studia Linguistica* 28:69-72 (1974).
413. "On Dating and Archaism in the *Pedeir Keinc*." *Transactions of the Honourable Society of Cymmrodorion* (Sessions 1972 and 1973), 95–103. Cf. 396 (1974); 709 (1982)
414. "Observations: Reduplications and monosyllables; Wortphonologie." *Child Language* 1:287-88 (1974).
415. "On false equations for OPruss. *seggīt*." *Baltistica* 10:87-9 (1974). Cf. 329 (1971)
416. "Features of Angas Syllables." *Journal of African Languages* 13:82-3 (1974).
417. "On **sm* in Gaulish and on the Prehistory of **cammīnu*." *RP* 28:17-20 (1974).

418. "Varia: (1) On the fundamental IE orientation (2) *enech*, ἐνῑπή (3) OW *enep* and the imperfect 3 sg. (4) *fíu, feb, ἧϋς, vásu-* (5) *escaid, aisc* (6) Lith. *nasraĩ*, Slav. *nozd(i)ri*, OIr. *srón*, Gk. ῥίς (7) Mod. Ir. *gead* and Slav. *zvězda* (8) On snow in Ireland (9) *asse* (10) *timme* (11) *anbal* (12) Copula of Possession (13) *dlūth*." *Ériu* 25:253–84 (1974). Cf. 405; 371 (1973); 364 (1972); 436 (1974); 448 (1975); 396 (1974); 493 (1975); 533 (1976); 538 (1976); 811 (1984); 911 (1986)
419. "The Mac Neill-O'Brien Law." *Ériu* 25:172–80 (1974). Cf. 375 (1973); 802 (1983)
420. "Albanian *thes* 'bag'." *Orbis* 23:128–9 (1974).
421. "*yrà*." *IJSLP* 17:7–8 (1974). Cf. 472 (1976); 579 (1977); 783 (1983); 836 (1984)
422. "*rattus*." *Rheinisches Museum für Philologie* 117:192 (1974).
425. "Something Fishy: *pysc pyscawt, Isca*." *Papers from the Tenth Regional Meeting, April 19–21, 1974*, eds. Michael LaGaly, Robert A. Fox, and Anthony Bruck. Chicago: Chicago Linguistic Society, 216–20 (1974). Cf. 386 (1973); 418 (1974); 438 (1975); 873 (1984)
426. "Reassignment of nasality in early Irish." *Papers from the Parasession on Natural Phonology*, eds. Anthony Bruck, Robert A. Fox, Michael LaGaly. Chicago: Chicago Linguistic Society, 127–30 (1974). Cf. 38 (1955); 242 (1969); 375 (1973); 418 (1974); 517 (1976)
429. "*biso*." *Actes du XIe Congres International des Sciences Onomastiques* (Sofia, 28 June–4 July 1972) 1:367–69 (1974). Cf. 167 (1961), 452 (1974).
430. "The element *-tamo-*." *EC* 14:187–92 (1974). Cf. 251 (1969), 367 (1973)
431. "Marginalia Lepontica." *EC* 14:193–94 (1974). Cf. 213 (1967); 587 (1979); 625 (1980)
432. "On some sources of Primitive Breton *l*." *EC* 14:195–99 (1974). Cf. 480 (1975); 658 (1981); 720 (1982)
433. "Bret. *gwazh, goah, goéh*, OIr. *féith*." *EC* 14:201–04 (1974).
434. "Nodiadau Amrywiol—Miscellaneous Notes: On the rounded character of British ǭ; *melltith; rhodd ac estyn; tyst*." *BBCS* 26:30–33 (1974). Cf. 455 (1975); 493 (1975)
435. "On Romansch and the Balkans." *Zeitschrift für Balkanologie* 10.2:33–38 (1974). Cf. 369 (1973), 397 (1974), 213 (1967)

436. "Sources of *šk* in Baltic." *Archivo Glottologico Italiano* 59: 31–36 (1974). Cf. 360 (1973); 418 (1973); 546 (1976); 436 (1974); 644 (1980)
439. "Palatized **l* in Umbrian." *Glotta* 52:231–33 (1974).
447. "An archaism in Slavic." *Zbornik za filologiju i lingvistiku* 27.1:241–44 (1974). Cf. 493 (1975); 572 (1978)
449. "Reply to Costa on *frost*." *JIES* 2:95–6 (1974). Cf. 373 (1973)
452. "Albanian and Baltic as clues to Thracian." *Primus congressus studiorum Thracicorum* (Sofia, 1972). Sofia, 1974. Pp. 367–8. Cf. 429 (1974)
459. "IE **su̯ergh-*." *IF* 79:154–55 (1974).
460. "Western Indo-European Notes: 1. German *deuten* OHG. *diuten*. 2. Welsh *blawdd*." *IF* 79:156–57 (1974).
461. "Welsh *maen*, Old Breton *main*." *IF* 79:158–60 (1974). Cf. 805 (1984)
464. "On **Ḱu̯* in Armenian: (1) *šun, skund, skesur*. (2) *ēš*." *REA* 10:23–25 (1973–74). Cf. 672 (1980)

Reviews
379. Review of Gordon B. Ford, Jr. *The Old Lithuanian Catechism of Martynas Mažvydas (1547)* (1971). *FL* 11:461–64 (1974). Cf. 465 (1975); 494 (1976); 545 (1976); 670 (1982); 842 (1984)

1975

Articles
424. "Letter on -oon." *Verbatim* 1. 4:6 (1975).
428. "Labial Continuant Graphs in Llanstephan 1 and Havod 2." *Archivum Linguisticum* 6:71–6 (1975).
437. "Old loans as tests for phonological abstractness." *Phonologica 1972*, eds. Wolfgang Dressler and F. V. Mareš. München/Salzburg: Wilhelm Fink Verlag, 1975. Pp. 323–25.
438. "*Alauno-, -ā*. Linguistic change and proper names." *Beiträge z. Namenforschungen* 10:173–78 (1975). Cf. 332 (1972); 425 (1974); 558 (1977); 571 (1976); 796 (1984)
440. "Current Tasks in Grammar and Phonology." *RRL* 20:93–103 (1975).
441. "Note on Ideal View." *Verbatim* 2.1:8 (1975).
442. "**dhugHtēr* in Irish." *Münchener Studien zur Sprachwissenschaft* 33:39–40 (1975). Cf. 263 (1970)

443. "IE *gʷreH₂uon-." *Münchener Studien zur Sprachwissenschaft* 33:41-43 (1975). Cf. 454 (1975); 755 (1983), 778 (1983)
444. "On the dual inflexions in Slovene." *Slavistična Revija* 23:67-70 (1975).
445. "The Gothic Rune name *Chozma*." *Ut Videam*. Lisse, The Netherlands: Peter de Ridder, 1975. Pp. 133-37.
446. "Latin *sīdus, sīdera*." *AJP* 96:64-66 (1975). Cf. 309 (1971); 521 (1977); 832 (1984); 896 (1985)
448. "The principal (?) Indo-European constellations." *Proceedings of the Eleventh International Congress of Linguistics* (Bologna, 1972). Bologna, 1975. II Pp. 1047-55. Cf. 365 (1973), 375 (1973), 418 (1974); 700 (1982) Arm. *amis*; 813 (1984)
451. "On Zuni-Penutian consonants." *IJAL* 41:310-12 (1975).
453. "*cut* and *meat* in Germanic." *Acta Philologica Scandinavica* 30:49-51 (1975). Cf. 613 (1979); 649 (1981); 754 (1983); 941 (1987)
454. "Indo-European *āu̯ before consonant in British and Indo-European *sun*." *BBCS* 26:97-102 (1975). Cf. 443 (1975); 578 (1977); 598 (1979); 700 (1982); 778 (1983)
455. "Nodiadau Amrywiol—Miscellaneous Notes: Welsh *dichlyn*; Welsh *cyd, y gyt, gyda*; OCorn. *chetua*; MBret. *quet-*; Welsh *at/ar* 'to'; Welsh *anant*, OIr. *anair*; Vagniacis." *BBCS* 26:138-40 (1975). Cf. 389 (1973); 434 (1974); 523, 530 (1977); 802 (1983); 955 (1987)
456. "Welsh *asswynaw* and Celtic legal idiom." *BBCS* 26:153-60 (1975). Cf. 434 (1974); 375 (1973); 530 (1977); 589 (1979); 786 (1983); 955 (1987)
457. "On the Disappearing English Relative Particle." *Akten der 1. Salzburger Frühlingstagung für Linguistik* (1974). Salzburg: Verlag Gunter Narr, 1975. Pp. 297-301.
458. "Nodiadau Amrywiol—Miscellaneous Notes: *diffoddi* and *differaf/diffryt*; *gwarther*; The ordinal forms of '4'." *BBCS* 26:308-11 (1975). Cf. 521 (1977); 734 (1982); 802 (1983)
462. "Old Irish *ed, id*." *ZCP* 34:20-9 (1975). Cf. 579 (1977); 807 (1983); 849 (1985), 877
463. "On some Romanian prepositions." *Studii și cercetări lingvistice* 26.4:365-7 (1975).
465. "*devjanosto* '90'." *Russian Linguistics* 2:219-22 (1975). Cf. 410 (1974); 379 (1974); 494 (1976); 524 (1977); 545 (1976); 678 (1981)

467. "Social Gradience in British Spoken Latin." *Britannia* 9:150-62 (1975). Cf. 555 (1978); 802 (1983)
468. "Varia II: (1) Syntactic Comparisons: (a) *airci(u)b* ~ argib ~ *ercib*, (b) *sraithi sraithius*, (c) Welsh *erbyn* (2) *do-s·n-áirthet*, *tárachtain* (3) **sek^w-* 'pronounce, speak' (4) *Femen* (5) Irish *óthath*, *tinaid*." *Ériu* 26:168-74 (1975). Cf. 471 (1976); 338 (1972); 377 (1973); 805 (1984)
469. "On the Nasal Presents of Armenian." *KZ* 89:100-9 (1975). Cf. 215 (1967); 499 (1976); 538 (1976); 639 (1979)
470. "*Abur*." *RRL* 20:499-500 (1975). Cf. 337 (1971); 474 (1976); 505 (1977); 569 (1979); 684 (1981)
473. "Labialization in Iruḷa." *Indo-Iranian Journal* 17:251-2 (1975).
480. "Welsh *dryll*, Breton *drailh*, Old Breton *drosion*, IE **dhrus*." *TPS* 1974: 128-45 (1975). Cf. 65 (1957); 432 (1974); 562 (1977); 589 (1979); 627 (1980); 637 (1979)
483. "Latin *flēmina* and *f* for *p*." *Glotta* 53:297-8 (1975).
484. "Etruscan *φersu*." *Glotta* 53:299-301 (1975). Cf. 371 (1973)
486. "Mini-Laws." *Papers from the Eleventh Regional Meeting*. Chicago Linguistic Society, Chicago, 1975. Pp. 257-9. Cf. 576 (1979)
487. "A Functional View of Bodily Functions." *Papers from the Parasession on Functionalism*. Chicago Linguistic Society, Chicago, 1975. Pp. 209-12. Cf. 531 (1977)
493. "Varia Etymologica: (1) Welsh *ffriw*, *ewin*, *tafod*, and Labiovelars; (2) Old Welsh *cant-* and Indo-European **k̑om*; (3) **dieu-* 'day' in Celtic." *EC* 14:461-77 (1975). Cf. 418 (1974); 359 (1973); 488 (1976); 447 (1974); 538 (1976); 594 (1979); 596 (1979); 625 (1980)
495. "Mabinogi." *Transactions of the Honourable Society of Cymmrodorion* (Sessions 1974 and 1975), 243-9 (1975). Cf. 567 (1978)
528. "*poton, poplon/poplun*." *LB* 18:69 (1975). Cf. 392 (1972); 576 (1979)
541. "Further on Buckra Blarney." *American Speech* 50:325 (1975). Cf. 457 (1975); 607 (1979)

Reviews
450. Review of Valerie Becker Makkai (ed.), *Phonological Theory: evolution and current practice* (New York: Holt, Rinehart & Winston, 1972). *JL* 11:372 (1975).

1976

Articles

466. "On Earlier Lenca Vowels." *IJAL* 42:78–79 (1976).
471. "*Barnu Brawd*." *Celtica* 11:68–75 (1976). Cf. 354 (1972); 123 (1965); 508 (1976); 538 (1976); 721 (1982); 798 (1983)
472. "Latin *inde*." *AJP* 97:20–21 (1976). Cf. 446 (1975); 309 (1970); 421 (1974); 481, 488 (1976); 615 (1980); 682 (1981); 690, 691 (1982); 783 (1983); 836 (1984)
474. "*u̯* and *b* before *u* and next to vowel." *RRL* 21:49–54 (1976). Cf. 467 (1975); 470 (1975); 505 (1977); 862 (1983)
475. "Some notes on *Istoria limbii române* by Al. Rosetti." *Studii și cercetări lingvistice* 27:181–4 (1976). Cf. 380 (1973); 198 (1967); 647 (1980)
476. "Some Romanian areal etymologies." *Studii și cercetări lingvistice* 27:33–6 (1976). Cf. 380 (1973); 440 (1975); 375 (1973); 569 (1979); 606 (1979); 623 (1980); 721 (1982); 836 (1984)
477. "On the Distribution and Origin of *vatra*." *Opuscula Slavica et Linguistica: Festschrift für Alexander Issatchenko*. Klagenfurt: Verlag Johannes Heyn, 1976. Pp. 201–210. Cf. 282 (1969); 324 (1971); 520 (1977); 650 (1980); 674 (1981), 665
478. "Ρουτούπιαι, *Rŭtŭpīnus* and Morphological Criteria." *BBCS* 26:395–8 (1976). Cf. 214 (1967); 371 (1973)
479. "Palatalization and Harmony in Gagauz and Karaite." *Festschrift Denis Sinor: Tractata Altaica*, eds. W. Heissig [et al.]. Wiesbaden 1976. Pp. 211–3. Cf. 646 (1980)
481. "Miscellanea Celtica: (1) The Transformation of British Inflection; (2) Lack of NP-VP Concord in British Celtic; (3) The British Interrogative Pronominals; (4) The British 2 pl. Ending and *-su̯-.*" *Studia Celtica* X–XI:54–73 (1975–6). Cf. 241 (1969); 371 (1973); 488 (1976); 472 (1976); 373 (1973); 648, 618 (1980); 690 (1982); 836 (1984) Important corrigendum to 357 (1972)
482. "Prenasalization in Eastern Oceanic." (First International Conference on Comparative Austronesian Linguistics), *Oceanic Linguistics* 12:295–301 (1976). Cf. 609 (1980)
485. "On Mon-Khmer, its kin, and principles." (First International Conference on Austro-Asiatic Linguistics), *Austro-Asiatic Studies*, eds. P. N. Jenner, L. C. Thompson, S. Starosta, University Press of Hawaii, Honolulu, 1976. Pp. 423–9.
488. "Why Syntax Needs Phonology." *Papers from the Parasession on Diachronic Syntax*. Chicago Linguistic Society, Chicago,

1976. Pp. 348-64. Cf. 421 (1974), 472, 481, 493 (1976); 611, 612 (1979); 615 (1980); 648 (1980); 781 (1983); 831 (1984), 836
489. "On Eskimo-Aleut and Luorevetlan." *Papers on Eskimo and Aleut Linguistics*, ed. Eric P. Hamp. Chicago Linguistic Society, Chicago, 1976. Pp. 81-92.
490. "*One* and *Single* in Ojibwa." *IJAL* 42:166-7 (1976).
491. "On Cumulative Criteria." *Acta Philologica Scandinavica* 31.2:191 (1976). Cf. 394 (1973)
492. "On Some Principles of Lexical-Phonological Comparison." *Papers from the Second International Conference on Historical Linguistics*. Amsterdam: North Holland, 1976. Pp. 203-9. Cf. 366 (1973); 409 (1974); 265 (1970); 451 (1975); 489 (1976); 711 (1982)
494. "Etymologies: OE *fēower*, OHG *niun*." *Michigan Germanic Studies* 2:1-2 (1976). Cf. 5 (1952); 379 (1974); 465 (1975); 534 (1976); 564 (1978)
496. "19th Century American Linguistics and Slovene Missionaries." *Society for Slovene Studies Newsletter*, 7 (Autumn 1976). Pp. 5-7.
497. "κρέας in Archaic Cretan." *Glotta* 54:98-9 (1976). Cf. 247 (1969); 561 (1977)
499. "*$g^w eiH_o$*- 'live'." *Studies in Greek, Italic, and Indo-European Linguistics Offered to Leonard R. Palmer*, eds. Anna M. Davies and Wolfgang Meid. Innsbruck: Innsbrucker Beiträge zur Sprachwissenschaft, 1976. Pp. 87-91. Cf. 117 (1960); 469 (1975)
500. "On Some Gaulish Names in *-ant-* and Celtic Verbal Nouns." *Ériu* 27:1-20 (1976). Cf. 521 (1977); 532 (1976); 517 (1976); 553 (1977); 555 (1978), 557; 629 (1980); 705 (1982); 754 (1983), 794; 833 (1984); 888 (1986)
501. "Shqipja me interes për studimin e gjuhësisë së përgjithshme." *Rilindja* 28 August 1976, 11. Cf. 547 (1978)
503. "On **HRC- in Latin." *Glotta* 54:261-3 (1976).
507. "ἄκος." *ŽA* 26:26 (1976). Cf. 123 (1965)
508. "προφέρω, φράζομαι." *ŽA* 26:30 (1976). Cf. 471 (1975); 617 (1979)
512. "Old Prussian *manga*, *mangoson*." *Baltistica* 12(1):24 (1976).
513. "The Accentuation of Lithuanian Compound Verbs." *Baltistica* 12(1):25-9 (1976).

514. "On the Baltic Verbal Ending -*ki*." *Baltistica* 12(1):29-30 (1976). Superseded by 726 (1978)
515. "*u̯el* and *u̯elH*." *Baltistica* 12(1):63-4 (1976).
517. "On the Celtic Names of Ig." *Acta Neophilologica* 9:3-8 (1976). Cf. 500 (1976); 426 (1974); 48 (1956); 3 (1952); 573 (1978)
518. "On the Importance of *os* in the Structure of the Runic Poem." *Studia Germanica Gandensia* 17:143-151 (1976).
519. "Latin *uastus*." *Rheinisches Museum für Philologie*, Neue Folge, 119:346-8 (1976). Cf. 562 (1977)
525. "Armenian *hariwr* again." *KZ* 90:128-130 (1976). Cf. 30 (1955).
526. "Βάτραχος." *ŽA* 26:333-334 (1976). Cf. 617 (1979)
527. "Latin *ārea* and Greek αἴνω." *ŽA* 26:362 (1976).
530. "Notes on Old Breton: 1. *a* 'depuis, de'; 2. *ad*; 3. *adac*; 4. *adas*; 5. *aen*; 6. *anre*; 7. *anteith*; 8. *antemeuetic*, Mod. Bret. *tañva*." *EC* 15:191-193 (1976-77). Cf. 375 (1973); 456 (1975); 555 (1978); 661 (1981); 954 (1987)
532. "Western Indo-European notes: 3. Gothic *hallus* ON. *hallr*, etc.; 4. Crimean Gothic, *knauen* ON. *knár*; 5. Crimean Gothic *ich*." *IF* 81:36-40 (1976). Cf. 500 (1976); 213 (1967); 615 (1980); 744 (1982); 784 (1983)
533. "φοῖβος, ἀφικτός." *IF* 81:41-42 (1976). Cf. 537 (1977); 546 (1976); 592 (1979)
534. "Illyrian *Neunt(i)us*." *IF* 81:43-44 (1976). Cf. 494 (1976); 314 (1971); 856 (1985)
538. "*śr̥nkhāṇikā*." *Philologia Orientalis* IV (In memoriam Academician George V. Tsereteli), Tbilisi 1976. 43-8. Cf. 418 (1974); 493, 469 (1975); 403, 419 (1974); 471 (1976)
546. "Slavic *ískra*." *Zbornik za filologiju i lingvistiku* 19:193 (1976). Cf. 436 (1974); 236 (1969); 533 (1976); 948 (1987)
545. "On Slavic *ev* < *eu̯*." *Zbornik za filologiju i lingvistiku* 19: 13-4 (1976). Cf. 744 (1982)
550. "Studime rreth *o*-së në gjuhën shqipe." *Gjurmime Albanologjike: Seria Filologjike* 6:41-6 (1976). [**ei* mbas **l*-së; *nye*; *sorrë*; *poshtë*, *përpsh*; *gjê*, *gjie*, *gjedh*; *gjollë*.] Cf. 344 (1972); 456, 462 (1975); 759 (1981)
571. "On the Role of Grammar in the Explanation of Variant Lexemes." *Makedonski jazik* 27:79-80 (1976). Cf. 438 (1975)

Reviews
498. Review of James W. Marchand, *The Sounds and Phonemes of Wulfila's Gothic* (The Hague/Paris: Mouton, 1973). *Foundations of Language* 14:431-2 (1976). Cf. 108 (1959); 309 (1970)

1977

Articles
502. "Romanian Etymologies: 1. *merge*, 2. Aromanian *orca*, 3. *păstra*—an autochthonous calque." *Studii și cercetări lingvistice* 28:73-7 (1977). Cf. 380 (1973); 282 (1969); 899 (1986)
504. "Slavic *kum* and Eastern Romance." *RRL* 22:11 (1977).
505. "Addenda on **b* before liquid." *RRL* 22:9-10 (1977). [1. *pătul*, 2. *faur*: Albanian *farkë*.] Cf. 470 (1975); 474 (1976)
506. Letter on *Schmuck* etc. *Comments on Etymology* 6(15):2 (1977).
509. "The Locative Pronominals in Romanian." *Studii și cercetări lingvistice* 28:167-70 (1977). Cf. 612 (1979); 691 (1982); 768 (1982)
510. "On XVIth Century *tomni*." *Studii și cercetări lingvistice* 28:197 (1977). Cf. 688 (1981)
511. "On Two Romanian Elements of Dubious Age." *RRL-CLTA* 14:35-7 (1977). (1. *copac*, 2. *daș*) Cf. 476 (1976)
516. "Old English *lēod-*." *English Studies* 58(2):97-100 (1977). Cf. 734 (1982); 886 (1984); 906 (1986)
520. "*Strunga*." *LB* 20:113-7 (1977). Cf. 477 (1976); 623, 636, 650 (1980); 674 (1981); 916 (1986)
521. "Notulae latinae: 1. *tandem, tam, utinam*; 2. *tam, -dam, nam*; 3. *quattuor*; 4. *quadru-, quadraginta*; 5. Romanian *mormînt* < *mon(i)mentum*." *Studii clasice* 17:147-52 (1977). Cf. 481, 488 (1976); 375 (1973); 458 (1975); 500 (1976); 652 (1979); 690, 691 (1982); 778 (1983); 853 (1985)
522. "On some questions of areal linguistics." *Berkeley Linguistics Society Papers* 3:279-82 (1977). Cf. 584 (1979); 616 (1980)
523. "The semantics of poetry in Early Celtic." *CLS* 13:147-51 (1977). Cf. 387 (1974); 636 (1980)
524. "On glottal stop + nasal." *CLS Book of Squibs* 46-8 (1977). Cf. 465 (1975); 564 (1978); 653 (1979); 727 (1980), 728 (1982)
531. "Ad *Słownik etymologiczny języka polskiego* IV 5(20): *łajno* and *gówno, łakomny, łania, łanitwa, łap!*." *Rocznik Slawistyczny* 38:83-4 (1977). Cf. 487 (1975); 391 (1973)

535. "Nodiadau Amrywiol ~ Miscellaneous Notes: Gaulish *aged-*, *agis-* Celtic *kumb-*; Celtic *banu̯o-*; Welsh *banw, benyw, banwy*; La Graufesenque *Circos.*" *BBCS* 27:213-6 (1977). Cf. 235 (1969); 553 (1977); 941 (1987), 955
536. "Crimean Gothic numerals." *Kwartalnik Neofilologiczny* 24: 275-7 (1977). Cf. 367 (1973); 331 (1972); 423 (1973); 145 (1961)
537. "Varia II: 1. *imb·said-, impuide*; 2. *$*H_a éndhi$ and *$*H_a mbhí$; 3. *$*H_e ńdhi$ and *$*H_e embhi$; 4. *$*i̯em-$; 5. *fairsing.*" *Ériu* 28: 145-8 (1977). Cf. 375 (1973); 309 (1970); 175 (1963); 400 (1974); 533 (1976); 610, 620 (1980); 667 (1981); 700, 736 (1982)
539. "The quality of nasal clusters in Prasun." *Acta Orientalia* 38:41-2 (1977).
542. "Notulae Daco-Iranicae." *Studia et acta orientalia* (Bucharest) 9:79-83 (1977). Cf. 438, 470 (1975); 477 (1976); 520 (1977); 929 (1987)
553. "Some Italic and Celtic Correspondences." *KZ* 91:240-5 (1977). [Welsh *adeg*; Welsh *asio, aseth*; Latin *gnāuos*; Latin *mortuus*; Welsh *rheg*; Irish *és*; Old Irish *maraid*, Latin *mora*]. Cf. 305 (1971); 535 (1977); 436 (1974); 735 (1981); 833 (1984); 899 (1986)
554. "On Polynesian NP and VP Determiners." *Journal of the Polynesian Society* 86:411-2 (1977).
558. "Indo-Celtica." *Lingua Posnaniensis* 20:9-11 (1977). Cf. 548 (1978); 579, 524 (1977); 727 (1980)
561. "Indo-European *$*kreuH$.*" *IF* 82:75-6 (1977). Cf. 497 (1976); 247 (1969); 621 (1980); 664 (1981), 668; 794, 801 (1983), 804 (1982), 805 (1984), 826; 860 (1985); 861 (1983), 873 (1984); 886 (1984)
562. "On Verbal Adjectives in *$*-ko-$*.*" *IF* 82:77-9 (1977). Cf. 519 (1976); 566, 572 (1978); 789 (1982); 906 (1986)
578. "Nodiadau Amrywiol ~ Miscellaneous Notes: Notulae Cornicae." *BBCS* 27:251-2 (1977). Cf. 454, 480 (1975); 319, 364 (1972); 418 (1974); 941 (1987)
579. "Celtic *$*dam-$ and vṛddhi and δᾶμος." *ZCP* 36:5-12 (1977). Cf. 558 (1977); 462 (1975); 326 (1972); 552 (1978); 662 (1981); 873 (1984)

Reviews
529. Review of Merrit Ruhlen, *A guide to the languages of the world* (Language Universals Project, Stanford University, 1976). *Journal of Linguistics* 13:355-6 (1977).

1978

Articles

540. Correspondence on *shyster*. *Comments on Etymology* VII No. 6/7:15-16; No. 13:1-3 (1978). Cf. 575 (1979)
543. Correspondence on St. Clair's review of Koo. *Conference on American Indian Languages Clearinghouse* (CAIL) *Newsletter* 6(2): 13-14 (1978).
544. "A note on 'pidgin'." *Language and Society* 6:389-90 (1978).
547. "Gjuha shqipe është thelb i studimeve ballkanike." *Rilindja* 2 September 1978, 12. Cf. 501 (1976)
548. "Sound change and the etymological lexicon." *Papers from the Parasession on the Lexicon*, Chicago Linguistic Society 1978: 184-95. Cf. 549 (1978); 275 (1970); 698 (1981); 804 (1982); 826 (1984); 853 (1985); 941 (1987)
549. "On Panoean sibilants." *Proceedings of the 4th Annual Meeting of the Berkeley Linguistic Society* 427-31 (1978). Cf. 548 (1978)
551. "Albanische Sprache." *Lexikon des Mittelalters* I:276-7 (1978). Cf. 378 (1974); 574 (1978)
552. "Slavic *Stryjь* 'Father's Brother'." *General Linguistics* 18:1-19 (1978). Cf. 203 (1966); 227 (1968); 579 (1977)
555. "Notes on Old Breton." *EC* 15:569-72 (1978). [9. *antunan*; 10. *a olguo*; 11. *apom*; 12. *arcoued*; 13. *ard*; 14. *a recter*; 15. *argent*; 16. *ari*; 17. *arimrot*; 18. *arm-*.] Cf. 530 (1976)
556. "Miscellanea Celtica." *Studia Celtica* 12-13:14-6 (1977-8). [*tân*, see now 924 (1987); *gwaddod*; article mutation in Swiss German]. Cf. 2 (1951)
557. "Intensives in British Celtic and Gaulish." *Studia Celtica* 12-13:1-13 (1977-8). [1. *ennyn, enynnu*; 2. Welsh *ach-, ech-*; 3. Welsh *ach, echenu*; 4. intensive *ad-*; 5. Welsh *affleu*; 6. Welsh **ande-*; 7. *an-* 'in, on'; 8. misc. *an-*; 9. *ar-*; 10. **ate*; 11. **u̯o*; 12. Gaulish and other intensives; 13. *gor-, ver-*; 14. *-m-, -s-*]. Cf. 375 (1973); 625, 633 (1980); 638 (1979) [NB]; 644 (1980); 651 (1981), 661; 705 (1982); 920 (1985)
559. "The British End of the Spectrum of Romania." *Contemporary Studies in Romance Linguistics*, ed. Margarita Suñer. Washington, D.C.: Georgetown University Press, 1978. Pp. 172-5. Cf. 364 (1972); 873 (1984); 892 (1986)
560. "Old Church Slavonic *veštĭ* 'thing'." *Comments on Etymol-*

ogy 8, No. 6:1-2 (1978). [Reprinted with corrections as *C on E* 8, No. 15:2-3, 1979.]

563. "**leudh-* 'obstruct'." *Münchener Studien zur Sprachwissenschaft* 37:65-8 (1978).
564. "On Greek 'Prothetic' Vowels." *Münchener Studien zur Sprachwissenschaft* 37:59-64 (1978). Cf. 494 (1976); 524 (1977); 845 (1984); 857 (1985)
566. "Nodiadau Amrywiol ~ Miscellaneous Notes: Breton *frig, froug.*" *BBCS* 28:94 (1978). Cf. 562 (1977)
567. "Varia II: 1. conjoining *os*; 2. *Gwion, Fer Fí*; 3. *iomna, udhacht.*" *Ériu* 29:149-54 (1978). Cf. 495 (1975); 683 (1981); 735 (1981); 881 (1985)
568. "Indo-European '6'." *Linguistic and Literary Studies in honor of Archibald A. Hill*, eds. M. A. Jazayery, E. C. Polomé, W. Winter. The Hague: Mouton (4 vols.) 3:81-90 (1978). Cf. 130 (1960); 143 (1961); 766 (1983); 842 (1984); 931 (1987)
572. "On **dei̯u̯o-* in Slavic." (*Studies in honor of Horace G. Lunt*, eds. E. A. Scatton, R. D. Steele, C. E. Gribble. Columbus, Ohio: Slavica Publishers, Inc.) *Folia Slavica* 2:141-3 (1978). Cf. 562 (1977); 447 (1974)
573. "Further Remarks on the Celtic Names of Ig." *Acta Neophilologica* (Ljubljana) 11:57-63 (1978). Cf. 517 (1976); 687 (1981)
574. "On Late Mediaeval Linguistic Contacts of Non-Slavs with Slavs in Southeastern Europe: The Quality of Evidence." *Les cultures slaves et les Balkans*. Sofia 2:313-22 (1978). Cf. 440 (1975); 147, 163 (1963); 230 (1968); 279 (1970); 520, 542 (1977); 477 (1976); 551 (1978)
581. "Indo-European 'duck'." *KZ* 92:29-31 (1978). Cf. 755 (1983)
591. "Hittite *ekt-* '(hunting) net'." *IF* 83:119-20 (1978). Cf. 588 (1979); 605 (1980); 709 (1982); 824 (1984)
597. "A Note on Some Non-Absolute Intransitives." *Te Reo* 21:82 (1978).
726. "On the Baltic Verbal Ending *-ki.*" *Baltistica* 14:110-1 (1978). Ad 514 (1976)

1979

Articles

565. (jointly signed) "Linguists Respond to Bohannan." *Anthropology Newsletter* 20:2 (1979).

569. "Romanian Etymologies: Ad DLR VI 3a." [*ma-* to *mă-*] *Studii și cercetări lingvistice* 30:89-90 (1979). Cf. 337 (1971); 470 (1975)
570. "*Horst* and Method." *Linguistic Method: Essays in honor of Herbert Penzl*, eds. I. Rauch and G. E. Carr. The Hague: Mouton, 1979. Pp. 175-81. Cf. 221 (1967); correction 648 (1980); 725 (1981)
575. "Correspondence on *shyster*." *Comments on Etymology* VIII No. 14:6-7 (1979). Cf. 540 (1978); 765 (1983)
576. "Romanian Etymologies: Ad DLR VIII partea A 3a." [*pî-* to *po-*] *Studii și cercetări lingvistice* 30:163-4 (1979). Cf. 486, 528 (1975)
577. "Methodological Light from Proto-Algonquian "Sun"." *Contributions to Canadian Linguistics* (National Museum of Man, Mercury Series Paper No. 50) Ottawa 1979. Pp. 1-6). Replaces 366 (1973)
580. "Letter on *skedaddle*." *Comments on Etymology* 8, No.15: 20-1 (1979).
582. "Tongass Tlingit and Na-Dene." *Proceedings of the 5th Annual Meeting of the Berkeley Linguistics Society*: 461-3 (1979). Cf. 904 (1985)
583. "Arin Ket Consonants." *The Elements: Papers from the Conference on Non-Slavic Languages of the USSR, CLS* 1979, 375-6. Cf. 133 (1960)
584. "Linguistic and Political Areas." *The Elements: Papers from the Conference on Non-Slavic Languages of the USSR, CLS* 1979: 371-4. Cf. 331 (1972); 522 (1977)
585. "Formy *tho/the* u Busbeka." *Ètimologija 1977* (Moskva 1979): 150.
586. "On Some Iranian Names Transmitted by Late Babylonian." *Indo-Iranian Journal* 21:189-90 (1979). Cf. 567 (1978)
587. "Indo-European *$g^w en$-H_a*." *KZ* 93:1-7 (1979). Cf. 431 (1974); 117 (1960); 955 (1987)
588. "**mi-t-* 'Journey': Unfinished Business." *AJP* 100:396-7 (1979). Cf. 591 (1978); 605 (1980)
589. "Notulae Etymologicae Cymricae." *BBCS* 28:213-7 (1979). [Welsh *gŵyl, gwyll, gwymon* = O.Ir. *fem(m)ain, gwyn* = O.Ir. *find, gwŷn, gwynn, Gwynedd, gwynias, gwyran* 'barnacle goose', *gwyran* 'grass', *gwŷs, gŵyth, gwyw* = O.Ir. *feo*,

gylf/gylyf, had, hadl, haeach, haidd, haeddel, haf.] Cf. 612 (1979); 745 (1982)
590. "On Nasal + Dental in Romanian." *Studii și cercetări lingvistice* 30:507 (1979). Cf. 688 (1981)
592. "ἀτρεκής, ἄτρακτος." *ŽA* 29:72 (1979). Cf. 533 (1976)
593. "νέφος." *ŽA* 29:90 (1979). Cf. 326 (1972); 470 (1975); 524 (1977)
594. "Welsh *nyf* ≠ O.Ir. *snigid*." *BBCS* 28:402 (1979). Cf. 493 (1975)
595. "IE *$ghreH_ou$-, *$ghrodh$-." *Münchener Studien zur Sprachwissenschaft* 38:83 (1979). Cf. 798 (1983)
596. "κοινός." *Münchener Studien zur Sprachwissenschaft* 38:86 (1979). Cf. 493 (1975); 877 (1985)
598. "On Pseudo-Suffixes in East Baltic." *Journal of Baltic Studies* 10:148-50 (1979). Cf. 285, 291 (1970); 454 (1975)
599. "Buxom and 1880." *Papiere zur Linguistik* 21:75-7 (1979).
600. "Towards the History of Slavic Scholarship." *Slovene Studies* 1979, 2:61-2. Cf. 927 (1987) for II
601. "Footnote on *thanatos*. *Comments on Etymology* 9, No. 6:5 (1979). Cf. 602 (1980)
603. "Supercalifragilisticexpialidocious Again." *American Speech* 51:124 (1976, actually 1979).
606. "On Ljubljana Old High German Glosses." *Acta Neophilologica* 12:59-60 (1979). Cf. 365 (1973); 355 (1973)
607. "Joinder and Rejoinder: III." *American Speech* 54:118-9 (1979). Cf. 541 (1975)
611. "On Syllabic Reduction and Syntax." *Festschrift for Oswald Szemerényi on the Occasion of his 65th Birthday* (Current Issues in Linguistic Theory: 11), ed. Bela Brogyani. Amsterdam: Benjamins (1979). 343-50. Cf. 612 (1979); 691 (1982) [correction]; 793 (1983); 908 (1986)
612. "Celtica Indogermanica." *ZCP* 37:169-73 (1979) 39:219 (1982). Cf. 488 (1976); 509 (1977); 632 (1980); 708 (1982); 882 (1985)
613. "The North European word for 'apple'." *ZCP* 37:158-66 (1979). Cf. 453 (1975); 808 (1983); 866 (1985), 878 (1985); 894 (1986); 919 (1985)
617. "βάτραχος again." *ŽA* 29:209-12 (1979). Cf. 526 (1976); 693 (1981); 741 (1982)

635. "Fjala *javë*, reduktimi i saj fonetik dhe sintaksa." *Gjurmime Albanologjike* (Seria e Shkencave filologjike) 8:121-9 (1979). Cf. 611 (1979)
637. "Albanian *drudhe* 'piece, crumb'." *IF* 84:201-2 (1979). Cf. 636 (1980)
638. "Western Indo-European Notes: 6. Welsh *echen* 'need'." *IF* 84:203-4 (1979).
639. "A Reshaped Irregularity." *IF* 84:255-8 (1979). Cf. 696 (1981)
652. "Lithuanian *keturì*, Latvian *četri*." *Baltistica* 15(1):44-5 (1979). Cf. 521 (1977); 672 (1980)
653. "On two Baltic etymologies: 1. *liežùvis*; 2. Old Prussian *kērmens* 'body'." *Baltistica* 15(2):144-5 (1979). Cf. 524 (1977)

1980

Articles

602. "Remarks on *thanatos*. *Comments on Etymology* 9, No. 10: 6-7 (1980). Cf. 601 (1979); 626 (1980)
604. "*ma-ri-ne-u* and *mallos*." *NESTOR* 7:2:1431 (1980). "μαλλός." *NESTOR* 7:3:1439 (1980). "μαλλός discontinued." *NESTOR* 7:5:1449 (1980). Cf. 481 (1976); 376 (1973); 299 (1970); 701 (1982)
605. "I. Vedic *upa-bhŕt-*; II. *sruvá-*." *Indo-Iranian Journal* 22:141-2 (1980). Cf. 588 (1979); 548, 591 (1978); 475 (1976); 368, 374 (1973); 198 (1967); 882 (1985); 901 (1986)
608. "Remarks on Latin *voltus*." *Comments on Etymology* 9, No. 10:22 (1980). Cf. 371 (1973); 418 (1974); 790 (1982); 811 (1984)
609. "On the Proto-Austronesian Spirants." *Austronesian Studies: Papers from the Second Eastern Conference on Austronesian Languages* (Michigan Papers on South and Southeast Asia #15), ed. Paz Buenaventura Naylor (1980). 195-201. Cf. 482 (1976)
610. "Albanian *është*." *American Indian and Indoeuropean Studies: Papers in Honor of Madison S. Beeler*, eds. K. Klar, M. Langdon, S. Silver. Mouton: The Hague (1980). 337-46. Cf. 537 (1977); 691 (1982) [correction]; 736 (1982); 847 (1985), 881 (1985)
614. "Russian Hospitality" (letter). *Physics Today* 33:7:69 (July 1980).

666. "An amendment to Fortunatov's Law." *Suniti Kumar Chatterji Commemoration Volume*, ed. Bh. P. Mallik. The University of Burdwan, West Bengal, India (1981). 106-12. Cf. 671 (1982); 770 (1983)
667. "Indo-European *(H_e)op-.*" *Münchener Studien zur Sprachwissenschaft*. 40:39-60 (1981). Cf. 661 (1981); 703; 736 (1982); 754 (1983); 831, 838, 812 (fn.2) (1984)
668. "Remarks on *ster-.*" *Münchener Studien zur Sprachwissenschaft* 40:35-8 (1981). Cf. 867 (1984)
674. "On the distribution and origin of *(h)urda.*" *LB* 24:47-50 (1981). Cf. 520 (1977); 665 (1981)
675. "*Hîrşova.*" *LB* 24:51 (1981).
676. "Culture contacts in English runes." *Papiere zur Linguistik* 25:91 (1981).
678. "Early Italic notes." *Glotta* 59:228-30 (1981). [1. *eu* in Early Italic; 2. Ardea *titoio*] Cf. 911 (1986)
679. "On **ri* in Latin and Albanian *krip.*" *Glotta* 59:230-1 (1981).
680. "'eat' in Greek." *Glotta* 59:155-7 (1981).
681. "πάθος." *Glotta* 59:157-9 (1981). Cf. 763 (1982); 855 (1985)
682. "Locatival -ου." *Glotta* 59:159-60 (1981). Cf. 832 (1984)
683. "Albanian *edhe* 'and'." *Bono Homini Donum: Essays in Historical Linguistics in Memory of J. Alexander Kerns*, eds. Y. L. Arbeitman and A. R. Bomhard. Amsterdam: Benjamins (1981). 127-31. Cf. 615 (1980); 735 (1981); 836 (1984)
684. "Romanian Etymologies." *Studii şi cercetări lingvistice* 32:425-8 (1981). [i ad DLR viii, 4:1. *potîrniche*; 2. *preot*; ii peripheral evidence on *calendae*: 1. Northwest Ardeal *corindă*; 2. Welsh *calan*; iii *arţar* 'érable'.] [Addendum *SCL* 32:536.] Cf. 650 (1980); 710 (1982)
686. "Latin *sūdus.*" *FLH* 2:149-50 (1981). Cf. 841 (1984)
687. "Latin *dextrata* and IE **deḱsi-no-.*" *Revue des Études Sud-Est Européennes* 19:141-5 (1981). [also *stolata* and *azi*]
688. "The chronology of a cluster type in Romanian." *RRL* 26:405-9 (1981). Cf. 590 (1979)
689. "Russu on *Illyrioi.*" *Studii şi cercetări lingvistice* 32:535-6 (1981). Cf. 856 (1985); 909 (1986)
. "Yet Again βάτραχος." *ŽA* 31:46 (1981). Cf. 617 (1979).
. "'ΑΓΟΣΤΟΣ, 'ΑΓΕΙΡΩ." *ŽA* 31:83-4 (1981). Cf. 696 (1981); 741 (1982); 617 (1979); 799 (1983), 800; 823 (1983)
. "Greek **g"hoitos.*" *ŽA* 31:92 (1981).

---

615. "Unrecognized Deixis in the Indoeuropean Pronouns." *Papers from the Parasession on Pronouns and Anaphora*. CLS (1980). 147-50. Cf. 472, 488, 481 (1976); 656 (1981), 683 (1981); 691 (1982); 743 (1982), 744
616. "Discussion on Inclusive/Exclusive." *Papers from the Parasession on Pronouns and Anaphora*. CLS (1980). 228-30. Cf. 522 (1977)
618. "Slovenski *koteri*, *katéri* in **saus-*, Briž. Slov. *v uzmazi* in *smag-.*" *Slavistična Revija* 28:97-101 (1980). [Alb. *thā-*, *i thātë* 'dry', *thi* 'pig'.] Cf. 306 (1971); 625 (1980); 749 (1982)
620. "Oscan Notes." *AJP* 101:190-3 (1980). [*dat* 'dē': o.Ir. *dē-*; *(p)únttram*?; : *ant.*] Cf. 493 (1975); 403 (1974)
621. "Lycian χahba." *JNES* 39:215-6 (1980).
622. "Latin *hālāre*, *anhēlāre.*" *AJP* 101:331-2 (1980). Cf. 382 (1974); 777 (1983); 902 (1985); 947 (1987)
623. "*burtă.*" *RRL* 25:335 (1980). Cf. 476 (1976); 520 (1977); 721 (1982)
624. "Latin *er* in British Celtic." *EC* 17:161-3 (1980)
625. "Varia." *EC* 17:165-7 (1980). [IE **sek*; dat.sg. of **ā-*stems; Welsh *eleni*.] Cf. 493 (1975); 260 (1970); 661 (1981)
626. Letter on Greek θνητός. *Comments on Etymology* 10, No. 1:5 (1980). Cf. 602 (1980)
627. "IE **k"eH_as-* 'cough'." *Ezikovedski proučvanija v čest na akad. V. I. Georgiev*. Sofija: BAN (1980). 130-4. Cf. 931 (1987)
628. "Latin *uolup(e).*" *KZ* 94:158 (1980). [*uolup est*] Cf. 141 (1960); 630 (1980); 752 (1982); 849 (1985); 877
629. "On IE **tu̯* > Hittite *z.*" *KZ* 94:64 (1980). [Verbal Noun **-tu-ēl*.]
630. "νῆϊς, H198, θ179." *Studii Clasice* 19:91-2 (1980). [**ne-u̯id-*, **nēsti-* Latv. *nav*.] Cf. 628 (1980)
631. "θαμά 'often', θάμνος, θάμνα." *Studii Clasice* 19:93-4 (1980). [Also Greek nouns in *m*-suffixes.]
632. "A Case of Paradigmatic Continuity in Italic and Romance." *Linguistic Studies in Honor of Ernst Pulgram* (Current Issues in Linguistic Theory: 18), ed. Herbert J. Izzo. Amsterdam: Benjamins (1980). 69-73. Cf. 481 (1976); 612 (1979); 509 (1977); 691 (1982) [revision, esp. fn.1], 708; 783 (1983)
633. "Varia VI: *álad* 'wound'." *Ériu* 31:172 (1980).

634. "Notes on Proto-Polynesian Colours from K. B. Branstetter, AL 19. 1–25, esp. 18–22, 1977." *Anthropological Linguistics* 22:390–1 (1980).

636. "On Participial *-do- and Verbs and Adjectives and Colours." *Wege zur Universalienforschung: sprachwissenschaftl. Beitr. zum 60. Geburtstag von Hansjakob Seiler*, eds. Gunter Brettschneider and Christian Lehmann. Tübingen: Narr (1980). 268–73. Cf. 634 (1980); 520 (1977); 637 (1979); 657, 686, 658 (1981); 745 (1982); 821 (1984); 875 (1985); 948 (1987)

640. "Latin *sucula*." *AJP* 101:458 (1980). Cf. 948 (1987)

641. "How can gen.-comp. classifications be based on typological considerations?: Discussion." *Typology and Genetics of Language* (Travaux du cercle linguistique de Copenhague 20), eds. Torben Thrane, Vibeke Winge, Lachlan Mackenzie, Una Canger and Niels Ege. Copenhagen: Linguistic Circle of Copenhagen (1980). 141–4.

642. "A grapho-phonemic confusion." *Beiträge zur Namenforschung* 15:360 (1980).

643. "Rezijansko *jïst* 'polenta'." *Slavistična Revija* 28:487–8 (1980).

644. "*imbolc, óimelc*." *Studia Celtica* 14–15:106–13 (1979–80). Cf. 557 (1978); 696 (1981); 906 (1986); 915 (1987); 920 (1985)

646. "Mongolian Vocalic Features and the Problem of Harmony." *Issues in Vowel Harmony* (Studies in Language Companion Series: 6), ed. Robert M. Vago. Amsterdam: Benjamins (1980). 101–11. Cf. 93 (1958); 479 (1976)

647. "*Łyżka*." *Rocznik Slawistyczny* 41:63 (1980). Cf. 475 (1976); 198 (1967)

648. "Nodiadau Amrywiol—Miscellaneous Notes: GPC *ef* I (b); 'hand' as a locative; Welsh *prys*; the Welsh Subjunctive." *BBCS* 29:83–7 (1980). Cf. 481 (1976); 570 (1979); 690 (1982); 735 (1981); 906 (1986) [GPC *ef* 1(b)—republished in error, *Studia Celtica* 16–17 (1981–2): 163–5.]

650. "*Codru*." *Studii și cercetări lingvistice* 31:663–6 (1980). Cf. 477 (1976); 520 (1977); 660 (1981), 684; 710 (1982); 909 (1986)

654. "On micro-syntactic change." *American Speech* 55:310–2 (1980).

672. "IE *( )ḱuon- 'dog'." *IF* 85:35–42 (1980). Cf. 789 (1982); 778 (1983)

677. "Germanic *blood/blut*." *FLH* 1:389–92 (1980). Cf. 664 (1981); 839 (1984), 851

727. "*nãmas, namiẽ*." *Baltistica* 16:44 (1980). Cf. 728 (1982); 558 (1977)

729. "Some remarks on Bright's 'Hispanisms in Cahuilla'." *Journal of California and Great Basin Anthropology, Papers Linguistics* 2:95–7 (1980).

Reviews

619. Review of Bojka Sokolova, *Albanski vъzroždenski pečа Bъlgarija* (Sofia: Izdatelstvo BAN, 1979, pp. 208). *Slavic East European Journal* 24:200–1 (1980).

1981

Articles

645. "On the Celtic Origin of English Slang *dig/twig* 'underst *Comments on Etymology* 10, No. 12–13:2–3 (1981).

649. "*Betulla* 'birch'." *Comments on Etymology* 10, No (1981).

651. "*VLPIA CASSA*." *Beiträge zur Namenforschung* (1981). [Ulpianum]

655. "¡Graphs, not punctuation!" Letter to *Science* 213 1981).

656. "Armenian *am* 'year'; Armenian *kʿez*." *Annual of Linguistics* 2:13–4 (1981). Cf. 142 (1961); 615 (1982); 835 (1985)

657. "Latin *cauda*." *AJP* 102:148 (1981). Cf. 946 (19

658. "*Vicus Cuprius*." *AJP* 102:149–50 (1981). Cf. 6

659. "Is the fibula a fake?" *AJP* 102:151–3 (1981). C

660. "'Bread' in Southeast Europe." *RP* 34:434 (1 (1980)

661. "Varia." *EC* 18:109–13 (1981). [iv (109–11) **isa* tic; v (111–2) Welsh *â ag*; vi (113) British *aᴸ-* 'a Cf. 719 (1982); 790 (1982); 802 (1983)

663. "On Leibniz's third Albanian letter." *Zeitschr ogie* 17:34–6 (1981).

662. "Comments on IE **orbho-*." *Zeitschrift f* 17:32–3 (1981).

664. "Two young animals." *Papiere zur Linguisti* [English *bird*; *pig*] Cf. 677 (1980)

665. "Autochthonous *vatră*." *RRL* 26:315 (198 520 (1977); 650 (1980); 674 (1981)

696. "Some Greek Forms in σ-." *ŽA* 31:93-6 (1981). Cf. 694 (1981); 943 (1986)
697. "*Anthrok*ʷ*os* once more." *ŽA* 31:133-4 (1981). Cf. 248 (1969)
698. "Refining Indo-European Lexical Entries." *KZ* 95:81-3 (1981). [1. I-E 'thrush'; 2. I-E *$H_a eḱs$- 'axle'.] Cf. 548 (1978); 776 (1983); 857, 898 (1985)
715. "I Nomi di Resia." *Ce Fastu? Sot la Nape* 33:11-16 (1981).
724. "Mycenaean -*da-a2* 'they contributed(?)'." *IF* 86:190 (1981).
725. "IE *$\underset{\smile}{u}res$- 'moisten' and Its Traces in Celtic." *IF* 86:191-3 (1981).
735. "Varia III." *Ériu* 32:158-62 (1981). [1. OIr *in·fét*, Welsh *dywedwyt*; 2. *és*; 3. *acus* ~ *ocuis*; 4. *geis*.] Cf. 553 (1977); 567 (1978); 763 (1982)
738. "Two Studies of Old English Poetic Discourse." *Zbornik Radova Katedre za anglistiku* (Filozofski fakultet Univerziteta u Nišu, Niš 1981) Papers in honor of Professor Vida E. Marković. 247-51.
739. "Lith. *vařdas*: Lat. *uerbum*." *Acta Baltico-Slavica* 14:143-4 (1981). Cf. 860 (1985)
758. "On the Columnar Accent of Slavic Postverbals in -ā." *Zbornik za filologiju i lingvistiku* 24.1:171 (1981).
759. "Slavic **slbzá*." *Zbornik za Filologiju i Lingvistiku* 24.1:171-2 (1981). Cf. 344 (1972); 550 (1976)
760. "Slavic **sъtъ* 'honeycomb'." *Zbornik za filologiju i lingvistiku* 24.1:172 (1981).

1982

Articles

669. Forum: Letter to the editors. *NESTOR* 9:1:1586-7 (1982). [πίσυρες] Cf. 672 (1980)
670. "*aśītí*- '80'." *Indo-Iranian Journal* 24:37-8 (1982).
671. "Brief Communication: 1. *kāla*- 'black'; 2. *kālá-ḥ* 'time'; 3. East Iranian **gaštra*- 'mouth, tooth'; 4. Avestan *staman*-." *Indo-Iranian Journal* 24:38-40 (1982). Cf. 753 (1982); 960 (1988) [ad § 1&2]
673. "Letter on *cheese it*. *Comments on Etymology* 11 No. 7-8:9 (1982).
685. "On Eminescu's poetic transcendence of meaning." *Tricolorul* (Toronto Canada) Nr. 10, p. 3 (March 1982).

690. "The anaphora *ei in Latin." *AJP* 103:98-9 (1982). Cf. 648 (1980); 691; 836 (1984); 900 (1986)
691. "*hīc* and *ibi* in Latin." *AJP* 103:99-101 (1982). Cf. 472 (1976); 615, 632 (1980).
692. "Addenda to Onomastica Nervosa." *Verbatim* 8. 4:4-5 (1982).
699. "Remnants of the Pronominal Genitive Singular *-l.*" *AJP* 103:214-6 (1982). Cf. 743 (1982); 896 (1985)
700. "Armenian Miscellanea." *Annual of Armenian Linguistics* 3: 53-6 (1982). [*eresk*ᶜ; *asełn*; *vaṙem*; *vaṙim*; locative *yamsean*; *ənd*, *ənto-cin*; *cnund*.] Cf. 736 (1982); 811 (1984); 850 (1983); 904 (1985)
701. "μαλλός: A Clarification." *Glotta* 60:61-2 (1982). Cf. 604 (1980)
702. " 'Arm, Shoulder'." *JIES* 10:187-9 (1982). Cf. 794 (1983)
703. "Gothic *inu*, Greek ἄνευ, OHG *ânu* 'OHNE'." *JIES* 10:189-90 (1982).
704. "On Greek ζ: *y-*." *JIES* 10:190-1 (1982).
705. "Nodiadau Amrywiol ~ Miscellaneous Notes." *BBCS* 29: 681-3 (1982). [*vch bob aelwyt*, *ffuruf*; *Corannyeit*; *cerennydd*.] Cf. 829 (1984)
706. "Old Spanish *sencido* Again." *RP* 36:28-31 (1982).
707. "The Oldest Albanian Syntagma." *LB* 25:77-9 (1982).
708. "Latin *ut/nē* and *ut* (. . . *nōn*)." *Glotta* 60:115-20 (1982). Cf. 632 (1980); 793 (1983)
709. "Indic *pṛtanā-* 'combat'." *Papers from the Parasession on Nondeclaratives*, CLS 63-5 (1982).
710. "From Latin to Romanian Deviously." *Proceedings of the 8th Annual Meeting of the Berkeley Linguistics Society* 33-5 (1982). Cf. 650 (1980); 684 (1981)
712. "Suffixal Sociology: *Stewardess* as a loanword." *American Speech* 57:234-5 (1982).
713. "Obiter Dicta: (*I*) *could care less*." *Verbatim* 9.1:8 (1982).
716. "OCS (*j*)*ešte*." *South Slavic and Balkan Linguistics* 2:91-4 (1982). Cf. 802 (1983); 831 (1984)
717. "The Loss of Declension and the Definite." *Bulgaria Past and Present* (Proceedings of the Second International Conference on Bulgarian Studies, Druzhba, Varna, 1978), Sofia 1982, 71-6. Cf. 785 (1983)
718. "Brief Communications: Skt. *prastha-*; Skt. *līlā*." *Indo-Iranian Journal* 24:295 (1982).

719. "Old Irish *biáil* 'axe'." *ZCP* 39:86–7 (1982). Cf. 661 (1981)
720. "Hispanic *Complūtum, Compleutica*." *ZCP* 39:204 (1982).
721. "The Indo-European Roots **bher-* in the Light of Celtic and Albanian." *ZCP* 39:205–18 (1982). Cf. 754 (1983); 787 (1983), 793; 833 (1984); 908 (1986) [**sani*]; 915 (1987); 960 (1988)
722. "Productive *to·*." *ZCP* 39:219 (1982). Cf. 908 (1986)
728. "**dmós* > **[ʔnmés]*." *Baltistica* 18:63–4 (1982). Cf. 727 (1980); 524 (1977)
730. "*thwaite*." *Language Form and Linguistic Variation: Papers dedicated to Angus McIntosh* (Current Issues in Linguistic Theory: 15), ed. John Anderson. Amsterdam: Benjamins (1982). 161–7. Cf. 753 (1982); 773 (1983); 826, 828 (1984)
731. "(Western) Indo-European **sel-* 'move'." *Münchener Studien zur Sprachwissenschaft* 41:49–59 (1982). Cf. 715 (1981)
732. "*Lloegr*: The Welsh Name for England." *Cambridge Medieval Celtic Studies* 4:83–5 (1982). Cf. 404 (1973); 867 (1984)
733. "Varia." *EC* 19:137–42 (1982). [vii (137–8) *cledr*, etc.; viii (138–40) Two Riddles of Breton Phonology; ix (140–1) Breton *riou, riv* and OIr *reód*; x (141) Ir. *síd* 'tumulus' and *síd* 'peace'; xi (141–2) OIr. *seir*, Welsh *ffer*, etc.] Cf. 740 (1982)
734. "**-og-* in British Celtic and Notes on *bro*." *EC* 19:143–9 (1982). [Welsh *Cymraeg, troed*, etc.]
736. "Varia VII." *Ériu* 33:178–83 (1982). [1. *Fer Diad*; 2. (178–80) The Collective Numerals; 3. (180–1) **H$_e$en* (+*i*); 4. (181–2) On post-syncope adjustment of quality; 5. (182–3) The neuter plural in *-a*.] Cf. 700 (1982); 754 (1983); 831 (1984); 847 (1985)
737. "*glōria*." *AJP* 103:447–8 (1982).
740. "ˮΗθος, ἔθος, Myc. *e-ti-we*." *ŽA* 32:33–4 (1982). Cf. 733 (1982)
741. "Two Prehellenic Possibilities." *ŽA* 32:37–8 (1982). [1. χλαμύς, χλαῖνα 2. ἄσιλλα.] Cf. 694 (1981)
742. "*Jad(e)r-, Dizéros* and *Drinus*." *ŽA* 32:104 (1982). Cf. 856 (1985)
743. "φίλος." *BSL* 77:251–62 (1982). Cf. 699; 896 (1985)
744. "Armenian and Baltic Personal Pronouns: Typology and History." *Folia Slavica* 5 (Papers from the Second Conference on the Non-Slavic Languages of the U.S.S.R., 1981):181–90 (1982). Cf. 615 (1980); 656 (1981)
745. "On Some Colour Terms in Baltic and Slavic." *Slavic Linguistics and Poetics: Studies for Edward Stankiewicz on his 60th*

Birthday, eds. K. E. Naylor, H. I. Aronson, B. J. Darden, A. M. Schenker = *IJSLP* 25/26:187-92 (1982). [1. SCr. *sȋv, sînjī*; Cz. *sivý, siný*; 2. SCr. *sȉjed*, Slovene *sęr*; Cz. *šedý, šerý*; 3. Lith. *rýtas*, Slavic *rano*]. Cf. 296 (1971); 589 (1979); 636 (1980); 948 (1987) ad #2

749. "Two Uncertain IE Roots." *FLH* 3:127-30 (1982). [1. **sleip-* or **ḱleip-*? 2. **reidh-*] Cf. 847 (1985)

750. "ἄεθλος, -ον." *FLH* 3:131-2 (1982). Cf. 754 (1983)

751. "*dulcis*." *FLH* 3:133-4 (1982).

752. "Latin *apis*." *Festschrift für Johannes Hubschmid zum 65. Geburtstag*, eds. O. Winkelman, M. Braisch. Bern-München: Francke (1982). 157-8. Cf. 628 (1980)

753. "Nodiadau Amrywiol ~ Miscellaneous Notes." *BBCS* 30:39-45 (1982). [*amygaf, amwyn*; *gorch(y)fygaf, gorch(y)fygu*; On Notable Trees; Welsh *safn*, Breton *staon*; An Indeterminacy.] Cf. 671 (1982); 802 (1983); 805 (1984); 829

757. "Two Roots **H̥bhel-*." *Glotta* 60:227-30 (1982). [1. ὀφείλω, εὑρίσκω; 2. ὀφέλλω.] Cf. 798 (1983)

761. "Old Irish *trog* = Serbo-Croatian *trâg*." *Zbornik za filologiju i lingvistiku* 25.1:70-1 (1982). Cf. 763

762. "Slavic **trьb(r̥)úxъ*." *Zbornik za filologiju i lingvistiku* 25.1:171-2 (1982). Cf. 847 (1985)

763. "Two Slavic *o*-grades." *Zbornik za filologiju i lingvistiku* 25.2:137-8 (1982). [1. *vaditi se*; 2. *padǫ, pasti*]. Cf. 735 (1981), 681 (1981)

767. "I nomi dei mesi a Resia." *Sot la Nape* 34.4:16-7 (1982).

768. "Old Romanian *iuo*." *Studii şi cercertări lingvistice* 33:493 (1982). Cf. 509 (1977); 612 (1979)

789. "Indo-European Notes." *IF* 87:70-5 (1982). [1. (70-2) IE **seik-* and its meaning; 2. (72-3) Indo-European **sH̥ei-* 'bind'; 3. (73-4) Thracian -σ(ο)υκος, -συχις; 4. (74-5) Ad *IF* 85, p. 35-42.] Cf. 562 (1977); 802 (1983) [ad **sH̥ei-*]; 833 (1984); 884 (1986) [ad § 3]; 950 (1987) [ad § 2]

790. "Western Indo-European Notes." *IF* 87:76-81 (1982). [7. (76-7) OHG *cnuosal*, OE *cnōsl*; 8. (77) *Kind* and **genetā*; 9. (77-9) **mesl(H)* "Amsel"; 10. (79-81) Germanic **wleit-*.] Cf. 375 (1973); 661 (1981); 608 (1980); 811 (1984)

791. (with Howard Berman) "Old Irish *allas*, Hittite *allaniya-*." *IF* 87:124-6 (1982).

795. "On the Justification of Ordering in *TYP*." *Studia Celtica* 16–17:104–9 (1981–2).
804. "Latin *dormiō*." *Bulletin of the Institute of History and Philology, Academia Sinica* 53 (Yuen Ren Chao Memorial Volume): 627–8 (1982). Cf. 794 (1983); 858 (1985); 956 (1987)
812. "On the Name *Ohrid*." *Makedonski Jazik* 32/33 [Festschrift for Blaže Koneski]:777–84
952. "Fraza nominale në gjuhët ballkanike." *Seminari Ndërkombëtar për Gjuhën, Letërsinë dhe Kulturën Shqiptare* (Prishtinë) 7:179–82.

Reviews
711. Review of M. D. Kinkade, K. L. Hale, and O. Werner eds., *Linguistics and Anthropology; In honor of C. F. Voegelin* (Lisse: Peter de Ridder Press, 1975). *IJAL* 48:327–32 and 344–56 (1982).
714. Review of J. T. Shipley, *Dictionary of Word Origins* (Philosophical Library, 1945, reprinted) Cf. 854 (1985) and P. Davies, *Roots: Family Histories of Familiar Words* (McGraw Hill, 1981). *Verbatim* 9.1:13–14 plus separate sheet of notes (1982).
723. Review of P. J. Hopper ed., *Studies in Descriptive and Historical Linguistics: Festschrift for Winfred P. Lehmann* (Amsterdam: Benjamins 1977). *ZCP* 39:343–6 (1982). Cf. 873 (1984)
756. Review of Demetrius J. Georgacas, *Ichthyological Terms for the Sturgeon and Etymology of the International Terms Botargo, Caviar, and Congeners* (Pragmateiai tēs Akadēmias Aθēnōn, Tom. 43. Athens: 1978). *JAOS* 102:656–7 (1982).

1983

Articles
746. "*Helluva*." *American Speech* 58:83–4 (1983).
747. "*Dozy*." *American Speech* 58:85 (1983).
748. "Noun Adjunction and *-ed*." *American Speech* 58:93 (1983).
754. "Some Italic and Celtic Correspondences II." *KZ* 96:95–100 (1983) [8. *$g^w eru$*; 9. Lat. *saec(u)lum*, Welsh *hoedl*; 10. Lat. *amita*; 11. Lat. *sacerdōs*; 12. Lat. *obscūrus*; 13. Collective Numerals]. Cf. 368 (1973); 721, 736, 750 (1982); 667 (1981); 833 (1984)

755. "On Latin stem alternations." *KZ* 96:101-2 (1983). [1. Lat. *hērēs*, Gk. χηρωσταί; 2. Lat. *ianitrīcēs*.] Cf. 581 (1978); 443 (1975)
764. "To the Discussion of *Mokh(e)* 'Armenian'." *Comments on Etymology* 12, Nos. 13-14:2-3 (1983).
765. "Letter on *shyster*." *Comments on Etymology* 12, Nos. 13-14:4 (1983). Cf. 540 (1978); 575 (1979)
766. "Brief Communications: East Iranian '6'; Skt. *ātāḥ*." *Indo-Iranian Journal* 25:102 (1983). Cf. 568 (1978)
769. "Brief Communications: *hu-* in Scythian." *Indo-Iranian Journal* 25:208 (1983). Cf. 362 (1972)
770. "Brief Communications: A Revised Amendment to Fortunatov's Law." *Indo-Iranian Journal* 25:275-6 (1983). Cf. 666 (1981); 859 (1985)
771. "Mi kʿani kisašpʿakanneri masin hayereni patmutʿyan mej." *Patma-banasirakan handes* 1983 (1) 38-42 ["On Some Affricates in the History of Armenian." 1. *ǵ* + liquid in Armenian; 2. *c* for *t*; 3. *cᶜ* as a complex. *Historical-Philological Journal*, Erevan.]
772. "On Prerequisites to Implications." *RRL* 28:11-3 (1983).
773. "Srbohrvaško *cèsta*, Slovensko *cę́sta*." *Slavistična Revija* 31:60-1 (1983).
774. "The Greek Chariot." *Zeitschrift für Balkanologie* 19:14-5 (1983).
775. "On the Helleno-Armenian Shared Lexicon." *Annual of Armenian Linguistics* 4:63-4 (1983). Cf. 798 (1983); 897 (1985)
776. "*Erastankᶜ*." *Annual of Armenian Linguistics* 4:64-5 (1983). Cf. 698 (1981); 904 (1985)
777. "Further on Latin *capillus* and *pullus* and Lautgesetze." *FLH* 4:133-5 (1983).
778. "Indo-European Disyllabic Nominal Bases: Word Formation by Reanalysis of Reconstruction." *FLH* 4:137-8 (1983). Cf. 443 (1975), 454; 521 (1977); 672 (1980)
779. "*e* before nasal clusters in Latin." *Proceedings of the 9th Annual Meeting of the Berkeley Linguistic Society*. Pp. 84-7. (1983). Cf. 820 (1984)
780. "A Morphological Law." *Lingua* 61:1-8 (1983). Cf. 798 (1983); 844, 873 (1984)
781. "A Morphological Comparison." *CLS* 19 (1983). Pp. 155-7. Cf. 488 (1976); 877 (1985)

782. "Animates in -g-." *Baltistica* 19:175 (1983). Cf. 937 (1987)
783. "*Pronoun + Clitic." *Baltistica* 19:176-8 (1983). Cf. 829 (1984); 903 (1985)
784. "*ja* = Runic *ek*." *IJSLP* 27:11-3 (1983). Cf. 532 (1976)
785. "On Continuity in Bulgarian and Noun Inflexions." *Proceedings of the Symposium on Slavic Cultures: Bulgarian Contributions to Slavic Cultures. An International Conference Dedicated to the Celebration of the Thirteen Hundredth Anniversary of the Founding of the Bulgarian State. Columbia University in the City of New York, November 14, 1980*, eds. Rado L. Lencek, Riccardo Picchio, Hristo A. Hristov, and Kujo Kuev. Sofia: Publishing House "Sofia Press" (1983). Pp. 155-61. Cf. 717 (1982); 901 (1986 for C(C)C)
786. "*imbúaruch, imbárach*." *Celtica* 15:53-4 (1983).
787. "Varia." *EC* 20:91-3 (1983). [xii. (91) OIr. *talam, tarathar*; xiii. (91-2) Welsh *hydref*, Breton *here*; xiv. (92-3) Etymologie croisée.] Cf. 721 (1982); 802 (1983); 892 (1986); 939 (1987) ad xii
792. "*for( )ever* and *ever-*." *American Speech* 58:374-6 (1983).
793. "ὄφρα, τόφρα." *AJP* 104:384 (1983). Cf. 708 (1982)
794. "Indo-European Substantives in **-mó-* and **-mā́-*." *KZ* 96:171-7 (1982-3). Cf. 804 (1982); 835 (1985); 858 (1985); 885, 906, 913 (1986); 947 (1987), 950, 956 (1987)
798. "Philologica Varia." *REA* 17:5-12 (1983). [I. Notulae Phonologicae 1. *pʿr̄nkam*; 2. *krcem*; 3. *eluk*; II. *mitkᶜ* III. Some Armenian Nouns 1. *ortᶜ*; 2. *lur*; 3. *merj*; 4. *argand*; IV. Some Archaic Armenian Nouns 1. *awr* 2. *asr*; 3. Stem of *jer̄n*; V. Some Archaic Armenian Verbs 1. *jnem, ganem*; 2. *henum ~ hanum ~ hinem*; 3. *erdnum*; 4. *epᶜem*; 5. *lucanem*; 6. *awelum*.] Cf. 775 (1983); 757 (1982); 816 (1983); 834, 846, 872 (1984); 835, 904 (1985)
799. "Prehellenic μύλη." *ŽA* 33:12 (1983). Cf. 694 (1981)
800. "Prehellenic ἄχυρον." *ŽA* 33:22 (1983). Cf. 694 (1981)
801. "Varia II." *Ériu* 34:18 (1983). [OIr. *slicht*]
802. "Nodiadau Amrywiol ~ Miscellaneous Notes: *(n)am(w)yn* 'except'; The genitive of *-oui̯os*; Notes to Armes Prydain; On Language Contact in Roman Britain; *trew* and *ystrew*; *dihaereb*; *-hwyfar, hud*; ad *BBCS* 28, 400-1; *egel*; On the Areal Treatment of ŋ; On the Phonology of Vowels in Welsh Verbal Nouns; Chamalières *eθθic*." *BBCS* 30:288-96 (1983). Cf. 787, 798 (1983)

803. "On Greek Verbs in -τάζω." *Essays in Honor of Charles F. Hockett*, eds. Frederick B. Agard, Gerald Kelley, Adam Makkai and Valerie Becker Makkai. Leiden: Brill, 1983. Pp. 171–9.
806. "ὀλισθάνω." *Glotta* 61:192 (1983).
807. "πεδά." *Glotta* 61:193 (1983).
808. "Zametki: *žába*; *žerebënok*." *Ètimologija* 1981:35–7 (1983).
816. "OIr. *ucht*, γένος." *IF* 88:92 (1983). Cf. 798 (1983); 275 (1970); 826 (1984)
817. "Three Pseudo-Problems." *IF* 88:93–5 (1983). [1. IE *tek^w-; 2. Eng. *seam*; 3. On the medial syllable of 'daughter'.]
822. "ἁδρός and ἅδην." *ŽA* 33:146 (1983). Cf. 948 (1987)
823. "Prehellenica 3. στιφρύς, στῖφος; 4. σμῖλη, σμῖνύη, σμίνθος." *ŽA* 33:147–8 (1983). Cf. 694 (1981); 941 (1987)
850. "IE *meH_enot- and the Perfect Participle." *JIES* 11:379–82 (1983).
861. "Indo-European *leugh*- in the Ponto-Baltic Region." *Ponto-Baltica* 2-3:7–8 (1982-3).
862. "On Inscriptions from Apulum." *Studii Classice* 21:95–6 (1983). Cf. 474 (1976)
917. "On the Sparseness of Greek Borrowings in Romanian." *Cercetări de Lingvistică* 28:7–9.

Reviews
788. Review of (microfiches) Margaret [Marged] Haycock, *Mynegair i Llyfr Taliesin/ Concordance to the Book of Taliesin (National Library of Wales MS Peniarth 2)* (Cardiff: University of Wales Press, 1979) and Jeremy Boreham and Morfydd E. Owen, *Mynegair i Ganu Aneirin/ Concordance of Canu Aneirin* (Cardiff: University of Wales Press, 1980). *Cambridge Medieval Celtic Studies* 6:108–9 (1983).

1984

Articles
796. "Grammar through Onomastics." *Names* 32:102 (1984). Cf. 438 (1975)
797. Letter cautioning against . . . reduplicated forms in Primitive Indo-European. *Comments on Etymology* 13, No. 11–2:1–3 (1984). More on reduplication in Primitive Indo-European. *Comments on Etymology* 13, No. 13–4:1–2 (1984). Cf. 725 (1981); 744 (1982); 568 (1978); 766 (1983); 810
805. "Varia I: 1. Irish *fert*, *fertae*; 2. Irish *serb* = Welsh *herw*;

Spanish *álamo*." *ZCP* 40:275-9 (1984). Cf. 753 (1982); 893 (1986)
809. (with Hilda Caton) "A Fresh Look at the Sign System of the Braille Code." *Journal of Visual Impairment & Blindness* 78:210-4 (1984).
810. Letter concerning Primitive Indo-European '4'. *Comments on Etymology* 13, No. 15:2 (1984). Cf. 670 (1982); 778 (1983)
811. "On the Meaning of Latin *uoltus* and IE 'face'." *Papers from the Twentieth Regional Meeting*, *CLS* 149-52 (1984). Cf. 608 (1980); 371 (1973); 418 (1974); 700 (1982)
813. "Remarks on *astuac*." *Annual of Armenian Linguistics* 5:87-9 (1984).
814. "*Nasz*." *NOWELE [North-western European Language Evolution]* 3:49-57 (1984).
815. "*to care*." *Journal of Historical Linguistics and Philology* I.2:186-90 (1984).
818. "Some Implications of Hittite *-z(a)*." *KZ* 97:58-9 (1984).
819. "Armenian *anurǰ*, ὀνειρο-." *KZ* 97:130 (1984). Cf. 138 (1960); 834 (fn. 8).
820. "Latin *in* before Dental." *Glotta* 62:73-4 (1984). Cf. 779 (1983)
821. "Latin *pulc(h)er*." *Glotta* 62:74-5 (1984). Cf. 636 (1980); 344 (1972); 906 (1986)
824. "IE **meH_a-*." *Münchener Studien zur Sprachwissenschaft* 43:45-6 (1984). Cf. 591 (1978)
825. "Albanian *thind* and IE **ḱent-*." *Münchener Studien zur Sprachwissenschaft* 43:47-8 (1984).
826. "Notes on Greek Noun Formation." *Münchener Studien zur Sprachwissenschaft* 43:49-53 (1984). [1. γωνία, ἀσχέδωρος; 2. θέσπις, θέσφατος; 3. κώπη 'handle'; 4. πρᾶΰς, πρᾶος.] Cf. 816 (1983)
827. "Indo-European and Balto-Slavic 'sheep'." *JIES* 12:192 (1984).
828. "*/Θw-/ in Modern English." *American Speech* 59:376-7 (1984). Cf. 730 (1982)
829. "Varia." *EC* 21:137-40 (1984). [xv. Bret. *amouc*; xvi. Welsh *hwde*; xvii. Celtic *-truks-*; xviii. *mech deyrn*; xix. Early Irish suffixed pronouns.] Cf. 877 (1985)
830. "Speyer Gothic *farwa*." *NOWELE* 4:51-2 (1984). Cf. 423 (1973)
831. "Avestan *aṭ*, *aṭčā*." *Indo-Iranian Journal* 27:290 (1984). Cf. 716, 736 (1982); 667 (1981); 488 (1976)

832. "Über das Deklinationssystem. . . ." *GL* 24:179–86 (1984). Cf. 682 (1981)
833. "Some Italic and Celtic Correspondences III." *KZ* 97:265–6 (1984). [Latin *asser* 'beam', *assis* 'plank'; Umbrian *afero, andersafust*.] Cf. 500 (1976); 553 (1977); 754 (1983)
834. "Indo-European 'bone' Reconsidered." *KZ* 97:197–201 (1984). Cf. 383 (1974); 857 (1985), 866, 875
836. "The Reconstruction of Particles and Syntax." *Historical Syntax*, ed. J. Fisiak, Mouton (1984) 173–82. [1. Slavic *i*, Lithuanian *ir̃* 'and'; 2. Albanian negatives.] Cf. 683 (1981); 690, 691 (1982); 421 (1974); 476, 488 (1976)
837. "On Myths and Accuracy." *GL* 24:238–9 (1984).
838. "Varia III." *Ériu* 35:200–2 (1984). [1. *líaig* 'physician' (better, *lïaig*); 2. *líach* 'ladle, spoon'; 3. ad *coll, coillid*; 4. *forrumai*; 5. Irish *forú, fora* 'eyelash'.] Cf. 198 (1967)
839. "On the Semantics of Blood." *FLH* 5:193 (1984). Cf. 677 (1980)
840. "Toward Indo-European Reflexive Reference." *FLH* 5:195–6 (1984).
841. "*sūda*, 'sterile'." *Quaderni Linguistici e Filologici*, Università di Macerata p. 43 (1982–84). Cf. 686 (1981)
842. "O. Pruss. *(w)uschts*: Lith. *ušės*." *Baltistica* 20:61–3 (1984). Cf. 568 (1978); 379 (1974)
843. "Lith. *ēžeras*." *Baltistica* 20:64 (1984). Cf. 287 (1970)
844. "On the Development of Oxytone *o*-grade Adjectives to *ú*-stems." *Baltistica* 20:141–2 (1984). Cf. 780 (1983); 636 (1980); 935 (1987), 937
845. "A Phonaesthetic Rule of Baltic." *Baltistica* 20:143–4 (1984). Cf. 564 (1978)
846. "A Note on Armenian *tesanem* 'see'." *REA* 18:315 (1984). [Memorial volume for R. Godel]
851. "Armenian *dalar* 'green', θαλερός 'moist'." *Die Sprache* 30:156–9 (1984).
867. "Final *Liquid + Laryngeal in Greek." *Glossología* 2-3:163–8 (1983-4). Cf. 904 (1985)
872. "Armenian *awr, awur-* '24-hour day'." *Papers from the Third Conference on the Non-Slavic Languages of the USSR*, ed. Howard I. Aronson. Columbus, Ohio: *Folia Slavica* 7 (1984). Pp. 150–2. Cf. 358 (1973), 798 (1983).
873. "Miscellanea Celtica: Welsh *gŵydd* 'wild' and IE guṇa; *Peryddon*; On Binchy and Others on Bergin's Rule." *Studia Celtica*

18-19:128-34 (1983-4). Cf. 860 (1985), 561 (1977), 723 (1982); 906 (1986); 956 (1987)
886. "*Župa.*" *Folia Slavica* 6, No. 3:308-9 (1984). Cf. 516, 561 (1977)

1985

Articles

835. "Greek πτ- and Armenian." *Annual of Armenian Linguistics* 6:51-2 (1985). [Papers presented to G. B. Djahukian.] Cf. 798 (1983); 910 (1986)
847. "Slavic *(ǫ)trъ-brúhъ.*" *Zbornik za Filologiju i Lingvistiku* 27/28:879-80 (1984-5). [Festschrift for Milka and Pavle Ivić.] Cf. 762, 749 (1982), 255 (1970)
848. "OED Suppl. *dreck.*" *NOWELE* 5:107-8 (1985).
849. "Some Archaic Greek Compounds." *AJP* 106:222-5 (1985). Cf. 628 (1980); 888 (1986)
852. "Transitive and Causative in Indo-European." *Papers from the Twenty-first Regional Meeting*, CLS (1985) pp. 64-6. [Alb. *vdes* 'die'.]
853. "Dissimilation of *rCr* to *nCr* in Latin." *RRL* 30:3-6 (1985). Cf. 344 (1972); 310 (1971); 521 (1977)
855. "Albanian *zbres* 'descend'." *Sprachwissenschaftliche Forschungen: Festschrift für Johann Knobloch* (*Innsbrucker Beiträge zur Kulturwissenschaft* 23), eds. H. M. Ölberg, Gernot Schmidt, and H. Bothien. Innsbruck (1985). Pp. 145-6. Cf. 332 (1972); 99 (1959); 167, 169 (1961)
856. "Latin *sica* 'dagger' and *sybina* 'spear'." *Studi linguistici e filologici per Carlo Alberto Mastrelli*. Pisa: Pacini (1985). Pp. 217-8. Cf. 200 (1967); 909 (1986)
857. "Indo-European 'Gerste, orge, barley'." *KZ* 98:11-2 (1985). Cf. 131 (1960); 698 (1981); 564 (1978); 834 (1984)
858. "Umbrian *stahmito.*" *KZ* 98:59 (1985). Cf. 804 (1982); 794 (1983)
859. "Latin *callum, callis*, Indic *kiṇa-.*" *KZ* 98:59 (1985). Cf. 770 (1983)
860. "Greek ἔργον, Armenian *gorc*, and ὄργανον." *Münchener Studien zur Sprachwissenschaft* 46 (*Festgabe für Karl Hoffmann, Teil III*): 103-9 (1985). [Also δράπανον; Gothic ghost *waurk*; ἔρδω and ῥέζω.] Cf. 873 (1984); 870, 891 (1985)
863. "Latin *altāria.*" *Glotta* 63:101-2 (1985).

864. "Latin *arr(h)a*." *Glotta* 63:109 (1985).
865. "Latin *pappa*." *Glotta* 63:110 (1985).
866. "German *Bein*, Old English *bān*; Slavic *kostь*." *NOWELE* 6:67-70 (1985). Cf. 613 (1979); 834 (1984).
868. "*dêsni*." *Mélanges Skok/Skokov Zbornik*. Zagreb: Jugoslavenska Akademija Znanosti i Umjetnosti (1985). Pp. 193-5. Cf. 920 (1985)
869. "*Like* over *as*." *American Speech* 60:376-7 (1985).
870. "Old English *bēacn* 'beacon', *beckon*, etc." *Comments on Etymology* 15, No. 5-6:9-10 (1985). [Also ON *vákn*, cf. 860 (1985)] Cf. 885 (1986); 889 (1984)
871. Notes on *now then, nobody but nobody*, and *what with. Comments on Etymology* 15, No. 5-6:10-1 (1985).
874. "Indo-European *$H_a ent$- 'kindle'." *IF* 90:65 (1985).
875. "Indo-European **bheHi-*, Latin *foedus*, and Balto-Slavic." *IF* 90:66-9 (1985). Cf. 834 (1984), 636 (1980)
876. "Notes on Indo-European Dialects." *IF* 90:70-1 (1985). [1. IE **ad-*; 2. IEW **bhili-*, **bhilo-*; 3. 'drive' in the IE dialects] Cf. 915 (1987)
877. "Varia." *EC* 22:199-202 (1985). [xx. OIr. *tánaise, imthánud*; xxi. Irish *cumm(a)e*; xxii. Welsh *hwre* and *hwdy*; xxiii. Welsh *mae* 'where is?'] Cf. 596 (1979), 829 (1984), 628 (1980)
878. "Ad *Słownik etymologiczny języka polskicgo* V 2(22): 1. *łatka*, 2. *łbica*, 3. *łbieniec*, 4. *Łekno*, 5. *łesktać*, 6. *łeż* 1, 7. *łęcina*, 8. *łeczek*, *łężek*, 9. *łęgi*, *łężny* 2, *łęk*, *łęczny*, 10. *łękawa*, *lękowaty*, 11. *(ty)łędzie*, 12. *łęp*, 13. *łepa*, *łępać*, 14. *łęt*, 15. *łężny* 1; OPol. *łonny* : *łonowy*; *Łozna*, 16. *łgacz*, 17. *łgać*, 18. *łkac*, 19. *łodzia*, *łodnia*, *łodny*, *łodziany*, *łodzienny*, *łodyga* 1, 20. *łokać*, 21. *łokieć*, 22. *(ł)okomę* : *(ł)okoma* : *łokami*." *Rocznik Slawisticzny* 45:81-86 (1985). Cf. 613 (1979); 892 (1986)
881. "Two Problems of Latin Alternation." *Symbolae Ludovico Mitxelena septuagenario oblatae*, ed. José L. Melena. Victorico Vasconum (Victoria) (1985). Pp. 223-5. [1. Latin *iēns/euntis*; 2. *sum, est, sont*.] Cf. 610 (1980), 567 (1978); 929 (1987)
882. "Varia IV." *Ériu* 36:181-4 (1985). [OIr. *tend*, W *tynn*; 2. *tí*; 3. *socair*; 4. *soirb*; 5. *sreb*, *srib*; 6. *slige*; 7. *se(i)che*; 8. *sech* 'cut'; 9. *sliss*; 10. *soss*; 11. *úam*; 12. *tlí*; 13. *segda*.] Cf. 362 (1972); 859 (1985) ad 6; 605 (1980); 612 (1979)
883. "Corinth." *Names* 33:289 (1985). Cf. 194 (1966)
890. "KN L 693 *qe-te-o* and ΜΑΝΤΙΣ." *Minos* 19:51-3 (1985). Cf. 194 (1966)

891. "ἕδρᾰνον and χόδᾰνον." *Glotta* 63:150 (1985). Cf. 860 (1985)
895. "An Archaic Poetic Statement." *ŽA* 35:85-6 (1985). Cf. 612 (1979); 167 (1961); 855
896. "Derivatives of **sue-* in Latin." *ŽA* 35:16 (1.), 20 (2., 3.) (1985). [1. *soleo*; 2. *suesco, suetus*; 3. *sodalis, socors, soluo.*] Cf. 699 (1982); 446 (1975)
897. "Two Etymological Remarks." *Eirene* 22:35-8 (1985). [1. στέλλω, Latin *locus*; 2. ἵημι.] Cf. 310 (1971); 904 (1985)
898. "Czech *dršt'ka*." *Wiener Slavistisches Jahrbuch* 31:135-8 (1985). Cf. 446 (1975)
902. "Slavic **vonja*." *Ètimologija* 1982:64-5 (1985). Cf. 622 (1980); 920 (1985)
903. "Slavic *tъg-d'a*." *IJSLP* 31-2 [*Slavic Linguistics, Poetics, Cultural History: In Honor of Henrik Birnbaum on his 60th Birthday, 13 December 1985.* Slavica]:175-6 (1985). Cf. 783 (1983)
904. "On Asymmetric Labial Loss and Armenian." *Journal of Turkish Studies* 9 [*Niguca Bicig: An Anniversary Volume in Honor of Francis Woodman Cleaves*] (Cambridge, Mass.: Harvard University):133-5 (1985). Cf. 259 (1970); 798 (1983); 867 (1984); 897 (1985)
918. "Baltic Infinitives and Verbal Nouns." *Proceedings of the Institute of Lithuanian Studies, 1981*, ed. Ina Čepėnaitė Užgirienė. Chicago Institute of Lithuanian Studies. Pp. 199-207.
919. "From the Northern IE Lexicon." *Lingua Posnaniensis* 28:77. [1. **treuk-* 'tug, hack'; 2. **tengh-* 'heavy'.] Cf. 613 (1979)
920. "Albanian Notes." *Lingua Posnaniensis* 28:78. [1. Alb. *(f)shâj* 'je soupire'; 2. Geg *dânë*, Tosk *darë* 'tongs'.] Cf. 902 (1985); 557 (1978); 644 (1980)

Reviews
854. Review of Joseph T. Shipley, *The Origins of English Words: A Discursive Dictionary of Indo-European Roots* (Baltimore: Johns Hopkins University Press, 1984). *Verbatim* 12.2:21 (1985). Cf. 714 (1982)

1986

Articles
880. "Alb. *vajzë, motrë*." *Studi Albanologici, Balcanici, Bizantini e Orientali in Onore di Giuseppe Valentini S.J.*, eds. P. Carlo Messori Roncaglia & G. B. Pellegrini. Firenze: Olschki (1986). Pp. 109-10.

884. "On Thracian Rounded Vowels." *LB* 29: 13-4 (1986). Cf. 789 (1982)
885. "German *Baum*, English *beam*." *Linguistics Across Historical and Geographical Boundaries*, eds. Dieter Kastovsky and Aleksander Szwedek, Mouton, pp. 345-6 [Festschrift for Jacek Fisiak] (1986). Cf. 332 (1972); 870 (1985); 889 (1984)
887. "*Ezn* 'ox'." *AAL* 7:63-4 (1986).
888. "On the Morphology of Indic Gerunds." *Indo-Iranian Journal* 29:103-8 (1986). Cf. 500 (1976); 901 (1986); 926 (1987), 954
892. "Notulae Praeromanicae." *ZCP* 41:251-5 (1986). [1. *ulwo-/a-;* 2. *durno-/a-* (253); 3. **lanka* (253-4); 4. *kukso-/a-* (254); 5. Gaulish **talu-* etc. (254-5).] Cf. 559 (1978); 787 (1983); 878 (1985) ad #3; 939 (1987) #2
893. "Early Irish *gert (a)* f." *ZCP* 41:256 (1986). Cf. 805 (1984)
894. "*Culhwch*, the Swine." *ZCP* 41:257-8 (1986). Cf. 613 (1979); 941 (1987)
899. "*Andāre*." *Aspects of Language Studies in Honor of Mario Alinei, I. Geolinguistics*, edited by a committee of the *ALE*, Amsterdam: Rodopi, pp. 99-104 (1986). Cf. 553 (1977)
900. "The Indo-European Anaphora **ei* in Umbrian." *AJP* 107:398-400 (1986). Cf. 690 (1982)
901. "Slavic Nomina Actionis from 'eat'," in *Festschrift für Wolfgang Gesemann*, vol. 3: *Beiträge zur slawischen Sprachwissenschaft und Kulturgeschichte* (*Slavische Sprachen und Literaturen* 8). München: Hieronymus, pp. 119-21 (1986). Cf. 888 (1986); 785 (1983); 605 (1980); 926 (1987)
905. "The Rebirth of Gaulish." *Celtic Studies Association of North America* 5.2:3 (*Samhain* 1986). Cf. 315 (1971)
906. "Varia." *EC* 23:47-51 (1986). [xxiv. ροκλοισιαβο (47); xxv. Notes on word formation: 1. Breton *dremm* (47); 2. Irish *brecc*, Welsh *brych* (48); 3. Irish *gu(s)* (48); 4. *orc* in Irish (49-50); 5. **brigantinos* (50-1).] Cf. 648 (1980); 941 (1987)
907. "On the Grammar and History of Two English Combining Forms." *Journal of English Linguistics* 19:2 (*In Memory of Raven I. McDavid, Jr.*):304-8 (1986). [1. Complex words in *electro-* (304-6); 2. Words in *equi-* (307-8).]
908. "Varia II." *Ériu* 37:183-4 (1986). [1. *turgaire*; 2. *taurráin*; 3. *turchlos*; 4. *súas, sís, sadess, fades*, etc.] Cf. 721, 722 (1982)
909. "Polish *bieszczad*, Ukrainian *béskyd*." *Zeitschrift für Balkanologie* 22/2:163 (1986). Cf. 689 (1981); 650 (1980)

910. "*Tellus* ('earth')." *Rheinisches Museum für Philologie* 129:360-1 (1986). Cf. 835 (1985)
911. "Notes on Latin Noun Formation." *Rheinisches Museum für Philologie* 129:362 (1986). Cf. 678 (1981); 343 (1972)
912. "More on the Vocative *-e.*" *General Linguistics* 26:258 (1986). Cf. 309 (1970)
913. "Greek ῥώμη, ῥῶσις." *Glotta* 64:246 (1986). Cf. 794 (1983)
916. "The Balkan Words for 'garlic'." *RRL* 31:503-4 (1986). Cf. 520 (1977); 221 (1967)
921. "Scottish Gaelic *morair.*" *Scottish Gaelic Studies* 14:138-41.
923. "Hey." *American Speech* 61.4:365-6 (1986).
930. "Armenian *yisun,*" in *Études arméniennes in memoriam Haig Berbérian*, ed. Dickran Kouymjian. Lisbon: Gulbenkian (1986). Pp. 293-4.
943. "Σπάθη. *ŽA* 36:44 (1986). Cf. 696 (1981)
953. "Subject Matter Entails Speech Situation and Style." *Philologica Pragensia* 29.2:109-10 (1986).

1987

Articles
914. "Bulgarian Dialectal *čùnka* and **(s)keub-.*" *LB* 30:21-2 (1987).
915. "OIr. ·*tab(a)ir* 'brings', ·*taít* 'comes'," in *Festschrift for Henry Hoenigswald on the Occasion of his Seventieth Birthday*, eds. George Cardona and Norman H. Zide. Tübingen: Gunter Narr, pp. 433-5 (1987). Cf. 644 (1980); 721 (1982)
924. "A Simple Exercise in the Importance of Word Morphology." *CLS* 23/1:116-7 (1987). [OIr. *tene, tan-* 'fire'.] Radical revision of 556 (1978).
925. "On the Settlement of the Americas: The Linguistic Evidence." *Current Anthropology* 28:101 (1987).
926. "Nekaj slovanskih glagolskih samostalnikov s *-t-.*" *Slavistična Revija* 35:223-4 (1987). Cf. 888, 901 (1986)
927. "K zgodivini slavistične znanosti II." *Slavistična Revija* 35:224 (1987).
928. "Albanian *xixë* and Balto-Slavic." *Acta Balto-Slavica* (Polska akademia nauk) 17:129-30 (1987). Cf. 392 (1972); 282 (1969); 293 (1971)
929. "*Fōns,*" in *Language, Literature, and History: Philological and Historical Studies Presented to Erica Reiner*, ed. Francesca

Rochberg-Halton (AOS 67). New Haven: American Oriental Society (1987). Pp. 155–6. Cf. 542 (1977); 881 (1985)
931. "On the Sibilants of Romani." *Indo-Iranian Journal* 30:103–6 (1987).
932. "*Bhadrá-* 'happy, favourable." *Indo-Iranian Journal* 30:175 (1987).
933. "Grooved Assimilation." *RRL* 32:51 (1987).
934. "North European IE 'bed'." *NOWELE* 9:89–90 (1987).
935. "On the History of Ѫже, Ѫз-, в Ѫз-." *LB* 30:131–2 (1987). Cf. 888 (1986)
936. "Archaic Evidence from the Septuagint." *LB* 30:133–4 (1987).
937. "Малжена и мѪжъ," *Bŭlgarski ezik* 37:305–7 (1987).
938. "Κιμμέριοι again." *Zeitschrift für Balkanologie* 23:108 (1987).
939. "Two Notes on Celtic Etyma." *Romance Philology* 41:150–1 (1987). [1. Old Occitan *dorn*; 2. *cadorn*.]
940. "On Making Choices." *RRL* 32:325–6 (1987).
941. "The Pig in Ancient Northern Europe." *Proto-Indo-European: The Archaeology of a Linguistic Problem, Studies in Honor of Marija Gimbutas*, eds. Susan Nacev-Skomal and Edgar C. Polomé. Washington, D.C.: 185–90 (1987). Cf. 894 (1986), 906
944. "A Friend of Mine." *Comments on Etymology* 17 no. 5–6:7 (1987).
946. "Ad *AJP* 102 (1981) 148." *AJP* 108:694 (1987). Cf. 657 (1981)
947. "Latin *animus, anima.*" *AJP* 108:695–6 (1987). Cf. 622 (1980); 794 (1983)
948. "On IE Formations in *-ró-* in Balto-Slavic." *Słavistyczne studia językoznawcze* 1987 (Festschrift F. Sławski):111–3 (1987). Cf. 822 (1983); 745 (1982); 636 (1980)
949. "The Athematic *s*-Subjunctive." *Ériu* 38:201 (1987).
950. "Derivatives of IE **sHei-*." *RRL* 32:107 (1987).
954. "Notes on Old Breton." *EC* 24:191–2 (1987). [19. *anroe.*] Cf. 530 (1976); 888 (1986)
955. "Varia." *EC* 24:185–9 (1987). [xxvi. Early Irish *abacc*; xxvii. **reg-* and **reig-*; xxviii. Terms for 'torch' and stems for 'kindle'; xxix. Welsh *cyd, y gyd, gyda*, MBret. *quet-*; xxx. Breton *bizou*; xxxi. Larzac *bnanom.*] Cf. 455 (1975); 587 (1979); 326 (1972)
956. "**Drěma, *drěmъ, *drěmati* (> дрѣмати)." *Bŭlgarski ezik* 37:471 (1987). Cf. 804 (1982); 794 (1983); 873 (1984)

Reviews
942. Review of Ian Press, *A Grammar of Modern Breton*, Berlin: Mouton/de Gruyter (1986), in *Celtic Studies Association of North America (CSANA) Newsletter* 6.2:7-9 (1987).

1988

Articles
945. "Observations on the *k*- in Some Words in *Leaves* . . . 1865." *Comments on Etymology* 17 no. 7-8:21-2 (1988).
951. "Old English *hæst*." *NOWELE* 11:89 (1988).
957. "Of *supportive of*." *American Speech* 63.1:95-6 (1988).
958. "Morpho-syntax as Proof in Etymology." (with addenda) *The Best of CLS: A Collection of Out-of-Print Papers from 1968 to 1975*, eds. E. Schiller, B. Need, D. Varley, and B. Eilfort. Chicago Linguistic Society (1988). Pp. 328-34. [Reprint with updating adenda of 260 (1970)]
959. "Indic *arí-* and *ā́rya-*." *Comments on Etymology* 17 no. 13-4: 1-3 (April 1988).
960. "Archaisms in Romani." *Papers from the Eighth and Ninth Annual Meetings Gypsy Lore Society, North American Chapter*, eds. Cara DeSilva, Joanne Grumet, and David J. Nemeth. New York (1988). Pp. 21-4. Cf. 721, 730, 671 (1982)
318. (Separate listing). "Brief Mention", *IJAL* (1971-   ).

37:2 (1971) 135-136
H. J. Uldall. *General Theory* (Part 1 of L. Hjelmslev and H. J. Uldall, *Outline of Glossematics*). 1967.
Wilga M. Rivers. *Teaching Foreign-Language Skills*. 1968.
George R. Stewart. *American Place Names: A Concise and Selective Dictionary for the Continental United States of America*. 1970.
Fred Tarpley. *Place Names of Northeast Texas*. 1969.
Edmond S. Meany. *Origins of Washington Geographic Names*. 1923 (Republished 1969).
A. Howry Espenshade. *Pennsylvania Place Names*. 1925 (Republished 1969).
Alfred A. Holt. *American Place Names*. 1938.
George A. West. *Tobacco, Pipes and Smoking Customs of the*

American Indians. 2 vols.: Part I: *Text*, Part II: *Plates.* 1934 (Reprint 1970).
Huron H. Smith. *Ethnobotany of the Menomini Indians.* 1923 (Reprint 1970).
James R. Jaquith. *The Present Status of the Uto-Aztecan Languages of Mexico: An Index of Data Bearing on Their Survival, Geographical Location and Internal Relationships.* 1970.

37:3 (1971) 210-212
Encyclopaedia of Linguistics, Information and Control. A. R. Meetham, editor-in-chief; R. A. Hudson, associate editor. 1969.
George Lakoff. *Irregularity in Syntax.* 1970.
Patricia L. Carrell. *A Transformational Grammar of Igbo.* (West African Monographs 8). 1970.
Jean-Michel Peterfalvi. *Introduction à la psycholinguistique.* 1970.
Joseph F. Kess. *A Bibliography of the Haida Language.* The Canadian Journal of Linguistics 14:1, 1968.
Óscar Uribe Villegas. *Un Mapa del Monolingüismo y el Bilingüismo de los Indígenas de México en 1960.* 1970.
Branislava Susnik. *Chamacocos. I: Cambio cultural (1969); II: Diccionario etnográfico* (1970).
Lidia N. Bruno and Elena L. Najlis. *Bibliográfia argentina de filología y lingüistica 1965-1968.* 1969.
Clemente Hermando Balmori. *Estudios de área lingüística indígena.* 1967.
Jehan A. Vellard. *Contribución al estudio de la lengua Uru.* CLI 4, 1967.
Elena L. Najlis. *Dialectos del mataco.* 1968.
Jehan A. Vellard. *Vocabulario toba.* CLI 6, 1969.

38:1 (1972) 78-79
Biennial review of *Anthropology* 1969. Benard J. Siegel, ed. 1970. Cf. 39.59
América indígena 31, 1 (January, 1971). Cf. 38.282
Iorgu Iordan, tr. John Orr. *An Introduction to Romance Linguistics: Its Schools and Scholars.* Revised, with a supplement thirty years on, by R. Posner. 1970.
La société roumaine de linguistique romane (see *Bulletin* 1969, vol. 6.).
C. H. Stevenson. *The Spanish Language Today.* 1970.

38:3 (1972) 221
Ives Goddard. *The Ethnohistorical Implications of Early Delaware Linguistic Materials. Man in the Northeast.* 1971.
Stig Wikander. *Maya and Altaic III.* 1972. Cf. 317 (1971)

38:4 (1972) 280-282 Chronicle and Theoretical
Main Trends of Research in the Social and Human Sciences (Preface by René Maheu). Part 1: *Social Sciences.* 1970.
Robert Borger and Frank Cioffi (eds.). *Explanation in the Behavioural Sciences.* 1970.
M. Gross and A. Lentin. *Introduction to Formal Grammars* (trans. M. Salkoff). 1970. (Fr. original 1967).
Noam Chomsky and George A. Miller. *L'analyse formelle des langues naturelles* (trad. Ph. Richard et N. Rowet). 1968.
Noam Chomsky. *Aspectos de la teoria de la sintaxis* (trans. C. P. Otero). 1970.
Johannes Bechert, Danièle Clément, Wolf Thümmel, Karl Heinz Wagner. *Einführung in die generative Transformationsgrammatik: Ein Lehrbuch.* 1970.

Varia
Robert Underhill (ed.). *Papers From the Seminar in American Indian Linguistics* (Vol. 3). 1970.
J. D. Kaye, G. L. Piggott, K. Tokaichi (eds.). *Odawa Language Project: First Report.* 1971.
T. S. T. Henderson. *Participant-Reference in Algonkin.* 1971.
E. R. Seary. *Place Names of the Avalon Peninsula of the Island of Newfoundland.* 1971.
Charles C. Adams. *Boontling: An American Lingo.* 1971.

From the Journals
América indígena 31(4). 1971.
Anales de la universidad de la Patagonia "San Juan Bosco".
Ciencas antropológicas tomo 1 nro. 1. 1967.
Andean Linguistics Newsletter.
Lingua. Master Index vols. 11-20 (1962-1968).
Conference on American Indian Languages NEWSLETTER of the Clearinghouse for Linguistic Information Helpful to Persons Helpful to Indians.
The Morning Star People (June, 1972).

39:1 (1973) 59-61 *Surveys*
Bernard J. Siegel (ed.). *Biennial Review of Anthropology* 1971. 1972. Cf. 38.78
Gordon R. Willey. *An Introduction to American Anthropology* Vol. 2: *South America*. 1971.
R. F. Heizer and M. A. Whipple (eds.). *The California Indians: A Source Book*. 1971.

From the History of Linguistics
Lidia Bruno. *Parentesco lingüístico*. 1969.
Maurice Leroy. *Les grands courants de la linguistique moderne* (2ᵉ éd.) 1971.
Eberhard Zwirner and Kurt Zwirner. *Principles of Phonometrics* (trans. H. Bluhme). 1970.
Ian Michael. *English Grammatical Categories and the Tradition to 1800*. 1970.
Otto Jespersen. *Linguistica: Selected Papers in English, French and German*. (Reprint 1970).

Varia
M. B. Emeneau. *Toda Songs*. 1971.
John B. Carroll, Peter Davies and Barry Richman. *Word Frequency Book*. 1971.
J. Akin, A. Goldberg, G. Myers, J. Stewart (eds.): *Language Behavior: A Book of Readings in Communication*. 1970.
R. A. Wisbey (ed.). *The Computer in Literary and Linguistic Research*. 1971.
Walter Shepherd. *Shepherd's Glossary of Graphic Signs and Symbols*. 1971.
The Minutes of the 6th International Conference on Salish Languages (Victoria, B.C. 16-18 August, 1971).

39:2 (1973) 129-131
Roderick A. Jacobs and Peter S. Rosenbaum, editors. *Readings in English Transformational Grammar*. 1970.
Paul M. Postal. *Crossover Phenomena*. 1971.
David M. Perlmutter. *Deep and Surface Constraints in Syntax*. 1971.
Charles J. Fillmore and D. Terence Langendoen, editors. *Studies in Linguistic Semantics*. 1971.
Danny D. Steinberg and Leon A. Jacobovits. *An Interdiscipli-*

nary Reader in Philosophy, Linguistics, and Psychology. 1971.
Pieter A. M. Seuren. *Operators and Nucleus.* 1969.
Olefia Kovacci. *Tendencias actuales de la gramática* (2a. ed.). 1971.
E. J. A. Henderson, editor. *The Indispensable Foundation: A Selection From the Writings of Henry Sweet.* 1971.
Nouvelles perspectives en phonétique: Conférences et travaux, volume 1. Institut de phonétique, Université de Bruxelles. 1970.
Dell Hymes, editor. *Pidginization and Creolization of Languages.* 1971.
Elizabeth Closs Traugott. *A History of English Syntax.* 1972.
Charles Jones. *An Introduction to Middle English.* 1972.
Charles A. Zisa. *American Indian Languages: Classification and List.* 1970.
Algonquian Linguistics Newsletter. Volume 1, 1972 (Department of Anthropology, Trent University, Peterborough, Ontario).
David Jones and Evelyn M. Todd. *A Revised Spelling List for Ojibwa.* 1971.
Conference on American Indian Languages Clearinghouse Newsletter, James L. Fidelholtz, editor, Volume 1, Number 2, September 1972. Cf. 38:282

Eric P. Hamp: Separate Publications

Glossary of American Technical Linguistic Usage 1925-1950. Utrecht: Spectrum, 1957. (3rd rev. ed., 1966).
Collaborator for Albanian: *The American Bibliography for Slavic and East European Studies* for 1956 through 1959 (Bloomington 1957-1960).
Author of articles in *Encyclopaedia Britannica* on Accent, Albanian language[3], Grammar, Sandawe[2], Secret Languages[2]; Holder, Jokl, Finck, Zeuss. (All except Grammar since ca. 1960 ed.; numbers indicate revisions. Grammar and Albanian language, new 1974 ed.). See 378, 399 (1974)
Introduction to Phoenix reprinting (1961) of E. H. Sturtevant, *Linguistic Change.*
Author of articles in *Grolier Encyclopedia* on Gaulish, Iberians, Indo-European, Italic, Lettish, Lithuanian (1963).
Moderator of panel discussion, "The Transformation Theory",

Report of the 13th Annual Round Table Meeting on Linguistics and Language Studies (ed. Elisabeth D. Woodsworth), Washington: Georgetown University Press, 1963, pp. 3-50.

(co-author) for Linguistic Society of America to *The Commission on the Humanities*, 1964 (152-8). Cf. 1985, report.

(with F. Householder and R. Austerlitz, eds.) *Readings in Linguistics II*. Chicago: The University of Chicago Press, 1966. Midway Reprint 1980.

(joint author, ALPAC) NAS-NRC, *Language and Machines*, 1966.

Author of grammar definitions, *The Random House Dictionary*. New York. 1966.

Chapter 22 (271-81): "American Schools of Linguistics". Voice of America *Linguistics*, 1969 (broadcast 1967). Cf. 148 (1964).

Participant Držić Symposium, Dubrovnik 1967. *Forum* 9-10 (Sept-Oct 1967) esp. 622-3.

Contributor to *MLA Bibliography* (Section Head for Historical Linguistics, Celtic, Albanian) 1968-81. Cf. 53 (1956); 345 (1972)

Sections on Albanian language, literature, folklore, ethnography in P. Horecky (ed.), *Southeastern Europe: A Guide to Basic Publications*, Chicago 1969. Cf. 345 (1972)

Chapter on Albanian in *Current Trends in Linguistics, Vol. 9: Western Europe*, ed. Thomas A. Sebeok. (1972) Written 1969 = 345

Consulting Editor, Aldus International Library of Knowledge, *Language and Communication*, London 1969.

31 Quileute tapes on file in the Library of the American Philosophical Society in Philadelphia. These tapes comprise all but approximately the last 15 pages of Manuel Andrade's and Leo Frachtenberg's Quileute texts, these being all the Quileute texts published to date. 1969-1970.

Advisor for Linguistics to *Encyclopaedia Britannica*, 15th ed. and revision (1980).

Editor, *History and Structure of Language Series*. University of Chicago Press.

Editor, *Languages and Areas Studies Presented to George V. Bobrinskoy*. Chicago: printed by the University of Chicago Press, 1967.

Editor, *Essays in Romance Philology* (in honor of the XII International Congress of Romance Philology, București, 15-20 April 1968). Chicago: Departments of Romance Languages and Literatures and of Linguistics, The University of Chicago, 1968.

Co-Editor with Jack Berry, *Hans Wolff Memorial Issues of International Journal of American Linguistics*: *IJAL* 35(4) October 1969 [p. 285 dedicatory note]; 36(2) April 1970; 36(4) October 1970.
Introduction to *The Chicago Which Hunt: Papers from the Relative Clause Festival*. Chicago Linguistic Society 1972.
Editor, *Papers on Italic Topics Presented to James Wilson Poultney*, Special Issue of the *Journal of Indo-European Studies*. Vol. 1, 1973.
Contributor, Harper & Row *Design for Reading* (Kindergarten through Grade 8), 1973.
Linguistic Consultant, and author of technical portions of teacher's edition, *Design for Reading* (Basic Program, Kindergarten through Grade 8) (10 vols.) Harper & Row 1973.
Editor, *Themes in Linguistics: the 1970s* (Janua Linguarum, series minor 172). The Hague-Paris: Mouton 1973.
Editor, *Papers in Philology and Romance Philology and Linguistics in Honor of Clarence E. Parmenter for his Eighty-Fifth Birthday*. (not published)
"A note on the Runes." Appendix C to *Mappae Clavicula: A little key to the world of medieval techniques*, Cyril S. Smith and John G. Hawthorne, eds. *Transactions of the American Philosophical Society* 64.4, 1974. Pp. 117-19. [On Phillipps-Corning MS.] Cf. 445 (1975); 518 (1976)
"On having a birthday." Preface to *Papers from the Tenth Regional Meeting of the Chicago Linguistic Society*. Chicago: Chicago Linguistic Society, 1974.
"On Bonaparte and the Neogrammarians as Field Workers." Chapter 16 (390-433) of *Studies in the History of Linguistics: Traditions and Paradigms*, Dell Hymes, ed. Bloomington, Ind.: Indiana University Press, 1974.
Editor, *Papers on Eskimo and Aleut Linguistics*, Chicago: Chicago Linguistic Society, 1976 [Preface and Acknowledgments] Cf. 489 (1976)
Contributor, Linguistic Consultant and author of technical portions, Harper & Row *Reading Basics Plus* (Kindergarten through Grade 8), 1976.
Contributor, Linguistic Consultant and author of technical portions, Harper & Row *Language Basics Plus*, 1979.
Consultant for revision, Harper & Row *Basic Language* (7-12), 1980.

"Anthropology and Linguistics, Fathers and Sons," paper for *Dilemmas of Focus in Linguistics* (Burg Wartenstein Symposium No. 77: Wenner-Gren Foundation) 1977. pp. 17.
Approaches to Language, eds. William C. McCormack and Stephen A. Wurm. The Hague: Mouton 1978, pp. 643-4. [Discussion to "Language Evolution" at IXth International Congress of Anthropological and Ethnological Sciences, Chicago 1973.]
"Problems of Multilingualism in Small Linguistic Communities"; ed. James E. Alatis, *Georgetown University Round Table on Languages and Linguistics* (1978) 155-64.
"A Glance From Here On"; eds. L. Campbell and M. Mithun, *The Languages of Native America: Historical and Comparative Assessment*. University of Texas Press, Austin 1979, 1001-15. Cf. 582 (1979); 212 (1967); 317 (1971); 925 (1987)
"Leksikata kako balkanistički aspekt na gramatikata." *Zbornik na trudovite od V Naučna Diskusija*, Ohrid 28-31. viii. 1978. Skopje 1979, 21-3.
"Thracian, Dacian and Albanian-Romanian correspondences." *Actes du IIe Congrès international de thracologie* (Bucarest, 4-10 Sept. 1976) III *Linguistique, ethnologie, anthropologie*, eds. Radu Vulpe, G. Mihăilă, R. Vulcănescu, D. Slușanski. București 1980, pp. 57-60. Cf. 429 (1974); 477 (1976); 520 (1977); 550 (1976); 380 (1973); 650 (1980); 687 (1981) [reprinted in *Le monde Thrace*. Volume selectif. Editrice Nagard, Milan, Paris, Roma, 1982, pp. 182-5.]
Linguistic Consultant for *Patterns: The Primary Braille Reading Program*. Louisville, Kentucky: American Printing House for the Blind.
Readiness Level 1980 (*go and do*; *letters and you*)
Pre-Primer Level (*Work and Play*; *Little and Big*; *Words and Games*)
Primer (*City and Farm*)
  Book 1. (*New Friends*) (3 braille volumes)
  Book 2. (*Old and New*) (3 braille volumes)
  Book 3. (*Far Away and Long Ago*) (3 braille vols. & glossary)
"*Gwyr a aeth*," in *Celtic Folklore and Christianity: Studies in Memory of William W. Heist*, ed. Patrick K. Ford. Los Angeles, Center for the Study of Comparative Folklore and Mythology, 1983, pp. 50-7. Cf. 795 (1981-2)

"*sh(ë) tun(ë).*" in *Studies in Kosova*, ed. Arshi Pipa and Sami Repishti. Boulder, East European Monographs, 1984, pp. 63-4.

"Problems of Archaic Features in Armenian Noun Inflexion," in *International Symposium on Armenian Linguistics (Yerevan, September 21-25, 1982): Reports.* Erevan, AN Armjanskoj SSR, 1984, pp. 107-113. Cf. 798 (1983); 579 (1977); 672 (1980); 443, 454 (1975); 587 (1979)

(Co-author) For Linguistic Society of America to "The State of the Humanities." American Council of Learned Societies, 1985, pp. 174-84.

(member of the editorial committee) *Atlas Linguarum Europae (ALE). Volume I: Commentaires: Deuxième fascicule.* Assen/Maastricht, The Netherlands: Van Gorcum (1986).

Obituary for George V. Bobrinskoy, University of Chicago *Record* (April 10, 1986) (pp. 64-6), and Linguistic Society of America *Bulletin* (March 1986).

Consultant for Etymology, *The Random House Dictionary of the English Language*, 2nd edition, unabridged. New York 1987 (Stuart Berg Flexner, ed.). Cf. 714 (1982), 854 (1985)

"Historical Sketch of the English Language." *Random House Dictionary, Unabridged* (1987) xv-xx.